BROADWAY
TRANSLATIONS

*" Age cannot wither her, nor custom stale
Her infinite variety."*

𝔅roadway 𝔗ranslations

SUETONIUS

HISTORY OF TWELVE CAESARS

Translated by

PHILEMON HOLLAND (ANNO 1606)

Edited by

J. H. FREESE, M.A.

FORMERLY FELLOW OF ST JOHN'S COLLEGE, CAMBRIDGE

With additional Notes and an Introduction

LONDON
GEORGE ROUTLEDGE & SONS LTD.
NEW YORK: E. P. DUTTON & CO.

PRINTED IN GREAT BRITAIN BY
THE EDINBURGH PRESS, 9 AND 11 YOUNG STREET, EDINBURGH

TABLE OF CONTENTS

PREFATORY NOTE

THIS edition of Holland's translation of Suetonius is not intended for the professed scholar. It is an attempt to make it simpler for the non-classical reader, at the same time preserving as far as possible the vigour and quaintness which constitute its great charm.

The spelling has been modernised throughout, and a few alterations made in the actual wording. One or two misprints and mistakes have been pointed out ; in some cases, as the editor did not see until later, Holland himself has corrected them in a list of Errata (" Faultes escaped in the Annotations "), printed in a manner which makes them difficult to read.

Except where the meaning was sufficiently obvious, a word or phrase now obsolete is explained in a note ; to have substituted a modern equivalent or paraphrase for, *e.g.* starting-holes or skarfires, would have destroyed a distinctive feature of the work. Murray's Dictionary, Skeat and Mayhew's Tudor and Stuart Glossary, and Nares's Glossary, ed. Halliwell and Wright, have been consulted throughout. The Annotations—not the original side-notes, " a marginal glosse," as Holland calls them—may be of interest even to the scholar or to one who has not kept up his knowledge of the Latin language or of Roman history and antiquities. The editor has done his best to verify the numerous references to classical and other authorities, but has not always been able to do so. One in Propertius, which he unaccountably failed to find, is due to the kindness of Prof. J. P. Postgate.

It is well to bear in mind that Holland most commonly uses nephew and niece for grandson and granddaughter, gentlemen of Rome for knights (*equites*), empire for reign.

For the notes in square brackets, except in a few cases

PREFATORY NOTE

where they are Holland's own, the editor is responsible. In the body of the text [12] indicates a reference to another chapter of the life in which the same word or allusion occurs ; [C. 18] a reference to another life. C. =Caesar, Aug. = Augustus, Tib. =Tiberius, Cal. =Caligula, Cl. =Claudius, N. = Nero, G. =Galba, O. =Otho, Vit. =Vitellius, Vesp. =Vespasian, T. =Titus, D. =Domitian. 8ᵃ means that there is an annotation as well as a note on a word or phrase.

ABBREVIATIONS OF LATIN PRAENOMINA

A. =Aulus, C. =Gaius, Cn. =Gnaeus, D. =Decimus, L. = Lucius, M. =Marcus, M'. =Manius, P. =Publius, Q. =Quintus, Ser. =Servius, Sex. =Sextus, Sp. =Spurius, T. =Titus, Ti. = Tiberius.

The editor desires to acknowledge assistance from the following in addition to the usual works of reference : Editions by I. Casaubon, 1691 edn., Baumgarten-Crusius, 1816, M. Ihm, 1908 (text only) ; translations by A. Thomson and T. Forester, 1855, in Bohn's Classical Library, and by J. C. Rolfe, 1914, in the Loeb Classical Library ; editions, with notes, of separate Lives : *Augustus*, E. S. Shuckburgh, 1896, *Claudius*, H. Smilda, 1896, *Galba, Otho, and Vitellius*, C. Hofstee, 1898. English Lives of *Augustus*, E. S. Shuckburgh, and *Nero*, B. W. Henderson, 1903. General : C. Merivale, *History of the Romans under the Empire*, 1850, etc.

It is hoped the Genealogical Table will be useful in checking the somewhat intricate family relationships. Attention may also be called to the Addenda (p. 392).

C. JULIUS CAESAR = MARCIA

1. Julia = C. Marius   2. C. Julius Caesar = Aurelia   3. Sextus Julius Caesar (cos. 91 B.C

1. C. JULIUS CAESAR = Cornelia   2. Julia = M. Atius Balbus

Julia = Cn. Pompeius Magnus   Atia = C. Octavius

(1)
1. Octavia minor = (a) C. Claudius Marcellus   = (b) M. Antonius (

(2)
1. Marcella major = (a) M. Vipsanius Agrippa   1. Antonia major = L. Dor
          = (b) Iullus (or Julius) Antonius
             (son of the triumvir)   1. Cn. Domitius Aheno
2. Marcella minor = (a) Paulus Aemilius Lepidus
          = (b) M. Valerius Messalla   NERO = (a) Clau
             Barbatus Appianus   = (b) Popp
                                         = (c) Stati

1. M. Valerius Messalla Barbatus = Domitia Lepida   Claudia Augusta
                                              2. Domitia = C. Passie
                                                    (stepfathe
Valeria Messalina = CLAUDIUS   3. Domitia Lepida = (a
2. Claudia Pulchra = P. Quintilius Varus   (Aunt of Nero)   (b
3. M. Claudius Marcellus = Julia, d. of Augustus   (c

(1) Octavius had another daughter Octavia (major) by Ancharia
(2) Authorities differ as to the Marcellas and their husbands. *See* Tacitus, *Ann.* ed. Furnea

---

TIBERIUS CLAUDIUS NERO = LIVIA DRUSILLA.

1. TIBERIUS = (a) Vipsania Agrippina   2. Drusus senior (38-9 B.C.) = Ant
         = (b) Julia, d. of Augustus
                                     1. Germanicus (B.C. 15–A.D. 19) =
(by a) Drusus junior (— A.D. 23) = Claudia Livilla
                                 1. Nero = Julia, d. of Drusus
1. Julia = (a) Nero, son of Germanicus   2. Drusus III (A.D. 7-33) = A
       = (b) C. Rubellius Blandus   3. Tiberius (died soon
2. Tiberius Gemellus   } twins   after birth)
3. Germanicus Julius Caesar   4. Gaius
                                         5. GAIUS (Caligula) = (a) Jur
                                                     = (b) Liv
                                                     = (c) Lo
                                                     = (d) Mi

                                                            Jul
                                   6. Julia Agrippina = (a) Cn
                                                  = (b) C.
                                                  = (c) CL
                                   7. Julia Drusilla I = L. Cas
                                   8. Julia Livilla   = M. Vi

iumvir) | 2. AUGUSTUS=(a) Claudia (Clodia)
=(b) Scribonia
=(c) Livia Drusilla

Ahenobarbus 2. Antonia = Drusus
minor senior Julia (by b)=(a) M. Claudius Marcellus
s=Julia Agrippina =(b) M. Vipsanius Agrippa
=(c) TIBERIUS (no issue by Julia)

tavia
abina C. Caesar=Claudia Livilla
ssalina L. Caesar
all by (b) Julia=L. Aemilius Paulus
Vipsania Agrippina=Germanicus,
ispus son of Drusus senior
ero) Agrippa Postumus
ssalla Barbatus
stus Cornelius Sulla
appius Junius Silanus

p. 170

inor

ia Agrippina 2. Claudia Livilla=(a) C. Caesar 3. CLAUDIUS=(a) Plautia Urgulanilla
=(b) Drusus =(b) Aelia Paetina
junior =(c) Valeria Messalina
Lepida =(d) Julia Agrippina

(by a) 1. Drusus IV (died quite young)
udilla (by b) 2. Claudia Antonia=(a) Cn. Pompeius
estilla Magnus
ulina =(b) Faustus Cornelius
Caesonia Sulla
(by c) 3. Claudia Octavia=NERO
silla II (by a) (by d) 4. Claudius Britannicus
itius
nus Crispus
s
onginus

INTRODUCTION

LITTLE is known of Gaius Suetonius Tranquillus. There is no certain information as to the dates of his birth and death, for which A.D. 75-160 or 69-141 have been suggested. His birth-place is equally uncertain ; it may have been Rome. From Otho (10) we learn that his father, Suetonius Laetus, was a tribune of the 13th legion, *Gemina,* and fought at the battle of Betriacum. It is doubtful whether C. Suetonius Paulinus, once governor of Britain and one of Otho's generals, belonged to the same family. In Nero (57) the author states that " twenty years after [Nero's death], when I was a young man, a person of uncertain rank appeared, who gave it out that he was Nero." As Nero died in 68, this passage would place Suetonius's youth during the reign of Domitian and the date of his birth not later than 75, though it may have been earlier.

The letters of the younger Pliny, with whom he was on intimate terms and whom he accompanied to Bithynia, of which Pliny was governor, throw more light on his later life. Four of these letters are directly addressed to Suetonius, while in three others he is referred to. From i, 18, we gather that he was in practice as an advocate, for which he hardly seems to have been fitted, as he was so alarmed by a dream that he asked Pliny to get a case postponed which he was afraid of losing. Nor does he seem to have had more taste for a public career, for he begs Pliny to transfer to a relative the military tribuneship which his friend had obtained for him (iii, 8). In v, 10, Pliny urges Suetonius to publish certain of his writings, although he does not specify which they were. Another letter (i, 24) is from Pliny to a friend, whose good offices he asks on behalf of Suetonius, here spoken of as *scholasticus* (a student) and *contubernalis meus* (my intimate friend), who is anxious to purchase a small estate. In the correspondence with Trajan (94) Pliny begs the emperor to grant Suetonius the *jus trium liberorum* (privileges bestowed upon those who had three children),[1] to which Trajan somewhat grudgingly assents (95).

Suetonius next appears as private secretary to the emperor Hadrian, a post which he owed to Septicius Clarus, praefect of the praetorian guard, 119-121. Both he and his patron, however, were deprived of their offices, because they had treated the empress Sabina disrespectfully during her husband's absence in Britain (Spartianus, *Hadrian*). Another reason suggested is that they were mixed up in one of the court intrigues so common during imperial times. After this, Suetonius devoted himself to literary work. Nothing further is known of him.

Of his numerous writings only two have been preserved in a more or less complete state. The first is the *Lives of the Emperors* from Julius Caesar to Domitian. It is divided into 8 books, Galba, Otho, and Vitellius making book 7, and Vespasian, Titus, and Domitian book 8. The abruptness with which the biography of Julius Caesar begins and a comparison with the method pursued in other biographies had long aroused the suspicion that the introduction had been lost. This was confirmed by the discovery (1785) and publication (1812) of a MS. (Greek) of the *Roman Magistracies* of Joannes Lydus (born A.D. 490). From this (ii, 6) we learn that the *Lives* was dedicated to Septicius Clarus when praefect of the praetorian guard, which fixes the date of publication. Lydus no doubt possessed the complete work, the lost portion probably containing the title; the dedication; a genealogical table; Caesar's childhood and early upbringing. The oldest and best MS. of Suetonius is the Memmianus of the 9th century.

An extant treatise *De Grammaticis et Rhetoribus* (on Scholars and Rhetoricians) formed the last section of a larger work *De Viris Illustribus* (on Famous Men), which in addition treated of poets, orators, historians, and philosophers, from Cicero and Sallust down to the time of Domitian. It was used by Jerome, as he himself states, as the model for a work bearing the same name, which dealt with the great ecclesiastical writers, and his Latin translation of the *Chronicle* of Eusebius contains extracts from the work of Suetonius. In addition,

---

[1] Those who had not were prohibited from taking more than half of a legacy or inheritance bequeathed to them.

we possess short lives of Terence, Horace, Lucan, and the elder Pliny, while the *De Grammaticis* contains an account of 25 out of 36 scholars.

Suïdas (10th century), in his encyclopaedic lexicon, under the heading Τράγκυλλος (Tranquillus) gives the following list of lost works by Suetonius : *On the Greek Pastimes ; On the Roman Shows and Contests ; On the Roman Year ; On Critical Marks in Books ; On Cicero's Republic*, a reply to an attack by the Alexandrian grammarian, Didymus ; *On the Proper Names and Different Kinds of Garments, Shoes, and Other Articles of Wearing Apparel ; On Words of Ill Omen* or *Terms of Abuse and their Origin ; On Rome and its Manners and Customs*. In addition to these, we hear of the following, also lost : *On Offices of State ; On Bodily Defects ; On Famous Courtesans ; On the Kings* (of Europe, Asia, and Africa) ; an *Encyclopaedia* called Pratum (=Gr. λειμών, meadow, miscellany) in 10 books, in which probably some in the first list were included. Among them may be those specially referring to Rome, unless they form part of a work of similar character called *Roma*. Some of these compositions were, no doubt, written in Greek, a language in which Suetonius like his imperial master was proficient.

Suetonius cannot be regarded as an historian in the modern sense of the word ; in this capacity he is inferior to Tacitus and Dion Cassius. This is partly to be accounted for by the fact that the personality of the ruler bulked so largely in the public eye that the writer was unable to take a comprehensive view of the condition of the empire as a whole, and the historian was lost in the biographer. Criticisms are few and far between, such as the discussion of the birthplace of Caligula (Cal. 8), or of the motives which led Augustus to appoint Tiberius his successor in spite of his unfavourable opinion of him (Aug. 21). Important military, political, and constitutional matters are briefly handled ; we are told little or nothing of prominent figures such as Agrippa and Maecenas, while the imperial vices and debaucheries meet with full recognition. The last, indeed, are described in a matter-of-fact, almost indifferent, way ; there is nothing of the burning indignation of Tacitus, nor of the outspoken invectives of Juvenal. Like Dion Cassius, Suetonius is superstitious and shows a fondness for signs and wonders and marvellous tales, from which even Tacitus is not exempt. Like Tacitus, he was a supporter of the senatorial party, and is severe on those who took the opposite side. Even as a biographer, his lack of psychological insight renders him inferior to Plutarch and Tacitus (*Agricola*). He may be best described as an indefatigable collector of notes, a retailer of anecdotes gathered from all sources and put together without critical examination.

While private secretary to Hadrian, Suetonius had access to the imperial archives, the records of the decrees of the senate and of the *Acta* or proceedings of the same body, the last, although their publication was forbidden by Augustus, being carefully preserved and drawn up by a senator specially appointed. Besides these official documents, among which may be included particulars of the imperial testaments, his position at court enabled him to pick up all kinds of information. Whether the stories and backstairs gossip retailed by him are true or not, it is hardly possible that he could have invented them, and the impression left on one's mind is that he has set down impartially, without fear or favour, anything that he considered worth recording or likely to be of interest to his readers. In spite of its defects the work is of great value, partly as confirming or supplementing Tacitus and Dion Cassius, and partly as a storehouse of information as to the private life of the first Roman emperors. The younger Pliny describes Suetonius as " a most worthy, honourable, and learned man, whose character and erudition I have long kept in view ; the more I know of him, the more I become attached to him." Vopiscus, one of the writers of the *Augustan History*, calls him (*Life of Firmus*, 1) " a most careful and impartial writer."

The Lives are arranged according to a uniform scheme. First comes an account of the origin and ancestors of the emperor's family ; the doings of some of its distinguished members, male and female ; omens presaging his future greatness ; his education and early years ; his natural disposition, whether vicious or such as held out hopes, too often disappointed, of a happy reign. Chronology is limited to the date of birth and death. The style is clear, simple, and unpretentious. It never attains to the liveliness and brilliancy of that of Tacitus, although the accounts of the death of Caligula, and especially of Nero are vivid and picturesque. The work of Suetonius was continued by Marius Maximus (*c.* 165-250), who wrote the lives of the emperors from Nerva to Elagabalus, which supplied the greater part of the material for the early part of the *Augustan History*.

There is apparently no English monograph on Suetonius. For further information the reader may consult : Teuffel-Schwabe's *History of Roman Literature*, Eng. trans. by G. C. Warr, 1900 (later German edition, 1910-16) ; *Prolegomena* (in Latin) to C. L. Roth's text, 1886 ; E. S. Shuckburgh, *Life of Augustus*, 1896 ; M. S. Dimsdale, *History of Latin Literature*, 1915 ; M. Schanz, *History of Roman Literature* (German : 1896, 1905) ; and, above all, A. Macé, *Essai sur Suétone* (1900).

More than three hundred years after its publication, Holland's spirited and vigorous, if at times somewhat diffuse translation, cannot be said to be superseded and is not likely to be. Though generally accurate, in some passages he seems to have misunderstood his author ; it should further be remembered that the text has been considerably improved since he wrote. Other versions by the indefatigable " translator-general of his age " are those of the whole of Livy, Pliny's *Natural History*, Plutarch's *Morals*, Ammianus Marcellinus, and Xenophon's *Cyropaedia*. The well-known epigram on his voluminousness may fitly be quoted here :

> *Philemon with translations does so fill us,*
> *He will not let Suetonius be Tranquillus.*

THE TWELVE CAESARS

Julius Caesar (102 or 100 B.C.–44 B.C.), dictator, —44 B.C. ; Augustus (63 B.C.–A.D. 14), emperor, 27 B.C.–A.D. 14 ; Tiberius (42 B.C.–A.D. 37), emperor, A.D. 14–37 ; Caligula (A.D. 12–41), emperor, 37–41 ; Claudius (10 B.C.–A.D. 54), emperor, 41–54 ; Nero (A.D. 37–68), emperor, 54–68 ; Galba (3 B.C.–A.D. 69), emperor, June 68–Jan. 69 ; Otho (A.D. 32–69), emperor, A.D. 69, Jan. 15–April 16 ; Vitellius (A.D. 15–69), emperor, 69, Jan. 2–Dec. 22 ; Vespasian (A.D. 9–79), emperor, 69–79 ; Titus (A.D. 39 or 41–81), emperor, 79–81 ; Domitian (A.D. 51–96), emperor, 81–96.

EPISTLE DEDICATORY

To the Right Honorable and Vertuous Ladie
THE LADIE HARINGTON

MADAME, the late pestilence in Coventrie, which occasioned my translation etc. of this Historie, moved me also, in part, to addresse the same unto your Honour.

For being altogether restrained then, from free practise of my profession abroad, and no lesse impatient of idlenesse at home, I could not readily thinke of a better course to spend that vacation, than in an Argument having a reference to mine old Grammaticall Muses, and according, in some sort, with my latter studies in Physick. What howres, therfore, either the doubtful or diseased estate of my neighbours, together with the meditations of mine owne mortalitie would afford, I employed gladly in the said Subject.

Againe, for as much as the selfe same cause debarred me from accesse unto your house at Combe (a dutie that otherwise the vicinitie of our aboad did require) I fully resolved at the finishing of those my Sedentary labours, to present the same to your view: therby to sheild my selfe (whom it pleased you beforetime to grace with kind entertainment) from the just imputation of rude negligence in that behalfe. But now, since the same citie so dangerous the yeare before, is become a retyring place of safety for your Houshold, and hath to mee alreadie yeelded fit opportunitie to excuse my former absence personally by word of mouth, I have presumed nevertheles to dedicate the same unto your Honour, as a token of my thankefulnesse for your bounteous favour, farre above the proportion of my deserts, and an earnest penny of that propense minde, which I carie to honour your name, in the best manner I could devise.

xv

EPISTLE DEDICATORY

And verily calling to my remembrance how courteously you have vouchsafed heretofore to accept even at second hand my travailes in this kinde, and with good words testified oftentimes the contentment you received therin, I had no reason to doubt the like acceptance of that which out of a loving and devote heart I offer first unto your selfe.

Lastly, when I consider, how together with sincere pietie, rare wisdome, and other eminent vertues, there is seated in your person a singular affection to advance good literature, with an extraordinarie respect of learned men, I knew no means out of my small fortunes to do you greater honour, than by entituling you as Patronesse of that, which may benefit young Scholers, my countrimen, that would be learned : to give knowledge unto the word, that all the profit or pleasure whatsoever, which shall grow unto them, from these endeavours of mine, are derived immediatly from you and for your sake bestowed upon them.

These motives, right Honorable, as well of my first enterprise, as of chusing your Patronage, if it please you to approve, (the onely thing that I humbly crave at your hand for this present) I shall not only thinke my pains well taken and choise as well made : prising your acceptance to the worth of a competent guerdon : but also continue my hearty prayers unto the Almightie for your perfect health, proceeding in a vertuous course of life, with increase of true Honour here upon earth, and after the revolution of many new yeares, for eternall happinesse in the highest Heaven.

Your Honours most readie at command,

PHILEMON HOLLAND.

SUETONIUS

A SUPPLEMENT TO THE BEGINNING OF GAIUS JULIUS CAESAR, DICTATOR

THE Julian lineage, as most men are persuaded, is descended
from Ascanius Iulus, the son of Aeneas by Creusa; which
Iulus, after he had left Lavinium, built Long Alba[1], wherein
also he reigned. Others, grounding upon a more assured
evidence, have thought it good to derive the same rather from
Iulus, the son of Ascanius. For when, after the death of this
Ascanius, the kingdom of the Latins was devolved again[2] upon
Silvius the son of Aeneas and Lavinia, the charge of religion and
sacred ceremonies of the Latin and Trojan nation both remained yet still in the race and progeny of Iulus, out of which
are sprung the Julii. These Julii, with certain other most
noble families of Latium, Tullus Hostilius, king of the Romans,
after he had razed Alba, translated to Rome, and ranged
among the nobility. Late it was ere they rose and mounted
to high place of magistracy, but were reckoned almost in the
last rank of the patricians of ancient nobility; and of them
the Julii bare the principal name. For C. Julius (son of
Lucius), surnamed also Iulus, was consul together with P.
Pinarius Mamercinus Rufus, in the year after the foundation of
Rome city 264[3]; and seven years after[4], his son[5], with Q.
Fabius Vibulanus (consul) the second time. Again, some
space of time coming between, Vopiscus Julius, son of Gaius
and nephew of Lucius, bore the consulship with L. Aemilius
Mamercinus[6], third time consul, in the year 280[7]. I find likewise, that in the year 302[8] Gaius Julius, son of Gaius, and
nephew of Lucius, was a decemvir for the enacting and penning
of laws, and that in the former election of that magistracy;

as also that Gaius Julius, son of Gaius and nephew of Gaius, became consul with Marcus Geganius Macerinus, in the year 306 [9], and the self-same man a second time, with Lucius Verginius Tricostus, in the year 318 [10]; and immediately in the year next following [11], a third time, with the same Verginius now twice consul. And thus much for the Julii. For to rehearse and collect all them of that family, together with the honourable places of every one, which were many in number and of sundry kinds, is not our purpose; and besides, the thing itself is apparent and upon record in the public registers.

Moreover, I have observed in the Julian line a certain house also of the Mentones: and among them one Gaius Julius, colleague in the consulship with T. Quintus Pennus Cincinnatus, in the 322nd year after the foundation of the city. I find likewise Gaius Julius Denter to be master of the horsemen, when Gaius Claudius Crassus Sabinus Regillensis was dictator, for to hold their solemn assembly of election, in the year 405. There were besides of these Julii others going under the name of Libones, and of the same race one triumphed; to wit, Lucius Julius, son of Lucius and nephew of Lucius, companion in the consulate with Marcus Atilius Regulus, in the year 486 [12]. But as touching Gaius Julius, son of Lucius and surnamed Caesar Strabo, whom Suetonius also meant in the 55th chapter of Julius Caesar and Cicero praiseth in his *Brutus*, and in the second book of his *Orator*, I doubt whether this addition Strabo should not be taken as a byname. For otherwise there is in our hands a piece of silver coin, with the inscription of Lucius Julius, son of Lucius, and surnamed Strabo. The epigram [13] of the former is extant among the antiquities of Rome city, in this manner:

C. Julius, L. F. Caesar Strabo, Aed. Cur. Q. Trib. Mil. bis
XVIR AGR. Dand. ADTR. IVD. Pontif.

To conclude, I have met with writers, who reckoned also among the Julii certain Annales [14]; which, for mine own part verily, I could never yet light upon, in searching the records and chronicles. But in the eighth book of the *Familiar Epistles* (of Cicero), and namely in the [eighth] letter there, of M. Caelius unto Cicero, there is mention made among others, of one L. Julius, son of Lucius, Pomp.[15] Annalis, where the

writing (as I suppose) is not very certain and clearly acknowledged. For besides that the better corrected copies call him
Villius (for Julius), Livy also hath expressly and plainly
written in his fortieth book, that one Lucius Villius, a tribune
of the commons, made a law which provided and ordained, in
what year of men's age they might sue for every kind of
magistracy, and be capable thereof. Whereupon unto that
family was given this surname, to be called Annales. Thus far
Livius. Hereunto may be added this moreover ; that the
kindred Julia is reckoned in the tribe Fabia (and not Pomptina), as we have noted in the fortieth chapter of Augustus. I
am of opinion therefore, that safer it is to account the Annales
among the Villii, and not the Julii. But thus much hereof,
by the way, and as it were passing by ; now proceed we to the
rest.

In the lineage Julia, then, there was a family also of the
Caesars. But what the reason should be of that surname, it is
not certainly known ; no more than who he was, that first bore
the said surname. For before Caesar the dictator, and his
father and grandfather, there were Julii named Caesares. As
for example, he who (as Livy witnesseth in his 27th book) was
in the second Punic war sent from the senate to Crispinus the
consul, about the nomination of a dictator. As for the term
Caesares, those usually the Roman tongue surnamed so, who
were born, either by ripping their mother's womb [16], or with a
bush of hair growing on their heads [17], or else grey-eyed [18]. Some
add, moreover, the tale of an elephant slain in Africa, which
the inhabitants there call caesar ; and upon that very cause
this surname first befell unto Caesar the dictator's grandsire.
But Spartianus and Servius, the authors hereof, are of the
meanest credit and authority. For not his progeny alone of
all the Julii had this surname, but many others besides of his
house and kindred, both long before and also together with
him.

Consuls before Julius Caesar the dictator there were,
Sext. Julius, son of Gaius, nephew of Lucius, together with
Lucius Aurelius Orestes, in the year after the foundation of
Rome 596 [19] : also Sext. Julius, son of Gaius, nephew of Sextus,
was colleague with L. Marcius Philippus in the beginning of
the Social war in the year after the city's foundation 662 [20], and

in the next year after, Lucius Julius, son of Lucius and nephew of Lucius, bore the consulate with Pub. Rutilius Lupus. Neither before these were any of the Caesars renowned or advanced to the highest office of state [21]. Many years after, out of the same family, Lucius Caesar, son of Sextus and cousin-german [22] to that C. Julius Caesar, who begat the dictator and attained only to the praetorship, who also died at Pisae without any evident sickness, even as he did his shoes on in a morning, that L. Caesar, I say, came to be consul.

Well, Caesar the dictator was born at Rome (when Gaius Marius and Lucius Valerius Flaccus were consuls) upon the fourth day before the ides of Quintilis, which month after his death was by virtue of the Antonian law called for that cause July. His bringing up he had with his mother Aurelia, daughter of Gaius Cotta, and his aunt by the father's side Julia, the wife of Marius. Whereupon grew the love that he took (a patrician though he were) to the plebeian faction, and the hatred he bore to Sulla. The Greek and Latin tongue, the precepts also and rules of oratory, he learned of M. Antonius Gnipho, a Frenchman born. Who, being of an excellent wit and singular memory, courteous besides in his behaviour and of a kind and gentle nature, taught the Greek and Latin grammar and rhetoric withal, first in the house of Gaius Caesar his father, afterwards in his own ; and got much thereby, such was the bounty of his scholars, considering that he never compounded with them for any wages or reward. Now was this Caesar wondrous docible [23] and apt to learn, yea, and framed naturally for eloquence.

His Latin speech was trimly garnished (through domestic acquaintance) by his mother Aurelia, a woman that spoke the Roman tongue purely and elegantly : like as the Muciae, Laeliae, Corneliae, and other right honourable dames did, in whose families there arose orators of great name.

4

THE HISTORY OF
GAIUS JULIUS CAESAR
DICTATOR

1. CAESAR in the sixteenth year of his age lost his father [a] ;
and in the year following [1], being elected flamen Dialis [b], he
cast off Cossutia (a gentlewoman born, but very wealthy),
affianced unto him during his childhood, and espoused Cornelia, the daughter of Cinna, four times consul, who bare unto
him soon after his daughter Julia ; neither could he by any
means be forced by Sulla the dictator to put her away [2] [c].
Whereupon, deprived of his sacerdotal dignity, losing the
dowry in the right of his wife, and forfeiting all his heritages [d]
descended unto him from his lineage and name, he was reputed one of the contrary faction [3], insomuch as he was constrained to hide his head [4], and, albeit the quartan ague hung
sore upon him, to change almost every night his starting-
holes [5] wherein he lurked, yea, and to redeem himself with a
piece of money out of the inquisitors' hands that made search
for him [e], until such time as, by the mediation of the religious
Vestal virgins [f], by the means also of Mamercus Aemilius and
Aurelius Cotta, his near kinsfolk [6] and allied unto him, he
obtained pardon.   Certain it is that Sulla, when he had denied
a good while the request of those right worshipful persons and
his singular good friends entreating in his behalf, and yet they
persisted earnest suitors still for him, being thus importuned
and at length overcome, broke forth aloud into these words,
either in a divine prescience, or some pregnant conjecture,
" Go to " (quoth he) " my masters ; take him to you, since ye
will needs have it so ; but know this withal, that he, whose life
and safety ye so much desire, will one day be the overthrow of
the nobles, whose side ye have maintained with me ; for in
this Caesar there be many Mariuses."

2. The first time that Caesar served in the wars was in Asia, and that in the domestic retinue [a] of Marcus Thermus the praetor[1]; by whom being sent into Bithynia for to levy a fleet, he made his abode with king Nicomedes, not without a foul rumour raised that he prostituted his body to be abused by the king; which rumour he augmented himself by coming again into Bithynia within few days, under a colour of calling for certain money, which should be due to a libertine[2][b] and client[c] of his. The rest of his soldiery he carried with better fame and reputation; and at the winning of Mytilenae Thermus honoured him with a civic garland[d].

3. He was a soldier also under Servilius Isauricus[1] in Cilicia, but it was not long; for upon certain intelligence given of Sulla his death, and the hope withal of the new dissension that was stirred and set on foot by M. Lepidus[a], he returned in all haste to Rome. And notwithstanding he was mightily solicited by many large offers and fair promises, yet forbare he to join in society with Lepidus, partly distrusting his nature, and in part doubting the present opportunity, which he found nothing answerable to his expectation.

4. Howbeit, when that civil discord and sedition was appeased[a], he judicially accused for extortion[1] Cornelius Dolabella, a man who had been consul and triumphed. But seeing that the defendant was found unguilty and acquitted, he determined to retire himself unto the city of Rhodes, as well to decline[2] the hatred of the world[3], as by occasion of that leisure and repose to learn the art of oratory under Apollonius Molo[4], a most renowned rhetorician in those days. As he crossed the seas thitherward (being now winter-time[5]) his fortune was, about the isle Pharmacusa, to be taken by rovers, and with them he remained in custody (not without exceeding indignation[6]) for the space well-near of forty days, accompanied with one physician and two grooms of his chamber. For his companions and the rest of his servants[7] belonging to his train, he had sent away[8] immediately at the very first to procure him money with all speed for his ransom. After this, upon the payment unto them of fifty talents[9], being set ashore, he delayed no time, but presently[10] put his fleet to sea again, embarked, and never gave over pursuing the said pirates, until he had overtaken them; and no sooner were they within his power but, as he oftentimes had threatened in mirth, he put them all to death. Now while Mithridates wasted the countries next adjoining, because he would not be thought to sit still and do nothing in this dangerous and doubtful state of confederate nations and allies to the Romans, he left Rhodes, whither he had directly bent his course, gathered a power of auxiliary soldiers, expelled the governor under the king out of the province, and so kept the cities and states in their allegiance, which were wavering and at the point of revolt.

5. In his military tribuneship [a], which was the first dignity after his return to Rome that befell unto him by the voices and election of the people, he assisted with all his might those patrons of the commons [1] who stood out for the restitution of their tribunes' authority, the force and strength whereof Sulla had abated. He effected moreover thus much, by virtue of an act proposed by Plotius [2][b], that L. Cinna, his wife's brother, and they who together with him in the time of the civil discord abovesaid took part with Lepidus, and after the consul's [3] death fled unto Sertorius, might return safely into the city and enjoy their freedom. As touching which matter himself made an oration before the body of the people.

6. Being quaestor [1], he made, as the ancient manner was, funeral orations out of the public pulpit called Rostra, in the praise of Julia, his aunt by the father's side and of his wife Cornelia, both late deceased. And in the commendation verily of his said aunt, speaking of the pedigree and descent by both sides, namely of herself and also of her father, he maketh report in these terms : " Mine aunt Julia " (quoth he) " by her mother is lineally descended from kings, and by her father united with the race of the immortal gods : for from Ancus Marcius are derived the Marcii surnamed Reges, that is, kings, which name my mother was styled with ; and from Venus the Julii draw their original, of which house and name is our family. So then in this stock there concur and meet together, as well the sanctity and sacred majesty of kings, who among men are most powerful, as the religious ceremonies and service of the gods, in whose power kings themselves are." In the place of Cornelia departed, he wedded Pompeia, daughter of Q. Pompeius, and niece to L. Sulla. But her afterward he divorced, suspecting that she had been naught[2] with P. Clodius, of whom there went so constant a report abroad, how at the celebration of certain public divine ceremonies he, being disguised in woman's apparel, had access secretly unto her, that the senate by decree directed a commission to justices inquisitors, for to sit upon the pollution of those sacred rites and mysteries[3].

7. During his quaestorship, it fell unto him by lot to execute his office in the farther province of Spain[1], where, whenas by the commandment of the lord-praetor[2] he rode his circuit to keep the assizes[3], and came to Gades, beholding advisedly the image or portrait of Alexander the Great in the temple of Hercules there, at the sight thereof he fetched a deep sigh; yea, and as one displeased and irked with his own slothfulness, in that he had performed yet no memorable act at those years[4], wherein Alexander had conquered the whole world, he presently made earnest suit for his discharge and licence to depart, thereby to take the first opportunity of all occasions to compass greater enterprises at home within the city. Being, moreover, much disquieted and dismayed with a dream the night before (for he imagined in his sleep that he had carnal company with his own mother) the diviners and wizards incited him to the hopes of most glorious achievements, making this exposition of his dream, that thereby was portended unto him the sovereignty of the whole world, considering that his mother whom he saw under him betokened naught else but the subjection of the earth, which is counted the mother of all things.

8. Departing therefore thence before his time was fully expired, he went unto the Latin colonies[a], which were now devising and in council to sue for the freedom of the city of Rome; and no doubt had solicited and excited them to attempt some tumult and trouble in the State, but that the consuls, for the avoiding of this very danger, kept back the legions for a while, which were enrolled for to be sent into Cilicia.

9. And yet, for all that, soon after he projected greater designs within the city. For not many days before he entered upon his aedileship, he was suspected to have conspired with M. Crassus (a man of consular degree[1]), with P. Sulla likewise and P.[2] Autronius (who, after they were consuls elect, stood condemned for suing indirectly and by corruption for that place), to set upon the body of the senate in the beginning of their year ; and that, after they had massacred whom it pleased them, M. Crassus should usurp the dictatorship ; himself be chosen by him master of the horsemen ; and so, when they had settled the State at their pleasure, Sulla and Autronius should be restored again unto their consulship. Of this conspiracy, Tanusius Geminus maketh mention in his story[3], M. Bibulus in his edicts, and C. Curio the elder[4] in his orations. Cicero likewise seemeth to signify as much in a certain epistle unto Axius, wherein he reporteth that Caesar established in his consulship that kingdom and royal government, which he plotted and thought upon when he was aedile. Tanusius writeth farther, that Crassus, either repenting himself, or else upon fear, was not present nor kept the day appointed for the said massacre, and therefore Caesar neither gave that signal, which by agreement he should have given. Now agreed it was, as Curio saith, that he should let his gown fall from his shoulders. The same Curio, yea, and M. Actorius Naso do write, that he conspired also with Cn. Piso, a noble young gentleman, who, being in suspicion for a conspiracy within the city, had the province of Spain extraordinarily and without his own suit bestowed upon him ; and complotted it was, that both he in foreign parts abroad and himself also at Rome should at once make an insurrection for to alter the State, and that by the occasion and means of the Lambranes[5] and inhabitants beyond the Po. But the design both of the one and the other was defeated and frustrated by reason of Piso his death[6].

10. When he was aedile, besides the comitium[a], the marketplace, and stately halls of justice, he beautified the Capitol also with fair open galleries built for the present occasion, to stand only during the public shows and plays ; wherein if the number of images, statues, and painted tables fell out to be greater than was needful, part of that furniture and provision might be set forth to the view of all men. As for the chasing and baiting of wild beasts, the stage-plays and solemn sights, he exhibited them both jointly with his companion in office and also severally by himself. Whereby it came to pass that, howsoever the

charges of these solemnities were borne in common by them
both, yet he alone went away with all the honour and thanks
thereof ; neither did M. Bibulus his colleague dissemble the
matter, but utter as much, when he said that the same befell
unto him which befell unto Pollux : " For like as " (quoth he)
" the temple erected in the common market-place of Rome unto
both the twin-brethren [1] beareth the name of Castor alone, even
so my munificence in expense and Caesar's together in setting
out these games and plays goeth under the name of Caesar
only." Caesar over and above did exhibit another show of
sword-fight even at the sharpe [2], but he brought into the place
fewer couples of champions by a good many than he purposed [3];
for, buying up (as he did) such a sort of fencers from all parts
out of every school, and putting his adversaries of the other
faction in great affright thereby, he gave occasion unto the
State to provide, by a special act in that behalf, for a certain
set number of sword-players, above which no man might
retain any at Rome.

11. Thus when he had gained the hearts and favour of the
people, he gave [1] the attempt by some of the tribunes [2] and
sued to have the province of Egypt by an act of the commons
conferred upon him, taking occasion to make suit for this
extraordinary government ; for that the Alexandrians had
driven their king [3] out of his realm, whom the senate had
styled with the title of ally and friend, an act of theirs generally
misliked. Howbeit, he could not carry it, by reason that the
faction of the nobles crossed him. Whose authority because
he would by way of quittance infringe and impair by all means
possible, the trophies and victorious monuments of C. Marius
for subduing king Jugurtha, the Cimbrians, and the Teutons,
which beforetime had been demolished and cast down by
Sulla, he erected and set up again [4]. Also, in sitting upon a
commission for the examination of murderers [5], he reckoned
those in the number of them, who in the time of the proscription had received money out of the public treasury for bringing
in the heads of Roman citizens [a], notwithstanding they were
excepted by virtue of the Cornelian laws [b] .

12. Moreover, he suborned one and set him on [a] to indict
C. Rabirius of high treason [b], by whose help especially, some
years before, the senate had repressed and restrained the

seditious tribuneship of L. Saturninus : and being by lot chosen a judge delegate[1] to pass sentence on the prisoner, so willing he was to condemn him that, when Rabirius appealed unto the people [c], nothing did him so much good as the rigour of the judge[2].

13. Having laid aside all hope of the aforesaid province[1], he stood to be the highest priest, not without excessive and most lavish largesse. Wherein, considering how deeply he engaged himself in debt, the same morning that he was to go unto the assembly for the election, when his mother kissed him he told her (by report) aforehand, that he would never return home but pontiff. And so far overweighed he two most mighty competitors[a], who otherwise for age and dignity much outwent him, that in their own tribes he alone carried more voices than both of them in all throughout[2].

14. Being created praetor[1], whenas the conspiracy of Catiline was detected, and all the senate generally awarded no lighter punishment than death[2] for as many as were parties and accessory in that action, he only gave his sentence : that their goods should be confiscate, and themselves put into several free cities and boroughs under the people of Rome, and there to be kept in ward ; and furthermore he put them in so great a fright that gave sharper censure (intimating eft-soons and setting before their eyes the exceeding great hatred of the Roman communalty, which in time to come they should incur) that Decimus Silanus, consul elect, was not abashed nor unwilling to mollify his own award[3], with a gentle exposition (because it had been a shame to alter it and eat his own words) as if it had been taken and construed in a harder sense than he meant it. And verily prevailed he had and gone clear away with it (for many there were already drawn to his side, and among the rest Cicero[4], the consul's[5] brother), but that a speech made by M. Cato emboldened the whole house, and confirmed all the senators in their former sentence, who now were at the point to yield unto him. And yet for all this he ceased not to hinder their proceedings, until such time as a troop of Roman knights, who stood round about the place in arms for guard and defence[6], threatened to dispatch him out of the way, in case he continued still in his obstinate contumacy, holding and shaking their drawn swords so near unto him, as that his next fellows forsook him as he sat with them, and very few, taking him in their arms and putting their gowns between [7], hardly and with much ado saved him from violence. Then was he scared indeed, insomuch as he not only condescended unto them, but also for the rest of that year [8] forbare to come into the senate-house.

15. The very first day of his praetorship, he convented [summoned] Q. Catulus before the body of the people to receive their order upon a matter to be discussed by them [a], as touching re-edification of the Capitol, having withal promulged a law [b], by virtue whereof he transferred the charge of that work unto another [1]. But not able to match the nobles and better sort [c], nor to make his part good with them drawing in one line [2], as they did, whom he saw in great frequency to run by heaps together, so fully bent to make resistance, that presently they left their officious [3] attendance upon the new consuls [d], he gave over this action.

16. But whereas Caecilius Metellus [1], a tribune of the commons, proposed most turbulent and seditious laws, malgré his colleagues with all their opposition, he showed himself a stout abetter and maintainer of him, most stiffly bearing him out in the cause, so long until both of them were by an injunction and decree of the senators removed from the administration of the commonwealth. Howbeit, presuming nevertheless to continue in his magistracy and to execute his jurisdiction, when he understood once that some were ready to prohibit him by force and arms, he sent away his serjeants [lictors], cast off his embroidered purple robe [a], and retired privily to his own house, minding there to keep himself quiet in regard of the troublesome time. And when, two days after, the multitude flocked unto him willingly and of their own accord, promising after a very tumultuous manner their help and assistance in the recovery of his former place and dignity, he repressed them. Which thing happening thus beyond all expectation, the senate, which was hastily met together about that riot and uproar, gave him hearty thanks, and that by the principal and noblest personages among them, sent for him into the Curia [b], and after they had in most honourable terms commended him, they restored him fully to his office, and reversed their former decree.

17. He fell again into another new trouble and danger, being called into question as one of Catiline's conspiracy, both before the quaestor Novius Niger in his house, and that by L. Vettius who impeached him [1]; and also in the senate, by [Q.] Curius, unto whom, for that he detected first the plots and designs of the conspirators, were rewards appointed by the State. Curius deposed that he knew so much by Catiline, and Vettius promised to bring forth even his own handwriting which he gave unto Catiline. But this was such an indignity as Caesar in nowise thought tolerable ; whereupon, craving the testimony of Cicero, by which he proved that himself merely of his own accord had given some information unto him of the said conspiracy, he prevailed so much that Curius went without those rewards. As for Vettius, after his goods were arrested and stresses taken [2], his household stuff rifled, himself evil entreated, beaten, and in the open assembly of the multitude even before the Rostra well-near pulled in pieces, him he clapt up in prison. After the same sort he served Novius the quaestor, because he suffered him, a superior magistrate of state [a], to be accused and defamed in his house.

18. After this praetorship of his [1], having the government of the farther province in Spain allotted unto him, he took order [2] with his creditors, that were in hand to stay him, by the means of certain sureties [a] who came in and undertook for him ; and before the governors of the provinces were disposed of by the State, with commissions sealed for their jurisdiction and other affairs, with allowance and furniture also set out for them accordingly, he, contrary to all right and custom, put himself in his journey. Were it for fear of some judicial proceeding intended against him whiles he was a private person, or because he might more speedily succour the allies of the Romans, who craved help, it is uncertain. Well, when he had settled the province in peace, he made as great haste to be gone ; and not expecting a successor he departed, as well to ride in triumph as to take upon him the consulship. But after the writs and proclamations were out for the great assembly to election (of consuls), when he might not be pricked nor propounded (consul) unless he entered the city in quality of a private citizen, and many withstood him [3], labouring as he did to be dispensed with for the laws, forced he was, for fear of being put by [4] the consulship, to forgo his triumph [b].

19. Of the two competitors with him for the consulship, to wit, L. Lucceius and M. Bibulus, he made choice of Lucceius to be his companion in office, upon this compact and condition that, since he was a man not so gracious, but better monied than himself, he should of his own purse pronounce in the name of both, and promise to deal moneys among the centuries [a]. Which device being known, the nobles [1] and great men, who were afraid that, being once a sovereign magistrate [2], and having a colleague ready at his beck to agree and consent with him, he would both dare and do any thing, persuaded with Bibulus to make promise of as great a donation as the other did, and the most part of them contributed their moneys thereunto. Yea, Cato himself verily was not against it, but said this largesse stood with the good of the weal public. Hereupon created consul he was with Bibulus. For the same cause, the said nobles and principal persons of the city gave order that the consuls for this year following should have the provinces [b] and commissions of least affair and importance, to wit, the looking unto forests and woods [c], unto lanes and paths [d]. Caesar, taking this wrong and disgrace most to the heart, made court all that ever he could unto Pompey, who had taken offence against the senators, for that, having vanquished king Mithridates, his acts and decrees were no sooner ratified and confirmed. He reconciled also unto Pompey M. Crassus, an old enemy ever since that consulship, which they bare together with exceeding much jarring and disagreement ; he entered likewise into a society [e] with them both, upon this contract, that nothing should be done or pass in the administration of the commonweal, that displeased any of them three.

20. When he was entered into this honourable place of consulship, he (first of all that ever were) ordained that all acts, as well of senate as people, should day by day, as they were concluded [a], be recorded also and published. He brought in likewise the ancient custom again, that in what month he had not the knitches of rods with axes borne before him [b], a public officer called accensus [c] should huisher [1] him before, and the serjeants or lictors follow after behind. Having promulged

an agrarian law, as touching the division of lands among the
commons, when his fellow-consul withstood and resisted his
proceedings, he drove him out of the common place[2], by
violence and force of arms. The morrow after, when the said
Bibulus had made his complaint in the senate of this outrage,
and there could not one be found that durst move the house
about so great a garboile[3] and hurly-burly as that was, nor
give his censure thereof (as oftentimes in lighter tumults[4]
and stirs there had passed many decrees), he drove him to such
a desperate fear that, until he went quite out of his magistracy,
he kept close within house and never prohibited any proceedings else[5] but by way of edict[6]. From that time forward,
Caesar alone managed all the affairs of state, even as he would
himself ; insomuch as divers citizens, pleasantly conceited,
whensoever they signed, subscribed, or dated any writings to
stand upon record, would merrily put it down thus, Such a
thing was done, not when Caesar and Bibulus, but when Julius
and Caesar were consuls, setting down one and the same man
twice, by his name and surname ; yea, and soon after these
verses were commonly current abroad :

> *Non Bibulo quidquam nuper, sed Caesare, factum est :*
> *Nam Bibulo fieri consule nil memini.*

> Caesar of late did many things, but Bibulus not one ;
> For naught by consul Bibulus can I remember done.

The Stellatine champaign fields, held consecrated and
religious by our ancestors, together with the Campanian
territory[7], reserved to yield rent and pay tribute for a subsidy
to the commonweal, he divided without casting lots[8], among
20,000 citizens who could show three children or more[d]. The
publicans[e] making request for some easement he relieved[9] by
striking off a third part of their rents, and warned them openly
that, in the setting and letting of the new commodities and
revenues of the city, they should not bid and offer too much.
All other things likewise he gave and granted, according as
every man's mind and desire stood thereto, and no man gainsaid him ; but went any about to thwart him, he was soon
frighted away. M. Cato, when he seemed to interrupt and
stop his proceedings, he caused to be haled violently out of
the senate-house by an officer, and committed to prison. As

L. Lucullus stoutly withstood his doings, he put him into so great a fear of sundry actions and criminations, that he was glad to come and fall down before him at his knees. When Cicero, pleading upon a time in court, had lamented the woeful state of those times, the very same day, at the ninth hour thereof [10], he brought P. Clodius his enemy to be adopted into the house and name of a commoner, one who long before had laboured in vain to go from the nobles and be incorporate among the commons. Last of all, it is credibly reported that he induced by rewards, against all those in general of the contrary faction, an impeacher [11] to profess that he was solicited by some for to murder Pompey ; who, being produced forth by him before the body of the people, nominated (as he had instructions, and as it was agreed between them afore) those that set him a-work. But when one or two of them were named to no purpose, nor without pregnant suspicion of some fraudulent practice, he, despairing the good success of so rash and inconsiderate a project, poisoned the party whom he had suborned [12], and made him away for telling any more tales.

21. About the same time, he took to wife Calpurnia, the daughter of L. Piso, who was to succeed him in the consulate, and affianced his own daughter Julia unto Pompey, rejecting and casting off her former spouse Servilius Caepio [1], by whose help especially a little before he had impugned Bibulus. After this new contracted affinity, he began (in council) to ask Pompey's opinion first [a], whereas before he was wont to begin with Crassus ; notwithstanding also the custom was, that the consul should observe that order all the year following, in asking the senators' sentences, which he began with the first day of January.

22. Being backed therefore by the favour and assistance of his wife's father [1] and son-in-law [2], out of all that choice of provinces he chose especially the Gauls, the wealth and commodity whereof might fit his hand, and minister matter sufficient of triumphs [a]. And verily at the first, by virtue of the Vatinian law [b], he took upon him the government of Gallia Cisalpina [c] together with Illyricum ; soon after, by the means of the senate, that also which was called Comata [d], for the nobility feared lest, if they had denied him it, the people would have bestowed the same also upon him. With joy whereof he grew so haughty and proud, that he could not hold and temper himself, but after some few days made his boast in a frequent [3] senate-house, that he had gotten now what he desired, in despite of his adversaries and full sore against their wills, and therefore from that time forward would insult upon all their heads [e] ; whereupon, when one by way of reproach denied that, and said that it was no easy matter for a woman so to do, he answered again, as it were alluding merrily to another sense, that even in Assyria there some time reigned queen Semiramis, and that the women named Amazons [f] held in times past a great part of Asia in subjection.

23. When he had borne his consulship, C. Memmius and L. Domitius, praetors for the time being, put to question his acts passed the former year [1] ; whereupon he referred the examination and censure thereof unto the body of the senate, but seeing they would not undertake the thing, after three days spent to no purpose in vain brables [2] and altercations, he departed into his province. And immediately his quaestor [3], for to prejudice him [a], was drawn into trouble and indicted upon certain crimes. Within a while himself also was brought judicially to his trial and accused by L. Antistius, a tribune of the commons ; but, by appealing unto the college of the tribunes, he prevailed through their favour thus much (in regard of his absence about the affairs of commonweal) that he should not be liable to the accusation. For his better security therefore against future times, he travailed much to oblige and make beholden unto him the magistrates every year ; and, of those competitors who sued for any honourable office, to help or suffer none other to come unto the place, but such as covenanted with him, and undertook to defend and maintain him in his absence [4]. For assurance of which their covenant, he stuck not to require of some an oath, yea, and a bill [5] of their own hands.

24. But when L. Domitius, a candidate for the consulship [a], threatened openly that, were he once consul, he would effect that which he could not while he was praetor, yea, and take from him his armies, he made means to draw Crassus and Pompey unto Luca, a city within his province ; with whom he dealt effectually that, for to give Domitius the repulse, they should both sue for themselves to be consuls the second time, and also labour that his government might be prorogued or

continued for five years longer ; and he effected both. Upon
this confidence he presumed to assume unto those legions,
which he had received from the State, others beside, maintained partly at the city's charges, and in part with his own
private purse. And one legion above the rest, enrolled from
out of the countries beyond the Alps, he termed by a French
word, for named it was Alauda[1]. Which, being trained in
military discipline, armed also and set out after the Roman
fashion, he afterwards enfranchised throughout and made free
of Rome. Neither from this time forward forbare he any occasion of war, were it never so unjust or dangerous, picking
quarrels as well with confederate nations as those that were
enemies, savage and barbarous, whom he provoked to take
arms ; insomuch as the senate one time decreed to send certain
ambassadors for to survey and visit the state of the Gauls ;
yea, and some were of opinion[2] that he should be delivered
unto the enemies' hands. But by reason that his affairs sped
well and had good success, he obtained in regard thereof
solemn supplications [b] both oftener and to hold more days than
ever any man did (before himself).

25. During the time of his provincial government, which
continued nine years' space, these, in manner, were the acts
which he performed. All that part of Gaul, which from the
forest and mountain Pyrenees, the Alps, and the hill Cebenna is
enclosed within the rivers Rhine and Rhone, containing in
circuit 3200 miles, not accounting the associate cities and
states who had deserved well of the people of Rome, he reduced
into the form of a province, and imposed upon them a payment
of tribute yearly. The Germans inhabiting beyond the Rhine
he of all the Romans first assailed by means of a bridge which
he built over the said river, and those he grievously plagued
and gave them many great overthrows. He set upon the
Britons also, a people beforetime unknown, whom he vanquished and compelled both to pay money and also to deliver
hostages. In so many prosperous battles and fortunate
exploits he tasted of adverse fortune thrice only and no more ;
once in Britain, when his fleet had like to have been lost and
cast away in a violent tempest ; a second time in Gaul, where
a legion of his was discomfited and put to flight, near unto
Gergovia ; and last of all, in the marches of Germany, when

Titurius and Aurunculeius his lieutenants were forelaid [1] by an ambush and put to the sword.

26. Within the compass of which very same time, he lost by death, first, his mother [1], then his daughter Julia, and not long after his niece [2] by the said daughter. And in this meanwhile, the commonwealth being much troubled and astonied at the murder of Clodius [3], when the senate thought good there should be but one consul created, namely, Pompey, he dealt with the tribunes of the commons (who intended that he should be the colleague in office with Pompey) to propose this rather unto the people : that they would grant leave unto him in his absence, whensoever the term of his government drew toward an end, to sue for his second consulship, because he might not be constrained upon that occasion, and whiles the war was yet unfinished, to depart out of his province. Which when he had once obtained at their hands, reaching now at higher matters and full of hopes, there was no kind of largesse, no manner of dutiful office, either in public to the whole city or privately unto any person, that he omitted and left undone. His forum or stately hall he began to build with the money raised of the spoils gotten in wars ; the very plot of ground whereon it should stand cost him *millies sestertium* [a] and above [4]. He pronounced also a solemn sword-fight and feast unto the people in the honour and memorial of his daughter, a thing that never any man did before him. And to cause an expectation of these solemnities in the highest degree, the viands and whatsoever pertained unto the feast, albeit he had agreed with butchers and victuallers for the same at a certain price, he provided nevertheless by his household servants. All the notable and well-known sword-players, when and wheresoever they fought so as, upon the mislike and displeasure of the beholders, they were in danger to be killed in the place at their commandment, he took order [18] and charged they should be had away by force and reserved for himself. As for new fencers and young beginners, he trained them neither in any public school, nor under professed masters of that faculty, but at home in private houses, by gentlemen of Rome [5], yea, and senators also, such as were skilful in their weapon and in feats of arms, praying and beseeching them earnestly (as appeareth in his epistles unto them) to take the charge of every one severally, and to have a special care to instruct each one, and give them rules in their exercises. The legionary soldiers' pay in money he doubled for ever. And so often as there was plenty of corn, he gave them their allowance of it without stint and measure, and otherwhile he bestowed upon every one a slave or bondservant, yea, and possessions by the poll[6].

27. Moreover, to retain still the bond of acquaintance, affinity, and good-will of Pompey, Octavia, his sister's niece[1], wedded unto C. Marcellus, he affianced and made sure unto him ; but withal he craved his daughter to wife, promised in marriage before unto Faustus Sulla. Having thus obliged and brought to his devotion all those about him, yea, and the greater number of senators, by crediting out his money unto them, either gratis, or upon a slight consideration, those also of other sorts and degrees, either invited kindly by himself or resorting unto him of their own accord, he gratified with a most magnificent and bounteous congiary[a]. The freedmen besides, yea, and the servants and pages belonging to every one, according as any of them were in favour with their lord and master[2], tasted of his liberality. Moreover, there was not a man sued in court judicially and in danger of the law ; there was not any deeply engaged and indebted unto his creditors ; there were no prodigal young spendthrifts, but he was their only supporter, and most ready at all assays[3] to help them, unless they were those that either had committed such grievous crimes, or were so low brought, or had been so excessive in riot as that they could not possibly be relieved by him. For such as these, he would say in plain terms and openly, there was no other remedy but civil war.

28. No less careful and studious was he to allure unto him the hearts of kings, yea, and whole provinces throughout the world ; unto some offering in free gift the delivery of captives and prisoners by thousands at a time ; unto others sending aid secretly and underhand without authority or commission of senate and people, whither and as often as they would ; and more than this, adorning with goodly building and excellent pieces of work the mightiest cities in Italy, Gaul, Spain, yea, and of Asia and Greece. This he did so long, until all men now were astonied thereat : and when they cast with themselves whereto this might tend, at last M. Claudius Marcellus the consul, after a preface and preamble made to his edict, namely, that he would speak as touching the main point of the commonweal, proposed unto the senate that, forasmuch as the war was now ended and peace abroad established, there might be one sent to succeed him, before his time was fully expired ; also, that the victorious army ought of right to be dismissed and have their discharge from warfare ; item, that in the high court and assembly for the consuls' election, his name should not be propounded, considering Pompey afterwards had annulled that act of the people a (by virtue whereof it was granted that he might be chosen consul in his absence). Now it had fallen out so, that he, making a law as touching the right of magistrates, in that chapter and branch thereof, wherein he disabled those who were absent for being capable of honours and dignities, forgat to except Caesar ; and soon after, when the said law was once engrossed and engraven in brass, and so laid up in the treasury, corrected his error and oversight. Neither was Marcellus content to deprive Caesar of his provinces, and to put him by [18] the privilege of a former act passed in especial favour of him, but he made a motion moreover, that those inhabitants, whom by the Vatinian law Caesar had planted in the colony of Novum Comum, should lose the freedom which they had as citizens of Rome ; for that this prerogative of theirs had been granted by ambitious means, and beyond that prescript number which was appointed and warranted by the decree in that behalf.

29. Caesar, highly displeased and troubled at these proceedings, and judging it (as he was heard by report many times to give out) a harder matter for him, a principal man of the city, to be deposed and thrust down from the highest and first place of degree into the second, then from the second into the lowest and last of all, withstood him with all his might and power, partly by the opposition and negative voice of the tribunes, and in part by Servius Sulpicius the other consul. Also, in the year following, when C. Marcellus, who succeeded his cousin-german by the father's side, Marcus, in the consulship, assayed to bring the same about, he bribed and made sure unto him, with a mighty sum of money, Aemilius Paulus, companion with him in office, and C. Curio [1], a most violent tribune, to stick unto him and defend his honour. But seeing all things carried still against him more obstinately than before, and the new consuls elect take the contrary side and bent another way, he wrote unto the senate, and by his letters humbly besought them, not to suffer the benefit granted unto him by the people to be taken from him ; or if they did, yet to give order that other generals likewise, as well as he, might leave their armies ; presuming confidently, as men think, upon this [that] himself should be able, whensoever he pleased, to assemble together his soldiers more easily then Pompey to levy new. But with his adversaries he would have treated by way of capitulation in these terms : that, after he had discharged and sent away eight legions, and given over the province of Gaul beyond the Alps, he might be allowed two legions with the province on this side the Alps ; or if not so, yet at leastwise one, together with Illyricum, until such time as he were created consul.

30. But perceiving that the senate came not between nor interposed their authority to stop the course intended against him, and his adversaries denied flatly to admit all manner of capitulating and composition concerning the commonwealth, he passed into the hither part of Gaul ; and having kept the assizes there and executed his provincial jurisdiction, stayed at Ravenna, with full resolution to be revenged by open war, in case there had passed from the senate any sharp and cruel decree, touching the tribunes of the commons opposing themselves in his behalf and quarrel ; and verily this was the colour and occasion which he pretended of civil war ; yet men think there were some other causes and motives thereto. Pompey was wont to give out that, forasmuch as Caesar was not able of himself and with his own private wealth, either to consummate and finish those stately works and edifices which he had begun, or to satisfy the expectation of the people which he had raised and wrought of his coming, therefore he intended to trouble the State and set all on a garboile [20]. Others say that he feared lest he should be compelled to give an account of those things which in his first consulship he had done against the sacred auspices, the laws, and prohibitions of the tribunes [a] (in the name of the people), considering that M. Cato had threatened and professed eft-soons, and not without

an oath, that no sooner should he and his army be parted, but
he would judicially call his name in question and bring him to
his answer ; also, for that it was commonly spoken abroad that,
if he returned once in quality of a private person, he should
after the example of Milo plead before the judges, with a guard
of armed men about the court and tribunal. And this seemeth
to be more probable by that which Asinius Pollio writeth, who
reporteth that, in the battle of Pharsalus, when he beheld his
adversaries before his face, slain and put to flight, he uttered
this speech word for word : " Lo ! this was their own doing ;
this would they needs have, and I, Gaius Caesar, after so many
worthy exploits achieved should have been a condemned man,
had I not craved help of mine army." Some are of opinion
that, being so long inured and acquainted with sovereign command, and weighing his own puissance and the power of his
enemies in balance one against the other, [he] took the occasion
and opportunity to usurp that absolute dominion, which in the
very prime of his years he aspired unto ; and of his mind it
seemeth Cicero was, who in his third book of Duties [1] writeth
that Caesar had always in his mouth these verses of Euripides [2] :

> Εἴπερ γὰρ ἀδικεῖν χρή, τυραννίδος πέρι
> Κάλλιστον ἀδικεῖν, τἄλλα δ᾽ εὐσεβεῖν χρεών.

Which Cicero himself translated thus :

> *Nam si violandum est jus, [regnandi] gratia*
> *Violandum est ; aliis rebus pietatem colas.*

> For if thou must do wrong by breach,
> Of laws, of right and equity,
> 'Tis best thereby a crown to reach,
> In all things else keep piety.

31. When word therefore was brought unto him, that the
tribunes' inhibition and negative voice was put down, and
themselves departed out of the city, having immediately sent
before certain cohorts privily, because no suspicion might
arise, he dissembled the matter, and was present in person to
behold a public game, viewed and considered the plotform [1]
according to which he was about to build a school of sword-
fencers, and according to his usual manner gave himself to
feast and banquet often. After this presently, upon the sunsetting, he took up certain mules from the next baker's mill-

house, set them in their gears to his wagon, and as closely [2] as possibly he could with a small retinue and company about him put himself in his journey ; and when, by reason that the lights were gone out, he had lost his way, after he had wandered a long time, at the length meeting with a guide by that time it was day, he passed on foot through most narrow cross-lanes and by-paths until he recovered the right way again. Now when he had once overtaken his cohorts at the river Rubicon, which was the utmost bound of his province, he rested and stood still a little while ; then casting in his mind, how great an enterprise he went in hand with, he turned unto them that were next unto him and said : " As yet, my masters, we may well return back ; but pass we once over this little bridge, there will be no dealing but by force of arms and dint of sword."

32. As he thus stayed and stood doubtful what to do, a strange sight he chanced to see in this manner. All of a sudden there appeared unto him a certain man of an extra-ordinary stature and shape withal, sitting hard by and piping with a reed. Now when, besides the shepherds and herdmen, many soldiers also from their standing wards [1] ran for to hear him, and among them the trumpeters likewise, he caught from one of them a trumpet, leapt forth to the river, and beginning with a mighty blast to sound the battle, kept on his pace to the very bank on the other side. Then Caesar : " Let us march on," quoth he, " and go whither the tokens of the gods and the injurious dealings of our enemies call us. The die be thrown ; I have set up my rest [2]. Come what will of it."

33. And thus having conveyed his army over the river, he joined with the tribunes of the commons, who, upon their expulsion out of the city were come unto him, and in a full and frequent [22] assembly, with shedding tears and rending his garment down the breast, besought the faithful help and assistance of his soldiers. It is supposed also that he promised unto every one of them a knight's living, which happened upon a vain and false persuasion ; for when, in his speech and ex-hortation unto them, he showed ever and anon the ring-finger of his left hand [a], and therewith avouched and promised, for the satisfaction and contentment of all those by whose means he should maintain his honour and dignity, that he would willingly pluck the ring from off his own finger [b], those that

stood hindmost in the assembly, who might better see than
hear him speak, took that for spoken which they imagined by
bare sight, and so the speech went for current, that he promised
them the dignity of wearing the ring of gold together with
400,000 sesterces [c].

34. The order, preceding a final complement [1] of those acts,
which from thenceforth he achieved, summarily goeth in this
manner. He seized into his hands and held Picenum, Umbria,
and Etruria. L. Domitius, who in a factious tumult was
nominated to be his successor and kept Corfinium with a
garrison, he subdued and forced to yield; and when he had
dismissed him, he marched along the coast of the Adriatic sea [2]
to Brundisium, whither the consuls and Pompey were fled,
intending with all speed to cross the narrow seas; whose
passage after he had assayed by all manner of lets to hinder and
stop (but in vain), he turned his journey and took the way
directly to Rome. And when he had courteously moved the
senators to give him meeting in the senate-house, there to
treat and consult as touching the state of the commonweal, he
set upon the most puissant forces of Pompey, which were in
Spain under the conduct of three lieutenants, M. Petreius, L.
Afranius, and M. Varro; having given out before among his
friends and openly professed, that he was going to an army
without a captain [a], and would return from thence to a captain
without an army [b]. And albeit the besieging of Massilia,
which city in his journey forward had shut the gates against
him, and exceeding scarcity of corn and victuals was some
impeachment [3] and stay unto him, yet within a short time he
overcame and subdued all.

35. From hence having returned to the city of Rome again
and passed over into Macedonia, after he had held Pompey
besieged for the space well-near of four months, and that
within most mighty trenches and strong rampiers [1], he discomfited [him] at the last in the Pharsalian battle and put him
to flight; and, following him hotly in chase as he fled to
Alexandria, so soon as he understood that he was slain, and
perceived likewise that king Ptolemy laid wait for his own
person also, he warred upon him; which, to say a truth, was a
most difficult and dangerous piece of work, by reason that he
managed it, neither in place indifferent nor time convenient,

but in the very winter season, and within the walls of a most wealthy and politic enemy, being himself in distress and want of all things, and unprovided besides to fight. Having achieved the victory, he granted the kingdom of Egypt unto Cleopatra and her younger brother, fearing to reduce it into the form of a province, lest at any time, being governed under some lord-president of a more stirring spirit and violent nature than others, it might give occasion and yield matter of rebellion. From Alexandria he went over into Syria, and so from thence into Pontus, upon the urgent news as touching Pharnaces ; whom, notwithstanding he was the son of the great Mithridates, and, taking the opportunity of the troubles and civil war among the Romans, made war, yea, and now bare himself presumptuous and overbold for his manifold victories and great success, yet within five days after his arrival thither, and four hours after he came into sight of the enemy, he vanquished and subdued in one only battle ; eft-soons and oftentimes recounting the felicity of Pompey, whose hap it was to win his principal name for warfare of so cowardly a kind of enemies. After this, he defeated Scipio and Juba ², repairing the relics of that side in Africa, and the children of Pompey in Spain.

36. In all the civil wars he sustained no loss or overthrow but by his own lieutenants, of whom C. Curio was slain in Africa ; C. Antonius yielded himself into the hands of his enemies in Illyricum ; P. Dolabella in the same Illyricum lost his fleet, and Cn. Domitius [Calvinus] his army in Pontus. Himself fought his battles always most fortunately and never was so much as in any hazard, save only twice ; once before Dyrrachium, where, being discomfited and put to flight, when he saw that Pompey followed not on in chase, he said of him, that he knew not how to use a victory ; a second time, in Spain, at the last battle that ever he fought, what time, being in great despair, he was of mind even to have killed himself.

37. Having finished all his wars, he rode in five triumphs : to wit, when he had vanquished Scipio, four times in one and the same month, but certain days between ; and once again, after he had overcome the children of Pompey. The first and most excellent triumph that he solemnised was that over Gaul ; then followed the Alexandrine ; after it the Pontic ; next thereunto the African ; and last of all the Spanish, every one set out diversely, with variety of ordinance, provision, and furniture. On the day of his Gallic triumph, as he rode along the Velabrum[1], he had like to have been shaken out of his chariot, by reason that the axle-tree broke. He mounted up into the Capitol by torchlight, having forty elephants on his right hand and left, bearing branches [a] and candlesticks. In his Pontic triumph, among the pageants and shows of that pomp[2], he caused to be carried before him the title and superscription of these three words, *Veni, vidi, vici*, I came, I saw, I conquered ; signifying, not the acts achieved by war, as other conquerors, but noting his expedition in dispatching the war.

38. Throughout the legions of old soldiers, he gave, in the name of pillage, unto every footman (over and above the 2000 sesterces [a], which he had paid at the beginning of the civil tumult) 4000 sesterces[1] [b], and to the horsemen 24,000 apiece[2] [c]. He assigned lands also unto them, but not lying all together, because none of the owners should be thrust out of their livings. Among the people of Rome, beside ten modii [d] of corn and as many pints of oil [e], he distributed and dealt 300 sesterces [f] also by the poll [26], which he had in times past promised, with an overdeal[3] of 100 [g] apiece to boot, for time[4]. He remitted moreover one year's house rent unto all tenants in Rome, if it amounted to 2000 sesterces [h] and not above ; but to those in Italy, if the said rent exceeded not 500[i]. Furthermore, he made them a general great feast, and distributed a dole of raw flesh[5], yea, and after his victory in Spain he gave them two dinners ; for, deeming the former of them to have been made niggardly and not beseeming his liberality, he bestowed upon them, five days after, another, and in most large and plenteous manner.

39. He exhibited shows of sundry sorts, as namely, a sword-fight of fencers at sharpe [10] ; he set forth stage-plays likewise in several quarters and regions [a] of the city throughout, and those verily acted by players in all languages[1] ; semblably[2], the solemn games in the circus [b] he showed ; and brought forth champions also to perform their devoir, and represented a naval fight. At the said solemnity of sword-players, there fought to the uttrance[3] in the market-place of

Rome, Furius Leptinus, descended from the race of praetors, and [Q.] Calpenus, one who had been sometime a senator and a pleader of causes at the bar. There danced the pyrrhic [c] warlike dance the children of the princes and potentates of Asia and Bithynia. During the stage-plays aforesaid D. Laberius [d], a gentleman of Rome, acted his own poem or interlude ; for which, being rewarded with 500,000 sesterces and a ring of gold, he passed directly from the stage by the orchestra [e] to take up his place among the knights in the fourteen foremost seats. At the games in the circus, against which the circus was enlarged on both sides and moated round about, there drove the steeds drawing chariots four and two together, yea, and mounted the vaunting [4] horses from one to another, the greatest gallants and bravest young gentlemen of the nobility. The warlike Trojan game [f] was performed by a twofold troop of greater boys and less. The hunting or baiting of wild beasts was presented five days together. And, the last day of all, there was a fight between two battles [5] of 500 footmen, 20 elephants, and 30 horsemen on a side, put to skirmish one against the other. For, to the end that they might have more scope to bicker together, the goals [g] were taken up and removed, but instead of them were pitched two camps confronting one another. As for the champions [h] abovesaid, they, having a place for to exercise their feats of activity set out and built for the present time, strove for the prize or best game three days together in the region of the Campus Martius. To set out the naumachia or naval battle, there was a place digged for a great pool, in the smaller Codeta [i] ; wherein certain galleys as well with two ranks of oars as with three, the ships of Tyre also and of Egypt encountered, being manned with a great number of fighting men. To behold these sights and shows, such a number of people resorted from all parts, as most of the strangers, either within the streets of the city or in the highways without, were fain to abide within booths pitched of purpose ; yea, and oftentimes very many were in the press crowded and crushed to death, among whom were two senators.

40. Turning after this to set the state of the commonweal in good order, he reformed the calendar, which long since, through the prelates' default, by their liberty of interlacing months and days at their pleasure, was so confused, that neither the festival holidays of harvest fell out in summer, nor those of the vintage in autumn. And he framed the whole year just unto the course of the sun, that it should contain 365 days, and, by abolishing the leap-month, one day every fourth year might be inserted between [a]. Now, to the end that the computation of the times to come might from the new kalends of January agree the better, between November and December he put two other months ; so as that year, wherein all this was ordained, had fifteen months, reckoning the ordinary interlaced month, which by course and custom fell just upon the said year.

41. He made up the full number of the senators [a], and chose unto that place new patricians [1] [b]. The number of praetors, aediles, quaestors, and of other inferior magistrates he augmented [c]. Such as were displaced and put down by virtue of the censor's office, or otherwise by sentence of the judges condemned for unlawful bribery and suing indirectly for any office, he restored to their former rooms. In the election of magistrates he parted with the people thus far forth ; as [2] (excepting the competitors of the consulship) for all the number besides of candidates, the one half should be declared those whom the people were disposed to propound, the other half, such as himself would nominate. Which nomination passed by certain bills sent about unto the tribes, in a brief kind of writ, after this manner : " Caesar dictator unto this or that tribe greeting. I commend unto you such an one and such an one, that by virtue of your voices and suffrages they may have and hold the dignity they sue for." He admitted unto honourable places the children of those who had been proscript and outlawed [3]. He reduced all judgments unto two sorts of judges, namely, of the knight's degree and the senators ; as for the tribunes of the treasury or chamber of the city, which had been the third, he utterly abolished [them] [4]. The general survey and numbering of the people he held neither after the accustomed manner [d] nor in the usual place, but street by street, and that by the landlords and owners of messuages and tenements standing together [5] ; and whereas [6] 3,020,000 citizens received allowance of corn from the State [e], he brought and reduced them to the number of 150,000. And to the end that no new conventicles and riots at any time might arise about this review, he ordained that every year, in the place of those that were deceased, the praetor should make a new supply and choice by casting lots, out of such as had not been reckoned and enrolled in the former survey.

42. Moreover, whenas to the number of 80,000 Roman citizens were bestowed in sundry colonies beyond the sea, he made a law for the more frequent inhabiting of the city of Rome, thus exhausted and dispeopled : that no citizen above 20 years of age, and under 40 (unless he were a sworn soldier to the State [a], and so bound by his oath) should remain out of Italy above three years together ; item, that no senator's son, except he lodged within the house or pavilion, or belonged to the familiar train of a chief magistrate [b], should travel forth of Italy ; item, that no graziers should keep and retain fewer than a third part of freeborn young men, among the keepers of their cattle. All professors of physic at Rome and teachers of the liberal arts, he enfranchised citizens, that both they themselves might more willingly dwell in the city, and others beside desire there to inhabit. As touching money lent out, when he had quite put down the expectation of cancelling debts [c] (a thing that was often moved [1]), he decreed at length : that all debtors should satisfy their creditors in this manner ; namely, by an estimate made of their possessions, according to the worth and value as they purchased them before the civil war, deducting out of the principal whatsoever had been paid or set down in the obligations for the use ; by which condition the fourth part well-near of the money credited forth was lost. All the societies and colleges, saving those that were of ancient foundation, he dissolved. The penalties of heinous crimes he augmented ; and whereas the rich and wealthier sort fell to wickedness so much the sooner, because they went into banishment [2], and saved their whole patrimonies and estates, parricides [d] therefore and wilful murderers (as Cicero writeth [3]) he deprived of all their goods ; other manslayers besides he fined with the loss of one half.

43. He ministered justice and decided matters in law most painfully and with passing great severity. Such as were attaint and convict of extortion [a] he removed even from their senator's place and degree. He broke the marriage of a man that had been praetor, marrying a wife presently after two days that she was divorced and went from a former husband, albeit there was no suspicion at all of adultery and naughtiness [6]. He ordained customs and imposts of foreign merchandise. The use of litters, likewise the wearing of purple clothes[1] and of pearl he took away, saving only in certain persons and ages, and upon special days. The sumptuary law [b], to repress excessive cost in fare, he executed most of any other ; and for this purpose, he set certain watchmen and warders in sundry places about the shambles and markets where victuals were sold, to lay hold upon all cates and viands contrary to the prescript rule of the law in that behalf, and to bring the same unto him. Otherwhiles also, he sent secretly his own officers and soldiers, to fetch away such meats out of the very dining-parlours and banqueting-rooms, even when they were set upon the board, if happily[2] they had any way escaped the hands of the aforesaid warders.

44. Now, as concerning his purpose to adorn and beautify the city of Rome with gallant works, as also to maintain and amplify the empire, he had more matters in his head and greater every day than other. Principally his intent and meaning was, to build so stately a temple in the honour of Mars, as the like was nowhere to be seen, having filled up and laid level that huge pit, wherein he had exhibited the show of a naval battle ; and also to erect an exceeding great theatre, fast adjoining to the Tarpeian mount ; item, to reduce the whole corpus of the civil law to a certain mean and mediocrity, and out of that huge and diffused number of laws, to choose out the best and necessary points, and those to bring into as few volumes as possibly might be ; item, to erect publicly the greatest libraries that he could, as well of Greek as Latin authors, committing unto M. Varro [a] the charge both to provide the said books, and also to digest and place them in order ; item, to lay the meres and fenny plashes Pomptinae[1] dry ; to draw and let forth the lake Fucinus ; to make a causey[2] or highway from the Adriatic sea, by the ridge or side of the Apennine hill, as far as to the river Tiber, and to dig through the isthmus [b] ; moreover, to bridle the Daci[3], who had invaded Pontus and Thracia ; and soon after to make war upon the Parthians by the way of Armenia the less, but not to give them battle before he had made trial of them [c]. Amid these purposes and designs death prevented him. Concerning which before I enter into speech, it shall not be impertinent to deliver summarily those points which concern the shape, feature, and proportion of his body ; his habit and apparel ; his fashions and behaviour ; and withal what may touch both his civil and also his martial affairs.

45. Of stature he is reported to have been tall ; of complexion white and clear ; with limbs well-trussed[1] and in good plight ; somewhat full-faced ; his eyes black, lively, and quick ; also very healthful, saving that in his latter days he was given to faint and swoon suddenly ; yea, and as he dreamed, to start and be affrighted ; twice also, in the midst of his martial affairs[2], he was surprised with the falling sickness[a]. About the trimming of his body he was over-curious[3] : so as he would not only be notted[4] and shaven very precisely, but also have his hair plucked, insomuch as some cast it in his teeth, and twitted him therewith. Moreover, finding by experience that the deformity of his bald head was oftentimes subject to the scoffs and scorns of backbiters and slanderers, he took the same exceedingly to the heart ; and therefore he both had usually drawn down his hair, that grew but thin, from the crown toward his forehead ; and also, of all honours decreed unto him from the senate and people, he neither received nor used any more willingly than the privilege to wear continually the triumphant laurel garland. Men say also that in his apparel he was noted for singularity[5], as who used to go in his senator's purple studded robe, trimmed with a jag or fringe at the sleeve hand, and the same so, as he never was but girt over it, and that very slack and loose ; whereupon arose (for certain) that saying of Sulla, who admonished the nobles oftentimes to beware of the boy that went girded so dissolutely[6] [b].

46. He dwelt at first in the Subura[1], but after he was high priest in the street Sacra[2], in an edifice of the city's. Many have written that he was exceedingly addicted to neatness in his house and sumptuous fare at his table. The manor-house, which he founded out of the very ground and with great charges finished in the territory Nemorensis[3], because it was not wholly answerable to his mind, he demolished and pulled quite down, although as yet he was but of mean estate and deeply indebted. Finally, this speech goeth of him, that in his expeditions he carried about with him pavements of checker-work made of quarrels square-cut [4], so as they might be taken asunder and set again together.

47. He made a voyage (as they say) into Britain, in hope of pearls ; and otherwhiles, in comparing their bigness, would with his own hand peise [1] them to find their weight. For to get and buy up precious stones, engraved and chased pieces, images, and painted tables of antique work, he was ever most eager and sharp-set. Slaves likewise, if they were anything fresh and new-come, trimly set out withal and fine, he procured at an exceeding price, such as himself also was ashamed of ; so as he forbade expressly the same should be brought in any of his reckonings and accounts.

48. It is reported of him, that in all the provinces which he governed he feasted continually, and furnished two halls or dining-chambers ordinarily ; the one, wherein either Gauls in their warlike habit [1], or Greeks in their cloaks ; the other, in which the gowned Romans, together with the more noble and honourable personages of the provinces, sat. The domestic discipline of his house he kept so duly, so precisely, and with such severity, in small matters as well as greater, that he bound with fetters and irons his baker for serving up secretly unto his guests other bread than to himself : and a freedman of his own (whom otherwise he did set very great store by) he put to death for dishonouring by adultery a Roman gentleman's wife, albeit no man made complaint thereof.

49. His good name for continency and clean life nothing verily blemished, save only the abode and inward familiarity with Nicomedes ; but a foul stain that was, which followed him with shame for ever, yea, and ministered taunting and reproachful matter unto every man. I omit [1] the notorious verses of Calvus Licinius :

> *Bithynia quicquid*
> *Et paedicator Caesaris unquam habuit.*

Look what it was that Bithyne land had ever more or less,
And he that Caesar did abuse, in filthy wantonness.

I let pass the invectives and accusatory actions of Dolabella and Curio the elder ; in which Dolabella, for his part, termeth him the king's concubine in the queen's place, and the inner room of his licter [2] ; and Curio nameth him Nicomedes, his filth and harlot[3], yea, and the Bithynian brothel-house. I overpass likewise those edicts of Bibulus, wherein he published his colleague and made him known by the name of the Bithynian queen ; saying, moreover, that before he had loved the king, and now cast a fancy[4] to the kingdom. At which very time, as M. Brutus makes report, there was one Octavius also, a man upon distemperature of his brain given to jest and scoff overbroadly, who, in a most frequent [22] assembly, after he had called Pompey king, saluted him by the name of queen. C. Memmius likewise laid in his dish[5], that he stood with the rest of the stale catamites as cupbearer, to serve Nicomedes with wine at a full feast, where sat at the table divers merchants and occupiers, citizens of Rome, whose names he putteth down. But Cicero [was] not contented herewith, that in certain epistles he had written, how by the guard or pensioners of the said king being conveyed into his bed-chamber[6], he lay down upon a bed of gold, arrayed in purple ; and so the flower of youth and maidenhead of him, who was descended from Venus[a], became defiled and distained in Bithynia. One time also, as Caesar in the senate-house pleaded to the cause and in the behalf of Nysa, Nicomedes his daughter, and therewith rehearsed up the gracious favours that the king had done unto him, " Let be " (quoth he) " these matters, I pray you, and away with them, since it is well-known, both what he bestowed upon you, and also what you gave to him." Finally, in the triumph over Gaul, his soldiers, among other sonnets such as they use to chant merrily when they follow the triumphal chariot, pronounced also these verses so commonly divulged :

Gallias Caesar subegit, Nicomedes Caesarem ;
Ecce Caesar nunc triumphat, qui subegit Gallias ;
Nicomedes non triumphat, qui subegit[b] Caesarem.

Caesar did subdue the Gauls, and him hath Nicomede.
Behold, now Caesar doth triumph, who did the Gauls subdue ;
But Nicomede triumpheth not, who Caesar had subdued.

50. An opinion there is constantly received, that he was given to carnal pleasures, and that way spent much ; also, that he dishonoured many dames, and those of noble houses, by name among others, Postumia, the wife of Servius Sulpicius ; Lollia, wife to A. Gabinius ; Tertulla, M. Crassus his wife ; and Mucia the wife of Pompey. For certain it is, that not only the Curios, both father and son, but many others also reproached Pompey, that for whose cause he had put away his own wife after she had borne him three children, and whom he was wont with a deep sigh and groan to call Aegisthus [1],— his daughter (I say) afterwards he espoused, upon a desire of power and greatness by that marriage. But above the rest he cast affection to Servilia, the mother of M. Brutus ; for whom both in his last consulship [2] he had bought a pearl that cost him six millions of sesterces [3] ; and also unto whom, during the civil war, over and above other free gifts, he sold in open port-sale [4], fair lands and most goodly manors at a very low price ; what time verily, when most men marvelled that they went so cheap, Cicero most pleasantly and conceitedly, " that ye may know " (quoth he) " she hath the better pennyworth in the purchase, *Tertia deducta est* " [a]. For it was thought that Servilia was bawd also to her own daughter Tertia, and brought her to Caesar his bed.

51. Neither forbare he so much as men's wives in the provinces where he was governor, as appeareth even by this his distich, taken up likewise by his soldiers at the Gallic triumph [a] :

> *Urbani, servate uxores ; maechum calvum adducimus ;*
> *Aurum in Gallia [effutuisti], hic sumpsisti mutuum.*

52. He was enamoured also upon queens, and among them he loved Eunoë, the Moor, wife of Bogudes, king of Mauritania, upon whom, as also upon her husband, he bestowed very many gifts and of infinite value, as [M. Actorius] Naso hath left in writing. But most especially he fancied Cleopatra ; for with her he both sat up many times and feasted all night long even until the break of day, and also in the same barge or galley [1] called *thalamegos* [a] had passed into Egypt almost as far as to Ethiopia, but that his army refused to follow ; and in the end, having trained [2] her into the city of Rome, he sent her back again, not without exceeding great honours, and enriched with many rewards ; yea, and suffered her to call the son she bare after his own name [3]. Whom verily some Greek writers have recorded to have been very like unto Caesar both in shape and also in gait [4], and M. Antonius avouched unto the

35

senate, that by the same resemblance he knew him to be his son, averring withal that C. Matius, Gaius Oppius, and the rest of Caesar's friends knew as much. Of whom C. Oppius (as if the thing were so pregnant, that it required some apology and defence) put forth a book entitled thus : *That he was not Caesar's Son, whom Cleopatra fathered upon him.* Helvius Cinna, a tribune of the commons, confessed unto many persons that he had a law drawn out in writing and in readiness, which Caesar, being absent himself, commanded him to propose, to this effect : that it might be lawful for him to marry what wives[5] and as many as he would[6], for to get children upon. And that no man need at all to doubt how infamous he was, both for uncleanness of body against kind[7][b], and also for adulteries, Curio the elder in a certain oration calleth him a woman for all men, and a man for all women.

53. That he was a most spare drinker of wine his very enemies would never deny. Whereupon arose this apophthegm of M. Cato : that, of all that ever were, Caesar alone came sober to the overthrow of the State. For about his food and diet C. Oppius showeth he was so indifferent and without curiosity[1] that, when upon a time his host set before him upon the board old rank oil instead of green, sweet, and fresh, so that other guests refused it, he only (by his saying) fell to it and eat thereof the more liberally, because he would not be thought to blame his host either for negligence or rusticity.

54. From other men's goods he held not his hands, neither when he had the command of armies abroad, nor when he was in place of magistracy at home ; for in Spain (as some have recorded) he took money of the proconsul[1], and the allies there, and that by way of begging, to help him out of debt : and certain towns of the Lusitanians[2] he sacked in hostile manner, albeit they denied not to do whatsoever he commanded them, and besides did set open their gates for him against his coming. In Gaul he robbed and spoiled the chapels and temples of the gods, full of rich gifts and oblations. As for cities, he put them to the sack, more often for booty sake and pillage, than for any trespass committed. Whereupon it came to pass that he got abundance of gold, so as of it which he had to spare and did set to sale, he sold[3] throughout Italy and in the provinces after[4] 3000 sesterces of silver the pound weight [a]. In his first consulship, when he had stolen out of the Capitol three thousand pound weight of gold, he bestowed in the place thereof as much brass gilt. The privileges of society and alliance with the Romans, as also kings' titles he gave for sums of money [b] ; as who (for example) from Ptolemy [5] that was but one, took away well-near 6000 talents [6], in the name of himself and Pompey. But afterwards, by most open pilling, polling [7], and sacrileges, he maintained the charges both of civil wars, and also of his triumphs and solemn shows exhibited to the people.

55. In eloquence and warlike feats together [1] he either equalled or excelled the glory of the very best. After his accusation of Dolabella, he was no doubt ranged in the rank of the principal advocates-at-law. Certes, Cicero, in his Catalogue of Orators to Brutus [lxxv, 261], saith he cannot see any one unto whom Caesar might give place ; affirming withal, that he holdeth an elegant and gay, a stately also, and in some sort a generous and gentleman-like kind of pleading : and unto Cornelius Nepos thus wrote he of the same Caesar : " What should a man say more ? which of all those orators that practised nothing else but oratory will you prefer before this Caesar ? who is there in sentences either quicker or coming thicker ? who for words, yielded more gallant or more elegant ? " He seemeth, whiles he was yet but young, to have followed that form of eloquence only, which Strabo Caesar professed ; out of whose oration also, entitled *Pro Sardis*, he transferred some sentences, word for word, into his own, called *Divinatio* [2]. It is said that in his pronunciation [3] he used a high and shrill voice, an ardent motion, and earnest gesture, not without a lovely grace. Some orations he left behind him in writing, among which certain go under his name, but untruly, as namely, that *Pro Q. Metello ;* which Augustus deemeth (and not without good cause) to have been written rather by notaries, who either took not his words aright or wrote not so fast as he delivered them, than penned by himself. For in certain copies I find that it had not so much as this inscription, *Pro Metello*, but *quam scripsit Metello* [4], being (as it is indeed) a speech coming from the person of Caesar, clearing Metellus and himself against the criminations and slanders of common backbiters to them both. The oration likewise *Ad Milites* [5] in Spain, the same Augustus hardly thinketh to be his, and yet there be two of them extant ; the one was pronounced at the former battle, the other at the latter, when, by the report of Asinius Pollio, he had not so much as any time to make a speech ; the enemies ran upon him and charged so suddenly.

56. He left commentaries also of his own acts, to wit, as touching the Gallic war, and the civil war with Pompey. For of the Alexandrine, African, and Spanish wars, who was the writer it is uncertain ; while some think it was Oppius, others, Hirtius, who also made up and finished the last of the Gallic war, which was imperfect. As concerning those commentaries aforesaid of Caesar, Cicero in the same book [1] writeth thus : " He wrote commentaries exceeding well, I assure you, to be liked ; naked they be, straight and upright, yea, and lovely too, being divested, as it were, of all ornaments and trim attire of style ; but while his mind was that other[s], disposed to write a complete history, should furnish and serve themselves with matter there ready to their hands, happily [2] to some foolish folk he did some pleasure, who are willing to curl and frizzle the same with their crisping pins, but surely the wiser sort he scared altogether from writing." Of the same commentaries, Hirtius giveth this report : " They are," quoth he, " in the judgement of all men so approved, that it seems he hath prevented writers, and not given them any help. And yet our admiration of this matter is more than all men's beside. For whereas others do know only how well and purely they were penned, we note also with [w]hat facility and expedition he wrote them." Asinius Pollio thinketh they were compiled with small care and diligence, with as little regard also of sound truth, seeing that Caesar received hand over head [3], and believed most things lightly, namely, such as were by others achieved ; and even those acts which himself exploited, either of purpose or for default of memory, he put down wrong ; he supposeth also that he meant to have written the same anew and corrected them. He left, moreover, two books, *de Analogia*, and as many *Anticatones* [4], besides a poem, entitled *Iter ;* of which books the foremost [5] he made in his passage over the Alps, what time as, having ridde [6] his circuits and finished the assizes, he returned out of the hither province of Gaul to his army ; those next following [7] [a], about the time of the battle at Munda ; and the last of all [8], whiles he travelled from the city of Rome into the farther province of Spain, and performed that journey within 24 days [9]. Extant there be also epistles of his written unto the senate, which (as it seemeth) he was the first that turned into pages and leaves, even to a form of a memorial [10] ; whereas beforetime the consuls and generals never sent any letters but written overthwart the paper. Missives likewise there be of his written to Cicero and to familiar friends as touching home affairs, in which, if any matters of secrecy were to be carried, he wrote them by private marks [11] ; that is to say, placing the letters in such order, as there could not one word be made of them. Which if a man would decipher and find out, he must of necessity exchange every fourth letter of the alphabet, to wit, d for a, and the rest likewise [12]. Furthermore, there be certain works of his abroad in men's hands, written when he was a boy and a very youth, as namely, *The Praises of Hercules*, *The Tragedy of Oedipus*, as also *Collects* [13] *of Sayings and Apophthegms ;* all which pamphlets Augustus forbade to be published, in a certain epistle of his ; which, being very brief and plain, he sent to Pompeius Macer, whom he had appointed for the disposing and ordering of his libraries.

57. In handling his weapon most skilful he was, and in horsemanship as cunning ; but what pains he would take, it is incredible. In the marching of his army, his manner was to be foremost, sometime on horseback, more often on foot : bareheaded, whether the sun shone or the clouds poured rain. He made exceeding long journeys with incredible speed ; even an hundred miles a day, riding in some hired wagon [1], if he were lightly appointed otherwise, and without carriages. Were rivers in his way to hinder his passage ? cross over them he would ; either swimming, or else bearing himself upon blown leather bottles [2], so that very often he prevented the letter-carriers and messengers of his coming.

58. In performing his expeditions and martial exploits, doubtful it is whether he were more wary or adventurous. He neither led his army at any time through ways dangerous for ambushments, before he had thoroughly viewed and descried the situation of the quarters ; nor put over his fleet into

Britain, until he had beforehand in proper person[1] sounded the havens, and tried the manner of sailing and arrival to the island. Howbeit, the same man (as circumspect as he was), upon news brought unto him, that his camp was beleaguered in Germany, passed through his enemies' corps de guard in French habit, and so came unto his own men. From Brundisium to Dyrrachium he sailed oversea in winter[2], between two fleets of the enemies riding opposite one to the other ; and whiles his own forces, which he had commanded to follow straight after him, lingered still behind, having sent messengers oftentimes to call them away, but all in vain, at last himself secretly in the night went aboard into a very small bottom, with his head hooded ; and neither discovered who he was, nor suffered the pilot to give way unto the tempest that came full afront the vessel, before he was well-near overwhelmed with the waves.

59. No religious fear of divine prodigies could ever fray[1] him from any enterprise, or stay him if it were once in hand. As he sacrificed upon a time, the beast made an escape and ran away, yet for all that deferred not he his journey against Scipio and Juba. He fortuned also to take a fall then, even as he went forth of the ship to land ; but turning this foretoken to the better presage, " I take possession," quoth he, " of thee, O Africa." Moreover, in very scorn, and to make but a mockery of these prophecies, whereby the name of Scipio was fatal to that province and held lucky and invincible there, he had with him in his camp the most base and abject fellow of all the Cornelian family, and who in reproach of his life was surnamed Saluito[2].

60. He fought not often[1] set fields appointed beforehand, but upon the present occasion offered ; many times he struck a battle immediately after his journey, otherwhiles in most foul and stormy weather, when no man ever thought he would once stir. Neither held he off and detracted fight, but in his latter days, being then of this opinion that, the oftener he had gotten victory, the less he was to venture and make trial of fortune ; also, that a victory could gain him nothing so much as some disastrous calamity might take from him. No enemy put he ever to flight, but he discamped him and drove him out of the field. By this means he gave them whom he had once

discomfited no time to bethink themselves. In any doubtful
and dangerous service, his manner was to send away the
horses, and his own with the first, to the end that, when all
means of flight were gone, they might of necessity be forced the
rather to stand to it and abide to the last.

61. The horse he used to ride upon was strangely marked,
with feet resembling very near a man's, and the hoofs cloven
like toes, which horse was foaled about home ; and when the
soothsayers of their learning had pronounced that he presaged
unto his owner the empire of the whole world, very careful he
was to rear him and nourish him. Now whenas the beast would
abide no man else to ride him, himself was he that backed
him first. The full portrait and proportion of which horse he
dedicated also afterwards before the temple of Venus Genetrix[a].

62. Many a time himself alone renewed the battle when it
was discomfited, standing in their way that fled and holding
them one by one back ; yea, and by wreathing[1] their throats
he turned them again upon the enemies. Thus dealt he I
say with his own soldiers, when they were many times verily
so fearfully maskered[2], that a standard-bearer threatened as
he stayed him[3] to smite him with the foot-point[4] of the
spear that carried the eagle [a], and another left behind him the
ensign in Caesar's hand as he detained it.

63. Of his constant resolution these be no less tokens, if not
greater (which I shall now rehearse). After the battle of
Pharsalus, when he had sent his forces before into Africa, and
himself crossed the seas through the strait of Hellespont in a
small passenger's bark[1], where he met with L. Cassius, one of
the adverse party, with ten strong warships armed with brazen
beak-heads, he avoided him not, nor gave way ; but, affronting him, began to exhort him for to yield, and so upon his
humble supplication received him aboard.

64. At Alexandria, being busy about the assault and winning of a bridge where, by a sudden sally of the enemies, he was
driven to take a boat, and many besides made haste to get
into the same, he leapt into the sea, and by swimming almost
a quarter of a mile recovered clear the next ship ; bearing up his
left hand all the while, for fear the writings which he held therein
should take wet and drawing his rich coat-armour after him
by the teeth [a], because the enemy should not have it as a spoil.

65. His soldiers he allowed for good in regard neither of manners and behaviour[1], nor of wealth and outward estate[2], but only of bodily strength ; and he used them all with like severity, with like indulgence also and sufferance. For he awed and chastised them not in all places nor at all times, but only when the enemy was very near at hand ; and then especially was he most severe and precise in exacting and executing of discipline, insomuch as he would not give them warning of the time, either of journey or of battle, but kept them ready, intentive[3] and prest[4] to be led forth upon a sudden every minute of an hour, whithersoever he would ; this did he also many times without any cause, especially upon rainy days and festivals. And admonishing his soldiers ever and anon to observe and have an eye unto him, he would suddenly in the daytime or by night withdraw himself out of the way ; yea, and stretch out his journey more than ordinary, even to tire them out who were late in following after.

66. As for his soldiers that were terrified with the rumour of their enemies, his manner was to animate and encourage them, not by denying or diminishing[1], but by augmenting the same to the highest degree, even above the truth. And thus, upon a time when the expectation of Juba his coming was terrible, he called his soldiers together, and in a public speech unto them, " Be it known unto you all," quoth he, " that within these very few days the king will be here with a power of ten legions of 30,000 men of arms[2], 100,000 light-armours[3] and 300 elephants. Forbear therefore some of you to inquire or imagine further of the matter, but give credit unto me, that know this for a truth ; or else verily I will embark you in the oldest ship I can get, and cause you to be carried away with any wind into what lands and countries it shall be your fortunes to fall upon."

67. As touching his soldiers' trespasses and delinquencies, he neither observed and took knowledge of them all, nor yet punished them fully to the proportion[1]. But as he made straight inquisition after those who traitorously forsook their colours and were mutinous, and proceeded against them with rigour, so at others he would wink. Sometimes also, after a great battle and victory obtained, he released them all of military duties, permitting them in all licentiousness to roist

and riot wantonly here and there ; being wont to give it out,
that his soldiers, perfumed though they were with odours, and
besmeared with sweet oils, could fight valiantly. Neither
called he them in his public oration plain soldiers, but by a
more pleasing name, fellow-soldiers. Furthermore he maintained them so trim and brave, that he stuck not to set them
out in polished armour, damasked with silver and gold ; as
well for goodly show as because they should in battle take
better hold and keep the same more surely, for fear of damage
and loss. Moreover, he loved them so affectionately that,
when he heard of Titurius his overthrow [2], he suffered the hair
of his head and beard to grow long, and would not cut the same
before he had revenged their death. By which means he both
had his soldiers most devoted unto him and also made them
right valorous.

68. When he was entered into the civil war, the centurions
of every legion presented unto him one horseman apiece, provided out of their own private stock [a] ; and generally all his
soldiers offered their service freely, without allowance of corn
or wages out of his purse, considering that the wealthier sort
had taken upon them the finding and maintenance of the
poorer. Neither all that long time of soldiery was there any of
them that once revolted from him ; and very many, being
taken prisoners by the enemies and having life granted unto
them upon condition they would serve as soldiers against him,
refused it. Hunger and other extremities which necessarily
follow war, not only whilst they were besieged, but also when
themselves beleaguered others, they endured so resolutely that,
during their strong siege and fortification against Dyrrachium,
Pompey, when he saw what kind of bread made of a certain
herb [b] they lived upon, said he had to deal with wild beasts,
commanding withal the same quickly to be had away, and not
shown to any one, for fear lest his own soldiers' hearts should
be utterly daunted, seeing once the patience and constancy of
their enemies. And how valiantly they bare themselves in
fight, this one thing may testify : that, having taken one foil
in a battle before Dyrrachium, they voluntarily offered to be
executed therefor [c], insomuch as their general was more
troubled about comforting than punishing them. In all other
battles they, fewer in number by many parts, easily van-

43

quished infinite forces of their enemies. To conclude, one cohort [d] and no more of the 6th legion, which had the keeping of a sconce [1], made good the place and held out for certain hours against four of Pompey's legions ; and were in manner all of them throughout shot into their bodies with a multitude of their arrows, of which were found 130,000 within their trench and rampiers [35]. And no marvel, if a man consider their several acts singly by themselves, either of Cassius Scaeva, a centurion, or of C. Acilius, a common soldier, to say nothing of many more. Scaeva, when his eye was smitten out, his thigh and shoulder shot through, and his buckler pierced likewise with the shot of 120 arrows [2], yet defended the guard of the fort committed to his charge, and kept it still. Acilius in a fight at sea before Massilia, after his right hand was quite cut off, wherewith he had caught the poop of his enemies' ship, following herein that memorable example of Cynegirus [3] among the Greeks, leapt notwithstanding into the said ship, shoving and driving before him with the boss and pike of his buckler those that he met in his way.

69. In ten years' space during the Gallic war they never so much as once mutinied ; in the civil wars sometimes they did, yet so as they were soon reclaimed and came again into order, not so much by the remiss indulgence as the authority of their captain. For never would he yield one jot unto them in these their seditious tumults ; nay, he always withstood and crossed them. And verily the 9th legion at Placentia (notwithstanding Pompey yet was in arms with his power in the field) he cashiered full and wholly, and sent away with shame : yea, and after many humble prayers and supplications with much ado restored he them to their places again, and not before execution done upon the offenders.

70. As for the soldiers of the 10th legion, whenas in Rome they earnestly called for their discharge from warfare, and required their rewards even with mighty threats, and that to the exceeding danger of the whole city, at what time also the war was very hot in Africa, he neither would admit them into his presence, nor yet dismiss them, albeit his friends seemed to scare him from taking that course ; but with one only word, whereby he named them *Quirites* [a] instead of *Milites*, he did so gently turn and wind, yea, and bring them to his bent, that forthwith they made answer, they would be his soldiers still ; and so of their own accord followed him into Africa, notwithstanding he refused their service. And yet for all this, he amerced and fined the most mutinous sort of them with the loss of a third part, both of the pillage and also of the lands appointed for them.

71. In affectionate love and faithful protection of his dependants he was not wanting in his very youth. When he had upon a time defended Masintha, a noble young gentleman, against king Hiempsal[1], so earnestly that, in the debate and altercation between them, he flew upon Juba, the king's son and caught him by the beard[a], after that the said Masintha was pronounced definitively the king's tributary[2], he forthwith both rescued him out of their hands that would have haled him away, and also kept him close a long time in his own lodging. And soon after his praetorship there expired, when he went into Spain, [he] took the young gentleman away with him in his own litter among others his followers and favourites, and those officers that attended upon him with their knitches of rods[3].

72. His friends he used at all times with so great courtesy and tender respect that, when C. Oppius, who accompanied him in his journey through a wild forest fell suddenly sick, he gave him room in the only inn that was, while himself lay all night upon the ground[1] without doors[2]. Moreover, being now become emperor and lord of all, some of them he advanced even from the lowest degree unto the highest place of honour. And when he was blamed and reproved therefor, he professed openly that, if he had used the help of robbers by the highway side, of cutters[3] and swashbucklers in maintaining of his own dignity, he would not fail but requite them and be thankful even to such.

73. He never entertained malice and hatred against any man so deeply, but willing he was to lay down the same upon occasion offered. Notwithstanding C. Memmius had made most bitter invectives against him, and he again written unto him as bitterly, yet soon after, when the said Memmius stood for the consulship, he friended him all that he could with his good word and procured him voices. When C. Calvus, after certain libels and defamatory epigrams against him, dealt by the mediation of friends for a reconciliation, he of his own accord wrote first unto him. As for Valerius Catullus[1], by whose verses concerning Mamurra he could not choose but take knowledge that he was noted and branded with perpetual infamy, when he excused himself unto him and was ready to make satisfaction[2], he bade him to supper that very day ; and, as he used beforetime, so he continued still to make his father's house his lodging.

74. Moreover, in his revengements he was by nature most mild. Those rovers by whom he was taken prisoner, after he had forced [them] to yield, because he had sworn before that he would hang them upon a cross, he commanded that their throats be first cut, and then be crucified. Cornelius Phagita, whose forelaying him by night he, lying sick and latitant, hardly had escaped (although he gave him a good reward[1]), but had like to have been brought unto Sulla, he never could find in his heart to hurt. Philemon, a servant and secretary of his, who had promised his enemies to take his life away by poison, he punished only by simple death, without any other torment. Being cited and called much upon to bear witness against P. Clodius, for being naught [6] with his wife Pompeia, who was accused besides for the same cause to have polluted the sacred ceremonies[2], he denied that he ever knew anything of the matter, or was able to bring in evidence, albeit both his mother Aurelia and Julia his sister had simply related all upon their credits, even before the same jury and judges. And being demanded thereupon, wherefore then he had put away his wife, " Because I deem," quoth he, " that those of my house ought to be clear as well of suspicion as of crime."

75. The moderation and clemency which he showed as well in the managing of the civil war, as in his victory, was admirable. When Pompey denounced in minatory terms that he would reckon him for an enemy, whosoever he was, that failed to maintain the commonwealth, he for his part pronounced openly that he would make sure account of them to be his, who stood indifferent between and were neuters. And so many as, upon the commendation of Pompey beforetime, he had given any charge or place of command unto in his army under him, he granted them all free leave and liberty to depart unto him. Upon articles and conditions of yielding moved and

propounded to Pompey at Ilerda, whiles between both parts there passed reciprocal dealing and commerce continually, when Afranius and Petreius had taken within their camp certain of Caesar's soldiers and (which they repented soon after) put them to the sword, he would in nowise imitate the same perfidious treachery of theirs practised against him. At the battle of Pharsalus he cried out, " Spare all citizens," and afterwards granted unto every one of his own soldiers (none excepted) this favour, to save each of them one of the adverse party, whom he would. Neither were any found or known slain, but in the very medley, except Afranius, Faustus, and L. Caesar the younger ; and even these verily, men think, were not with his good will put to death. Of whom, notwithstanding, both the former, to wit, Afranius and Faustus, after pardon obtained had rebelled and entered into arms again, and L. Caesar for his part, when in cruel manner by fire and sword he had made havoc of his freedmen and bondservants, spitefully slew the very wild beasts also, which Caesar had provided against the solemnity of a public show to be exhibited before the people. To conclude, in his very latter day he permitted all those also, whom beforetime he had not pardoned, to return into Italy, to govern as magistrates in the city, and to command as generals in the field. Yea, the very statues of L. Sulla and Pompey, which the commons had overthrown and cast up and down, he erected again in their due places. And if after this there was any plot intended or word spoken against him by his adversaries to his hurt, he chose rather to repress than to revenge the same. And so, diverse conspiracies detected and night conventicles he found fault with no farther than thus, by giving notice in some edict and proclamation that he had intelligence thereof. And as for such as gave out bitter speeches of him, he thought it sufficient in an open assembly to give them an admonition not to persist therein. Finally, when in a most slanderous book written by A. Caecina and certain verses as railing and reproachful as it, devised by Pitholaus, his credit and reputation was much cracked and impaired, he took the matter no more to the heart than one citizen would have done at another's hand.

76. Howbeit, the rest of his deeds and words overweigh and depress his good parts down, so as he might be thought both to have abused his sovereignty, and worthily to have been murdered. For he not only took upon him excessive honours, to wit, continued consulship, perpetual dictatorship, and presidency of manners [1], and, more than so, the forename of emperor [2], the surname father of his country, his statue among the kings, an eminent seat of estate [3] raised above the rest in the orchestra among the senators ; but he suffered also more stately dignities than beseeming the condition of a mortal wight to be decreed and ordained for him : namely, a golden throne in the Curia and before the tribunal [4] ; a sacred chariot [a], and therein a frame carrying an image [5], at the solemn pomp of his games in the circus ; temples, altars, his own images placed near unto the gods ; a sacred bed-loft [6] [b] for such images to be bestowed upon ; a flamen [c], certain Luperci [7] [d] ; and the denomination of one month [e] after his own name. Besides, no honourable offices there were but he took and gave at his own pleasure. His third and fourth consulship in name only and title he bare, contenting himself with the absolute power of dictatorship decreed unto him with his consulares [8] all at one time, and in both years he substituted two consuls under him for the three last months, so as, in the meantime, he held no election but of tribunes and aediles of the commons. Instead of praetors he ordained provosts [9], who should administer the affairs of the city even whiles he was present [10]. And upon the very last day of the year, to wit, next before the kalends of January [11], the place of a consulship being vacant by the sudden death of a consul he conferred upon one that made suit to enjoy the same but a few hours [f]. With semblable licentiousness [12] despising the custom of his country, he ordained magistrates to continue in office many years together. To ten men of praetor's degree he granted the consular ornaments. Such as were but enfranchised citizens, and divers mongrel Gauls no better than half-barbarians, he admitted senators [13]. Furthermore, over the mint and receipt of the city revenues he set certain peculiar servants of his own to be rulers. The charge and command of three legions which he left in Alexandria he committed wholly to a son of Rufinus his freedman, a stale youth and catamite of his own.

77. Neither did some words of his which he openly delivered bewray less presumptuous lordliness, as T. Ampius [1] writeth,

For example, that the Commonwealth was now no more any real thing [a], but a name only, without form and shape ; that Sulla was altogether unlettered and no grammarian [2] [b], in giving over his dictatorship ; that men ought now to speak with him more considerately, and to hold every word that he saith for a law. Nay, he proceeded to this point of arrogance that, when upon a time, in a certain sacrifice, the soothsayer brought him word of unlucky inwards in the beast and such as had no heart at all, he made answer and said that those which were to follow afterwards should prove more joyful and fortunate, if it pleased him [3] ; neither was it to be taken for a prodigious and strange token, if a beast wanted a heart.

78. But the greatest envy and inexpiable hatred he drew upon himself by this occasion most of all [1]. What time as all the senators in general came unto him with many and those most honourable decrees, he received them sitting still [2] before the temple of Venus Genetrix. Some think that, when he was about to rise up, Cornelius Balbus stayed and held him back ; others are of the mind that he never went about it. But when C. Trebatius advertised him to arise unto them [3], he looked back upon him with a strange kind of look ; which deed of his was thought so much the more intolerable, for that himself, when Pontius Aquila, one of the college of tribunes [a], stood not up nor did reverence to him as he rode in triumph and passed by the tribunes' pews [4], took such snuff [5] and indignation thereat, that he broke out aloud into these words : " Well done, tribune Aquila ! recover thou then the commonwealth out of my hands " ; and for certain days together never promised aught unto any man without this proviso and exception, " If Pontius Aquila will give me leave [b]."

79. To this contumelious and notorious behaviour of his toward the senate thus despised he adjoined a deed much more arrogant. For whenas, in his return from the solemn sacrifice of the Latin holidays, among other immoderate and new acclamations of the people, one out of the multitude had set upon his statue a coronet of laurel tied about with a white band [1] ; and Epidius Marullus, a tribune of the commons together with his colleague Caesetius Flavus commanded the said band to be plucked off and the man to be had away to prison, he, taking it to heart, either that

this overture to a kingdom sped no better, or (as he made
semblance and pretended himself) that he was put by [18] the
glory of refusing it, sharply rebuked the tribunes, and deprived
them both of their authority. Neither for all this was he
willing afterwards to put away the infamous note [2] of affecting
and seeking after the title of a king ; albeit he both made
answer unto a commoner [a], saluting him by the name of a king,
that he was Caesar and no king, and also at the Lupercalia [3],
when Antonius the consul imposed the diadem oftentimes upon
his head before the Rostra, did put it back again, and send it
into the Capitol to Jupiter Optimus Maximus [b]. Moreover,
sundry rumours ran rife abroad that he would depart (for ever)
to Alexandria [c] or to Ilium [d], having at once translated and
removed thither the puissance and wealth of the empire, dispeopled Italy with mustering of soldiers, and withal betaken [4]
the administration of Rome city unto his friends ; as also that,
in the next session of the senate, L. Cotta, one of the quindecemvirs [e], would move the house to this effect : that, forasmuch
as it was contained in the fatal books of the Sibyl, that the
Parthians could not possibly be vanquished but by a king,
therefore Caesar should be styled king.

80. This gave occasion to the conspirators for to hasten the
execution of their design, lest of necessity they should be
driven to assent thereto. Their counsels therefore and con-
ferences about this matter, which beforetime they held dispersed here and there, and projected oftentimes by two and
three in a company, they now complotted all together, for
that by this time the very people joyed not in the present
state, seeing how things went ; but both in secret and openly
also distasted such sovereignty, and called earnestly for protectors and maintainers of their liberties. Upon the admission
of aliens into the order of senators, there was a libel [1] proposed
in this form ; *Bonum factum* [a] : that no man should show the
senate-house to any new senators. And these verses were
commonly chanted :

> *Gallos Caesar in triumphum ducit, iidem in Curia* [2]
> *Galli bracas* [3][b] *deposuerunt, latum clavum sumpserunt.*

The French in triumph Caesar leads ; in senate they anon
No sooner laid their breeches off, but purpled robes put on.

As Q. Maximus, substituted by Caesar to be a consul for

three months, entered the theatre, and the serjeant [lictor] commanded, as the manner was, that the people should observe and regard him according to his place [c], they all with one accord cried out that he was no consul. After that Caesetius and Marullus, the tribunes aforesaid, were removed out of their office, at the next solemn assembly held for election, very many voices were found declaring them two consuls. Some there were who subscribed under the statue of L. Brutus these words, " Would God thou were alive " [d] ; likewise under the statue of Caesar himself :

> Brutus, for expelling the kings, was created consul the first [e] :
> This man, for expelling the consuls, is become king, the last [4].

There conspired against him more than threescore, the heads of which conspiracy were C. Cassius, Marcus [5] and Decimus Brutus. Who, having made doubt at first whether, by dividing themselves into parties [6], they should cast him down the bridge [f], as he called the tribes to give their voices at the election in Mars' Field, and so take him when he was down and kill him right out ; or set upon him in the high street called Via Sacra [7] [46], or else in the very entrance to the theatre ; after that the senate had summons to meet in council within the Court of Pompey upon the ides of March [8], they soon agreed of this time and place before all others.

81. But Caesar surely had fair warning of his death before it came, by many evident prodigies and strange foretokens. Some few months before, when certain new inhabitants, brought by virtue of the Julian law [1] to dwell in the colony [of] Capua, overthrew most ancient sepulchres for to build them houses to their lands, and did the same so much the more diligently and with better will, for that in searching they lighted upon manufactures and vessels, good store of antique work, there was found in that very monument, wherein by report Capys, the founder of Capua, lay buried, a brazen tablet with a writing upon it in Greek words and Greek letters to this effect : " When the bones and relics of Capys happen to be discovered, it shall come to pass that one, descended from Iulus, shall be murdered by the hands of his near kinsfolk, and his death soon after revenged with the great calamities and miseries of all Italy." And lest any man should think this to be a fabulous

tale and forged matter, know he that Cornelius Balbus, a very
inward and familiar friend of Caesar, is the author thereof.
And the very day next preceding his death, those troops of
horses, which in his passage over the river Rubicon he had
consecrated and let go loose, ranging here and there without a
keeper (as he understood for certain), forbare their meat and
would not, to die for it, touch any, yea, and shed tears abundantly. Also, as he offered sacrifice, the soothsayer Spurinna
warned him to take heed of danger toward him, and which
would not be deferred after the ides of March. Now, the very
day before the said ides, it fortuned that, as the bird Rega-
liolus [2] [a] was flying with a little branch of laurel into the Court
of Pompey, a sort [3] of other birds of divers kinds from out of
the grove hard by pursued after and there pulled it in pieces.
But that night next before the day of his murder, both himself
dreamed as he lay asleep, one while, that he was flying above
the clouds ; another while, that Jupiter and he shook hands ;
and also his wife Calpurnia imagined that the finial of his house
fell down, and that her husband was stabbed in her very
bosom ; and suddenly withal the chamber door of itself flew
open. Hereupon, as also by reason of sickliness, he doubted
a good while whether he should keep at home and put off those
matters which he had purposed to debate before the senate or
no. At the last, being counselled and persuaded by Decimus
Brutus not to disappoint the senators, who were now in frequency [22] assembled and stayed for his coming long since, he
went forth when it was well near eleven of the clock. And
when one met him by the way, and offered him a written
pamphlet, which laid open the conspiracy, and who they were
that sought his life, he shuffled the same among other skroes [4]
and writings which he held in his left hand, as if he would have
read it anon. After this, when he had killed many beasts for
sacrifices and could speed of [5] the gods' favour in none, he
entered the Curia [6] in contempt of all religion ; and therewith
laughed Spurinna to scorn, charging him to be a false prophet,
for that the ides of March were come, and yet no harm befell
unto him ; albeit he answered, that come indeed they were,
but not yet past.

82. When they saw [1] once that he had taken his place and
was set, they stood round about him as serviceable attendants

ready to do him honour; and then immediately Cimber Tullus[2], who had undertaken to begin first, stepped nearer unto him, as though he would have made some request. When Caesar seemed to mislike and put him back, yea, and by his gesture to post him off unto another time, he caught hold of his gown at both shoulders; whereupon, as he cried out, " This is violence," one of the two Cassii[3a] came full afront, and wounded him a little beneath the throat[4]. Then Caesar catching Cassius by the arm thrust it through with his style or writing punch[b]; and with that, being about to leap forward[5], he was met with another wound and stayed. Now when he perceived himself beset on every side and assailed with drawn daggers, he wrapped and covered his head with his gown; but withal he let down the large lap[6] with his left hand to his legs beneath, hiding thereby the inferior part also of his body, that he might fall more decently[c]. And so with three and twenty wounds he was stabbed, during which time he gave but one groan, without any word uttered, and that was at the first thrust; although some have written that, as M. Brutus came running upon him, he said, Καὶ σὺ, τέκνον, " And thou, my son "[d]. When all others fled sundry ways, there lay he a good while dead, until three of his own pages bestowed him in a litter, and so, with one arm hanging down[7], carried him home. Neither in so many wounds was there, as Antistius his physician deemed, any one found mortal, but that which he received second, in his breast[8]. The conspirators were minded to have dragged his corpse, after he was thus slain, into the river Tiber, confiscated his goods, and repealed all his acts; but for fear of M. Antonius the consul, and Lepidus, master of the horsemen, they held their hands and gave over those courses.

83. At the demand therefore of L. Piso, whose daughter he married, his last will and testament was opened and read in the house of Antonius: which will, upon the ides of September[1] next before, he had made in his own house at Labicum and committed to the keeping of the chief Vestal virgin[a]. Q. Tubero writeth that, from his first consulship unto the beginning of the civil war, he was ever wont to write down for his heir Cn. Pompeius, and to read the said will unto his soldiers in their public assembly. But in this last testament of his he ordained three co-heirs, the nephews all of his sisters[2] ; to wit, C. Octavius[3], of three fourth parts, L. Pinarius, and Q. Pedius of one fourth part remaining. In the latter end and bottom of this testamentary instrument he adopted also C. Octavius into his house and name ; and many of those that afterwards murdered him, he nominated for guardians to his son[4], if it fortuned he had any born ; yea, and Decimus Brutus to be one of his second heirs in remainder. He bequeathed in his legacies unto the people[5] his hortyards[6] about Tiber to lie common ; and three hundred sesterces[7] to them by the poll [26].

84. The solemnity of his burial being proclaimed, there was a pile of wood for his funeral fire reared in Mars' Field, near unto the tomb of Julia[1]. Before the Rostra was placed a chapel[2] all gilt, resembling the temple of Venus Genetrix, and within it a bedstead[3] of ivory, richly spread with cloth of gold and purple, and at the head thereof a trophy, supporting the robe wherein he was slain. Now, because it was thought that those should not have day enough who came to his offerings and brought their oblations, commandment was given that, without observing the strict order[4], every man might bring, which way and by what street of the city he would, his gift into Mars' Field abovesaid. During the games and plays then exhibited there were chanted certain verses, fitly applied as well to move pity as hatred withal of his death, and namely out of the tragedy of Pacuvius, entitled *The Judgement of Armour*[a] :

> *Men' Men' servasse, ut essent qui me perderent?*

> Alas the while, that I these men should save,
> By bloody death to bring me to my grave[b] ;

as also another out of that of Accius[5] to the same sense. Instead of a laudatory oration, Antonius the consul pronounced by the public crier the act of the senate, wherein they decreed for him all honour, both divine and human ; likewise the solemn oath, wherewith they all obliged themselves to defend the life and person of him and none but him, whereunto he added some few words of his own. The aforesaid bed[6] the magistrates for the time being and such as had borne office of state already had conveyed into the Forum before the Rostra.

Which when some intended to burn within the cell of Jupiter Capitolinus, others in the Court of Pompey [7], all of a sudden there were two fellows with swords girt to their sides and carrying two javelins, who with light-burning [Aug. 82] tapers set it on fire ; and with that immediately the multitude that stood round about gat dry sticks together and heaped them thereupon, with the tribunal seats and other pews [78] of inferior magistrates, and whatsoever beside was ready and next at hand [c]. After them, the minstrels and stage-players disrobed themselves of those vestments which out of the furniture of his triumphs they had put on for the present use and occasion, rent the same in pieces, and flung all into the flaming fire. The old legionary soldiers also did the like by their armour, wherein they bravely went to solemnise his funeral. Yea, and most of the city dames did no less by their jewels and ornaments which they had about them, their children's pendant brooches also, and rich coats embroidered and bordered with purple. In this exceeding sorrow and public mourning, a number there were besides from foreign nations, who every one, after their country manner, lamented round, one after another, by companies in their turn ; but above all other the Jews [8], who also for many nights together frequented the place of his sepulture and where his body was burnt.

85. The common people, straight after his funeral obsequies, went with burning firebrands and torches to the dwelling-houses of Brutus and Cassius ; from whence being hardly repelled, they, meeting with Helvius Cinna by the way, and mistaking his name, as if he had been Cornelius Cinna (one who the day before had made a bitter invective as touching Caesar and whom they sought for), him they slew, set his head upon a spear, and so carried it about with them. After this they erected in the forum a solid column almost 20 feet high, of Numidian marble, with this title graven thereupon : *Parenti Patriae,* " to the Father of his Country." At which pillar for a long time they used still to sacrifice, to make vows and prayers, to determine and end certain controversies, interposing always their oath by the name of Caesar.

86. Caesar left behind him, in the minds of certain friends about him, a suspicion that he was neither willing to have lived any longer, nor cared at all for life, because he stood not well

to health, but was evermore crasie[1], and thereupon neglected
as well all religious warnings from the gods, as also what
reports soever his friends presented unto him. There be that
think how, trusting upon that last act of the senate and their
oath aforesaid, he discharged the guard of Spaniards from
about him, who, armed with swords, gave attendance upon his
person. Others contrariwise are of opinion that, seeing, as he
did, how he was forelaid [25] on every side, and confessing it
were better once for all to undergo those imminent dangers,
than always to stand in fear thereof, he was wont to say[2] : it
concerned not himself so much as it did the State, that he
should live and be safe ; as for him, he had gotten long since
power and glory enough : marry, the commonwealth (if aught
but well came to him) should not be at quiet, but incur the
troubles of civil war, the issue whereof would be far worse
than ever it had been.

87. This one thing verily all men well-near are agreed upon,
that such a death befell unto him as himself in manner wished.
For not only upon a time when he had read in Xenophon[1],
how Cyrus, being at the point of death, gave some order for his
funeral, he, setting light by so lingering and slow a kind of
death, had wished to die quickly and of a sudden ; but also the
very day before he was killed, in a certain discourse moved at
supper in Marcus Lepidus' house upon this point, What was the
best end of a man's life ? preferred that which was sudden and
unlooked for.

88. He died in the fifty-sixth[1 a] year of his age, and was
canonised among the gods, not only by their voice who decreed
such honour unto him, but also by the persuasion of the common people. For at those games and plays which were the
first that Augustus his heir exhibited for him thus deified,
there shone a blazing star for seven days together, arising about
the eleventh hour of the day ; and believed it was to be the
soul of Caesar received up into heaven. For this cause also
upon his image there is a star set to the very crown of his head.
Thought good it was to dam up the court wherein he was
murdered [b] ; to name the ides of March parricidium [c] ; and
that the senate should never meet in council upon that
day.

89. Of these murderers, there was not one in manner[1] that

either survived him above three years, or died of his natural
death. All stood condemned, and by one mishap or other
perished ; some by shipwreck, others in battle ; and some
again [2] shortened their own days with the very same dagger
wherewith they had wounded Caesar.

THE HISTORY OF
OCTAVIUS CAESAR AUGUSTUS

1. THAT the principal name and lineage of the Octavii dwelt in times past at Velitrae [1], there be many evidences to show ; for both a street in the most frequented place of the said town long since carried the name Octavius, and also there was to be seen an altar there consecrated by one Octavius [2], who, being general of the field in a war against the borderers, when he happened to be sacrificing to Mars, upon news brought that the enemy gave a sudden charge, caught the inwards of the beast sacrificed, half-raw as they were, out of the fire [3], cut and offered them accordingly, and so entered into battle and returned with victory. There is, besides, a public act extant upon record, wherein decreed and provided it was that, every year after, the inwards in like manner should be presented unto Mars, and the rest of the sacrifice remaining carried back unto the Octavii.

2. These Octavii, being by king Tarquinius Priscus naturalised Romans, soon after translated and admitted by Servius Tullius into the senate among the patricians and nobles, in process of time ranged themselves with the commons, and with much ado at length, by the means of Julius of sacred memory returned to the patrician degree again. The first of these that by the people's election bare any magistracy was C. Rufus, who having been quaestor begat Gnaeus and Gaius. From them descended two families of the Octavii, and those for their estate of life far different. For Gnaeus and all the rest from him one after another attained to places of highest honour ; but Gaius and his posterity every one, even unto the father of Augustus (such was either their fortune or their will), stayed in the order and degree of gentlemen, [1] and rose no higher. The great-grandfather of Augustus, in the second Punic war [2], served in quality of a military tribune [3] in Sicily, under Aemilius Papus, lord-general [4]. His father, contenting himself with bearing office like another burgess in his own borough, being left wealthy by his father, grew to a good estate, and lived to be an old man, in much peace and tranquillity. But of these matters let others make report. Augustus himself writeth no more but thus, that the house from whence he came was of Roman gentlemen, wealthy and ancient withal, wherein the first that ever came to be senator was his father. M. Antonius hitteth him in the teeth with his great-grandfather, saying he was but a libertine [C. 2] born, and by occupation a roper [5], and come out of a village of the Thurines [6] ; also that his grandfather was no better than a very banker [7]. Neither have I found any more as touching the ancestors of Augustus by the father's side.

3. Octavius his father, from the very beginning of his age, was of great wealth and reputation, so that I cannot but marvel, that he also hath been reported by some a banker or money-changer, yea, and one of the dealers of money [a] and servitors employed in the Campus Martius by those that stand for offices ; for, having been from his very cradle brought up in wealth highly and plentifully, he both attained unto honourable dignities with facility, and administered the same with credit and reputation. Presently upon [1] his praetorship, the province of Macedonia fell unto his lot. And in his journey thither, the fugitives, to wit, the relics of Spartacus' and Catiline's forces, who then held the Thurine territory, he defeated, having commission extraordinarily given unto him in the senate so to do. This province he governed with no less justice than fortitude ; for, having discomfited in a great battle the Bessi and the Thracians, he dealt so well with the allies and confederates of that kingdom, that there be certain letters of M. Tullius Cicero extant, wherein he exhorteth and admonisheth his brother Quintus [2] (who at the same time, little to his credit and good name, administered the proconsulship of Asia) for to imitate his neighbour Octavius, in doing well by the allies, and winning their love thereby.

4. As he departed out of Macedonia before that he could profess himself to be a suitor for the consulship, he died a sudden death, leaving these children behind him alive ; namely, two daughters, Octavia the elder, which he had by Ancharia,

Octavia the younger, and Augustus likewise, by Atia. This Atia was the daughter of M. Atius Balbus and Julia, the sister of C. Caesar. Balbus by his father's side was an Aricine[1], a man that showed senators' images and arms in his house, by his mother linked to Pompey the Great in the nearest degree of consanguinity. And having borne the office of praetorship he among the twenty commissioners divided, by virtue of the Julian law, the lands in the territory of Capua [C. 20] among the commons. But M. Antonius[2], despising the parentage and pedigree of Augustus by the mother side also, twitteth him and layeth in his dish, [C. 49] that his great-grandsire was an African born ; saying one while, that he kept a shop of sweet oils, ointments and perfumes, another while, that he was a baker in Aricia. Cassius verily of Parma, in a certain epistle, taxeth Augustus as being the nephew, not of a baker only, but also of a banker, in these terms : " Thou hast meal for thy mother ; and then comes a banker of Nerulum, who out of a most painful bakehouse in Aricia kneadeth and mouldeth it, with his hands sullied by telling and exchanging money[3]."

5. Augustus was born when M. Tullius Cicero and Antony were consuls, the ninth day before the kalends of October[1], a little before the sunrising, in the Palatine quarter [a] of the city, at a place called Capita Bubula[2], where now it hath a sacred chapel, built and erected a little after he departed out of this world. For, as it is found in the records of the senate, when C. Lectorius, a young gentleman of the patrician order, pleaded to have some easier punishment for his adultery, and alleged, over and besides his young years and parentage, this also in his plea before the senators, that he was the possessor and, as it were, the warden and sexton[3] of that ground or soil, which Augustus of happy memory touched first [b] ; and requested that it might be given and granted unto the said Augustus as to his domestic and peculiar god, decreed it was that the same part of the house should be consecrated to that holy use.

6. There is yet to be seen the place of his nursery, within a suburban house belonging to his ancestors, near unto Velitrae, a very little cabin, about the bigness of a larder or pantry ; the neighbours are possessed with a certain conceit, as if he had been there also born. To enter into this room, unless it be of necessity and with devout chastity[1], men make it scrupulous and are afraid ; upon an old conceived opinion, as if unto as many as came thither rashly and inconsiderately, a certain horror and fearfulness were presented. And, verily, this was soon after confirmed by this occasion. For when the new land-lord and possessor of that farm-house, either by chance and at unawares, or else to try some experiment [2], went into it, there to take up his lodging, it happened that in the night, within very few hours after, being driven out from thence by some sudden violence (he knoweth not how), he was found in manner half-dead, together with bed and all, before the door.

7. Being yet an infant, surnamed he was Thurinus, in memorial of the beginning of his ancestors ; or else because in the country about Thurii, when he was newly born, his father Octavius fought a battle against the fugitives. That he was surnamed Thurinus, myself am able to report by a good and sufficient evidence, as having gotten an old little counterfeit in brass representing him being a child, which had in iron letters, and those almost worn out, this name engraven. This said counterfeit, being given by me unto the prince [1], is now devoutly kept and worshipped among other his bed-chamber images. Moreover, called he is oftentimes in taunting wise, by M. Antonius in his epistles, Thurinus and himself writeth unto him back again, as touching that point, nothing but this : that he marvelleth why that former name of his should be objected unto him as a reproach. Afterwards, he assumed the surname of Gaius Caesar, and, after it, of Augustus ; the one by the last will of his great-uncle by the mother side, the other by the virtue of Munatius Plancus' his sentence [2] ; for when some gave their opinion that he ought to be styled Romulus, as if he also had been a founder of the city, Plancus prevailed that he should be called rather Augustus ; not only for that it was a new surname, but also greater and more honourable, because religious and holy places, wherein also anything is consecrated by bird-flight and feeding of them, be called augusta, *ab auctu*, from growing, or else *ab avium gestu gustuve*, from birds' gesture and feeding. Like as Ennius [*Annales*, i. 116] also teacheth, writing in this manner :

Augusto augurio postquam inclita condita Roma est,
After that noble Rome was built by sacred flight of birds.

8. He was four years old when his father died ; and in the twelfth year of his age he praised in a public assembly his grandmother Julia, deceased. Four years after, having put on his virile robe[a], he had military gifts[b] bestowed upon him at the African triumph of Caesar, albeit by reason of his young years he had not once served in the wars. Soon after, when his uncle (Caesar) was gone into Spain against Pompey's children, he followed within a while (being as yet not well recovered out of a grievous sickness), even through ways infested by enemies, with very few in his train to accompany him, and having suffered shipwreck besides ; whereby he mightily won his uncle's love, who quickly approved his towardly behaviour and disposition, over and above his diligence in travel. When Caesar, after he had recovered Spain and brought it to his subjection, intended a voyage against the Daci[1], and from thence against the Parthians, he, being sent afore to Apollonia, became a student there and followed his book. And so soon as he had certain intelligence that Caesar was slain, and himself made his heir, standing in doubt and suspense a long time, whether he should implore the help of the legions or no, at length he gave over that course verily, as too hasty and untimely ; but when he was returned again to Rome, he entered upon his inheritance, notwithstanding his mother made some doubt thereof and his step-father, Marcius Philippus[2], a man of consular degree, much dissuaded him therefrom. And from that time, having levied and assembled his forces, he governed the commonwealth, first jointly with M. Antonius and M. Lepidus[c] for the space almost of twelve years, and at the last for forty-four years by himself alone.

9. Having thus laid open the very sum, as it were, of his life, I will go through the parts thereof in particular ; not by the times, but by the several kinds thereof, to the end the same may be shown and known more distinctly. Five civil wars he made, to wit, at Mutina, Philippi, Perusia, in Sicily, and at Actium, of which the first and last were against M. Antonius ; the second against Brutus and Cassius ; the third against L. Antonius, brother to the triumvir ; the fourth against Sextus Pompeius, Pompey the Great's son. Of all these wars he took the occasion and quarrel from hence, namely, reputing and judging in his mind nothing more meet and convenient than the revenge of his uncle's death and the maintenance of his acts and proceedings.

10. No sooner was he returned from Apollonia, but he purposed to set upon Brutus and Cassius at unawares ; and (because upon foresight of danger they were fled secretly out of the way) to take the course of law, and in their absence to indict them of murder. As for the plays and games for Caesar's victory, because they durst not exhibit them, whose lot and office it was so to do, himself set them forth. And to the end that he might go through all other matters also more resolutely, he professed himself to labour for the tribuneship [1] in the room of one who fortuned to die, albeit he was one of the nobility, though not of the senate. But seeing that M. Antonius the consul withstood his attempts, whereas he hoped he would have been his principal friend in that suit, and vouchsafed not unto him so much as the assistance of his own public authority or help procured from others in any thing [2], without he agreed and covenanted to yield unto him some exceeding consideration, he betook himself unto the protection of those nobles and chief senators, unto whom he perceived that Antony was odious ; in this regard especially, that he [3] endeavoured all that he could by force of arms to expel Decimus Brutus, besieged at Mutina, out of that province, which by Caesar was granted and by the senate confirmed unto him. And thereupon, by the advice and persuasion of some, he set certain persons privily in hand to murder Antony ; which perilous practice of his being detected, and fearing still the like danger to himself, he waged the old soldiers with as bountiful a largesse as possibly he could, for the defence as well of his own person as of the State. And being appointed to lead this army thus levied, in quality of propraetor and together with Hirtius and Pansa, who had entered upon the consulship, to aid D. Brutus, he made an end of this war committed unto him within three months, in two fought fields. In the former of which Antony writeth that he fled, and without coat-armour or horse appeared at length after two days and showed himself. But in the battle next following, well-known it is that he performed the part not only of a captain, but also of a soldier ; and in the very heat and midst of the medley, by occasion that the standard-bearer of his own legion was grievously hurt, he supported the eagle with his own shoulders [4], and so carried it a good while.

11. During this war, when Hirtius had lost his life in the conflict, and Pansa soon after of his wound, it was bruited rifely abroad, that both of them were by his means slain, to the end that, having defeated Antony, and the commonwealth being bereft of both consuls, he alone might seize upon the victorious armies. And verily the death of Pansa was so deeply suspected, that Glyco the physician was committed to ward and durance, as if he had put poison into his wound. Aquilius Niger [1] added moreover and saith, that the one [2] of the consuls, to wit, Hirtius, was in the very confused medley of the battle killed by Augustus himself.

12. But so soon as he understood that Antony after his flight was entertained by M. Lepidus, that other captains also and armies consented to take part with the side [1], he forsook without all delays the cause of the nobles and principal senators ; and, for the better pretence of this change and alteration of his mind, craftily and unjustly alleged the words and deeds of certain of them ; as if some [a] had given it out of him, that he was a boy, others [b], that he was to be adorned and honoured [2], that neither himself nor the old beaten [3] soldiers might be rewarded according to their deserts. And the better to approve his repentance of the former side and faction that he took, he fined the Nursians [4] in a great sum of money, and more than they were able to pay ; for that upon the monuments or tomb of those citizens that were slain in the battle at Mutina (which at their common charges was reared) they wrote this title, " That they died for the Liberty and Freedom of their City."

13. Being entered into society with Antony and Lepidus, he finished the Philippian war also (although he was but weak and sickly), and that with two battles ; in the former, being discamped and driven out of the field, hardly he escaped by flight and recovered [1] the regiment or wing of Antony. Neither used he moderately the success of his victory, but, when he had sent the head of Brutus to Rome for to be bestowed under the statue of Caesar, he dealt cruelly with the noblest and most honourable prisoners, and not without reproachful words ; so far forth verily, that to one of them, making humble suit and

prayer for his sepulture, he answered (by report) in this wise :
that it would be anon at the disposal of the fowls of the air ; and
when others, to wit, the father and son [a] together, entreated
for their lives, he commanded them either to cast lots or try by
combat whether of them should have life granted ; and so
beheld them both as they died, while the father who offered
himself to die was slain, and the son voluntarily took his
death.   Whereupon the rest, and amongst them M. Favonius,
that worthy follower of Cato, when they were brought forth
with their irons and chains to execution, after they had in
honourable terms saluted Antony by the name of emperor [2],
openly reviled and let fly at him [Octavian] most foul and railing words.   Having parted between them their charges and
offices after this victory, when Antony undertook to settle the
East in good order, and himself to bring the old soldiers back
into Italy, and to place them there in the lands and territories •
belonging to the free towns and boroughs, he kept himself in
favour neither with the said old soldiers, nor the former pos-
sessors of those lands ; while the one sort complained that they
were disseized, and the other, that they were not well-entreated
according to their hope for so good deserts.

14. At which very time he forced L. Antonius (who, confidently presuming upon the consulship which he then bare, and
his brother's power withal, went about to make an insurrection
and alteration in the State) to flee unto Perusia, and there for
very hunger compelled him to yield, but yet not without great
jeopardy of his own person, both before and after the war.   For
when, at a certain solemn sight of stage-plays, he had commanded an ordinary and common soldier, who was set within
the fourteen ranks [a], to be raised [1] by an officer, and thereupon
a rumour was carried and spread by his malicious ill-willers and
backbiters, as if presently [4] after torture he had put the same
soldier to death, there lacked very little but that, in the concourse and indignation of the military multitude, he had come
to a mischief and been murdered.   This only saved his life ;
that the man, for a while missed, suddenly was to be seen again
alive and safe without any harm done unto him.   About the
walls of Perusia, as he sacrificed, he had like to have been intercepted by a strong company of sword-fencers that sallied out
of the town.

15. After he had forced Perusia, he proceeded to the execution of very many, and ever as any went about either to crave pardon or to excuse themselves, with this one word he stopped their mouths, " Die ye must." Some write, that 300 of both degrees (to wit, senators and knights) chosen out of them who had yielded, were killed as sacrifices [1] upon the ides of March [2], at the altar built in the honour of Julius Caesar of famous memory. There have been others who wrote, that of very purpose he took arms and made this war, to the end that his close [C. 31] adversaries and those who rather for fear than of good-will held in [3], upon occasion given and opportunity by L. Antonius their leader, might be detected [4], that, having once vanquished them and confiscated their goods, the rewards promised unto the old soldiers he might the better perform.

16. The war in Sicily he began betimes and with the first, but drew it out a long time, as being often intermitted : one while, for the repairing and rigging of his fleet, which by two shipwrecks in tempest (and that in summer-time [1]) he had lost ; another while, by occasion of peace made at the earnest cry of the people, for the provision of their victuals cut off and kept from them, and the famine thereby daily growing ; until such time as, having built new ships, manumitted, and set free 20,000 slaves, and those put to the oar for to learn to row galleys, he made the haven Julius at Baiae by letting the sea into the lakes Lucrinus and Avernus. In which when he had trained and exercised his sea-forces whole winters, he overcame [Sextus] Pompeius between Mylae [2] and Naulochus [3] ; at the very hour and instant time of which naval battle he was suddenly surprised with such a sound sleep, that his friends were fain to waken him and raise him out of bed for to give the signal. Whereupon occasion and matter was ministered (as I think) to Antony [4] for to cast this in his teeth, that he could not so much as with his eyes open see directly before him the battle set in array, but lay like a senseless block on his back, looking only into the sky aloft [5], nor once arose and came in sight of his soldiers, before that M. Agrippa had put his enemies' twelve ships to flight. Others blame and charge him both for a speech and deed also of his, as if he should cry out [6] and say that, seeing his own regiment of ships were cast away by tempests, he would even against the will of Neptune obtain victory. And verily, the next day of the games in the circus [a], he took out of the solemn pomp there shown the image of the said god [7] ; neither in any other war lightly [8] was he in more and greater dangers. For, having transported one army into Sicily, when he sailed back again for to waft over the rest of his forces from the continent and firm land [9], he was at unawares overtaken and surprised by Demochares and Apollophanes, the lieutenants and admirals of Pompeius, but at the length, with very much ado, he escaped with one only bark.   In like manner as he travelled by land unto Rhegium [b] near Locri, kenning afar off Pompeius' [10] galleys sailing along the coasts and weening them to be his own, he went down to the shore, and had like to have been caught and taken by them.   And even then, as he made shift to flee and escape through by-ways and blind lanes, a bondservant of Aemilius Paulus, a companion of his, taking it to the heart that his master's father Paulus was in times past by him proscribed and outlawed, and embracing, as it were, the good occasion and opportunity of revenge now offered, gave [made] the attempt to kill him.   After the flight of Pompeius [11], when M. Lepidus, one of his colleagues [12], whom he had called forth of Africa to his aid, bearing himself proud upon the confidence of twenty legions, challenged a sovereignty over the rest, and that with terror and menaces, he stript him of all his army, and upon his humble submission and supplication pardoned his life, but confined him for ever to Circeii.   The society [13] of M. Antonius, wavering always in doubtful terms and uncertain, and, notwithstanding many and sundry reconciliations, not well-knit and confirmed, he broke off quite in the end ; and the better to prove and make good that he had degenerated [c] from the civil behaviour and modesty of a Roman citizen, he caused the last will and testament of the said Antony, which he had left at Rome [d], and therein nominated even the children of Cleopatra among his heirs, to be opened and read in a public assembly.   Howbeit, when he was judged by the State an enemy, he sent back unto him those of his nearest acquaintance and inward friends, and among others, C. Sosius and T. Domitius [14][e], being consuls at that time still.   The Bononians [15] also, for that of old they were dependants of the Antonii and in their retinue and protection, he by a public act acquitted and pardoned for not entering into a confederacy with all Italy on his side [f]. Not long after, he vanquished him in a naval battle before Actium [g], what time, by reason that the fight continued until it was late in the evening, he was forced to lodge all night, conqueror as he was, on shipboard.

17. When he had retired himself from Actium into the island [of] Samos for his winter harbour, being disquieted with the news of his soldiers' mutiny demanding rewards and discharge from service, those I mean, whom after the victory achieved he had from out of the whole number sent before to Brundisium, he went again into Italy; but, in crossing the seas thither, twice was he tossed and troubled with tempests, first, between the promontories or capes of Peloponnesus and Aetolia, again, about the mountains or cliffs called Ceraunii. In both which places part of his pinnaces were cast away and drowned; and withal the very tackling of that ship wherein he embarked was rent and torn asunder, yea, and the rudder thereof quite broken. Neither stayed he at Brundisium above twenty-seven days, that is to say, until he had settled his soldiers and contented them in their desires and requests, but fetching a compass [1] about Asia and Syria, sailed into Egypt. Where, after he had laid siege unto Alexandria, whither Antony and Cleopatra were together fled, he soon became master of that city. And as for Antony, who now (all too late) made means [2] for conditions of peace, he enforced to make himself away, and saw him dead [3]. And to Cleopatra, whom most gladly he would have saved alive for to beautify his triumph, he set the Psylli [a] to suck out the venom and poison within her body; for that supposed it was she died with the sting of the serpent aspis [b]. This honour he did unto them both, namely, to bury them in one sepulchre; and the tomb by them begun, he commanded to be finished. Young Antony, the elder of those twain whom he had by Fulvia, he caused to be violently haled from the statue of Julius Caesar of famous memory, unto which, after many prayers but all in vain, he was fled as to sanctuary, and so killed him. Likewise Caesario, whom Cleopatra gave out openly that she had conceived by his father Caesar [4], he fetched back again from the place whither he was fled, and put him to death. The rest of the children of Antony and the queen together he both saved (no less than if they had been linked in near alliance unto himself), and also, according to the state of every one of them, he maintained and cherished respectively.

18. About the same time, when he beheld the tomb together with the corpse of Alexander the Great, taken newly forth of the vault or secret chapel where it was bestowed, he set upon it a coronet of gold, and strewing flowers thereupon worshipped it ; and being asked the question, whether he would look upon the Ptolemies [1] also, he answered that he was desirous indeed to see a king, but not the dead [a]. When he had reduced Egypt in the form of a province, to the end that he might make it more fruitful and fit to yield corn and victuals for the city of Rome, he scoured and cleansed, by help of soldiers, all those ditches whereinto the Nile overfloweth, which by long time had been choked with mud. And that the memory of his victory at Actium might be more renowned among posterity, he built the city of Nicopolis over against Actium, and ordained certain games and plays there, every five years ; and, having enlarged the old temple of Apollo [2] and the place wherein he had encamped, he beautified with naval spoils and then consecrated it to Neptune and Mars.

19. After this, sundry tumults and the very beginnings of commotions and insurrections, many conspiracies also detected before they grew to any head, he suppressed, and those, some at one time, and some at another ; namely, first one of Lepidus the younger ; then, another of Varro Murena and Fannius Caepio ; soon after that, of M. Genatius [1], and so forward of Plautius Rufus and L. Paulus, his niece's [2] husband; and besides all these, that of L. Audasius, accused of forgery and counterfeit seals, a man neither for years able nor body sound ; likewise of Asinius Epicadus, descended from the Parthinian nation, a mongrel [3][a] ; and last of all, of Telephus, a base nomenclator [4], servant to a woman ; for free was not Augustus from the conspiracy and danger, no, not of the most abject sort of people. As for Audasius and Epicadus, they had intended to carry away Julia, his daughter, and Agrippa, his nephew, out of those islands wherein they abode confined, unto the armies ; and Telephus purposed, upon a deep conceit that the sovereignty of dominion was by the destinies and will of God due unto him, even to lay upon him and the senate violent hands. And more than that, one time there was taken, near

unto his bed-chamber by night, a camp-slave belonging to the
Illyrian army, who had deceived the porters and gotten thither
with a wood-knife at his side, but whether he were out of his
wits, or feigned himself mad, it was uncertain ; for nothing
could be wrung out of him by examination upon the rack and
torture.

20. Foreign wars he made in his own person, two in all and
no more ; that is to say, the Dalmatian [a], when he was yet a
very youth ; and the Cantabrian, after he had defeated
Antony. In the Dalmatian war, he was wounded also ; for
in one battle he gat a blow upon his right knee with a stone,
and in another, not his leg only, but also both his arms were
hurt with the fall from a bridge [1] [b]. The rest of his wars he
managed by his lieutenants, yet so as that in some of them,
namely, the Pannonian and the German, he would either come
between times, or else remain not far off, making his progress
from the city of Rome as far as to Ravenna, or Mediolanum
[Milan] or to Aquileia.

21. He subdued, partly by his own conduct in proper per
son, and in part by his lieutenants having commission immediately from him and directed by his auspices, Cantabria,
Aquitania, Pannonia, and Dalmatia, together with all Illyricum,
Rhaetia likewise, the Vindelici, the Salassi and the nations
inhabiting the Alps [1]. He repressed also the incursions of the
Daci [C. 44], having slain three of their generals with a great
number of them besides. And the Germans he removed and
set further off, even beyond the river Albis [Elbe]. Howbeit,
of these the Suevi and the Sicambri, because they yielded themselves, he brought over into Gaul, and placed them in the lands
next unto the Rhine. Other nations being malcontent, he
reduced unto his obedience. Neither made he war upon any
people without just and necessary causes ; and so far was he
from desire of enlarging his empire, or advancing his martial
glory, that he compelled certain princes and potentates of the
barbarians to take an oath in the temple of Mars the Revenger [a],
for to continue in their allegiance, and in the protection and
peace which they sued for ; yea, and from some of them he
assayed to exact a new kind of hostages, even women [2], for that
he perceived that they neglected the pledges of the males ; and
yet he gave them liberty, as often as they would, to receive

their hostages again. Neither proceeded he at any time against those, who either usually or treacherously above the rest took arms and rebelled, to any punishment more grievous than this, even to sell them as captives; with this condition, that they should not serve in any neighbour country, nor be manumitted and made free within the space of thirty[3] years. By which fame of virtue and moderation that went of him, he induced and drew the very Indians and Scythians, nations known by report and hearsay only, to make suit of their own accord by ambassadors, for amity of him and the people of Rome. The Parthians also, whenas he laid claim unto Armenia, yielded soon unto him; and those military ensigns which they had taken from M. Crassus[4] and M. Antonius, they delivered unto him again at his demand, and moreover offered hostages unto him. And finally, when there were many competitors together at one time claiming a title to the kingdom, they would not allow of any but one by him elected.

22. The temple of Janus Quirinus[a], which from the foundation of the city before his days had once and twice been shut, he in a far shorter space of time (having peace both by sea and land) shut a third time[1]. Twice he rode on horseback ovant[2][b] into the city; once presently [3] upon the Philippian war, and again, after the Sicilian. He kept three triumphs riding in his chariot; to wit, the Dalmatian, the Actian, and the Alexandrian, and these continued all for three days together.

23. Of shameful foils and grievous overthrows he received but two in all, and those in no place else but in Germany; namely, when Lollius and Varus[1] were defeated. That of Lollius was a matter of dishonour more than loss and damage; but the other of Varus drew with it in manner utter destruction, as wherein three legions with their general, the lieutenants, and auxiliaries[a], all were slain. Upon the news of this misfortune, he proclaimed a set watch both day and night through the city of Rome for fear of some tumult and uproar; and the commissions of presidents and deputies over provinces he renewed and enlarged their time of government, to the end that the allies of the people of Rome might be kept in allegiance by governors, such as were both skilful and also acquainted with them. He vowed also the great Roman games and plays to the honour of Jupiter Optimus Maximus, if the commonwealth turned to better state. This[2] happened during the time of the Cimbrian and Marsian wars[3]. For therewith (by report) he was so troubled and astonied, that for certain months together he let the hair of beard and head grow still and wore it long, yea, and otherwhiles would run his head against the doors[4], crying out, " Quintilius Varus, deliver up thy[5] legions again." And the very day[b] of this unfortunate calamity he kept every year mournful, with sorrow and lamentation.

24. In warfare and feats of arms he both altered and also instituted many points ; yea, and some he reduced to the ancient manner. Military discipline[a] he exercised most severely. He permitted not so much as any of his lieutenants, but with much ado and discontentment, to visit otherwhiles their wives, and never but in the winter months[b]. A Roman knight, for cutting off the thumbs[c] of two young men his sons, to avoid the military oath and war service, he set in open port-sale [C. 50], himself (I say) and all his goods. Whom notwithstanding, because he saw the publicans[d] about to buy and bid very well for him, he appointed and delivered to his own freedman, that, being confined and sent away unto his living and lands in the country, he might permit him to live as free. The 10th legion, for being stubborn and unwilling to obey, he dismissed all and whole with ignominy ; other legions likewise, requiring malapertly their discharge, he cassed[1] without allowance of rewards due for their service. Whole bands or cohorts, if any of them gave ground and reculed[2], he tithed, that is to say, executed every tenth man of them : and the rest, he allowed barley instead of wheat to feed upon. Those centurions who forsook their stations he punished with death, even as well as the common soldiers of their bands ; and for other kinds of delinquency he put them to shame sundry ways, as commanding them to stand all the day long before the praetorium[3], sometimes in their single coats[4] and ungirt, otherwhiles with ten-foot perches[5] in their hands, or else carrying turfs of earth.

25. After the civil wars, he called none of his soldiers either in any public speech, or by way of edict or proclamation, by the name of fellow-soldiers[a], but plain soldiers. Nay, he would not suffer them otherwise to be termed so much as by his sons, or his step-sons, thinking it was a more affected

manner [1] of appellation than stood either with martial law, or
the quietness of those times [a], or the majesty of himself and
his house.   Libertines [b] he employed in soldiery, unless it were
at Rome about skarfires [2] by night (notwithstanding there was
feared some tumult and uproar by occasion of great dearth and
scarcity), but twice only ; once, in garrison for defence of those
colonies which bounded fast upon Illyricum, a second time, for
keeping the banks of the river Rhine.   And those, being as
yet bond, imposed upon men and women [3] of the wealthier sort
for to set out, but without delay manumitted, he kept with him
to serve under one of the foremost banners [4] in the van-guard,
neither intermingled with such as were freeborn, nor in the
same manner armed.   As for military gifts, he gave unto his
soldiers trappers [5], collars, and whatsoever stood upon gold or
silver [6], much sooner than vallar [7] or mural coronets [c], which
were more honourable.   These he bestowed most sparingly,
and when he did, it was without suit [8] made therefor ; and many
times upon the common and base soldiers [d].   He gave unto M.
Agrippa, after a naval victory in Cilicia, a blue streamer.
Those captains only who had triumphed, albeit they were both
companions with him in his expeditions and also partakers of
his victories, he thought not meet to be rewarded with any
gifts at all, because they also had power to bestow the same
upon whom they would.   Moreover, he deemed nothing less
beseeming a perfect and accomplished captain than haste-
making and rashness.   And therefore, these mots and sen-
tences were rife in his mouth. $\Sigma\pi\epsilon\hat{v}\delta\epsilon$ $\beta\rho\alpha\delta\acute{\epsilon}\omega s$ [e].

'Ασφαλὴs γὰρ ἐστ' ἀμείνων ἢ θρασὺs στρατηλάτηs [f] :

As also, *Sat celeriter fieri, quicquid fiat satis bene* [g].   His saying
was that " neither battle nor war was once to be undertaken,
unless there might be evidently seen more hope of gain than
fear of damage " ; for such as sought after the smallest commodities, not with as little danger [9], he likened unto those that
angle or fish with a golden hook ; for the loss whereof, if it
happened to be knapt or broken off, no draught of fish whatsoever was able to make amends.

26. He managed magistracies and honourable places of
government before due time [1], some of them also of a new kind [2];
and others in perpetuity [3].   The consulship he usurped and

entered upon in the twentieth year of his age [a], presenting
forcibly and in hostile manner his legions before the city, sending some of purpose to demand it, even in the name of the
army, for him. What time verily, when the senate made some
doubt and stay of the matter, Cornelius, a centurion and the
chief man of that message, casting off [4] his soldier's jacket and
showing his sword's haft, stuck not to say thus openly in the
senate-house, " This here shall do the deed, if ye will not " [b].
His second consulship he bare nine years after ; the third, but
one year between ; the rest ensuing he continued one after another unto the eleventh. Afterwards having refused many
consulships when they were offered unto him, his twelfth
consulship a greater while after, even seventeen years, himself
made suit for ; so did he again, two years after it, for his thirteenth, to the end that, being himself in place of the sovereign
and highest magistrate, he might bring honourably into the
common hall [5] Gaius and Lucius his adopted sons [6] ; each of
them to commence and perform their first pleadings at their
due time [7] in virile gowns. The five middle consulships
between, to wit, from the sixth to the eleventh, he held the
whole years through ; the other, for the space of six, or nine,
four, or three months, but the second, very few hours ; for
upon the very kalends of January [8], when he had sat awhile
upon his curule chair of estate [C. 76] before the temple of
Jupiter Capitolinus, he resigned up the office, and substituted
another in his place. Neither entered he upon all his consulships at Rome, but the fourth in Asia, the fifth, in the island of
Samos ; the eighth and ninth at Tarraco.

27. The triumvirate for settling of the commonwealth [1] he
administered for the space of ten years, wherein, verily, he
stood against his colleagues' proceedings for a good while, that
there might be no proscription ; but when it was once on foot,
he executed it more sharply than they both. For, whereas
they were exorable [2] and would be oftentimes entreated by
favour and prayer to respect the persons of many, he alone was
very earnest, that none might be spared ; among the rest, he
proscribed C. Toranius also, his own tutor and guardian, yea,
and the companion in the office of aedileship with his father
Octavius. Junius Saturninus [3] writeth moreover that, after
the proscription was ended, when M. Lepidus had in the senate-

house excused all that was past and given good hope of clemency for the time to come, because there had been execution enough done already, he on the contrary side professed openly, that he had determined no other end of the said proscription, but that he might have liberty still to proceed in all things as he would. Howbeit, in testimony of repentance for this rigour and obstinacy of his, he honoured afterward with the dignity of knighthood T. Junius Philopoemen[4], for that he was reputed to have in times past hid his own patron that was proscribed. In the same triumvirate he incurred many ways the ill-will and heartburning of the people ; for he commanded that Pinarius, a gentleman of Rome (what time as he himself made a public speech in an assembly whereunto he had admitted a multitude of pagans[5], that is to say, such as were no soldiers, and espied him there to take notes of something that he delivered before the soldiers, supposing him to be overbusy[6] and a spy), should be stabbed to death even in his sight ; yea, and he terrified Tedius Afer, consul elect (because he had maliciously in some spiteful terms depraved[7] something that he had done) with so great menaces, that in a melancholy he cast himself headlong and broke his own neck. Likewise, as Q. Gallius the praetor held under his robe a pair of duple writing-tables[8], when he came of course to do his duty and salute him, he, suspecting that he had a short sword hidden underneath, and not daring straightways to search him farther, for fear something else than a sword should be found about him, within a little while after caused him to be haled out of the tribunal seat of judgement by the hands of certain centurions of soldiers, and put to torture like a bondslave ; yea, and seeing he would confess nothing, commanded him to be killed, having first with his own hands plucked his eyes out of his head. Howbeit Augustus writeth, that the said Gallius, by pretending to parley secretly with him, laid wait for his life ; whereupon he committed him to prison, and afterwards dismissed and enlarged[9] him only to dwell in Rome ; and that in the end he perished either by shipwreck, or else by the hands of thieves who forelaid [C. 25] him. He received and held the tribunate in perpetuity. Therein, once or twice, he chose and assumed unto him a colleague, for several lustra[10]. He took upon him likewise the government of manners and laws as a perpetual censor ; in full right whereof, although he had not the honourable title of censorship, yet he held a survey and numbering of the people thrice, the first and third with a companion in office, the middle by himself alone.

28. Twice he was in mind to have resigned up his absolute government ; first, immediately upon the suppressing of Antony, mindful of that which oftentimes he had objected against him [1], namely, as if it had been long of him [2] that it was not resigned, and the commonwealth brought to a free state again ; and secondly, by reason that he was weary of a long and lingering sickliness, what time he sent also for all the magistrates and the senate [3] home to his house, and delivered up an account-book or register of the whole empire [4]. But considering better with himself that, were he once a private person, he could not live without danger ; and withal, that it would greatly hazard the commonwealth to be put into the hands and dispose of many, he continued in the holding thereof still. And whether the event ensuing, or his will herein were better, it is hard to say. Which will of his, as he pretended oftentimes when he sat in place, so he testified also by a certain edict in these words : " O that I might establish the commonwealth safe and sound in her own proper seat [5], and thereof reap that fruit which I desire ; even that I may be reported the author of an excellent estate, and carry with me when I die this hope, that the groundwork and the foundations of the commonwealth which I shall lay may continue and abide steadfast in their place." And verily, what he wished himself effected and brought to pass [6], having endeavoured and done his best every way, that no man might repent of this new estate. For the city, being not adorned according to the majesty of such an empire and subject to the casualties of deluges and fires, he beautified and set out so, as justly he made his boast, that where he found it built of brick, he left it all of marble. And for the safety thereof, he performed as much for future posterity as could be foreseen and provided for by man's wit and reason.

29. Public works he built very many, whereof the chief and principal was his Forum or stately hall of justice, together with the temple of Mars the Revenger ; the temple of Apollo in Palatium [1] ; the temple likewise of Jupiter the Thunderer in the Capitol. The reason why he built the said Forum was the multitude of men and their suits, which, because two would not suffice [a], seemed to have need of a third also. And therefore with great speed erected it was for that public use, even before the temple of Mars was finished. And expressly provided it was by law, that in it public causes should be determined apart, and choosing of judges or juries by itself. The temple of Mars he had vowed unto him in the Philippian war, which he took in hand for the revenge of his father's death. He ordained therefore by an act, that here the senate should be consulted with, as touching wars and triumphs ; that from hence those praetors or governors, who were to go into their provinces, should be honourably attended and brought onward on their way ; and that hither they should bring the ensigns and ornaments of triumph, who returned with victory. The temple of Apollo he reared in that part of the Palatine house, which, being smitten with lightning, was by that god required, as the soothsayers out of their learning had pronounced ; hereto was adjoined a gallery, with a library of Latin and Greek books. In which temple he was wont in his old age both to sit oftentimes in counsel with the senate, and also to oversee and review the decuries [2] of the judges. He consecrated the temple unto Jupiter the Thunderer, upon occasion that he escaped a danger, what time as in his Cantabrian expedition, as he travelled by night, a flash of lightning glanced upon his litter, and struck his servant stone-dead, that went with a light before. Some works also he made under other folks' names, to wit, his nephews, wife, and sister ; as the gallery and stately palace [basilica] of Lucius and Gaius [3], likewise the gallery or porches [colonnades] of Livia and Octavia ; the theatre also of Marcellus. Moreover, divers other principal persons he oftentimes exhorted to adorn and beautify the city, every man according to his ability, either by erecting new monuments, or else by repairing and furnishing the old. By which means many an edifice was by many a man built ; as namely, the temple of Hercules and the Muses by Marcius Philippus ; the temple of Diana by L. Cornificius ; the Court of Liberty [4] by Asinius Pollio ; a temple of Saturn by Munatius Plancus ; a theatre by Cornelius Balbus ; and an amphitheatre [b] by Statilius Taurus ; but many, and those very goodly monuments, by M. Agrippa.

30. The whole space of the city he divided into wards [a] and streets. He ordained that, as magistrates or aldermen yearly by lot should keep and govern the former, so there should be masters or constables elected out of the commons of every street, to look unto the other. Against skarfires [25] he devised night-watches and watchmen. To keep down inundations and deluges, he enlarged and cleansed the channel of the river Tiber, which in times past was full of rammell [1] and the ruins of houses, and so by that means narrow and choked. And that the avenues on every side to the city might be more passable, he took in hand himself to repair the highway or causey [C. 44] Flaminia, so far as to Ariminum ; and the rest he committed to sundry men who had triumphed, for to pave ; and the charges thereof to be defrayed out of the money raised of spoils and sackage. The sacred churches and chapels decayed and ruinate by continuance of time, or consumed by fire, he re-edified, and those, together with the rest, he adorned with most rich oblations ; as who brought into the cell, or tabernacle of Jupiter Capitolinus at one donation 16,000 pound weight of gold, besides precious stones valued at 50 millions of sesterces [2].

31. But after that he entered now at length upon the high priesthood, when Lepidus was once dead, which he never could find in his heart to take from him whiles he lived, what books soever of prophecies and destinies went commonly abroad in Greek and Latin, either without authors, or such as were not authentic and of credit, he caused to be called in from all places, to the number of 2000 and above ; and when he had burnt them, he retained those only of the Sibyl's prophecies. [1] And even of those also he made some special choice, and bestowed them close [C. 31] in two little desks or coffers under the base and pedestal of Apollo Palatinus. The year's revolution, reduced as it was into order by Julius of sacred memory, but afterwards through negligence troubled and confused, he brought again to the former calculation. In the dispose whereof, he called the month Sextilis (rather than September, wherein he was born) by his own name, because in it there befell unto him both his first consulship and also notable victories. Of all the Religious and priests, but especially of the Vestal virgins he augmented the number, the dignity, and the commodities also. And whereas, in the room of any Vestal nun deceased, there must another of necessity be chosen and taken, he, perceiving many to make suit that they might not put their daughters to the lottery, protested and bound it with an oath that, if any one of his own nieces or daughters' daughters were of competent age, he would present her to the place. Divers ancient ceremonies also, which by little and little were disused and abolished, he restored again, as namely, the augury [a] of Salus [2], the flamenship of Jupiter, the sacred Lupercal, the secular plays [b] and the Compitalicii [3]. At the Lupercal solemnities, he commanded that no beardless boys should run. Likewise, at the secular plays, he forbade young folk of both sexes to frequent any show exhibited by night, unless it were in the company of some ancient person of their kindred. The tutelar images of cross-ways called Lares Compitales he was the first that ordained to adorn twice in the year with flowers of the spring and summer seasons. The principal honour next unto the immortal gods he performed to the memorial of those worthy captains, who had raised the Roman empire from a small thing to so high and glorious a state. And therefore both the works and monuments of every one of them he repaired and made again, reserving their titles and inscriptions still; and all their statues also, in triumphant form and shape, he dedicated in both the porches or galleries of his hall of justice. And in a public edict he professed thus much, that he devised it to this end, that both himself whiles he lived, and the princes or emperors his successors for the ages to come, might be called upon and urged by their subjects and citizens to conform themselves as it were to their pattern and example. The statue likewise of Pompey, translated out of the court wherein C. Caesar was murdered, he placed over against the princely palace of his theatre under an arch of marble in manner of a thoroughfare [4].

32. Many most dangerous enormities and offensive abuses, which either had continued by custom and licentious liberty during the civil wars, or else crept in and began in the time of peace to the utter ruin of the commonwealth, he reformed. For a number of bold roisterers and professed robbers jetted [1] openly with short swords and skenes [2] by their sides, under colour of their own defence; passengers and wayfaring men, as they travelled through the country, were caught up by them, as well freeborn as slaves without respect, and kept hard to work in the prisons of landed men [3]. Many factious crews also, under the title of a new college, had their meetings and joined in fellowship to the perpetrating of mischief whatsoever. Whereupon he disposed strong guards, and set watches in convenient places ; he repressed those robbers and hacksters, [4] he visited and surveyed the aforesaid prisons ; and all colleges or guilds, save only those of ancient foundation and by law erected, he dissolved and put down. The bills [5] of old debts due to the chamber of the city [the treasury], he burnt [6], as being the chief matter and occasion of malicious accusations. The public places and houses in the city, whereof the tenure and hold was doubtful, he adjudged unto those who were in present possession. The debts and actions commenced against such as had been troubled and sued a long time in the law, by whose mournful habit and distressed estate their adversaries sought for nothing but pleasure and the fulfilling of their wills, he annulled and denounced this condition withal, that if any one would needs bring them into new trouble again, he should be liable to the like danger of punishment or penalty as the molested party was. And to the end that no lewd [7] act might escape with impunity, nor business [8] in court be shuffled over by delays, he added unto the term-time [9] thirty days [a] over and above, which days the honorary games [10] and plays took up before. To three decuries of judges he added a fourth out of a lower and meaner degree, which went under the name of ducenarii [11], and were to judge of smaller sums. As for those judges, he enrolled and elected them into the decuries after they were once thirty years of age [12], that is to say, five years sooner than they were wont. But seeing that most of them refused, and were loath to execute this burdensome office of judging, he hardly granted that each decury should have their year's vacation [13] by turns ; and that the law matters, which were wont to be pleaded and tried in the months of November and December [14], should be let pass and omitted quite.

33. Himself sat daily in judgement, yea, and otherwhiles until it was dark night, lying, if he had not his health, in a litter which was of purpose set before the tribunal seat, or else in his own house ; and he ministered justice not only with exceeding severity, but also with as great lenity. For when upon a time there was one accused for a manifest parricide, because he should not be sewn up in a leather male or[1] budget[a] (a punishment that none suffered but such as had confessed the fact) he examined (by report) upon interrogatives in this manner, " Certes, thou never murdered'st thy father, did'st thou ? " Again, whenas a matter was handled before him as touching a forged will, and all the witnesses that set their hands and seals thereto were attaint by the Cornelian law[b], he delivered unto the commissioners who had the hearing and deciding together of the cause, not only the two ordinary tables of condemnation and acquittal, but a third also, whereby they might have their pardon, who were certainly known to have been seduced and brought to be witnesses, as is before said, either by fraudulent practice or error and oversight. As for the appeals in court, he yearly assigned those which were for the city suitors unto praetors of the city ; but if they were for provincial persons, unto certain men of the consul's degree, such as he had ordained, in every province one, for to be in commission and to determine provincial affairs.

34. The laws made beforetime he revised and corrected ; some also he ordained and established anew, as namely, Sumptuaria[a], as touching expenses at the board ; of adulteries[b] and unnatural filthiness committed with the male kind[1] ; of indirect suit for offices[c] ; of the mutual marriages of senators and gentlemen with commoners[d]. This act last-named, when he had amended and reformed somewhat more precisely and with greater severity than the rest, he could not carry clearly and go through with, for the tumult of those that refused so to do, but that part of the penalties at length was quite taken away or else mitigated, an immunity[2] also and toleration (of widowhood) granted for three years[3], and the rewards besides augmented. And notwithstanding all that, when the order of gentlemen stood out stiffly and stoutly, calling in open sight and publicly for the repealing of the said statute, he sent for Germanicus his children, and taking some of them himself, and bestowing the others in their father's arms, showed and presented them unto their view ; signifying, as well by the gesture of his hand as by countenance, that they should not be loath nor think much to imitate the example of that young gentleman. Moreover, perceiving that the force and vigour of that law was dallied with and avoided by the immaturity of young espoused wives[4], as also by often changing of marriages[5], he brought into a narrower compass the time of wedding and having such spouses, and also limited divorcements.

35. The number of senators growing still to a shameful and confused company (for there were not of them so few as 1000, and some most unworthy ; as who after Caesar's death were taken into the house for favour or bribes, whom the common people termed abortive[1], as it were untimely births or born before their time) he reduced to the ancient stent[2] and honourable reputation, and that in two elections ; the former, at their own choice, will, and pleasure, whereby one man chooseth his fellow ; the second, according to his own and Agrippa's mind. At which time he is thought to have sat as president, armed with a shirt of mail or privy coat under his gown, and a short sword or skene [32] by his side ; having a guard also standing about his chair of estate [C. 76], to wit, ten of the stoutest and tallest men that were of senator's degree, and all his friends. Cordus Cremutius[3] writeth, that there was not so much as admitted then into the senate-house any senator but singly, one alone by himself, and not before his clothes were well-searched and felt, for having any weapon under them. Some of them he brought to this modesty as to excuse themselves[4] ; and yet for such as thus made excuse he reserved still the liberty to wear a senator's habit[a], the honour also to sit and behold the games and plays in the orchestra[5], together with privilege to keep their place at the solemn public feasts. Now to the end that, being thus chosen and allowed (as is above said), they might with more religious reverence and less trouble execute the functions belonging to senators[b], he ordained that, before any one sat him down in his chair, he should make devout supplication and sacrifice with frankincense and wine, at the altar of that god[6], in whose temple they assembled for the time ; and that ordinarily the senate should not be holden oftener than twice in a month, to wit, upon the kalends[c] and ides[d] of the same ; and that in the months September and October[7] none else should be bound to give attendance, save those that were drawn by lot, by whose number decrees might pass. Furthermore, he devised to institute for himself, and that by casting lots, a privy council for six months, with whom he might treat beforehand of businesses and affairs to be moved unto a frequent [C. 22] senate-house fully assembled. As touching matter of greater importance put to question, he demanded the opinion of the senators, not after the usual manner and in order, but as it pleased himself ; to the end that every man should bend his mind so intentively [C. 65] thereto, as if he were to deliver his own advice, rather than give assent unto another.

36. Other things there were besides, whereof he was the author and beginner, and among the rest ; that the acts of the senate[1] should not be published nor appear upon record ; item, that no magistrates, after that they had left or given up their honourable places, should eft-soons presently be sent as governors into any provinces ; that, for proconsuls or presidents, there should be a certain rate in money set down and allowed, for their sumpter-mules, for their tents and hales[2], which were wont really beforetime to be sent out and allowed for them, at the public cost of the city ; item, that the charge of the city's treasure should be translated from the quaestors or treasurers of the city unto those that had been praetors, or to the praetors for the time being ; lastly, that certain decemvirs[3] should summon and assemble the centumviral court[a] and call the centumvirs to the spear, which they only were wont to do, that had borne the office of quaestorship.

37. And to the end that more men might bear their part in administration of the commonweal, he devised new offices ; to wit, the overseeing of the public works, the surveying of the ways, streets, and causeys [C. 44], of the watercourses or conduits, of the channel of Tiber, and distributing corn among the people ; also the provostship of the city[1] ; one triumvirate[2] for choosing senators, and another for reviewing and visiting the troops or cornets of horsemen, so often as need required. The censors, whose creation was forelet[3] and discontinued, after a long time between, he created again. The number of praetors he augmented. He required also and demanded that, so often as the consulship was conferred upon him, he might have, for one, two colleagues or companions in office, but he could not obtain it ; whilst all men with one voice cried out, that his majesty was abridged enough already, in that he bare not that honourable office by himself, but with another.

38. Neither was he more sparing in honourably rewarding martial prowess, as who gave order that, to thirty captains and above, there should be granted by public decree full triumphs, and to a good many more triumphal ornaments [a]. Senators' children, to the end they might be sooner acquainted with the affairs of state, he permitted to put on even at the first their virile gown ; to wear likewise the senator's robe powdered with broad-headed purple studs ; and to have their places in the senate-house. Also, at their first entrance into warfare, he allowed them to be not only military tribunes in the legions [1], but also captains over the horsemen in the wings [2] ; and that none of them might be unexpert of the camp affairs, he ordained for the most part over every wing or cornet, two such senators' sons to be provosts. The troops and companies of Roman gentlemen he often reviewed ; and after a long space of time between, brought into use again the manner of their muster [3] or riding solemnly [b] on horseback, to show themselves. Neither would he suffer any one of them, during this solemnity, to be unhorsed and arrested by his adversary, that pretended any matter in law against him, a thing that was usually done. And to as many as were known to be aged or to have any defect or imperfection of body, he gave leave to send their horses before, and to come on foot to answer whensoever they were cited. And soon after he did those this favour to deliver up their public horses, who, being above thirty-five years of age, were unwilling to keep them still.

39. Having obtained also by the senate [1] ten coadjutors, he compelled every gentleman (that served with the city's horse) to render an account of his life. And of such as were blamable and could not approve their living, some he punished, others he noted with shame and ignominy, the most part of them with admonition, but after sundry sorts. The easiest and lightest kind of admonition was the tendering unto them, in open place and all men's sight, a pair of writing-tables [2], to read unto themselves presently [3] in the place where they stood. Some also he put to rebuke and disgrace for taking up of money upon small interest for the use, and putting it forth again for greater gain and usury.

40. At the election of tribunes of the commons, if there wanted senators [a] to stand for that office, he created them out of the degree of Roman gentlemen ; so as, after they had borne that magistracy, they might remain ranged in whether degree [1] they would themselves. Now, whenas many of the Roman gentlemen, having wasted and decayed their patrimony and estate in the civil wars, durst not out of the fourteen foremost seats behold the public plays and games, for fear of the penalty by the law (Roscia and Julia) called *theatralis*, he pronounced openly and made it known, that such gentlemen were not liable thereto, if either themselves or their fathers [2] before them were ever at any time valued to the worth of Roman gentlemen [3]. He made a review [4] of the people of Rome, street by street ; and, to prevent that the common people should not be often called away from their affairs by occasion of the dole and distribution of corn, he purposed to give out, thrice a year, tickets or tallies for to serve four months ; but when the people were desirous of the old custom, he granted them again to receive the same upon the nones [b] of every month. The ancient right and liberty also in elections and parliaments he brought in again ; and having restrained the indirect suing for dignities by manifold penalties, upon the day of such elections, he distributed out of his own purse, among the Fabians and Scaptians [c], who were of the same tribes wherein himself was incorporate, a thousand sesterces apiece, because they should not look for aught at any of their hands who stood for offices. Moreover, supposing it a matter of great consequence to keep the people incorrupt and clear from all base mixture of foreign and servile blood, he both granted the freedom of the city of Rome most sparingly, and also set a certain gage and limitation of manumitting and enfranchising slaves. When Tiberius made request unto him by letters, in the behalf of a Grecian, his client, to be free of Rome, he wrote back unto him, that he would not grant it unless he came personally himself, and could persuade him what just causes he had of his suit ; and what time as Livia entreated the like for a certain Frenchman, tributary to the Romans, he flatly denied the freedom of the city, but offered in lieu thereof immunity and remission of tribute ; avowing that he would more easily abide that somewhat went from the public treasure and chamber of the city than have the honour of the Roman city to be made vulgar and common. Nor content that he had by divers strait edicts and provisos kept many slaves from all manner of freedom, but more a great deal from full freedom in the best condition, as having precisely and with much curiosity [5] put in caveats both for the number and also for the condition and respect otherwise of those that were to be made free, he added thus much moreover ; that no slave, who had ever been bound and imprisoned, or examined by torture, should obtain the freedom of the city, in any kind of enfranchisement whatsoever. The old manner of going and wearing apparel also he endeavoured to bring into use again. And having seen, upon a time assembled to hear a public speech, a number of citizens clad all in black cloaks [6] or sullied gowns [7], taking great indignation thereat, crying out withal : " Behold," quoth he,

" *Romanos rerum dominos gentemque togatam* [8],

The Romans, lords of all the world, and long-rob'd nation."

He gave the aediles in charge not to suffer any person from thenceforward, to abide or stay, either in the common place or the circus, but in a gown [d], laying aside all cloaks or mantles thereupon.

41. His liberality unto all degrees of citizens he showed oftentimes as occasions and opportunities were offered ; for both by bringing into the city in the Alexandrine triumph the treasures of the Egyptian kings [1], he caused so great plenty of money, that usury fell, but the price of lands and lordships arose to a very high reckoning ; and also afterwards, so often as out of the goods of condemned persons there was any surplusage of money remaining above their fines, he granted for a certain time the free loan and use thereof to as many as were able to put in security for the principal, by an obligation in duple the sum. The substance and wealth of senators he augmented and, whereas the value thereof before amounted to the sum of 800,000 sesterces [2], he taxed or sessed them at 1,200,000 ; and look, who had not so much, he supplied and made it up to the full. He gave congiaries oftentimes to the people, but lightly [3] they were of diverse sums, one while 400, another while 300, and sometimes 250 sesterces ; and he left not so much as boys under age, whereas they had not wont to receive such congiaries, unless they were above eleven years old. He measured out also to the people by the poll [C. 26] corn in times of scarcity, oftentimes at a very low price, and otherwhiles freely, without paying therefor ; and as for the tickets of money, he doubled the sum in them contained.

42. And that you may know, he was a prince more respective[1] of thrift and wholesomeness[2] than desirous of popularity, praise, and honour. When the people complained of the want and dearth of wine, he checked and snubbed them with this most severe speech : " that his son-in-law Agrippa had taken order[3] good enough that men should not be athirst, by conveying so many waters into the city." Unto the same people demanding the congiary, which indeed was by him promised, he answered : " that his credit was good, and he able to perform his word " ; but when they earnestly called for one which he had never promised, he hit them in the teeth by an edict or proclamation with their dishonesty and impudence, assuring them that give it he would not, although he had intended it.

And with no less gravity and resolution, when, upon his proposing and publishing of a congiary, he found that many in the meantime were manumitted and inserted into the number of citizens, he rejected such, and said they should not receive any, unto whom he had made no promise ; and to all the rest he gave less than he promised, that the sum which he had appointed might hold out and be sufficient. When upon a time there was great barrenness and scarcity of corn, being put to a hard exigent[4] and to seek a difficult remedy, insomuch as he was driven to expel out of the city all the sort of young slaves pampered and trimmed up for sale, as also whole schools and companies of novice-fencers and sword-players, all strangers and foreigners, except physicians and schoolmasters, yea, and some of the ordinary household servants ; so soon as the market began to mend and victuals grew plentiful, he writeth, that it took him in the head to abolish those public doles of corn for ever, because upon the trust and confidence of them tillage was clean laid down. Howbeit, he continued not in that mind long, as being assured that the same doles might be set up again one time or other by the ambitious humour (of princes his successors). And therefore, after this he ordered the matter so indifferently, as that he had no less regard of the city's farmers of tillage and other undertakers and purveyors of the public corn than of the people and commons of the city.

43. In number, variety, and magnificence of solemn shows exhibited unto the people he went beyond all men. He reporteth of himself that he set forth plays and games in his own name four and twenty times ; and for other magistrates, who either were absent or not sufficient to bear the charges, three and twenty times. Divers times he exhibited plays by every street, and those upon many stages, and acted by players skilful in all languages, not in the common Forum only, nor in the ordinary amphitheatre, but also in the circus. In the enclosure called Septa [1], he never represented any sports but the baiting and coursing of wild beasts and the shows of champions-sight, having built wooden scaffolds and seats for the nonce in Mars' field. In like manner, he made the show of a naval battle about the river Tiber, having digged of purpose a spacious hollow pit within the ground, even there whereas now is to be seen the grove of the Caesars. On which days he bestowed warders in divers places of the city, for fear it might be endangered by sturdy thieves and robbers, taking their vantage that so few remained at home in their houses. In the circus he brought forth to do their devoir charioteers, runners, and killers of savage beasts, otherwhiles out of the noblest young gentlemen of all the city. As for the warlike riding or tournament called Troy, he exhibited it oftenest of all other, making choice of boys to perform it, as well bigger as smaller ; supposing it a matter of antiquity, a decent and honourable manner besides, that the towardly disposition and proof of noble blood should thus be seen and known. In this solemnity and sport, he rewarded C. Nonius Asprenas, weakened [2] by a fall from his horse, with a wreath or chain of gold, and permitted both himself and also his posterity to bear the surname of Torquatus. But afterwards he gave over the representation of such pastimes, by occasion that Asinius Pollio, the orator, made a grievous and invidious complaint in the senate-house of the fall that Aeserninus his nephew took, who likewise had thereby broken his leg. To the performance of his stage-plays also and shows of sword-fight, he employed sometimes even the gentlemen and knights of Rome ; but it was before he was inhibited by virtue of an Act of the senate. For after it, verily, he exhibited no more, save only a youth called L. Icius, born of worshipful parentage, only for a show, that being a dwarf not two feet high, and weighing³ seventeen pounds, yet he had an exceeding great voice. One day of the sword-fight that he set forth, he brought in for to behold the solemnity, even through the midst of the show-place, the Parthians' hostages, who then were newly sent to Rome, and placed them in the second rank or row of seats above himself⁴. His manner was moreover, before the usual days of such spectacles and solemn sights, and at other times, if any strange and new thing were brought over unto him and worthy to be known, to bring it abroad for to be seen upon extraordinary days, and in any place whatsoever. As for example, a rhinoceros within the empaled or railed enclosure called Septa ; a tiger upon the stage : and a serpent 50 cubits long, within the hall Comitium. It fortuned that, during the great Circensian games which he had vowed before, he fell sick, whereby he lay in his litter and so devoutly attended upon the sacred chariots called tensae. Again, it happened at the beginning of those plays, which he set out when he dedicated the temple of Marcellus, that his curule chair became unjointed, and thereby he fell upon his back. Also, at the games of his nephews, when the people there assembled were mightily troubled and astonied, for fear that the theatre would fall, seeing that by no means he could hold them in, nor cause them to take heart again, he removed out of his own place, and sat him down in that part thereof which was most suspected. The most confused and licentious⁵ manner of beholding such spectacles, he reformed and brought into order, moved thereto by the wrong done to a senator, whom at Puteoli, in a frequent [C. 22] assembly sitting at their right solemn games, no man had received to him ⁶ and vouchsafed a rowne.⁷

44. Hereupon, when a decree of the senate was passed, that, so often as in any place there was aught exhibited publicly to be seen, the first rank or course of seats should be kept clear and wholly for senators, he forbade the ambassadors of free nations and confederates to sit at Rome within the orchestra, because he had found that even some of their libertines' kind were sent in embassage. The soldiers he severed from the other people. To married men that were commoners he assigned several rows by themselves ; to noblemen's children under age his own quarter[1] ; and to their teachers and governors the next thereto. He made an act also, that not one of the base commons wearing black and sullied gowns should sit so near as the midst of the theatre [a]. As for women, he would not allow them to behold so much as the sword-fencers (who customarily in the time past were to be seen of all indifferently) but from some higher loft above the rest[2], sitting there by themselves. To the Vestal nuns he granted a place apart from the rest within the theatre, and the same just over against the praetor's tribunal. Howbeit, from the solemnity of champions'-show, he banished all the female sex ; so far forth as that, during the pontifical games[3], he put off a couple of them, who were called for to enter into combat, until the morrow morning [b], and made proclamation that his will and pleasure was, that no woman should come into the theatre before the fifth hour of the day[4].

45. Himself beheld the Circensian games, for the most part from the upper lofts and lodging of his friends and freedmen, sometimes out of the pulvinar[1], sitting there with his wife only and children. From these shows and sights he would be absent many hours together, and otherwhiles whole days, but first having craved leave of the people and recommended those unto them, who should sit as presidents of those games in his turn. But so often as he was at them, he did nothing else but intend[2] the same ; either to avoid the rumour and speech of men, whereby his father Caesar (as he said himself) was commonly taxed, namely, for that in beholding those solemnities he used between-whiles to give his mind to read letters and petitions[3], yea, and to write back again ; or else upon an earnest desire and delight he had in seeing such pastimes, his pleasure and contentment wherein he never dissembled, but oftentimes frankly professed. And therefore he proposed and gave of his own, at the games of prize and plays even of other men, coronets and rewards, both many in number, and also of great worth ; neither was he present at any of these Greek games and solemnities [a], but he honoured every one of the actors and provers of maisteries[4] therein according to their deserts. But most affectionately of all other he loved to see the champions at fist-fight[5], and the Latins especially ; not those only who by lawful calling were professed[6] and by order allowed (and even those he was wont to match with Greeks), but such also as out of the common sort of townsmen fell together by the ears pell-mell in the narrow streets, and though they had no skill at all of fight, yet could lay on load[7], and offend their concurrents[8] one way or other. In sum, all those in general, who had any hand in those public games or set them forward any way, he deigned good rewards and had a special respect of them. The privileges of champions he both maintained entire, and also amplified. As for sword-fencers, he would not suffer them to enter into the lists, unless they might be discharged of that profession, in case they became victors[9]. The power to chastise actors and players[10] at all times and in every place (granted unto the magistrates[11] by ancient law) he took from them, save only during the plays and upon the stage. Howbeit, he examined straitly nevertheless at all times, either the matches or combats of champions called *Xystici*[b], or the fights of sword-fencers. For the licentiousness of stage-players he so repressed, that when he had for certain found out that Stephanio, an actor of Roman plays, had a man's wife waiting upon him, shorn and rounded[12] in manner of a boy, he confined and sent him away as banished, but well beaten first with rods through all the three theatres[13]. And Hylas the pantomime[14], at the complaint made of him by the praetor, he scourged openly in the courtyard before his house, and excluded no man from the sight thereof ; yea, and he banished Pylades out of the city of Rome and Italy, because he had pointed with his finger at a spectator who hissed him out of the stage, and so made him to be known[15].

46. Having in this manner ordered the city and administered the civil affairs therein, he made Italy populous and much frequented with colonies[a] to the number of twenty-eight, brought thither and planted by him ; yea, he furnished the same with public works and revenues in many places. He equalled it also after a sort, and in some part, with the very city of Rome, in privileges and estimation, by devising a new kind of suffrages, which the decurions or elders of colonies gave every one in their own township, as touching magistrates to be created in Rome, and sent under their hands and seals to the city against the day of the solemn elections. And to the end there should not want in any place either honest and worshipful inhabitants, or issue of the multitude ; look, who made suit to serve as men-of-arms on horseback upon the public commendation of any township whatsoever, those he enrolled and advanced unto the degree of gentlemen. But to as many of the commoners as could by good evidence prove unto him, as he visited the countries and regions of Italy, that they had sons and daughters, he distributed a thousand sesterces apiece for every child they had.

47. As for those provinces, which were more mighty than other, and the government whereof by yearly magistrates was neither easy nor safe, he undertook himself to rule [a] ; the rest he committed to proconsuls by lot, and yet otherwhiles he made exchange of such provinces ; and of both sorts he oftentimes visited many in person. Certain cities, confederate and in league with Rome, howbeit by overmuch liberty running headlong to mischief and destruction, he deprived of their liberties. Others again, either deeply in debt, he eased ; or subverted by earthquake, he re-edified ; or able to allege their merits and good turns done to the people of Rome, he endowed with the franchises of Latium, or else with freedom of Rome. There is not, I suppose, a province (except Africa only and Sardinia), but he went unto it. Into these provinces, after he had chased Sextus Pompeius thither, he prepared to sail out of Sicily and to cross the seas, but continual storms and extreme tempests checked him ; neither had he good occasion or sufficient cause afterwards to pass over unto them.

48. All those kingdoms which he won by conquest and force of arms, unless some few, he either restored unto those princes from whom he had taken them, or else made them over to other kings, mere aliens. Princes his associates he conjoined also together among themselves by mutual bonds of alliance, as being a most ready procurer and maintainer of affinity and amity of every one ; neither had he other regard of them all in general than of the very natural members and parts of his own empire. Moreover, he was wont to set guardians and governors over the said princes, when they were either young and under age, or lunatic and not well in their wits, until such time as they were grown to ripe years, or began to come again to themselves. The children of very many of them he both brought up and also trained and instructed together with his own.

49. Out of his military forces he distributed both legions and auxiliaries by provinces. He placed one fleet at Misenum, and another at Ravenna, for the defences of the upper [1] and nether [2] seas. A certain number of soldiers he selected for a guard, partly of the city, and in part of his own person, having discharged the regiment of the Calagurritanes [3], which he had retained about him, until he vanquished Antony, and likewise of the Germans, which he had waged [4] among the squires of his body, unto the disastrous overthrow of Varus. And yet he suffered not at any time to remain within the city more than three cohorts, and those without their pavilions. The residue his manner was to send away to wintering places and summer harbours about the neighbour-towns. Moreover, all the soldiers that were in any place whatsoever, he tied to a certain prescript form and proportion of wages and rewards, setting down, according to the degree and place of every one, both their times of warfare, and also the commodities [5] they should receive after the term of their service expired and their lawful discharge ; lest that, by occasion of old age, or for want, they should, after they were freed from warfare, be solicited to sedition and rebellion. And to the end that for ever, and without any difficulty, there might be defrayed sufficient to maintain and reward them accordingly, he appointed a peculiar treasury for soldiers, with new revenues devised for their maintenance [6]. And that with more speed and out of hand word might be brought, and notice taken what was doing in every province, he disposed along the road highways, within small distance one from another, first, certain young men as posts, and afterwards, swift wagons to give intelligence. This he thought more commodious and better to the purpose, that they who from a place brought him letters might be asked questions also, if the matters required aught.

50. In charters, patents, writs, bills and letters he used for his seal, at the first, the image of sphinx [a] ; soon after, that of Alexander the Great ; and last of all, his own, engraven by the hand of Dioscurides [1], wherewith the princes and emperors his successors continued to sign their writings. To all his missives his manner was, to put precisely the very minutes of hours, not of day only but of night also, wherein it might be known they were dated.

51. Of his clemency and civil courtesy [a], there be many, and those right great proofs and experiments [1]. Not to reckon up, how many and who they were of the adverse faction, that he vouchsafed pardon and life, yea, and suffered to hold still a principal place in the city, he was content and thought it sufficient to punish Junius Novatus and Cassius Patavinus, two commoners, the one with a fine of money, and the other with a slight banishment ; notwithstanding that Junius Novatus, in the name of young Agrippa, had divulged a most biting and stinging letter touching him, and Cassius Patavinus, at an open table and full feast, gave out in broad terms that he wanted neither hearty wishes nor good-will to stab him. Moreover, in a certain judicial trial, when among other crimes this article was principally objected against Aemilius Aelianus of Corduba, that he was wont to have a bad conceit [2] and to speak but basely of Caesar, himself turned unto the accuser, and as if he had been sore offended, " I would," quoth he, " thou wert able to prove this unto me ; in faith Aelianus should well know, that I also have a tongue, for I will not stick [3] to say more by him." And farther than this he neither for the present nor afterwards inquired into the matter. Likewise, when Tiberius grieved and complained unto him of the same indignity in a letter, and that incessantly and after a violent manner, thus he wrote back again : " Do not, my good Tiberius, in this point follow and feed the humour of your age [4], neither set it too near your heart, that there is any man who speaketh evil of me ; for it is enough for us, if no man be able to do us harm."

52. Albeit he wist well enough that temples were usually granted by decree even unto proconsuls, yet in no province accepted he of that honour, but jointly in the name and behalf of himself and of Rome. For in Rome, verily, he forbare this honour most resolutely ; yea, and those silver statues which in times past had been set up for him, he melted every one. Of which [1] he caused golden tables [2] to be made, and those he dedicated to Apollo Palatinus. When the people offered and instantly forced upon him the dictatorship, he fell upon his knees, cast his gown from off his shoulder, bared his breast, and, with detestation of the thing, besought them not to urge him farther.

53. The name and title of Lord [1] [a] he always abhorred as a contumelious and reproachful term. When, upon a time as he beheld the plays, these words were pronounced out of a comedy [2], " O good and gracious Lord " [3], whereupon the whole assembly with great joy and applause accorded thereto, as if they had been spoken of him, immediately, both with gesture of hand and show of countenance, he repressed such indecent flatteries, and the next day reproved them most sharply by an edict. Neither would he ever after suffer himself to be called dominus, no, not of his own children and nephews either in earnest or boord [4]. And that which more is, such fair and glavering [5] words he forbade them to use among themselves. Lightly [6] you should not have him depart forth of the city or any town, nor enter into any place but in the evening, or by night, for disquieting [7] any person in doing him honour by way of dutiful attendance. In his consulship he went commonly in the streets on foot ; out of his consulship oftentimes in a close chair or litter [8] [b]. In general salutations and duties done unto him he admitted the very commons, entertaining the suits and desires of all comers with so great humanity [9] as that he rebuked one of them merrily, because, in reaching unto him a supplication, he did it so timorously, as if he had raught [10] a small piece of coin [11] to an elephant. On a senate-day, he never saluted his nobles but in the Curia [c], and those verily as they sat, every one by name, without any prompter [12] ; and at his departure out of the house, he used to bid them farewell, one by one as they were set, in the same manner. With many men he performed mutual offices, yielding one kindness for another interchangeably. Neither gave he over frequenting their solemnities and feasts [13] until he was far stept in years ; and by this occasion that, once upon a day of espousals [14], he was in the press and throng of people sore crowded. Gallus Terrinius, a senator and none of his familiar acquaintance, howbeit fallen blind and purposing resolutely to pine himself to death [d], he visited in proper person, and by his consolatory and comfortable words persuaded him to live still.

54. As he delivered a speech in the senate, one said unto him, " I conceived [1] you not " ; and another, " I would gainsay you, if any place were left for me to speak " [2]. Divers times, when upon occasion of excessive altercation and brabling [C. 23] among the senators in debating matters, he was about to whip out of the senate apace in a great chafe, some of them would choke him with these words : " Senators ought to have liberty to speak their minds concerning the commonweal." Antistius Labeo, at a certain election of senators, when one man chooseth another [3], made choice of M. Lepidus, who sometime was Augustus' mortal enemy, and then in exile. Now when he demanded of the said Antistius, if there were not others more worthy to be chosen, he returned this answer, that every man had his own liking and judgement by himself. Yet for all this did no man's free speech, or froward self-will turn him to displeasure or danger.

55. Moreover, the defamatory libels of him cast abroad and dispersed in the Curia, he neither was affrighted at, nor took great care to refute, making not so much as search after the authors. Only this he opined, that from thenceforth there should be inquisition made, and examination had of those that, either in their own name or under other men's, did put forth libels, rhymes, or verses to the infamy of any person. Furthermore, to meet with the spiteful taunts and scurrilous scoffs of some, wherewith he was provoked, he made an edict against such. And yet, to the end that the senate should pass no act for the inhibition of their licentious liberty [a] in their last wills and testaments [1], he interposed his negative voice.

56. Whensoever he was present himself at the general wardmotes for election of magistrates, he went with his own candidates [a] round about to the tribes, and humbly craved their voices according to the usual custom. Himself also gave a voice in his own tribe [1] as one of the ordinary people. When he appeared as witness in judicial courts, he suffered himself right willingly to be examined upon interrogatives, and also to be impleaded against and confuted. His common hall of justice [2] he made less and of narrower compass [3], as not daring to encroach upon the next houses and dispossess the owners. He never recommended his sons unto the people but with this clause added thereto, " If they shall deserve." When, being yet under age and in their purpled child's habit, all the people generally that sat in the theatre rose up unto them, and the standers below clapped their hands, he took it very ill and complained grievously thereof. His minions and inward friends he would have to be great and mighty men in the city ; yet so as they should have no more liberty than other citizens, but be subject to laws and judgements as well as the rest. When Asprenas Nonius ᵇ, a man of near alliance and acquaintance with him, was accused by Cassius Severus for practising poison, and pleaded for himself at the bar, he asked counsel of the senate, what they thought in duty he was to do ? " For I stand in doubt," quoth he, " lest, being here present as an advocate, I should acquit the prisoner defendant ⁴ and so hinder the course of law ; again, if I be absent and fail him, lest I might be thought to forsake and prejudice my friend." Whereupon, by all their consents, he sat there in the pews [C. 78] ⁵ certain hours, but spake never a word nor afforded so much as a commendatory speech in the defendant's behalf, as the manner of friends was to do in the trial of such cases. He pleaded the causes even of his very clients, and, by name, of a certain shield-bearer ⁶ ᶜ, whom in times past he had called forth to serve him in the wars ; he spake, I say, in his defence, when he was sued in an action for insult. Of all those that were thus in trouble, he delivered one and no more from making his appearance in court ; and him verily no otherwise but by earnest prayers and entreating the accuser before the judges ; and him he persuaded at length to let fall his action. And Castricius it was, a man by whose means he came to the knowledge of Murena's conspiracy.

57. How much and for what demerits¹ of his he was beloved, an easy matter it is to make an estimate. The acts and decrees of the senate concerning his honours I pass over, as which may be wrested from them either upon mere necessity or bashful modesty. The gentlemen of Rome, of their own accord and by a uniform consent, celebrated his birth-feast always for two days together. All states and degrees of the city, yearly upon a solemn vow that they made, threw small pieces of brass coin into Curtius' lake ² for the preservation of his life and health. Semblably [C. 39], at the kalends of January every year, they offered a New-year's gift in the Capitol unto him, although he were absent. Out of which mass and gross sum he disbursed as much money, as wherewith he bought the most precious images of the gods, and dedicated them in divers streets ; as namely, Apollo Sandaliarius[3], and Jupiter Tragoedus[4], and others besides. For the re-edification of his house in Palatine[5] consumed by fire, the old soldiers, the decuries of the judges, the tribes, and many several persons by themselves of all sorts, willingly and according to each one's ability, brought in their moneys together. Howbeit, he did no more but slightly touch the heaps of such money as they lay, and took not away out of any one above one single denier[6]. As he returned out of any province, they accompanied him honourably, not only with good words and lucky osses[7], but also with songs set in musical measures. This also was duly observed, that, how often soever he entered Rome, no punishment that day was inflicted upon any person.

58. The surname[1] in his style of Pater Patriae they all presented unto him with exceeding great and unexpected accord. The commons, first, by an embassage which they sent unto Antium ; then, because he accepted not thereof, at Rome as he entered the theatre to behold the plays, they tendered it a second time themselves in great frequency, dight with laurel branches and coronets. Soon after, the senate did the like, not by way of decree nor acclamation, but by Valerius Messalla [Tib. 70], who had commission from them all to relate their minds in this manner : " That," quoth he, " which may be to the good and happiness of thee and thy house, O Caesar Augustus (for in this wise we think that we pray for perpetual felicity and prosperity to this commonwealth) : the senate, according with the people of Rome, do jointly salute thee by the name of Pater Patriae[2]." Unto whom Augustus, with tears standing in his eyes, made answer in these words (for I have set the very same down, like as I did those of Messalla) : " Now that I have, mine honourable Lords, attained to the height of all my vows and wishes, what remaineth else for me to crave of the immortal gods, but that I may carry with me this universal consent of yours unto my life's end ? "

59. Unto Antonius Musa his physician, by whose means he was recovered out of a dangerous disease, they erected a statue, by a general contribution of money, just by the image of Aesculapius. Some householders[1] there were, who in their last wills and testaments provided that their heirs should lead beasts for sacrifice into the Capitol and pay their vows with this title, carried before them containing the reason of so doing, Because they [2] had left Augustus living after them. Certain cities of Italy began their year that very day, on which he first came to them. Most of the provinces, over and above temples and altars, ordained, almost in every good town, solemn games and plays every fifth year in his honour [3].

60. Kings his friends and confederates, both severally every one in his own kingdom, built cities calling them Caesarea, and jointly altogether intended, at their common charges, fully to finish the temple of Jupiter Olympius at Athens, which long time before was begun, and to dedicate it unto his Genius. And oftentimes the said princes, leaving their realms, going in Roman gowns, without diadems and regal ornaments, in habit and manner of devoted clients, performed their dutiful attendance unto him day by day ; not at Rome only, but also when he visited and travelled over the provinces.

61. Forasmuch as I have shown already what his public carriage was in places of command and magistracies, in the managing also and administration of the commonweal throughout the world, both in war and peace ; now will I relate his more private and domestic life, as also what behaviour he showed and what fortune he had at home and among his own, even from his youth unto his dying day. His mother he buried during the time of his first consulship, and his sister Octavia in the fifty-fourth year of his age. And as he had performed unto them both, whiles they lived, the offices of piety and love in the best manner, so, when they were dead, he did them the greatest honours he possibly could.

62. He had espoused, being a very youth, the daughter of P. Servilius Isauricus ; but upon his reconciliation unto Antony after their first discord, at the earnest demand of both their soldiers, that they might be conjoined and united by some near affinity, he took to wife Antonius' step-daughter Claudia, the lawful daughter of dame Fulvia by P. Clodius, a young damosel, scarce marriageable. And upon some displeasure, falling out with Fulvia, his wife's mother, he put her away, as yet untouched and a virgin ; soon after, he wedded Scribonia, the wife before of two husbands, both men of consular dignity, and by one of them a mother. This wife also he divorced, not able to endure, as he writeth himself, her shrewd [1] and perverse conditions : and forthwith took perforce from Tiberius Nero Livia Drusilla, his lawful wife and great with child. Her he loved entirely, her he liked only, and to the very end.

63. Upon Scribonia he begat Julia ; by Livia he had no issue, although full fain he would. Conceive once she did by him, but she miscarried, and the infant was born before time. As for Julia, he gave her in marriage first to Marcellus, the son of his sister Octavia, even when he was but newly crept out of his child's age. Afterwards, when Marcellus was departed this life, he bestowed her upon M. Agrippa, having by entreaty obtained of his sister to yield up unto him her right and interest in her son-in-law [1]. For at the same time Agrippa had to wife one of the Marcellas [2] (her daughters) and of her body [had] begotten children. When this Agrippa was likewise dead, he cast about and sought for divers matches a long time, even out of the ranks of Roman gentlemen, and chose for her his step-son Tiberius [3] ; whom he forced to put away a former wife then with child, and by whom he had been a father already. M. Antonius writeth, that he had affianced the said Julia, first, to Antony his son, and afterwards to Cotiso, king of the Getae, what time Antony himself required to have a king's daughter [4] likewise to wife.

64. By Agrippa and Julia he had three nephews [C. 26], Gaius, Lucius, and Agrippa ; nieces likewise twain, Julia and Agrippina. Julia he bestowed in marriage upon Lucius Paulus, the censor's son, and Agrippina upon Germanicus, his sister's nephew [1 a]. As for Gaius and Lucius, he adopted them for his own children at home in his house, having bought them of Agrippa their father by the brazen coin and the balance [b]. Whom being yet in their tender years, he employed in the charge of the commonweal ; and no sooner were they consuls elect, but he sent them abroad to the government of provinces and conduct of armies. His daughter and nieces above-named he brought up and trained so as that he acquainted them with housewifery, and set them even to card, spin, and make cloth, forbidding them straitly either to say or do aught but openly in the sight and hearing of all men, and that which might be recorded in their day-books. Certes, so far forth he prohibited and forewarned them the company of strangers, that he wrote upon a time unto L. Vinicius, a noble young gentleman and a personable, charging him that he passed the bounds of modesty, in that he came once to Baiae for to see and salute his daughter. His nephews himself for the most part taught to read, to write, and to swim [2] [c], besides the rudiments and first introductions to other sciences. But in nothing travailed he so much as in this, that they might imitate his handwriting. He never supped together with them, but they sat at the nether end of the table; neither went he any journey, but he had them either going before in a wagon, or else about him riding by his side.

65. But as joyous and confident as he was in regard both of his issue and also of the discipline of his house, fortune failed him in the proof of all. His daughter and niece, either of them named Julia, distained with all kind of lewdness and dishonesty [1], he sent out of the way as banished. Gaius and Lucius [2] [a] both, he lost in the space of eighteen months; Gaius died in Lycia, Lucius at Massilia. His third nephew Agrippa, together with his wife's son Tiberius, he adopted [b] his sons in the forum of Rome by an act of all the curiae [3]. But of these twain within a small time he cast out of his favour, yea, and confined aside unto Surrentum, Agrippa, for his base disposition and fell nature [4]. Moreover, he took much more patiently the death than the reproachful misdemeanours of his children. For at the misfortune of Gaius and Lucius he was not extremely dismayed and cast down; marry, of his daughter and her lewd pranks, he gave notice in his absence to the senate, and that in writing, which his quaestor [c] read openly before them; and for very shame he absented himself a long time and avoided the company of men, yea, and that which more is, once he was of mind to put her to death. And verily, whenas about the same time a freedwoman of his named Phoebe, one of them that were privy to her naughtiness [C. 6], knit her own neck in a halter, and so ended her days, he gave it out that he wished with all his heart he had been Phoebe's father. Confined thus when she was, he debarred her wholly the use of wine, and all manner of delicate trimming and decking her body; neither would he permit any man, one or other, bond or free, to have access unto her without his privity and leave asked, nor unless he might be certified before, of what age, of

what stature and colour he was, yea, and what marks and
scars he carried about him [d].   After five years' end, he removed
her out of the island [5] into the continent, where she abode at
more liberty somewhat, and not so straitly looked unto, for,
to call her home again once for all, he could by no means be
entreated ; as who, many a time, when the people of Rome
besought him earnestly and were very instant with him in her
behalf, openly before a frequent [C. 22] assembly of them
cursed such daughters and such wives, saying, " God bless [6]
ye all from the like."   The infant that his niece Julia bore after
she was condemned, he forbade expressly to take knowledge
of and to give it the rearing.   As touching his nephew Agrippa,
seeing him to prove nothing more tractable, but rather brain-
sick every day more than other, he transported him from Surrentum into an island and enclosed him there besides with a
guard of soldiers.   He provided also by an act of the senate,
that in the same place he should be kept for ever.   And so
often as there was any mention made either of him or the two
Julias, he used to fetch a sigh and groan again, and withal to
break out into this speech,

αἴθ' ὄφελον ἄγαμός τ'ἔμεναι, ἄγονός τ' ἀπολέσθαι,

Would God I never had wedded bride
Or else without any child had died [e].

66. Friendship with any person as he did not easily entertain [a], so he maintained and kept the same most constantly ;
not honouring only the virtues and deserts of every man
according to their worth, but enduring also their vices and
delinquencies, at leastwise if they exceeded not.   For out of all
that number of his dependants there will hardly be any found,
during his friendship, to have been plunged in adversity and
thereby overthrown, except Salvidienus Rufus, whom he had
before advanced to the dignity of consul, and Cornelius Gallus,
promoted by him to the provostship of Egypt, raised both
from the very dunghill.   The one of these for practising seditiously an alteration in the State, and the other for his unthankful and malicious mind he forbade his house and all his
provinces.   But as for Gallus, whenas both by the menaces of
his accusers, and also by the rigorous acts of the senate passed
against him, he was driven to shorten his own life, Augustus

commended verily their kind hearts to him for being so wroth
and grieving so much in his behalf ; howbeit for Gallus' sake
he wept, and complained of his own hard fortune, in that he
alone might not be angry with his friends within that measure
as he would himself.   All the rest of his favourites flourished in
power and wealth to their lives' end, as chief persons every one
in their rank, notwithstanding some discontentment and mis-
likes came between.   For otherwhiles he found a want in M.
Agrippa of patience, and in Maecenas of taciturnity and
secrecy ; whenas the one[1], upon a light suspicion of his cold
love and affection[2], with a jealousy besides that Marcellus
should be preferred before him, left all and went to Mitylenae ;
the other[3] unto his wife Terentia revealed a secret[b], as touching
the detection of Murena's conspiracy.   Himself also required
semblably [C. 39] mutual benevolence of his friends, as well
dead as living.   For although he was none of these that lie in
the wind to mung[4] and catch at inheritances, as who could
never abide to reap any commodity by the last will and testament of an unknown person, yet weighed he most strictly and
precisely the supreme[5] judgements and testimonies of his
friends concerning him, delivered at their deaths ; as one who
dissembled neither his grief, in case a man respected him
slightly and without honourable terms, nor his joy, if he remembered him thankfully and with kindness.   As touching
either legacies or parts of heritages, as also portions left unto
him by any parents whatsoever, his manner was either out of
hand to part with the same unto their children, or if they were
in their minority, to restore all unto them with the increase
upon the day that they put on their virile gowns, or else whereon they married.

67. A patron he was to his freedmen and a master to his
bondservants no less severe than gracious and gentle.   Many
of his enfranchised men he highly honoured and employed
especially, by name Licinius, Enceladus, with others.   His
servant Cosmus, who thought and spake most hardly of him,
he proceeded to chastise no farther than with hanging a pair of
fetters at his heels.   As for Diomedes, his steward, who, walking together with him, by occasion of a wild boar running full
upon them, for very fear put his master between himself and
the beast, he imputed unto him rather timidity than any fault

else ; and although it were a matter of no small peril, yet because there was no prepensed malice, he turned all into a jest. Contrariwise, the self-same man forced to death Polus a freedman of his and whom he set greatest store by, because he was detested [1] for abusing men's wives. Thallus, his scribe [2], had received 500 deniers [57] for making one privy unto a letter of his hands, but he caused his legs to be broken for his labour. The pedagogue and other servitors attendant upon Gaius his son, who, taking the vantage of his sickness and death, bare themselves proudly and insolently in his province [3] and therein committed many outrages, he caused to be thrown headlong into a river, with heavy weights about their necks.

68. In the prime and flower of his youth he incurred sundry ways the infamous note of a vicious and wanton life. Sextus Pompeius railed upon him as an effeminate person. M. Antonius laid to his charge, that he earned his uncle's adoption by suffering the filthy abuse of his body. Semblably [C. 39], Lucius, brother to the said Marcus, inveighed against him, as if he had abandoned and prostituted his youth, deflowered and tasted first by Caesar, unto A. Hirtius also in Spain for 300,000 sesterces ; and that he was wont to singe his legs with red-hot walnut-shells [1], to the end the hair might come up softer. The very people also in general, one time on a day of their solemn stage-plays, both construed to his reproach, and also with exceeding great applause verified of him a verse pronounced upon the stage, as touching a priest of Cybele, mother of the gods, playing upon a timbrel :

Videsne, [ut] cinaedus orbem digito temperat [a].

69. That he was a common adulterer his very friends did not deny, but they excuse him forsooth, saying, that he did it not upon filthy lust, but for good reason and in policy ; to the end he might more easily search out the plots and practices of his adversaries, by the means of women and wives, it skilled not [1] whose. M. Antonius objected against him, besides his over-hasty marriage with Livia [2], that he fetched a certain noble dame, the wife of one who had been consul, forth of a dining-parlour, even before her husband's face, into his own bed-chamber, and brought her thither back again, to make an end of the banquet, with her hair all ruffled, even while her ears were yet glowing red ; also that he put away Scribonia [3], because she was too plain and round [4] with him, upon grief she took that a concubine was so great and might do so much with him ; as also that there were bargains and matches sought out for him by his friends upon liking, who stuck not to view and peruse [5] both wives and young maidens of ripe years, all naked, as if Toranius the bawd were a-selling of them. Moreover, he writeth thus much to himself, after a familiar sort, as yet being not fallen out flatly with him, nor a professed enemy : " What hath changed and altered you ? Is it because I lie with a queen, she is my wife ? And is this the first time ? Did I not so nine years since ? Alas ! good sir, you that would have me company with Octavia my wife only, tell me true : know you for your part none other women but Drusilla ? Go to : so may you fare well and have your health, as, when you shall read this letter, you be not ready to deal carnally with Tertulla [6], or Terentilla, or Rufilla, or Salvia Titisenia, or with all of them. And think you it skilleth not [7], where and whom you lust after and meddle with ? "

70. Moreover, much talk there was abroad of a certain supper of his, more secret I wis than the rest, and which was commonly called δωδεκάθεος [a] ; at which, that there sat guests in habit of gods and goddesses, and himself among them adorned instead of Apollo, not only the letters of Antony, who rehearsed most bitterly the names of every one, do lay in his reproach, but also these verses without an author, so vulgarly known and rife in every man's mouth :

> *Cum primum istorum conduxit mensa choragum,*
> *Sexque deos vidit Mallia sexque deas ;*
> *Impia dum Phoebi Caesar mendacia ludit,*
> *Dum nova divorum cenat adulteria :*
> *Omnia se a terris tunc numina declinarunt,*
> *Fugit et auratos Iuppiter ipse thronos :*

> When first the table of these (guests) hired one the dance to
>   lead,[1][b]
> And Mallia [2][c] six goddesses and gods as many saw ;
> Whiles Caesar Phoebus conterfeits profanely [d], and, instead
>   Of supper, new adultries makes [e] of gods against all law ;
> All the heavenly powers then from the earth their eyes quite
>   turned away,
> And Jupiter himself [f] would not in gilt shrines [3] longer stay.

The rumour of this supper was increased by the exceeding dearth and famine at that time in Rome ; and the very next morrow there was set up this cry and note within the city, that the gods had eaten up all the corn, and that Caesar was become Apollo indeed[4], but yet Apollo the Tortor[g], under which surname that god was worshipped in one place of the city. Furthermore, taxed he was for his greedy grasping after precious house-furniture and costly Corinthian vessels, as also for giving himself much to dice-play. For, as in time of the proscription, there was written over his statue :

Pater argentarius, ego Corinthiarius,

My father was a banking-money-changer,
And I am now a Corinth-vessel-monger.

Because it was thought he procured some to be put into the bill of those that were proscribed, even for the love of their Corinthian vessels, so afterwards, during the Sicilian war, this epigram of him went current abroad :

Postquam bis classe victus naves perdidit,
Aliquando ut vincat, ludit assidue aleam,

Since time he lost his ships at sea in fight defeated twice,
That win he may sometime, he plays continually at dice.

71. Of these criminous imputations or malicious slanders (I wot not whether) the infamy[1] of his unnatural uncleanness he checked and confuted most easily by his chaste life both at the present and afterward. Semblably [C. 39], the invidious opinion of his excessive and sumptuous furniture, considering that, when he had by force won Alexandria, he retained for himself out of all the king's household stuff and rich implements, no more but one cup of the precious stone myrrha[2] ; and soon after, all the brazen vessels which were of most use, he melted every one. Marry, for fleshly lust otherwise and wantonness with women he went not clear, but was blotted therewith. For afterwards, also as the report goes, he gave himself overmuch to the deflowering of young maids, whom his wife sought out for him from all places. As for the rumour that ran of his dice-playing he bashed[3] no whit thereat ; and he played simply without art and openly for his disport, even when he was well-stricken in years, and besides the month

December [a], upon other play-days also, yea, and work-days too. Neither is there any doubt to be made thereof. For in a certain epistle written with his own hand : " I supped," quoth he, " my Tiberius, with the same men ; there came moreover to bear us company these guests, Vinicius, and Silius the father. In supper-time [4] we played like old men, both yesterday and to-day. For when the dice [5] were cast [b], look, who threw the chance, canis or senio, for every die he staked and laid to the stock a denier ; which he took up and swooped all clean, whose luck it was to throw Venus." Again in another letter : " We lived full merrily, my Tiberius, during the feast Quinquatria [c] ; for we played every day, we haunted, I say, and heated [6] the dicing-house. Your brother [7] did his deed with many great shouts and outcries ; howbeit, in the end he lost not much, but after his great losses gathered up his crumbs prettily well [8] by little and little, beyond his hope and expectation. I for my part lost 20,000 sesterces in mine own name ; but it was when I had been overliberal in my gaming, as commonly my manner is. For, if I had called for those losing-hands which I forgave my fellow-gamesters, or kept but that which I gave clean away, I had won as good as 50,000 clear. But I choose rather thus to do ; for my bounty exalteth me unto celestial glory." Unto his daughter thus he writeth : " I have sent unto you 250 deniers, just so many as I had given to my guests apiece, if they would have played together in supper-time, either at cockeal [9], or at even and odd." For the rest of his life, certain it is that in every respect he was most continent, and without suspicion of any vice.

72. He dwelt at first hard by the Forum of Rome above the winding stairs Anulariae [1], in a house which had been Calvus the orator's ; afterwards on the mount Palatium, howbeit in a mean habitation, belonging sometime to Hortensius, and neither for spacious receite [2] nor stately setting out, and trim furniture, conspicuous ; as wherein the galleries were but short, standing upon pillars made of soft Alban stone, and the refection-rooms without any marble or beautiful pavements. For the space of forty years and more, he kept one bed-chamber winter and summer ; and albeit he found by experience the city not very wholesome in the winter for his health, yet continually he wintered there. If he purposed at any

OCTAVIUS CAESAR AUGUSTUS

time to do aught secretly and without interruption, he had a
special room alone by itself aloft, which he called Syracuse[3][a].
Hither would he withdraw himself orderly, or else make a step
to some country-house, near the city, of one of his libertines
[C. 2]. Was he sick at any time? Then he used to lie in
Maecenas his house. Of all his retiring places of pleasure, he
frequented these especially that stood along the maritime tract,
and the isles of Campania; or else the towns near adjoining to
the city of Rome, to wit, Lanuvium, Praeneste, and Tibur,
where also, within the porches of Hercules' temple, he sat very
often to minister justice. Large palaces and full of curious
works he misliked, and verily, those that were sumptuously
built he razed down to the very ground; his own, as little as
they were, he adorned and beautified, not so much with trim
statues and gay painted tables as with open walks[4], pleasant
groves[5], and such things, as for their antiquity and rareness
were notable; of which sort were at Capreae the huge members
of monstrous fishes[6] and wild beasts, the bones that are said
to be of giants, and the armour of the demi-gods and worthies
in old time.

73. How slenderly provided he was of household stuff and
furniture otherwise appeareth by his dining-pallets and tables
yet remaining, the most part whereof be scarce answerable to
the elegance of a mere private person. Neither slept he by
men's saying otherwise than upon a low bed[1], and the same
but meanly spread and laid with coverlets. He wore not
lightly[2] any apparel but of housewife's cloth, made within
house by his wife, his sister, his daughter, and nieces. His
gowns were neither strait[3] and scant, nor yet wide and large;
his senator's robe neither with overbroad studs of purple
guarded, nor with narrow; his shoes underlaid somewhat with
the highest, that he might seem taller than he was. As for the
raiment which he used abroad, and his shoes, he had them at all
times laid ready within his bed-chamber, against all sudden
occurrents and unlooked for occasions whatsoever.

74. He feasted daily, and never otherwise than at a set
table[1], not without great respect and choice of degrees and
persons. Valerius Messalla [Tib. 70] writeth, that he never
entertained any of his libertines at supper except Menas, and
him naturalised first[2], even after the betraying of Sextus

Pompeius' fleet. Himself writeth, that he invited one, in whose farm he would make his abode, and who in times past had been a spy [3] [a] of his. He came to the board himself, when he made a feast, sometimes very late, and otherwhiles left the same as soon ; and then his guests would both fall to their suppers before he sat down, and also continued sitting still after he was gone. The suppers he made consisted ordinarily of three dishes of meat [4] and when he would fare most highly, of six at the most ; and as he entertained his guests in no exceeding sumptuous manner, so he welcomed them with all the kindness and courtesy that might be. For he would provoke them, if they either sat silent or spake softly, to the fellowship of discourse and talk ; yea, and interpose either acroames [5] and players, or else trivial fellows [6] out of the circus, but most commonly these discoursing poor threadbare philosophers [7].

75. Festival and solemn days he celebrated sometimes with unmeasurable expenses, otherwhiles with mirth and sport only ; as [1] the Saturnalia, and at other times when it pleased him, he used to send abroad as his gifts, onewhiles apparel, gold, and silver, otherwhiles money of all stamps, even old pieces current in the kings' days, and strange coins ; sometime nothing but hair clothes, sponges, cole-rakes [2], cizars [3], and such-like stuff, under obscure and doubtful titles symbolising somewhat else. He was wont also to offer sale by marting [4], in the time of a banquet to his guests, of such things as were in price most unequal [5], yea, and to tender blind bargains unto them also of painted tables, with the wrong side outward, and so, by uncertain venturing upon their hap, either to frustrate and disappoint, or fully to satisfy the hope of the chapmen ; yet so as the cheapening of the thing should always pass through every bourde [6], and the loss or gain grow to them all as common.

76. As touching diet (for I may not overpass so much as this), he was a man of very little meat, and feeding for the most part gross. Second bread [1] and small fishes, cheese made of cow's milk and the same pressed with the hand [2], and green figs, especially of that kind which bear twice a year, his appetite served unto. His manner was to eat even just before supper, when and wheresoever his stomach called for food. His very words out of his own epistles show no less, which are these : " Whiles we were in a British wagon [3], we tasted of bread and

dates." Again : " As I returned homeward in my litter from
the palace, I eat an ounce weight of bread with a few hard-
coated grapes [4]." And once more : " The very Jew, my
Tiberius, observeth not his fast upon the Sabbath [a] so precisely
as I have this day, who in the baines [5], not before the first hour
of the night was past, chewed two morsels of bread, even before
I began to be anointed." Upon this retchless neglect of diet [6],
he used divers times to take his supper alone, either before his
other guests were set and fell to meat, or else after all was taken
away, and they risen, whereas at a full board he would not
touch a bit.

77. He was by nature also a very small drinker of wine.
Cornelius Nepos reporteth of him, that his usual manner was,
during the time he lay encamped before Mutina, to drink at a
supper not above thrice. Afterwards, whensoever he drank
most liberally, he passed not six sextants [1] ; or if he went
beyond, he cast it up again. He delighted most in Rhaetian
wine ; and seldom drank he in the daytime [2]. Instead of
drink he took a sop of bread soaked in cold water ; or a piece
of cucumber, or a young lettuce head, or else some new-
gathered apple, sharp and tart [3], standing much upon [4] a
winish liquor within it.

78. After his noon's repast he used to take his repose and to
sleep awhile, in his clothes as he was, with his shoes on [a],
stretching out his feet [b], and holding his hand before his eyes.
After supper he retired himself into a little closet or study [c],
and there continued he by a candle far in the night, even until
he had dispatched the rest of that day's business, either all or
the most part. From thence he went directly to his bed,
where he slept at the most not above seven hours, and those
verily not together, but so as in that space of time he would
awake three or four times : and if he could not recover his
sleep thus broken and interrupted (as it happened otherwhiles),
he would send for some to read or tell tales, and by their means
catch a sleep again, and draw the same out often after daybreak. Neither would he ever lie awake without one sitting by
his bedside. Much offended he was with want of sleep or wak-
ing early in a morning ; and if he were to be awakened sooner
than ordinary, either about some worldly affairs of his friends,
or service of the gods, because he would not prejudice thereby

his own good or health, he used to stay in some of his familiar friends'[1] upper rooms and loft, next to the place where his occasions[2] lay. And even so, many a time for want of sleep, both as he was carried through the streets, and also when his litter was set down, he would between-whiles take a nap and make some stay.

79. He was of an excellent presence and personage, and the same throughout all the degrees of his age most lovely and amiable, negligent though he were in all manner of pikedness[1], for combing and trimming of his head so careless, as that he would use at once many barbers, such as came next hand, it skilled not [69] whom ; and onewhile he clipped, anotherwhile he shaved his beard, and yet at the very same time he either read, or else wrote somewhat. His visage and countenance, whether he spake or held his peace, was so mild, so pleasant, and lightsome, that one of the nobles and potentates of Gaul confessed unto his countrymen, he was thereby only stayed and reclaimed[2], that he did not approach near unto him under colour of conference, as he passed over the Alps, and so shove him down from a steep crag to break his neck, as his full intent was. He had a pair of clear and shining eyes, wherein also (as he would have made men believe) was seated a kind of divine vigour ; and he joyed much, if a man, looking wistly[3] upon him, held down his face, as it were against the brightness of the sun. But in his old age he saw not very well with the left eye. His teeth grew thin in his head, and the same were small and ragged ; the hair of his head was somewhat curled and turning downward, and withal of a light-yellow colour. His eyebrows met together ; his ears were of a mean bigness ; his nose both in the upper part[4] bearing out round, and also beneath somewhat with the longest[5]. Of colour and complexion, he was between a brown and fair white[6]. His stature but short ; and yet Julius Marathus his freedman writeth in the history of his life, that he was five feet and nine inches high[a]. But as low as the same was, the proportionable making and feature of his limbs hid it so as it might not be perceived, unless he were compared with some taller person than himself standing by.

80. His body, by report, was full of spots, having upon the breast and belly natural marks which he brought with him into the world, dispersed, for the manner, order, and number, like unto the stars of the celestial bear[1]; as also certain hard risings of thick brawny skin, occasioned in divers places by the itching of his body, and the continual and forcible use of the strigil[2] in the baines [76]; which callosities resembled a ring-worm[a]. In his left huckle-bone[3][b], thigh, and leg, he was not very sound, insomuch as many times for grief thereof he halted on that side; but by a remedy that he had of sand and reeds[c] he found ease and went upright again. Also, the forefinger of his right hand he perceived otherwhiles to be so weak that, being benumbed and shrunk by a cramp upon some cold, he could hardly set it to any writing, with the help of a hoop and finger-stall of horn. He complained also of the grief[4] in his bladder[d], but voiding at length little gravel-stones by urine, he was eased of that pain.

81. All his lifetime he tasted of certain grievous and dangerous sicknesses, but especially after the subduing of Cantabria; what time, by reason of his liver diseased and corrupted by distillations[1], he was driven to some extremity, and thereby of necessity entered into a contrary and desperate course of physic[a]; for, seeing that hot fomentations did him no good, forced he was, by the direction and counsel of Antonius Musa his physician, to be cured by cold. He had the experience also of some maladies which came yearly[b] and kept their course at a certain time. For about his birthday[c], most commonly he was sickish and had a faintness upon him; likewise in the beginning of the spring[d], much troubled he was with the inflation of the midriff and hypochondrial parts[2]; and whensoever the wind was southerly, with the murr and the pose[3]. By occasion whereof, his body being so shaken and crasie [C. 86], he could not well endure either cold or heat.

82. In winter-time clad he went against the cold with four coats, together with a good thick gown, and his waistcoat or petticoat body of woollen, well-lapped[1] also about the thighs and legs[a]. During summer he lay with his bed-chamber doors open, and oftentimes within a cloister supported with pillars, having water walming out[2] of a spring[b], or running from a spout in a conduit, or else some one to mak wind hard by him[c]. He could not away [94] so much as with the winter sunshine; and therefore, even at home, he never walked up and down in the air without a broad-brimmed hat[3] upon his head. He travelled in a litter, and never lightly[4] but in the night. The journeys that he made were soft[5] and small, so as if he went from Rome but to Tibur or Praeneste, he would make two days of it. Could he reach to any place by sea, he chose rather to sail thither than go by land[d]. But as great infirmities as he was subject unto, he maintained and defended his body with as much care and regard of himself, but principally by seldom bathing[6][e]; for anointed he was very often and used to sweat before a light[7] fire, and then upon it to be doused in water lukewarm, or else heated with long standing in the sun. And so often as he was to use the sea-waters hot, or those of Albula[8] for the strengthening of his sinews, he contented himself with this, namely, to sit in a wooden bathing-tub, which himself by a Spanish name called dureta[f], and therein to shake up and down his hands and feet, one after another by turns.

83. The exercises in Mars' field of riding on horseback and bearing arms, he laid aside immediately after the civil wars, and took himself, first, to the little tennis-ball[a], and the handball blown with wind[b]. Soon after, he used only to be carried[1] and to walk, but so as that in the end of every walk he would take his run by jumps, lapped [82] and wrapped within a light garment called sestertius[2] or a thin veil and sheet of linen[c]. For his recreation and pastime, his manner was sometime to angle or fish with the hook, otherwhiles to play with cockall bones[d], or trundling round pellets[3][e], or else with nuts even among little boys ; whom he would lay for and seek out from all parts, if they were of an amiable countenance and could prattle prettily with a lovely grace[4], but principally those of the Moors' and Syrians' kind. As for dwarfs, crooked and misshapen elves and all of that sort, he could not put up with such, as being the very mockeries of nature's work, and of unlucky presage.

84. Eloquence and other liberal professions he exercised from his very childhood right willingly, and therein took exceeding great pains. During the war at Mutina, notwithstanding that huge heap of affairs and occurrents, by report he read, he wrote, he declaimed every day. For afterwards, neither in the senate-house, nor before the people, nor unto his

soldiers made he ever speech, but it was premeditate and composed before, albeit he wanted not the gift to speak of a sudden
and extempore. Now, for fear lest his memory at any time
should fail him, lest also he might spend too much time in
learning by rote, he began to read and rehearse all out of his
written copy. His very speeches also with folk by themselves,
even with Livia his wife, about any grave and serious matters
were never but penned and put down in writing ; out of which
he would rehearse the same, that he might not speak otherwise
extempore or more or less than was meet. His pronunciation
and utterance was sweet, carrying with it a peculiar and proper
sound of his own, and continually he used the help of a phonascus [1] to moderate his voice ; but sometimes, when his throat
was weakened [2], he delivered his orations to the people by the
mouth of a crier.

85. Many compositions he made in prose, of sundry arguments. Of which he would read some in a meeting of his
familiars, as it were in an auditory ; as namely, a rejoinder,
called *Rescripta*, unto Brutus, against Cato [1]. Which volumes
when for the most part he had rehearsed, being now well-
stricken in years and growing weary, he made over to Tiberius
for to be read through. In like manner he wrote certain
Exhortations unto Philosophy, and somewhat of his own life,
which he declared [2] in thirty books [3], even unto the Cantabrian
war, and no farther. As for poetry, he dealt in it but superficially. One treatise there is extant, written by him in hexameter verses, the argument whereof is *Sicily*, and so it is
entitled. There is another book also, as little as it, *Of Epigrams :* which for the most part he studied upon and devised
whiles he was in the baines [76]. For, having in a great and
ardent heat begun a tragedy [4], when he saw his style would not
frame thereto and speed no better, he defaced and wiped it
quite out. And when some of his friends asked him how Ajax
did, he answered, that his Ajax was fallen upon a sponge [5 a].

86. The eloquence that he followed was of an elegant and
temperate kind ; wherein he avoided unapt and unfit sentences, as also the stinking savours, as himself saith, of dark
and obscure words, but took especial care how to express his
mind and meaning most plainly and evidently. For the
better effecting whereof, and because he would not in any

place trouble and stay reader or hearer, he stuck not either to put prepositions unto verbs, or to iterate conjunctions very oft ; which being taken away bred some obscurity, although they yield a greater grace. As for those that affect new-made words [a], such also as use old terms past date, he loathed and rejected alike, as faulty, both the sorts of them in a contrary kind. Those he shook up divers times, but especially his friend Maecenas, whose *myrobrechis cincinnos* [1] [b], for these were his terms, he evermore curseth and taxeth, yea, and by way of imitation [c] merrily scoffeth at. Neither spared he so much as Tiberius for hunting otherwhiles after old words out of use, and such [as] be obscure and hardly understood. As for Marcus Antonius, he rateth him as if he were frantic, for writing that which men may rather wonder at than understand. And proceeding to mock his lewd and inconstant humour in choosing a kind of eloquence by himself, he added thus much moreover : " And are you in doubt to imitate Cimber Annius and Veranius Flaccus [d], so that you might use the words which Crispus Sallustius gathered out of Cato's *Origines* [2] ? or rather transfer the rolling tongue of Asiatic orators, full of vain words and void of pithy sentences, into our language and manner of speech ? " And in a certain epistle, praising the ready wit of Agrippina his own niece [3] [grand-daughter], " But you have need," quoth he, " to endeavour that, neither in writing nor in speaking, you be troublesome and odious."

87. In his daily and ordinary talk certain phrases he had, which he used very often and significantly, as the letters of his own handwriting do evidently show ; in which, ever and anon, when he meant some that would never pay their debts, he said, " They would pay *ad kalendas Graecas* [1]." And when he exhorted men to bear patiently the present state whatever it was : " Let us content ourselves," quoth he, " with this Cato [2]." To express the speedy expedition of a thing done hastily, " Quicker," would he say, " than asparagus can be sodden [3]." He putteth also continually for *stultus* [4], *baceolus* [5] : for *pullus* [6], *pulleiaceus :* and for *cerritus, vacerrosus* [7] ; and instead of *male se habere, vapide se habere* [8] : and for *languere, betizare* [9], which commonly we mean by *lachanizare* [10]. Sem-blably [C. 39], for *simus, sumus ;* and *domos,* in the genitive case singular, for *domus*. And never used he these two words otherwise, that no man should think it was a fault rather than a custom. Thus much also have I observed, especially in his manuscripts, that he never cutteth a word in sunder ; nor in the end of any rewes [11] transferreth the overplus of letters unto those next following, but presently putteth them down even there underneath, and encloseth them within a compass line.

88. Orthography, that is to say, the form and precise rule of writing set down by grammarians, he did not so much observe, but seemeth to follow their opinion rather, who think men should write according as they speak. For, whereas oftentimes he either exchangeth or leaveth clean out not letters only, but syllables also, that is a common error among men. Neither would I note thus much, but that it seemeth strange unto me, which some have written of him, namely, that he substituted another in the place of a consular lieutenant (as one altogether rude and unlearned) because he had marked in his handwriting, ixi for *ipsi*. And look how often himself writeth darkly by way of ciphering ; he putteth *b* for *a*, *c* for *b*, and so forth after the same manner, the letters next following instead of the former, and for *x* a duple *a a*.

89. Neither verily was he less in love with the study of Greek literature ; for even therein also he highly excelled, as having been brought up and taught under the professed rhetorician Apollodorus of Pergamum, whom, being now very aged, himself as yet but young had forth of Rome with him to Apollonia. Afterwards also, when he was well furnished with variety of erudition and learning of Sphaerus [a], he entered into familiar acquaintance with Areus the philosopher and his two sons, Dionysius and Nicanor ; yet so as for all that he neither could speak readily, nor durst compose any thing [1]. For if occasion required aught, he drew it in Latin, and gave it unto another for to be translated into Greek. And, as he was not altogether unskilful in poems, so he took delight even in the old comedy [b] also, which he exhibited oftentimes to be acted in public solemnities. In reading over and perusing authors of both languages, he sought after nothing so much as wholesome precepts and examples, serving to public or private use ; and those, when he had gathered out of them word for word, he sent either to his inward friends and domestic servitors, or to the commanders of armies and governors of provinces, or else for the most part to the magistrates of the city, according as any of them needed admonition. Moreover, whole books he both read from one end to the other unto the senate, and also published oftentimes to the people by proclamation; as namely, the orations of Q. Metellus [c], touching the propagation and multiplying of children; those likewise of Rutilius, concerning the model and form of buildings [2], thereby the rather to persuade them, that he was not the first that looked into both these matters, but that their forefathers in old time had even then a care and regard thereof. The fine wits flourishing in his days he cherished by all means possible. Such as rehearsed before him their compositions he gave audience unto courteously and with patience; not only verses and histories, but orations [3] also and dialogues. Marry, if anything were written of himself, unless it were done with serious gravity and by the best, he took offence thereat; and gave the praetors in charge not to suffer his name to be made vulgar and stale, in the trivial contentions of orators, poets, etc., when they were matched one with another.

90. For religious scrupulosity and superstition, thus by hearsay he stood affected. Thunder and lightning he was much afraid of, insomuch as always and in every place he carried about him for a preservative remedy a seal's skin [1]; yea, and whensoever he suspected there would be any extraordinary storm or tempest, he would retire himself into a close secret room underground [a], and vaulted abovehead; which he did, because once in times past he had been frighted with a flash of lightning, crossing him in his journey by night, as we have before related [29].

91. As for dreams, neither his own nor other men's of himself he neglected. At the battle of Philippi, albeit he meant not to step out of his pavilion by reason of sickness, yet went he forth, warned so to do by the dream of his physician [1]. And it fell out well for him, considering that, after his camp forced and won by the enemies, his litter was in that concourse [2] of theirs stabbed through and all rent and torn, as if he had remained there behind lying sick. Himself every spring was wont to see many visions most fearful, but the same proved vain illusions and to no purpose; at other times of the year he dreamed not so often, but yet to more effect. Whenas he ordinarily frequented the temple dedicated to Jupiter the Thunderer in the Capitol, he dreamed that Jupiter Capitolinus complained how his worshippers were taken from him perforce, and that he answered that he had placed Thundering Jupiter hard by him, instead of a porter[3] ; whereupon soon after he adorned the lantern[4] of that temple with a ring[5] of bells, because such commonly do hang at men's gates[6]. By occasion of a vision by night, he begged yearly upon a certain day money of the people[a], and held out his hand hollow[7] to those that brought and offered unto him brazen dodkins[8] or mites called asses.

92. Certain foretokens and ominous signs he observed as infallible presages ; to wit, if in a morning his shoes were put on wrong, and namely, the left for the right, he held it unlucky; again, when he was to take any long journey by land or sea, if it chanced to mizzle of rain, he took that for a lucky sign, betokening a speedy and prosperous return. But moved he was especially with uncouth[1] and supernatural sights. There happened a date-tree to spring forth between the very joints of the stones before his door, which he removed and transplanted in the inward court of his domestic gods[2], taking great care that it might get root and grow there. He joyed so much in the island [of] Capreae, [where] the boughs of a very old holm-tree, hanging and drooping now for age down to the ground, became fresh again at his coming thither, that he would needs make an exchange with the state of Naples, and in lieu of that island give them Aenaria [mod. Ischia]. Certain days also he precisely observed ; as for example, he would not take a journey anywhither, the day after the nundinae[a], nor begin any serious matter upon the nones of a month ; herein verily avoiding and eschewing naught else, as he writeth unto Tiberius, but the unlucky ominousness of the name[b].

93. Of foreign ceremonies and religions, as he entertained with all reverence those that were ancient, and whereof he conceived good reason, so he despised the rest. For, having been instituted and professed in the sacred mysteries of Ceres at Athens, when afterwards he sat judicially upon the tribunal at Rome to hear and determine a controversy as touching the privilege of Ceres' priests in Attica, and perceived that certain points of great secrecy were proposed there to be debated, he

dismissed the assembly and multitude of people standing all about in the court, and himself alone heard them plead the cause. But contrariwise, not only when he rode in visitation all over Egypt, himself forbare to turn a little out of his way for to see Apis [a], but also commended his nephew Gaius, because, in riding through Judaea, he did not so much as once make supplication in Jerusalem [b].

94. And seeing we have proceeded thus far, it would not be impertinent to annex hereto, what befell unto him before he was born ; what happened upon his very birthday, and what presently ensued thereupon, whereby that future greatness and perpetual felicity of his might be hoped for and observed. At Velitrae, part of the town wall in old time had been blasted by lightning ; upon which occasion answer was given by oracle, that a citizen of that town should one day be ruler of the world. The Velletrians, in confidence hereof, both then immediately and afterwards also, many a time warred with the people of Rome, even well-near to their own final ruin and destruction. At length (though late it was) by good proofs and evidences it appeared that the said strange accident portended the mighty power of Augustus.

Julius Marathus [79] reporteth, that some six months before Augustus' nativity, there happened at Rome a prodigy publicly known, whereby foreshown and denounced [1] it was, that Nature was about to bring forth a king over the people of Rome [a] ; at which the senate, being affrighted, made an act, that no man-child that year born should be reared and brought up. But they, whose wives then were great-bellied (for every one was ready to draw the hope unto himself), took order [2] that the said act of the senate should not be brought into the city chamber [3] and there enrolled. I read in the books of Asclepiades Mendes [4] entitled *Theologoumena* [5], how Atia [6], being come at midnight to celebrate the solemn sacrifice and divine service of Apollo, while other dames slept, fell fast asleep also ; and suddenly a serpent [b] crept close unto her, and soon after went forth from her ; she, therewith being awakened, purified herself, as she would have done upon her husband's company with her ; and presently there arose to be seen upon her body a certain mark or speck representing the picture of a serpent, which never after could be gotten out, insomuch as immediately thereupon she forbare the public baines [76] for ever ; also, how in the tenth month after she was delivered of Augustus, and for this cause he was reputed to be the son of Apollo. The same Atia, before she was brought to bed of him, dreamed that her entrails were heaved up to the stars, and there stretched forth and spread all over the compass of earth and heaven. His father Octavius likewise dreamed that out of the womb of Atia there arose the shining beams of the sun.

The very day on which he was born, what time as the conspiracy of Catiline was debated in the senate-house, and Octavius, by occasion of his wife's childbirth came very late thither, well-known it is and commonly spoken, that P. Nigidius [7], understanding the cause of his stay, so soon as he learned the hours also when she was delivered [8], gave it out confidently, that there was born the sovereign lord of the world. Afterwards, when Octavius, leading an army through the secret parts of Thrace, inquired in the sacred grove of Liber pater [father Bacchus] (according to the rites and ceremonies of that barbarous religion) concerning his son, the same answer he received from the priests there ; for that when the wine was poured upon the altars, there arose from thence so great a shining flame, as surmounted the lantern [91] of the temple, and so ascended up to heaven ; and that in times past the like strange token happened to Alexander the Great, and to none but him, when he sacrificed upon the same altars. Moreover, the night next following, he presently thought he saw his son, carrying a stately majesty above the ordinary proportion of a mortal wight, with a thunder-bolt and a sceptre [9] in his hand, with the triumphant robes also of Jupiter Optimus Maximus upon his back and a radiant coronet on his head over and besides his chariot dight with laurel and drawn with twelve steeds exceeding white. While he was yet a very babe (as C. Drusus hath left in writing extant), being by his nurse laid in the evening within a cradle in swaddling bands, beneath upon a low floor, the next morning he could nowhere be seen ; and after long seeking was found at last, lying upon a very high turret just against the sun rising.

So soon as he began to speak, he commanded the frogs to keep silence, that about the manor of his grandsires by the city side chanced to make a foul noise : and thereupon ever after the frogs in that place are not able to croak.   About four miles from Rome, as ye go directly to Capua [10], it fell out that suddenly an eagle snatched a piece of bread out of his hand as he took his dinner within a pleasant grove ; and when he had mounted up a very great height, came gently down of a sudden again and restored unto him the same.   Q. Catulus, after the dedication of the Capitol, dreamed two nights together ; in the former, him thought that Jupiter Optimus Maximus, while many young boys, noblemen's sons, were playing about his altar, severed one of them from the rest and bestowed in his bosom the public broad seal [c] of the State to carry in his hand. And the next night following he saw in another dream the same boy in the bosom of Jupiter Capitolinus ; whom when he commanded to be pulled from thence, prohibited he was by the admonition of the god, as if the same boy should be brought up for the defence and tuition of the commonweal.   Now the morrow after, chancing to meet with young Augustus (whom erst he had not known before), he beheld him wistly [79], not without great admiration, and withal openly gave it out, that he was for all the world like unto that boy of whom he dreamed. Some tell the former dream of Catulus otherwise ; as if Jupiter (whenas a number of those boys required of him a tutor) pointed out one of them, unto whom they should refer all their desires ; and so, lightly touching his lips, and taking as it were an assay thereof with his fingers, brought that kiss back to his own mouth.   M. Cicero, having accompanied Gaius Caesar into the Capitol, happened to report unto his familiar friends the dream he had the night before ; namely, how a boy of an ingenious [11] face and countenance was let down from heaven by a golden chain, and stood at the door of the Capitol, unto whom Jupiter delivered a whip [d] : hereupon, espying at unawares Augustus, whom (as yet altogether unknown to most men) his uncle Caesar had sent for to the sacrifice, he avouched plainly that this boy was very he, whose image was represented unto him in a vision as he lay asleep.

When he was putting on his virile gown, it fortuned that his broad-studded coat [12] with purple, being unstitched in the seams of both shoulders, fell from about him down to his feet. There were who made this interpretation, that it betokened nothing else but that the degree [13], whereof that robe was a badge, should one day be subjected unto him. Julius of sacred memory, being about to choose a plot of ground for to encamp in about Munda, as he cut down a wood, chanced to light upon a date-tree, which he caused to be spared and reserved as the very presage of victory ; from the root of it there sprung immediately certain shoots, which in few days grew so fast, that they not only equalised, but overtopped also and shadowed their stock : yea, and doves [14] haunted the same, therein to nestle and breed, notwithstanding that kind of bird cannot of all others away with [15] any hard leaves and rough branches. Upon this strange sight especially, Caesar by report was moved to suffer none other to succeed him in the empire but his sister's nephew.

Augustus, during the time that he was retired to Apollonia, went up in the company of Agrippa into the gallery [16] of Theogenes the mathematician [17]. Now when Agrippa (who inquired first what his own fortune should be) had great matters and those in manner incredible foretold unto him, Augustus himself concealed the time of his own nativity, and in nowise would utter the same, for fear and bashfulness lest he should be found inferior to the other. But when, hardly after many exhortations and much ado, he had delivered [18] the same, Theogenes leapt forth and worshipped him. Augustus then anon conceived so great a confidence in his fortunes, that he divulged his horoscope and the ascendant of his nativity ; yea, and also stamped a piece of silver coin with the mark of the celestial sign Capricornus, under which figure and constellation he was born.

95. After Caesar's death, being returned from Apollonia, as he entered Rome city, suddenly, when the sky was clear and weather very fair, a certain round coronet in form of a rainbow compassed the circle of the sun, and therewith soon after the monument of Julia, Caesar's daughter, was smitten with lightning. Moreover, in his first consulship [a], whiles he attended to take his augury, there were presented unto him, like as to Romulus, twelve geirs [1] ; and as he sacrificed, the livers of all the beasts then killed appeared in open view enfolded double, and turned inwardly from the nether fillet ; and no man of skill conjectured otherwise but that prosperity and greatness hereby was portended.

96. Furthermore, the very events also of all his wars he foresaw. What time as all the forces of the triumvirs[1] were assembled together at Bononia, an eagle, perching over his tent, all to-beat[2] two ravens that assailed and fell upon her on either side, and in the end struck them both down to the ground ; which sight the whole army marked very well, and presaged thereby that one day there would arise between the colleagues of that triumvirate such discord, and the like end ensue thereof, as after followed. At Philippi there was a certain Thessalian[3], who made report of the future victory, alleging for his author Caesar of famous memory, whose image[4] encountered him as he journeyed in a desert and by-way. About Perusia, when he offered sacrifice and could not speed[5], but demanded more beasts[a] still to be killed, behold, the enemies made a sudden sally forth, caught up and carried away the whole provision of the sacrifice. The soothsayers then agreed upon this point, that those perilous and adverse calamities which had been threatened and denounced to him that sacrificed, should light all and return upon their heads, who gat the inwards ; and so it fell out indeed. The day before he fought the battle at sea near Sicily, as he walked upon the shore, a fish leapt out of the sea and lay at his feet. At Actium, as he was going down to fight the battle, there met him in the way an ass with his driver ; the man's name was Eutychus, and the beast's Nicon[b]. After victory obtained, he set up the images of them both in brass within that temple, into which he converted the very place where he encamped.

97. His death also (whereof from henceforth I will write) and his deification after death was known before by many signs most evident. When he had taken a review of the city, and was about the solemn purging[1] thereof within Mars' field before a frequent [C. 22] assembly of people, an eagle there was that soared oftentimes round about him and, crossing at length from him unto a house thereby, settled upon the name of Agrippa, and just upon the first letter of that name ; which when he perceived, the vows which the manner was to be made until the next lustrum[a], he commanded his colleague Tiberius to nuncupate[2] and pronounce. For, notwithstanding the tables and instruments[b] containing them were now written and in readiness, yet denied he to undertake those vows which he should never pay. About the same time the first letter [3] of his own name, upon a flash and stroke of lightning, went quite out of the inscription that stood upon his statue ; answer was made by the soothsayers, that he was to live but just one hundred days after, which number that letter did betoken ; and that it would come to pass that he should be canonised and registered among the gods, because aesar, the residue of the name Caesar, in the Tuscan language signified god. Being about therefore to send Tiberius away into Illyricum and to company him as far as Beneventum, when divers suitors for one cause or other interrupted him, yea, and detained him about hearing and determining matters judicially, he cried out aloud (which also within a while was reckoned as a presaging osse [57]), that were he once out of Rome, he would never after be there again, what occasion soever might make him stay. And so, being entered upon his journey, he went forward as far as to Astura [4] : and so presently from thence (contrary to his usual manner [c]), with the benefit of a fore-wind and gentle gale, took water by night and sailed over [5].

98. The cause of his sickness he caught by a flux of the belly. And for that time having coasted Campania and made circuit about the islands next adjoining, he bestowed also four days within a retiring place of pleasure at Capreae, where he gave his mind to all ease and courteous affability. It happened, as he passed by the bay of Puteoli, certain passengers and soldiers out of a ship of Alexandria [a], which then was newly-arrived, all clad in white, dight also with garlands and burning frankincense, had heaped upon him all good and fortunate words, chanting his singular praises in these terms : that by him they lived, by him they sailed, by him they enjoyed their freedom, and all the riches they had. At which he took great contentment and was cheered at the heart, insomuch as thereupon he divided to every one of his train about him 40 pieces of gold [b], but he required an oath again and assurance of each one, that they should not lay out that money otherwise than in buying the wares and commodities of Alexandria [c]. For certain days together that remained, among diverse and sundry gifts, he distributed among them over and above gowns and cloaks, with this condition, that Romans should use the Greek habit and speak likewise Greek, the Greeks also wear

Roman attire and use their language. He beheld also continually the youths exercising themselves (of whom there remained yet some store at Capreae) according to the ancient custom[1]. And even unto them he made a feast in his own sight, permitting them or rather exacting of them their old liberty of sporting, of snatching apples and cates, and of skambling[2] for such small gifts and favours as were sent or scattered abroad. In one word, he forbare no manner of mirth and pastime.

The isle[3] hard by Capreae[d] he called Apragopolis[e], of the idleness of such as out of his train retired themselves thither. But one of his beloved minions named Masgabas[f] he had wont merrily to call κτίστης, as one would say, the founder of that island. The sepulchre of this Masgabas (who died a year before) when he perceived [it] one time out of his dining-chamber to be frequented with a sort [C. 81] of people and many lights, he pronounced this verse aloud, which he made extempore :

Κτίστου δὲ τύμβον εἰσορῶ πυρούμενον,

I see the tomb of Ktistes all on fire.

And therewith turning to Thrasyllus, a companion of Tiberius sitting over against him, and not wotting what the matter was, he asked him of what poet's making he thought that verse to be ? And when he stuck at the question and made no answer, he came out with another to it :

Ὁρᾶς φάεσσι Μασγάβαν τιμώμενον ;

See'st thou with lights Masgabas honoured ?

Of this verse also he demanded whom he thought to be the maker. But when Thrasyllus returned no other answer but this that, whosoever made them, right excellent they were, he laughed a-good[4] and made himself exceeding merry. Soon after he crossed over to Naples, albeit even then his guts were greatly enfeebled and the disease[5] grew variable[g] : yet for all that, the quinquennial gymnastic games[h] instituted in the honour of him he beheld to the very end, and so together with Tiberius went to the place appointed. But in his return from thence, his disease increased more and more, so as at length he yielded to it at Nola ; where, having sent for Tiberius and called him back from his journey, he held him a great while in secret talk, neither from that time framed he his mind to any greater affair.

99. Upon his dying day, inquiring ever and anon whether there was as yet any stir and tumult abroad as touching him, he called for a mirror, and commanded the hair of his head to be combed and trimmed, his jaws also, ready for weakness to hang or fall, to be composed and set straight. Then, having admitted his friends to come unto him and asked of them, whether they thought he had acted well the interlude[1] of his life, he adjoined withal this final conclusion for a plaudite[2] :

Κρότον δότε, καὶ πάντες ὑμεῖς μετὰ χαρᾶς κτυπήσατε[3],
Now clap your hands and all with joy resound a shout.

After this he dismissed them all, and whiles he questioned with some that were new-come from the city, concerning the daughter of Drusus then sick, suddenly, amidst the kisses of Livia and in these words, he gave up the ghost : " Live mindful, Livia, of our wedlock, and so farewell." Thus died he an easy death and such as he had ever wished to have. For lightly[4], so often as he heard of anybody to have departed this life quickly and without all pangs, he prayed unto God that he and his might have the like euthanasia ; for that was the very word he was wont to use. One sign only and no more he showed of a mind disquieted and distracted, before he yielded up his vital breath ; in that he suddenly started as in a fright and complained, that he was harried away[5] by forty tall and lusty young men. And even that also was rather a pregnant presage of his mind, than a raving fit and idle conceit of light brain ; for so many soldiers they were indeed of the praetorian band, who carried him forth dead into the street upon their shoulders.

100. He died in that very bed-chamber wherein his father Octavius left his life before him, when Pompeius and Appuleius, having both their forename Sextus, were consuls, fourteen days before the kalends of September[1], at the ninth hour[2] of the day, being seventy-six years old wanting five and thirty days. His corpse was conveyed and borne by the decurions[3] of the free boroughs and colonies from Nola to Bovillae by night, for the hot season of the year ; whereas till the daytime it was bestowed in the hall of every town, or else in the greatest

temple [a] thereof. From Bovillae the degree of Roman gentlemen took charge of it, and brought it into the city of Rome,
where they placed it within the porch of his own house. The
senate, both in setting out his funeral and also in honouring his
memorials, proceeded so far in striving who should show
greater affection, that, among many other compliments, some
were of mind, that the pomp and solemn convoy of his obsequies should pass forth at the triumphal gate with the image of
Victory, which is in the Court Julia, going before, and the chief
noblemen's children of both sexes singing a doleful and lament-
able song; others opined that, upon the very day of the
funeral, their rings of gold [b] should be laid away and others of
iron put on. Again, divers gave advice that his bones should
be gathered up [4] by the priests [c] of the most ancient societies.
And one above the rest would have had the name of the month
August [5] to be shifted and transferred unto September, for that
Augustus was born in this and died in the other. Another
persuaded that all the time from his very birth unto the dying
day, should be named *Seculum Augustum* [6], and so recorded in
the calendars and chronicles.

But thought best it was, to keep a mean in the honours done
unto him. Whereupon, twice and in two several places,
praised he was in a funeral oration; once before the temple of
Julius late deceased, of sacred memory, by Tiberius, and
again at the Rostra [d] under the Veteres [7] by Drusus the son of
Tiberius; and so upon senators' shoulders was he borne into
Campus Martius, and there committed to the fire and burnt.
Neither wanted there a grave personage [8], one that had been
praetor, who affirmed and bound it with an oath, that he saw
his very image [9], when he was burnt, ascending up to heaven.
The chief gentlemen of the knights' order, in their single
waistcoats [10], ungirt and barefooted, gathered up his relics [e]
together, and bestowed them in a stately monument [f]; which
piece of work himself had built between the street Flaminia and
the bank of Tiber in his sixth consulship, and even then given
the groves growing about it and the walks adjoining to be
common for the use of the people of Rome for ever.

101. His last will and testament, made by him when L.
Plancus and C. Silius were consuls, the third day before the
nones of April [1], a year and four months before he died, and the

same in two books, written partly with his own hand, and in part with the hands of Polybus and Hilarion his freedmen, the Vestal virgins [a], who had the keeping thereof upon trust, brought forth, together with three other rolls or volumes sealed alike ; all which instruments were opened and read in the senate. He ordained for his six [2] heirs ; in the first place, Tiberius of the one half and a sixth part [b], and Livia of a third [c] ; whom also he appointed to bear his own name [d]. In a second rank [3], he appointed Drusus the son of Tiberius to inherit one third part, and Germanicus with his three male children the other parts remaining. In a third degree [4], he nominated of his own kinsfolk, allies and friends, very many.

He bequeathed as a legacy to the people of Rome [e] 400,000 sesterces [5] an hundred times told ; to the soldiers of the guard [6] a thousand sesterces apiece ; among the cohorts of the city soldiers 500 ; and to those of the legionary cohorts 300 apiece. Which sum of money he commanded to be paid presently [7] ; for he had so much in store at all times, put up in bags and coffers, lying by him. Sundry parcels gave he besides by legacy parole [8]. And of some thereof he deferred the payment [9], if the same were above 20,000 sesterces. For paying of which he set a year's day at the farthest, alleging for his excuse his mean estate ; and protesting, that by this account there would not come to his heirs' hands above 150 millions [10], albeit, within the compass of twenty years immediately going before, he had received by the wills and testaments of his friends 1400 millions [11]. All which mass of treasure, together with two patrimonies by his two fathers [12] and other inheritances, he had spent well-near every whit upon the commonweal. The two Julias, to wit, his daughter and niece [13] (if aught happened to them) he forbade expressly to be interred in his own mausoleum. Of those three rolls or instruments abovenamed, in the first he comprised his own directions as touching his funeral ; the second contained a register or index [14] of those acts which he had achieved ; and his pleasure was that the same should be engraven in brazen tables [15] and erected before his mausoleum. In the third he represented a breviary and abstract of the whole empire : to wit, how many soldiers were enrolled and in pay, in any place whatsoever ; as also, how much money was in the common treasury of the city and in his own coffers ; lastly, what the arrierages [16] were of such revenues and tributes as were due to the State and unpaid.   Whereto he annexed also a schedule, containing the names of freedmen and bond, his receivers, at whose hands the reckoning might be exacted.

THE HISTORY OF
TIBERIUS NERO CAESAR

1. THE patrician family Claudia (for there was likewise another, plebeian, of that name, neither in power nor dignity inferior) had the first beginning out of Regilli, a town of the Sabines. From thence they came with a great retinue of vassals to Rome newly-founded, there to dwell, induced thereto by the counsel of T. Tatius, fellow in government of the kingdom with Romulus; or (which is the more received opinion) through the persuasion of Atta ᵃ Claudius [1], a principal person of that house, about the sixth year after the kings were expelled; and so, by the senators of Rome, ranged they were among the patricians. Upon this, soon after, they received by virtue of a grant from the whole city, for their clients and vassals, lands to occupy beyond the river Anio, and for themselves a place [2] of sepulture under the Capitol; and so forth [3], in process of time obtained 28 consulates, five dictatorships, censorships seven, triumphs six, and two ovations. This family, being distinguished by sundry forenames and surnames both, in a general consent rejected the forename of Lucius, after that two of their lineage bearing that name were convict, the one of robbery, the other of murder. Among surnames it assumed the addition of Nero ᵇ, which in the Sabine tongue signifieth strong or stout.

2. Many of these Claudii, as they deserved many ways passing well of the commonwealth, so, in as many sorts, they faulted and did amiss. But to relate the principal examples only in both kinds: Appius surnamed Caecus [blind] was he who dissuaded the entering into league and society with king Pyrrhus, as prejudicial unto the State; Claudius Caudex ᵃ was the first man that passed over the narrow seas with a fleet, and drove the Carthaginians out of Sicily; Claudius Nero surprised

131

and defeated Hasdrubal, coming out of Spain with a very great and puissant army, before he could join with his brother Hannibal. Contrariwise, Claudius Appius Regillanus, being decemvir[1] chosen to frame and pen the Roman laws, went about by violence (for the satisfaction of his fleshly lust) to enthrall[2] a virgin freeborn ; and thereby gave occasion to the commons for to fall away and forsake the nobles a second time. Claudius Drusus, having his own statue erected with a diadem in a town called Forum Appii[b], attempted with the help of his favourites and dependants to hold all Italy in his own hands. Claudius Pulcher[3], whenas, in taking of his auspicia[c] before Sicily, the sacred pullets would not feed, caused them, in contempt of religion, to be plunged into the sea, " that they might drink, seeing they would not eat," and thereupon struck a battle at sea ; in which, being vanquished and commanded by the senate to nominate a dictator, scorning, as it were, and making but a jest at the public danger and calamity of the State, named a base serjeant of his own, called Glycia[4]. There stand likewise upon record the examples of women, and those as diverse and contrary. For two Claudiae there were of the same house ; both she that drew forth[5] the ship with the sacred images of the Idaean mother[6] of the Gods sticking fast and grounded within the shelves[7] of Tiber, having before made her prayer openly that, as she was a true and pure virgin, so the ship might follow her, and not otherwise ; as also another, who, after a strange and new manner, being a woman[8], was arraigned before the people of high treason, for that, when her coach wherein she rode could hardly pass forward by reason of a thick throng and press of people, she had openly wished that her brother Pulcher were alive again, and might lose a fleet the second time, to the end there might be by that means a less multitude at Rome. Moreover, very well-known it is, that all the Claudii, excepting only that P. Clodius who, for expelling Cicero out of Rome, suffered himself to be adopted by a commoner[9][d] and one younger also than himself, were always optimates, the only maintainers or patrons of the dignity and power of the patricians ; yea, and in opposition of the commons so violent, stubborn, and self-willed, that not one of them, although he stood upon his trial for life and death before the people, could find in his heart so much as to change his

weed [10,e], or to crave any favour at their hands. Nay, some
of them there were, who in a brawl and altercation stuck not to
beat the very tribunes of the commons [f]. Furthermore, a
virgin Vestal [11] there was of that name, who, when a brother of
hers triumphed without a warrant from the people, mounted
up with him into the chariot, and accompanied him even into
the Capitol, to this end that none of the tribunes might lawfully oppose themselves and forbid the triumph [12].

3. From this race and lineage Tiberius Caesar deriveth his
genealogy, and that verily in the whole blood and of both
sides ; by his father, from Tiberius Nero, by his mother from
Appius Pulcher, who were both of them the sons of Appius
Caecus. Incorporate he was besides into the family of the
Livii, by reason that his grandfather by the mother's side [1] was
adopted thereinto ; which family (commoners though they
were) flourished notwithstanding and was highly reputed, as
being honoured and graced with eight consulships, two censorships, and three triumphs, with a dictatorship also and master-
ship of the horsemen ; renowned likewise and ennobled for
brave and notable men, Salinator [a] especially and the Drusi [2].
As for Salinator, in his censorship he noted and taxed all the
tribes, every one and whole body of the people, for unconstant
levity ; for that, having upon his former consulship condemned him and set a fine upon his head, yet afterwards they
made him consul a second time and censor besides. Drusus,
upon the killing of one Drausus, the general of his enemies, in
close combat and single fight, purchased unto himself and his
posterity after him that surname. It is reported also, that
this Drusus, being propraetor, recovered and fetched again
out of his province of Gaul that gold which in times past had
been given unto the Senones, when they besieged the Capitol ;
and that it was not Camillus (as the voice goeth) that wrested
the same perforce out of their hands. His son [3] in the fourth
degree of descent, called, for his singular employment against
the Gracchi, patron of the senate, left behind him a son, whom,
in the like variance and debate[4], as he was busy in devising and
putting in practice sundry plots, the adverse faction treacherously slew.

4. But the father of this Tiberius Caesar, being treasurer
unto C. Caesar [1], and admiral of a fleet in the Alexandrine war,

performed very good service for the achieving of victory, whereupon he was both substituted pontifex instead of Scipio, and also sent with commission to plant colonies in Gaul, among which were Narbo [Narbonne] and Arelate [Arles]. Howbeit, after that Caesar was slain, whenas all men for fear of troubles and uproars decreed a final abolition and oblivion [2] of that act (and all other quarrels thereupon depending) he proceeded farther and opined, that they should consult about the rewards of such tyrant-killers. After this, having borne his praetorship (in the end of which year there arose some discord between the triumvirs) he retained by him still the ensigns [3] and ornaments of that office after the time fully expired ; and following L. Antonius, the consul and the triumvir's brother, as far as to Perusia, when the rest yielded themselves, continued alone fast, and stuck to the faction (that sided against Octavius), and first escaped to Praeneste, then to Naples ; where when he had proclaimed (but in vain) freedom for all bondslaves [4], he fled into Sicily. But taking it to the heart that he was not immediately admitted to the presence of Sextus Pompeius, but debarred the use of his knitches of rods to be borne before him [a], he crossed the seas into Achaia, and went to M. Antonius. With whom, by occasion that, shortly after, an atonement and peace was made between all parties, he returned to Rome ; and at the request of Augustus yielded unto him his own wife Livia Drusilla, who both at that time was great with child, and also had already before brought him a son named Tiberius in his own house. Not long after, he departed this life, and left his children surviving him, namely, Tiberius Nero and Drusus Nero.

5. Some have thought that this Tiberius Caesar was born at Fundi, grounding upon a light conjecture, because his mother's grandam [1] was a Fundane born, and for that soon after the image of Felicity [2], by virtue of an act of the senate, was there publicly set up [a]. But, as the most authors and those of better credit do write, born he was at Rome in the Mount Palatium, the sixteenth day before the kalends of December [3], when M. Aemilius Lepidus was consul the second time together with Munatius Plancus, even after the war at Philippi ; for so it stands upon record and in the public registers. Yet there want not some who write otherwise :

partly, that he was born a year before in the consulship of
Hirtius and Pansa, and partly, the year next following, wherein
Servilius Isauricus and Antonius were consuls.

6. His infancy and childhood both were exceeding forward[1][a] and the same full of toilsome travail and danger, by
occasion that everywhere he accompanied his parents still, in
their flights and escapes. And verily, twice he had like to have
descried[2] them with his wrawling[3] at Naples, what time as, a
little before the forcible and sudden entry of the enemy, they
made shift secretly to get into a ship ; namely once, when he
was taken hastily from his nurse's breast, and a second time
out of his mother's lap and arms, by those who, as the necessity
of the time required, did their best to ease the poor women of
their burden and load. He was carried away with them likewise through Sicily and Achaia ; yea, and being recommended
to the Lacedaemonians (who were under the protection of the
Claudii, their patrons) for to take the charge of him in public,
as he departed from thence by night, he was in danger of his
life by reason of a light [Aug. 82] flaming fire, which suddenly
from all parts arose out of a wood, and compassed all the company in his train, so as that some part of Livia's apparel and
the hair of her head was scorched and singed therewith. The
gifts bestowed upon him in Sicily by Pompeia, the sister of
Sextus Pompeius, to wit, a little cloak with a button or clasp
to it, likewise studs and bosses of gold, continue and are yet
shown to be seen at Baiae. After his return into the city of
Rome, being adopted by M. Gallius, a senator, in his last will
and testament, he accepted of the inheritance and entered
upon it ; but within a while forbare the name, because Gallius
had sided with the adverse faction and taken part against
Augustus. Being nine years old, he praised his father deceased openly from the Rostra. Afterwards, as he grew to be a
springall[4], he accompanied in the Actian triumph the chariot
of Augustus, riding upon the steed drawing without the yoke[5]
on the left hand, whenas Marcellus, the son of Octavia, rode
upon the other on the right hand[b]. He was president also at
the Actian games[6] and plays, yea, and the Trojan tournament
in the Circensian solemnities, where he led the troop of the
bigger boys.

7. After he had put on his virile robe[1], his whole youth and all the time besides of the age next ensuing, even unto the beginning of his empire, he passed for the most part in these affairs following. He exhibited one sword-fight, performed by fencers to the outrance [C. 39], in memorial of his father, likewise another in the honourable remembrance of his grandfather Drusus, and those at sundry times and in diverse places ; the former in the Forum [2] of Rome, the second in the amphitheatre, having brought again into the lists even those that were freed beforetime and discharged from that profession ; whom he now hired and bound to fight with the sum of 100,000 sesterces. He did set forth stage-plays also, but whiles himself was absent, all with great magnificence, and also at the charges of his mother [3] and step-father [4]. Agrippina [5], the daughter also of M. Agrippa and niece to Pomponius Atticus, a gentleman of Rome, him I mean, unto whom Cicero wrote his epistles, he took to wife. And when he had begotten of her a son named Drusus, albeit she fitted him well enough and was besides with child again, enforced he was to put her away, and forthwith to wed Julia, the daughter of Augustus ; not without much grief and heart-break, considering that he both desired still the company of Agrippina and also misliked the conditions and demeanour of Julia, as whom he perceived to have had a mind and fancy unto him whiles she was the wife of a former husband, which verily was thought also abroad. But as he grieved, that after the divorce he had driven away Agrippina, so when he chanced but once (as she met him) to see her, he followed her still with his eyes so bent [6], so swelling, and staring [7], that strait order was given, and a watch set, she should never after come in his way nor within his sight. With Julia he lived at the first in great concord and mutual love ; but afterwards he began to estrange himself, and (that which was the more grief) he proceeded to part beds and to lie from her continually, namely, after that the pledge of love, their son begotten between them, was untimely taken away, who being born at Aquileia died a very infant. His own brother Drusus [8] he lost in Germany, whose body he conveyed throughout to Rome, going before it all the way on foot.

8. In his first rudiments and beginnings of civil offices, he pleaded at the bar in defence of Archelaus, of the Trallians and Thessalians, all of them in sundry causes whiles Augustus sat in judgement to hear their trial ; in the behalf also of the Laodiceans, Thyatireans and Chians, who had suffered great loss by earthquake, and humbly sought for relief, he entreated the senate. As for Fannius Caepio, who together with Varro Murena had conspired against Augustus, he arraigned [him] of high treason before the judges, and caused him to be condemned ; and amid these affairs he executed a duple charge and function[1], to wit, the purveyance of corn and victuals, whereof there happened to be scarcity : and the skouringe[2] or riddance of the workhouse prisons[3], the lords and masters whereof were become odious, as if they had caught up and held to work not only wayfaring persons, but those also who, for fear of taking a military oath and to be enrolled, were driven to shroud themselves[4] in such corners and starting-holes [C. 1].

9. His first service in the wars was in the expedition of Cantabria, what time he had the place of a tribune military[1]. Afterwards, having the conduct of an army into the East parts, he restored the kingdom of Armenia unto Tigranes, and from the tribunal seat did put the diadem upon his head. He recovered also those military ensigns which the Parthians had taken from M. Crassus. After this he governed as regent that part of Gaul beyond the Alps, called Comata, which was full of troubles, partly by the incursions of barbarous nations, and in part through the intestine discord of princes and nobles of the country. Then warred he upon the Rhaetians and Vindelicians, and so forward upon the Pannonians and Germans (whom he vanquished all). In the Rhaetian and Vindelician wars he subdued the nations inhabiting the Alps ; in the Pannonian, he conquered the Breuci and Dalmatians. In the German war he brought over into Gaul 40,000 that yielded unto him, and placed them near unto the Rhine bank, where they had their habitations assigned. For which acts, he entered the city of Rome both ovant [Aug. 22] riding on horseback, and also triumphant mounted upon a chariot, being the first[2] (as some think) that was honoured with triumphal ornaments, a new kind of honour and never granted to any man before. To bear magistracy he both began betimes, and also ran through them all in manner jointly and without intermission, namely, his quaestorship, praetorship, and consulate. After some space between, he became consul a second time, yea, and also received the tribunician authority for five years together.

10. In this confluence of so many prosperous successes, in the strength also of his years and perfect health, he had a full purpose suddenly to retire himself and remove out of the way as far as he could. Whether it were for the weariness he had of his wife, whom neither he durst plainly charge or put away, nor was able to endure any longer, or to the end that, by avoiding contempt [a] incident to daily and continual residence, he might maintain and increase his authority by absenting himself, if at any time the State stood in need of him, it is uncertain. Some are of opinion that, considering Augustus his children were now well-grown, he of his own accord yielded up unto them the place and possession, as it were, of the second degree [1], which himself had usurped and held a long time ; following herein the example of M. Agrippa, who, having preferred [2] M. Marcellus to be employed in public affairs, departed unto Mitylenae, lest by his presence he might seem to hinder [3] them or deprave [Aug. 27] their proceedings. Which cause even himself, but afterwards, alleged ; marry, for the present, pretending the satiety that he had of honourable places, and rest from his travails, he made suit for licence to depart ; neither gave he any ear to his own mother humbly beseeching him to stay, nor to his step-father, who complained also that he should be forsaken thereby and left desolate in the senate. Moreover, when they were instant still to hold him back, he abstained from all kind of meat four days together. At length, having obtained leave to be gone, he left his wife and son behind him at Rome, and forthwith went down to Ostia, giving not so much as one word again to any that accompanied him thither, and kissing very few of them at the parting.

11. As he sailed from Ostia along the coast of Campania, upon news that he heard of Augustus' weakness, he stayed awhile and went not forward ; but when a rumour began to be spread of him (as if he lingered there, waiting some opportunity of greater hopes), he made no more ado, but even against wind and weather sailed through and passed over to Rhodes, having taken a delight to the pleasant and healthful situation of that island, ever since he arrived there in his return from Armenia. Contenting himself here with a mean and small habitation, with a farm-house[1] likewise by the city side not much larger nor of greater receite [Aug. 72], he purposed to lead a very civil and private life ; walking otherwhile in the gymnasium[2] without lictor[3] or other officer, performing acts and duties in manner one for another with the Greeks conversing there. It happened upon a time, when he disposed of the businesses which he would dispatch one day, that he gave it out beforehand, He was desirous to visit all the sick[4] in the city. These words of his were mistaken by those next about him. Whereupon all the lazars and diseased persons were by commandment brought into a public porch or gallery and placed there in order, according to the sundry sorts of their maladies. At which unexpected sight, being much troubled and perplexed, he wist not for a good while what to do ; howbeit, he went round about from one to another, excusing himself for this that was done even to the meanest, poorest, and basest of them all. This only thing and nothing else beside was noted, wherein he seemed to exercise the power of his tribune's authority.

Being daily and continually conversant about the schools and auditories of professors, by occasion that there arose a great brawl among the sophisters[5] opposite in arguing cases and declaiming one against other, there chanced to be one who, perceiving him coming between and inclining to favorise one party above the other, railed bitterly at him. Withdrawing himself therefore by little and little, and retiring home to his house, he came forth suddenly again and appeared with his lictors ; where he cited by the voice of his crier, to appear judicially before his tribunal, that foul-mouthed railing fellow, and so commanded him to be had away to prison. After this, he had certain intelligence given him that Julia his wife was convict and condemned for her incontinence and adulteries ; also that in his name (by a warrant directed from Augustus) she had a bill of divorce sent unto her. And albeit he was glad of these tidings, yet he thought it his part, as much as lay in him, by many letters to reconcile the father unto his daughter ; yea, and however she had deserved badly at his hands, yet to suffer her for to have whatsoever he had at any time given unto her in free gift. Now, after he had passed through the time of his tribune's authority, and confessed at last that, by this retiring of his out of the way, he sought to

avoid naught else but the suspicion of jealousy and emulation
with Gaius and Lucius, he made suit that, seeing he was now
secured in this behalf, and they strengthened enough and able
with ease to manage and maintain the second place in government, he might be permitted to return and see his friends and
acquaintance again, whose presence he missed and longed
after.   But he could not obtain so much ; nay, admonished he
was and warned beforehand, to lay aside all regard of his
friends and kinsfolk, whom he was so willing to leave and
abandon before.

12. He abode therefore still at Rhodes, even against his
will ; and hardly by the means and intercession of his own
mother wrought thus much that, for to cover his ignominy and
shame, he might be absent under this pretence, as if he were
Augustus his lieutenant.   And then, verily, lived he not only
private to himself, but also exposed to danger and in great fear
of some hard measure ; lying close and hidden in the up-
landish and inward parts of the island, and avoiding the
offices [1] of them that made sail by those coasts, who had frequented him continually ; forasmuch as no man went into any
province that way, as lord-general or magistrate [2], but he
struck aside and turned to Rhodes.   Besides, other causes
there were of greater fear and trouble presented unto him.
For whenas he crossed the seas to Samos for to visit Gaius, his
wife's son [3], president of the East parts, he perceived him to be
more estranged than beforetime through the slanders and
criminous imputations which M. Lollius, companion and
governor to the said Gaius, had put into his head.   He was
drawn also into suspicion by certain centurions, whom his
favour had advanced, and who at the day limited in their
passport were returned to the camp [4], that he had delivered
unto many (of them [5]) mandates [6] of an ambiguous and duple
construction, such as might seem to sound the minds of every
one and solicit them to rebellion.   Of which suspicion being
certified by Augustus, he never rested [7] to call for and require
to have some one of any degree and order whatsoever, to
observe all his deeds and words.

13. He neglected also his wonted exercises of horse and
armour ; yea, and having laid by the habit [1] of his native
country, he betook himself to a cloak and slippers [2].   In such

a state and condition as this continued he almost two years
throughout, more despised and hateful every day than other,
insomuch as the [Nemausians] [3] overthrew his images and
statues ; and upon a time, at a certain feast, where familiar
friends were met together, by occasion that mention was made
of him, there was one stood up who promised Gaius that, in
case he did but command and say the word, he would immediately sail to Rhodes and fetch unto him the head of that
exiled person, for so was he commonly called.   And chiefly
upon this, which was now no bare fear, but plain peril, enforced
he was by most earnest prayers, not only of his own but also
of his mother, to require and seek for to return ; which he
obtained at length with the help somewhat of good fortune.
Augustus had fully set down with himself to resolve upon
nothing as touching that point, but with the will and good-
liking of his elder son [4].   Now was he, as it happened at that
time, much offended and displeased with M. Lollius, but to his
step-father [5] (Tiberius) well-affected, and easy to be by him
entreated.   By the permission therefore and good leave of
Gaius called home he was, but with this condition, that he
should not meddle one jot in the affairs of state.

14. Thus, in the eighth year after his departure, returned
he full of great hopes and nothing doubtful of future fortunes,
which he had conceived as well by strange sights, as also by
predictions and prophecies even from his very birth.   For
Livia whiles she went with child of him, among many and
sundry experiments which she made, and signs that she
observed (and all to know whether she should bring forth a
man-child or no), took closely [1] an egg from under a hen that
was sitting, and kept it warm sometime in her own, otherwhiles in her women's hands by turns one after another, so
long until there was hatched a cock-chicken with a notable
comb upon the head.   And when he was but a very babe,
Scribonius the astrologer gave out and warranted great matters
of him, and namely, that he should one day reign as monarch,
but yet without the royal ensigns [2].   For as yet, ye must wot,
the sovereign power of the Caesars was unknown.   Also, as he
entered into his first expedition and led an army into Syria
through Macedonia, it chanced that the consecrated altars of
the victorious legions [3] in time past at Philippi shone out

suddenly of themselves all on a light [Aug. 82] fire [4]. And soon after, when in his journey toward Illyricum he went to the oracle of Geryon near unto Padua and drew forth his lot, whereby he was advised that, for counsel and resolution in such particulars as he required after, he should throw golden dice [5] [a] into the fountain Aponus, it fell out so that the dice thus cast by him showed the greatest number [6]; and even at this very day these dice are seen under the water. Some few days likewise before he was sent for home, an eagle (never seen aforetime at Rhodes) perched upon the very top and ridge of his house; and the very day before he had intelligence given him of his return, as he was changing his apparel, his shirt was seen on fire. Thrasyllus also the astrologer [b], whom for his great profession of wisdom and cunning he had taken into his house to bear him company, he made then most trial of; namely when, upon kenning a ship afar off [7], he affirmed that joyful news was coming, whereas, at the very same instant as they walked together, Tiberius was fully purposed to have turned him headlong down into the sea, as being a false prophet (for that things fell out untowardly and contrary to his former predictions) and one besides who chanced for the most part to be privy unto him of all his secrets.

15. Being returned to Rome, and having brought his son Drusus solemnly into the Forum [1], he removed immediately out of [the] Carinae and the house of Pompey [2] unto Esquiliae [3] and the hortyards [C. 83] of Maecenas; where he gave himself wholly to quietness, performing private duties only and not meddling at all in public offices. After that Gaius and Lucius were dead within the compass of three years [4], he, together with their brother M. Agrippa, was adopted by Augustus, but compelled first himself to adopt Germanicus his brother's son. Neither did he aught afterwards as a householder [5], nor retained one jot of that right which he had forgone by his adoption. For he gave no donations, he manumitted no person; nor yet made benefit of any inheritance or legacies [6] otherwise than in the nature of *peculium* [7]: and so he did put them down in his book of receipts. But from that time forward was there nothing pretermitted for the augmentation of his state and majesty, and much more after that Agrippa once was in disfavour and sent away; whereby the world took knowledge for certain, that the hope of succession rested only in him.

16. Now was the tribunician authority conferred a second time upon him, and that for the term of five years ; the honourable charge and commission likewise, for to pacify the state of Germany, was assigned unto him ; and the Parthian ambassadors, after they had declared their message at Rome unto Augustus, were commanded to repair unto him also into his province[1]. But upon the news that Illyricum revolted, he removed from thence to the charge of a new war[2], which, being of all foreign wars the most dangerous since those with the Carthaginians, he managed, with the power of fifteen legions and equal forces of auxiliaries, for the space of three years in great extremity of all things, but especially in exceeding scarcity of corn. And notwithstanding that he was oftentimes revoked from this service, yet persisted he unto the end, fearing lest the enemy, so near a neighbour and so puissant withal, should make head and come upon them, if they first did quit the place and retire. And verily, passing well-paid and rewarded was he for this perseverance of his, as having thereby fully subdued and brought under his subjection all Illyricum as far as reacheth and spreadeth between Italy, the kingdom of Noricum, Thracia, and Macedonia, between the river Danube also and the gulf of the Adriatic sea.

17. Which glorious exploit of his was yet more amplified and increased by the opportunity of an occurrent that fell between. For about the very same time Quintilius Varus, together with three legions, was overthrown and defeated in Germany ; and no man made any doubt but that the Germans, following the train of this their victory, would have joined with Pannonia, in case Illyricum had not been subdued before. For these his noble acts a triumph with many great honours was decreed for him ; some also delivered their sentence, that he should be surnamed Pannonicus ; others would have had the addition of Invincible ; and some again of Pius, in his style. But as touching any such surname, Augustus interposed his negative voice, promising and undertaking in his behalf, that he should rest contented with that[1], which he was to assume after his death. As for the triumph, himself did put it off unto a further day, by occasion that the whole state sorrowed for the overthrow and loss abovesaid of Varus ; nevertheless, he entered the city in his rich praetexta or embroidered purple robe, with a chaplet of laurel upon his head, and so mounted up to the tribunal erected for him in the Septa [a], whiles the senate stood to give attendance ; and there, together with Augustus, in the midst between the two consuls, he took his place and sat down. From whence, after he had saluted the people, he was honourably conducted round about all the temples.

18. The next year following, being returned into Germany, when he perceived that the Varian defeat aforesaid happened through the rashness and negligence of the general, he did nothing at all without the opinion of his council of war. And whereas he had used also before to stand upon his own bottom, and to rest in his self-judgement alone, then, contrary to his manner, he conferred with many as touching the management of the war ; yea, and he showed more care and preciseness in every point than his wont was aforetime. Being about to pass over the Rhine, all his provision of victuals strictly reduced to a certain rate and stint he would not send over the water before he had considered (standing upon the very bank of the river) the load of every wagon, that no carriages might be discharged or unloaded [1], but such as were by him allowed and thought necessary. When he was once on the other side of the Rhine this course and order of life he held ; namely, to sit upon a bare bank of turf, and so to eat his meat ; to lie abroad all night, and take his rest oftentimes without tent ; to deliver all directions for the day following, as also what sudden service or business was to be enjoined, by writing ; with this caveat and admonition that, whereof any man doubted, he should repair unto him at all hours of the night, and seek for no other expositor but himself.

19. Martial discipline he required most sharply, bringing again into use and execution certain kinds of chastisements and ignominious disgraces which had been used in ancient times ; insomuch as he branded with open shame the lieutenant of a legion, for sending a few soldiers with his own freedman over the other side of the river a-hunting. As for battles, albeit he did put as little as might be upon the hazard of fortune and chance, yet entered he upon them with much more resolution, so often as whiles he watched or studied by a candle, the light

suddenly fell down and went out, when nobody forced it ; trusting confidently (as he said) upon this sign, which both he and all his ancestors had tried and found to be infallible during all their warlike conducts and regiments [1].   But howsoever he sped well and had good success in this province, he escaped very fair [2] that he had not been killed by a certain Rhutene [3] [a], who, being among those that were next about his person, and detected by his timorous gesture, was apprehended, and with torture forced to confess his prepensed design.

20. Being after two years returned out of Germany to Rome, he rode in that triumph which he had deferred, accompanied with his lieutenants, for whom he had obtained triumphal ornaments [Aug. 36, Annot.].   And ere he turned into the Capitol he alighted from his chariot, and bowed himself to the knees of his father [1], sitting then before him as president.   A captain and commander of Pannonia named Bato, he rewarded first with exceeding great presents, and then removed him to Ravenna, in thankful requital for suffering him, upon a time when with his army he was enclosed within the straits [2], to pass forward and escape.   After this he bestowed upon the people of Rome a solemn dinner, where they sat at a thousand tables, and gave besides to them three thousand[3] sesterces apiece for a congiary.   He dedicated also the temple of Concord, likewise that of Pollux and Castor in his own name and his brother's, all out of the spoil won from the enemies.

21. And not long after, when, by virtue of an act preferred by the consuls, that he should administer the provinces jointly with Augustus and likewise hold the general review and muster of the people, he had performed the same and finished it with a solemn purging called lustrum, he took his journey into Illyricum.   And being incontinently [1] called back out of the very way, he came and found Augustus dangerously sick, howbeit yet breathing and alive, with whom he continued in secret talk one whole day.   I wot well it is commonly received and believed that, when Tiberius after private conference was gone forth, these words of Augustus were overheard by the chamberlains : *Miserum populum Romanum, qui sub tam lentis maxillis erit :* " O unhappy people of Rome, that shall be under such a slow pair of jaws [a]."   Neither am I ignorant of this also, that some have written and reported of Augustus, how openly and in plain terms without dissembling, he disliked his churlish behaviour and harshness of manners so much, as divers times, being in pleasant discourse and merry talk, he would break off when Tiberius came in place ; howbeit, overcome by his wife's entreaty and earnest prayer, he refused not to adopt him, or rather, was induced so to do, upon an ambitious humour and conceit of his own that, leaving such a successor, himself might another day be more missed and wished for again.   Yet cannot I be persuaded otherwise but to think that Augustus, a right circumspect, considerate, and prudent prince did nothing, especially in so weighty a business, hand over head [C. 56] and without advise [2], but, having duly weighed the vices and virtues of Tiberius, esteemed his virtues of more worth ; and namely, seeing that both he swore solemnly in a general assembly of the people, that he adopted him for the good of the commonweal [b], and also commendeth him in certain epistles for a most expert and martial warrior, yea, the only defender and protector of the people of Rome.

Out of which I have thought good to quote some places here and there for example.   " Farewell, most sweet Tiberius, and God bless your conduct and proceeding, warring as you do for me and the Muses [3]."   Again : " O most pleasant, and (as I desire to be happy) right valiant man, and accomplished captain, with all perfections, adieu."   Also : " As touching the order and manner of your summer camp, for mine own part verily, my Tiberius, I am of this mind that, considering so many difficulties and distresses, in regard also of so great sloth and cowardice of soldiers, no man in the world could perform the service better than you have done.   And even they of your train who were with you do all confess, that this verse may be applied fitly unto you :

Unus homo nobis vigilando restituit rem [c],
One man alone by watchful sight
Our tott'ring state hath set upright.

And whether (quoth he) there fall out any occurrent to be considered upon with more care and diligence, or whether I be displeased and angry at anything, I have a great miss, I assure you, of my Tiberius, and evermore that verse of Homer cometh into my remembrance :

Τούτου δ' ἐσπομένοιο, καὶ ἐκ πυρὸς αἰθομένοιο
ἄμφω νοστήσαιμεν, ἐπεὶ περίοιδε νοῆσαί [d],

Whiles this man bears me company (so well he doth foresee)
We may ev'n out of flaming fire return, both I and he.

When I hear say and read that you are weakened and grown
lean with incessant and continual labour, God confound me, if
my body do not quake and tremble. I pray you, therefore,
spare yourself : lest, if it come to our ears that you are sick,
both I and your mother also die for sorrow, and the people of
Rome beside hazard the empire. It makes no matter, whether
I be in health or no, if you be not well [4]. The Gods I beseech to
preserve you for us and vouchsafe your health both now and
ever, unless they hate the people of Rome to death."

22. The death of Augustus he divulged not abroad, before
that young Agrippa was slain. This Agrippa was killed by a
military tribune [1], set and appointed to guard him, so soon as
he had read the writ [2], whereby he was commanded to do the
deed. This writ, whether Augustus left behind him when he
died, thereby to take away all matter that might minister
tumult after his death ; or whether Livia in the name of
Augustus indited it, and that with the privity of Tiberius, or
without his knowledge, it resteth doubtful. Certain it is that,
when the said tribune brought him word, that the thing was
dispatched which he had commanded, he made answer, that he
gave no such commandment, and added moreover, that he
should answer it before the senate, declining [C. 4] no doubt the
envy [3] and hard conceit [4] of men for the present ; for within a
while after he buried the matter in silence.

23. Having now assembled the senate by virtue and
authority of his tribuneship [a], and begun to make a speech [1]
unto them by way of consolation [2], all on a sudden, as unable
to master his grief, he fell into a fit of sighing and groaning ;
yea, he wished that not only his voice, but his vital breath also
might fail him, and therewith gave the book unto his son
Drusus to read it out. After this, when the last will or testament of Augustus was brought in and none of the witnesses
admitted to come in place, but those only who were of senator's
degree, the rest standing without the Curia and there acknow-
ledging their hands and seals, he caused it to be read and pronounced by his freedman. The will began in this manner :

" Forasmuch as sinister fortune hath bereft me of Gaius and Lucius, my sons, I will that Tiberius Caesar be mine heir, in the one moiety and a sixth part[3]." By which very beginning their suspicion was augmented who thought thus, that, seeing he forbare not after this sort to make his preface, he ordained Tiberius to be his successor upon necessity, rather than any judgement and discretion.

24. Albeit he made no doubt[1] to enter upon his imperial government immediately and to manage the same, and that by taking unto him a strong guard of soldiers about his person, that is to say, main force and the very form of absolute rule and dominion, yet notwithstanding he refused it a long time ; and putting on a most impudent and shameless mind, onewhile he seemed to rebuke his friends that encouraged him thereto, as those who knew not what a monstrous and untamed beast an empire was ; and otherwhiles with ambiguous answers and crafty delays holding the senate in suspense, when they besought him to take it upon him, yea, and humbly debased themselves before his knees, insomuch as some of them, having their patience moved therewith, could endure him no longer ; and one among the rest in that tumult cried aloud, " Let him either do it at once, or else give over quite," and another openly to his face upbraided him in these words, " Whereas other men be slack in doing and performing that which they have promised, he was slack in promising that which he did and performed." In the end, as if forsooth he had been compelled, and complaining withal that there was imposed upon his shoulders a miserable and burdensome servitude, he took the empire upon him ; and yet no otherwise, than giving hope that one day he would resign it up. His very words are these : " Until I come unto that time, wherein ye may think it meet to give some rest unto mine aged years."

25. The cause of this holding off and delay that he made was the fear of imminent dangers on every side, insomuch as he would often say he held a wolf by the ears. For there was one of Agrippa's slaves named Clemens, who had levied and gathered together no small power for to revenge his master's death, and L. Scribonius Libo, a nobleman, secretly complotted sedition and rebellion ; yea, and a twofold mutiny of the soldiers arose, in Illyricum and in Germany. Both the armies called hard upon him for performance of many matters extraordinarily, but above all, that they might have equal pay with the praetorian soldiers [a]. And as for the Germanician [b] soldiers, they verily refused him for their prince and sovereign, as not by them ordained ; and with all their might and main urged Germanicus, who then was their general, to take upon him the government of the State, albeit he withstood and denied them stoutly. Fearing therefore the issue and danger of this occurrent most of all, he required for himself to have that part of the commonweal in charge, which it should please the senate to lay upon him, seeing that no man was sufficient to wield the whole, unless he had another, or many assistants rather, joined with him. He feigned himself also to be sickly, to the end that Germanicus might with the better will and more patience abide in expectance either of speedy succession after him, or at leastways of fellowship [1] in the empire with him. Well, after he had appeased those mutinies, Clemens likewise by a fraudulent wile he overraught [2], and brought to his devotion. As for Libo, because he would not be thought at his entrance newly into the empire for to proceed rigorously, two years after, and not before, he charged and reproved him before the senate, contenting himself all that mean space to beware of him only, and to stand upon his guard. For, as the said Libo was together with him among other pontiffs sacrific-ing, he took order [C. 18], that instead of the iron cleaver there should be closely laid for him a chopping-knife of lead ; and when the same Libo requested upon a time to have secret talk and conference with him, he would not grant it, without his son Drusus might be by ; and so long as he walked up and down with Libo he seemed to lean upon his hand, and so held it sure enough all the while until their communication was ended.

26. But being once delivered from this fear, he carried him-self at the beginning very orderly and after a civil sort, yea, and somewhat under the port of a private person [1]. Of very many dignities and those right honourable, which by public decree were presented unto him, he accepted but few, and those of the meanest kind. His birthday-mind [Aug. 53], falling out in the time of the plebeian games and plays exhibited in the circus [a], he hardly would suffer to be celebrated and honoured so much as with the addition extraordinarily of one chariot drawn with two steeds. He forbade expressly any temples, flamens, or priests, to be ordained for him, yea, and the erection of statues and images in his honour, without his leave and permission ; the which ran with this only clause and condition, that they should not be set up among the images of the gods, but stand with other ornaments of the house. He prohibited also by his negative voice the solemn oath of observing and keeping his acts inviolably ; as also to call the month September [2] Tiberius, or October [3] Livius. The forename also in his style of imperator [b] ; the surname likewise of Pater Patriae ; as also a civic coronet [C. 2] [c] at the foregate or porch of his palace he refused. Nay, the very name of Augustus, hereditary though it were, he would not put as an addition to any of his epistles, but those only which he sent unto kings and great potentates. Neither bare he more than three consulships ; the first but a few days ; the second three months ; the third, in his absence, no longer than unto the ides of May [4].

27. He detested flattery and obsequious compliments, so much as that he would admit no senator to his litter side, either by way of dutiful attendance, or otherwise about any business whatsoever. When a certain consular [1] person was about to make satisfaction unto him, and humbly to entreat and crave pardon by a reverent touching of his knees, he started and fled from him so as he fell therewith and lay along upon his back [2]. Yea, and that which more is, if in any talk or continued speech there passed words of him smelling of flattery, he would not stick to interrupt the speaker, to check him, and presently [Aug. 3] to alter and correct such terms. One there was who called him *Dominus*, that is, Sir [3], but he gave him warning not to name him any more by way of contumely [4]. Another chanced to say, His sacred businesses ; and a third again, That he went into the senate, *auctore se*, by his warrant or authority. He caused them both to change those words, and for *auctore* to say *suasore*, that is, by his advice and counsel, and instead of sacred to put in laborious and painful.

28. Moreover, against railing taunts, bad reports, and rumours, as also slanderous libels, verses, and songs cast out either of himself or those about him, he stood so firm and patient, as that ever and anon he would give out that, in a free state, folk ought to have both tongue and thought free. And when upon a time the senate called earnestly unto him, that such crimes, and the offenders themselves, might be brought judicially into question, " We have not," quoth he, " so much leisure as to entangle ourselves in many affairs. If ye open this window once, ye will suffer nothing else to be done ; for under pretence hereof ye shall have the quarrels of every man preferred unto you [1]." There is besides a passing civil apophthegm [2] of his extant, which he uttered in the senate. " If so be," quoth he, " that he speak otherwise of me than well, I will endeavour to give an account of my deeds and words, but in case he continue so still, I will hate him for it again [3]."

29. And these things were so much the more remarkable in him, for that, in speaking to them either one by one severally [1] or to all at once in general, yea, and in reverencing them, himself exceeded in a manner the measure of all humanity [2]. When he dissented one day in opinion from Q. Haterius in the senate : " Pardon me, I beseech you," quoth he, " if I as a senator shall speak aught overfrankly against you " ; and then, directing his speech unto the whole house, " Both now," quoth he, " and many times else, my lords, this hath been my saying ; that a good and gracious prince, whom ye have invested in so great and so absolute a power, ought to serve the senate and all the citizens generally, oftentimes also, yea, and for the most part, every [one] of them particularly. Neither repent I that I have so said, for I have ever found you, and do so still, to be my good, my gracious and favourable lords."

30. Furthermore, he brought in a certain show of the common liberty, by preserving entire for the senate and magistrates both their ancient majesty and also their authority ; neither was there any matter so small or so great, pertaining to public or private affairs, but proposed it was at the counciltable before the senators, as namely, about tributes, customs, and revenues of the State ; of monopolies ; of building and repairing any public works ; of enrolling or discharging soldiers ; of setting down the number as well of legions as of auxiliary forces ; finally, who should have their place of command and government continued by a new commission, or take the charge of extraordinary wars ; as also what, and in what form, they thought it good to write again, and to answer letters sent by kings. A certain captain over a cornet [1] of horsemen, being accused for an outrage and for robbery, he compelled to make his answer before the senate [2]. He never entered the Curia but alone. And being one time brought in sick within his litter, he caused all his train and company to void [3] [a].

31. That some decrees were enacted against his mind and sentence, he never once complained, nor found himself grieved. Notwithstanding he opined that magistrates appointed to any charge ought not to be absent, to the end that by their presence they might the better intend [1] their function and calling, yet one praetor elect obtained the favour of a free embassage [a]. Again, when he advised in the Ocriculans' [2] behalf a grant, that they might bestow the money in paving a causey [C. 44] or highway, which was by legacy given to the building of a new theatre, he could not prevail but that the will of the testator should stand and be fulfilled. When it fortuned upon a time that an act of the senate should pass by going to a side [3], and himself went over to the other part where the fewer in number were, there was not one that followed him. Other matters also were handled and debated by the magistrates and the ordinary course of law, and not otherwise ; wherein the consuls bare so great sway and authority, that certain ambassadors out of Africa repaired unto them for dispatch, as complaining that they were put off and delayed by Caesar, unto whom they had been sent. And no marvel ; for evident it was, that himself also would arise up unto the said consuls and give them the way.

32. He rebuked generals of armies, even such as had been consuls, for not writing unto the senate of their war exploits, also for consulting with him and asking his advice as touching the grant of military gifts [1], as if it lay not in their own power to give and dispose all. He commended a praetor for bringing up again the ancient custom, in the entrance of his government, to make an honourable mention and rehearsal of his ancestors before a frequent [C. 22] assembly of the people. The funeral obsequies of certain noble personages he accompanied with the common multitude to the very fire [a]. The like moderation he showed in meaner persons and matters both. When he had called forth unto him the magistrates of the Rhodians, for delivering unto him public letters from the State without the due subscription [b], he gave them not so much as one hard word, but only commanded them to subscribe, and sent them away. Diogenes, the professed grammarian, who was wont to dispute [2] and discourse at Rhodes every Sabbath [3], had put him back and would not admit him into his school, coming of purpose extraordinarily to hear him, but by his page posted him off until the [next] seventh day. Now, when the same Diogenes stood waiting before his gate at Rome to do his duty and to salute him, he quit him no otherwise than thus, namely, by warning him to repair thither again seven years after. When the presidents and governors abroad gave him counsel to burden the provinces with heavy tributes and taxes, he wrote back unto them, that it was the part of a good shepherd to shear his sheep, and not to slay [4] them.

33. By little and little he put himself forth and showed his princely majesty, however for a long time in some variety, yet for the most part rather mild and gracious than otherwise, and more inclined to the good of the commonwealth ; and at the first, thus far forth only interposed he his absolute power and inhibition, that nothing should be done unjustly. Therefore he both repealed certain constitutions [1] of the senate, and also very often, when the magistrates were sitting judicially upon the bench to decide matters, he would offer himself to join as it were in counsel, and to be assistant with them, or else just over against them in the forepart of the tribunal. And if the rumour went that any defendant were like by favour to escape clear, all on a sudden he would be in place, and either on the ground below, or else from the tribunal seat of the lord chief justice [a], put the other judges and jury in mind of the laws, of their conscience and religion, and of the crime whereupon they sat. Also, if any thing were amiss and faulty in the public ordinances and manners of the city, forelet [Aug. 37] by occasion of idleness or taken up through evil custom, he undertook to reform the same.

34. He abridged and restrained the expenses of stage-plays and games [1] exhibited unto the people, by cutting short the wages paid to actors upon the stage, and reducing the couples of sword-fencers to a certain number. That Corinthian vessels and manufactures grew to an exceeding high rate, and that three barbels were sold for 30,000 sesterces, he grievously complained, and gave his opinion that there should be a gage [2] set, and a mediocrity kept in household furniture [3] ; as also that the price of victuals in open market should be ordered yearly at the discretion of the senate, with a charge given unto the aediles for to inhibit victualling-houses, taverns, and thus far forth, as they should not suffer any pastry-works to be set out to sale [a] : and to the end that, by his own example also, he might put forward the public frugality, himself, at his solemn and festival suppers, caused oftentimes to be served up to the board viands dressed the day before and those half-eaten already, saying, that the side of a wild boar had in it all the same that the whole. He forbade expressly by an edict the usual and daily kisses commonly given and taken ; likewise the intercourse of New-year's gifts sent to and fro, namely, that it should not continue after the kalends of January. He had wont to bestow for his part a New-year's gift fourfold worth that which he received, and to give the same with his own hand; but being offended that a whole month together he was in his other affairs troubled with such as had not been with him, nor felt his liberality upon the very feast, he never gave any again after the said day.

35. Wives of lewd and dishonest life, if there wanted accusers to call them publicly into question, his advice and sentence was, that their next kinsfolk should, *more majorum* [1], agree together in common, for to chastise and punish. He dispensed with a gentleman of Rome for his oath [2] (who had sworn before never to divorce his wife), and gave him leave to put her away, being taken in adultery with her son-in-law. Certain women infamous for whoredom and filthiness began to profess before the aediles bawdery, to the end that, having by this base trade and occupation lost the right privilege and dignity of matrons, they might delude [3] the laws [4] and avoid the penalties thereof [a]. Semblably [C. 39], out of the youth of both degrees [5], the lewdest spendthrifts of all other, because they would not be liable to an act of the senate in that behalf, for performing their parts in acting upon the stage, or their devoir within the lists [6], wilfully underwent the ignominious note of infamy. But as well them, as those light women aforesaid, he banished all, that none ever after should by such delusion of the law seek evasion. He took from a senator his robe [7], after he knew once that just before the kalends of July [b], he removed out of his dwelling-house into certain hortyards [C. 83] and gardens [8], to the end that, when the said day was past, he might take his house again within the city at a lower rent. Another he deprived of his quaestorship for that, having (as it were) by lottery chosen and married a wife the one day, he dismissed her on another [9].

36. All foreign ceremonies in religion, the Egyptian also and the Jewish rites he prohibited, compelling those [1] who were given to that superstition for to burn all their religious vestments, the instruments likewise, and furniture whatsoever thereto belonging. The serviceable youth of the Jews, under colour of a military oath he sent into sundry provinces, which were in a pestilent and unwholesome air above others [a]; the rest of that nation or such as were addicted to the like religion, he banished out of Rome, upon pain of perpetual bondage if they obeyed not. He expelled also astrologers; but upon their earnest entreaty and promise to give over the practice of that art, he permitted them there to remain.

37. A special care he had to keep the peace, and to preserve the State from outrages and robberies, as also from licentious mutinies and seditions. The set guards and garrisons of soldiers he disposed thicker than the wonted manner was, throughout all Italy. He ordained a standing camp at Rome [1], wherein the praetorian cohorts, wandering up and down before that time and dispersed in diverse inns and hostelries [2], might be received. All insurrections of the people he punished most sharply; he took likewise much pains to prevent such commotions. There happened upon some discord and variance to be a murder committed in the theatre; but [3] the principal heads of the faction, as also the actors themselves for whose sake the quarrel and fray began, he exiled, neither could he ever be brought for any prayer and entreaty of the people to revoke and restore them. When the commons of Pollentia would not suffer the dead corpse of a certain principal centurion to be carried with funeral obsequies out of their market-place, before they had forcibly extorted out of his heirs' hands a piece of money to the setting out of a game of fencers with unrebated swords [4], he took one cohort from Rome, and another out of king Cottius' [5] kingdom, dissembling the cause of this journey;

and suddenly discovering their arms and weapons which they closely [C. 31] carried, and giving alarum with sound of trumpets, all at once he put them into the town with banners displayed at sundry gates and so cast into perpetual prison the greater part of the commons and decurions [6].

The privilege and custom of sanctuaries, wherever they were, he abolished. The Cyzicenes [7], who had committed some notorious outrage and violence upon Roman citizens, he deprived generally of their freedom, which in the war against Mithridates they had by their good service gotten. The rebellions of enemies he repressed ; not undertaking therefor any expedition afterwards himself, but by his lieutenants only, and not by them verily without lingering delays, and driven thereto of necessity. Kings that rebelliously took arms, or were suspected to break out, he kept down with threats rather and complaints, than otherwise by force and open hostility. Some of them, whom he had trained out of their own realms unto him with fair words and large promises he never sent home again : as by name Maroboduus the German, Thrascypolis [8] a Thracian, and Archelaus the Cappadocian, whose kingdom also he reduced into the form of a province.

38. For two years together after he came unto the empire, he never set foot once out of Rome gates. And the time ensuing, he absented not himself in no place unless it were in towns near adjoining, or as far as Antium when he travelled farthest, and that was very seldom and for a few days, albeit he promised and pronounced openly oftentimes that he would visit the provinces also and armies abroad ; yea, and every year almost he made preparation for a journey, taking up all the wains and wagons that were to be gotten, and laying provision of corn and victuals in all the good boroughs and colonies by the way, yea, and at the last suffered vows to be made for his going forth and return home ; insomuch as commonly, by way of a jest and byword, he was called Callippides [1 a], who in a Greek proverb is noted to be always running, and yet never gaineth ground one cubit forward.

39. But being bereft of both his sons, of which Germanicus [1] died in Syria and Drusus [2] at Rome, he withdrew himself into Campania, as to a retiring place ; and all men well-near were fully persuaded and spake it as constantly, that he would never return but die soon after. Both which had like indeed to have come to pass. For in truth he never came again to Rome; and within some few days, near unto Tarracina, in a certain part of his manor-house, built especially for his own lodging and called spelunca [cave], as he sat there at supper, a number of huge stones from above chanced to fall down, whereby many of his guests at the table and servitors there waiting were crushed and squeezed to death; but he himself beyond all hope escaped.

40. Having made his progress over Campania, when he had dedicated a capitol at Capua, and the temple of Augustus at Nola, which he pretended to have been the motive of his journey, he betook himself to Capreae; delighted especially with that island, because there was but one way of access unto it and the same by a small shore and landing-place, as being otherwise enclosed round about, partly with craggy rocks and steep cliffs of an exceeding height, and in part with the deep sea. But soon after, when the people called him home and incessantly besought him to return, by occasion of an unhappy and heavy accident, whereby at Fidenae 20,000 folk [1] and more, at a solemn fight of sword-players, perished by fall of an amphitheatre, he passed over into the main and firm land, permitting all men to come unto him; the rather for that, when he first set forth and went out of Rome, he had given strait commandment by an edict that no man should trouble him, and all the way voided [2] as many as were coming towards him.

41. Being retired again into the said isle, he cast aside all care verily of commonweal, so far forth [1] as never after he did so much as repair and make up the broken decuries of horsemen; he changed no military tribunes nor captains; no, nor any presidents and governors of provinces. He held Spain and Syria both for certain years without consular lieutenants; he neglected Armenia and suffered it to be overrun and possessed by the Parthians; Moesia to be wasted and spoiled by the Daci [C. 44] and Sarmatians, as also Gaul by the Germans, to the great shame and no less danger of the whole empire.

42. To proceed, having now gotten the liberty of this secret place, and being, as one would say, removed from the eyes of people, at length he poured forth and showed at once all those vices which with much ado for a long time he had cloaked and dissembled. Of which I will particularise and make relation from the very beginning. In the camp, when he was but a new and untrained soldier, for his excessive greediness of wine-bibbing, he was for Tiberius named Biberius [a] ; for Claudius, Caldius ; for Nero, Mero. After being emperor, even at the very time when he was busy in reforming the public manners and misdemeanour of the city he spent with Pomponius Flaccus and L. Piso one whole night and two days in gluttony and drunkenness ; unto the former of these twain he presently [Aug. 3] gave the government of the province of Syria ; upon the other he conferred the provostship [prefecture] of Rome, professing even in all his letters and writings, that they were most pleasant companions and friends at all assays[1]. To Sextus Claudius[2], a *senex* fornicator and prodigal dingthrift[3], who had in times past been by Augustus put to ignominy and shame, yea, and by himself some few days before rebuked before the senate, he sent word that he would take a supper with him : upon this condition, that he altered nothing, nor left aught out of his ordinary and customed manner, and namely, that wenches all naked should serve at the table. He preferred one to be a competitor for the quaestorship, who was a most base and obscure person, before others that were right noble gentlemen, only for carousing and drinking up at a banquet a whole amphora [b] of wine when he drank unto him. Unto Asellius Sabinus he gave 200,000 sesterces for a dialogue of his making, in which he brought in a combat or disputation between the mushroom, the ficedula [c], the oyster, and the thrush [d]. To conclude, he instituted a new office forsooth, *a voluptatibus*[4], wherein he placed Priscus a gentleman of Rome, and one who had been censor [e].

43. But during the time of his private abode in Capreae, he devised a room with seats and benches in it, even a place of purpose for his secret wanton lusts. To furnish it there were sought out and gathered from all parts a number of young drabs and stale catamites, sorted together ; such also as invented monstrous kinds of libidinous filthiness, whom he termed *spintriae, [qui] triplici serie conexi, in vicem incestarent coram ipso, ut aspectu deficientes libidines excitaret.* He had bed-chambers besides in many places, which he adorned

with tables and petty puppets, representing in the one sort
most lascivious pictures, and in the other as wanton shapes
and figures. He stored them likewise with the books of
Elephantis, that none might be to seek for a pattern of the
semblable form and fashion, in that beastly business performed
in every kind. He devised in the woods also and groves here
and there certain places for lechery and venereous acts;
*prost[r]antesque per antra et cavas rupes ex utriusque sexus
pube Paniscorum et Nympharum habitu, quae palam jam
et vulgo nomine insulae abutentes Caprineum dictitabant* a.

44. He incurred yet the infamy of greater and more shameful filthiness, such as may not well be named or heard, and
much less believed; to wit, that he should train up and
teach fine boys, the tenderest and daintiest that might be
had (whom he called his little fishes), to converse and play
*ut natanti sibi inter femina versarentur ac luderent lingua
morsuque sensim appetentes; atque etiam quasi infantes
firmiores, necdum tamen lacte depulsos, inguini ceu papillae
admoveret pronior sane ad id genus libidinis et natura et
aetate.* Therefore, whereas a certain painted table of Par-
rasius' making (*in qua Meleagro Atalanta ore morigeratur*)
was given unto him as a legacy, upon condition that, if he were
offended with the argument or matter represented therein, he
might in lieu thereof receive 1,000,000 sesterces, he not only
preferred the said picture before such a sum of money, but also
dedicated it in his own bed-chamber. It is reported besides
that, being at sacrifice upon a time, he, casting a fancy to the
beautiful and well-favoured face of a youth and servitor as he
carried before him the censer, *nequisse abstinere, quin paene
vixdum re divina peracta ibidem statim seductum constupraret
simulque fratrem ejus tibicinem; atque utrique mox, quod
mutuo flagitium exprobrarant, crura fregisse.*

45. Moreover, in what sort he was wont to offer abuse unto
the very heads of women [1], and those nobly born and of good
reputation, appeared most evidently by the woeful end of one
dame named Mallonia. For when she was by force brought
unto his bed, and most resolutely, to die for it, refused to suffer
any more than naturally a woman was to suffer, he suborned
certain promoters [2] falsely to accuse her; and evermore as she
pleaded in her own defence, asked her still, whether she re-

pented not yet of her obstinacy ? which he followed so long, until at length she left the court, made haste home to her house, and there ran herself through with a sword, after she had openly and aloud reproached the shag-haired and rammish old churl with his filthy and beastly mouth. Whereupon, in a by-interlude called *Atellanicum Exodium,* this infamous and shameful note[3], received with exceeding great accord, was rife and current abroad in every man's mouth, that the old buck-goat was licking the nature[4] of the does (or females).

46. Being a very niggard of his purse and one that would part with nothing, he never maintained those of his train in all his journeys and expeditions with any wages or set salaries[1], but found their meat and victuals only ; yet must I need say, that once, out of his step-father's indulgence and bounty, he bestowed upon them a piece of liberality ; when, having ranged them according to the worthiness of every one into three ranks, he dealt among those of the first 600,000 sesterces, of the second 400,000, of the third 200,000. And the same called he the company[2], not of his friends but *gratorum*[3], that is, of his thankful favourites.

47. All the while he was emperor, neither built he any stately works (for the very temple of Augustus[1] and the re-edification of Pompey's theatre, which only and none else he had undertaken, after so many years he left unfinished) nor exhibited so much as one solemn show unto the people ; and at those which were by any other set out he was very seldom present, and all for fear lest something should be demanded at his hands ; and namely[2], after that he was compelled once to manumit the comedian Actius. Having relieved the want and poverty of some senators, because he would not help more of them, he denied to succour any other than those who alleged before the senate good and just causes of their necessities. By which deed of his he frighted the most part upon a modesty and bashfulness in them ; and among the rest one Hortalus, the nephew of Q. Hortensius, the professed orator, who, being of a very mean estate, had begotten four children, by the means and persuasion of Augustus[3].

48. As touching his public munificence, he never showed it but twice ; once, when he purposed and published[1] a free loan for three years of 100,000,000 sesterces ; and again, when unto certain landlords of fair houses and tenements, which, situate upon mount Caelius, were consumed with fire, he restored the full price and worth of them. One of these boons he was forced to grant, by reason that the people in great want of money called earnestly for his help ; what time as, by virtue of an act of the senate, he had ordained, that usurers should lay out two (third) parts of their stock [2] in lands, tenements, and appurtenances immovable [3], the debtors likewise make present payment of two parts of their debts, and yet the thing was not done and dispatched accordingly [4] ; the other, for to mitigate the grievousness of those heavy times [5]. Howbeit this later beneficence of his he so highly prized, that he commanded the name of mount Caelius to be changed and called Augustus. The legacies given by Augustus in his last will unto the soldiers being once published [6], he never after bestowed any largesse upon them, saving that among those of the praetorium [7] he dealt one thousand deniers apiece [and] in and to the legions in Syria certain gifts, for that they alone among all their ensigns in the field honoured no image at all of Sejanus [8]. Moreover, he made very seldom any discharges of old soldiers [9], as expecting upon age their death, and by death gaping for some gain and vantage. Neither succoured he the very provinces with his bountiful hand, except it were Asia, by occasion that certain cities therein were by earthquake overthrown [10].

49. Afterwards and in process of time he gave his mind wholly even to rapine and plain pillage. It is for certain known, that Cn. Lentulus the augur, a man of exceeding great wealth, for very fear and anguish of mind was by him driven to a loathing and weariness of his own life, and at his death to make no other heir but himself ; that dame Lepida likewise, a right noble lady, was condemned by him to gratify Quirinus [1], one that had been consul, but passing rich [a] and childless [2] withal, who, having beforetime put her away being his wedded wife, twenty years after called her judicially into question, and laid to her charge that long ago she had bought and provided poison for to take away his life. Besides, as well-known it is, that certain princes and potentates of Gaul, Spain, Syria, and Greece, forfeited their estates upon so slight a slander and impudent imputation, that against some of them naught else was objected but this, that they had part of their substance and wealth lying in money[3][b] ; yea, and that many cities and private persons lost their ancient immunities and privileges, as also their right in mines and metals, tolls, and customs ; and finally, that Vonones, a king of the Parthians, who, being driven out of his kingdom by his own subjects, retired himself with a huge mass of treasure into Antioch, under the protection, as it were, of the people of Rome, was perfidiously stript out of all and killed.

50. The hatred that he bare to his kinsfolk and near allies he bewrayed, first, in his brother Drusus, by disclosing a letter of his, wherein he dealt with him about compelling Augustus to restore the common liberty ; afterwards, in others also. As for his wife Julia, so far was he from showing any courtesy or kindness unto her when she stood confined (which had been the least matter of a thousand), that, whereas by an ordinance of her father's she was shut up within one town, he gave strait order that she should not step out of doors, and enjoy the society of people and worldly commerce ; nay, he proceeded so far as to bereave her of that little stock and household stuff which her father allowed her ; yea, and defrauded her of the yearly pension and exhibition for her maintenance, and all, forsooth, under a colour of common right and law, because Augustus in his last will and testament had not expressly provided in this behalf. Being not able well to endure his mother Livia, as challenging to herself equal part with him in power and authority, he avoided both to keep ordinary and daily company, and also to entertain long speech or secret conference with her ; because he might not be thought ruled and directed by her counsels, which otherwhiles notwithstanding he was wont both to stand in need of and also to use. Semblably [C. 39], he took to the very heart the passing of this act in the senate : " That, in his style, as he had the title son of Augustus, so this addition should run withal, son of Livia." And therefore it was, that he would not suffer her to be named Parens Patriae[1], nor to receive any remarkable honour in open place and by public decree. Oftentimes also he admonished her to forbear intermeddling in greater affairs, and such as were not meet for women ; especially after he perceived once, that when the temple of Vesta was on fire, she also came thither in person among others, and there encouraged the people and soldiers both to do their best and help all what they could, as her manner was to do in her husband's days.

51. By these degrees he proceeded even to secret rancour and malice against her, but chiefly upon this occasion, as men report. She had been very earnest with him many a time to enrol one in the decuries of the judges [a], who was made free denizen and citizen of Rome ; but he denied flatly to choose and admit the party, unless it were upon this only condition, that she would suffer a clause to be written and annexed to the instrument or roll [1], in these words : " This grant was by my mother wrung and wrested from me." Whereat she, highly displeased and offended, brought forth out of her closet and cabinet certain old letters of Augustus written unto her, as touching his perverse, bitter, and intolerable manners ; and those she openly read. He again took the matter so grievously, that she had both kept those writings so long by her, and also cast them in his dish [C. 49] so spitefully, that some think this was the greatest cause of his departure from the city. And verily, for the space of three years complete, during which time he was absent and his mother living, he saw her but once, and that was no more than one day, and very few hours of the same. And afterwards as little mind he had to be by her lying sick ; and when she was dead, suffering her corpse by staying so long above ground (whiles men hoped still of his coming) to corrupt at length and putrefy, after she was interred, he forbade that she should be canonised and registered in the catalogue of saints ; pretending as if she herself had given that order. Her will he annulled, all her friends and familiars, even those unto whom upon her deathbed she had committed the charge of her funeral, within a short time he persecuted and plagued, yea, and one of them, to wit, a worshipful gentleman of Rome, he condemned to the pump [2].

52. Of his two sons, he loved neither Drusus that was his own son, nor Germanicus by adoption, as a father should, as taking offence at the vices of the one [1]. For Drusus was of an effeminate mind, given to a loose and idle life. Therefore was not Tiberius so nearly touched and grieved for him being dead, but presently after [Aug. 3] his funeral returned to his ordinary and accustomed business, prohibiting vacation of justice [2] to continue any longer. Moreover, when the ambassadors of

Ilium came somewhat with the latest to comfort him, he (as if now by this time the memory of his sorrow had been clean worn out) scoffed at them and made this answer, that he likewise was sorry in their behalf for the loss they had of Hector, so noble and brave a citizen. As for Germanicus, he depraved [Aug. 27] and disgraced him, so as that not only he did extenuate and diminish all his worthy exploits as mere vain and needless, but also blamed his most glorious victories, as dangerous and hurtful to the commonwealth. Also, for that without his advice he went unto Alexandria (by occasion of an extreme and sudden famine), he complained of him in the senate ; yea, and it is verily believed he was the cause of his death, and used the means of Cn. Piso, lieutenant of Syria ; who soon after, being accused of this crime, would (as some think) have uttered abroad those directions and warrants that he had so to do, but that Sejanus secretly withstood it [3]. For which Tiberius was oftentimes and in many places much blamed [4], and in the night-season commonly called upon with this cry and note, *Redde Germanicum*, " Give us Germanicus again." The suspicion whereof himself afterwards confirmed and made good, by afflicting in cruel manner the wife also and children of the said Germanicus.

53. Furthermore, his daughter-in-law [1] Agrippina, for complaining over-boldly of him after the death of her husband, he took by the hand, and recited unto her a Greek verse [a] to this effect : " If thou hast not sovereign rule and dominion," quoth he, " thinkest thou, pretty daughter, that thou art wronged ? " and so vouchsafed her no speech at all after. Also, because upon a time when she durst not at supper taste of those apples which he had reached unto her, he forbare to invite her any more, pretending that she charged him with the crime of attempting her with poison ; whenas indeed it was of purpose plotted and packed [2] aforehand, both that himself should by the offering of such fruit tempt her, and she again beware [3] most present and assured death. At the last, having untruly accused her, as if she minded to flee one-while to the statue of Augustus, and another-while to the armies, he confined and sent her away to the isle of Pandataria ; and as she railed at him, he by the hands of a centurion, with whipping and lashing her over the face, struck out one of her eyes.

Again, whenas she was fully determined to pine herself to death, he caused her mouth perforce to be opened, and meat to be crammed into her throat ; yea, and after that, by continuance in this mind, she consumed quite away and died in the end, he inveighed against her in most odious and reproachful terms, having opined [4] first in the senate that her birthday also should be reckoned among the dismal and unlucky days. Furthermore, he expected thanks, as for a high favour done unto her, in that he strangled her not before with a cord, and so flung her to the Gemoniae [5] [b] ; and in regard of such a singular clemency as this, he suffered a decree to pass, that thanks should be given unto him, and a present of gold consecrated unto Jupiter Capitolinus.

54. Whereas by Germanicus he had three nephews, Nero, Drusus, and Gaius, by Drusus one, to wit Tiberius, when he was left destitute and fatherless by the death of his children, the two eldest sons of Germanicus, namely Nero and Drusus, he recommended to the lords of the senate ; and celebrated the day of both their commencement [1] with giving a congiary [2] to the people. But no sooner understood he that upon New-year's day there had been public vows made by the city for their life also and preservation, but he gave the senate to understand, that such honours ought not to be conferred upon any persons but those that were experienced and far stept in years. Thereby having discovered the inward character and canker of his heart, from that day forward he exposed them to the slanders and imputations of all men ; when also by sundry subtle devices he had wrought so that they might be both provoked to give railing taunts, and also, being so provoked, come to mischief and destruction, he accused them in his letters, heaped most bitterly upon them heinous reproaches, caused them to be judged enemies to the State, and so hunger-starved them to death ; Nero, within the isle of Pontia, and Drusus at the very foot and bottom of Palatium [3]. Men think that Nero was driven to work his own death [4], what time as the hangman, as sent by a warrant from the senate, presented unto him halters and hooks [5]. As for Drusus, kept he was from all food and sustenance, insomuch as he gave [made] the attempt to eat the very flocks that stuffed the mattress [6] whereupon he lay. The relics [7] of them both were so dispersed and scattered abroad, that hardly they could be ever gathered together.

55. Over and above his old friends and familiars, he had demanded twenty out of the number of the best and principal citizens as counsellors and assistants unto him in public affairs. Of all these he could hardly show twain or three at the most alive ; the rest, some for one cause and some for another, he brought to confusion and killed, among whom (with the calamity and overthrow of many more) was Aelius Sejanus, whom he had to the highest place of authority advanced, not so much for any good-will, as to be his instrument and right hand, by whose ministry and fraudulent practices he might circumvent the children of Germanicus, and so establish as heir apparent in succession of the empire the nephew he had by Drusus as his [own] son.

56. No milder was he one jot unto the Greek professors and artists living and conversing daily with him, and in whom he took most contentment. One of them named Zeno, as he reasoned and discoursed very exactly [1] of a question, he asked, What harsh dialect [a] that was, wherein he spake ? and when he answered, It was the Doric, he confined him for his labour into Cinaria, supposing that he twitted and reproached him for his old vacation and absence from Rome, because the Rhodians spake Doric. Semblably [C. 39], whereas his manner was, out of his own daily readings to propound certain questions as he sat at supper, having intelligence that Seleucus the grammarian inquired diligently of his ministers and servitors what authors at any time he had in hand, and so came prepared to assoil [2] the said questions, first he forbade him his house and ordinary society, afterwards he forced him even to death.

57. His cruel, close, and unpliable nature was not hidden, no not in his very childhood ; the which Theodorus of Gadara [1], his teacher in rhetoric, seemed both at first to foresee most wisely, and also to express and resemble [2] as fitly, when by way of chiding and rebuke he called him ever and anon Πηλὸν αἵματι πεφυραμένον (*Pēlon haimati pephuramenon*), that is, clay [3] soaked in blood [4]. But the same broke out and appeared somewhat more, when he became emperor, at the very beginning ; what time as yet he lay [5] for to win the love and favour of men, with a pretence of civil moderation. A certain

buffoon [6] there was, who, as a funeral passed by, had willed the
party whose body was carried forth [7], to report unto Augustus,
that his legacies were not yet paid and delivered, which he had
left for the commons of Rome.   Him he caused to be haled
and brought unto his presence, to receive also the debt which
was due : and then commanded him to be led to execution, and
so to relate the truth unto his father Augustus.   Not long
after, as he threatened to send unto prison one Pompeius, a
Roman knight, for stoutly [opposing] something [8], he assured
him, that of a Pompeius he would make him a Pompeianus,
glancing by this bitter and biting taunt both at the
man's name and also at the old ill-fortune of that
side [9].

58. About the same time, when the praetor came to know
of him, whether his pleasure was to hold the judicial assizes as
touching the case of majesty [1], or no, he made answer, that the
laws must have their course and be put in execution ; and in
very truth he executed them with extreme rigour.   There was
one who from the statue of Augustus had taken away the head,
for to set upon the same the [head] of another.   The matter
was debated in the senate, and because some doubt arose who
did the deed, inquisition was made by torture.   The party
delinquent being condemned, this kind of calumniation by
little and little proceeded so far that such points as these also
were made capital crimes : namely, to have beaten a slave
about the image of Augustus [2] ; item, if a man had shifted his
apparel [a] and put on other clothes (about the same image) ;
item, to have brought into any privy or brothel-house his
image [3] imprinted either in money or ring ; lastly, to have
impaired any word or deed of his, in the least credit and reputation that might be.   To conclude, it cost one his life, for suffering in his own colony honours to be decreed unto him, upon the
same day that they had in times past been decreed for
Augustus.

59. Many parts besides, under the colour of gravity and
reformation, but rather indeed following the course of his own
nature, he used to play, so cruelly and with such rigour, that
some there were, who in verses both upbraided by way of
reproach the calamities present, and also gave warning of the
future miseries, in this manner [1] :

TIBERIUS NERO CAESAR

Asper et immitis.   Breviter, vis omnia dicam?
Dispeream, si te mater amare potest.

Harsh and unkind (in brief wilt thou I should say all?) thou art:
God me confound, if mother thine can love thee in her heart.

Non es eques; quare? non sunt tibi millia centum;
Omnia si quaeras, et Rhodos exilium est.

No knight thou art; and why? for hundred thousands none;
(Search all) thou hast in store[2]: and now at Rhodes exil'd do'st
wone [dwell].

Aurea mutasti Saturni saecula Caesar;
Incolumi nam te, ferrea semper erunt.

Of Saturn king thou changed hast that age resembling gold,
For while thou, Caesar, liv'st, the world of iron shall ever hold.

Fastidit vinum, quia iam sitit iste cruorem;
Tam bibit hunc avide, quam bibit ante merum.

Wine doth he loathe, because that now of blood he hath a thirst,
He drinketh that as greedily, as wine he did at first.

Aspice felicem sibi, non tibi, Romule, Sullam:
Et Marium, si vis, aspice, sed reducem,
Nec non Antoni civilia bella moventis
Nec semel infectas aspice caede manus.
Et dic, Roma perit.   Regnabit sanguine multo,
Ad regnum quisquis venit ab exilio [a].

See Sulla, happy for himself, O [Roman], not for thee:
And Marius, in case thou wilt, but new-returned, see;
Likewise behold of Antony those hands in blood imbrued
Not once, I mean of Antony, who civil war renew'd.
Then say, Rome goes to wrack.   And he with bloodshed much
     will reign
Who to a kingdom's state is come from banishment again.

Which verses at first he would have had to be taken and construed as made by them who were impatient of any lordly rule
and absolute dominion at Rome, and as if they had been framed
and devised, not so much with any considerate judgement, as
upon stomach and choler.   And evermore his saying was,
Oderint dum probent, Let them hate me, so long as they suffer
my proceedings to pass.   But afterwards, even himself proved
them to be very true and most certain.

60. Within few days after he came to Capreae, when a
fisherman suddenly and unlooked for presented unto him (as
he was in a secret place doing somewhat by himself) a barbel
of an extraordinary bigness[1], he caused his face to be rubbed

all over with the same fish : as put in a fright, no doubt, for that from the back-side of that island, he had made means through the rough thickets and by-ways, to creep and get unto him where he was. And when the poor fellow amid this punishment seemed to rejoice yet, and said, it was happy [2] that he had not offered unto him a lobster also (which he had caught) of a huge greatness, he commanded that his face should be grated and mangled likewise with the said lobster. A soldier, one of his own guard, for filching and stealing a pea-cock out of an orchard [3] he put to death. In a certain journey that he made, the litter wherein he was carried chanced to be entangled and somewhat stayed with briars and brambles ; whereupon a centurion of the foremost cohorts in the vaward [4], that had in charge to try and clear the ways, he caused to be laid along upon the ground, and there he all to-beat him [5] until he was well-near dead.

61. Soon after, he broke out into all kinds of cruelty, as one who never wanted matter to work upon ; persecuting the familiar friends and acquaintance of his own mother first, then of his nephews and daughter-in-law, and at the last, of Sejanus, after whose death he grew to be most cruel. Whereby especi-ally it appeared, that himself was not wont so much to be provoked and set on by Sejanus, as Sejanus to serve his turn and feed his humour, seeking as he did all occasions ; howso-ever, in a certain commentary, which he composed summarily and briefly of his own life, he durst write thus much, that he executed Sejanus, because he had found that he raged furiously against the children of Germanicus his son. Of whom, to say a truth, the one himself murdered, after he had first suspected Sejanus, and the other, not before he had killed him. To prosecute in particular all his bloody deeds would require a long time. It shall suffice therefore to rehearse in general the patterns as it were and examples of his cruelty. There passed not a day over his head, no, not so much as any festival and religious holiday, without execution and punishment of folk [a]. Some suffered even upon New-year's day. Accused and con-demned there were many together, with their children and very wives. Strait commandment and warning was given, that the near kinsfolk of such persons as stood condemned to die, should not mourn and lament for them.

Especially rewards were by decree appointed for their
accusers, otherwhiles also for bare witnesses. No informer and
promoter was discredited, but his presentment taken. And
every crime and trespass went for capital, and so was received,
were it but the speaking of a few simple words. Objected it
was against a poet, that in a tragedy he had reviled and railed
upon Agamemnon[1][b]; as also it was laid to an historian's[2]
charge, for saying that Brutus and Cassius[3] were the last of all
the Romans[c]. Presently were the authors and writers
punished, and their writings called in and abolished; notwithstanding certain years before they had been recited even in the
hearing of Augustus, with his good liking and approbation.
Some, committed to ward, were deprived not only of their
solace and comfort in studying, but also of the very use of
talking with others. Of such as were cited peremptorily by
writ and process to answer at the bar, some gave themselves
mortal wounds at home in their houses as sure to be condemned, only to avoid torments and ignominy, others in the
open face and midst of the court drank poison; and yet were
they, with their wounds bound up, and whiles they yet panted
between alive and dead, haled away to prison. There was not
one executed but he was thrown also into the Gemoniae, and
drawn with the drag. In one day were there twenty[d] so
thrown and drawn, and among them boys and women.

As for young girls and maidens of unripe years, because by
ancient custom and tradition unlawful it was to strangle
virgins, first deflowered they were by the hangman and afterwards strangled[e]. Were any willing of themselves to die?
such were forced violently to live. For he thought simple
death so light a punishment, that when he heard how one of the
prisoners, Carnulius[4] by name, had taken his death voluntarily before, he cried out in these words, " Carnulius hath
escaped my hands." Also, in overseeing and perusing [Aug.
69] the prisoners in gaol, when one of them besought to have
his punishment with speed, he made him this answer : " Nay
marry, thou art not yet reconciled unto me, that I should
show thee such favour." A certain consular writer[5] hath
inserted this in his Annals : That, upon a time at a great feast
(where himself also was present), Tiberius, being on a sudden
asked, and that openly, with a loud voice by a dwarf

standing at the table among other buffoons [6] and jesters,
wherefore Paconius being attaint of treason lived so long ?
for that instant verily chid the party for his saucy and
malapert tongue ; but after a few days wrote unto the
senate, to take order [C. 18] with all speed for the execution
of Paconius.

62. He increased and strained still more and more this
cruelty, by occasion that he was galled and fretted at the news
of his son Drusus his death : for, having been of opinion that he
died upon some sickness and intemperate life, so soon as he
understood at length that he was poisoned and so made away
by the villainous practice of his wife Livilla [1] and Sejanus together, he spared not to torment and execute any one whomsoever. So bent and addicted [was he] whole days together to
the inquisition and trial of this only matter, as that when word
came unto him how a host of his, an inhabitant of Rhodes
(whom by familiar letters he had sent for to Rome), was come,
he commanded him out of hand to be put to torture [2], as if he
had been some near friend present at the foresaid examination.
But afterwards, when his error was discovered, and seeing how
he had mistaken, he caused him also to be killed, because he
should not divulge and make known the former injury. The
place is yet to be seen at Capreae of his butcherly carnage,
from which he caused condemned persons, after long and
exquisite torments, to be flung headlong before his face into
the sea ; where were ready to receive them a number of
mariners, who with their sprits, poles, and oars should beat and
batt their carcasses, to the end that none of them might have
any breath or wind remaining in the body. He had devised
moreover, among other kinds of torment, what time as men by
deceitful means had their load [3] with large drinking of strong
wine, suddenly to knit fast and tie their privy members with
lute-strings, that he might cause them to swell and be pent in
most dolorous pains, occasioned at once as well by the strait
strings, as the suppression and stoppage of urine. And had it
not been that both death prevented and Thrasyllus [4] also enforced him of purpose (as men say) to put off some designs in
hope of longer life, he would have murdered a good many more
(as it is fully believed), and not spared those very nephews of
his that remained yet alive ; considering he both had Gaius in

171

suspicion, and also cast off Tiberius, as conceived in adultery. And it soundeth to truth, that he was minded thus to do. For ever and anon he called Priam happy in that he overlived all his sons and daughters.

63. But how amid these pranks he lived not only odious and detested, but exceeding timorous also and exposed to the contumelious reproaches of the world, there be many evidences to show. That any soothsayers should be sought unto and consulted with apart without witnesses by, he forbade ; as for the oracles near adjoining to the city of Rome, he attempted to subvert them all. But being terrified with the majesty of those answers [1] which were delivered at Praeneste [2], he gave over ; namely, whenas he could not find them (sealed up though they were and brought down to Rome) within the chest, until the same was carried back again unto the temple [3]. And not daring to send away and dismiss from him one or two [4] consular lord-deputies [5], after he had offered provinces unto them, he detained them so long until, after certain years expired, he ordained others to succeed them, whiles the others remained present with him ; whereas, in the meantime, reserving still the title of the office, he assigned unto them many commissions and matters of charge, and they continually gave order for execution thereof, by the ministry of their legates, lieutenants and coadjutors.

64. His daughter-in-law [1] and nephews, after they were once condemned, he never removed from place to place otherwise than chained and in a close covered litter sewn up fast, setting his soldiers to prohibit all passengers that met with them, and wayfaring persons travelling by, once to look back thither [2], or to stay their pace and stand still.

65. When Sejanus went about seditiously to work alteration in the State, albeit he saw now that both his birthday was publicly solemnised, and also his images of gold worshipped everywhere, he overthrew him (I must needs say) at length, but with much ado, by crafty sleights and guile, rather than by his princely authority and imperial power. For first, to the end that he might dismiss the man in show of honour, he assumed him to be his colleague in the fifth consulship, which in his long absence [1] he had taken upon him for that very purpose. Afterwards, when he had deceived him with hope of

affinity[2] and the tribunes' authority, he complained of the
man (looking for no such matter) in a shameful and piteous
oration[3]; beseeching the lords of the senate, among other
requests, to send one of the consuls to conduct him, an aged
and desolate man, with some guard of soldiers, into their sight.
And yet nevertheless, distrusting himself and fearing an uproar[4], he had given commandment that his nephew Drusus,
whom still he kept in prison at Rome, should be set at liberty
(if need did so require), and ordained general captain. Yea,
and whiles his ships were ready rigged and prepared to what
legions soever he meant for to flee, he stood looking ever and
anon, from the highest cliff that was, toward the marks and
signs, which he had appointed (lest messengers might stay too
long) for to be reared a great way off, thereby to have intelligence, as any occurrent (good or bad) fell out. Nay, when the
conspiracy of Sejanus was now suppressed, he was never the
more secure and resolute, but for the space of nine months
next ensuing he stirred not out of the village[5] called
Jovis.

66. Beside all this, divers and sundry reproachful taunts
from all parts nettled and stung his troubled mind. For there
was not a person condemned, that reviled him not in all sorts
openly to his face, yea, and discharged upon him opprobrious
terms by libels laid for the nonce in the very orchestra[1], with
which contumelies verily affected he was after a most diverse
and contrary manner; so that one-while he desired, for very
shame of the world, that all such abuses might be unknown and
concealed; other-whiles, he contemned the same, and of his
own accord broached and divulged them abroad. Furthermore, rated he was and railed at in the letters also of Artabanus,
king of the Parthians, who charged him with parricides,
murders, cowardice, and luxurious riot[2], who gave him
counsel likewise, with all speed possible to satisfy with a
voluntary death the hatred of his citizens, conceived against
him in the highest degree and most justly. At the last, being
even weary of himself, in the beginning of such an epistle as
this he declared and confessed in manner the very sum of all
his miseries: " What shall I write, my lords of the senate, or
how shall I write ? Nay, what is it, at a word, that I shall not
write at this time ? The gods and goddesses all plague and

confound me utterly at once, feeling as I do myself daily to perish."

67. Some think that he foreknew all this by the skill he had of future events [1], that he foresaw also long before how great a calamity and infamy both would one day betide him ; and therefore it was that he refused most obstinately to take upon him the empire [a] and the name of Pater Patriae, as also stood against the oath to maintain his acts [2], for fear lest within a while after, to his greater disgrace and shame, he might be found inferior and unworthy of such special honours, which verily may be gathered out of the speech he made as touching both those points, when he saith but thus : " That he would be always like to himself and never change his manners, so long as he continued in his sound wits. Howbeit, for example sake provided it would be, that the senate bind not themselves to keep and ratify the actions of any one, who by some chance might be altered." And again : " Marry, if at any time," quoth he, " ye shall make doubt of my loyal behaviour and devoted mind unto you (which before it ever happen, I wish my dying day to take me from this mind and opinion of yours, once conceived of me and afterwards changed), the bare title of Pater Patriae will add no honour unto me, but upbraid you either with inconsiderate rashness, for imposing that surname upon me, or else with inconstancy, for your contrary judgements of me."

68. Corpulent he was, big-set and strong, of stature above the ordinary [a], broad between the shoulders and large-breasted; in all other parts also of the body (from the crown of his head to the very sole of his foot) of equal making and congruent proportion. But his left hand was more nimble and stronger than the right ; and his joints so firm, that with his finger he was able to bore through a green and sound apple, with a fillip also to break the head of a boy, yea, of a good stripling and big youth. Of colour and complexion he was clear and white, wearing the hair of his head long behind, insomuch as it covered his very neck ; which was thought in him to be a fashion appropriate to his lineage and family [1]. He had an ingenuous and well-favoured face, wherein notwithstanding appeared many small tumours or risings [b], and a pair of very great goggle eyes in his head, such as (whereat a man would

marvel) could see even by night and in the dark ; but that
was only for a little while and when they opened first after
sleep, for in the end they waxed dim again [2].   His gait [3] was
with his neck stiff and shooting forward [4] [c], with a countenance
bent [5] and composed lightly [Aug. 41] to severity.   For the
most part he was silent ; seldom or never should you have
him talk with those next about him, and if he did, his speech
was exceeding slow, not without a certain wanton [6] gesticula-
tion and fumbling with his fingers.   All which properties being
odious and full of arrogance, Augustus both observed in him,
and also went about to excuse and cloak for him before the
senate and people, assuring them they were the defects and
imperfections of nature, and not the vices of the mind.   He
lived most healthful, and verily all the time well-near that he
was emperor not once in manner crasie [C. 86] ; albeit from that
he was thirty years old he governed his health after his own
order and direction, without any help or counsel at all of
physicians [d].

69. As little respect as he had of the gods, or sense of any
religion (as one addicted to astrology and calculation of
nativities, yea, and fully persuaded that all things were done
and ruled by fatal destiny [1]) yet feared he thunder exceedingly ;
and were the air or weather any whit troubled, he ever carried
a chaplet or wreath of laurel about his neck [2], because that kind
of green branch is never, as they say, blasted with lightning [3].

70. The liberal sciences of both sorts [1] he loved most
affectionately.   In the Latin speech [2] he followed Corvinus
Messalla [3], whom, being an aged professor, he had observed
from his very youth ; but with overmuch affectation and
curiosity [4] he marred all and darkened his style, so as he was
thought to do somewhat better extempore, than upon study
and premeditation.   He composed also a poem in lyric verses [a],
the title whereof is, *A complaint of L. Caesar's Death* [5] [b].   He
made likewise Greek poems in imitation of Euphorion, Rhianus,
and Parthenius [6] ; in which poets being much delighted, their
writings and images he dedicated in the public libraries among
the ancient and principal authors.   A number therefore of
learned men strove a-vie [7] to put forth many pamphlets of
them [8], and to present him therewith.   But above all he
studied for the knowledge of fabulous history, even unto mere

fooleries, and matters ridiculous. For the very grammarians (which kind of professors, as we have said, he affected especially) he would assay and appose [9] commonly with these and suchlike questions: namely, Who was Hecuba's mother? What name Achilles had among the virgins [10]? What it was that the mermaids [Sirens] were wont to sing? The very first day (after the death of Augustus) that he entered into the Curia, as if he minded once for all to perform the duty of piety and religion, following the example of Minos, he sacrificed indeed, as the manner was, with frankincense and wine, but without a minstrel, as the said Minos sometime did at the death of his son [11].

71. In the Greek tongue, howsoever, he otherwise was ready enough and spake it with facility, yet he used it not everywhere, but most of all forbare it in the senate-house; insomuch verily, as when he came to name *monopolium* [a], he craved leave beforehand, for that he was to use a strange and foreign word. Yea, and in a certain decree of the senators, when this word *emblema* [b] was read, he gave his opinion that the said word should be changed, and instead of that strange term some Latin vocable sought out; and if such a one could not be found, then to utter and declare the thing, though it were in more words and by circumlocution. A certain Greek soldier also [1], being required for to depose and deliver his testimony, he forbade to make answer, unless it were in Latin [c].

72. All the time that he was retired and lived from the city of Rome, twice and no more he assayed to return thither. Once he came by water, embarked in a galley [1], as far as to the hortyards [C. 83] and gardens adjoining to the Naumachia [a], but he had set guards along the banks of the Tiber, for to void [2] and put back such as went forth to meet him; a second time, by the street or part of the Appian way so far as the seventh mile's end from Rome [b], but when he had only seen the walls afar off, without approaching nearer unto the city he returned. For what cause he did so at first [3], it was not certainly known; afterwards, affrighted he was with this prodigious picture and strange sight [4]. Among other delights he took great pleasure in a serpent dragon [c], which when, according to his usual manner, he would have fed with his own hand and found eaten by pismires, he was warned thereupon to beware the violence

of a multitude. In his return therefore speedily into Campania he fell sick at Astura, but, being eased a little of that malady, he went forward as far as to Circeii ; and because he would give no suspicion of sickness, he was not only present himself at the games exhibited by the garrison soldiers there, but also, when there was a wild boar put forth into the open show-place for to be baited, he launched darts at him from above where he was ; and presently therewith, by occasion of a convulsion in his side, and for that he had taken the cold air upon an exceeding heat, he fell back by relapse into a more dangerous disease [d]. Howbeit, he bare it out a pretty while, notwithstanding that, after he was come down so far as to Misenum, he pretermitted nothing of his ordinary and daily manner, no, not so much as his feasting and other pleasures ; partly upon an intemperate humour of his own, and in part to dissemble and palliate his weakness. For when Charicles, his physician, who by virtue of a passport was licensed to depart and be absent, went forth from the table and took hold of his hand to kiss it, he, supposing that he had felt his pulse [5], desired him to stay and sit down again, and so drew out the supper longer. Neither gave he over his usual custom, but even then, standing in the midst of the banqueting-room with a lictor [6] by him, he spake to every one by name [7] as they took their leave.

73. Meanwhile, when he had read among the proceedings of the senate, that certain prisoners were enlarged [1] and dismissed, but not so much as once heard, concerning whom he had written very briefly and no otherwise than thus, that nominated they were by an impeacher ; chafing and frowning hereat, as if he had been held in contempt, he fully purposed to go again into Capreae [2], as one who lightly would attempt nothing, but where he was sure enough and without all danger. But being kept back, as well by tempest as the violence of his disease that grew still upon him, he died soon after in a village [3] bearing the name Luculliana [4] [a], in the seventy-eighth year of his age, the three and twentieth of his empire, and the seventeenth day before the kalends of April [5], when Cn. Acerronius Proculus and C. Pontius Niger were consuls. Some think that Gaius [6] had given him a poison of slow operation, which should by little and little consume him. Others are of opinion that,

when he desired meat in the remission of an ague fit wherein he had swooned, it was denied him [7], and therewith a pillow [8] thrown upon his face to smother him and stop his breath ; some again, that it was when, coming soon to himself, he called for his ring, which was plucked from his finger whiles he fainted. Seneca writeth that, perceiving himself drawing on and ready to die [9], he took off his ring, as if he minded to give it unto some one, and so held it a pretty while, then afterwards did it upon his finger again ; and so, keeping down and gripping close his left hand [10], lay still a long time without once stirring ; but suddenly calling for his grooms and servitors, when none made answer, rose up, and not far from his pallet, his strength failing him, fell down dead.

74. Upon the last birthday feast of his that ever he saw, him thought, as he lay asleep, that Apollo Temenites (an idol of exceeding bigness and most artificially wrought) which was newly brought from Syracuse to be set up in the library of his new temple, assured him that he could not possibly by him be dedicated. And some few days before his death, the watchtower that gave light [1] at Capreae by an earthquake fell down in the night ; and at Misenum, the ashes remaining of the embers and coals brought in to heat his refection-parlour, being quenched quite and continuing cold a long time, suddenly broke forth into a light fire [Aug. 82], at the shutting in of the evening, and so shone out a great part of the night and gave not over.

75. The people joyed so much at his death that, running up and down at the first tidings thereof, some cried out in this note, " (Fling) Tiberius into the Tiber [1] " ; others in their prayers besought mother earth and the infernal gods to vouchsafe him now dead no place, but among impious wretches ; and a sort there were, who threatened his lifeless carcass [with] the drag and the Gemoniae, as who, over and above the remembrance of his former cruelty in times past, were provoked to anger with a fresh outrage newly committed. For whereas by an act of senate it was provided, that the execution of condemned persons should be put off unto the tenth day after sentence given, it happened so that the day on which some of them were to suffer fell out to be the very same, wherein news came of Tiberius' death. These poor souls, notwithstanding they piteously called for man's help (because in the absence yet of Gaius no man was known, who might in such a case be repaired unto and spoken with) the gaolers, for that they would do nothing against the constitution [33] aforesaid, strangled them and flung their bodies into the Gemoniae.   Hereupon, I say, the people's hatred against him increased, as if the tyrant's cruelty remained still after his death.   His corpse, so soon as it began to be removed from Misenum, notwithstanding the most part cried with one voice, to carry it rather to Atella ª, and there to half-burn it ᵇ in the amphitheatre ᶜ, yet was brought to Rome by the soldiers and burnt in a public funeral fire.

76. A twofold will [1] he made two years before, the one written with his own hand, the other by his freedman, but both of them were of the same tenor, and signed he had them with the seals of most base persons.   By virtue of which will and testament he left co-heirs and equal in portion Gaius, his nephew by Germanicus, and Tiberius by Drusus.   These he substituted and appointed to succeed one another.   He gave legacies also to many more and among the rest unto the Vestal virgins, and to the soldiers of all sorts in general, as also to the commons of Rome by the poll [C. 26] : yea, and to the masters of every street by themselves severally.

THE HISTORY OF
GAIUS CAESAR CALIGULA

1. GERMANICUS, father of Gaius Caesar, son of Drusus and
Antonia [1], no sooner was adopted by his uncle Tiberius, but
forthwith he bore the office of quaestorship five years before
he might by the laws [2] [a], and after it the consulate [3]. And being
sent into Germany to the army, when, upon news brought of
Augustus' death, the legions all throughout stood out most
stiffly and refused Tiberius for their emperor, offering unto him
the absolute government of the State (whether their [4] constant
resolution or kind affection herein were greater it is hard to
say) he stikled [5] and repressed them, yea, and soon after, having
subdued the enemy triumphed. After this, being created
consul the second time, and driven forth perforce [6] [b] (before
he entered into that honourable place) to compose the troubles
and to quiet the state in the East parts, when he had deposed [7]
the king of Armenia, and brought Cappadocia into the form
of a province, in the thirty-fourth year of his age, he died of a
long disease at Antioch, not without suspicion of poison [8].
For besides the blackish and swart spots which were to be
seen all over his body and the frothy slime that ran forth at
his mouth, his heart also (after he was burnt) they found
among the bones all sound and not consumed, the nature
whereof is thought to be such that, if it be infected with poison,
it checks all fire and cannot possibly be burnt.

2. But, as the opinion of the world went, his death, con-
trived by the wicked plot of Tiberius, was effected by the
ministry and help of Gnaeus Piso ; who about the same time
being president of Syria, and not dissembling that he was
to offend either father or son [1] (as if there were no other
remedy but needs he must so do) made no spare [2], but beyond
all measure dealt with Germanicus (sick as he was) most

rigorously, both in word and deed. For which, so soon as he was returned to Rome, he had like to have been pulled in pieces by the people ; and by the senate condemned he was to die.

3. It is for certain known and confessed, that there were in Germanicus all good parts and gifts, as well of body as mind, and those in such measure, as never to any man befell the like. To wit, for show, full of passing beauty, favour, and feature, with strength and valour answerable thereto, and for wit, excellently well-seen in eloquence and learning of both kinds [1] ; the very attractive object, he was of singular benevolence [2], endowed with a wonderful grace and effectual desire to win men's favour and deserve their love. The only defect that he had in his making and personage were his slender shanks ; and yet the same also by little and little became replenished with continual riding on horseback [3] after his meat [a]. Many a time wounded he his enemy in close fight hand to hand. He pleaded causes of great importance, even as touching the decree of triumph [4]. And among other monuments of his studies he left behind him in Greek comedies also [5]. Both at home and abroad civil [b] he was, insomuch as he would go to free and confederate cities without any lictors. Wherever he knew any sepulchres of brave and worthy men to be, there his use was to offer unto their ghosts. Being purposed to inter in one tomb the old relics and bones dispersed of those that were slain in that great overthrow with Varus, he first gave the assay [6] with his own hand to gather and carry them together into one place. Moreover, to his slanderers and backbiters (if he lighted upon them), of what quality soever the persons were, or how great cause soever they gave, so mild, so remiss and harmless he was that, notwithstanding Piso reversed and cancelled his decrees, plagued and persecuted a long time his dependants, yet could he not find in his heart to be angry with him, before he had for certain known, that he attempted his person with poisons and sorcerous execrations [7], and even then verily, he proceeded no farther against him but *more majorum* to renounce all friendship with him, and to give his domestic friends in charge to be revenged, if aught happened to himself otherwise than well.

4. Of these virtues he reaped most plentiful fruit ; so liked and loved of his kinsfolk and friends (for I let pass all other affinities and acquaintance of his) as that Augustus, after he had continued a long time in suspense, whether he should ordain him for his successor or no, recommended him at length unto Tiberius for to be adopted ; so highly favoured of the common people, as that many do report and write, whensoever he came unto a place or departed from thence, divers times by reason of the multitude flocking to meet him and to bear him company, he endangered his own life in the press. As he returned out of Germany, after the suppressing of seditious tumults and mutinies there, all the praetorian cohorts every one went out to encounter him upon the way, albeit warning was given beforehand by proclamation, that no more than twain of them should go forth. But as for the people of Rome, of all sexes, ages, and degrees, they ran out by heaps to meet him twenty miles from Rome.

5. Howbeit, far greater and more assured testimonies of men's judgement touching him appeared at and after his death. The very day wherein he left this life, the temples [1] were pelted with stones [a] ; the altars of the gods cast down ; the domestic Lares [b] by some flung out of doors into the street, yea, and new-born babes of wedded parents thrown forth to be destroyed [c]. And that which more is, the report goeth that the very barbarians, notwithstanding they were at variance and civil war among themselves, yea, and had taken arms against us, yet, as it were in some domestic and common sorrow [2], agreed all to make truce and a cessation of arms for a time. Some of their princes also and potentates, to declare their extraordinary mourning and regret, did cut off their own beards and shaved their wives' heads. Yea, the very king of kings [d] himself gave over his exercise of hunting, and dissolved the society of his great peers and princes at his table, which among the Parthians is as much as a law-steed [3] [e].

6. At Rome verily, whenas the city, upon the first rumour of his sickness, in amazedness and heavy cheer [1] expected the messengers that came after, and all of a sudden in the evening the voice went current (although the authors were unknown) that now at length he was recovered, running there was

everywhere from all parts with lights [2] and sacrifices [3] into the
Capitol ; yea, the very doors of the temple were like to have
been burst open, that nothing might stand in their way and
hinder them, so desirous and earnestly bent with joy to pay
their vows ; insomuch as Tiberius was awakened out of his
sleep with the shouts and voices of the people rejoicing, and
from every side with one accord resounding this note,

> *Salva Roma, salva patria, salvus est Germanicus.*
> Safe is Rome, safe is our country, safe is Germanicus.

Also, when now at the last it was known abroad that he
was departed this life, the public sorrow by no comfortable
words nor edicts and proclamations could be repressed, but
continued still even all the festival days of the month of
December [a]. His glory and the miss of him thus deceased
was much augmented also by the outrages of the times
ensuing ; whiles all men were of opinion (and not without
good reason) that the fierceness of Tiberius, which soon
after broke forth, was held in and kept down by the reverent
respect and fear that he had of him.

7. He wedded Agrippina, daughter to Marcus Agrippa and
Julia, by whom he had nine children, of which fair issue twain,
being yet infants, were taken away by untimely death ; one
died when he was now waxen a jolly boy, passing full of
lovely mirth and pretty talk, whose counterfeit in the habit
of Cupid Livia Augusta dedicated in the chapel of Venus
Capitolina, and the same Augustus was wont to kiss while
it stood in his bed-chamber, so often as he entered into it.
The rest survived their father ; three of the female sex,
Agrippina, Drusilla, and Livilla, born all one after another
in the space of three years, likewise as many male children,
Nero, Drusus, and Gaius Caesar. As for Nero and Drusus, the
senate, upon imputations laid by Tiberius, judged them to
be enemies unto the State [Tib. 54].

8. Gaius Caesar was born the day next preceding the
kalends of September [1], when his father and Gaius Fonteius
Capito were consuls. The place of his nativity, by the dis-
agreement of writers, is left uncertain. Gnaeus Lentulus
Gaetulicus [2] writeth that he was born at Tibur [3] ; Plinius
Secundus, within the country of the Treviri, in a town called

Ambiatinum [4], upon the very confluents [5]. For evidence and proof whereof he further saith that certain altars are there to be seen carrying this inscription : For the childbirth and delivery of Agrippina. But these verses following, divulged soon after that he came to be emperor, do plainly show that born he was in the very camp, where the legions wintered :

In castris natus, patriis [a] nutritus in armis,
Jam designati principis omen erat :

Born in the camp, in father's war with soldiers rear'd was he ;
A sign that then ordain'd he was an emp'ror for to be.

I myself do find among the records, that Antium was the place of his birth. Pliny refelleth [6] Gaetulicus, as if he made a lie by way of flattery, because, to the praise of a young and glorious prince, he would fetch some argument and matter even out of a city consecrated to Hercules ; and was the bolder, as he saith, to abuse the said lie, for that, indeed, a year almost before, Germanicus had a son born at Tibur, named likewise Gaius Caesar, of whose amiable child-hood and untimely death we have spoken before [7]. And as to Pliny himself, confuted he is by the calculation of the times ; for they who have recorded the acts of Augustus do all agree that Germanicus was sent into Germany after the time of his consulship expired, whenas Gaius was already born. Neither can the inscription of the altar one jot make good his opinion, considering that Agrippina was delivered of daughters twice in that country. And what childbirth soever it was, without respect and difference of sex, called it is *puerperium ;* for that in old time folk used to name little girls also *puerae*, like as little boys *puelli*.

There is besides an epistle of Augustus, written not many months before he died unto Agrippina, his niece [7], as touching this Gaius (for there was not now living any other infant of the like name), in these words : " I have no longer ago than yesterday taken order [8] with Talarius and Asillius that, with the leave of God, they bring the boy Gaius upon the fifteenth day before the kalends of June [9]. I send besides with him of mine own servants a physician whom Germanicus (as I have written unto him) may, if he will, retain and keep with him still. Farewell, my Agrippina, and endeavour to come well and in health to thy Germanicus." It appeareth I suppose sufficiently that Gaius could not in that place be born, unto which he was conveyed from Rome not before he was well-near two years old. And as for those verses, these self-same evidences likewise discredit them ; and the rather, because they have no author. We are to follow therefore the only authority that remaineth, of the records and public instrument, seeing especially that Gaius evermore preferred Antium before all other retiring places, and loved it no otherwise than his native soil ; yea, and by report was fully minded once (upon a tedious weariness that he had of Rome city), to transfer thither even the very seat and habitation of the empire.

9. He got his surname Caligula by occasion of a merry word taken up in the camp, because he was brought up there in the habit of an ordinary and common soldier among the rest [a]. With whom how much besides he was able to do in love and favour by means of his education and daily feeding with them, was most of all known when, after the death of Augustus, he only (no doubt) with his very sight and presence quieted them [1], what time they were in an uproar and at the very point of furious outrage. For they ceased not to mutiny, until they perceived that he was about to be sent out of the way for danger of the sedition and appointed to the next city adjoining. Then and not before, turning to repentance, they stayed and held back his coach, and so by prayer averted the displeasure that was toward them.

10. He accompanied his father also in the expedition into Syria ; from whence being returned, first he abode in house with his mother, and after that she was banished and sent away, he remained with his great-grandmother Livia Augusta ; whom, deceased, he praised in a funeral oration at the Rostra, when he was as yet but a very youth in his *praetexta*, and then removed he to his grandmother Antonia. From her, in the twentieth year of his age, he was sent for to Capreae by Tiberius, and upon one and the self-same day he did on [1] his virile gown [a] and withal cut the first down of his beard, without any honourable solemnity, such as his brethren before him had at their commencements [2]. Here, notwithstanding he was tempted by all the deceitful trains [3] that they could devise, who

would have drawn and forced him to quarrels [4], yet gave he
never any occasion, having rased out and quite forgotten the
fall and calamity of his mother, brethren, and near friends,
as if nothing had befallen to any of them ; passing over all
those abuses which himself had endured with incredible dis-
simulation so obsequious and double diligent besides to his
grandfather and those about him, that of him it was said
and not without good cause : " A better servant and a worse
master there never was [5]."

11. Howbeit, the cruel disposition and villainous nature of
his own he could not even then bridle and hold in, but both
at all castigations and punishments of such as were delivered
over to execution, most willing he was to be present ; and also
would haunt taverns and brothel-houses, men's wives also
suspected for adultery, going about from place to place disguised under a peruke of false hair [a], and in a side (woman's)
garment ; yea, and most studiously gave his mind to learn
the artificial feat of dancing and singing upon the stage.
And verily Tiberius was well content to wink hereat and
suffer all, if haply thereby his fierce and savage nature might
have been mollified and become tractable. Which the old
man (as he was a prince right prudent and one most quick of
scent) had foreseen well enough long before ; insomuch as
divers times he gave out and said openly, that Gaius lived to
the destruction of him and them all ; likewise, that he cherished and brought up a very *natrix* [1], which is a kind of serpent,
for the people of Rome, and another Phaëthon [b] to the whole
world.

12. Not long after he took to wife Junia Claudilla [1], the
daughter of Marcus Silanus, a right noble gentleman. And
then, being nominated to succeed augur in the room of his
brother Drusus, before his investure and installation therein
he was advanced to the sacerdotal dignity of a pontiff [2], a
notable testimony of his piety and towardness, whenas,
the royal line and imperial court being desolate and destitute
of all other helps [3], Sejanus also suspected and soon after
overthrown, he should thus by small degrees arise to the hope
of succession in the empire. Which hope the rather to confirm, after his wife aforesaid Junia was dead in childbirth, he
solicited unto filthy wantonness dame Ennia, the wife of

Naevius Macro[4], then captain of the guard and praetorian cohorts, having promised her marriage also, in case he ever attained to the empire ; and for assurance hereof he bound it with an oath and a bill[5] of his own hand. By her means being insinuated once into the inward acquaintance of Macro[6], he attempted, as some think, Tiberius with poison ; and whiles he was yet living, but labouring for life, commanded his ring to be plucked from his finger, but perceiving that he gave some suspicion of holding it fast, he caused a pillow to be forced upon his mouth, and so with his own hands stifled and strangled him ; yea, and when his freedman[7] made an outcry at this cruel and horrible act, he gave order immediately to crucify him. And verily this soundeth to truth, considering there be some authors who write, that himself afterwards professed[8], if not the murder done, yet at leastwise his intention one day to do it. For he made his boast continually, in reporting his own piety[9], that to revenge the death of his mother and brethren, he entered with a dagger[10] into Tiberius' bed-chamber whiles he lay asleep ; and yet upon mere pity and commiseration bethought himself, flung away the weapon, and so went back again. Neither durst Tiberius, although he had an inkling and intelligence of his design, make any inquisition at all of the matter or proceed to revenge.

13. Thus having obtained the empire, he procured unto the people of Rome, or (as I may so say) to all mankind their heart's desire ; being a prince, of all that ever were, most wished for of the greatest part of provincial nations and of the soldiers, because most of them had known him an infant, and generally of the whole commonalty of Rome, in remembrance of his father Germanicus, and upon compassion they took of that house in manner ruinated and extinct. As he removed therefore from Misenum, albeit he was clad in mourning weed[1] and reverently did attend the corpse of Tiberius, yet went he among the altars, sacrifices, and burning torches[a] in a most thick throng and joyful train of such as met him on the way, who beside other lucky and fortunate names called him *sidus*, their star, *pullum*, their chick, *pupum*, their babe[2], and *alumnum*, their nursling.

14. No sooner was he entered into the city of Rome, but

incontinently, with consent of the senate and the multitude rushing into the Curia, after they had annulled the will of Tiberius, who in his testament had adjoined co-heir unto him another of his nephews [8] under age [1], and as yet in his *praetexta* [2], permitted he was alone to have the full and absolute power of all, and that with such a universal joy, that in three months' space next ensuing and those not fully expired, there were by report above 160,000 beasts slain for sacrifice.

After this, whenas within some few days he passed over by the water but to the next islands of Campania, vows were made for his safe return ; and no man there was who did let slip the least occasion offered, to testify what pensive care he took as touching his health and safety. But so soon as he was once fallen sick, they all kept watch by night about the palace ; neither wanted some, who vowed to fight armed to the very outrance [3] for his life thus lying sick, yea, and devoted their very lives for him if he recovered [4 a], professing no less in written bills set up in public places. To this surpassing love of his own citizens and countrymen was adjoined the notable favour also of foreign states. For Artabanus, king of the Parthians, professing always his hatred and contempt of Tiberius, sought of his own accord to him for amity : yea, he came in person to a conference with one of his legates that had been consul, and, passing over Euphrates, adored the eagles [5] and other military ensigns of the Romans, as also the images of the Caesars.

15. Himself also enkindled and set more on fire the affections of men by all manner of popularity. When he had with many a tear praised Tiberius in a funeral oration before the body of the people, and performed the complement of his obsequies most honourably, forthwith he hastened to Pandataria and Pontiae, for to translate from thence the ashes of his mother and brother, and that in foul and tempestuous weather, to the end that his piety and kindness might the more be seen. And being come to their relics, very devoutly himself with his own hands bestowed them in several pitchers. And with no less show in pageant wise, having wafted them first to Ostia with a flag (or streamer) pitched in the poop or stern of a galley guided by two ranks of oars and so forth to Rome up the Tiber, by the ministry of the most worshipful gentlemen of Rome he conveyed them within two fercules (or frames)[1] devised for the purpose into the mausoleum, even at noonday, when people were assembled there in great frequency[2]. In memorial likewise of them he ordained yearly dirges and sacrifices to be performed with religious devotion to their ghosts by the whole city. And more than that, he instituted for his mother solemn games within the circus and a sacred chariot withal, wherein her image to the full proportion of her body should be carried in the pomp[3]. But in remembrance of his father he called the month September Germanicus.

These ceremonial duties done, by virtue of one sole act of the senate, he heaped upon his grandmother Antonia whatsoever honours Livia Augusta had received in her whole time. His uncle Claudius, a knight of Rome until that time and no better, he assumed unto him for his colleague in the consulship. His brother Tiberius[4] he adopted the very day that he put on his virile gown, and styled him prince of the youth[5]. As touching his sisters, he caused in all oaths this clause to be annexed[6]: "Neither shall I prize myself and children more dear than I do Gaius and his sisters." Item, he ordained that, in moving and propounding of matters by the consuls unto the senators, they should begin in this form, *Quod bonum*, etc., That which may be to the good and happy estate of Gaius Caesar and his sisters, etc. In the semblable [C. 39] vein of popularity, he restored all those that had been condemned, confined, and exiled, yea, he freely dispensed with them[7], pardoning whatsoever crimes or imputations remained still behind from beforetime[8]. All the books and registers pertaining to the causes of his mother and brethren, because no informer or witness should afterwards need to fear, he brought together into the Forum; where, protesting beforehand and calling the gods to record with a loud voice, that he had neither read aught nor meddled once therewith, he burnt them. A certain pamphlet presented unto him concerning his life and safety he received not, but stood upon this point, that he had done nothing wherefore he should be odious to any person; saying withal that he had no ears open for informers and tale-bearers.

16. The *spintriae* [Tib. 43], inventors of monstrous forms in perpetrating filthy lust, he expelled forth of Rome, being hardly and with much ado entreated not to drown them in the deep sea. The writings of Titus Labienus[1], Cordus Cremutius[2], and Cassius Severus[3], which had been called in and abolished by divers acts of the senate, he suffered to be sought out again, to be in men's hands extant and usually to be read ; seeing that it concerned him principally and stood him upon most[4], to have all actions and deeds delivered unto posterity. The breviary[5] of the empire, that by Augustus had been wont to be proposed openly, but was by Tiberius intermitted, he published. Unto the magistrates he granted free jurisdiction and that there might be no appealing to himself. The gentry and knighthood of Rome he reviewed with severity and great preciseness, yet not without some moderation of his hand. He openly took from them their horses[6], in whom was found any foul reproach or ignominy ; as for those who were culpable in smaller matters, he only passed over their names in reading the roll. To the end that the judges might be eased of their labour, unto the four former decuries he added a fifth. He gave the attempt likewise to bring up again the ancient manner of elections and to restore unto the people their free voices.

The legacies due by the last will and testament of [Tiberius] (although the same was abolished), as also of Livia Augusta, which Tiberius had suppressed, he caused faithfully and without fraud to be tendered and fully paid. The exaction called *ducentesima*[7][a] of all bargains and sales he remitted throughout Italy. The losses that many a man had sustained by fire he supplied ; and if to any princes he restored their kingdoms, he adjoined withal the fruit and profits also of their rents, customs, and imposts growing to the Crown in the middle time between ; as namely, unto Antiochus Commagenus who had been confiscate and fined in a hundred million sesterces[8]. And that he might the rather be reputed a favourer of all good examples, he gave unto a woman (by condition a libertine) 800,000 sesterces[9], for that she, being under most grievous and dolorous torments, concealed yet and would not, to die for it, utter a wicked act committed by her patron. For which things, among other honours

done unto him there was decreed for him a shield of gold [b],
which upon a certain day every year the colleges of the
priests should bring into the Capitol, with the senate accompanying them, and noblemen's children as well boys as girls,
singing the praises of his virtues in musical verse tuned
sweetly in metre. Moreover, there passed a decree, that the
day on which he began his empire should be called Parilia [c],
implying thereby as it were a second foundation of the city.

17. He bore four consulships : the first, from the kalends of
July for two months ; the second, from the kalends of January,
for thirty days ; the third, unto the ides of January ; and
the fourth, unto the seventh day before the said ides [1]. Of
all these, the two last he held jointly together ; the third
he alone entered upon at Lugdunum [Lyons], not, as some
deem, upon pride or negligence, but because, being absent, he
could not have knowledge that his colleague died just against
the very day of the kalends. He gave a largesse to the people
twice, to wit, 300 sesterces to them apiece, and a most plenteous
dinner he made as oft unto the senate and degree of gentlemen, as also to the wives and children of them both. In the
latter dinner of the twain, he dealt over and above among
the men, garments to be worn abroad ; unto the women and
children, guards, welts [2], or laces, of purple and violet colour.
And to the end he might augment the public joy of the city
with perpetuity also, he annexed unto the feast Saturnalia
one day more, and named the same Juvenalis.

18. He set forth games of sword-fencers, partly in the
amphitheatre of Taurus, and partly within the Septa in
Mars' Field, into the which he inserted and brought in certain troops of African and Campanian pugilists to skirmish
by companies, even the very best, selected out of both countries. Neither was he always himself president at these
solemnities and public shows, but otherwhiles enjoined the
magistrates or else his friends to take the charge of presidency. As for stage-plays, he exhibited them continually
in divers places and in sundry sorts, once also in the night-
season, burning lights throughout the city. He scattered
likewise and flung among the common people missiles [1] of
many and sundry kinds to scramble for, and dealt, man by
man, panniers with viands therein. At which feasting, to

a certain gentleman of Rome who over against him plied
his jaws full merrily and fed right heartily with a greedy
stomach, he sent his own part ; as also to a senator, for
the same cause, his letters patent, wherein he declared him
extraordinarily praetor. He represented besides many circus-
games, which held from morn to even, interposing one while
the baiting of panthers[2], another while the Troy-jousting
[C. 39] and tournament. But some especial sports there
were above the rest, and then the circus was laid all over
with vermilion and borax mineral[3], where none but of senator's
degree ruled and drove the chariots. Some also he put
forth upon a sudden, namely, whenas he beheld from out
of the house Gelotiana[4] the preparation and furniture of
the circus, some few from the next open galleries jettying
out [5] [a] called unto him for the same.

19. Furthermore he devised a new kind of sight, and such
as never was heard of before. For over the middle space[1]
between Baiae and the huge piles or dams at Puteoli, containing three miles and 600 paces well-near he made a bridge,
having got together from all parts ships of burden, and placed
them in a duple course at anchor, with a bank of earth cast
thereupon, direct and straight after the fashion of the highway
Appia. Upon this bridge he passed to and fro for two days
together ; the first day mounted on a courser richly trapped,
himself most brave and goodly to be seen with a chaplet of
oak branches, armed with a battle-axe, a light target and a
sword, clad also in a cloak of gold ; the morrow after he
appeared in the habit of a charioteer, riding in a chariot
drawn with two goodly steeds of an excellent race, carrying
before him Dareus a boy, one of the Parthian hostages, with a
train of the praetorian soldiers marching after in battle array,
and accompanied with the cohort of his minions in British
wagons[2]. Most men, I wot well, are of opinion that Gaius
invented such a kind of bridge in emulation of Xerxes, who
not without the wonder of the world made a bridge of planks
over the Hellespont, an arm of the sea somewhat narrower
than this ; others, that by a bruit blazed abroad of some huge
and monstrous piece of work, he might terrify Germany and
Britain, upon which countries he meant to make war. But I
remember well that, being a boy, I heard my grandfather

report and tell the cause of this work, as it was delivered by his own courtiers, who were more inward with him than the rest ; namely, that Thrasyllus, the great astrologer, assured Tiberius, when he was troubled in mind about his successor, and more inclined to his natural and lawful nephew [3] indeed by lineal descent, that Gaius should no more become emperor than able to run a course to and fro on horseback through the gulf of Baiae.

20. He set forth shows also even in foreign parts, to wit, in Sicily at Syracuse, the games called Actiaci [1], likewise at Lugdunum in Gaul, plays of a mixed nature and argument ; as also a solemn contention for the prize in eloquence both Greek and Latin. In which trial of masteries, the report goeth that those who were foiled and overcome conferred rewards upon the winners, yea, and were forced to make compositions in their praise. But look, who did worst, they were commanded to wipe out their own writings, either with a sponge or else with their tongues, unless they would choose rather to be chastised with ferulars [2] or else to be ducked over head and ears in the next river [3].

21. The buildings left half-undone by Tiberius, namely, the temple of Augustus and the theatre of Pompey, he finished. He began moreover a conduit in the Tiburtine territory, and an amphitheatre near unto the enclosure called Septa ; of the two works the one [1] was ended by his successor Claudius, the other was forelet [Tib. 33] and given over quite. The walls at Syracuse by the injury of time decayed and fallen down were by him re-edified, and the temples of the gods there repaired. He had fully purposed also to build anew the palace of Polycrates at Samos, to finish Apollo's temple called Didymeum at Miletus, as also to found and build a city upon the top of the Alps ; but, before all, to dig through the isthmus in Achaia, and thither had he sent already one of purpose, who had been a principal captain of a cohort in the vaward [2], to take measure of the work.

22. Thus far forth as of a prince ; now forward relate we must as of a monster. Having assumed into his style many surnames, for called he was *pius*, kind, *castrorum filius*, the son of the camp, *pater exercituum*, father of hosts, and *optimus maximus Caesar*, the most gracious and mighty

Caesar [1], when he happened to hear certain kings [2] (who were come into the city for to do their duties and to salute him) contend, as they sat with him at supper, about the nobility of their birth and parentage, he cried forth

Εἷς κοίρανος ἔστω, εἷς βασιλεὺς.

One Sovereign Lord, one King let there be [a]:

and there lacked not much but that presently [3] he had taken the diadem upon him and converted wholly the show of empire into the form of a kingdom [4][b]. But being told that he was mounted already above the height and state both of emperors and also of kings [5], thereupon from that time forward he began to challenge unto himself a divine majesty ; and having given order and commission that the images of the gods, which, either for devout worship done unto them or for curious workmanship seen upon them, excelled the rest (among which was that of Jupiter Olympius), should be brought out of Greece unto Rome, that, when their heads were taken off he might set his own in the place [6], he enlarged the Palatium [7] and set out one part thereof as far as to the Forum. Transfiguring likewise and turning the temple of Castor and Pollux into a porch or entry [8], he stood many times in the middle between the said two gods, brethren, and so exhibited himself to be adored of all comers. And some there were who saluted him by the name of Jupiter Latiaris.

Moreover he ordained a temple peculiarly appropriate to his own godhead, as also priests and most exquisite osts [9]. In his said temple stood his own image all of gold, lively portrayed and expressing his full proportion, the which was daily clad with the like vesture as himself wore. The masterships of the priesthood by him instituted the richest men that were every time of vacancy purchased, such as made greatest suit and offered most therefor. The osts or sacrifices aforesaid were these fowls, phoenicopteri [c], peacocks, tetraones [wood-cocks] [d], numidicae [e], meleagrides [f], and pheasants [g], and those to be sorted by their kinds, and so every day killed. And verily, his usual manner was in the night to call unto the moon, when she was at full and shining bright out, for to come and lie with him in his arms, but in the daytime he talked secretly and apart with Jupiter Capitolinus, one while by whispering and rounding [10] one another in the ear, otherwhiles speaking more loud and not without chiding; for he was heard in threatening wise to utter these words, Εἰς γαῖαν Δαναῶν περάω σε,[11] I will remove and translate thee into the land of the Greeks, until such time as, being entreated (according as he told the tale himself) and invited first by him for to cohabit, he made a bridge over the temple of Augustus of sacred memory, and so joined the Palatium and Capitol together[12]. And soon after, to the end that he might be nearer unto him, he laid the foundation of a new house in the void base-court of the Capitol.

23. He could in no wise abide to be either reputed or named the nephew of Agrippa by reason of his base and obscure parentage; yea, and angry he would be, in case any man, either in oration or verse, inserted him[1] among the images of the Caesars. But he gave it out openly, that his own mother[2] was begotten by incest which Augustus committed with his own daughter Julia. And not content with this infamous imputation of Augustus, the Actian and Sicilian[3] victories by him achieved he straitly forbade to be celebrated yearly with solemn holidays, as being unlucky and hurtful to the people of Rome. As for Livia Augusta his great-grandmother, he called her ever and anon Ulysses in a woman's habit; yea, and in a certain epistle unto the senate he was so bold as to lay unto her ignobility[4], as descended from a decurion of Fundi[5] who was her grandsire by the mother's side, whereas it is evident and certain by public records that Aufidius Lingo bore honourable offices in Rome. When his grandam Antonia[6] requested secret conference with him, he denied her, unless Macro, captain of the guard, might come in between to hear their talk. And so by such indignities and discontentments as these he was the cause of her death; and yet, as some think, he gave her poison withal. Neither when she was dead deigned he her any honour, but out of his dining-chamber beheld her funeral fire as it was burning.

His brother Tiberius he surprised suddenly at unawares, sending a tribune of soldiers, who rushed in upon him and so slew him[a]. Likewise Silanus, his father-in-law, he forced to death, even to cut his own throat with a razor, picking quarrels to them both and finding these causes: to wit, that the one[7] followed him not when he took sea being very rough and much troubled, but stayed behind in hope to seize the city of Rome into his own hands, if aught happened but well unto him [8] by occasion of tempests ; the other [9] smelled strongly of a preservative or antidote, as if he had taken the same to prevent his poisons. Whereas in very truth Silanus avoided thereby the insufferable pain of being sea-sick and the grievous trouble of sailing ; and Tiberius for a continual cough that grew still upon him used a medicine. For [10] his uncle Claudius he reserved for nothing else but to make him his laughing-stock.

24. With all his sisters he used ordinarily to be naught [C. 6] ; and at any great feast he placed evermore one or other of them by turns beneath himself, while his wife sat above. Of these sisters (as it is verily thought) he deflowered Drusilla being a virgin, when himself also was yet under age and a very boy ; yea, and one time above the rest he was found in bed with her and taken in the manner [1] by his grandmother Antonia, in whose house they were brought up both together. Afterwards also, when she was bestowed in marriage upon Lucius Cassius Longinus, a man of consular degree, he took her from him and kept her openly, as if she had been his own lawful wife. Also when he lay sick, he ordained her to be both heir of all his goods and successor also in the empire. For the same sister deceased he proclaimed a general cessation of law [2] in all courts. During which time, a capital crime it was for any man to have laughed, bathed, or supped together with parents, wife, or children. And being impatient of this sorrow, when he was fled suddenly and by night out of the city and had passed all over Campania, to Syracuse he went ; and so from thence returned speedily again with his beard and hair of head overgrown. Neither at any time ever after, in making a speech before the people or to his soldiers concerning any matters, were they never so weighty, would he swear otherwise than by the name of Drusilla [3]. The rest of his sisters (Livia and Agrippina) he loved neither with so tender affection nor so good respect, as whom he oftentimes prostituted and offered to be abused by his own stale catamites. So much the more easily therefore condemned he them in the case of Aemilius Lepidus, as adulteresses and privy to his treasons and wait-layings ad-

dressed against his person. And he not only divulged the
hand-writings which were sought out by guile and adulteries,
but also consecrated unto Mars Revenger those three daggers
prepared for his death[4], with a title over them, containing
the cause of his so doing.

25. As for his marriages, a man may hardly discern whether
he contracted, dissolved, or held them still with more dishonesty.   Livia Orestilla, what time she was wedded unto
Gaius Piso, himself (being one who came in person to the
solemnisation of the marriage) commanded to be brought
home unto him as his own wife ; and having within few days
cast her off, two years after he banished and sent her away,
because in the middle time between she was thought to
have had the company[1] again of her former husband.   Some
report that, being an invited guest at the nuptial supper, he
charged Piso, sitting over against him, in these terms ; " Sirrah, see you sit not too close unto my wife," and so presently [22] had her away with him from the table ; and
the next day published by proclamation that he had met
with a marriage after the example of Romulus and Augustus[a].
As touching Lollia Paulina, married already to Gaius Memmius,
a man of consular degree and ruler of armies, upon mention
made of her grandmother as the most beautiful lady in her
time, he all of a sudden sent and called her home out of the
province[2] and, taking her perforce from her husband, wedded
her and shortly turned her away, forbidding her straitly for
ever the use of any man's body whatsoever.

Caesonia, for no special beauty and favour of her own
above others, nor yet because she was in the flower of her
youth (considering she had been the mother already of three
daughters by another man), but only for that she was a most
lascivious woman and of insatiable lust, he loved with more
ardent affection and constancy ; insomuch as many a time he
would show her to his soldiers in her hair[3], clad in a soldier's
cassock[4] with a light target and a helmet, riding close unto
him, but to his friends stark-naked also[5].   When she brought
him a child[6], he vouchsafed her then the name of his wife and
not before ; professing and making it known, that in one and
the self-same day he was become both her husband and also
father of the infant of her body born.   This babe he named

Julia Drusilla, whom he carried about with him through the temples of all the goddesses, and bestowed at length in the lap of Minêrva[7], recommending it to her for to be nourished, brought up, and taught. Neither had he any surer sign and evidence to believe she was his own and of his natural seed conceived than her curstness[8] and shrewdness[9] : and that quality had she even then at the first, in such measure as that with her perilous[10] fingers she would not stick[11] to lay at the face and eyes of other small children playing together with her.

26. Vanity it were and mere folly to adjoin hereunto, how he served his kinsfolk and friends, to wit, Ptolemy, king Juba's son and his own cousin german[1] (for he also was the nephew of Marcus Antonius by his daughter Selene [a]), but especially Macro himself, yea, and Ennia likewise, who were his chief helpers and advanced him to the empire. All of them, in right of their near affinity and in consideration of their good deserts, were highly rewarded, even with bloody death. No more respective[2] was he one whit of the senate, nor dealt in gentler wise with them ; some, after they had borne the highest honours, he suffered to run by his wagon[3] side in their gowns for certain miles together, and, as he sat at supper, to stand waiting one while at the head, another while at the foot of the table, girt with a white linen towel about them. Others, whom he had secretly murdered, he continued nevertheless calling for, as if they were alive, giving it out most untruly some few days after, that they had wilfully made themselves away. The consuls had forgot by chance to publish by proclamation his birthday, for which he deprived them of their magistracy ; and so for three days' space the commonwealth was without the sovereign authority [b]. His own quaestor, who happened to be nominated in a conspiracy against him, he caused to be scourged, and the clothes out of which he was stripped to be put under the soldiers' feet, that they might stand more steadily while they were whipping him.

In semblable [15] pride and violence he handled other states and degrees of citizens. Being disquieted with the stir and noise that they kept, who by midnight took up their standings in the circus, which cost them nothing, he

drove them all away with cudgels ; in which tumult and
hurly-burly, there were twenty knights of Rome and above
crowded and crushed to death, as many matrons and wives
also, besides an infinite number of the common multitude.
At the stage-plays, being minded to sow discord and minister
occasion of quarrel between the commons and gentlemen of
Rome, he gave his tallies [4] forth sooner than ordinary [c], to the
end that the *equestria* [5] might be possessed aforehand, even by
the basest commoners that came. At the sword-fight, he
otherwhiles commanded the curtains to be folded up and
drawn together during the most parching heat of the sun, and
forbade that any person should be let forth [6] ; and then, removing and sending quite away the ordinary furniture of
shows provided to make pastime, he put forth unto the people
for to behold, poor wild beasts and carrion-lean [7], to be baited,
the basest sword-fencers also and worn with age, to combat ;
yea, and appointed householders [8], such as were of quality and
well-known, but yet noted for some special feebleness and
imperfection of body, to go under the *pegmata* [9] [d] and carry
them. And divers times he brought [10] a dearth and famine
among the people, by shutting up the garners and storehouses from them.

27. The cruelty of his nature he showed by these examples
most of all. When cattle, which were to feed wild beasts
prepared for baiting, grew to be sold very dear, he appointed
malefactors found guilty to be slaughtered for that purpose. And in taking the review of gaols and prisoners
therein, as they were sorted according to their offences, he,
without once looking upon the title and cause of their imprisonment, standing only within a gallery, commanded all
in the midst *a calvo ad calvum* [1] [a], from one bald-pate to
another, to be led forth to execution. He exacted of him
the performance of a vow, who had promised to do his devoir
in public sword-fight for the recovery of his health, and
him he beheld fighting at sharpe [2] ; neither dismissed he
him before he was victor, and after many prayers. Another
there was who for the same cause had vowed to die. This
man, being not very forward to pay his vow, he caused to
be dight with sacred herbs, and adorned with infules [3], like
a sacrifice ; and so delivered him into the hands of boys,

who, calling hard upon him for the discharge of his vow, should course and drive him through the streets of the city, until he were thrown headlong down the steep rampier [4]. Many honest citizens of good calling and estate, after he had first disfigured [them] with marks of branding irons, he condemned to dig in mines, and to make highways, or to encounter with beasts; or kept them creeping with all four [5] like brute beasts within a cage for the nonce, or else slit them through the midst with a saw. And those whom he thus served were not all of them guilty of any grievous offences; but sufficient it was, if they had a base conceit [6] and spake but meanly of some show that he exhibited; or because they had never sworn stoutly by his genius [7] [b].

Parents he forced to be present at the execution of their own children. And when one father excused himself by reason of sickness, he sent a litter for him; another of them, immediately after the heavy spectacle of his son put to death, he invited to his own board [c], made him great cheer, and by all manner of courtesy provoked him to jocoseness and mirth. The master of his sword-fights and beast-baitings he caused for certain days together to be beaten with chains [d] in his own sight; but killed him not quite, before himself could no longer abide the stench of his brain by this time putrefied. A poet, the author of Atellane Interludes, for a verse that he made, implying a jest which might be doubly taken, he burnt at a stake in the very middle show-place of the amphitheatre. A gentleman of Rome, whom he had cast before wild beasts, when he cried out that he was innocent, he commanded to be brought back; and after he had cut out his tongue, sent him among them again (to fight for his life or to be devoured).

28. Having recalled one from exile who had been long banished, he demanded of him what he was wont to do there; who made answer thus by way of flattery, " I prayed," quoth he, " to the gods always that Tiberius [1] (as now it is come to pass) might perish, and you become emperor." Hereupon Caligula, weening that those whom he had banished prayed likewise for his death, sent about into the islands [2], to kill them every one. Being desirous to have a senator torn and mangled piecemeal, he suborned certain of purpose, who all on a sudden, as he entered into the Curia, should call him enemy to the State, and so lay violent hands upon him : and when they had with their writing-irons ᵃ all to-pricked ³ and stabbed him, deliver him over to the rest, for to be dismembered and cut in pieces accordingly. Neither was he satisfied, until he saw the man's limbs, joints, and inwards drawn along the streets, and piled all on a heap together before him.

29. His deeds, most horrible as they were, he augmented with as cruel words. His saying was, That he commended and approved in his own nature nothing more than (to use his own term) *adiatrepsia* ¹, immovable rigour. When his grandmother Antonia seemed to give him some admonition, he (as though it were not enough to disobey her), " Go to, dame," quoth he, " remember I may do what I will against all persons whomsoever." Being minded to kill his own brother, whom for fear of poison he imagined to be fortified aforehand with preservatives ² : " What ! " quoth he, " is there any antidote against Caesar ? " When he had banished his sisters, he threatened them in these terms, saying that he had not islands ᵃ only at command, but swords also. A certain citizen of praetor's degree desired oftentimes, from the retiring place where he was at Anticyra ³ ᵇ (into which isle he went for his health sake) to have his licence continued ⁴. But he gave order he should be killed outright, adding these words therewith, that bloodletting was necessary for him, who in so long time had found no good by hellebore ⁵. Once every ten days his manner was to subscribe and write down a certain number out of the gaol to be executed, and said withal, that he cast up his reckonings and cleared the book of accounts. When he had at one time condemned a sort [C. 81] of Gauls and Greeks together, he made his boast that he had subdued Gallograecia ⁶.

30. He would not lightly [36] permit any to suffer death but after many strokes given and those very softly, with this rule and precept evermore, which now became rife and well-known, " Strike so as they may feel that they are dying." He executed on a time one whom he had not appointed to die, by error only and mistaking his name : " But it makes no matter," quoth he, " for even he also hath deserved death." This speech of the tyrant ¹ out of a tragedy he often repeated :

Oderint dum metuant, " Let them hate me, so they fear me."
Many a time he inveighed bitterly against all the senators
at once, as the dependants and adherents of Sejanus, or the
informers against his mother and brethren, bringing forth
those evidences which he had made semblance before [15]
were burnt ; and therewith excused and justified the cruelty
of Tiberius as necessary, seeing he could not otherwise choose
but believe so many that made presentments unto him.
The degree of gentlemen he railed at continually, as devoted
wholly to the stage and show-place. Being highly displeased
upon a time with the multitude, favouring as they did the
contrary faction[2] to his[3] : " Would God," quoth he, " that
the people of Rome had but one neck." And when Tetrinius
Latro[a] was by them called for to fight at sharpe [27] he
said that they also who called for him were Tetrinii[4] every
one. It fortuned that five of these retiarii[5], fighting in
their single coats, and together by companies[6], had without
any combat yielded themselves as overcome to as many other
champions or fencers called secutores[7]. Now when command was given by the people that they should be killed, one
takes me up his trout-spear again into his hand and slew all
the other five who were thought the conquerors. This
slaughter he both bewailed in an edict as most cruel, and also
cursed them that endured to see the sight.

31. He was wont moreover to complain openly of the condition of his time wherein he lived, as not renowned by any
public calamities ; whereas the reign of Augustus [Aug. 23]
was memorable for the overthrow of Varus, that of Tiberius
[Tib. 40] ennobled by the fall of scaffolds in the theatre at
Fidenae. As for himself, like he was to be forgotten (such was
the prosperity in his days). And evermore he wished the
carnage and execution of his armies, famine, pestilence, and
skarfires[1], or some opening chinks of the ground.

32. Even whiles he was at his recreations and disports,
whiles he set his mind upon gaming and feasting, the same
cruelty practised he both in word and deed. Oftentimes, as
he sat at dinner or banqueted, were serious matters examined
in his very sight by way of torture ; and the soldier that had
the skill and dexterity to behead folk then and there used
to cut off the heads of any prisoners indifferently without

respect. At Puteoli, when he dedicated the bridge which, as we noted before [19], was his own invention, after he had invited many unto him from the shore and strand, suddenly he turned them all headlong over the bridge into the water. And seeing some of them taking hold of the helms[1] for to save themselves, he shoved and thrust them off with poles and oars into the sea. At a public feast in Rome, there chanced a servant[2] to pluck off a thin plate[3] of silver from the table[4]; and for this immediately he delivered him to the hangman for to be executed, namely, to have his hands cut off and hung about his neck just before his breast, with a written title carried before him, declaring the cause of this his punishment, and so to be led round about all the companies as they sat at meat. One of these fencers called mirmillones[5] coming out of the fence-school played at wooden wasters[6] with him, and there took a fall for the nonce[7], and lay along at his feet; him he stabbed for his labour with a short iron skene[8] that he had, and withal, after the solemn manner of victors, ran up and down with his garland of palm-tree branches. There was a beast brought to the altar ready to be killed for sacrifice; he comes girt in habit of these beast-slayers[9], and with the axe-head that he lifted up on high knocked down the minister himself, who was addressed to cut the said beast's throat, and so dashed his brains out. At a plenteous feast where there was great cheer he set up all at once an immeasurable laughter; and when the consuls who sat just by him asked gently and with fair language whereat he laughed so, "At what else," quoth he, "but this, that with one nod of my head I can have both your throats cut immediately."

33. Among divers and sundry jests and merry conceits of his, as he stood once hard by the image of Jupiter, he demanded of Apelles, an actor of tragedies, whether of the twain he thought to be the greater and more stately, Jupiter or himself. And whiles he made some stay ere he answered, he all to-tare [28] and mangled him with whipping cheer[1], praising ever and anon his voice, crying unto him for mercy, as passing sweet and pleasant, even when he groaned also under his lashes. So often as he kissed the neck of wife or concubine, he would say withal, " As fair and lovely a neck

as this is, off it shall go if I do but speak the word." Moreover, he gave it forth many a time, that he would himself
fetch out of his wife Caesonia, though it were with lute-
strings[2], what was the reason that he loved her so entirely[a].

34. Neither raged he with less envy and spiteful malice
than pride and cruelty, against persons, in manner[1], of all
times and ages. The statues of brave and worthy men,
brought by Augustus out of the Capitol courtyard for the
straitness of the place into Mars' Field, he overthrew and
cast here and there in such sort as they could not be set
up again with the titles and inscriptions whole ; forbidding
that ever after there should be anywhere statue or image
erected unto any person living, without his advice asked and
grant passed. He was of mind also to abolish Homer's
verses : " For why may not I," quoth he, " do that which
Plato lawfully did, who banished him[2] out of the city that he
framed and ordained ? " The writings likewise and images
of Virgil and Livy he went within a little of removing out of
all libraries. The one[3] of these he carped as a man of no
wit and very mean learning ; the other[4] for his verbosity
and negligence in penning his history. Moreover, as touching
lawyers (as if he meant to take away all use of their skill and
knowledge) he cast out these words many times, that he would
surely bring it to pass they should be able to give none other
answer nor counsel than according to reason and equity[a].

35. He took from the noblest personages that were the
old arms and badges[1] of their houses ; from Torquatus the
collar[2] ; from Cincinnatus the curled lock of hair ; and
from Gnaeus Pompeius[3], of an ancient stock descended, the
surname of Magnus belonging to that lineage. As for king
Ptolemy (of whom I made report before [26]), when he had
both sent for him out of his realm and also honourably entertained him he slew [him] all of a sudden, for no other cause
in the world but for that, as he entered into the theatre to
see the shows and games there exhibited, he perceived him
to have turned the eyes of all the people upon him, with the
resplendent brightness of his purple cassock. All such as
were fair and carried a thick bush of hair grown long, so
often as they came in his way, he disfigured by shaving their
heads all behind. There was one Aesius Proculus (whose

father had been a principal captain of the foremost cohort) for his exceeding tall personage and lovely favour withal named Colosseros [a]. Him he caused suddenly to be pulled down from the scaffold where he sat, and to be brought into the plain within the lists, where he matched him in fight with a sword-fencer of that sort which be called *threces* [b], and afterwards with another all-armed [4]. Now when he had given the foil twice [5] and got the upper hand, he commanded him forthwith to be pinioned and bound fast, and being put into foul and overworn clothes to be led round about the streets to be shown unto women, and so to have his throat cut in the end. To conclude, there was none of so base and abject condition, nor of so mean estate, whose commodities and good parts he depraved [Aug. 27] not.

Against the great prelate styled by the name Rex Nemorensis [c], because he had many years already enjoyed his sacerdotal dignity he suborned underhand a concurrent [6] and adversary mightier than himself. Whenas, upon a certain day of public games [7], there was greater applause and more clapping of hands than ordinary at Porius the fencer [8] manumitting his slave for joy of the fortunate combat which he had made, he flung out of the theatre in such haste that, treading upon his own gown-skirt, he came tumbling down the stairs with his head forward, chafing and fuming, yea, and crying out that the people of Rome, lords of all nations, yielded more honour, and that out of a most vain and frivolous occasion, unto a sword-fencer, than to consecrated princes, or to himself there in personal presence.

36. No regard had he of chastity and cleanness, either in himself or in others. Marcus Lepidus, Mnester the pantomime [1], yea, and certain hostages he kept and loved, as the speech went, by way of reciprocal commerce in mutual impurity, doing and suffering against kind [2]. Valerius Catullus, a young gentleman descended from a family of consul's degree, complained and openly cried out that he was unnaturally by him abused, and that his very sides were wearied and tired out with his filthy company. Over and above the incests committed with his own sisters and his love so notorious of Pyrallis, that common and prostitute strumpet, there was not lightly [3] a dame or wife of any worship and reputation that

he forbare. And those for the most part would he invite
together with their husbands to supper, and as they passed
by at his feet peruse [4] and consider curiously ; taking leisure
thereto, after the manner of those that cheapen and buy
wares in overt market, yea, and with his hand chuck them
under the chin and make them to look up, if happily [5] any
of them in modesty and for bashfulness held down their faces.
And then, so often as he listed, out he goes from the refection-
room, and when he had called her unto him apart that liked
him best, he would within a little after (even whiles the
tokens were yet fresh testifying their wanton work) return,
and openly before all the company either praise or dispraise
her ; reckoning up every good or bad part of body and action
in that brutish business. To some of them himself sent bills
of divorcement in the name of their husbands absent, and
commanded the same to be set upon the file and stand in
public record.

37. In riotous and wasteful expense [a] he outwent the wits
and inventions of all the prodigal spendthrifts that ever
were, as having devised a new-found manner and use of
baines [Aug. 76], together with most strange and monstrous
kinds of meats and meals ; namely, to bathe with hot and cold
ointments [1], to drink off and quaff most precious and costly
pearls dissolved in vinegar, to set upon the board at feasts
loaves of bread and other viands to them before his guests
all of gold, saying commonly withal, that a man must either
be frugal or else Caesar. Moreover, for certain days together
he flung and scattered among the common people from the
louver of the stately basilica Julia, money in pieces of no mean
value. He built, moreover, tall galliasses of cedar timber [b],
with poops and sterns beset with precious stones, carrying
sails of sundry colours, containing in them baines, large
galleries, walking-places, and dining-chambers of great receit [2],
with vines also and trees bearing apples and other fruit in as
much variety ; wherein he would sit feasting in the very daytime among choirs of musicians and melodious singers, and so
sail along the coasts of Campania. In building of stately
palaces and manor-houses in the country he cast aside all
rules and orders, as one desirous to do nothing so much as
that which was thought impossible to be done. And therefore

he laid foundations of piles where the sea was most raging and
deep withal, and hewed rocks of most hard flint and rag[3] ;
plains also he raised even with mountains and by digging down
hill-tops levelled them equal with the plains, all with incredible
celerity, as punishing those who wrought but slowly even with
death.   In sum (and not to reckon up everything in particular) that infinite wealth and mass of treasure which Tiberius
Caesar left behind him, valued at 2700 millions[4] of sesterces,
he consumed to nothing before one whole year was gone
about.

38. Being exhausted therefore and grown exceeding bare,
he turned his mind to rapine and polling[1] by sundry and most
nice points of forged calumniation, of sales, of imposts, and
taxes.   He affirmed plainly that those held not by law and
rightfully the freedom of Rome city, whose ancestors had
obtained the grant thereof in these terms to them and their
posterity, unless they were sons ; for " by *posteri* (posterity),"
quoth he, " ought to be understood none beyond this degree of
descent."   And when the letters patent and grants of Julius
and Augustus (late emperors of sacred memory) were brought
forth as evidence, he bewailed[2] the same as old, past-date and
of no validity.   He charged those also with false valuation
and wrong certificate of their estates, unto whom there had
accrued afterward (upon what cause soever) any increase of
substance.

The last wills and testaments of such as had been principal centurions of the foremost cohorts, as many, I say, as
from the beginning of Tiberius' empire, had left neither the
said Tiberius nor himself heir, he cancelled for their un-
thankfulness ; of all the rest likewise he held the wills as
void and of none effect, in case any person would come forth
and say that they purposed and intended at their death to
make Caesar their heir.   Upon which fear that he put men
in, being now both by unknown persons unto him nominated[3]
heir among their familiar friends and also by parents among
their children, he termed them all mockers and cozeners, for
that after such nuncupative wills they continued still alive ;
and to many of them he sent certain dainties[4] empoisoned.
Now such causes as these abovesaid he heard judicially debated,
having beforehand set down a certain rate and sum of money,

for the raising whereof he sat judicially in court; and when that sum was fully made up, then, and not before, he would arise. And (as he was one who in no wise could abide any little delay) he condemned upon a time, by virtue of one definitive sentence, above forty persons, liable to judgement for divers and sundry crimes; making his boast withal unto his wife Caesonia, newly wakened out of her sleep, what a deal he had done while she took her noon's repose.

Having published an open port-sale [C. 50] of the residue remaining of furniture provided to set out all shows and games, he caused the said parcels to be brought forth and sold; setting the prices thereof himself and enhancing the same to such a prick[5], that some men, enforced to buy certain things at an extreme and exceeding rate (whereby they were impoverished and stripped of all their goods) cut their own veins and so bled to death. Well-known it is that, whiles Aponius Saturninus took a nap and slept among the seats and stalls where these sales were held, Gaius put the bedel[6] in mind not to let slip and overpass such an honourable person of praetor's degree as he was, "considering," quoth he, "that with his head he had so often nodded and made signs unto him"[7]; and thus taking that occasion, he never rested raising the price whiles he sat and nodded still, until there were fastened upon the man (ignorant, God wot, altogether of any such matter) thirteen sword-fencers, at 9,000,000 sesterces.

39. In Gaul likewise, when he had sold the jewels, ornaments, and household-stuff of his sisters[1] by him condemned, their servants also and very children[2] at excessive high prices, finding sweetness in the gain growing thereupon and thereby drawn on to proceed in that course, look, what furniture belonged to the old imperial court, he sent for it all from the city of Rome; for the carriage whereof he took up even the passengers' wagons that usually were hired, yea, the very jades which served mills and bake-houses[3], insomuch as many times there wanted bread in Rome; and a number of termers[4], such as had matters depending in law, for that they could not make their appearance in court at their days appointed, by absence lost their suits. For the selling of which furniture, there was no fraud, no guile, no deceitful allurement to be devised that he used not; onewhile checking each one for their avarice, and rating them because they were not ashamed to be richer than he ; otherwhiles making semblance of repentance, in that he permitted persons to have the buying of such things as belonged to the empire. Intelligence was given unto him that a certain wealthy and substantial man in that province had paid 200,000 sesterces unto his officers (who had the bidding of guests unto his own table) that by some subtle shift himself might be foisted in among other guests, neither was he discontented that the honour of supping with him was prized so high. The morrow after, therefore, as this provincial man was sitting at a public port-sale, he sent one of purpose to tender and deliver unto him some frivolous trifle (I wot not what) at the price of 200,000 sesterces, and withal to say unto him that take a supper he should with Caesar, as a guest invited by his own self.

40. He levied and gathered new tributes and imposts such as never were heard of before, at the first by the hands of publicans, and afterwards (by reason of the excessive gains that came in) by the centurions and tribunes of the praetorian cohorts. For he omitted no kind of thing, no manner of person, but he imposed some tribute upon them. For all cates that were to be sold throughout the city there was exacted a certain taxation and set payment. For actions, for suits, for judgements wheresoever commenced or drawn in writing, the fortieth part of the whole sum in suit went to his share in the name of a tribute, not without a penalty, in case any one were convinced[1] to have either grown to composition[2] or given the thing in question. The eighth part of the poor porters' and carriers' day's wages, out of the gets[3] also and takings of common strumpets, as much as they earned by once lying with a man, was paid *nomine tributi*. Moreover, to the chapter of the law this branch was annexed, that there should be liable to this tribute not only the parties themselves that by trade of harlotry got their living, but even they likewise who kept houses of bawdry ; as also that wedded persons should pay for their use of marriage.

41. After these and such-like taxes were denounced by proclamation, but not yet published abroad in writing, whenas through ignorance of the written law many trespasses and transgressions were committed [a], at length, upon instant demand of the people, he [published] indeed the act, but written in very small letter and within as narrow a place so that no man might exemplify [1] the same or copy it out. And to the end that there might be no kind of spoil and pillage which he attempted not, he set up a stews and brothel-house in the very palace, with many rooms and chambers therein distinguished asunder, and furnished according to the dignity and worth of that place. In it there stood to prostitute themselves married wives, youths, and springals [Tib. 6] freeborn. Then sent he all about to the frequented places, as well markets as halls of resort [2], certain nomenclators [3] to invite and call thither by name young men and old for to fulfil and satisfy their lust. All comers at their entrance paid money (as it were) for usury and interest [4]. Certain persons also were appointed to take note in open sight of their names, as of such as were good friends increasing the revenues of Caesar. And not disdaining so much as the lucre and vantage arising out of hazard and dice-play, he gained the more by cogging [5], lying, yea, and forswearing (of gamesters). And upon a time, having put over to his next fellow-gamester his own course, to cast the dice for him in his turn, out he goes into the courtyard and foregate of the house ; where, having espied two wealthy gentlemen of Rome passing by, he commanded them to be apprehended incontinently [6], and condemned in the confiscation of their goods, which done he returned in again, leaping for joy and making his vaunt, that he never had a luckier hand at dice.

42. But when he had once a daughter born, complaining then of his poverty and the heavy charges that lay upon him not only as emperor but also as a father, he gently took the voluntary contributions and benevolence of men toward the finding of the girl her food, as also for her dowry another day. He declared also by an edict that he would receive New-year's gifts ; and so he stood, the first day of January, in the porch or entry of his house Palatine, ready to take what pieces soever of money came, which the multitude of all sorts and degrees with full hands and bosoms [1] poured out before him. Finally, so far was he incensed with the desire of handling money, that oftentimes he would both walk bare-

footed up and down, yea, and wallow also a good while with his whole body upon huge heaps of coined gold pieces, spread here and there in a most large and open place.

43. In military matters and warlike affairs he never dealt but once, and that was not upon any intended purpose ; but what time as he had made a progress to Mevania, for to see the sacred grove and river of Clitumnus[1], being put in mind to supply and make up the number of the Batavians whom he had about him for his guard, it took him in the head to make an expedition into Germany. Neither deferred he this design, but, having levied from all parts a power consisting of legions and auxiliary forces, and taken musters most rigorously in every quarter, as also raised and gathered together victuals and provision of all sorts in that quantity as never any other before him the like, he put himself on his journey. Wherein he marched, one while in such hurry and haste, as that the praetorian cohorts were forced (against the manner and custom) to bestow their ensigns upon the sumpter beasts' backs and so to follow after ; otherwhiles, after such a slow and delicate manner, as that he would be carried in a litter upon eight men's shoulders, and exact of the common people inhabiting the neighbour cities adjoining that the highways might be swept and watered for the dust against his coming.

44. After that he was arrived once at the camp, to the end that he might show himself a sharp and severe captain, those lieutenants who had brought aid with the latest[1], out of divers and dissituate[2] parts, he discharged with ignominy and shame. But in the review of his army the most part of the centurions who had already served out their complete time, yea, and some whose term within very few days would have been fully expired, he deprived of their places, to wit, the leading of the foremost bands, finding fault forsooth with the old age and feebleness of every one. As for the rest, after he had given them a rebuke for their avarice, he abridged the fees and avails[3] due for their service performed, and brought that same down to the value of 6000 sesterces. And having achieved no greater exploit than taken to his mercy Adminius, the son of Cynobellinus, king of the Britons[4], who, being by his father banished, was fled over sea with a small power and train about him, he sent magnificent and glorious letters to Rome, as if the whole isle had been yielded into his hands; warning and willing the couriers ever and anon to ride forward in their wagon directly into the market-place and the Curia, and in no wise to deliver the said missives but in the temple of Mars unto the consuls, and that in a frequent [15] assembly of the senate.

45. Soon after, when there failed matter of war, he commanded a few Germans of the corps de guard[1] to be transported and hidden on the other side of the Rhine, and that news should be reported unto him after dinner in most tumultuous manner, that the enemy was come; which done, he made what haste he could, and together with some of his friends and part of the praetorian horsemen he entered the next wood, where, after he had cut off the heads of trees and adorned their bodies in manner of trophies, he returned into the camp by torch-light. As for those verily who followed him not in this service, he reproved and checked them for their timorousness and cowardice; but his companions and partners in this doughty victory he rewarded with a new kind and as strange a name of coronets, which being garnished and set out with the express form of Sun, Moon, and stars he called *exploratoriae*[a]. Again, whenas certain hostages were had away perforce out of the grammar school and privily sent before, he suddenly left his supper and with his men of arms pursued them as runaways, and being overtaken and caught again he brought them back as prisoners bound in chains, showing himself even in this interlude also beyond all measure insolent and intemperate. Now after he was come back to supper, those who brought him word that the battles[2] were rallied and come forward in safety he exhorted to sit down to meat, armed as they were, in their corslets; yea, and advertised them out of that most vulgar[3] verse of Virgil: *Durarent, secundisque rebus se servarent*[4],

> Still to endure in all assays
> And keep themselves for better days.

Moreover, amid these affairs, he rebuked most sharply in a proclamation the senate and people both in their absence;

for that whiles Caesar fought battles and was exposed to
so many perils, they could so unseasonably celebrate feasts,
haunt also the circus, the theatres, and their retiring places of
solace and pleasure.

46. Last of all, as if he meant now to make a final dispatch
for ever of the war, having embattelled his army upon the
Ocean shore, planted his ballistas and other engines of artil-
lery in their several places (and no man wist the while or
could imagine what he went about), all at once he commanded them to gather fish-shells, and therewith to fill their
headpieces and laps, terming them the spoils of the Ocean,
due to the Capitol and the Palatium. In token also and
memorial of this brave victory, he raised an exceeding high
turret, out of which, as from a watch-tower, there might
shine all night long lights and fires for the better direction
of ships at sea in their course. And after he had pronounced
publicly a donative to his soldiers, even a hundred good
deniers apiece, as if thereby he had surmounted all former
precedents of liberality, " Now go your ways," quoth he,
" with joy. Go your ways I say, enriched and wealthy [1]."

47. Turning his mind after this to the care of his triumph,
he selected and set apart for the pomp [15] (over and above
the captives and runnagate [1] barbarians) the tallest men of
stature also that were to be found in Gaul, and every one
that (as he said himself) was *axiothriambeutos*, that is, worthy
to be seen in a triumph, yea, and some of the nobles and
principal persons of that nation ; whom he compelled not
only to colour the hair of their heads yellow like burnished
gold and to wear the same long, but also to learn the Germans'
language, and to bear barbarous names. He gave command
also, that the galleys with three ranks of oars, wherein he had
embarked and entered the Ocean, should be conveyed to
Rome, a great part of the way by land. He wrote likewise
unto his procurators and officers to provide the furniture of
his triumph with as little cost as might be, but yet the same in
as ample manner as never before was the like, seeing they had
both might and right to seize all men's goods into their hands.

48. Before his departure out of that province, he intended
the execution of a horrible and abominable design, even
to put to sword those legions, which long ago upon the decease

of Augustus had made a commotion, because, forsooth, they had beset both his father Germanicus their captain and himself also, then an infant. And being hardly and with much ado reclaimed from such a rash and inconsiderate project, yet could he by no means be stayed, but stiffly persisted in a full mind and will to tithe them[1]. When he had summoned them therefore to a public assembly unarmed and without their swords, which they had put off and bestowed here and there, he environed them with his cavalry all-armed. But seeing once that many of them, suspecting whereabout he went, slipped away in sundry places for to resume their weapons if any violence were offered, himself abandoned the assembly and fled, taking his direct way immediately to the city of Rome, diverting all his bitterness and cruelty upon the senate, whom, to avert from himself the odious rumours of so great and shameful villainies, he openly threatened ; complaining among other matters that he was by them defrauded and put by [C. 28] his just and due triumph, whereas himself but a little before had intimated and denounced[2] upon pain of death, that they should not make nor meddle in any matter about his honours.

49. Being encountered therefore and met upon the way by ambassadors from that most honourable order[1], entreating him to make speed, with a most loud voice, " Come I will," quoth he, " I will come, I say, and this with me here," beating oft upon the sword's hilt, which he wore by his side. He made it known also by an edict that he returned indeed, but it was to them alone who wished it, namely, the degree of gentlemen and the common people, for himself would be no longer a citizen or prince to the senate. He commanded moreover that not one of the senators should meet him. And thus, either omitting quite or putting off his triumph, he entered the city riding ovant [Aug. 22], upon his very birthday, and within four months after came to his end, having attempted and done notable outrages and very great villainies, but plotting still and practising much greater. For he had purposed to remove his imperial court to Antium, and afterwards to Alexandria[2], but having massacred first the most choice and chief persons of both degrees[3]. And that no man may seem to doubt hereof, there were in his secret cabinet[4] found two books bearing divers titles. The one had for the inscription *Gladius*, the sword, the other, *Pugio*, that is to say, the dagger ; they contained, both of them, the marks and names of such as were appointed to death. There was found besides a big chest full of divers and sundry poisons, which, soon after being by Claudius drowned in the seas, infected and poisoned the same, not without the deadly bane of fishes killed therewith, which the tide cast up to the next shores.

50. Of stature he was very tall, pale, and wan-coloured, of body gross and without all good-making ; his neck and shanks exceeding slender ; his eyes sunk in his head, and his temples hollow, his forehead broad, and the same furrowed and frowning ; the hair of his head growing thin, and none at all about his crown ; in all parts else hairy he was and shaggy. It was therefore taken for a heinous and capital offence, either to look upon him as he passed by from a higher place, or once but to name a goat upon any occasion whatsoever. His face and visage, being naturally stern and grim, he made of purpose more crabbed and hideous, composing and dressing it at a looking-glass all manner of ways to seem more terrible and to strike greater fear.

He was neither healthful in body nor stood sound in mind. Being [as] a child much troubled with the falling sickness, in his youth [he was] patient of labour and travail, yet so as that ever and anon, upon a sudden fainting that came upon him, he was scarce able to go[1], to stand, to arise, to recover himself, and to bear up his head. The infirmity of his mind both himself perceived, and oftentimes also was minded to go aside (unto Anticyra[2]), there to purge his brain thoroughly. It is for certain thought that poisoned he was with a potion given unto him by his wife Caesonia, which indeed was a love medicine, but such a one as cracked his wits and enraged him. He was troubled most of all with want of sleep ; for he slept not above three hours in a night, and in those verily he took no quiet repose, but fearful and scared with strange illusions and fantastical imaginations ; as who, among the rest, dreamed upon a time that he saw the very form and resemblance of the sea talking with him. And hereupon, for a great part of the night, what with tedious wakefulness and weariness of lying, one while sitting up in his bed, another while roaming and wandering to and fro in his galleries (which were of an exceeding length), he was wont to call upon and look still for the daylight.

51. I should not do amiss if unto this mind's sickness of his I attributed the vices which in one and the same subject [1] were of a most different nature, to wit, excessive confidence, and contrariwise overmuch fearfulness. For he that set so light by the gods and despised them as he did, yet at the least thunder and lightning used to wink close with both eyes, to enwrap also and cover his whole head ; but if the same were greater and somewhat extraordinary, to start out of his bed, to creep and hide himself under the bed-stead [a]. During his peregrination verily and travel through Sicily, after he had made but a scorn and mockery at the miracles and strange sights in many parts there, he fled suddenly by night from Messana, as affrighted with the smoke and rumbling noise of the top of Aetna. And he that against the barbarians was so full of threats and menaces, whenas beyond the river Rhine he rode in a German chariot between the straits [2], and the army marched in thick squadrons together, by occasion only that one said there would be no small trouble and hurly-burly, in case the enemy from any place appeared in sight, forthwith he mounted on horseback and turned hastily to the bridges ; but finding them full of camp-slaves and carriages wherewith they were choked [3], as one impatient of any delay, he was from hand to hand and over men's heads conveyed to the other side of the water.

Soon after likewise, hearing of the revolt and rebellion of Germany, he provided to flee, and for the better means of flight prepared and rigged ships, resting and staying himself upon this only comfort ; that he should yet have provinces beyond sea remaining for him, in case the conquerors, following the train of their victory, either seized the hill-tops of the Alps (as sometimes the Cimbrians), or possessed themselves of the very city of Rome, as the Senones in times past did. Hereupon I verily believe that the murderers of him afterwards devised this shift, namely, to hold up his soldiers with a loud lie when they were in an uproar, and to bear them in hand[4] that he laid violent hands on himself, affrighted at the fearful news of the field lost.

52. As for his apparel, his shoes and other habit, he wore them neither after his own country guise, nor in a civil fashion[1], no, nor so much as in manlike manner, nor yet always, I may tell you, sorting with the state and condition of a mortal wight. Being clad oftentimes in cloaks of needlework and embroidered with divers colours, and the same set out with precious stones ; in a coat also with long sleeves, and wearing bracelets withal, he would come abroad into the city. Sometime you should see him in his silks, and veiled all over in a loose mantle of fine sendal[2] with a train[3] ; onewhile going in Greek slippers[4], or else in buskins, otherwhiles in a simple pair of brogues or high shoes, such as common soldiers employed in espial used. Now and then also was he seen shod with women's pumps[5]. But for the most part he showed himself abroad with a golden beard[a], carrying in his hand either a thunder-bolt or a three-tined mace[6][b], or else a warder[7] or rod called caduceus[c] (the ensigns all and ornaments of the gods), yea, and in the attire and array of Venus. Now for his triumphal robes and ensigns, he used verily to wear and bear them continually, even before any warlike expedition, and sometime the cuirass withal of Alexander the Great, fetched out of his sepulchre and monument.

53. Of all the liberal sciences he gave his mind least to deep literature and sound learning, but most to eloquence, albeit he was by nature fair-spoken and of a ready tongue[1]. Certes, if it had been to plead and declaim against one, were he angered once, he had both words and sentences at will. His action, gesture, and voice also served him well, insomuch as for very heat and earnestness of speech uneth[2] was he able to stand his ground and keep still in one place, yet might he be heard nathless of them that stood afar off. When he was about to make an oration, his manner was to threaten in these terms, namely, that he would draw forth and let drive at his adversary the keen weapon and dart of his night-study by candlelight ; contemning the milder and more piked[3] kind of writing so far forth as that he said of Seneca, a writer in those days most accepted, that his compositions which he made were plain exercises to be shown only, and was no better him-

self than sand without lime. His wont was also to answer by
writing the orations of those orators who had pleaded well and
with applause ; to meditate and devise as well accusations and
defences of great persons who were impeached in the senate,
and, according as his style framed, either to overcharge and
depress, or to ease and relieve every man with his sentence,
having called thither by virtue of his edicts the degree also of
gentlemen to hear him speak.

54. The arts moreover and masteries[1] of other kinds he
practised right studiously, even those of most different
nature. A professed sword-fencer[2] he was and a good
charioteer, a singer withal and a dancer. Fight he would
even in earnest with weapons at sharpe [27], and run a race
with chariots in the open circuses, which he built in many
places. As for chanting and dancing, he was so hotly set
thereupon that he could not forbear so much as in the public
theatres and show-places but that he would both fall a-
singing with the tragedian as he pronounced, and also counterfeit and openly imitate the gesture of the player, as it were by
way of praise or correction. And verily, for no other cause
proclaimed he (as it is thought) a wake or vigil all night long,
that very day on which he was murdered, but that by taking
the opportunity of the night's licentiousness he might therewith begin to enter upon the stage. And divers times danced
he by night ; but once above the rest, having raised out of
their beds three honourable persons that had been consuls
and sent for them at the relief of the second watch into
the palace, whiles they were much afraid and doubted some
extremity, he caused them to be placed aloft upon a scaffold,
and then suddenly, with a great noise of hautboys and sound
of shawms or cymbals[3], out cometh he leaping forth with
a pall and cassock reaching down to his ankles ; and after
he had danced out the measures to a song, vanished and
went his way again. Now this man, so apt a scholar as
he was to learn all other feats, had no skill at all in swimming[4].

55. Look, whom he took a love and liking unto he favoured
them all exceedingly and beyond all reason. Mnester the
famous pantomime[1], he affected so much, as that he bashed[2]
not to kiss him even in the open theatre ; and if any, whiles
he[3] was dancing or acting a part, made never so little noise

and interrupted him, he commanded the party to be pulled out of his place and with his own hand scourged him. A gentleman of Rome chanced to keep some stirre [4] whiles the said Mnester was upon the stage ; unto him he sent word peremptorily by a centurion to depart without delay and go down to Ostia (there to take sea) and so to carry unto king Ptolemy as far as into Mauritania his letters in writing-tables, the tenor whereof was this : " To this bearer, whom I have sent hither to you, see you do neither good nor harm." Certain fencers called *Thraces* [5] he made captains over those Germans that were of his guard and squires to his body. As for the *mirmillones* [6], he deprived them of their armour. One of them named Columbus fortuned to foil his concurrent [35], howbeit he had gotten before some small hurt ; he made no more ado but put poison into the wound, which thereupon he called Columbinum [7]. So much addicted and devoted was he to the green faction [8] of charioteers that day by day he would take his suppers and make his abode in their hostelry [9]. Upon Eutychus a chariot-driver [10] he bestowed in hospital gifts [11] at a certain banquet two millions of sesterces. To one of their chariot-steeds named Incitatus [12], for whose sake (because he should not be disquieted) he was wont, the day before the games in the circus, by his soldiers to command the neighbours there adjoining to keep silence, besides a stable all-built of marble stone for him, and a manger made of ivory, over and above his caparison also and harness of purple, together with a brooch or pendant jewel of precious stones at his poictrel [13], he allowed a house and family of servants, yea, and household-stuff to furnish the same, all to this end that guests invited in his name might be more finely and gaily entertained. It is reported, moreover, that he meant to prefer him unto a consulship.

56. As he rioted thus and fared outrageously, many there were who wanted no heart and good-will to assault his person. But after one or two conspiracies detected, when others for default of opportunity held off and made stay, two at length complotted and imparted one unto the other their design, yea, and performed it, not without the privity of the mightiest freedmen about him and the captains of his guard. The reason was for that they also, being nominated (although untruly) as accessory to a certain conspiracy, perceived themselves suspected and odious unto him therefor. For, even immediately, by sequestering them apart into a secret place he brought upon them great hatred, protesting with his sword drawn, that die he would upon his own hand, if they also thought him worthy of death. Neither ceased he from that time forward to accuse one unto the other, and to set them all together by the ears. Now when these conspirators were resolved and agreed to assail him during the Palatine games [a], as he departed thence out of the theatre at noontide, Cassius Chaerea, tribune of the praetorian cohort, took upon him to play the first part in this action ; even he whom, being now far stept in years, Gaius [1] was wont to frump [2] and flout in most opprobrious terms as a wanton and effeminate person, and one while, when he came unto him for a watchword, to give him Priapus or Venus, another while, if upon any occasion he rendered thanks, to reach out unto him his hand, not only fashioned but wagging also after an obscene and filthy manner.

57. Many prodigious signs were seen, presaging his future death and murder. The image of Jupiter at Olympia, which his pleasure was to be disjointed and translated to Rome, did set up all on a sudden such a mighty laughter that the workmen about it let their engines and vices slip and so ran all away. And straightway came there one in place whose name also was Cassius, that avouched he had warning and commandment in a dream to sacrifice a bull unto Jupiter. The Capitol [a] in Capua upon the ides of March was smitten with lightning ; likewise at Rome the porter's lodge belonging to the prince's palace. And there wanted not some who gave their conjecture that by the one prodigy was portended danger to the master of the house from his guard and the squires of his person ; by the other some notable murder again, such as in times past had been committed upon the same day [b]. Also Sulla the astrologer, when Gaius asked his counsel and opinion as touching the horoscope of his nativity, told him plain that most certain and inevitable death approached near at hand. Semblably [15] the oracle at Antium gave him a caveat to beware of Cassius. For which very cause he had taken order [8] and given express commandment that Cassius

Longinus, proconsul then in Asia, should be killed, not remembering that the foresaid Chaerea had to name Cassius.

The day before he lost his life he dreamt that he stood in heaven close unto the throne of Jupiter, and that Jupiter spurned him with the great toe of his right foot, and therewith threw him down headlong to the earth. There went also for current prodigies and foretokens of his fall even those occurrents that happened unto him that very day, a little before he was murdered. As himself sacrificed, besprinkled he was with the blood of the fowl phoenicopterus [22]. And Mnester, the skilful actor abovenamed, represented that very tragedy [1], which whilom Neptolemus the tragedian acted at the solemnity of those games, wherein Philip, king of the Macedonians [2], was killed. And whenas in the show or interlude entitled *Laureolus* [c], wherein the chief player, making haste to get away out of the ruin [3], vomited blood, many more of the actors in a second degree strove [4] a-vie to give some trial and experiment of the like cunning, the whole stage by that means flowed with blood. Prepared there was likewise against night another show, wherein the dark fables reported of hell and the infernal spirits there were to be exhibited and unfolded by Egyptians and Aethiopians [5].

58. Upon the ninth day before the kalends of February [1], about one of the clock after noon, doubting with himself whether he should rise to dinner or no (for that his stomach was yet raw and weak upon a surfeit of meat taken the day before), at last by the persuasion of his friends he went forth. Now, whenas in the very cloister [2] through which he was to pass certain boys of noble birth sent for out of Asia (to sing hymns and to skirmish martially upon the stage) were preparing themselves, he stood still and stayed there to view and encourage them ; and but that the leader and chieftain of that crew said he was very cold, he would have returned and presently [22] exhibited that show. But what befell after this is reported two manner of ways. Some say that, as he spake unto the said boys, Chaerea came behind his back, and with a drawing blow grievously wounded his neck with the edge of his sword, giving him these words before, *Hoc age* [3], Mind this ; whereupon Cornelius Sabinus, another of the conspirators, encountered him afront and ran him through in the breast. Others write that Sabinus, after the multitude about him was voided [4] by the centurions (who were privy to the conspiracy), called for a watchword, as the manner is of soldiers, and when Gaius gave him the word, Jupiter, Chaerea cried out aloud, *Accipe ratum*, Here take it sure [5] : and with that, as he looked behind him, with one slash cut his jaw quite through. Also, as he lay on the ground and drawing up his limbs together cried still that he was yet alive, the rest of their complices with thirty wounds dispatched and made an end of him. For this mot, *Repete*, Strike again, was the signal of them all ; some of them also thrust their swords through his privy members. At the very first noise and outcry, his litter-bearers came running to help with their litter-staves ; soon after, the Germans that were the squires of his body came in, and as they slew some of the murderers, so they killed certain senators also that were mere innocent.

59. He lived twenty-nine years and ruled the empire three years ten months and eight days. His dead corpse was conveyed secretly into the Lamian hortyards [1], where, being scorched only or half-burnt in a tumultuary and hasty funeral fire, covered it was with a few turfs of earth lightly cast over it, but afterwards by his sisters now returned out of exile taken up, burnt to ashes, and interred. It is for certain known and reputed that, before this complement [2] was performed, the keepers of those hortyards were troubled with the walking of spirits and ghosts ; and in that very house [3] wherein he was murdered there passed not a night without some terror or fearful object, until the very house itself was consumed with fire. There died together with him both his wife Caesonia, stabbed with a sword by a centurion, and also a daughter of his, whose brains were dashed out against a wall.

60. What the condition and state was of those days, any man may gather even by these particulars. For neither when this massacre was divulged and made known abroad, men gave credit by and by thereto, but there went a suspicion that Gaius himself had feigned and given out a rumour of this murder, by that means to sound men's minds and find how they stood affected unto him ; nor yet had those conspirators destined the empire to any one. And the senators,

in recovering their ancient freedom again, accorded so as that
the consuls assembled them not at the first into the Curia[1],
because it bore the name Julia[2], but into the Capitol ; yea,
and some of them, when their turns came to speak, opined
that the memory of the Caesars should be utterly abolished and
rased out, giving advice to pull down their temples. Moreover, this hath been observed and noted especially, that the
Caesars, who had to their forename Gaius[3], beginning at him
first who was slain in the troublesome days of Cinna, died all of
them a violent death.

THE HISTORY OF TIBERIUS
CLAUDIUS DRUSUS CAESAR

1. As touching Drusus, father to this Claudius Caesar, which
Drusus was in times past forenamed Decimus and afterwards
Nero, dame Livia, wedded unto Augustus even when she was
great with child, brought him into the world within three
months after the said marriage, and folk suspected that
begotten he was in adultery by his (supposed) step-father
himself[1]. Certes, presently [Cal. 22] after his birth, this
verse went rife in every man's mouth, τοῖς εὐτυχοῦσι καὶ
τρίμηνα παιδία,

> On persons great this fortune doth attend,
> That children they may have at three months' end.

This Drusus, in the honourable place of quaestor and praetorship, being lord-general of the Rhaetian and so forth
of the German war, was the first Roman captain that sailed
in the northern Ocean, and on the farther side of the Rhine
cast those trenches of a straung and infinite work which
yet at this day be called Drusinae[2]. Many a time he put
the enemy to sword, and when he had driven him as far as
to the inmost deserts, gave not over chasing and pursuing
until there appeared unto him the likeness of a barbarian
woman[3], more portly than a mortal wight, which in the
Latin tongue forbade him to follow the train of victory
any farther. For which acts achieved he enjoyed the honour
of a petty triumph[4] and had the triumphal ornaments granted
unto him. After his praetorship he entered immediately
upon the consulate, and having enterprised a second expedition thither, fell sick and died in his summer camp, which
thereupon took the name of *Castra scelerata*[5][a]. His corpse
by the principal citizens and burgesses of the free boroughs
and colonies, by the decuries also and orders of the scribes[6]
(who met them in the way and received it at their hands)

was conveyed to Rome and buried in Mars' Field. Howbeit the army reared in honour of him an honorary tomb [7] (or stately hearse), about the which, every year afterwards upon a certain set day, the soldiers should run at tilt, keep jousting and tournament, the cities likewise and states of Gaul sacrifice and make public supplications to the gods. Moreover the senate, among many other honours, decreed for him a triumphal arch of marble, with trophies thereto, in the street [8] Appia, as also the surname of Germanicus to him and his posterity for ever.

Furthermore he is thought to have carried a mind no less glorious than civil and popular [9]. For over and above the conquests gained of his enemies, he won also from them royal spoils [10], and oftentimes to the uttermost hazard of his life coursed and chased the general of the Germans all over the field ; neither dissembled he, but gave it out that one day he would restore unto the commonwealth their ancient state and liberty again. Whereupon, I suppose, some presume to write that Augustus had him in jealousy and suspicion, called him home out of his province, and because he lingered and delayed his return, made him away by poison. Which verily put down I have, because I would not seem to pretermit such a matter, rather than for that I think it either true or probable ; considering that Augustus both loved him while he was alive so entirely, as that he always ordained him fellow-heir with his sons (like as he openly professed upon a time in the senate-house), and also commended him after his death so highly, that in a solemn oration before the body of the people he prayed unto the gods to vouchsafe his own Caesars to be like unto him, and to grant himself one day such an end as they had given him. And not contented with this, that he had engraven upon his tomb an epitaph in verse which he himself composed, he wrote also the history of his life in prose. By Antonia the younger he became father verily of many children, but three only he left behind him at his death, namely, Germanicus, Livilla, and Claudius.

2. This Claudius was born at Lugdunum, in the year when Julius Antonius and Fabius Africanus were consuls, upon the kalends of August, that very day on which the altar was first dedicated there unto Augustus, and named he was

Tiberius Claudius Drusus; and a while after, when his elder
brother was adopted into the family Julia, he assumed into
his style the surname of Germanicus. Being left an infant
by his father, all the time in manner of his childhood and
youth, piteously handled he was with sundry diseases, and
those tough and such as stuck long by him; insomuch as,
being dulled and enfeebled thereby both in mind and body,
he was not thought in the very progress of riper age sufficient and capable of any public office or private charge;
yea, and many a day after that he came to full years and
had sued out his livery[1], he was at the dispose of another,
even under a pedagogue and governor, whom in a certain
book himself complaineth of, terming him a barbarous fellow
and no better sometime than a muleteer[2], set over him of
purpose to chastise and punish him most cruelly for every
light cause and occasion whatsoever. By reason of this his
sickness, both at the sword-play which he and his brother
jointly exhibited in memorial of their father, he sat as president
(not after the accustomed manner) lapped in a cloak; and
also upon his commencement day [Cal. 10], when he was to
put on his virile gown, about midnight, without any honourable attendance and solemn train, brought he was in a litter
into the Capitol[a].

3. Howbeit, from his very childhood, he employed no mean
study in the liberal sciences, and oftentimes gave good proof
even in public place of his proceedings in them all; yet
could he never for all that reach to any degree of dignity,
or yield better hope of himself for the time to come. His
mother Antonia was wont to call him *Portentum hominis*,
a monster and fantastical show of a man, as if he had not
been finished but only begun by Nature; and if she reproved
any one for his foolishness she would say he was more sottish
than her son Claudius. His grandmother Augusta[1] thought
always most basely of him, as who used neither to speak unto
him but very seldom, nor to admonish him, unless it were in
some sharp and short writing, or else by messengers going between. His sister Livilla, when she heard that he should
be one day emperor, openly and with a loud voice detested[2]
and wished far from the people of Rome so hard and miserable a fortune.

4. And no marvel : for to the end that it might be more certainly known what opinion his great-uncle Augustus [1] had of him both ways [2], I have set down certain articles and principal points gathered out of his own epistles. " I have," quoth he, " my good Livia, talked and conferred with Tiberius as you charged me, about this, namely, What is to be done to your nephew [Cal. 8] Tiberius, at the solemnity of the games in honour of Mars [3] ?   Now, we are both agreed that it must be determined and set down once for all what course we should take and follow with him ; for, if he be ἄρτιος [4], and as I may so say ὁλόκληρος [5], what doubt need we to make but that he is to be trained and brought by the same opportunities of time and degrees [6] by which his brother was ?   But if we perceive him ἠλαττῶσθαι καὶ βεβλάφθαι καὶ εἰς τὴν τοῦ σώματος καὶ εἰς τὴν τῆς ψυχῆς ἀρτιότητα [7] : we must not minister matter to men, τὰ τοιαῦτα σκώπτειν καὶ μυκτηρίζειν εἰωθόσι [8], for to deride both him and us. For we shall ever find trouble and vexation enough, in case of every occasion of time presented unto us we should deliberate, μὴ προϋποκείμενον ἡμῖν [9], whether we think him able to manage honourable offices in the State or no.   Howbeit for the present (concerning such things whereof you ask my advice), I mislike it not that he have the charge of the priests' dining-chamber during these games of Mars aforesaid, so that he will suffer himself to be admonished and schooled by Silvanus' son, a man allied unto him, that he do nothing which may be noted [10] or derided. That he should behold the games in the circus from out of the pulvinar [11] in no wise can I allow ; for, being exposed so to the sight of men in the very forefront of the theatre, he will be eyed and observed.   Neither like we in any hand [12] that he should go up the Alban mount or abide at Rome during the Latin holidays [13]; for if he be able to accompany and follow his brother to that mountain, why is he not as well made provost of the city the while [14] ?   Thus, my Livia, you have our opinions delivered, as who are fully resolved that once for all somewhat must be put down as touching the whole matter, lest we be evermore wavering between hope and fear.   You may also, if it please you, impart unto our (niece) Antonia thus much of this our letter."

Again, in another epistle : " As for young Tiberius[15], I for my part, while you are absent, will daily invite him to supper, that he may not sup alone with his Sulpicius and Athenodorus. And I could wish with all my heart that he would more soundly and less μετεώρως [16] make choice of some special one, whose gesture, habit, and gang he might, silly soul as he is, imitate :

'Ατυχεῖ λίαν ἐν τοῖσι σπουδαίοις πάνυ.
He comes far short (when he is matched) with men of deep understanding.[17]

But look, when his mind is not wandering out of the way, the generosity [18] of his heart appeareth sufficiently." Likewise in a third letter : " Your nephew Tiberius, my sweet Livia, if I do not wonder that, when he declaimed, that he could please and content me, I pray God I be dead. For how he that in his daily talk speaketh so ἀσαφῶς [19] should be able, when he declaimeth, to deliver his mind and what he hath to say σαφῶς [20] I cannot see." Neither is there any doubt to be made but that after all this Augustus ordained and left him endowed with no honourable office, save only the sacerdotal dignity of augur ; nay, he nominated him not so much as his heir but in a third degree and descent, even among those that were well-near strangers, and that in a sixth part only of his substance ; and by way of legacy bequeathed unto him not above 800,000 sesterces.

5. Tiberius his uncle conferred upon him, when he sued for honourable dignities, the ornaments of consuls [1]. But when he instantly demanded still not imaginary but true magistracies indeed, he wrote back unto him in his writing-tables thus much only, that he had sent unto him forty pieces of gold [2] to spend at the feast Saturnalia, and to bestow in puppets and trifling gauds [3] at the same time. Then, and not before, casting aside all hope of preferment and real dignities, he betook himself to rest and quietness of life, lying close onewhile within hortyards of pleasure and in a manor-house without the city, and lurking otherwhiles in a withdrawing place out of the way in Campania. And by his daily acquaintance and company-keeping with most base and abject persons, besides the old infamous note [4] of sluggishness and foolishness he incurred an ill name for drunkenness and dice-play; notwithstanding that, all the while he thus led his life, he never wanted the public attendance and reverent regard of men seeking unto him.

6. The order of gentlemen elected him twice for their patron in an embassy that was to be sent and delivered in their own behalf; once when the consuls required to have the carriage of Augustus his corpse upon their own shoulders to Rome, a second time when they were to congratulate with the same consuls for the suppressing of Sejanus. Moreover, they were wont in shows and in the theatre, when he came in place, to arise up and lay off their mantles[1] in respective [Cal. 26] honour of him. The senate also ordained that to the ordinary number of the priests or guild-brethren called Augustales, who were by lot chosen, he should be admitted extraordinarily; and soon after, that his house, which by misfortune of a skarfire [Aug. 25] he had lost, should at the city's charges be re-edified; as also the privilege to deliver his mind and opinion in the senate among those who had been consuls. Which decree of theirs was reversed and annulled, whiles Tiberius[2] alleged by way of excuse his imbecility, and promised to repair the foresaid loss out of his own private purse and liberality. Yet when he lay upon his death-bed, he both named him among his heirs in a third range and in a third part of his estate, and also bequeathed him a legacy of 2,000,000 sesterces; yea, recommended him besides by name unto the armies, to the senate likewise and people of Rome, in the rank of other his especial friends and kinsfolk.

7. At length under Gaius[1] his brother's son, who at his first coming to the empire sought by all manner of enticing allurements to gain the good opinion of a bountiful and gracious prince, he began first to bear office of state, and continued consul together with him for the space of two months; and it fortuned at his first entrance into the Forum with his knitches of rods, that an eagle, soaring thereby, settled upon his right shoulder. He was pricked also and allotted unto a second consulship against the fourth year following. Divers times he sat as president of the solemn shows in Gaius his turn, what time the people cried *Feliciter*[2], partly to the emperor's uncle, and in part to Germanicus his brother.

8. Yet lived he nevertheless subject to the contumelious reproaches of the world ; for if at any time he came somewhat with the latest and after the hour appointed to a supper, hardly and with much ado was there any room made for to receive him, and not before he had gone round about the tables where guests were set, for to find a place. Likewise, whensoever he took a nap and fell asleep after meat (which was an ordinary thing with him) the buffoons [1] and jesters about him made good sport, pelting him with olive- and date-stones ; otherwhiles also they would by way of merriment awaken him with the clap of a ferula or lash of some whip. They were wont likewise to glove his hands (as he lay snorting asleep) with his shoes [2], that as he suddenly awaked he might rub his face and eyes therewith.

9. Neither verily could he avoid divers dangerous troubles. First in his very consulship ; for, being behindhand and over-slack in taking order [Cal. 8] with the workmen for the making and erecting of Nero and Drusus' statues, who were Caesar's [1] brethren, he had like to have been removed and put out of that honourable office : afterwards, as either any stranger or one of his own house informed aught against him, he was continually and sundry manner of ways molested. But whenas the conspiracy of Lepidus and Gaetulicus [2] came to light, being sent among other ambassadors to congratulate Gaius in the name of the city, he was in jeopardy of his very life, whiles Gaius chafed and fumed with great indignation that his uncle chiefly of all others was sent unto him, as it were to govern a child ; insomuch as some have not stuck [Cal. 25] to report in writing that he was turned also headlong into the river in his clothes and all as he came apparelled. From which time forward never spake he to any matter proposed in the senate but last of all those that had been consuls, as being in reproachful wise and to his disgrace asked his opinion after them all. There was received [3] likewise against him the examination of a forged will, wherein himself also had been a witness and put to his seal. Last of all, he was forced to disburse 8,000,000 sesterces for a fine or income [4] at his entrance into a new priesthood ; by occasion whereof

his estate being so much decayed, driven he was to those
straits that, for his disability to keep credit and satisfy the
debt due unto the chamber of the city [5], by an edict of the
city treasurers [a] according to the law *praediatoria* he hung
[it] up [6] to be sold in *vacuum* [7].

10. Having passed the greatest part of his time in running
through these and such-like troubles, at length, in the fiftieth
year of his age, he attained to the empire, and that by a
strange and wonderful hap. Being among others excluded
by the conspirators that laid wait for Gaius' life, what time
they voided [Cal. 58] all the company about his person, under
a colour as if he desired to be apart himself alone in some
by-place, this Claudius had stept aside and retired into a
lodging or parlour called Hermaeum ; and not long after,
being affrighted at the rumour of that murder, slyly crept
forth and conveyed himself up into a solar [1] next adjoining,
and there hid himself between the hangings that hung before
the door. Whiles he lurked close there, a common soldier,
chancing to run to and fro that way, espied his feet, and by
earnest inquiry and asking who he was happened to take
knowledge of him ; who having drawn him forth of the place
(whenas for fear he fell down humbly at his feet and took hold
of his knees) saluted him by the name of emperor. From
thence he brought him immediately to his other fellow-
soldiers, who as yet stood wavering and wist not what to do
but fare and fume [2]. By them was he bestowed in a litter
and, for that his own servants were fled scattering here and
there, they also by turns one after another supported the said
litter upon their shoulders ; and so was he brought into the
praetorian camp, all sad and amazed for fear, pitied also by the
multitude that met him on the way, as if some innocent had
been haled to execution.

Being received within the trench and rampire [C. 35],
lodged he was all night among the soldiers' watch with less
hope of his a good deal than confidence [3]. For the consuls,
together with the senate and the cohorts of the city-soldiers,
seized the Forum and the Capitol, with a purpose to claim and
recover the common liberty ; and when himself was sent for by
tribunes of the commons into the Curia, to sit in consultation
and give his advice about those matters that were thought

good to be propounded, he made answer that detained he was perforce and by constraint. But the next morrow, whenas the senate grew more cold and slack in following and executing their foresaid projects (by reason of their tedious trouble and discord who dissented in opinion), whiles the multitude also, standing round about, demanded by this time one ruler and him by name, he called the soldiers in armour[4] to an assembly and suffered them to take their oath of allegiance and swear to maintain his imperial dignity ; [and] therewith promised unto them 1500[0] sesterces[5] apiece, the first of all the Caesars that obliged unto him the soldiers' fealty by a fee and reward.

11. Having once established his empire, he thought nothing more dear and behoveful[1] than to abolish the remembrance of those two days, wherein there was some doubtful question about the change and alteration of the State. Of all deeds and words therefore which had passed during that time he made an act there should be a general pardon and perpetual oblivion ; which also he made good and performed accordingly. Only some few colonels and centurions, out of that crew which conspired against Gaius, he put to the sword, as well for example sake, as for that he had certain intelligence they required to have him also murdered. Then presently turning and bending his mind to the duties of piety and kindness, he took up no form of oath, either with more devout religion or oftener, than by the name of Augustus. He gave order that for his grandmother Livia there should by decree be granted divine honours, as also in the stately pomp [Cal. 15] of the circus solemnities a chariot drawn with elephants, like unto that of Augustus ; semblably [15], for the souls of his own parents departed, public dirges and funeral feasts, and more than so, particularly in the honour of his father circus-plays and games every year upon his birthday ; and in memorial of his mother, a coach to be led and drawn along through the circus, and the surname of Augusta, which by his grandmother was refused. In remembrance of his brother[2] (to celebrate whose memorial he omitted no occasion) he exhibited a Greek comedy at the solemn games held in Naples, where by sentence of the umpires and judges he received a coronet therefor. He suffered not so much

as M. Antonius[3] to pass unhonoured, nor without a thankful
mention and remembrance, protesting one time, and that by
an edict, that so much the more earnest he was to have men
celebrate the birthday of his father Drusus, because upon the
same day his grandfather Antony also was born. The marble
arch, decreed verily in times past by the senate to be erected
for Tiberius[4] near unto the theatre of Pompey, but forelet
[Cal. 21], he finished. And albeit he abrogated and repealed
all the acts of Gaius, yet the day of his death, although it were
the beginning of his empire, he forbade to be registered among
feasts in the calendar.

12. But in honouring himself he was sparie[1] and carried a
civil [Cal. 52] modesty. The forename of emperor he forbare ;
excessive honours he refused ; the espousals[2] of his own
daughter, the birthday also of his nephew her son he passed
over in silence, only celebrating it with some private ceremony and religious complements [5] within [the] house. He
restored no banished person but by the authority and warrant of the senate. That he might bring with him into
the Curia the captain of the guard and tribunes of the soldiers ;
item, that those acts might be ratified and stand in force,
which his procurators had set down in judging of causes, he
obtained by entreaty. He made suit unto the consuls for a
licence to hold fairs and markets for his own private manors
and lands. In commissions and examinations of causes held
by the magistrates, he would oftentimes be personally present
and sit as one of the commissioners. To the same magistrates,
when they exhibited any plays or games, himself also with the
rest of the multitude would arise up and both with hand and
voice[3] do them honour. When the tribunes of the commons repaired unto him before the front of his tribunal,
he excused himself unto them for that, by reason of strait
room, he could not give audience unto them otherwise than
standing upon their feet. Therefore within a small time
he purchased so much love and favour, as that, when news
came to Rome that forelaid [C. 25] and slain he was in his
journey to Ostia, the people in a great tumult and uproar
fell to banning and cursing both the soldiers as traitors,
and the senate also as parricides ; neither ceased they thus
to force[4] against them, until first one messenger, and then

another, yea, and soon after many more were produced by
the magistrates to the public Rostra, who assured them
that he was alive and approached homeward.

13. Yet continued he not for all this secured every way
from the danger of secret practices and wait-laying ; but
assailed he was as well by private persons as by whole factions
and conspiracies, yea, and sore troubled in the end with civil
wars. For there was a man, one of the commons, taken about
midnight near unto his bed-chamber with a dagger. Found
there were likewise twain of the gentlemen's degree in the
open street with a staff having a blade in it [1], and a hunter's
wood-knife waiting for him ; the one to assault his person
when he was gone forth of the theatre, the other as he sacrificed at the temple of Mars. Now there had conspired to
make an insurrection and to alter the State, Gallus Asinius
and Statilius Corvinus, the nephews of Pollio and Messalla [2]
the orators, taking unto them for their complices many of
his own freedmen and servants. As for civil war, kindled it
was and begun by Furius Camillus Scribonianus, lieutenant-
general of Dalmatia, but within five days quenched clean and
suppressed ; by reason that the legions which had changed
their oath of allegiance in remorse of conscience and touch of
religion repented, after that, upon signification given of a
journey to their new general, neither the eagles could be dight
and trimmed, nor the military ensigns plucked up and removed [3].

14. To his first consulship he bore four more, of which the
two former jointly and immediately one after another ; the
rest ensuing, with some time between, to wit, each one in
the fourth year ; and as for the third, he had no precedent
for it in any other prince, as being substituted in the void
place of a consul deceased. A precise justicer he was, ministering justice, both when he was consul and also being out
of that office, most painfully, even upon the solemn days
instituted for him and his, yea, and otherwhiles upon the
ancient festival days and such as were religious. He followed
not always the prescript rule of laws, moderating either the
rigour or the lenity of penalties by equity and reason, according as he stood affected to a cause ; for both unto those he
restored their actions and gave leave to commence them

anew, who in the court before private judges [1] had once lost
their suits, by claiming more than was due, and also such as
were convict of some greater deceit and cozenage, he condemned to be cast unto wild beasts, exceeding therein the
ordinary punishment by law appointed.

15. Moreover, in the examination, trial, and deciding of
controversies he was wondrous variable ; onewhile circumspect, wary, and of great insight, otherwhiles as rash and
inconsiderate, now and then also foolish, vain, and like to
one without all reason. When he reviewed upon a time
the decuries of judges, and put whom he thought good from
their jurisdiction, one of them, who had answered to his
name and concealed the immunity and privilege that he
had by the benefit of children, he discharged quite, as a man
desirous to be a judge [1]. Another of them, being molested
and called into question by his adversaries before him, as
touching a matter between him and them, and pleading
withal for himself that it was a case to be tried not extraordinarily by Caesar but by the common course of law and in
an ordinary court of deputed judges, he compelled immediately to handle and decide his own cause before him ; as who in
his proper business [2] should give proof how indifferent a judge
he would be hereafter in the matter of another.

There was a woman that would not acknowledge her own
son. Now when by evidences and arguments alleged *pro et
contra* on both sides, the question rested in equal balance doubtful, he awarded that she should be wedded to the young man [3],
and so forced her to confess the truth and to take him for her
child. Most ready he was to give judgement on their side,
who made appearance in court when their adversaries were
absent, without any respect and consideration whether a
man slacked and stayed by his own default or upon some
necessity. One cried out upon a forger of writings, and
required that both his hands might be cut off. He made
no more ado, but forthwith called instantly to have the
hangman sent for, with his chopping-knife and butcher's
block, to do the deed. There happened one to be called
judicially to the bar, for that, being a foreigner, he bare
himself as a Roman citizen ; and when the advocates of
both sides grew to some little variance about this circum-

stance, namely, whether the party defendant ought to make his answer and plead his own cause in a gown [4] or a cloak [5], he then, as if he would make exceeding show of pure and uncorrupt equity, commanded him to shift and change his habit often in the place, according as he was either accused or defended. Moreover, sitting in judgement to decide a certain controversy, when he had heard what could be said, he pronounced sentence out of a written table, as it is verily thought, to this effect, that he judged on their side who had alleged the truth.

For which pranks he became base and contemptible, insomuch as everywhere and openly he was despised. One, to excuse a witness whom Caesar had called for out of a province, alleged in his behalf and said he could not possibly come in time and be present, dissembling the cause thereof a great while ; at length, after many long demands what the reason might be, " Why," quoth he, " the man is dead at Puteoli [6]." Another, when he gave him thanks for suffering a person accused to have the benefit of a trial and to be defended, added moreover these words, " And yet this is a usual and ordinary thing." Furthermore, I myself have heard old folk say that these lawyers and barristers were wont to abuse his patience so much that, as he was going down from the tribunal [7], they would not only call upon him to come back again, but also take hold of his gown-lappet and skirt, yea, and otherwhile catch him fast by the foot, and so hold him still with them. And that no man need to marvel hereat, there was one of these Greek lawyers, who pleading before him happened in earnest altercation to let fall these words, Καὶ σὺ γέρων εἶ καὶ μωρός, Thou art both old and a fool besides. And verily it is for certain known that a gentleman of Rome, accused before him for his obscene filthiness and unnatural abuse of women, although untruly (as having an indictment framed against him by his enemies that were mighty), when he saw common strumpets cited and their depositions heard against him, flung his writing-steel and the books which he had in his hand, with great upbraiding of him also for his foolishness and cruelty, even at his very face, so as he rippled [8] and hurt therewith his cheek not a little.

16. He bore also the censorship, an office that a long time had been discontinued after Paulus and Plancus the censors, but even this very place he held with an uneven hand and as variable a mind as the event and success ensuing. In the review taken of Roman gentlemen he dismissed without shame and disgrace a young man charged with many infamous villainies, howbeit one whom his own father testified upon his knowledge and trial to be right honest, saying withal that he had a censor of his own. To another youth, who was in a very bad name for spoiling of maidens and adulteries committed with wives, he did no more but give warning, either more sparily [12] to spend himself in those young and tender years of his, or else more warily at leastwise to go to work, adding thus much beside, " For why know I," quoth he, " what wench thou keepest ? " And when upon the entreaty of his familiar friends he had taken off the infamous note [5] which was set upon the name of one, " Well," quoth he, " let the blot yet remain still to be seen [1]." An honourable man and a principal personage of the province of Greece, howbeit ignorant in the Latin tongue, he not only [e]rased out of the rank and roll of judges, but also deprived of his freedom in Rome and made him a mere alien. Neither suffered he any man to render an account of his life otherwise than with his own mouth, as well as every one was able, and without a patron to speak for him. He noted [2] many with disgrace, and some of them without their knowledge as mistrusting no such thing, yea, and for a matter that had no precedent, namely, because without his privity and a passport obtained they went forth of Italy ; one also among the rest, for that in the province he accompanied a king in his train, alleging for example that in his ancestors' days Rabirius Postumus [3], for following king Ptolemy into Alexandria to save and recover the money which he had lent him, was accused before the judges of treason to the State.

Having assayed to put many more to rebuke with great imputation of the inquisitors' negligence, but with greater shame of his own, look, whomsoever he charged with single life, with childless estate, or poverty [4], those lightly [5] he found guiltless as who were able to prove themselves husbands, fathers, and wealthy. Certes, one there was who, being accused to have laid violent hands upon himself and wounded his own body with a sword, stripped himself naked and showed the same whole and sound, without any harm in the world. Many other acts he did of special note whiles he was censor, as namely these : he commanded a silver chariot sumptuously wrought and set out to sale in the street Sigillaria, for to be bought and broken all to pieces openly ; item, in one day he published twenty edicts or proclamations, and two among the rest, in the one whereof he gave the people warning that, when their vineyards bare grapes plentifully, they should pitch[6] their vessels very well within, in the other, he did them to understand that there was nothing so good against the stinging of a viper as the juice of the yew-tree.

17. One expedition and no more he undertook, and that was very small. When the senate had by decree allowed him triumphal ornaments, he, supposing that a bare title of honour was inferior to the majesty of a prince and emperor, willing also to enterprise some exploit whereby he might win the due glory of a complete triumph, made choice before all other provinces of Britain ; attempted by none since Julius Caesar of famous memory and at that time in a tumultuous uproar, for that certain revolts and rebels fled from thence were not rendered[1]. As he sailed from Ostia thitherward, twice had he like to have been cast away and drowned, by reason of the strong blustering southern[2] wind Circius, near unto Liguria, hard by the Stoechades[a] islands. Having therefore travelled by land from Massilia as far as to cape Gesoriacum[3], he crossed the seas from thence into Britain ; and in a very few days[4], without battle or bloodshed, part of the island yielded to his devotion[5]. So in the sixth month after his first setting forth he returned to Rome, and triumphed with most sumptuous pomp therefor prepared. To the sight of which solemnity he suffered not only the presidents and governors of provinces to have recourse[6] into the city, but also certain banished persons. And among the enemy's spoils he set up a naval coronet and fastened it to the finial of his house [on the] Palatine, hard by another civic garland, in token and memorial of the Ocean by him sailed over and subdued. After his triumphant chariot rode Messalina his wife in a coach, then followed those gallants also, who in the same war had attained to triumphal orna-

ments ; the rest went on foot and in their rich robes guarded with purple, only Crassus Frugi mounted upon a brave courser trimly trapped and arrayed himself in a triumphant mantle of estate[7], for that now twice he had achieved that honour.

18. He was at all times most careful and provident for the city[1], especially that the market might be well-served with victuals. What time the Aemilian edifices (or tenements) were on fire and continued still burning, he remained two nights together in the place called diribitorium[2], and when the multitude of soldiers and household servants failed, he called together by means of the magistrates the commons of the city out of all the streets and parishes to come in and help, setting before [them] his chests full of money, exhorting them to do their best for the quenching of the fire, and ready for to pay presently [Cal. 22] every one a good reward according to the pains he took. Now when corn and victuals were grown very scarce (such was the continual unseasonable weather that brought barrenness), he was upon a time in the middle of the market-place[3] detained by the multitude and so assailed and pelted what with reviling taunts and what with pieces of broken bread, that hardly and with much ado he was able to escape and no otherwise than by a postern gate unto the palace. Whereupon he devised all the means he possibly could to bring into the city provision of corn and victuals, even in the winter season. For he not only proposed certain set gains to all corn-masters that would venture for grain, undertaking himself to bear all the loss that should happen unto any of them by tempest, but ordained also great fees and avails [Cal. 44] for those that would build ships for such traffic and merchandise, according to the condition and quality of each one ;

19. Namely, for every Roman citizen exemption from the law Papia Poppaea ; for enfranchised Latins the freedom of Roman citizens ; and for women, the privilege and benefit of those that had four children, which constitutions stand in force and be observed at this day.

20. Many works he finished and those rather for greatness, huge, than for use, needful[1]. But the chief and principal were these ; the conduit of water begun by Gaius ; item, a scluse[2] to let out and drain the lake Fúcinus, and the haven[3]

at Ostia ; although he knew well enough that the one[4] of
the twain Augustus had denied unto the Marsians who continually entreated him about it, and the other[5], intended
oftentimes in the design of Julius Caesar of sacred memory,
was for the difficulty thereof laid aside. The two cold and
plenteous fountains of the water Claudia, of which the one
beareth the name of Caeruleus, the other of Curtius or Albu-
dignus, as also the new river of Anio[6] he conveyed and brought
to Rome all the way, within stonework, and then derived and
divided the same into many and those right beautiful pools[7].
He went in hand with the mere Fucinus in hope of gain as well
as of glory, when some there were who would have bound
themselves in covenant and promise to drain the said marsh
at their own private charges, in case the grounds being once
made dry might be granted unto them in freehold. Now
for the length of three miles, partly by digging through the
hill, and partly by hewing out the rock before him, he finished
the channel at last with much ado and after eleven years'
labour, albeit thirty thousand men were at work continually
about it and never rested between. The pier at Ostia before-
said he made by drawing an arm of the sea about on the left
and right hand both, and withal at the mouth and entrance
thereof, where now the ground lay deep, raising a huge dam
or pile against it. For the surer foundation of which pile he
drowned beforehand that ship[8], wherein the great obelisk had
been transported out of Egypt ; and when he had supported it
with buttresses of many stones, he planted aloft upon the same
an exceeding high watch-tower to the pattern of that pharos
at Alexandria, to the end that by the fires burning there in
the night season vessels at sea might direct their course.

21. He dealt often among the people great doles and congiaries. Many shows and games likewise he exhibited, and
those magnificent ; not such only as were usual and in accustomed places, but those that were both newly devised and
also brought into use again, whereas they had of ancient time
been discontinued, yea, and where no man else before him
had ever set forth any. The games for the dedication of
Pompey's theatre, which being half-burnt he had re-edified[1],
he gave a signal to begin from out of his tribunal[2] erected in
the orchestra, seeing that beforetime, when he had sacrificed

and done his devotions in the houses above and came down
from thence through the midst of the theatre and assembly,
not one would once arise and give applause, but sat still and
kept silence. He set out also the secular games and plays[3],
as if they had been exhibited by Augustus over-soon, and not
reserved unto their full and due time ; and yet himself in his
own histories writeth that, whereas the said solemnities had
been intermitted, Augustus long after by a most exact calculation of the years reduced them into order again. By occasion
whereof the voice of the crier was then ridiculous and laughed
at, when after the solemn manner he called the people to behold
those games and plays, which no man had once seen already,
or should ever see again ; whereas there survived yet many
who had seen them before, yea, and some of the actors, who in
times past had been produced, were then likewise brought
forth upon the stage. Oftentimes also he represented the
Circensian games in the Vatican[4], and otherwhiles after every
five courses[5] he brought in the baiting of wild beasts. But in
the greatest circus of all[6], which was beautified with bar-gates
of marble-stone and goals[7] all gilded (whereas beforetime they
had been made of soft sandstone and wood), he appointed
proper and peculiar places for the senators, who had wont
beforetime to behold the same sports here and there. Beside
the races for the prize[8] of chariots drawn with four steeds he
represented also the warlike Troy pastime and the baiting of
leopards, which the troop of the praetorian horsemen slew,
having for their leaders the tribunes and the captain himself.
Moreover, he brought into the show-place Thessalian men of
arms, whose manner is to chase about the circus wild bulls
until they be tired, then to mount them and by the horns to
force them down to the ground.

As for shows of sword-fencers, he exhibited them in many
places and after divers and sundry sorts. One, that was kept
every year within the praetorian camp without any baiting
and sumptuous provision of furniture, as for that[9], which was
ordinarily set out and formally with baiting and other prepara-
tions in Mars' Field, at the Septa ; in the same place likewise,
another extraordinary one and of short continuance, which he
began to call Sportula [Aug. 74], because he proclaimed at
first when he exhibited it, that he invited the people thereto,

as it were to a sudden supper and short pittance, such as men use to bid themselves unto. And in no kind of sport or gaming represented unto them was he more civil [Cal. 52], familiar, and better disposed to pass the time away, insomuch as putting forth his left hand, he together with the common sort would both by word of mouth tell and with his fingers also number the pieces of gold as he tendered them unto the winners ; and many a time by way of exhortation and entreaty provoke the people to mirth, ever and anon calling them Sirs [10], yea, and between-whiles intermingling bald and far-fetched jests. As for example, when the people called for one Palumbus [11 a] to play his prizes, he promised to let them have him, if he were once caught. This also was but a simple plain jest, although to good purpose and in season delivered ; when he had by a special indulgence granted unto a champion, who fought out of a British chariot (for whom his four children made earnest suit and entreaty), that he should be freed from that profession of sword-fight [12], and that with the great favour and liking of all men, he sent presently an admonition in writing, wherein he advertised the people how much they should endeavour to get children, seeing, as they did, in what good stead they served, and how they procured grace even unto a sword-fencer.

He represented also in Mars' Field a warlike show of the winning and sacking of a town, likewise the yielding of the princes of Britain, where he sat himself as president in his rich coat-armour. When he was about to let out the water of the mere Fucinus, he exhibited in it a naval fight before ; and as they who were to fight this battle cried out unto him, " *Ave Imperator, morituri te salutant !* All hail, O Emperor, they salute thee and wish thy life who are ready to die," he again made answer, " *Avete* [13] *vos.*" After which word given, as if he had pardoned them this skirmish, there not one of them would fight ; he, sitting a good while in doubt and suspense with himself, whether he should destroy them all with fire and sword, at length leapt forth of his throne, and running to and fro about the circuit of the said lake (not without foul faltering of his legs under him), partly with threats, and in part by way of exhortation, constrained them to skirmish. At this brave show, the Sicilian and

Rhodian fleets encountered, either of them consisting of twelve [14] galleys ruled with three ranks of oars apiece. To give the signal of battle, there was a triton of silver [15] arising out of the midst of the lake by a fabric artificially devised to sound the trumpet and set them together.

22. Certain points about religious ceremonies, touching the state likewise of civil and military affairs, as also concerning all degrees of persons both at home and abroad, he either reformed, or after long disuse forgotten brought into practice again, or else instituted and ordained new. In the election and admission of priests throughout their several colleges he nominated not one but he took his oath first. He observed also precisely that, so often as there was an earthquake in the city, the praetor for the time being should call a public assembly of the people and proclaim certain holidays; semblably [Cal. 15], that upon the prodigious sight of an unlucky fowl [1] in the Capitol there should be held a solemn procession and supplication, wherein himself personally in the right of high priest, after warning given unto the people from the Rostra, did read and pronounce a form of prayers and they say after him. But from this congregation he sequestered and removed the base multitude of mechanical labourers and slaves.

23. The handling of causes and judicial pleading in courts, divided beforetime into certain months for winter and summer, he conjoined all together. The jurisdiction as touching feoffments upon trust, which was wont year by year and only within the city to be committed unto the magistrates, he ordained to hold by patent for ever, and betook the charge thereof unto the rulers and governors also of state in every province. That branch annexed to the law Papia Poppaea [1 a], which implieth thus much, that men threescore years of age are disabled for generation, he altered by an edict [2]. He ordained that unto pupils [3] the consuls should extraordinarily appoint tutors and guardians; that they also who by the head-magistrates were forbidden to make abode within any provinces should be debarred likewise from the city of Rome and Italy. Himself confined some after a strange fashion and without any precedent, inhibiting them to depart above three miles from the city. When he was to treat of any

great affair in the Curia, his manner was to sit in the tribune's pew[4] just in the midst between the consuls' chairs. As for passports[5] which the consuls were wont to be sued unto for, he would have the citizens to be beholden unto himself only therefor and to crave the same at his hands.

24. The badges and ornaments belonging unto the consuls he granted unto the ducenary procurators and seneschals of provinces[1]. From as many as refused the honourable dignity of senators he took away also the worship of the gentlemen's degree. The right to wear the laticlave[2] (although he promised at first not to choose any one senator who could not reckon four lineal descents from a citizen of Rome) he allowed also to a libertine's [C. 2] son, but with this condition, if he were adopted before by a gentleman of Rome. And fearing for all that lest he should be blamed, he proved and showed that even Appius Caecus, the chief ancestor and auctor[3] of his own race, being censor elected and admitted into the senate the sons of libertines ; ignorant as he was that in the days of the said Appius and in the times long after ensuing those were called libertines, not only who themselves were manumitted and enfranchised, but such also as were freeborn of their progeny. The college of quaestors, instead of paving the streets and highways, he enjoined to exhibit a game or show of sword-fencers ; and in the lieu of the provinces Ostia and Gaul[4], which he took from them, he restored the charge of the public treasure in the temple of Saturn, which office, in the mean space between[5], the praetors for the time being or those verily who had been praetors before had borne. Unto Silanus, espoused and betrothed unto his daughter, before he was undergrown[6] and fourteen years of age he granted triumphal ornaments ; but of elder persons to so many, as there is an epistle extant written in the common name of the legions, wherein they make petition that unto the consuls-lieutenants there might be granted together with the conduct of the army the said triumphal honours, to the end that they should not pick quarrels and seek occasions of war, they cared not how nor what way. Moreover to A. Plautius he gave by a decree the petty triumph ovatio [Aug. 22], and as he entered so into the city himself met him upon the way, and both when he went into the Capitol and returned also from thence again, gave him the better hand[7]. Unto Gabinius Secundus, who had vanquished the Cauchi, a nation in Germany, he permitted and gave leave to assume the surname Cauchius in his style.

25. The horsemen's service and their places he ordered so by degrees, as that after the charge of a cohort he granted the leading of a wing, and after the command thereof the tribuneship or regiment of a legion. He ordained their stipends also, and a kind of imaginary warfare[1] called *supra numerum*, which they that were absent might execute, and in name or title only. By virtue of a decree that passed even from the nobles themselves he prohibited all soldiers professed to enter into any senators' houses for to do their duty and salute them. Those libertines who bore themselves for Roman gentlemen he caused to forfeit their goods and bodies to the State. Such of them as were unthankful and of whom their patrons complained he deprived of freedom and made them bound again; yea, and denied unto their advocates for to hear any plea and to sit in judgement against their own freedmen. When some masters there were that put forth their sick and diseased slaves into the isle of Aesculapius[2], for to avoid the tedious trouble of their cures at home, he made an act and ordained that all such slaves should be free and not return again into the hands of their masters, in case they ever recovered; and if any master chose to kill them outright rather than thus to put them forth, they should be guilty of murder. He gave warning by an edict that no wayfaring men should travel through any town in Italy but either on foot, or borne in a chair, or else carried in a litter[a]. In Puteoli and in Ostia he placed several cohorts to put by all mischances of skarfires [Aug. 25].

He forbade all persons by condition aliens and foreigners to take upon them Roman names, those I mean only that distinguished houses and families. As many of them as usurped the freedom of Rome he beheaded in the Esquiline field[3]. The two provinces Achaia and Macedonia, which Tiberius the emperor had appropriated to himself[4], he yielded up again into the hands and dispose of the senate. The Lycians he deprived of their freedom, by occasion of the mortal discord and variance among them. To the Rhodians, who repented for their old trespasses, he restored their liberty which they had lost. He forgave all tributes to the people of Ilium for ever, as to the first founders and stock-fathers of the Roman nation ; and to that purpose he read an old letter in Greek written unto king Seleucus by the senate and people of Rome, wherein they promised to entertain amity and league with him upon this condition that he would grant unto the people of Ilium, their natural kinsfolk, immunity from all taxes and tributes. The Jews [5] [b], who by the instigation of one Chrestus were evermore tumultuous, he banished Rome. The ambassadors of the Germans he permitted to sit in the orchestra [c] with the senators, being moved so to do at their simplicity and confident boldness ; for that, being brought into the *popularia* [d] and perceiving Parthians and Armenians sitting among the senators, they of their own accord had removed and passed to that quarter, giving out these words withal, that their valour and condition of estate was nothing inferior to the others.

The religion of the Druids among the Gauls, practising horrible and detestable cruelty and which under Augustus Roman citizens only were forbidden to profess and use, he quite put down and abolished. Contrariwise, the sacred rites and holy ceremonies called Eleusinia he attempted to transfer out of Attica to Rome. The temple likewise of Venus Erycina [e] in Sicily, which in continuance of time was decayed and fallen down, he caused to be repaired and built again at the common charges of the people of Rome ; he made covenants and league with foreign kings, by the complements [Cal. 59] of killing a sow in the Forum and using withal the sentence or preface that the heralds [6] in old time pronounced. But both these affairs and others besides, the whole empire also in a manner or a great part thereof he managed not so much after his own mind, as by the direction and will of his wives and freedmen, being verily affected and framed for the most part so as stood either with their profit or good pleasure.

26. When he was a very youth, he had espoused two maidens, namely, Aemilia Lepida, niece [1] to Augustus once removed, likewise Livia Medullina, surnamed also Camilla, a lady descended from the ancient house of Camillus the dictator.

The former of these twain, because her parents had offended
Augustus, he cast off remaining as yet a virgin ; the latter he
lost by occasion of sickness upon that very day which was
appointed for the marriage. After this, he wedded these
wives ; to wit, Plautia Herculanilla [2], whose father had
triumphed, and not long after, Aelia Paetina, whose father
had been consul. Both these he divorced, Paetina upon
light offences and small displeasures ; marry, Herculanilla he
put away for her filthy lust and whorish life, as also for
suspicion of a murder. After these he took to wife Valeria
Messalina, the daughter of Barbatus Messala his cousin
german ; whom when he found once, over and beside the rest
of her abominable vices and dishonesties, to have been wedded
to Gaius Silius [3], and that with a dowry assured unto her
and signed among the [diviners] [4], he put to death. And
in a speech that he made openly before his praetorian soldiers
[he] avowed that, because his marriages proved so bad, he
resolved to remain unmarried and live a single life, and if
he did not continue so for ever, he would not refuse to be
stabbed by their very hands. Neither could he endure but
forthwith [5] treat upon conditions of marriage even with
Paetina, whom long before he had put away, yea, and with
Lollia Paulina, wife sometime to Gaius Caesar. But through
the enticing allurements of Agrippina [6], the daughter of Germanicus his own brother, what by the means of kissing cour-
tesies, what by the opportunities of other dalliances, being
drawn into love and fancy with her, at the next session of the
senate he suborned certain of purpose to opine and give advice
to compel him for to make her his wife, as being a matter of
right great consequence, and which most of all concerned the
State ; that other men also might be dispensed with [7] and
licensed to contract the like marriages [8] which until that time
were reputed incestuous. And so himself stayed hardly one
day between before he dispatched the wedding ; but none
were found that followed the precedent, except one libertine
and another who had been a principal centurion in the foremost
cohort, at whose marriage even himself in person together
with Agrippina was present to do him credit and honour.

27. Children he begat of three wives. By Herculanilla he
had Drusus and Claudia ; by Paetina he was father of Antonia ;

and Messalina bare unto him Octavia and a son, whom first he named Germanicus and afterwards Britannicus. As for Drusus, he lost him at Pompeii before he was fourteen years of age by occasion that he was choked with a pear, which in play and pastime, being tossed aloft into the air, fell just into his mouth as he gaped wide for it ; unto whom also but few days before he had affianced in marriage the daughter of Sejanus, which maketh me more to marvel that some have written he was treacherously killed by Sejanus. His (supposed) daughter Claudia, who indeed was conceived by his freedman Boter, although she was born before the fifth month after the divorce and began to be nursed and reared, yet he commanded to be laid at her mother's door and starknaked to be cast forth. Antonia his daughter he gave in marriage to Gnaeus Pompeius Magnus, afterwards to Faustus Sulla, two right noble young gentlemen ; and Octavia he bestowed upon Nero[1], his wife's son, notwithstanding she had been promised and betrothed before unto Silanus. His son Britannicus, whom Messalina bare unto him the twentieth day after he came to the empire and in his second consulship, being yet a very babe he recommended continually both to the soldiers in open assembly, dandling him in his own hands, and also to the common people at the solemnities of games and plays, holding him either in his bosom or just before him, whiles the multitude with great acclamations, all good words, and fortunate osses [Aug. 57] seconded him. Of his sons-in-law who matched with his daughters he adopted Nero ; Pompeius and Silanus he not only cast off and rejected but murdered also.

28. Of all his freedmen he esteemed especially Posides the eunuch, unto whom also in his triumph over Britain, among martial men and valiant soldiers, he gave a spear without an iron head[1]. And no less account made he of Felix[2], whom first he ordained captain over the cohorts and cornets of horsemen, yea, and ruler of the province of Judaea, the husband of three queens[a] ; as also of Harpocras, unto whom he granted a privilege to be carried in a litter through the city of Rome and to set out games and plays in public[b] ; and besides these he affected with much respect Polybius, the guide and director to him in his studies, who oftentimes would walk cheek by jowl between the two consuls. But above all these he held in greatest esteem Narcissus, his secretary or inditer of epistles, and Pallas, the keeper of his books of accounts ; whom by virtue of a decree also which went from the senate he suffered willingly to be not only rewarded with rich fees, but also to be adorned with the honours of quaestor and praetor, likewise to get, to pill and poll[3] by hook and crook so much as that, when himself complained upon a time how little treasure he had in his coffers, one made answer unto him not absurdly[4], that he might have store enough and plenty, in case his two freedmen[5] would admit him to share with them.

29. To these freedmen and to his wives, as I said before, being wholly addicted and enthralled, he bare himself not as an absolute prince, but as their minister and servitor[a]. According as it was behoveful [11] and commodious to any of these, or stood with their affection and pleasure, he granted honourable dignities, conferred the conducts of armies, and awarded impunities and punishments ; yea, and for the most part, I assure you, when himself was altogether ignorant and wist not what he did. And not to reckon up particularly every small thing, to wit, his liberalities and gifts revoked, his judgements reversed, his patents and writings concerning the grants of offices either foisted in or plainly altered or changed by them, he slew his brother Appius Silanus[1] ; the two Julias, the one daughter of Drusus[2], and the other of Germanicus[3], upon bare imputation of a crime without any ground, not allowing them so much as lawful trial and liberty to plead in their own defence ; likewise Gnaeus Pompeius, husband to his elder daughter, and Lucius Silanus espoused to the other (and all through their suggestions and informations)[4]. Of which, Pompeius was stabbed even as he lay in bed with a beloved youth and catamite of his ; Silanus was forced to resign up his praetorship four days before the kalends of January and to lose his life[5] in the beginning of the year on the very wedding day of Claudius and Agrippina.

To the execution of thirty-five senators and more than 300 Roman gentlemen so easily was he induced as that, when the centurion brought word back as touching the death of one who had been consul, saying that the deed was done which he had commanded, he flatly denied that he gave any such warrant. Nevertheless the thing he allowed, while his freedmen aforesaid standing by avouched that the soldiers had done their devoir, in that they ran willingly of their own heads to revenge their emperor. For[6] it would be thought incredible if I should relate, how even for the very marriage of Messalina with the adulterer Silius his own self sealed the writings for assurance of the dowry, being persuaded and brought thereunto as though the said wedding was but colourably of purpose pretended to avert forsooth and translate the danger, that by certain prodigies were portended to hang over his own head.

30. Right personable he was and carried a presence not without authority and majesty, whether he stood or sat, but especially when he was laid and took his repose ; for of stature he was tall and nathless his body not lank and slender. His countenance lively, his grey hairs beautiful, which became him well, with a good fat and round neck under them. Howbeit, both as he went his hams, being feeble, failed him, and also whiles he was doing aught, were it remissly or in earnest, many things disgraced him ; to wit, indecent laughter and unseemly anger, by reason that he would froth and slaver at the mouth and had evermore his nose dropping ; besides, his tongue stutted[1] and stammered, his head likewise at all times, but especially if he did anything, were it never so little, used to shake and tremble very much.

31. Concerning his bodily health, as beforetime he used to be grievously sick, so being once emperor exceeding healthful he was and stood clear of all diseases save only the pain of the stomach[a], in a fit whereof he said he thought to have killed himself.

32. He made feasts, and those very great and ordinarily[1] ; yea, and in most open and large places, such as for the most part would receive six hundred guests at one sitting. He feasted also even upon the sluice of the lake Fucinus, what time he had like to have been drowned, whenas the water let out with a forcible violence reflowed back again. At every supper his manner was to have also his own children, who together with other noblemen's children, as well boys as girls, should after the old manner sit and feed at the tables' feet[2]. One of his guests, who was thought to have closely[3] stolen away a cup of gold the day before, he re-invited against the morrow, and then he set before him a stone-pot[4] to drink in. It is reported moreover that he meant to set forth an edict, wherein he would give folk leave to break wind downward and let it go even with a crack at the very board[a], having certain intelligence that there was one who for manners and modesty sake, by holding it in endangered his own life.

33. For appetite to meat and drink his stomach served him passing well always and in every place. Sitting upon a time judicially in Augustus' hall of justice[1] to hear and determine causes, and scenting there the steam of a dinner, that was a-dressing and serving up for the priests Salii[a] in the temple of Mars[2] next adjoining, he forsook the tribunal, went up to the said priests, and there sat down with them to meat. Lightly [Cal. 36] you should never have him go out of any dining-room but with his belly strutting[3] out, well whittled[4] also and drenched with wine : so as straitway, while he laid him down along upon his back and took a sleep gaping, there was a feather put ordinarily into his mouth wide open for to discharge his stomach. He took very short sleeps, for commonly before midnight he awaked ; yet so as other-whiles he would catch a nap in the daytime, as he sat to minister justice, and scarcely could be awakened by the advocates at the bar, who of purpose raised their voices and pleaded the louder. He was excessively given to the wanton love of women ; as for the preposterous abuse of male kind, he was altogether unacquainted therewith. He played at dice most earnestly (concerning the art and skill whereof he published also a little book), being wont to ply that game even whiles he was carried[5] up and down, having his carroch and dice-board so fitted as there might be no confusion nor shuffling at all in play.

34. That cruel he was and given to bloodshed naturally appeared in great and very small matters. As for tortures used in examinations and the punishments that parricides suffered [Aug. 33][a], he exhibited and exacted the same to be done without delay and openly in his own presence. Being desirous upon a time to behold an execution performed after the ancient manner [1] at Tibur, whenas (the malefactors standing bound already to a stake) there wanted the butcherly executioner to do the feat, he stayed there still in the place and waited until evening for one that was sent for out of Rome. At all sword-fights, whether they were set forth by himself or by others, he commanded as many of the champions as chanced only but to stumble and fall therewith to have their throats cut, especially the fencers called retiarii [2]; and why? because forsooth he would see their faces as they lay gasping and yielding up their breath. It fortuned that a couple of these fighting at sharpe [Cal. 27] wounded and killed one another; thereupon he commanded little knives to be made of both their blades for his own proper use. He took such pleasure in those that fought with wild beasts [3] [b], as also in the sword-fights ordinarily about noon [4], that he would by break of day go down to the theatre for to behold the one, and at noon dismiss the people to their dinners, and sit it out himself to see the other; yea, and besides those that were appointed to such combats, upon any slight and sudden occasion set some to fight for their lives, even out of the number of carpenters, servitors, and such-like employed about these games, if happily [Cal. 36] any of those artificial motions [c] that go by vices, or a pageant in frame, or some such fabric proved not well. He fetched in also one of his own nomen-clators [5] even in his gown as he went to fight for his life [6].

35. But it passed [1] how timorous and diffident he was. At his first coming to the empire (however, as we said before, he bragged and stood upon his civil and familiar behaviour) he durst not for certain days go to any feast, dinner, or supper, without pensioners [2] standing about him with their spears and javelins and his soldiers waiting at the table; neither visited he any sick person unless the bed-chamber where the party lay were first searched, the beds, bolsters, pillows, coverlets and other clothes were groped, felt, and thoroughly shaken beforehand. All the time after, he appointed evermore certain searchers for them all that came to salute him, sparing not one, and such searchers as were most cruel. For long it was first and that with much ado, ere he granted that women, young boys in their embroidered coats, and maidens should not be handled and felt in this manner, that any man's attendants likewise or clerks might not have their pen-sheaths and pen-knife-cases taken from them [a]. In a civil commotion, when Camillus (making no doubt but that without any war at all he might be terrified) willed him in a contumelious, menacing, and malapert letter to resign up the empire and to lead a quiet life in private estate, he called his nobles and chief personages about him to counsel and put to question, whether it were best to hearken unto him or no.

36. At the headless [1] report and flying news of some treason that should be practised against him he was so affrighted that he went about to lay down his imperial dignity. By occasion that one (as I related before) was taken with a weapon upon him about his person as he sacrificed [13], in all haste he sent out the beadles [2] and called the senate together ; before whom with tears and loud outcries he bewailed his own piteous case, as who nowhere could make account of any safety, and thereupon for a long time forbare to come abroad. His affectionate love also to Messalina, most fervent though it were, he renounced and cast clean from her, not so much for any indignity of the dishonourable wrongs she offered unto him, as upon very fear of danger, as fully persuaded that she practised to bring the empire into Silius the adulterer's hands. At which time in a great fright he fled in shameful manner to the camp, asking and inquiring all the way nothing else but whether the empire remained still safe to his behoof [Cl. 11].

37. There arose no suspicion, there came forth no author [1] so light and vain, but gave him a bone to gnaw upon [2], and put no small toys [3] in his head, whereby he was forced to beware and seek revenge. One of those that had a matter depending in court before him, taking him aside, when he came by way of salutation to do his duty, avowed unto him that he dreamed how he was killed by one. Then within a while after the same party (as if he had now taken knowledge who that one was that should murder him) pointed unto his own adversary, even as he tendered a supplication unto Claudius, and said " This is he." Whereupon immediately apprehended he was and haled to execution. After the semblable [Cal. 15] manner, by report, came Appius Silanus to his death. For when Messalina and Narcissus had conspired to work his overthrow and final destruction, they complotted thus, that Narcissus betimes in a morning before daylight rushed like a man amazed and astonied into the bed-chamber of his patron, relating unto him his dream, namely, that Appius had laid violent hands upon him ; and Messalina for her part, composing and framing herself as if she wondered greatly thereat, reported how she likewise had seen already the same vision for certain nights together. And not long after this word came (as it was before agreed between them) that Appius was coming to rush in among them, who indeed had been bidden the day before to be present at the same instant. Whereupon, as if the said dream had now proved true and been plainly represented in effect, order was given for Appius to be indicted, arraigned, and to suffer death. Neither doubted Claudius the morrow after to report the whole story and the order thereof unto the senate, and withal to give thanks unto his freedman [4] for being so vigilant and watchful in his very sleep for his sake.

38. Being privy to himself [1] of passionate anger [2] and bearing malice he excused them both in an edict, distinctly promising that the one of them verily should be but short and harmless, the other not unjust nor causeless. Having sharply rebuked the men of Ostia, because they had not sent boats and barges to meet him as he came upon the river Tiber, and that in such odious terms as these, that he was now become base and abject in their eyes, all on a sudden he pardoned them upon the submission and readiness to make satisfaction. Some there were whom in the very open street he thrust from him with his own hand, coming unto him somewhat out of season. Semblably [Cal. 15] he confined and banished the court a scribe who had been quaestor [3] ; a senator likewise that had borne the praetorship, both of them without their cause heard and altogether guiltless ; for that the one [4], pleading in court as an advocate against him when he was a private person, had carried himself not so modestly as he should, and the senator in his aedileship had amerced and fined certain tenants of his dwelling upon his lands for selling boiled meats contrary to the law expressly forbidding so to do, and withal whipped his bailiff coming between [5]. For which cause also he took from the aediles their authority to punish the disorder of those that kept taverns and victualling houses. But as touching his own foolishness, he concealed it not, but gave it out and protested in certain short orations that he counterfeited himself a fool for the nonce during Gaius' days, because otherwise he should not have escaped nor attained to that place [6] which he aimed at and was now entered upon. Howbeit he could not make the world believe so much, until [7] there was a book put forth within a short time after, entitled Μωρῶν Ἀνάστασις, *The Resurrection (or Exaltation) of Fools*, the argument and matter whereof was, that no man feigneth folly [a].

39. Among other things men wondered at him for his oblivion and unadvisedness, or (that I may express the same in Greek) his μετεωρίαν καὶ ἀβλεψίαν, his gross oversight or forgetfulness and inconsiderate blindness. When Messalina was (by his own command) killed, within a while after he was set in his dining-parlour he asked why his lady [1] came not. Many of those whom he had condemned to death, the very morrow immediately after he commanded to have warning both to sit in counsel with him and also to bear him company at dice-play ; yea, and by a messenger chid and checked them as drowsy and slothful for staying so long and making no better haste. Being minded to take Agrippina to wife against all law of God and man, he ceased not in all his speech to call her his daughter [2] and nursling, to give out also that she was born and brought up in his bosom. Having a purpose to admit Nero into the very name of his own house and family, as if he had not incurred blame enough already for adopting (him) his wife's son, having a natural son [3] of his own who was now of ripe years, he eft-soons divulged that never any one had been by adoption inserted or incorporated into the family of the Claudii.

40. He showed oftentimes so great negligence and carelessness what he said or did, that he was thought not to know nor consider, either who made any speech, or among whom, or at what time, and in what place. When there was some question and debate about butchers and vintners, he cried out in the senate-house, " I beseech you [1], my masters, who is able to live without a little piece or morsel of flesh ? " and withal described the abundance [2] of the old taverns [a], from whence himself also in times past was wont to be served with wine. As touching a certain quaestor, who was a candidate of his and by him recommended, among other reasons why he favoured him he alleged this, because his father had quickly and in due time given him, lying sick, cold water to drink. Having in the senate brought in a woman to depose : " This," quoth he, " was my mother's freedwoman and she that kept her ornaments and used to deck and dress her, but she always took me for her patron. This have I," quoth he, " delivered of purpose, because there be some yet in mine house who think me not to be her patron." Moreover, sitting upon the tribunal, when he was in a great chafe and the men of Ostia requested at his hands (I wot not what) in the name of their town, he cried out aloud that he knew nothing wherefore he should oblige them unto him : " And if any man else," quoth he, " I also am free and at mine own liberty." As for these words of his which now I will relate, they were rife in his mouth daily, yea, every hour and minute thereof : " What ! dost thou take me for Theogonius[3] and λογιώτατος [4] [b] ? " beside many such foolish terms, not beseeming private persons, much less a prince otherwise not uneloquent nor unlearned, nay, rather one eagerly given to his book and a great student in the liberal sciences.

41. In his youth he attempted to write a history, exhorted thereto by Titus Livius[1], and having the help besides of Sulpicius Flavus. And when he put the same first to the trial and judgement of men in a frequent [Cal. 15] auditory, hardly and with much ado he read it through, being often in the while coldly heard by an occasion that himself gave. For, when (as he began his reading) there was set up a laughter, by reason that many of the seats broke with the weight of a certain corpulent and fat swad[2], he was not able to hold[3], no, not after the tumult appeased, but eft-soons ever and anon call to mind that accident and fall afresh to immeasurable laughing. During his empire likewise he both wrote much and also rehearsed the same continually by his reader[4]. The beginning of his foresaid history he took from the time presently ensuing[5] the murder of Caesar dictator, but he passed over to the later days, and began again at the civil pacification ; perceiving that it was not left in his power and liberty to write of the occurrents in those former times, as who was often checked both by his mother[6] and also by his grandam[7]. Of the former argument [N. 12] he left behind him two volumes, of the latter forty-one.

He compiled of his own life eight books, a report not so wisely and discreetly put down as otherwise elegantly penned ; item, an apology or defence of Cicero against the books of Asinius Gallus[8], a piece of work full enough of learning. He devised moreover three new characters or letters[9] in the Latin alphabet[a], and put them to the number of the old as most necessary. And having published, whiles he was yet a private person, concerning the reason of those letters one book, soon after being emperor he easily effected that they should be brought into use also indifferently with the rest. And verily such manner of writing with those characters is now extant to be seen in many books of records in journals and titles or inscriptions of works.

42. With no less diligence studied he the Greek disciplines[1], professing, as any occasion was offered, his affectionate love to that tongue and the excellency thereof. When a certain barbarian[2] discoursed in Greek and Latin, " See, you be skilful," quoth he, " in both our languages " ; and in recommending Achaia unto the lords of the senate, he said it was a province that he affected well and delighted in for the commerce and society of studies common to him and them ; and many a time he answered their ambassadors in the senate with a long and continued oration in Greek. But upon the tribunal he used very much verses also out of Homer. Certes, whensoever he had taken revenge of enemy or traitor, he lightly gave unto the tribune over the sentinels and guard of his person, calling unto him after the usual manner for a watchword, none other but this [*Iliad*, xxiv, 369] :

> Ἄνδρ᾽ ἀπαμύνασθαι, ὅτε τις πρότερος χαλεπήνῃ
> Resist, revenge with main and might,
> When one provokes thee first to fight.

To conclude, in the end he wrote Greek histories also, to wit, twenty books entitled *Tyrrhenicon*[3], and eight entitled *Carchedoniacon*[4]. In regard of which histories, unto the ancient school at Alexandria he adjoined another bearing his own name[5] ; and ordained it was, that every year in the one of them his books *Tyrrhenicon*, and in the other his *Carchedoniacon* upon certain days appointed therefor should (as it were in a frequent auditory) [6] be read whole through by several single readers in their turns.

43. Toward the end of his life he showed certain signs, and those evident enough, that he repented both his marriage with Agrippina and the adoption also of Nero. For by occasion that his freedmen made mention and gave their commendation of a judicial proceeding of his, wherein he had condemned the day before a woman in the case of adultery, he avouched that the destinies likewise had so ordained that all his marriages [1] should be unchaste, howbeit not unpunished ; and soon after, meeting his son Britannicus and embracing him harder and more closely than his manner was, " Grow apace," quoth he, " and take account of me for all that I have done," using withal these Greek words, ὁ ἔρως δ᾽ ἐπείγεται, love enforced me [2]. And when he had fully purposed to give him, being as then very young and of tender years, his virile robe, seeing that his stature and growth would bear and permit it [a], he uttered these words moreover, " to the end that the people of Rome may yet at last have a true and natural Caesar."

44. And not long after this he wrote his will and signed it with the seals of all the head-magistrates. Whereupon, before that he could proceed any further, prevented he was and cut short by Agrippina, whom they also who were privy to her and of her counsel [1], yet nevertheless informers, accused besides all this of many crimes. And verily it is agreed upon generally by all, that killed he was by poison, but where it should be, and who gave it, there is some difference [a]. Some write that as he sat at a feast in the Capitol castle with the priests, it was presented unto him by Halotus, the eunuch, his taster ; others report that it was at a meal in his own house by Agrippina herself, who had offered unto him a mushroom empoisoned, knowing that he was most greedy of such meats. Of those accidents also which ensued hereupon the report is variable. Some say that straight upon the receipt of the poison he became speechless, and continuing all night in dolorous torments died a little before day. Others affirm that at first he fell asleep, and afterwards, as the meat flowed and floated aloft, vomited all up, and so was followed again with a rank poison[2]. But whether the same were put into a mess of thick gruel (considering he was of necessity[3] to be refreshed with food being emptied in his stomach), or conveyed up by a clyster, as if being overcharged with fulness and surfeit he might be eased also by this kind of egestion[4] and purgation, it is uncertain.

45. His death was kept secret until all things were set in order about his successor. And therefore both vows were made for him as if he had lain sick still, and also comic actors were brought in place colourably to solace and delight him, as having a longing desire after such sports. He deceased three days before the ides of October[1], when Asinius Marcellus and Acilius Aviola were consuls, in the sixty-fourth year of his age and the fourteenth of his empire. His funeral was performed with a solemn pomp and procession of the magistrates, and canonised he was a saint in heaven ; which honour, forelet [Cal. 21] and abolished by Nero, he recovered afterwards by the means of Vespasian.

46. Especial tokens there were presaging and prognosticating his death : to wit, the rising of a hairy[1] star which they call a comet ; also the monument[2] of his father Drusus was blasted with lightning ; and for that in the same year most of the magistrates of all sorts were dead[a]. But himself seemeth not either to have been ignorant that his end drew near or to have dissembled so much ; which may be gathered by some good arguments and demonstrations. For both in the ordination of consuls he appointed none of them to continue longer than the month wherein he died, and also in the senate, the very last time that ever he sat there, after a long and earnest exhortation of his children to concord, he humbly recommended the age of them both to the lords of that honourable house ; and in his last judicial session upon the tribunal once or twice he pronounced openly that come he was now to the end of his mortality, notwithstanding they that heard him grieved to hear such an osse [Aug. 57], and prayed the gods to avert the same.

THE HISTORY OF
NERO CLAUDIUS CAESAR

1. OUT of the Domitian stock and name, there sprung two
famous families, to wit, the Calvini and the Ahenobarbi.
These Ahenobarbi have for the first author of their original and
surname likewise Lucius Domitius, whom, as he returned in
times past homeward out of the country, two young men
twins[1], carrying with them a venerable presence and countenance more than ordinary, encountered by report and commanded to relate unto the senate and people of Rome news of
that victory[2] whereof as yet they stood in doubt ; and for the
better assurance of their divine majesty stroked his cheeks so
that therewith they made the hair of black, red[3], and like in
colour to brass[4]. Which mark and badges continued also in
his posterity, and most of them have such red[5] beards. Moreover, having borne seven consulships, triumphed likewise,
and been censors twice, and therewith been chosen into the
rank of the patricians, they remained all in the same surname.
Neither were they known by any other forenames than Gnaeus
and Lucius, and the same in variety worth the noting and
observation ; onewhile continuing either of the said names in
three persons together, otherwhiles changing alternatively[6]
one after another in every descent. For we have heard say
that the first, second, and third of these Ahenobarbi were forenamed Lucii, and again the three next following them in order
were Gnaei. All the rest no otherwise than by turns one after
another had their forenames first Lucii and then Gnaei. That
many persons of this house descended should be known I
suppose it very pertinent and material ; whereby it may the
better appear that Nero degenerated from the virtues of his
ancestors so as yet he carried away and resembled the vices of
them all, as infused into him and inbred by nature.

2. To fetch the beginning therefore of this our discourse somewhat farther off, his great-grandfather's grandfather [1], Gnaeus Domitius, being in his tribunate much offended at the pontiffs [2] for electing any other but himself into his father's place, transferred the right and power of subrogating priests in the room of those that were deceased from their colleges to the body of the people. But in his consulship having vanquished the Allobroges and the Arverni, he rode through his province [3] mounted upon an elephant, whiles the whole multitude of his soldiers attended upon him in a train after the manner of a solemn triumph [4]. This Domitius it was, of whom Licinius Crassus the orator in a certain declamation said, It was no marvel he had a brazen beard, whose face was made of iron and heart of lead. His son, being praetor, was the man who, as Caesar [5] went out of his consulship (which he was thought to have borne against the auspicia [6] and the laws), convented [7] him before the senate to be by them examined, tried, and censured. Afterwards, when he was consul, he attempted to fetch him back, lord-general as he was of an army, from his forces in Gaul ; and being by the adverse faction [8] nominated his successor in that province, was in the beginning of the civil war taken prisoner before Corfinium. From whence being dismissed and set at liberty, after he had by his coming to the Massilians, straitly beleaguered, much strengthened them, suddenly he forsook them, and in the end at the battle of Pharsalus lost his life ; a man not very constant and resolute, but withal of a fell and savage nature. Being driven to utter despair, he was so much afraid of death, which for fear he had desired, that after a draught of poison he repented the taking thereof and cast it up again ; yea, and enfranchised his physician, who wittingly and of purpose had so tempered it that it might do him no great harm. And what time as Gnaeus Pompeius put to question what should be done to those neuters that stood indifferent and stuck to no party, he alone opined that they were to be reckoned enemies and proceeded against accordingly.

3. He left behind him a son, worthy without question to be preferred before all others of his name and lineage. This man, being among those that were privy to Caesar's death and of that conspiracy, standing condemned (though

guiltless) by the law Paedia[1], when he had betaken himself
to Cassius and Brutus his near kinsfolk, after the end of
them both held still in his hand the fleet committed beforetime to his charge, yea, and augmented the same ; neither
yielded he it up to Mark Antony before his own side was
everywhere quite overthrown, which he then did of his
own accord and so as that Antony took himself highly beholden unto him therefor. He only also of all those who
by virtue of the like law stood condemned, being restored
into his native country, went through the most honourable
offices of state ; soon after likewise, when civil dissension
was kindled again and renewed, being in quality of lieutenant to the said Antony, what time the sovereign empire
was offered unto him by those who were ashamed of Cleopatra[2], not daring to accept thereof nor yet to refuse it resolutely, by occasion of sudden sickness wherewith he was
surprised, [he] went and sided with Augustus, and within
a few days after departed this life. He himself was also noted
with some infamy, for Antony gave it commonly forth that
for the love of one Servilia Nais, whom he kept, he fled to
Augustus' side.

4. From him came that Domitius, who soon after had the
name abroad to have been the chapman of Augustus' goods
and substance left by his will and testament[1], a man no less
renowned in his youth for good skill in ruling of chariots and
running with them a race, as afterwards for the triumphant
ornaments achieved by the German war, but arrogant of
spirit, wasteful in expense, and therewith cruel. When he
was aedile he forced Lucius Plancus that had been censor[2]
to give him the way. Bearing the honourable offices of
praetor and consul, he produced upon the stage, to act a
comic and wanton interlude, the gentlemen and dames of
Rome. He exhibited baiting of wild beasts both in the
circus and also in every quarter of the city, yea, and a show
of sword-fight, but with so great cruelty that Augustus was
compelled of necessity to restrain him by an edict, since that
no secret warning nor admonition at his hands would prevail.

5. Of Antonia the elder he begat the father of Nero, an
imp[1] in all the parts of his life ungracious and detestable.
For accompanying Gaius Caesar[2] in his youth into the East

parts, where he killed a freedman of his own because he refused to quaff as much as he was commanded, being discharged therefore out of the cohort of his friends he led his life never a whit more modestly ; but both within a village standing upon the Appian Way, suddenly put his horses to gallop and not unwittingly rode over a little child and trod him to death, and also at Rome, in the midst of the Forum, plucked a Roman gentleman's eye out of his head, for chiding him somewhat over-boldly. So false and perfidious besides [he was], that he defrauded not only the bankers and money-changers of the prices of such commodities as they had bought up[3], but also when he was praetor put the runners with chariots besides[4] the prizes of their victories. For which pranks reproved he was merrily even by his own sister Lepida, and upon complaint made by the masters of the four factions[a] he enacted that from thenceforth ever after the said prizes should be presently [Cal. 25] paid. Being accused likewise for treason to the State and many adulteries, as also for incest committed with his sister Lepida a little before the decease of Tiberius, yet escaped he the danger of law by the alteration of the times and died at Pyrgi of the dropsy[5][b], when Agrippina, daughter to Germanicus, had brought him a son named Nero.

6. This Nero was born at Antium, nine months after that Tiberius departed this world, eighteen days before the kalends of January, just as the sun was newly risen, so as his beams lighted well-near upon him before they could touch the earth[1]. As touching his horoscope, many men straightways gave many guesses and conjectures of fearful events, and even a very word that his father Domitius spake was taken to be a presaging osse [Aug. 57]. For when his friends by way of gratulation wished him joy of his son new-born, he said that of himself and Agrippina there could nothing come into the world but accursed, detestable, and to the hurt of the weal public. Of the same future infortunity [Aug. 23] there appeared an evident sign upon his naming day[a] : for Gaius Caesar Caligula, when his sister Agrippina requested him to give the infant what name[2] he would, looking wistly[3] on Claudius his uncle (by whom afterwards being emperor the child was adopted), said he gave him his name. Neither spake he this in earnest but merrily in boord [4], and Agrippina scorned and rejected it, for that as then Claudius went for a fool and one of the laughing-stocks of the court.

At three years of age he became fatherless, and being his father's heir but of one-third part, yet could not he touch so much as that full and whole by reason of Gaius his co-heir, who had seized upon and caught up beforehand all the goods ; and for that his mother also was soon after confined and packed away, he, being in manner destitute of all help and very needy, was fostered in his aunt Lepida's house under two pedagogues, a dancer and a barber.   But when Claudius was come once to the empire, he not only recovered his patrimony, but also was enriched by the inheritance of Crispus Passienus, his mother's husband, that fell unto him.   And verily through the grace and power of his mother now called home again and restored to her estate, he flourished and grew so great that commonly it was bruited abroad that Messalina, the wife of Claudius, sent some of purpose to take the opportunity of his noon's sleep and so to smother and strangle him, as the only concurrent [Cal. 35] of Britannicus [5] and one that eclipsed the light of his glory.   Now in the tale it went besides that the said parties took a fright at a dragon issuing out of his pillow, whereupon they fled back and forsook the enterprise.   Which fable arose upon this, that there was indeed found the slough of a serpent in his bed about the bolsters.   And yet this slough he enclosed within a bracelet of gold (as his mother willed him) and wore it a good while after upon his right arm ; and at length, weary of any memorial and monument of his mother, flung it away, but in his extremity and despair of his estate sought for the same again in vain.

7. In his tender years and whiles he was yet a boy of no full growth, he acted at the circus games the warlike Troy fight most resolutely, with great favour and applause of the people.   In the eleventh [1] year of his age adopted he was by Claudius and put to school unto Annaeus Seneca, even then a senator, for to be trained up in good literature.   The report goes that Seneca the next night following dreamed as he lay in bed that he was teaching Gaius [2] Caesar ; and shortly after Nero proved his dream true, bewraying the fell stomach and shrewd [3] nature of the said prince by the first experiments that

he could give thereof. For when his brother Britannicus saluted him after he was once adopted (as his wonted manner was before) by the name of Ahenobarbus, he went about to lay this imputation upon him before his father, that he was some changeling and no son of his as he was reputed. His aunt Lepida likewise being in trouble he deposed against in the open face of the court, thereby to gratify his mother her heavy friend[4], and who followed the suit hotly against her. Being honourably brought into the Forum[5], the day of his first plea and commencement [Cl. 2], he promised publicly for the people a congiary and a donative for the soldiers. Having proclaimed also a solemn jousting[6], himself rode before the praetorian soldiers bearing a shield in his own hand. After this he solemnly gave thanks to his father in the senate, before whom being then consul he made a Latin oration in the behalf of the Bononians, and for the Rhodians and inhabitants of Ilium another in Greek. His first jurisdiction he began as provost [*praefectus*] of the city[a] during the celebration of the Latin holidays, what time the most famous advocates and patrons in those days strove a-vie [Cal. 57] who could bring before him most accusations and longest[7], not (as the manner was) such as were ordinary and brief, the express command of Claudius forbidding the same notwithstanding. Not long after he took to wife Octavia, and for the good health of Claudius exhibited the circus games and baiting of wild beasts.

8. Being seventeen years old, so soon as it was known abroad that Claudius was dead, he came forth to those of the praetorian cohort that kept watch and ward, between the sixth and the seventh hour of the day[1], for by reason that the whole day beside was ominous and dismal there was no time thereof thought more auspicious and convenient than it to enter upon the empire ; and so, before the palace stairs being proclaimed and saluted emperor, he was in a litter brought to the camp[2], and hastily from thence, after a short speech made unto the soldiers, conveyed into the Curia. From whence he departed home in the evening, and of those exceeding and infinite honours which were heaped upon him, he refused only the title in his style of Pater Patriae[3], in regard of his young years.

9. Beginning then with a glorious show of piety [1] and kindness at the funeral of Claudius, which was most sumptuously performed, he praised him in an oration and consecrated him a god. In the memorial of his own father Domitius he did him right great honour. His mother he permitted to have the whole regiment [2] of all matters as well public as private. The very first day also of his empire, when the tribune of the sentinels [3] asked of him a watchword, he gave unto him this mot, *Optima mater* (my best mother), and afterwards many a time she accompanied him through the streets in his own litter. He planted a colony at Antium, enrolling therein the old soldiers out of the praetorian cohort and joining with them (by translating their habitations) the richest centurions who had been leaders of the foremost bands ; where also he made a pier [4], a most sumptuous piece of work.

10. And to show a surer proof still of his towardness [1], after profession made to govern the empire according to the prescript rule of Augustus, he omitted no occasion to show either bountifulness or clemency, no, nor so much as to testify his gentleness and courtesy. Those tributes and taxes which were anything heavy he either abolished quite or abated. The rewards due unto informers as touching the Papian law he reduced to the fourth part only of the penalty. Having dealt among the people 400 sesterces [2] for every poll [C. 26], to as many senators as were most nobly descended (howbeit decayed and weakened in their estates) he allowed yearly salaries [3], and to some of them 500,000 sesterces [4]. Likewise for the praetorian cohorts he ordained an allowance of corn monthly gratis. And whensoever he was put in mind to subscribe and set his hand to a warrant (as the manner is) for the execution of any person condemned to die, he would say, " Oh, that I knew not one letter of the book ! " [5] Many times he saluted all the degrees of the city one after another by rote and without book. When the senate upon a time gave him thanks, he answered " (Do so) when I shall deserve [them]." To his exercises in Mars' Field he admitted the commons also, yea, and declaimed often publicly before them. He rehearsed his own verses likewise, not only within house at home but also in the theatre, and that with so general a joy of as many as heard him, that for the said rehearsal there was a solemn procession decreed, and some of his said verses written in golden letters were dedicated to Jupiter Capitolinus.

11. Many and sundry kinds of shows he set forth, to wit, the juvenal[1] sports[a], the circus games, and the stage-plays, also a sword-fight. In the juvenal pastimes he admitted old men, even those of consul's degree, aged women also and matrons to disport themselves. At the circus games, he appointed places for the gentlemen of Rome apart by themselves, where he put also to run a race for the prize chariots drawn with four camels. In the stage-plays (which being instituted for the eternising and perpetuity of his empire he would have to be called Maximi) very many of both degrees[2] and sexes played their parts upon the stage. A Roman gentleman of very good note and especial mark mounted upon an elephant ran down a rope[3]. There was brought upon the stage to be acted the Roman comedy of Afranius entitled *Incendium*, and granted it was unto the actors therein to rifle all the goods and implements of the house as it burned and to take the same as their own. Scattered also abroad there were for the people missiles [Aug. 98][4] during the whole time of those plays ; to wit, a thousand birds every day of all kinds, cates and viands manifold, tickets and tallies for corn, apparel, gold, silver, precious stones, pearls, pictures upon tables, slaves, labouring garrons[5], and beasts also[6] tamed ; last of all, ships, isles[7], lands and possessions, according to their tallies.

12. These games he beheld from the top of the proscenium[1]. At the sword-fight, which he exhibited in the amphitheatre built of timber in one year's space within the ward of Mars' Field he suffered not one man to be killed, no, not so much as a guilty malefactor. Moreover, he brought into the lists for to fight at sharpe [Cal. 27] even 400[2] senators and 600[3] gentlemen of Rome. Some of good wealth and reputation out of the same degrees he caused to come forth into the show-place, for to kill wild beasts and perform sundry services thereto belonging. He represented also a naval fight upon salt water from the sea, with a device to have sea-beasts swimming therein. Semblably, certain Pyrrhic[4] dances in armour, sorted out of the number of young springals [Tib. 6] ; and after their devoir done he gave freely unto every one of them patents and grants to be enfranchised citizens of Rome. Between [5] the arguments [6] of these Pyrrhic dances, devised it was that a bull should leap Pasiphae [a], hidden within a frame of wood resembling a heifer [7], which was acted so lively that many of the beholders believed verily it was so indeed. As for Icarus, at the first attempt to fly he fell presently [Cal. 25] down hard by his own [8] bed-chamber [9] [b], so that he besprinkled him with blood. For very seldom had he used to sit as president at these games, but his manner was to behold them as he lay upon his bed [10], first through little loopholes, but afterwards setting the whole gallery [11] open from whence he looked.

He was the first moreover that instituted at Rome, according to the Greek fashion, quinquennial games of three kinds, to wit, of music and poetry, of gymnastic masteries [Cal. 54] and of horsemanship, which games he called Neronia. After he had dedicated the baines [Aug. 76] and a place therein for gymnastic exercises [c], he allowed the oil that went thereto both for the senate and also for the gentlemen. He ordained masters and wardens of all this solemnity, especial persons of consular degree, chosen by lot to sit as overseers in the place of praetors [12], and then came down himself into the orchestra [13] and the senators' quarter. And verily the victorious coronet for the Latin tongue, both in prose and verse, about which the best and most worshipful persons had contended, when it was granted unto him with their own consents he received ; and the harp presented unto him [14] by the judges he adored, and commanded that it should be carried to the statue of Augustus. At the gymnastic games which he exhibited in the Septa, during the solemn preparation of the great sacrifice Buthysia [Βουθυσία], he cut off the first beard that he had, which he bestowed within a golden box, adorned it with most precious pearls and then consecrated it in the Capitol [15]. To the show of wrestlers and other champions he called also the Vestal virgins, because at Olympia the priestesses likewise of Ceres are allowed to see the games there.

13. I may by good reason among other shows by him exhibited reckon also the entrance into Rome city of Tiridates, whom, being king of Armenia, he had solicited by large promises. Now, when he meant to show him unto the people upon a set day appointed by an edict, and was driven to put it off (the weather was so cloudy), he brought him forth before them to be seen upon the best and most opportune day that he could find, having bestowed about the temples situate in the Forum[1] cohorts of soldiers armed, and sitting himself upon his ivory curule chair of estate [C. 76] before the Rostra in triumphal habit, among the military ensigns, banners, guidons, and streamers. And as the king came up towards him by the ascent of the steep pulpit, he admitted him first to his knees, and then raising up with his right hand kissed him ; afterwards, as he was making his prayer unto him, having taken off his tiara[2], he did the diadem on[3], whiles one who had been praetor pronounced unto the multitude the suppliant's words, as they were by an interpreter delivered unto him. Being brought after this into the theatre and making supplication again, he placed him on his right side next to himself. For which he was with one accord saluted emperor ; and so bringing with him the laurel branch into the Capitol, he shut both doors of double-faced Janus' temple, as if no relic of war remained behind [Aug. 22].

14. Four consulships he bore, the first for two months, the second and last for [six], the third for four. The middle twain he continued without any intermission, the rest he varied with a year's space between.

15. In his ordinary jurisdiction he lightly gave no answer to the proctors before the day following, and that was by writing. In extraordinary commissions and trials this course he held, namely, to decide every cause by itself one after another upon certain days of the session, and to surcease quite the huddling up and debating of matters one in the neck of another[1] ; so often as he went aside to consult, he did deliberate and ask advice of nothing either in common or openly, but reading secretly to himself the opinions written by every counsellor, what liked his own self that pronounced he, as if many more thought well of the same. For a long time he admitted not the sons of libertines into the Curia, and to those that were admitted by the emperors his predecessors he denied all honourable offices. If there sued for magistracies more than could speed [2] or were places void, to comfort their hearts again for delaying and making them to stay longer, he gave unto them the conduct of legions. He granted for the most part all consulships for six months' term. And if one of the two consuls happened to die about the kalends of January [3], he submitted none in his stead, as misliking altogether the old precedent of Caninius Rebilus, who was consul but one day [4]. Triumphal ornaments he gave even unto those that had borne quaestor's dignity only, yea, and to some of the gentlemen's degree, and verily not always for any military service [5]. His orations [6] sent into the senate concerning certain matters he caused for the most part to be read and rehearsed by the consuls, passing by the quaestors' office [7].

16. He devised a new form of the city buildings ; and namely, that before the edifices standing by themselves [1] and other houses likewise there should be porches [2], from the solars whereof all skarfires [Aug. 25] might be put by [C. 18] and repelled [3] ; and those he built [4] at his own charges. He had an intention once to set out and enlarge the walls of Rome even as far as to Ostia, and from thence by a fosse to let the sea into old Rome [5]. Many matters under him were both severely punished and also restrained, yea, and likewise newly ordained. Expenses in his days had a gage [Tib. 34] and stint set upon them [6]. The public suppers [a] were brought down to small collations [7]. Forbidden it was that anything sodden [8], but only pulse and worts [9] should be sold in taverns and cooks' houses, whereas beforetimes there was no manner of viands but it was set out to sale. The Christians, a kind of men given to a new, wicked, and mischievous superstition, were put to death with grievous torments. The sports of charioteers, wherein by an old and licentious custom they had been allowed to range up and down, to beguile folk, to pilfer and steal in merriment, were prohibited. The factions [b] of the pantomimi [10] together with the actors themselves were banished and sent away.

17. Against forgers of writings then first came up this invention, that no books or instruments should be signed unless they were bored and had a thread three times drawn through the holes. Provided it was that in wills the two first [1] parts [2] thereof should be shown as blanks unto those that came to seal the same, having the testator's name only written therein ; item, that no clerk or notary, who was to draw and write another man's will should put down any legacy for himself ; item, that they who had suits depending in court should pay the certain due fee set down by law for pleading of their causes : but for the benches [3][a] nothing, considering the chamber of the city [the treasury] allowed the same gratis and to be free ; item, that in the pleading and deciding of controversies all causes debated aforetime before the masters of the exchequer or city chamber should be removed unto the common hall [4], to be tried before the commissioners and delegates called recuperatores [5], finally, that all appeals from the judges should be made unto the senate.

18. Having no will, no motion, nor hope at any time, to propagate and enlarge the empire, he thought once to have withdrawn the forces even out of Britain ; neither gave he over that intent of his but only for very shame, lest he might be thought to deprave [Aug. 27] the glory of his father Claudius. Only the realm of Pontus with the leave of Polemon [a], as also the kingdom of the Alps by the death of king Cottius, he reduced into the form of a province.

19. Two voyages and no more he undertook, the one to Alexandria, the other into Achaia. But his journey to Alexandria he gave over the very day of his setting forth, by occasion that he was disquieted at once, both with a religious scruple and also with some peril. For when he had gone in procession about all the temples and sat down within the chapel of Vesta, as he was rising up, first the hem [1] or edge of his gown stuck to the seat, and after this arose so dark a mist before his eyes that uneth [Cal. 53] he could see and look about him. In Achaia he attempted to dig through [the] isthmus [a], and in a frequent [C. 22] assembly made a speech unto the praetorian soldiers, exhorting them to begin the work ; and having given the signal by sound of trumpet, himself first broke up the ground with a little spade [2], and when he had cast up the earth, carried it forth upon his own shoulders in a scuttle. He prepared also an expedition to the Caspian Gates, for which he enrolled a new legion of

Italian young soldiers six feet high[3] ; this legion he called the phalanx or squadron of Alexander the Great. These particulars premised, partly deserving no blame, and in part worthy even of no mean praise, have I collected together, that I might sever and distinguish them from his villainies and wicked acts, whereof from henceforward I will make report.

20. Among other arts and sciences, being in his childhood trained up in the skill also of music, no sooner attained he to the empire but he sent for Terpnus the harper, renowned in those days for his cunning above all other. Sitting by him as he played and sung, day by day after supper until it was far in the night, himself likewise by little and little began to practise and exercise the same, yea, and not to let pass any means that expert professors in that kind were wont to do, either for preserving or the bettering and fortifying of their voices ; even to wear before him upon his breast a thin plate or sheet of lead ; to purge by clyster or vomit ; to abstain from apples and fruit, with all such meats as were hurtful to the voice : so long until, his [improvement] still drawing him on (a small and rusty[1] voice though he had), he desired to come forth and show himself upon the open stage, having among his familiar companions this Greek proverb evermore in his mouth, that hidden music was naught worth[a].

The first time that he mounted the stage was at Naples, where he gave not over singing (albeit the theatre was shaken and ready to fall by a sudden earthquake) before he had finished the song begun. In the same place he chanted often and many days together. Moreover, after some short time between taken to repair his voice (as one impatient of keeping within house) from the baines [Aug. 76] there he passed directly to the theatre[2] ; and having in the midst of the orchestra before a frequent multitude of people feasted and banqueted, made promise in the Greek tongue, that if he had sippled a little and wet his whistle he would ring out some note more fully and with a stronger breast. Now, being much delighted with the Alexandrians' praises[3] in prick-song[4], who newly in a second voyage had with their fleet conflowed [C. 39] to Naples[b], he sent for more of them out of Alexandria. And never the later[5] he chose from all parts youths of gentlemen's degree and not so few as 5000 of the lustiest and strongest young men out of the commons, who being sorted into factions [6] should learn certain kinds of shouts and applauses, which they termed *bombos* [c], *imbrices* [d] and *testas* [e] ; also that deft and trim boys, such as had the thickest bush of hair upon their heads [f] and were set out in most excellent apparel, and not without a ring on their left hands [7], should give their attendance upon him as he sang. The chieftains and leaders of these had for their stipend 400,000 sesterces [8].

21. Esteeming so highly as he did of singing, he solemnised at Rome also again the foresaid games called Neroneum before the day and time by order appointed [1]. And when all the people called upon him for his celestial voice [a], he made answer that he verily would do them that pleasure (being so willing and desirous as they were to hear him), but it should be in his hortyards [Cal. 59]. Howbeit, when the corps de guard of the praetorian soldiers, which at that time kept watch and ward, seconded the prayers of the common people, willingly he promised to fulfil their minds [2] out of hand in the very place ; and without any further delay caused his own name to be written in the roll of other professed minstrels and singers to the harp. Thus having put his lot into the pitcher with the rest, he entered the stage when his turn came, and withal the captains of the guard supporting his harp, after them the tribunes military [3], and close unto them his most inward friends and minions. Now when he had taken up his standing and ended his proem, he gave public notice and pronounced by the voice of Cluvius Rufus (no meaner man than of consul's degree) that he would sing and act the story of Niobe [4], and so continued he well-near unto the tenth hour of the day [5] ; which done he deferred the music coronet due for the present victory together with the residue of that gaming [contest] unto the next year following, and all because he might have occasion oftener to chant. But bethinking himself that the time was long, he ceased not to come ever and anon abroad to show his skill in open place. He stuck not [Cal. 25] also in private shows and games [6] to do his devoir, even among common actors and stage-players, and namely, when one of the praetors [7] made offer of a 1,000,000 sesterces. He sung moreover, disguised, tragedies of the worthies and gods; of noble ladies likewise in old time and of goddesses, having their visards[8] framed and made to the likeness of his own face and of some woman whom he loved. Among the rest he chanted the tale of Canace travailing in childbirth[b]; of Orestes who killed his own mother[c]; of Oedipus that plucked out his own eyes[d]; and of Hercules enraged[e]. In the acting of which tragedy, the report goes that a novice[9] placed to keep and guard the entry of the stage, seeing him dressed and bound with chains (as the argument of the said tragedy required) ran in a good [haste] to help him.

22. Exceedingly given he was of a boy to delight in horsemanship and with the love of charioting mightily inflamed, and very much would he be talking (forbidden though he were) of the Circensian games. And one time as he was making moan and bewailing among his schoolfellows the hard fortune of a chariot-driver, one of the green-coat faction, drawn and dragged by his steeds[1], being chidden therefor by his schoolmaster, he had a lie ready and said that he spake of Hector[2]. But as about his first entrance to the empire his custom was daily to play upon a chessboard with ivory horses[3] drawing in chariots, so he used to resort also from his retiring place of pleasure[4] to all the Circensian games, even the very least and meanest of them, first by stealth and privily, afterwards in open sight; so as no man made doubt but at such a day he would be sure always there to be. Neither dissembled he that he was willing to augment the number of the prizes; and therefore the show of chariot-running was drawn out in length and held until late in the evening, by occasion of many more courses than ordinary, so as now the masters of every faction deigned not to bring forth their crews and companies[5] unless they might run the whole day through[6]. Soon after himself also would needs make one and be seen oftentimes to play the charioteer. And when he had tried what he could do and performed, as it were, his first acts in private hortyards among very slaves and the base commons, he proceeded to show himself in the Circus Maximus in all men's eyes, appointing one of his freedmen to put out a white towel for a signal from the place where magistrates are wont to do it.

But not content with this, that he had given good proof of his progress in these feats at Rome, he goes, as I said before [19], into Achaia, moved especially upon this occasion. Those cities and states, where solemn gamings of music are usually held, had brought up a custom to send all the coronets of harp-players unto him. This he accepted so kindly, that he not only admitted at the very first to his presence the ambassadors who brought the same, but also placed them among his familiar guests at the table. And being requested by some of them to sing at supper-table, and highly praised with excessive applause, he came out with this speech, that Greeks were the only skilful hearers, and the men alone worthy of his studies. Neither made he any longer stay, but took his voyage; and no sooner was he passed over the sea to Cassiope[7], but presently he began to sing at the altar there of Jupiter Cassius.

23. After this, he went to all the games of prize [Cl. 21], one after another; for even those that usually are celebrated at most remote and distant times he commanded to be reduced all into one year[1], and some of them also to be iterated[2]. At Olympia likewise he caused (contrary to the manner and custom of that place) a game of music to be held. And lest, whiles he was busied about these matters, anything might either call him away or detain him, when he was advertised by his freedman Helius that the city affairs required his presence, he wrote back unto him in these words: " Albeit your counsel to me at this present and your willing desire is that I should return with all speed, yet ought you to advise me and wish rather that I may return worthy myself, that is to say, Nero." All the while he was singing, lawful it was not for any person to depart out of the theatre, were the cause never so necessary. Whereupon reported it is that some great-bellied women falling into travail were delivered upon the very scaffolds; yea, and many men besides, weary of tedious hearing and praising him, when the town-gates were shut, either by stealth leaped down from the walls, or counterfeiting themselves dead were carried forth as corpses to be buried. But how timorously, with what thought and anguish of mind, with what emulation of his concurrents [Cal. 35] and fear of the umpires he strove for the mastery, it is almost incredible.

His manner was to deal with his adversaries, as if they had been but his equals and of the same condition with him, in this sort ; namely, to observe, watch, and mark their behaviours, to lie in the wind for to catch advantage, to defame them underhand, otherwhiles to rail at them and give them hard terms as they came in his way, yea, and to corrupt with bribes[3] and gifts such as excelled in skill and cunning. As for the judges and umpires aforesaid, he would speak unto them in all reverence before he began to sing, using these terms : that he had done whatsoever was to be done, howbeit, the issue and event was in the hand of Fortune ; they therefore, as they were wise men and learned, ought to except and bar all chances and mishaps. Now upon their exhortations unto him for to be bold and venturous, he would indeed go away from them better appaied[4], but yet for all that not without pensive care and trouble of mind ; finding fault also with the silence and bashful modesty of some, as if the same argued their discontented heaviness and malicious repining, saying withal that he had them in suspicion.

24. During the time that he strove for to win any prize, so strictly obeyed he the laws of the game that he never durst once spit and reach up fleame[1], and the very sweat of his forehead he wiped away with his arm only[2]. Moreover in the acting of a tragedy, when he had quickly taken up his staff again[a], which he happened to let fall, being much dismayed and in great fear lest for that delinquency he should be put from the stage, by no means took he heart again until an under-actor[3] or prompter standing by swore an oath that it was not espied and marked for the shouts and acclamations of the people beneath. Now whensoever he won the victory, he used to pronounce himself victor ; for which cause he contended also in every place for the crier's coronet[4][b]. And to the end there should remain extant no memorial or token of any other victors in these sacred games beside himself, he commanded all their statues and images to be overthrown, drawn with a drag, and so flung into sinks and privies.

Furthermore, he ran with chariots for the best game in many places, and at the Olympic solemnities with one that had a team of ten steeds, notwithstanding he reproved the very same in king Mithridates, as appeared by certain verses

of his own making. But being once shaken and hoisted
out of his chariot and set therein again, howbeit not able
to hold out he desisted and gave over, before he had run
the race through, yet was he crowned nevertheless. After
this, at his departure from thence he enfranchised the whole
province throughout, and withal the judges of these games he
endowed with the freedom of Rome and rewarded with great
sums of money. Which benefits of his himself published
with his own voice from the middle of the race[course], upon
a day of the Isthmian games.

25. Being returned out of Greece he entered Naples,
mounted upon a chariot drawn with white horses, for that
in the said city he had made profession first of his skill in
music, and a part of the wall was cast down against his coming (as the manner is of all victors in those sacred games).
Semblably [C. 39] rode he into Antium, and from thence into
Albanum, and so forward into Rome. But he entered Rome
in the very same chariot wherein sometime Augustus had
rode in triumph, clad in a purple cloak[1], and the same garnished with stars embroidered in gold, wearing upon his head
the Olympic coronet[2], and bearing in his right hand the
Pythian[3], with a pomp and gallant show of the rest before
him[4], together with their titles and inscriptions, testifying
where, and whom, in what kind of song or fabulous argument,
he had won ; not without a train also of applauders[a], following
his chariot, after the manner of those that ride ovant [Cal. 49]
in petty triumph setting up a note, and crying with a loud
voice that they were Augustians and the soldiers of his triumph.
From thence he rode forward, and having thrown down
the arch of the Circus Maximus, he passed on through the
Velabrum and market-place [Forum], up to the Palatium and
so to the temple of Apollo. To do him honour all the way as he
went were beasts killed for sacrifice and saffron eft soons
strewn along the streets. Birds were let fly, ribbons also
and labels, yea, and sweet banqueting junkets cast among.
As for the sacred coronets and garlands aforesaid, he bestowed them in his own bed-chamber round about his beds,
likewise his own statues portrayed in the habit of an harper[5],
and with that mark stamped he his money. And after all
this so far was he from letting slack and remitting one jot

his ardent study of his music profession, that for the preservation of his voice he would never make speech unto his soldiers but absent [6] or having another to pronounce his words for him [7] ; nor yet do aught in earnest or mirth without his phonascus [8] by, to put him in mind for to spare his pipes and hold his handkerchief to his mouth ; and to many a man he either offered friendship or denounced enmity, according as every one praised him more or less.

26. His unruly wildness, unbridled lust, wasteful riotousness, avarice, and cruelty, he practised verily at first by leisure closely [Cl. 32], as the tricks of youthful folly ; yet so as even then no man might doubt that they were the inbred vices of nature and not the errors of young age. No sooner was it twilight and the evening shut in, but presently [Cal. 22] he would catch up a cap [1] [a] on his head, and so disguised go into taverns and victualling houses, walk the streets playing and sporting all the way, but yet not without shrewd [Cal. 25] turns and doing mischief. For he used to fall upon those that came late from supper and knock them soundly, yea, and if they struggled with him and made resistance, to wound and drown them in the sinks and town ditches [2] ; to break into petty shops also and rifle them ; for he had set up in his house at home a fair [3] [b], there to receive the price of the booty which he had gotten, and was to be sold to who would give most and bid best therefor. But many a time at such brawls and scufflings aforesaid he endangered his eyes, yea, and his life too ; being once beaten well-near to death by a certain young gentleman of senator's degree [c], whose wife he had misused with unclean handling. Whereupon never after durst he go abroad into the streets at that hour of the night without his military tribunes following after him aloof and secretly. In the daytime also, being carried close in a chair [4] into the theatre, he would be present in person, and from the upper part [5] of the proscenium [6] both give a signal to the seditious factions of players (setting them together by the ears) and also behold them how they bickered. Now when they were come once to plain fight, skirmishing with stones and fragments of broken seats [and] scaffolds, himself stuck not [Cal. 25] to fling apace at [7] the people, insomuch as once he broke the praetor's head.

27. But as his vices grew by little and little to get head, he laid aside these wild tricks by way of sport and in secret, and without all care of concealing and dissembling the matter broke out openly to greater outrages. His meals he drew out at length [a], eating and drinking from noon to midnight, doused and fomented oftentimes in cisterns of hot waters, and in summer season within baths altered and made cold with snow. His suppers he took divers times abroad also in public place, to wit, in the naumachia [1] shut up and enclosed, or in Mars' Field, or else in the Circus Maximus, where he was served and attended upon by all the common queans of the city and stinking strumpets [b] of the stews. So often as he went down the Tiber to Ostia, or sailed along the Baian creek [2], there were provided in divers places of the strand and banks booths to bait in, conspicuous brothel-houses and taverns, where stood married dames after the manner of hostesses and victualling wives [c] calling unto him, some here, some there on both sides of the banks, entreating him to land and turn in to them. His manner was also to give warning unto his familiar friends and bid himself to supper ; and one of them it cost in sweetmeats four millions of sesterces [d], and another a good deal more in rose-water and odoriferous oils or perfumes of roses from Syrtium [e].

28. Over and besides the unnatural abusing of boys free-born and the keeping of men's wives as his concubines, he forced also and deflowered Rubria, a Vestal virgin. Acte, a freedwoman, he went very near to have wedded as his lawful wife [1], suborning certain men who had been consuls to avouch and forswear that she was of royal blood descended. A boy there was named Sporus [a], whose genitals he cut out and assayed thereby to transform him into the nature of a woman. Him he caused to be brought unto him as a bride, with a dowry, in a fine yellow veil, after the solemn manner of marriage, not without a frequent and goodly train attending upon him, whom he maintained as his wife. Hereupon there goes abroad a pretty conceited jest of a pleasant fellow, that it might have been well and happy with the world, if his father Domitius had wedded such a wife. This Sporus, trimly set out with the jewels, decked with the ornaments of the empresses, and carried in a litter, he accompanied all about the shire-towns of great resort and market boroughs of Greece, yea, and afterwards at Rome up and down the street Sigillaria [Cl. 16], many a time sweetly kissing him by the way. For that he had a lust to lie with his own mother and was frighted from it by some depraving [Aug. 27] backfriends[2] of hers, for fear lest the proud and insolent dame might by this kind of favour grow too mighty, no man ever made doubt, especially after that he entertained among his concubines a harlot, most like in all points (by report) unto Agrippina. It is affirmed moreover that in times past, so often as he rode in a litter together with his mother, he played the filthy wanton and was bewrayed by the marks and spots appearing upon her vesture.

29. As for his own body, certes he forfeited the honour thereof, prostituting it to be abused so far forth[1] as, having defiled in manner all the parts of it, at the last he devised a kind (as it were) of sport and game ; that, being covered all over in a wild beast's skin, he should be let loose forth of a cage[2] and then give the assault upon the privities of men and women both, as they stood tied fast to a stake, and when he had shown his rage to the full, be killed, forsooth by Doryphorus[a] his freedman, unto whom himself also was wedded like as Sporus unto him, insomuch as he counterfeited the noise and cries of maidens when they be forced and suffer devirgination[3]. I have heard of divers that he was fully persuaded no man nor woman was honest or in any part of their bodies pure and clean, but most of them dissembled their uncleanness and craftily hid it. As many therefore as professed[4] unto him their obscene filthiness, he forgave all other faults and trespasses whatsoever.

30. The fruit of riches and use of money he took to be nothing else but lavish expense, thinking them to be very base niggards and mechanical pinch-pennies, that kept any account of reckoning what they spent and laid out, but such only passing rich and right magnificoes, who misspent and wasted all. He praised and admired his uncle Gaius in no respect more than for that he had lashed out and consumed in a short space a huge mass of wealth left unto him by Tiberius ; he kept therefore no mean nor made any end of prodigal giving and making away all. He allowed unto

Tiridates [a] (a thing almost incredible) 800,000 sesterces day by day for his expenses, and at his departure bestowed upon him not so little as 100,000,000. Menecrates the harper and Spicillus the sword-fencer he enfeoffed in the livings, patrimonies, and houses of right noble personages who had triumphed. Cercopithecus, whom he had enriched with the lands and houses (as well within the city as country) of Paneros the usurer [1], he honoured like a prince at his funeral, and interred with the charges well-near of a royal sepulture. No garments did he on his back twice. At hazard, when he played he ventured no less than 400,000 sesterces at a cast, upon every point or prick of the chance [2] [b]. He fished with a golden net [3] (drawn and knit) with cords twisted of purple and crimson silk in grain [4]. He never, by report, when he made any journey, had under a thousand carroches in his train. His mules were shod with silver, his muleteers arrayed in fine red Canusian cloth [5], and attended he was with a multitude of Mazaces [6] and couriers gaily set out with their bracelets and rich phalers [c].

31. In no one thing was he more wasteful and prodigal than in building. He made a house that reached from the Palatium to the Esquiliae, which at first he called his transitory [1], but when it had been consumed with fire and was re-edified he named his golden edifice. As touching the large compass and receit [Cal. 37], the rich furniture and setting out thereof, it may suffice to relate thus much. The porch [2] was of such a height as therein might stand upright the giant-like image representing his own person, a hundred and twenty feet high. So large was this house as that it contained three galleries of a mile apiece in length [3]. Item, a standing pool like unto a sea, and the same enclosed round about with buildings in form of cities. It received moreover granges with cornfields, vine or garden pastures and woods to them, stored with a multitude of divers and sundry beasts, both tame and wild of all sorts. In all other parts thereof all was laid over with gold, garnished with precious stones and shells of pearls [4]. As for the parlours, framed they were with embowed roofs, seeled [5] with panels of ivory, devised to turn round and remove so as flowers might be scattered from thence, with a device also of pipes and spouts to cast and sprinkle

sweet oils from aloft. But of all these parlours [or] banqueting-rooms the principal and fairest was made round, to
turn about continually both day and night in manner of the
world [6]. The baines within this house flowed with salt water
derived from the sea and with fresh from the rivers Albulae [7].
This edifice, finished after such a fashion as this, when he
dedicated [8] [it], thus far forth only he liked as that he said
he now at length began to dwell like a man. Furthermore,
he began a pool [9] reaching from Misenum to the mere [10]
Avernus, covered all above-head, enclosed and environed
with cloisters [11], into which all the hot waters that were
in the baths of Baiae might be conveyed. Likewise he cast
a fosse [12] from the said Avernus as far as to Ostia, and the same
navigable, that men forsooth might sail in ships and yet not
be upon the sea. This carried in length 160 miles, and bare
that breadth as galleys with five ranks of oars might pass to
and fro thereupon. For the performing of these works he
had given command that all prisoners wheresoever should
be transported into Italy, and that no person attaint and
convict of any wicked act should be condemned otherwise
but to work thereat.

32. To these outrageous expenses, besides the trust and
confidence he had in the revenues of the empire, put forward
he was upon a certain unexpected hope also that he conceived of finding a world of wealth ; and that through intelligence given unto him by a gentleman of Rome, who assured
him upon his knowledge that the rich treasure and old store
of silver and gold both, which queen Dido fleeing out of Tyre
carried away with her, lay buried in Africa within most huge
and vast caves under the ground and might be got forth with
some small labour of those that would go about it. But
when this hope failed him and came to nothing, being now
altogether destitute and so far exhausted and bare of money,
that of necessity even soldiers' pay and the fees due unto old
servitors in the wars for their service must run on still and be
deferred, he bent his mind to promoting of false imputations,
to pilling also and polling [C. 54].

First and foremost he brought up this order, that out of the
goods of freedmen deceased, instead of the one half, three-
fourth parts [1] should be exacted and gathered for him, of as

many, I say, as without justification bore that name, which
any of those families did whereunto himself was allied; afterwards, that their wills should be forfeit and confiscate, who
were unthankful to the prince[2]; item, that lawyers should
not escape free and go clear away, who had drawn and written
such wills; as also that all deeds and words should be brought
within the compass of treason, if there could be found but any
promoter[3] to give information. He called moreover, after a
long time passed, for the rewards and coronets due to victors,
which ever at any times the cities and states had presented
or decreed unto him at the games of prize [23]. And whereas
he had prohibited the use of the amethyst[4] and purple colours,
he suborned one of purpose underhand to sell upon a market
day[5] some few ounces thereof, and thereupon made stay of
all occupiers and chapmen[6] whatsoever and laid them fast[7].
Furthermore, having espied once (as he was singing) a dame
of Rome from the scaffolds in the theatre, arrayed in purple
forbidden by the law[8], himself pointed at her (as it is verily
thought) and showed her to his procurators,[9] and presently
caused the woman to be haled from thence and turned out
not only of her garments but also of all the goods she had.
He assigned an office to no man but he used these words
withal: "Thou knowest what I have need of." Also: "Let
us look to this, that no man may have[10] anything." To
conclude, he robbed the temples of many gifts and oblations;
the images likewise therein made of gold or silver he melted
into a mass, and among the rest, even those of the tutelar
gods of Rome[11], which soon after Galba restored and erected
again in their places.

33. As touching his parricides and murders he began them
first with Claudius, of whose death, although he were not
principal author, yet he was privy and accessory thereto.
Neither dissembled he so much, as who afterwards was wont
by a Greek byword[1] to praise mushrooms (in which kind
of meat Claudius had taken his bane[2]), as the food of the
gods[3]. Certes, he abused him after he was dead in most
spiteful and contumelious manner, both in word and deed
every way, taunting and twitting him, one while with his
folly, another while with his cruelty. For in scoffing wise he
would say of him that he had left now *morari*[a] any longer

among mortal men, using the first syllable of the said word long ; and many of his decrees and constitutions he annulled as the acts of a doltish and doting man. Finally, he neglected the place of his funeral fire [4] [b], suffering it to be empaled [5], but with slight stuff and low rails of timber.

As for Britannicus, [just as] much for envy that he had a sweeter and pleasanter voice than himself as for fear lest another day he should be more gracious [6] than he among men in remembrance of his father, he attempted to make him away by poison. This poison Nero had received at the hands of one Locusta, a woman who impeached and brought to light divers confectioners of poisons ; and seeing it wrought later than he looked it should do and proved not to his mind, by reason that it moved Britannicus to the stool only and caused a lask [7], he sent for the said woman and beat her with his own hands, laying hardly to her charge that instead of a poison she had given him a remedy and wholesome medicine. Now when she alleged for her excuse that she gave him the less dose thereby to colour and cloak the odious fact, which would have bred much anger and hatred : " Why ! then belike," quoth he, " I am afraid of the Julian law [8]." And so he forced her before his face in his own bed-chamber to compound and seethe a poison that should be most quick and of present operation [9]. And then having made trial thereof on a kid, after he saw once that the beast continued five hours before it died, he caused the same to be boiled again and many times more, and so he set it before a pig. And when the pig died presently upon the taking thereof, he commanded it should be brought into his refection chamber and given unto Britannicus as he sat at supper with him. No sooner had he tasted it but he fell down dead. Nero readily made a lie and gave it out among the rest of his guests that Britannicus was surprised by a fit of the falling sickness, as his manner was to be. But the next morrow in all haste he took order [Cal. 8] for his corpse to be carried forth to burial with no better funeral than ordinary, and that in an exceeding great storm of rain. Unto the said Locusta for her service done he granted impunity [10] ; he endowed her also with fair lands, yea, and allowed her to have scholars for to be trained up under her in that feat.

34. His own mother, for looking narrowly into him and

examining his words and deeds somewhat straitly, for seeming also to correct and reform the same, thus far forth [29] only at the first he was grieved and offended with, as that eftsoons he made her odious to the world, pretending that he was about to resign up the empire and depart to Rhodes [1]. Soon after he deprived her of all honour, dignity, and authority, and removing from about her the guard of German soldiers [2] that attended upon her person, he banished her out of the same house with him and so forth out of the precincts of the palace ; neither cared he what he did, so he might molest and trouble her, suborning some of purpose both to disquiet her while she abode in Rome with suits and actions, and also when she was desirous of repose and ease in a retiring place out of the way, to course [3] her with reproachful taunts and flouting scoffs as they passed that way either by land or sea. But being terrified with her threats and violent shrewdness [Cal. 25], he determined to kill and dispatch her at once.

Having attempted it with poison thrice and perceiving that she was defended with antidotes and preservatives, he provided a bed-chamber for her with so ticklish an arched roof over her head as, being easily unjointed, the frame thereof might fall in pieces in the night and light upon her as she lay asleep. When this design could not be kept close but was revealed by some of the complices privy thereto, he devised a ship so made as that quickly it should cleave asunder, that either by the wreck or fall of the fore-deck [4] aloft she might come to a mischief and perish. And so, making a semblance of a love-day [5] and reconciliation, he sent for her by most sweet and kind letters, training [6] her unto Baiae, there to celebrate with him the solemnity of the Quinquatrus [7]. And having given order beforehand to certain masters of galleys for to split the foist [8] wherein she was embarked, as if by chance they were run full upon her, he made it late ere he went to the feast and sat long at it. Now when she was to return back again unto Bauli, in lieu of that vessel thus shaken and cracked he put unto her the other abovesaid made with joints and vices, easy to fall in pieces ; and so with a cheerful countenance accompanied her (to the water-side [9]) and at the parting also kissed her paps. All the time after he lay awake in great trouble and fear, waiting for the issue of these

enterprises. But when he understood that all went cross and
that she was escaped to land by swimming, being altogether
to seek what course to take, as Lucius Agerinus, her freedman,
brought word with great joy how she was escaped alive and
safe, he conveyed privily a dagger close by him [10] ; and as if
he had been suborned and hired secretly by her to kill him,
caused the said Agerinus to be apprehended and bound with
chains, and withal his mother aforesaid to be murdered, pretending as if by voluntary death she had avoided the odious
crime thus detected, and so made herself away.

Worse matter yet than all this and more horrible is reported beside, and that by authors of good credit who will
stand to it ; namely, that he ran in all haste to view the
dead body of his mother when she was killed, that he handled
every part and member of it, found fault with some and commended others, and being thirsty in the meantime [11] took a
draught of drink. Howbeit, notwithstanding he was heartened
by the joyous gratulation of soldiers, senate, and people, yet
could he not either for the present or ever after endure the
worm and sting of conscience for this foul act, but confessed
many a time that haunted and harried he was with the appari-
tion of his mother's ghost, tormented also with the scourges
and burning torches of the Furies. Moreover, with a sacrifice
made by direction of magicians, he assayed to raise up her
soul and spirit and to entreat the same to forgive him. Verily,
as he travelled through Greece, at the sacred Eleusinian ceremonies (from the institution and professing therein all impious,
godless, and wicked persons are by the voice of a crier debarred [a]) he durst not be present.

To this parricide of his mother he adjoined also the murder
of his aunt [12]. For when upon a time he visited her lying sick
of a costive belly [13], and she, a woman now well stept in years,
in handling the tender down of his beard new budding forth,
chanced (as the manner is) by way of pleasing speech, to say,
" Might I but live to take up this soft hair when it falls [14], I
would be willing to die," he, turning to those that stood next
unto him, in derision and scoffing manner said, " Marry and
even straightway I will cut it off (for her sake)," and so
made no more ado but gave order [15] unto the physician to
ply the sick woman still with stronger purgatives [16]. For

even before she was through dead, he laid sure hold of her goods and suppressed her last will, that nothing might escape his clutches.

35. Besides Octavia [1], he married afterwards two wives, to wit, Poppaea [2] Sabina, the daughter of one [3] who had been quaestor and the wedded wife before of a Roman knight [4], then Statilia Messallina, niece [5] in the third degree removed of Taurus [6], twice consul, who had once triumphed. For to have and enjoy her he murdered her husband Atticus Vestinus then consul, even during the time of that honourable magistracy. Soon weary he was of Octavia's company and forsook her bed, and when some friends reproved him for it, he made answer that the jewels and ornaments only of a wife ought to content her. Soon after when he had assayed many times (but in vain) to strangle her, he put her away, pretending she was barren. But when the people misliked this divorce and forbare not to rail upon him for it, he proceeded even to confine and banish her quite. In the end he murdered her under a colourable imputation of divers adulteries, charged upon her so impudently and falsely, that when all generally who were by torture examined upon the point stood stoutly to the very last in denial, he suborned and brought in Anicetus [7] his own pedagogue against her, who should slander himself with her and confess that by a wile he had abused her body. The twelfth day after the said divorcement of Octavia he espoused and married the aforesaid dame Poppaea, whom he loved entirely ; and yet even her also he killed with a kick [8] of his heel, for that, being big with child and sickly withal, she had reviled him and given him shrewd [Cal. 25] words for coming home so late one night after his running with chariots. By her he had a daughter named Claudia Augusta, whom he buried when she was a very infant.

There was no kind of affinity and consanguinity, were it never so near, but it felt the weight of his deadly hand. Antonia, the daughter of Claudius, refusing after the death of Poppaea to be his wife, he slew under a pretence as if she went about to conspire against him and to alter the State. Semblably [C. 39] he killed all the rest that were either allied unto him or of his kindred. Among whom Aulus Plautius, a young gentleman, was one, whose body after he had by force filthily against kind [C. 52] abused before his death, " Let my mother go now," quoth he, " and kiss my successor's sweet lips," giving it out that he was her well-beloved darling and by her set on to hope and gape after the empire. His step-son Rufinus Crispinus, the son of Poppaea[9], being yet of tender years and a youth under age, because the report went of him that in game he would play for dukedoms[10] and empires, he gave order unto his own servants for to drown in the sea whiles he was there fishing. Tuscus his nurse's son he confined and sent away, for that, being his procurator in Egypt, he had bathed in those baines [Aug. 76] which were built against his coming. His preceptor and school-master Seneca he compelled to die[11], albeit he had sworn unto him very devoutly (when he made suit many times for a licence to depart the court and yielded up therewith all his goods into his hands) that he[12] had no cause to suspect him, for he would rather lose his own life than do him any harm. Unto Burrus, captain of the guard[13], he promised a medicine to heal his swollen throat[14], and sent him the rank poison toxicum for it. His freedmen[15] that were rich and old, whose favour, friendship, and directions had stood him in good stead for procuring unto him in times past adoption and afterwards the imperial rule, he cut short every one by poison, partly put into their meats and partly mingled with their drinks.

36. With no less cruelty raged he abroad even against strangers and mere foreigners. A blazing hairy star, commonly thought to portend death and destruction to the highest powers, began to arise and had appeared many nights together. Being troubled therewith, and informed by Babillus the astrologer that kings were wont to expiate such prodigious signs with some notable massacre, and so divert the same from themselves and turn all upon the heads of their peers and nobles, he thereupon projected the death of all the noblest personages in the city ; and verily, so much the rather, and as it were upon just cause, by reason of two conspiracies by him published and divulged abroad, of which the former and the greater bearing the name of Piso[1] was plotted and detected at Rome, the latter going under the name of Vinicius[2]

at Beneventum. The conspirators had their trial and pleaded
bound with threefold chains ; and as some of them confessed
the action of their own accord, so others[3] said moreover, that
he was beholden unto them for it, because they could not
possibly do a cure upon him by any other means (distained as
he was and dishonoured with all kind of wicked acts) but only
by death. The children of the condemned were expelled the
city, and then dispatched with poison or hunger-starved. It is
for certain known that some of them with their pedagogues
and book-keepers[4] took their bane [33] all at one dinner
together, others were restrained from seeking and earning
their daily food.

37. After this, without all choice and respect, without
all measure in his hand, he spared none ; he put to death
whomsoever it pleased him and for what cause it skilled[1] not.
But not to make long relation of many, it was laid to Salvidienus Orfitus' charge that he had set and let three shops out of
his house about the Forum unto the cities and states abroad
for their ambassadors for to make their abode and converse
in ; to Cassius Longinus the lawyer (a man bereft of both his
eyes) objected it was that in the ancient pedigree of his own
house and lineage he had set up again[2] the images of Gaius
Cassius, one of them that murdered Caesar ; to Paetus
Thrasea, for having a stern and severe countenance like a
pedagogue. When these with other were appointed once
to die, he allowed them no more than one hour's respite to
live after, and because no further delay might come between,
he put unto them chirurgeons (in case they lingered and made
no haste) to cure them out of hand (for that was the term
he used), meaning thereby to cut their veins and let them
bleed to death. It is verily thought also, that to a certain
great eater[3] (an Egyptian born), that used to feed on raw
flesh and whatsoever was given him, he had a great desire to
cast men alive, for to be quartered, cut in pieces, and devoured
by him[a]. Being lifted and puffed up with these as it were
so great successes, he said that no prince ever knew[4] what
he might do ; and oftentimes he cast out many words, betokening very significantly that he would not spare the
senators remaining behind, but one day utterly rase[5] that
order and degree out of the commonwealth, and permit the

gentlemen of Rome and his freedmen only to rule provinces and have the conduct of armies. Certes, neither at his coming home nor going forth anywhither vouchsafed he to kiss any one of them, no, nor so much as once to resalute them; and when with formal compliments he entered upon his work of digging through [the] isthmus [6], he wished and prayed aloud before a frequent audience, that the enterprise might speed well and turn to the weal of himself and the people of Rome, concealing and suppressing all mention of the senate [7].

38. But yet for all that he spared not the people nor forbare the very walls and buildings of his country the city. When one in common talk upon a time chanced to say,

> Ἐμοῦ θανόντος γαῖα μιχθήτω πυρί [a],
> When vital breath is fled from me,
> Let earth with fire imingled be,

"Nay, rather," quoth he, "'Ἐμοῦ ζῶντος,"

> Whiles vital breath remains in me.

And even so he did indeed: for being offended as it were with the ill-favoured fashion of the old houses as also with the narrow, crooked, and winding streets, he set the city of Rome on fire so apparently that many citizens of consul's degree, taking his chamberlains [1] in the manner [2] with matches, touchwood, and hurds [3] in their messuages within the city would not once lay hand on them but let them alone; yea, and certain garners and storehouses about his golden edifice (for that the plot of ground on which they were situate his mind stood most unto) were by war-engines forcibly shaken, thrown down, and fired, by reason they were built with stone walls. For six days and seven nights together raged he in this wise, making havoc of all and driving the common people to take up their inns [4] and shrowd themselves [5] the while about the tombs and monuments of the dead. During this time, beside an infinite number of houses standing apart from others [b], the goodly edifices and buildings of noble captains in old time, adorned still and beautified with the spoils of enemies, the stately temples also of the gods, vowed and dedicated by the ancient kings first and afterwards in the

Punic [6] and Gallic wars, burned all on a light fire [Aug. 82] ; and in one word, whatsoever remained from old time worth the seeing and memorable was consumed. This fire beheld he daily out of Maecenas' high tower [c], and taking joy (as he said himself) at the beautiful flame that it made, chanted the winning and destruction of Troy in that musician's habit wherein he was wont to sing upon the stage. And because he would not miss, but lay fast hold upon all the booty and pillage which possibly he could come by even from thence also, having promised free leave to cast forth dead carcasses and rid away the rammel of the ruins, look, what relics remained of all their goods and substance unburnt, he permitted not one to go unto it. Finally, not only by receiving, but also by exacting contributions from all parts, he beggared well-near the provinces and consumed the wealth of private persons.

39. To amend the matter well, unto these harms and reproachful dishonours of the State so great as they were, arising from the prince, there happened also some other calamities by chance and fortune ; to wit, a pestilence continuing one autumn, whereby thirty thousand burials were reckoned in the record [1] of Libitina [2][a] ; an unfortunate loss in Britain, wherein two principal towns of great importance were sacked [3], with great slaughter besides of Roman citizens and allies ; a shameful disgrace received in the East by reason that the Roman legions in Armenia were put under the yoke as slaves, and Syria was hardly and with much ado kept in terms of allegiance. But a wonder it was to see, and a thing especially to be noted, that amid all these misfortunes he took nothing less to the heart than the shrewd [35] checks [4] and reviling taunts of men, and was to none more mild than to such as had provoked him, either with hard speeches or opprobrious verses.

Many infamous libels and defamatory words both in Greek and Latin were publicly written or otherwise cast and spread abroad against him [b], as for example these :

Νέρων, Ὀρέστης, Ἀλκμέων, μητροκτόνοι.
Νεόνυμφον, Νέρων ἰδίαν μητέρα ἀπέκτεινε.

Nero, Orestes [c], Alcmæon [d], did shorten mother's life :
  Nero slew his [5], when newly her he wedded [6] as his wife.

Quis neget Aeneae magna de stirpe Neronem?
Sustulit hic matrem, sustulit ille patrem.

Who can deny, of great Aeneas our Nero sprung to be
  That rid his mother of her life, as Sire [7] from fire did he [e] ?

Dum tendit citharam noster, dum cornua Parthus,
Noster erit Paean, ille Hecatebeletes.

Whiles our Nero bendeth his harp [8] while Parthian his bow ;
  Our prince shall be Paean, he Hecatebeletes [f].

Roma domus fiet : Veios migrate, Quirites,
Si non et Veios occupat ista domus.

Rome will become a dwelling house [g] : to Veii flit apace,
  Quirites, lest this house before ye come take up the place.

But no search made he after the authors hereof, and some of them, being by the impeacher convented [2] before the senate, he would not suffer to sustain any grievous punishment. As he passed by in the open street, Isidorus the Cynic [9] had checked him aloud in these terms, that he used to chant the calamities of Nauplius [h] very well, but disposed of his own goods as badly. And Datus, a player of the Atellane comedies [10] in a certain sonnet singing these words [i], Ὑγίαινε πάτερ, Farewell, father, Ὑγίαινε μῆτερ, Farewell, mother, had acted the same so significantly as that he feigned the one drinking and the other swimming, to express thereby the end of Claudius [11] and Agrippina [12] ; and in the last conclusion of all, with these words

Orcus vobis ducit pedes,

Now Pluto leadeth forth your feet [k],

in plain gesture noted the senate. The actor and philosopher Nero did no more unto but banish them Rome and Italy, either for that he set light by all shame and infamy, or else, lest in bewraying any grief [13] he might stir up and provoke pregnant wits to work upon him.

40. Well, the world having endured such an emperor as this little less than fourteen years, at length fell away and forsook him clean. And first the Gauls began, following as the ringleader of their insurrection Julius Vindex, who that very time governed the province [1] as propraetor. Foretold it had been long ago unto Nero by the astrologers that one day he should be left forlorn. Whereupon this saying was most rife in his mouth,

Τὸ τεχνίον πᾶσα γαῖα τρέφει[2],

An artisan of any kind
In every land will living find,

so that he might the better be excused and borne withal for studying and practising the art of minstrelsy and singing to the harp, as a skill delightful unto him now a prince, and needful for him another day a private person. Yet some there were who promised unto him so forsaken the government of the East parts, and others by special name the kingdom of Jerusalem ; but most of them warranted him assuredly the restitution of his former estate. And being inclined rather to rest upon this hope, when he had lost Britain and Armenia and recovered them both again, he thought himself discharged then and quit from the fatal calamities destined unto him. But sending one time to the oracle of Apollo at Delphi and hearing this answer from thence, that he must beware of the year seventy-three [a], as who would say he was to die in that year (of his own age) and not before, and divining no whit of Galba's years, with so assured confidence he conceived in his heart not only long life but also a perpetual and singular felicity, that when he had lost by shipwreck things of exceeding price, he stuck not [Cal. 25] to say among his familiars that the fishes would bring the same again unto him [3].

At Naples advertised he was of the rebellion in Gaul, which fell out to be the very same day of the year on which he had killed his mother. But he took this news so patiently and carelessly that he gave suspicion even of joy and contentment, as if occasion had been offered and presented thereby to make spoil (by the law of arms) of those most rich and wealthy provinces ; and straightways going forth into the gymnasium [4], he beheld with exceeding great earnestness and delight the wrestlers and champions striving for the prize. At supper-time also, being interrupted with letters importing more tumults and troubles still, thus far forth only he grew into choler and indignation as that he threatened mischief [5] to them who had revolted [6]. To conclude, for eight days together he never went about to write back unto any man nor to give any charge or direction at all, but buried the matter quite in silence.

41. At the last, thoroughly moved and nettled with the contumelious edicts of Vindex coming so thick one in the neck of another [15], he exhorted the senate in a letter written unto them to revenge him and the commonwealth, alleging for an excuse the quinsy [1] whereof he was sick and therefore could not himself be present in person. But nothing vexed him so much as this ; that he was by him blamed for an unskilful musician [2], and because instead of Nero he called him Ahenobarbus [3]. And verily, as touching this name appropriate to his house and family, wherewith he was thus in contumelious manner twitted, he professed to resume the same and to lay away the other that came by adoption [4]. All other reviling taunts and slanders he confuted as mere false by no other argument than this, that unskilfulness, forsooth, was objected unto him in that very art, which he had so painfully studied and brought to so good perfection, and therewith asked them eft-soons one by one, whether they had ever known a more excellent musician than himself. But when messengers came still one after another, in great fear he returned to Rome. And having his heart lightened but a little in the way with a vain and foolish presage, by occasion that he espied and observed engraven upon a monument a certain French soldier with a Roman knight overmatched in fight and trailed along by the hair of the head, he at this sight leaped for joy and worshipped the heavens. Neither then, verily, did he so much as consult in public with the senate or assemble the people, but only call forth home to his house some of the chief and principal persons among them. And having dispatched in great haste this consultation, the rest of that day he led them all about to his musical water-instruments of a strange device and fashion not before known ; and showing every one by itself unto them, discoursing also of the reason and difficult workmanship of each one, he promised even anon to bring them all forth into the open theatre, if Vindex would give him leave [5].

42. After that he understood besides how Galba likewise and the provinces of Spain were revolted, he fell down at once ; his heart was then daunted and clean done ; and so he lay a good while speechless in a trance and ready, as one would say, to go out of the world. And so soon as he came again to himself, he rent his clothes, beat and knocked his head; saying plainly that he was utterly undone ; yea, and when his nurse came about him to comfort his poor heart, telling him that the like accidents had befallen to other princes also before him, he answered again, that he above all the rest suffered miseries never heard of nor known before, thus in his life-time to forgo and lose his empire. Neither yet for all this struck he sail one whit in laying away or leaving out one jot of his ordinary riot and supine slothfulness ; nay, when some little inkling was given of good news out of the provinces as he sat at a most sumptuous and plentiful supper, he pronounced even with express gesture like a player certain ridiculous rhymes, and those set to lascivious and wanton measures, against the chieftains of rebellion ; and what were those ? even stale stuff and commonly known already. Being also secretly conveyed into the theatre, he sent word unto a certain player acting his part with great contentment of them that saw and heard him, that he did but abuse his occupations[1].

43. Immediately upon the beginning of this fearful tumult[1] it is credibly thought that he intended many designs and those very cruel and horrible, yet such as agreed well enough with his natural humour ; namely, to send underhand successors and murderers of all those that were commanders of armies and regents of provinces, as if they all had conspired and drawn in one and the selfsame line[2] ; item, to massacre all banished persons wheresoever and the Frenchmen every one that were to be found in Rome, those because they should not band and combine with them that revolted, these as complices with their own countrymen and their abetters ; item, to permit the armies for to make spoil and havoc of the provinces in Gaul ; item, to poison all the senate generally at some appointed feast ; last of all, to fire Rome and let wild beasts loose among the people, that thereby there might be more ado and greater difficulty to save the city.

But being scared from these designs, not so much upon any repentance as despair of their accomplishment, and persuaded withal that necessary it was to make a voyage and warlike expedition, the consuls then in place he deprived of

their government before the due time and himself alone
entered upon the consulship in their rooms, as if forsooth the
destinies had so ordained that Gaul could not be subdued but
by a (sole) consul[3]. Having then taken into his hands the
knitches of rods[4], when after meat he withdrew himself aside
out of his dining-chamber, leaning upon the shoulders of his
familiar friends, he protested that so soon as ever he was come
into the province he would show himself unarmed before
the armies and do nothing else but weep ; and after he had
once by that means reclaimed the authors of the revolt and
brought them to repentance, sing merrily the day following
songs of triumph with them that rejoiced with him, " which
songs," quoth he, " ought with all speed even now to be composed for me."

44. In the preparation of this warlike voyage his special
care was to choose forth meet wagons for the carriage of his
musical instruments ; to cut and poll the concubines which
he carried out with him like men, and to furnish them with
battle-axes and little bucklers after the Amazonian fashion.
This done, he cited the city tribes to take the military oath ;
and when no serviceable men would answer to their names, he
enjoined all masters to set forth a certain number of bondservants, neither admitted he out of the whole family and
household of every man but such only as were most approved,
excepting not so much as their stewards or clerks and secretaries. He commanded likewise all degrees to allow and con-
tribute towards this expedition part of their estate according
as they were valued in the censor's book ; and more than so,
the tenants inhabiting private messuages and great houses
standing by themselves to pay out of hand[1] in yearly pension
to his exchequer. He exacted also, with great scornfulness[2]
and extremity[3], good money rough and new-coined, silver fine
and full of risings[4], gold pure and red as fire[5], insomuch as
most men openly refused the payment of all contributions,
demanding in a general consent, that what money soever promoters [32] had received for their informations should rather
be required back again at their hands.

45. By the dearth likewise of corn, look, what hatred was
conceived against the gainers[1], the same grew heavy upon
him. For it fell out by chance that in this public famine

word came of a ship[2] of Alexandria[a], how it was arrived
freighted with a kind of dust for the wrestlers of Nero his
court. Having thus stirred up and kindled the hatred of
all the world against him, there was no contumelious despite
but he sustained. To one statue of his, just behind the crown
of the head, was set a chariot[3] with an imprese[4] in Greek
to this effect : Now in truth, and not before, is the combat[b] ;
and again, Now or never hale and draw[c]. To the neck of
another there was tied a leather-bag[5], and therewith this
title : What could I do[6][d] ? But thou hast deserved a very
leather budge[7][e] indeed. This writing also was fastened
upon the columns : Now with his chanting he hath awakened
the Gauls[8][f]. And by this time many there were who, in the
night season making semblance of chiding and brawling with
their servants, called often for a Vindex[g].

46. Besides all this, he took affright at the manifest por-
tents as well new as old, of dreams, of prodigies[a], and of osses
[Cl. 27]. For whereas before time he was never wont to
dream, when he had murdered his mother[b] once[1] there
appeared visions in his sleep, him thought he saw the helm
of a ship wrested out of his hand as he steered it ; and that
by his wife Octavia he was haled into a very narrow and blind
place, one while that he was covered all over with a multitude
of winged ants, another while that the images of brave men
descended of noble houses dedicated in Pompey's theatre
went round about him and debarred him from going forward.
Also, that his ambling gelding wherein he took most delight
was in most parts transfigured into the form of an ape, but
having his head only sound and entire did set up a loud and
shrill-voiced neighing. Out of the mausoleum[2], when all the
doors thereof flew of their own accord open, a voice was heard
calling him by name. Upon the kalends of January, his
domestic gods, garnished and adorned (as they were) at the
very time when the sacrifice was in preparing, fell all down[3].
And as he was observing the signs by bird-flight, Sporus
presented him with a ring for a New-year's gift, in the precious
stones whereof was engraven the ravishing and carrying away
of Proserpina. At the solemn nuncupation [Aug. 97] of his
vows, whenas a great and frequent number of all degrees were
already assembled together, the keys of the Capitol could

hardly be found. What time as out of his invective oration against Vindex these words were rehearsed in the senate, that such wicked persons should suffer punishment, they all cried out with one voice, *Tu facies, Auguste*, Thou shalt so do, O Augustus. This also had been observed, that the last tragedy which he acted and sang in public place was *Oedipus the Banished*, and just as he pronounced this verse,

Θανεῖν μ' ἄνωγε σύγγαμος, μήτηρ, πατήρ.
How can I chuse but death desire,
Thus bidden by wife, by mother and sire ?

he fell down[4].

47. In this meanwhile, when news came that all the other armies also [had] rebelled, the letters delivered unto him as he sat at dinner he tore in pieces, overthrew the table, and two cups of crystal, out of which he took the greatest pleasure to drink and which he called Homeric for certain verses of Homer[1][a] engraven and wrought upon them, he dashed against the paved floor. Then, after he had received a poison of Locusta and put it up in a golden box, he went directly into the hortyards of the Servilii[2], where, having sent before his most trusty freedmen unto Ostia for to rig and prepare a fleet to sea, he sounded the tribunes and centurions of the guard, whether they would bear him company and flee with him, or no. But when some of them made it coy[3] and kept some hafting[3], others in plain terms refused, and one also cried out aloud,

Usque adeone mori miserum est ?[b]
What! is it such a misery
To leave this life and so to die ?

he cast about and thought of many and sundry shifts ; whether he should go as a humble suppliant unto the Parthians or to Galba, or whether it were best for him, arrayed all in black, to come abroad into the city and there in open place before the Rostra, with all the rueful and piteous moan that he could possibly make, crave pardon for all that was past, and unless he could turn the people's hearts unto mercy[4], make suit to have if it were but the deputyship [prefecture] of Egypt granted unto him[c]. Certes, found there was afterwards in his cabinet a speech of his own penning, as touching this

argument ; but men think he was scared from this enterprise,
as fearing lest before he thither could come [5] he should be
pulled in pieces.

Thus, putting off all farther cogitation of this matter unto
the next day, and awakened about midnight [6], when he understood that the guard of his soldiers was retired and gone,
he leaped forth of his bed and sent all about to his friends.
But because no word was brought back from any of them,
himself accompanied with a few about him went to every
one of their lodgings ; where finding all doors shut and no
body to make him answer he returned to his bed-chamber,
by which time his keepers also and warders were slipped from
thence, but they had stolen away first the hangings and
furniture of his chamber, yea, and sent out of the way the
box aforesaid with the poison. Then straightway he sought
for Spicillus the sword-fencer, or any other common hackster [7],
he cared not who, by whose hand he might receive his death's
wound, but finding none, " Well," quoth he, " and have I
neither a friend nor a foe ? " And so he runs forth as if he
would have thrown himself headlong into [the] Tiber.

48. But having reclaimed [1] once again that violent mood, he
desired some more secret retiring place, wherein he might
lurk awhile and recall his wits together. And when Phaon
his freedman made offer unto him of a farm-house [villa]
of his, that he had by the city side about four miles off, between the highways Salaria and Nomentana, bare-footed
as he was and in his shirt [2], he cast over it a cloak all sullied
and which had lost the colour ; and so, covering his head and
holding a handkerchief before his face, to horseback he went,
having not above four persons in his company, of which
Sporus made one [3]. And being by and by affrighted with an
earthquake and lightning that flashed against his face, he
heard withal as an outcry and shout (from the camp hard by)
of the soldiers ossing [46] all mischief at him and all good unto
Galba ; yea, and one of the passengers that he met, saying,
These be they that pursue Nero, as also another asking, What
news in Rome of Nero ? Now by occasion that his horse
under him, scenting a dead carcass that was thrown out in the
way, started and flung at one side, his face was discovered and
himself known of one Missicius [4] a praetorian soldier, who

saluted him by his name. When they were come to the next lane turning out of the roadway, their horses they forsook and turned them up; and so among thickets of shrubs, rough bushes and briers, with much ado through a narrow path within a reed-plot and not without clothes[5] spread under foot, he got at length as far as to the wall of the country-house abovesaid over and against him. There when the said Phaon persuaded him to bestow himself the mean-while within a pit, from whence sand had been cast forth, " Nay," quoth he, " I will never go quick underground "[6]; and so, after he had stayed a little (while there was a secret way a-making to let him into the farm-house), he ladled up water with his own hand out of a ditch under him, minding to drink : " and this," quoth he, " is Nero's decocted[7] water." After this, because his cloak was torn among the bushes and briers aforesaid he rid it from the prickly sprigs that were run through and stuck therein, and so creeping upon all fours through a straight and narrow hole digged in the wall for him, received he was into the next back room[8], where he laid him down on a pallet made of a simple scant mattress, and an old overworn cloak cast over it for a coverlet. Now when hunger came upon him and thirst withal the second time, the brown and coarse bread verily which was offered unto him he refused, but of warm water he drank a pretty draught.

49. Whenas each one called then instantly on every side upon him to deliver himself with all speed from the reproachful contumelies and abuses whereto he was hourly[1] subject, he commanded a grave to be made before his face, and gave a measure therefor according to the just proportion of his body ; and therewith, if any pieces of marble stone might be found about the house, to be laid in order ; that water also and wood should be got together for his dead body to be washed anon therewith, weeping at every word he spake and inserting ever and anon this pitiful speech, *Qualis artifex pereo !*[2] What an excellent artisan am I ! and yet now must I die[3].

While some stay was made about these complements[4], Phaon's courier[5] brought certain letters which he intercepted and snatched out of his hands. And reading therein that he had his doom by the senate, to be an enemy to the State, that he was laid for all about to be punished, *More majorum* [in the old-fashioned way]. "*More majorum!*" quoth he, "what kind of punishment is that?" and when he understood it implied thus much, that the man so condemned should be stripped all-naked, his head locked[6] fast in a fork[7], and his body scourged with rods to death, he was so terrified therewith that he caught up two daggers which he had brought with him; and trying the points of them both how sharp they were, he put them up again, making this excuse, that the fatal hour of his death was not yet come. And one while he exhorted Sporus to begin for to lament, weep, and wail; another while he entreated hard that some one of them would kill himself first, and by his example help him to take his death. Sometime also he checked and blamed his own timorousness in these words, "I live shamefully," and in reproach, Οὐ πρέπει Νέρωνι, οὐ πρέπει· νήφειν δεῖ ἐν τοῖς τοιούτοις· ἄγε, ἔγειρε σεαυτόν, "It becomes not Nero, it becomes him not. In such cases as these he had need to be wise and sober; go to, man! pluck up thy heart and rouse thyself!" Now by this time approached the horsemen near at hand, who had a warrant and precept to bring him alive. Which when he perceived, after he had with trembling and quaking uttered this verse,

ἵππων μ' ὠκυπόδων ἀμφὶ κτύπος οὔατα βάλλει[8],

The trampling noise of horses swift resoundeth in mine ears,

he set a dagger to his throat, while Epaphroditus his secretary[9] lent him his hand to dispatch him. When he was yet but half-dead, a centurion broke in upon him, and putting his cloak upon the wound, made semblance as if he came to aid and succour him; unto whom he answered nothing but this, "Too late. And is this your loyalty and allegiance?" In which very word he yielded up his breath, with his eyes staring out and set in his head, to the great fear and horror of all that were present. He had requested of the company which attended upon him no one thing more earnestly than this, that no man might have his head severed from the body, but that in any wise he might be burnt whole. And Icelus, a freedman of Galba, who not long before was delivered out of prison (into which he was cast [10] at the beginning of the first tumult [11]) permitted so much [12].

50. His funeral was performed with the charges of 200,000 sesterces ; his corpse was carried forth to burial enwrapped within white clothes of tinsel woven with gold-wire between, the very same that he had worn upon the kalends of January. His relics [1] Ecloge and Alexandra, his two nurses, together with Acte his concubine, bestowed within the monument belonging to the house of the Domitii his ancestors, which is to be seen out of Mars' Field, situate upon the knap of a hill within their hortyards. In which sepulchre his chest [2], made of porphyrite marble, with an altar (as it were) or table of white marble of Luna [3] standing upon it, was enclosed round about with a fence of Thasian [4] marble-stone.

51. He was for stature almost of complete height [1], his body full of specks and freckles and foul of skin besides, the hair of his head somewhat yellow, his countenance and visage rather fair than lovely and well-favoured [2], his eyes grey and somewhat with the dimmest, his neck full and fat, his belly and paunch bearing out, with a pair of passing slender spindle-shanks, but withal he was very healthful. For being as he was so intemperate and most riotously given, in fourteen years' space he never fell sick but thrice, yet so as he neither forbare drinking of wine nor anything else that he used to do. About the trimming of his body and wearing of his clothes [he was] so nice as it was shameful, insomuch as he would always have the bush of his head laid and plaited by curls in degrees [3], but what time as he travelled in Achaia he drew it backward also from the crown of his head and wore it long [4]. For the most part, he wore a dainty and effeminate pied garment called synthesis, and with a fine lawn neckerchief bound about his neck he went abroad in the streets, ungirt, untrussed [5], and unshod.

52. Of all the liberal sciences in manner [Cal. 34] he had a taste when he was but a child ; but from the study of philosophy his mother turned his mind, telling him it was repugnant to one who another day was to be a sovereign, and from the knowledge of ancient orators his master Seneca withdrew him, because he would hold him the longer in admiration of himself. And therefore, being of his own accord readily inclined to poetry, he made verses voluntarily and without pain, neither did he (as some think) set forth other men's poems as his own. There have come into my hands writing-tables and books containing verses very famous and well-known abroad, written with his own hand ; so as a man may easily see they were not copied out of other books, nor yet taken from the mouth of any other that indited them, but plainly penned, as a man would say, by one that studied for them, and, as they came in his head, so put them down ; so many blots and scrapings out, so many dashes and inter-linings were in them.

53. No small delight he had beside in painting, and most of all in forging and moulding counterfeits. But above all he was ravished and lifted up with popularity and praise of men, desirous therefore to imitate and equal them who by any means pleased the humours and contented the minds of the common people. There went an opinion and speech of him that, after he had gained the coronets for his musical feats performed upon the stage, he would at the next five years' revolution [1] go unto the Olympic games and contend for the prize among the champions there, for he practised wrestling continually. Neither beheld he the gymnastic games throughout all Greece otherwise than sitting below within the stadium [2], [in] the manner of the judges and um-pires of such masteries ; and if any pairs [3] of them drew too far back out of the appointed place, to pluck [4] them with his own hands into the middle again. He had intended moreover (since he was reputed to have equalled Apollo in singing and matched the sun in charioteering) to imitate also the worthy acts of Hercules. And men say there was a lion prepared, which he, all-naked, should either with his club brain or else with straight clasping between his arms throttle and crush to death within the amphitheatre in the sight of all the people.

54. Certainly, a little before his end he had openly made a vow that in case he continued still in good and happy estate, represent he would likewise at the games, in his own person after victory obtained, an organist and player upon water-instruments, upon the flute also and hautboy, yea, and a bag-piper, and on the last day (of the said games) an actor of interludes, what time he would dance and gesture Turnus in Virgil. And some write that Paris the actor was by him killed, as a concurrent [Cal. 35] that stood in his way and eclipsed his light.

55. A desire he had (foolish and inconsiderate though it were) of eternity and perpetual fame. And therefore, abolishing the old names of many things and places, he did upon then new after his own. The month April also he called Neroneus. He meant moreover to have named Rome Neropolis [1].

56. All religions wheresoever he had in contempt, unless it were that only of the Syrian goddess [1]. And yet soon after he despised her so far that he polluted her [2] with urine, by occasion that he was wonderfully addicted to another superstition, wherein alone he continued and persevered most constantly. For having received in free gift a little puppet representing a young girl at the hands of a mean commoner and obscure person, as a remedy, forsooth, or defensative [3] against all treacheries and secret practices, and thereupon straightways chancing to discover a conspiracy, he held it for the sovereign deity above all, and persisted honouring and worshipping it every day with three sacrifices. Nay, he would have men believe that he foreknew things to come by advertisement and warning given from her. Some few months before he lost his life, he took regard also of the skill in prying into beasts' entrails, which he observed indeed, but never sped well [15] therewith, nor gained thereby the favour of the gods.

57. He died in the two-and-thirtieth year of his age, that very day of the year on which in times past he had murdered his wife Octavia, and by his death brought so great joy unto the people generally, that the commons wore caps [1], and ran sporting up and down throughout the city. Yet there wanted not some who a long time after decked his tomb with gay flowers that the spring and summer do afford, and who one while brought forth his images clad in robes embroidered with purple guards before the Rostra, otherwhile published his edicts, as if he had been yet living and would shortly return to the great mischief of his enemies. Moreover, Vologaesus, king of the Parthians, when he sent his ambassadors unto the senate for to treat about the renewing of league and alliance with them, requested this also very earnestly, that the memorial of Nero might be still solemnized. To conclude, when twenty years after his decease (while I myself was but a young man) one arose among them (no man knew from whence, nor of what condition), who gave it out that he was Nero (so gracious [33] was his name among the Parthians) he was mightily upheld and maintained, yea, and hardly delivered up again [2].

THE HISTORY OF
SERVIUS SULPICIUS GALBA

1. The progeny[1] of the Caesars ended in Nero. Which that
it would so come to pass appeared verily by many signs,
but by two of all other most evident. As Livia in times past,
immediately after her marriage with Augustus, went to see
a manor-house and land of her own in the Veientine territory,
it fortuned that an eagle soaring over her head let fall into her
lap a white hen, holding in her bill a laurel branch even as
she had caught it up. And thinking it good to have both the
fowl kept and the said branch set in the ground, behold
there came of the one such a goodly brood of chickens[2],
that even at this day the very house aforesaid is called *Ad
Gallinas*[3], and sprung of the other so fair a row of bay-trees,
that all the Caesars when they were to ride in triumph gathered
from thence their laurel garlands[4]. And as the manner was,
that when any of them triumphed they should prick down[5]
straightways others in the same place, so it was observed likewise that a little before the death of every one the tree by him
planted did mislike[6] and die. In the last year therefore of
Nero not only the whole grove of bay-trees withered to the
very root, but all the hens there died every one. And anon
after the temple of the Caesars being[7] struck with lightning,
the heads withal of their statues fell down all at once and the
sceptre of Augustus was shaken out of his hands[8][a].

2. After Nero succeeded Galba, in no degree allied unto the
house of the Caesars, but without all question a right noble
gentleman of a great and ancient race[1], as who in the titles
and inscriptions over his own statues wrote himself always
the nephew[2] once removed of Quintus Catulus Capitolinus;
and being once emperor, did set up also in his hall[3] the lineal
process[4] and race of his house, wherein he deriveth his descent

306

by the father's side from Jupiter, and by his mother from
Pasiphaë, the wife of king Minos.

3. To prosecute the images and laudatory testimonials
belonging to the whole stock and lineage in general were
a long piece of work; those only of his own family will I
briefly touch. The first of all the Sulpicii why and whereupon he bore the surname of Galba, there is some doubtful
question. Some think it came by occasion of a town in Spain,
which after it had been a long time in vain assaulted, he at
length set on fire with burning brands besmeared all over
with galbanum [1]; others, for that in a long sickness which he
had, he used continually galbeum, that is to say, a cure with
remedies enwrapped within wool [2]; some again, because he
seemed to be very fat, and such a one the French do name
galba; or contrariwise, in regard that he was as slender as
are those creatures (or worms) [3] which breed in the trees called
aesculi [4], and be named galbae.

This family one Servius Galba, who had been consul and in
his time most eloquent, ennobled first and made renowned,
who, by report, ruling the province of Spain as praetor, having
treacherously [5] put to sword 30,000 [6] Lusitanians, was the cause
of the Viriathian [7] war. His nephew being maliciously bent
against Julius Caesar (whose lieutenant he had been in Gaul)
for a repulse that he took in suing to be consul, joined in the
conspiracy with Cassius and Brutus, for which condemned
he was by the Paedian law. From this man descended
immediately the grandsire and father of this Galba the
emperor. His grandfather for his book and learning was
more famous than for any dignity in commonweal that ever
he attained unto; for he arose no higher than to the degree
of a praetor, but many histories he wrote, and those not
slightly nor negligently composed. His father bore the
honourable office of consul, a man very low of stature and
withal crowch-backed [8], and having but a mean gift in oratory
yet used he to plead causes industriously. Two wives he had,
Mummia Achaica, the niece of Catulus and once removed of
Lucius Mummius, who razed and destroyed Corinth; likewise
Livia Ocellina, an exceeding wealthy lady and a beautiful.
Of whom for his noble blood sake it is thought he was wooed [a];
yea, and somewhat the more hotly, after that (upon her im-

portunate suit) he stripped himself once out of his clothes in a secret place before her, and revealed the imperfection of his body, because he would not seem to deceive her for want of knowledge. By Achaica he had issue Gaius and Servius. Of whom Gaius, the elder, having wasted his estate and spent all, left the city of Rome, and was by Tiberius prohibited to put in his lot for to be chosen proconsul in his year [9], whereupon voluntarily he killed himself.

4. To come now unto Servius Galba the emperor, born he was when Marcus Valerius Messalla and Gnaeus Lentulus were consuls, the ninth day before the kalends of January, in a country-house situate under [1] a little hill near unto Tarracina, on the left hand as men go to Fundi. Being adopted by his stepmother [2], he assumed the name of Livius, and the surname Ocella [3], changing his forename withal; for afterwards, even unto the time of his empire, he was forenamed Lucius instead of Servius. It is for certain known that Augustus (what time as little Galba among other boys like himself saluted him) took him by his pretty cheek [4] and said, Καὶ σὺ, τέκνον, τῆς ἀρχῆς ἡμῶν παραγεύσῃ, [5] "And thou also, my child, shalt have a taste one day of our sovereign rule." Tiberius likewise, when he had knowledge once that he [6] should be emperor, but not before old age, "Go to," quoth he, "let him live, a God's name, seeing it is nothing to us." Also, as his grandfather was sacrificing for the expiation of an adverse flash of lightning [7] (what time an eagle caught out of his hands the inwards of the beasts, carried them away, and bestowed them in an oak bearing mast [8]), answer was given unto him by the soothsayers out of their learning, that thereby was portended and foreshown unto his house sovereign government, but it would be late first. Then he again, by way of irrision, "Ye say very true indeed; that will be," quoth he, "when a mule shall bring forth a foal." Afterwards, when this Galba began to rebel and aspire unto the empire, nothing heartened him in this design of his so much as the foaling of a mule; for when all men besides abhorred this foul and monstrous prodigy, he alone took it to be most fortunate, calling to remembrance the foresaid sacrifice and the speech of his grandfather.

When he had newly put on his virile gown, he dreamt that

Fortune spake these words unto him, namely, how she stood before his door all-weary, and unless she were let in the sooner, she should become a prey unto whomsoever she met. No sooner awakened he and opened his port hall-door[9], but he found hard by the entry[10] a brazen image of the said goddess about a cubit long; which he carried away with him in his bosom to Tusculum where he was wont to summer, and having consecrated it in one part of his house there, worshipped the same from that time forward with monthly supplications, and a vigil[11] all night long once every year. And albeit he was not yet come to his middle and staid age, yet retained he most constantly this old manner of the city (which was now worn out of use, but that it continued still in his house and lineage) that his freedmen and bondservants should duly twice a day present themselves all together before him, and one by one in the morning salute him with a good morrow, and in the evening take their leave likewise with a farewell and also good night.

5. Among the liberal sciences he gave himself to the study of the civil law. He entered also into the state of wedlock; but having buried his wife Lepida and two sons that he had by her, he led always after a single life. Neither could he ever by any offer or condition be persuaded to marriage again, no, not of dame Agrippina, who by the death of Domitius[1] became a widow, and had by all means solicited Galba even while he was the husband of a wife and not yet a single man, and insomuch as at a great meeting of ladies and matrons the mother of his wife Lepida [abused] her roundly, yea, and knocked her well for it with her own fists. He honoured and affected above all others Livia Augusta the empress, through whose grace and favour while she lived he became mighty, and by whose will and testament when she was dead he had like to have been enriched. For whereas, among others whom she remembered in her will, he had a special legacy to the value of 50,000,000 sesterces bequeathed unto him[2]; because the said sum was set down in figures and ciphers and not written out at large, her heir Tiberius brought it down unto half a million[3], and yet even that he never received.

6. Having entered upon the honourable offices of state

before due time by law set down, when he was praetor, during the plays and games called Floralia[1], he showed a new and strange kind of sight, to wit, elephants walking upon ropes. After that he governed the province of Aquitania almost one whole year. Soon after he bore the ordinary consulship in his due time[2] for the space of six months. And it fell out so that, as himself therein succeeded Domitius, the father of Nero, so Salvius, the father of Otho, followed immediately after him ; a very presage of the event ensuing, whereby he came to be emperor just in the middle between the sons of them both. Being by Gaius[3] Caesar substituted lord-general for Gaetulicus, the very next day after he was come to the legions, whenas the soldiers at a solemn show which happened then to be exhibited clapped their hands, he restrained them with this precept[a], that they should keep their hands within[4] their cloaks[5] ; whereupon this byword anon ran rife through the camp :

> *Disce miles militare,*
> *Galba est, non Gaetulicus.*

> Learn, soldiers, service valorous[6],
> Galba is here, and not Gaetulicus[b].

7. With semblable [C. 39] severity he inhibited all petitions for placards[1] and passports. The old beaten[2] soldiers as well as the new and untrained he hardened still with continual work and labour ; and having soon repressed the barbarians, who by their rodes[3] and incursions had now by this time broken in violently and set foot within Gaul, he quit himself so well and showed such good proof of his army unto Gaius[4], also then and there present in proper person, as that among an infinite number of forces levied and assembled out of all provinces there were none went away with greater testimonies of prowess nor received larger rewards than he and his regiments. Himself above them all was most bravely beseen[5] in this that, marching with his target before him he marshalled the gallants jousting and running at tilt in the plain field, and for that he ran also by the emperor's chariot side for the space of twenty miles.

When tidings came that Gaius was murdered, and many pricked him forward to take the opportunity then offered, he preferred quietness and rest. For which cause he stood

in especial favour with Claudius, and was admitted into the
rank of his inward friends ; a man of that worth and reputation as that, when he fell suddenly sick (although not very
grievously), the day appointed for to set forth in the British
expedition was deferred. He governed Africa as proconsul
two years, being elected without lots drawing for to settle and
bring into order that province, far out of frame and disquieted
as well with the civil mutinies among the soldiers as tumultuous commotions of the barbarous inhabitants. Which commission he discharged with great regard of severe discipline
and execution of justice even in very small matters. A soldier
of his there was who, during the expedition abovesaid, in a
great dearth and scarcity of corn was accused to have sold a
residue remaining of his own allowance, to wit, a modius[6] of
wheat for one hundred deniers[7] ; whereupon he gave strait
commandment that when the said soldier began once to want
food, no man should be so hardy as to relieve him ; and so for
hunger he pined to death. As for his civil jurisdiction and
ministering justice, when there grew some question and
debate about the proprietary[8] and right owner of a labouring
beast[9], and slight evidences and presumptions on both sides
were alleged, as simple witnesses also produced, and therefore[10] hard to divine and guess of the truth, he made this
decree, that the beast should be led hoodwinked[11] unto the
pool where it was wont to be watered ; and when it was
unhooded again, he awarded and pronounced the said beast
to be his, unto whom of its own accord it returned directly
after it had drunk.

8. For his brave exploits achieved both in Africa then
and also in Germany aforetime he received the honour of
triumphal ornaments and a triple sacerdotal dignity, being
admitted among the quindecemvirs[1], into the guild and con-
fraternity of the Titii[a], and the college or society of the
priests of Augustus[b]. And from that time unto the midst
well-near of Nero's empire he lived for the most part private
in some retiring place out of the way ; yet so as he never went
forth any journey (were it but for exercise by way of gestation[2]) but he took forth with him in a wagon going hard by
to the value of 1,000,000 sesterces in gold, until such time
as, making his abode in a town called Fundi, the regency of a

province in Spain named Tarraconensis was offered unto him.
And it fortuned that when he was newly arrived and entered
into that province, as he sacrificed within a public temple, a
boy among other ministers holding the censer suddenly had all
the hair of his head turned grey. Now there wanted not some
who made this interpretation, that thereby was signified a
change in the states [3] and that an old man should succeed a
young, even himself in Nero's stead. And not long after there
fell a thunderbolt [4] into a lake [5] of Cantabria, and found
there were immediately twelve axes, a doubtless token presaging sovereign rule.

9. For eight years' space he governed that province variably and with an uneven hand. At the first sharp he was,
severe, violent, and in chastising verily of trespasses beyond
all measure extreme. For he caused a banker, for unfaith-
ful handling and exchange of money, to lose both his hands
and to have them nailed fast unto his own shop-board ;
a guardian also he crucified for poisoning his ward, whose
heir he was in remainder. Now, as the party delinquent
called for the benefit of law and avouched in his plea that
he was a Roman citizen [1], Galba, as if he would allay his
punishment with some comfort and honour [2], commanded
the cross already made to be changed, and another to be
reared far higher than the ordinary, and the same laid over
with a white colour. By little and little he grew to be slothful, careless, and idle, because he would minister no matter
unto Nero for to work upon, and for that (as himself was wont
to say) no man was compelled to render an account of his own
idleness [3].

As he held the judicial assizes at New Carthage, he had
intelligence that Gaul was in a tumult. And while the ambassador [4] of Aquitania besought him earnestly to send aid,
the letters of Vindex came in the very nick, exhorting him to
frame and carry himself as the deliverer and protector of
mankind, even to take upon him to be their general captain.
He, making no longer stay upon the point, accepted the offer,
partly for fear and in part upon hope. For he had both found
out the warrants of Nero sent privily unto his agents and procurators there as touching his death ; and also much confirmed and strengthened he was, as well by most lucky

auspices and [Aug. 57] osses as by the prophecy of an honest [5] virgin, so much the rather because the very same verses containing the prophecy the priest of Jupiter at Clunia, two hundred years past (by warning and direction given him in a dream), had fetched out of an inward and secret vault of the temple, delivered then likewise by a maiden which had the spirit of prophecy. The meaning and effect of which verses was that one day there should arise out of Spain the sovereign prince and lord of the whole world.

10. Therefore, when he had mounted the tribunal, as if he intended then the manumitting[1] of slaves, and set before him in open sight very many portraits and images of such as had been condemned and killed by Nero, while there stood also in his presence a boy of noble blood[2], whom he had sent for of purpose out of one of the Balearic islands hard by, where he was exiled[3], he bewailed the state of those times. Whereupon being with one accord saluted emperor[4], yet he professed himself to be the lieutenant only of the senate and people of Rome. After this, having proclaimed a cessation of judicial pleas for the time, out of the commons verily of that province he enrolled both legions and auxiliaries over and above the old army, which contained one legion, two cornets of horsemen, and three cohorts ; but out of the better sort, to wit, the nobility and gentry, such I mean as for wisdom and age went before the rest, he ordained a body of a senate, unto whom men should have recourse touching matters of greater importance, as need required. He chose forth also young gentlemen for the knights' degree, who, continuing still the wearing of gold rings, should be called *evocati*[5], and kept watch and ward instead of sworn soldiers[6] about his lodging and bed-chamber. He sent out his edicts also in every province, counselling and persuading all and some to join with him in these designs, and (proportionally to the means that every one had) to help and promote the common cause.

Much about the same time, in the fortification of a town which he had chosen to be the capital seat of the war, a ring was found of antique work, in the gem or stone whereof was engraven the express resemblance of Victory [a] together with a trophy [b] ; and soon after a ship of Alexandria, freighted with armour, arrived before Dertosa[7], without pilot, without

mariner or passenger, that no man might make any doubt
but that this war was just, lawful, and undertaken with the
favour and approbation of the gods. But lo! suddenly and
unlooked for, all in manner was dashed and put out of frame.
One of the two cornets of horsemen above-mentioned, as
bethinking themselves and repenting that they had changed
their military oath, was at the point to fall away and forsake
him as he approached the camp, yea, and hardly kept in their
allegiance to him ; certain slaves also, whom (being prepared
aforehand to do him a mischief) he had received as a present
at the hands of a freedman of Nero's, missed but little of
killing him, as he passed through a cross-lane to the baines for
to bath. And surely done the deed they had, but that as they
exhorted and encouraged one another not to overslip[8] the
opportunity presented, they were overheard ; who, being
examined and asked upon what occasion they spake such
words, were by torture forced to confess the truth.

11. Besides these dangers so great there fell out (to help
the matter well) the death of Vindex ; wherewith, being most
of all amazed and like to a man utterly forlorn, he went
within a little of renouncing this world and forgoing his own
life. But by occasion of messengers coming with news from
the city in the very instant, no sooner understood he that
Nero was slain and all men in general had sworn allegiance unto
him, but he laid away the name of lieutenant and took upon
him the style of Caesar. So he put himself on his journey clad
in his coat-armour, with his dagger hanging down from about
his neck just before his breast ; neither took he to the use of a
gown and long robe again before they were surprised and suppressed, who made insurrections and rose up in arms against
him[1] ; namely, at Rome Nymphidius Sabinus, captain of
the praetorian guard, in Germany, Fonteius Capito, and
in Africa Clodius Macer, two lieutenants.

12. There had a rumour been raised before of his cruelty
and covetousness both ; for punishing the cities of Spain,
which were somewhat slack in coming to side with him,
by laying very heavy tributes and taxes upon them, some
of them also by dismantling and razing their walls ; likewise for putting to death certain presidents and procurators together with their wives and children ; as also for

melting a coronet of gold weighing fifteen pounds, which the
men of Tarraco from out of the old temple of Jupiter had
presented unto him, and commanding that the three ounces
which wanted of the full weight should be exacted and made
good [1]. This report was both confirmed and also increased
upon his first entrance into Rome. For when he would have
compelled the servitors at sea (whom Nero had made of
mariners and oarsmen full and lawful soldiers) to return
again to their former state and condition, when they made
refusal and besides called malapertly for their eagle and other
military ensigns, he not only sent in among them a troop of
horsemen and so trod them under foot, but also executed with
death every tenth man of them. Semblably the cohort of
Germans, which in times past had been by the Caesars ordained for the guard of their persons and by many good proofs
were found most trusty, he dissolved, and without any avails
[Cal. 44] and recompense for their service sent them home
again into their country, pretending that they stood better
affected unto Gnaeus Dolabella (near unto whose hortyards
and gardens they quartered) than to him. Moreover, these
reports also (whether truly or falsely I wot not) went commonly of him by way of mockery ; that when there was a more
plentiful supper than usual served up before him, he gave a
great groan thereat. His steward verily in ordinary [2] cast
up his books and rendered unto him a breviary of all reckonings and accounts ; for his great care and serviceable diligence he reached unto him a dish of pulse [3]. But when Gaius [4]
the minstrel played upon the hautboy and pleased him
wondrous well, he bestowed liberally upon him for his labour
five good deniers [5], and those he drew with his own hand out
of his privy purse.

13. At his first coming therefore he was not so welcome,
and that appeared at the next solemnity of public shows [1].
For whenas in the Atellane comedies some had begun a most
vulgar [2] canticle with this verse,

> *St! venit, Io Simus a villa,*
> St: See [3], our Simus that country clown
> Is from his farm now come to town,

the spectators all at once with one accord and voice sung
out the rest in manner of a respond, and repeating withal

the said verse oft, as the fore-burden of the song, acted (and with gesture) noted him [4].

14. Thus verily with far greater favour and authority obtained he the empire than managed it when he was therein, notwithstanding he gave many proofs of an excellent prince ; but nothing so acceptable were his good acts as those were odious and displeasant wherein he faulted and did amiss. Ruled he was according to the will and pleasure of three persons, whom, dwelling as they did together and that within the Palatium (ready evermore at his elbow and in his ear), men commonly called his pedagogues. These were Titus Junius [1], his lieutenant in Spain, a man infinitely covetous ; Cornelius Laco, who being of his counsel and assistance [2] was advanced by him to be captain of the guard, one for his arrogance and luskishness [3] intolerable ; and a freedman of his, Icelus, who but a little before, being honoured with the golden ring [4] and endowed with the surname Marcianus, looked now for to be the provost and captain of the praetorian gentlemen and knight's degree [5]. Unto these men, I say, playing their parts and committing outrages correspondent to their vices in divers kinds, he yielded and wholly gave himself to be abused so much, as that scarcely he was like himself, but always variable ; onewhile precise and near, otherwhiles as remiss and careless, more, I wis, than became a prince elected and a man of these years [6].

Some honourable persons of both degrees [7] he condemned upon the least suspicion before their cause was heard. The freedom of Rome city he seldom granted to any. The privilege and immunity due to those who had three children he gave to one or two at most with much ado, not to them verily but for a certain time limited and set down. The judges making suit for to have a sixth decury adjoined unto them, he not only denied flatly, but also this benefit of vacation granted unto them by Claudius [Cl. 23], that they should not be called forth to sit in the winter season [a] and at the beginning of the year, he took from them.

15. It was thought also that he purposed to determine and limit the offices belonging to senators and gentlemen within the compass of two years, and not to bestow the same but upon such as were unwilling and refused to take them. The

liberalities and bountiful donations of Nero[1] he took order
[Cal. 8] by a commission directed unto fifty gentlemen of
Rome[2] for to be revoked, yea, and the same to be exacted
for his behoof, allowing out thereof not above the tenth part ;
with this strait condition moreover, that if actors upon the
stage or wrestlers and champions otherwise had sold any
such donation given unto them aforetime, the same should
be taken from the buyers, since that the parties who had sold
the same had spent the money and were not sufficient[3] to
repay it.   Contrariwise, there was not anything but by the
means of his followers, favourites and freedmen, he suffered
either to be purchased for money or granted freely for favour ;
as for example, customs, imposts, immunities, punishments of
the innocent and impunity of malefactors.   Moreover, whenas
the people of Rome called upon him for justice, and namely
to have Halotus and Tigellinus executed, the only men of all
the bloodhounds and instruments of Nero that wrought
most mischief, he saved them from danger, and besides advanced Halotus to a most honourable procuratorship, and
in the behalf of Tigellinus rebuked the people by an edict
for their cruelty unto him.

16. Having hereby given offence and discontentment to
the states and degrees in manner all[1], yet he incurred the
displeasure and ill-will most of the soldiers.   For when his
provosts had promised and pronounced unto them (what
time they swore allegiance unto him) a greater donative
than usually had been given, he would not make good and
ratify the same, but eft-soons gave it out, that his manner
had ever been to choose and not buy his soldiers.   And
as upon that occasion verily he angered all his soldiers wheresoever, so the praetorians and those of his guard he provoked moreover with fear and nettled with offering them
indignities ; namely, by removing and displacing most of
them one after another as suspected persons and the adherents
of Nymphidius.   But the forces of Upper Germany grumbled
and fumed most of all for being defrauded of their rewards for
service performed against the Gauls and Vindex.   They were
the first therefore that durst break out into open disobedience,
and upon New-year's day refused to take an oath and bind
themselves in allegiance unto any other than the senate of

Rome. They intended also to dispatch forthwith an embassy unto the praetorian guard, with these advertisements and messages from them, namely, that they were displeased with an emperor made in Spain, and therefore themselves should elect one whom all the armies in general might allow and approve.

17. No sooner heard he this news but, supposing that he was become contemptible not so much for his old age as his childless estate, he presently, out of the thick throng and middle[1] multitude that came to salute him, caught hold of Piso Frugi Licinianus, a noble young gentleman and of excellent parts, one whom in times past he had made right great account of and always[2] in his will remembered as inheritor to succeed in his goods and name ; him he now called son, him he presented unto the praetorian camp, and there before a public assembly adopted. But of the foresaid donative not a word all this while, no, not at that very time ; whereby he ministered unto Marcus Salvius Otho better occasion and readier means to accomplish his enterprises within six days after this adoption.

18. Many prodigious sights and those presented continually even from the very first beginning had portended unto him such an end as ensued. When all the way as he journeyed beasts were sacrificed to do him honour in every town on both sides, it chanced that a bull, astonied with the stroke of the butcher's axe, broke the bond wherewith he stood tied and ran full upon his chariot, and rising up with his forefeet, all to-bespreinct[1] and drenched it with blood. As he alighted out of it, one of the guard and pensioners about him, with the thrusting of the throng, had like with his spear to have wounded him. As he entered also the city of Rome and so passed forward up to the Palatium, he was welcomed with an earthquake and a certain noise resembling the lowing of a beast.

But there followed after these greater prodigies still and more fearful. He had selected and laid by itself out of all his treasure a jewel set thick with pearls and precious stones, for to beautify and adorn his goddess Fortune at Tusculum. This jewel (as if it had been worthy of a more stately and sacred place) all of a sudden he dedicated to Venus in the

Capitol, and the next night following he dreamt that he saw Fortune making her moan and complaining how she was defrauded of the gift intended and meant unto her, threatening withal that she herself also would take away what she had given him. Now being affrighted with this vision, when in great haste he was gone apace to Tusculum, and had by break of day sent certain before of purpose to provide an expiatory sacrifice for this dream[2], he found nothing there but warm embers upon the altar hearth and an old man all in black[3] sitting hard by, holding in a dish of glass frankincense and in an earthen cup wine[4]. Observed also it was that upon the kalends of January while he sacrificed his coronet fell from his head. As he took his auspices, the pullets flew away. And upon the solemn day of the foresaid adoption, when he should make a speech unto the soldiers, the camp-throne[5] stood not (as the manner was) before his tribunal (such was the forgetfulness of his ministers), and in the senate his curule chair was placed wrong, with the back toward him.

19. But before he was slain, as he sacrificed that morning, the soothsayer oftentimes warned him to beware of danger, for murderers were not far off. And not long after he took knowledge that Otho was possessed of the camp[1]. And when most of those about his person persuaded him still to make what speed he could and go forward thither (for why ? by his authority and presence he might bear sway and prevail), he resolved to do no more but keep close within house, to stand upon his guard, and to fortify himself with the strength of his legionary soldiers, in many and divers places quartered. Howbeit he put on a good linen jack[2 a], although he seemed to acknowledge that in small stead it would stand him against so many sword-points. But being borne in hand[3] and seduced with rumours which the conspirators had of purpose spread abroad to train [N. 34] him out into the open street, while some few rashly affirmed that all was dispatched, the rebels and seditious persons defeated, and the rest coming in great frequency with joy and gratulation, ready to do him all the obsequious service they could, he to meet them went forth ; and that with so great confidence, as that unto a soldier who made his boast he had slain Otho he answered, " And by whose warrant[b] ? " Thus advanced he as far as into the market-place. There the horsemen having commission and commandment to kill him, when they had voided [Cal. 58] the common people out of the way, and put their horses forward through the streets, and espied him afar off, stayed a while but afterwards, setting spurs to again, fell upon him and slew him outright, forsaken as he was of all his train and followers.

20. There be that report how at the first uproar he cried aloud : " What mean ye, my fellow-soldiers ? I am yours, and ye are mine," and withal promised to pay the donative. But many more have left in writing, that of himself he offered them his throat and willed them (since they thought so good) to mind that only which they came for, even to strike and spare not. A strange and wonderful thing it was, that of those who were there present not one went about to help their emperor, and all that were sent for rejected the messenger, saving only a guidon[1] of German horsemen. These, in regard of his fresh demerit [Aug. 57], in that he had tenderly cherished and made much of them being sick and feeble, hastened to the rescue ; howbeit they came too late, by occasion that, being ignorant of the streets and places, they took a wrong way and were hindered.

Killed he was at the lake Curtius[2], and there left lying even as he was, until such time as a common soldier, as he returned from foraging and providing of corn, threw down his load and cut his head off. Now, because he could not catch hold of the hair of his head (so bald he was) he hid it in his lap, and anon thrust his thumb into his mouth and so brought it to Otho, who gave it to the scullions, lackeys, and varlets[3] that follow the camp. These, sticking it upon a spear carried it, not without reproachful scorn, all about the camp, setting up ever and anon this note, " Galba, thou lovely Cupid, take thy time, and make use of thy fresh and youthful years " ; provoked they were especially to such malapert frumps [Cal. 56] and flouts, because some days before there ran a rife report abroad, that unto one who commended that visage and person of his, as continuing still fresh, fair, and vigorous, he made this answer,

ἔτι μοι μένος ἔμπεδόν ἐστιν,

I have yet still
My strength at will.[4]

At their hands a freedman of Patrobius Neronianus bought the same for one hundred pieces of gold [a] and flung it into that very place [b] where beforetime his patron [5] by the command of Galba had been executed. At length (late though it was) his steward Argivus buried both it and the trunk of his body within his own private hortyards in the Aurelian Way.

21. Of full stature he was, his head bald, his eyes grey, and his nose hooked ; his hands and feet by reason of the gout grown exceeding crooked, insomuch as uneth [Cal. 53] he was able either to abide shoes on the one, or to turn over, or so much as hold his books with the other. There was an excrescence [1] also of flesh in the right side of his body, and the same hung downward so much, as hardly it could be tied up with a truss [2].

22. A great feeder and meat man by report he was. For in winter-time he used to eat before daylight, and at supper to be served so plentifully that the relics and reversion of the board, being gathered together into heaps, he commanded to be carried round about and distributed among those that stood waiting at his feet [1]. Given he was overmuch to the unnatural lust of male-kind, but such chose he (and none else) for his darlings, as were stale thick-skins and past growth. It was reported that in Spain, when Icelus, one of his old catamites, brought him word of Nero's end, he not only received him in open sight with most kind kisses, but entreated him without delay to be plucked [2] and so led him at one side out of the way.

23. He died in the seventy-third year of his age and the seventh month of his empire. The senate, as soon as lawfully they might, had decreed for him a statue standing upon a column adorned with the stems and beak-heads of ships, in that part of the mercate-steed [1] of Rome where he lost his life ; but Vespasian repealed that decree, as being thus conceited of him [2], that he had suborned and sent underhand out of Spain into Judaea certain of purpose to murder him.

THE HISTORY OF
MARCUS SALVIUS OTHO

1. THE ancestors of Otho had their beginning in a town called
Ferentinum, extract[1] out of an ancient and honourable
family, even from the princes of Etruria. His grandfather,
Marcus Salvius Otho, having for his father a gentleman of
Rome and for his mother a woman of base condition (and
whether she was freeborn or no, it is uncertain), through the
favour of Livia Augusta, in whose house he had his rising and
growth, was made a senator [but] exceeded not the degree of a
praetor.

His father, Lucius Otho, by his mother's side of right
noble blood descended, and thereby allied to many great
kindreds, was so dear and in face so like unto Tiberius the
emperor, that most men believed verily he was his own
son. The honourable offices within the city, the proconsulship of [Africa], and other extraordinary places of conduct
and command he managed most severely. He adventured
also in Illyricum to proceed so far as to put certain soldiers
to death, for that, in the commotion of Camillus, upon a
touch of conscience they had killed their captains and provosts[2]
as authors of the revolt and rebellion against Claudius, and
verily this execution himself in person saw performed in the
camp even before the principia[a], notwithstanding that he
knew they were for that service advanced to higher places by
Claudius. By which act of his as he grew in glory so he de-
creased in favour ; and yet the same he soon recovered again,
by detecting the perfidious plot of a Roman knight, whom
by the impeachment of his own servants he found to have
attempted the death of Claudius. For both the senate
endowed him with an honour most rare and seldom seen,
to wit, his own statue erected in the Palatium ; and also
Claudius, when he ranged him among the patricians and in

most honourable terms praised him, added these words withal, " He is a man, than whom I would not wish, I assure you, to have better children of mine own." Of Albia Terentia, a right noble and gallant lady, he begat two sons, Lucius Titianus and a younger forenamed Marcus, and carrying the surname of his father[3]; a daughter also he had by her, whom as yet not marriageable, he affianced unto Drusus, the son of Germanicus.

2. This Otho the emperor was born the fourth day before the kalends of May[1], when Camillus Arruntius and Domitius Ahenobarbus were consuls. From the very prime of his youth he was riotous, wild, and wanton, insomuch as his father swindged[2] him well and soundly for it; reported also to use night-walking, and as he met any one either feeble or cup-shotten or overcome with drink, to catch hold of him, lay him upon a soldier's gaberdine, and so to toss and hoist him up into the air[a]. Afterwards, upon his father's death, a certain libertine [C. 2] woman of the court, a dame very gracious[3] (because he would make the more benefit by following and courting her as his mistress) he pretended love unto, albeit an old trot she was, in manner doting for age. By her means winding himself into the favour of Nero, he easily obtained the chief place among his minions and favourites (such was the congruence of their humours and dispositions) and, as some write, by mutual abusing also of one another's body against kind [C. 52]. But so mighty he waxed and bare such a side[4], as that in consideration of a great piece of money agreed upon he presumed to bring into the senate-house for to give thanks[5] a man of consular degree, who stood condemned for extortion, even before he had fully obtained his restitution[6].

3. Being now, as he was, privy and party to all the counsels and secret designs of Nero, to avert all manner of suspicion, that very day which Nero had appointed for the murdering of his mother he entertained them both at supper with most exquisite and the kindest welcome that might be. Semblably, dame Poppaea Sabina, being as yet but the paramour of Nero, whom he had newly taken from her husband[1] and committed in the meanwhile unto himself upon trust for to keep[2], under a colour of marriage[3] he received; and not content herewith that he alienated her heart from Nero and used her body, he loved her so entirely that he could not endure Nero himself to be his co-rival [4]. Certes, it is thought of a truth that not only the messengers who were sent to fetch her came again without her, but also that one time he kept Nero himself without doors standing there and cooling his heels, with threats also and prayers intermingled, demanding his pawn [5] which he had left with him, but all in vain. Whereupon after the said marriage [was] broken and dissolved, sent out of the way he was under a pretence of an embassage into Lusitania, which course was thought sufficient, for fear lest his proceeding to any sharper punishment might have told tales [6] abroad and marred all the play [7], howbeit, as secretly conveyed as it was, out it came and was made known by this distich :

> *Cur Otho mentito sit, quaeritis, exsul honore ?*
> *Uxoris moechus coeperat esse suae.*
>
> Exil'd in show of embassage was Otho. Ask ye, why ?
> With his own wife begun he had to act adultery [a].

Having been aforetime in no higher place than quaestor [8], yet governed he a province for the space of ten years with singular moderation [9] and abstinence [10].

4. As occasion at length and opportunity of revenge [1] was offered, he was the first that combined with Galba in his attempts. At which very instant himself also conceived hope of the empire, and great the same was, no doubt, considering the condition and state of those times, but greater somewhat by reason of Seleucus the astrologer's words ; who, having long before warranted him that he should survive Nero, was then of his own accord come unlooked for and promised again [2] that shortly also he should be emperor. Omitting therefore no kind of obsequious office and ambitious popularity even to the very meanest, look, how often he invited the emperor [3] to supper, he would deal throughout the cohort that then warded to every man a piece of gold [4] ; and no less careful was he to oblige unto him one way or other the rest of the soldiers. And when one of them went to law with his neighbour about a parcel of ground in the skirts and confines of both their lands, being chosen arbitrator, he bought the whole land for the said soldier and enfeoffed him in it ;

so as now by this time there was scarce one but both thought and said that he alone was worthy to succeed in the empire.

5. Moreover, he had fed himself with hopes to have been adopted by Galba, and that looked he for daily ; but after that Piso was preferred and himself disappointed of his hope, he turned to plain violence, pricked thereto, over and beside the discontentment of his mind, by occasion that he was so deeply indebted. For he stuck not [Cal. 25] to profess he was not able to stand, unless he were emperor, and it skilled not [N. 37] whether he were overthrown by his enemy in the field, or fell under his creditors' hands at the bar. Some few days before he had fetched over[1] one of the emperor's servants in a million of sesterces for the obtaining of a stewardship, and with the help of this sum of money enterprised he so great a project. At the first he committed the matter to five soldiers employed in espial[2] ; then to ten others whom they had brought forth with them, to wit, every man twain. To each one of these he paid in hand 10,000 sesterces[3], and promised 50,000 more. By these were the rest solicited, and those not very many, as making no doubt, but presuming confidently of this, that a number besides would be ready in the very action to second it.

6. He had minded once, presently after [Cal. 25] the adoption of Piso, to seize their camp into his own hands, and so to set upon Galba as he sat at supper in the palace ; but the respective [Cal. 26] regard he had of the cohort, which then kept watch and ward, checked this intent of his, for fear lest the same should incur the intolerable hatred of the world ; considering by the guard of that very cohort Gaius had been slain before and Nero perfidiously betrayed afterwards. Moreover, exception was taken against the middle time between, partly upon a superstition[1] that he had, and in part by direction from Seleucus.

Well then, upon a day[2] appointed, after warning given aforehand unto those that were privy to the conspiracy for to attend him in the market-place at the golden milliarium[a] under the temple of Saturn, he saluted Galba in the morning, and (as the manner was) being received with a kiss, was present also as he sacrificed and heard the soothsayer's predictions. Which done, a freedman of his brought him word that the architects were come (this was the watchword agreed upon between them), whereupon, as if forsooth he were to look upon a house that was to be sold, he departed, gat him quickly away through the back-side of the palace, and hied apace toward the place appointed. Others say that he feigned himself to have an ague and willed those that stood next to him to make that excuse in case he were asked for. Then, lying hidden within a woman's litter [3], he hastened to the camp, and for that the litter-bearers were tired and faint, he alighted on the ground and began to run afoot ; but by occasion that his shoe's latchet was slack he stayed behind, until such time as without any further delay he was taken up on men's shoulders and by the train and company there present saluted emperor ; and so with lucky acclamations among drawn swords came as far as to the principia [4], whiles every one all the way he went adhered unto him, as if they had been all privy and party in the conspiracy. There, after he had dispatched certain away to kill both Galba and Piso, to win the soldiers' hearts by fair promises, he protested before them all assembled together, that himself would have and hold no more than just that which they would leave for him.

7. This done, as the day drew toward evening, he entered into the senate ; and briefly laying before them a reason of his proceeding, as if he had been carried away perforce out of the market-place and compelled to take the empire upon him (which he would administer according to the general will and pleasure of them all), to the palace he goeth. Now, whenas beside other sweet and plausible words delivered by such as did congratulate and flatter him, he was by the base common people called Nero, he gave no token at all that he refused it ; nay rather, as some have reported, ever in his patents, grants, and missives which he first wrote unto certain presidents and governors of provinces, he added unto his style the surname of Nero. This is certain, he both suffered his images [1] and statues [2] to be erected again in their own places, and also restored his procurators and freedmen to the same offices that they had enjoyed before. Neither by his imperial prerogative and absolute power subscribed he anything before a warrant for 50,000,000 sesterces to the finishing of Nero's Golden House. It is said that the same night, being affrighted in his sleep, he groaned very sore and was by his servitors that ran thick into the chamber found lying on the bare floor before his bed ; also that he assayed by all kind of propitiatory sacrifices and peace-offerings to appease the spirit[3] of Galba, whom he had seen in his sleep to thrust and drive him forth ; semblably, the morrow after, as he was taking his auspices[4], there arose a sudden tempest, whereupon he caught a grievous fall, and oftentimes he mumbled this to himself :

Τί γάρ μοι καὶ μακροῖς αὐλοῖς ;

For how can I (whose blast is short)
With these long hautboys fitly sort[a] ?

8. And verily about the same time the forces and armies in Germany[a] had sworn fealty and allegiance unto Vitellius ; which when he understood, he propounded unto the senate that an embassage might be sent thither, to advertise them that there was an emperor chosen already and advise them withal to peace and concord ; yet by intercourse of messengers and letters between he made offer unto Vitellius to partake equally with him in the empire and accept of a marriage with his daughter. But when there was no way but one and that by open war, seeing that now already the captains and forces which Vitellius had sent before approached[1], he had good proof what loyal and faithful hearts the praetorian soldiers carried towards him, even to the utter ruin and destruction well-near of the most honourable degree of senators. Now decreed it had been[2], that by the sea-servitors[3] the armour[4] should be conveyed over and sent back to Ostia by shipping. And as the said armour was in taking forth out of the armoury in the camp at the shutting of the evening, some soldiers, suspecting treachery and treason, raised a tumult and gave an alarum ; wherewith suddenly all of them[5] without any certain leader to conduct them, ran to the palace, calling hard to have the senate[6] massacred. And when they had repelled some of the tribunes who assayed to repress their violence and killed other of them, all imbrued in blood as they were and asking still where the emperor was they rushed in as far as into his banqueting-room, and never rested until they had seen him[7].

Then set he forward his expedition lustily, and began with more haste than good speed, without any care at all of religion and the will of God, as having only stirred and taken those sacred shields [8] called *Ancilia* [b] and not bestowed them quietly again in their due place (a thing in old time held ominous and ever presaging ill-luck) ; besides, the very same day it was [March 24] upon which the priest and ministers [9] of Cybele the mother of the gods begin to lament, weep, and wail : to conclude, when all signs and tokens were as cross as possibly they might be. For not only in the beast killed for sacrifice unto father Dis [10] he found the inwards propitious (whereas in such a sacrifice as that the contrary had been more acceptable), but also at his first setting out stayed he was by the inundation and swelling of the river Tiber. At the twenty miles' end [11] likewise, he found the highway choked and stopped up against him with the ruins of certain houses fallen down.

9. With like inconsiderate rashness, albeit no man doubted but that in good policy the war ought to have been protracted, because the enemy was distressed as well with famine as the strait wherein he was pent, yet resolved he with all speed to hazard the fortune of the field and to try it out by fight ; as one either impatient of longer thought and pensiveness, hoping that before the coming of Vitellius most part of the business might be dispatched, or else because he could not rule his soldiers calling so hotly upon him to give battle. Yet was not he present in that conflict but stayed behind at Brixellum.

And verily in three several skirmishes, which were not great, to wit, upon the Alps, about Placentia, and at Castoris [1] (a place so called) he won the victory, but in the last battle of all (which was the greatest) [2] he lost the day, and was by a treacherous practice vanquished ; namely, when upon hope of a parley pretended, as if the soldiers had been brought out of the camp to treat of conditions of peace, suddenly and unlooked for, even as they saluted one another [3], there was no remedy but fight it out they must. And straightway in a melancholy he conceived a resolution to make himself away (as many are of opinion and not without cause), rather for shame that he would not be thought to persevere in the maintenance of his sovereign dominion with so great jeopardy of the State and loss of men than upon any despair or distrust of his forces.   For still there remained a puissant army whole and entire, which he had detained with him for trial of better fortune, and another power [4] was coming out of Dalmatia, Pannonia, and Moesia.   Neither verily were they, discomfited, so much daunted and dejected but that, for to be revenged of this disgrace and shameful foil, ready they were of themselves and alone without help of others to undergo any hard adventure whatsoever.

10. In this war served my own father Suetonius Lenis [1], in quality of a tribune [2] of the 13th legion and by degree a senator of the second rank [3].   He was wont afterwards very often to report that Otho, even when he lived a private person, detested all civil wars so far forth [N. 29] that as one related at the table the end of Cassius and Brutus, he fell a-quaking and trembling thereat.   Also, that he never would have been Galba's concurrent, but that he confidently thought the quarrel might have ended without war.   Well then, upon a new accident incited he was to the contempt of this present life, even by the example of a common and ordinary soldier who, reporting this overthrow of the army, when he could of no man have credit, but was charged one while with the lie, another while for his fear and cowardice (as who was run away out of the battle), fell upon his own sword at Otho's feet. At which sight he cried out aloud and said that he would no more cast so brave men and of so good desert into danger. Having exhorted therefore his own brother, his brother's son, and every one of his friends severally to make what shift they could for themselves, after he had embraced and kissed them each one he sent them all away ; and retiring himself into a secret room, two letters he wrote full of consolation to his sister, as also to Messalina, Nero's widow, whom he had purposes to wed, recommending the relics of his body and his memorial.   And look, what epistles soever he had in his custody, he burnt them all, because they should breed no man any danger, loss, or displeasure with the conqueror. And out of that store of treasure which he had about him he dealt money to his domestic servitors.

11. Being now thus prepared and fully bent to die, perceiving by occasion of some hurly-burly, which while he made delay arose, that those who began to slip away and depart [1] were (by his soldiers) rebuked as traitors and perforce detained, " Let us," quoth he, " prolong our life yet this one night." Upon which words and no more he charged that no violence should be offered to any ; but suffering his bed-chamber door to stand wide open until it was late in the evening, he permitted all that would to have access unto him. After this, having allayed his thirst with a draught of cold water he caught up two daggers, and when he had tried how sharp the points of them both were, he laid one of them under his pillow ; and so, the doors being fast shut, he took his rest and slept most soundly. Wakening then at last about daylight and not before, with one only thrust under his left pap he stabbed himself. And when at the first groan that he gave his servants broke in, he, one while concealing and another while discovering the wound, yielded up his vital breath and quickly [2] (as he had given charge before) was brought to his funeral fire, in the thirty-eighth year of his age and on the ninety-fifth day of his empire.

12. Unto so great a mind and generous courage of Otho neither was his person nor habit answerable ; for he was by report of a mean and low stature, feeble feet he had besides, and as crooked shanks. As for his manner of attire, as fine and nice he was well-near as any woman ; his body plucked and made smooth ; wearing by reason of thin hair a peruke [1], so fitted and fastened to his head, that no man there was but would have taken it for his own. Nay, his very face he was wont every day to shave and besmear all over with soaked bread [a], which device he took to at first when the down began to bud forth, because he would never have a beard. It is said, moreover, that many a time he openly celebrated the divine service and sacred rites of Isis in a religious vestment of linen. Whereby I would think it came to pass that his death nothing at all consonant to his life was the more wondered at. Many of his soldiers who were present about him, when with plentiful tears they had kissed his hands and feet dead as he lay, and commended him withal for a most valiant man and the only emperor that ever was, presently in the place and not far from his funeral fire killed themselves. Many of them also who were absent, hearing of the news of his end, for very grief of heart ran with their weapons one at another to death. Finally, most men who in his life-time cursed and detested him, now when he was dead highly praised him ; so as it came to be a common and rife speech abroad, that Galba was by him slain, not so much for that he affected to be sovereign ruler, as because he desired to restore the state of the republic and recover the freedom that was lost.

THE HISTORY OF
AULUS VITELLIUS

1. As touching the original and beginning of the Vitellii some write this, others that, and all as contrary as may be ; reporting it partly to be ancient and noble, and in part new start-up and obscure, and very base and beggarly. Which I would suppose to have happened by means of the flatterers and backbiters both of Vitellius the emperor, but that I see there is sometime variance and diversity about the very condition of that family. A little book there is extant of one Quintus Eulogius [a] his making, written unto Quintus Vitellius, quaestor to Augustus Caesar of sacred memory, wherein is contained thus much, that the Vitellii, descended from Faunus, king of the Aborigines [1], and lady Vitellia (who in many places was worshipped for a goddess) reigned over all Latium ; that the offspring remaining of them removed out of the Sabine country to Rome and were taken into the rank of the patricians ; that many monuments giving testimony of this race continued a long time, to wit, the highway [2] Vitellia reaching from Janiculum [3] to the sea, likewise a colony of the same name, the defence and keeping whereof against the Aequiculi they in times past required with the strength only and puissance of their own family ; moreover, that afterwards in the time of the Samnite war, when a garrison was sent into Apulia [4], some of the Vitellii remained behind at Nuceria, and their progeny many a year after returned to Rome and recovered their senator's degree.

2. Contrariwise, more authors there be who have left upon record that their stock-father was a libertine [C. 2]. Cassius Severus [Aug. 56] and others as well as he do write, that the same man was also a very cobbler [1 a], whose son, having got more by chaffering [2] at a price for the confiscated goods of men condemned[3] and by gains arising of undertaking men's suits, of a common naughty pack [D. 22], the daughter of one Antiochus a baker, begat a son, who proved afterwards a gentleman of Rome. This dissonance of opinions I leave indifferent for men to believe which they will.

But, to the purpose : Publius Vitellius, born in Nuceria [4] (whether he were of that ancient lineage or descended from base parents and grandfathers), a Roman gentleman doubtless and a procurator under Augustus of his affairs, left behind him four sons, men of quality all and right honourable persons, bearing also their father's surname[5], and distinguished only by their forenames Aulus, Quintus, Publius, and Lucius. Aulus died even when he was consul, which dignity he had entered upon with Domitius, the father of Nero Caesar, a man very sumptuous otherwise in his house and much spoken of for his magnificent suppers. Quintus was displaced from his senator's estate, what time as by the motion and persuasion of Tiberius there passed an act that such senators as were thought insufficient should be culled out and removed[6]. Publius, a companion and dependant of Germanicus, accused and convicted Gnaeus Piso, his mortal enemy[7] and the man who murdered him, and after the honourable place of praetor being apprehended among the complices of Sejanus' conspiracy and committed to the keeping of his brother[8], with a penknife cut his own veins ; and after that, not so much repenting that he sought his own death as overcome with the earnest entreaty of his friends about him, suffered his wounds to be bound up and cured, but in the same imprisonment [9] he died of sickness.

Lucius, after his consulship being provost[10] of Syria, with passing fine slights and cunning devices trained [N. 34] and enticed forth Artabanus, king of the Parthians, not only to parley with him but also to worship and adore the standard of the Roman legions. Soon after, together with Claudius the emperor, he bore two ordinary consulates, one immediately upon another, and the censorship also. Likewise the charge of the whole empire, while Claudius was absent in the expedition to Britain, he sustained ; a harmless person, active and industrious, howbeit blemished with a very bad name for the love he bore unto a libertine woman [b], whose spittle mixed with honey he used as a remedy [11] (and that not closely [C. 31] and seldom, but every day and openly), washing therewith his pipes [12] and throat. He was besides of a wonderful glavering [13] nature and given to flatteries. He it was that first by his example brought up the order to adore [14] Gaius Caesar [15] as a god, what time as, being returned out of Syria, he durst not come into his presence otherwise than with his head covered [16], turning himself about and then falling down prostrate before him at his feet. And because he would omit no artificial means to curry favour with Claudius, a prince so addicted to his wives and freedmen, he made suit unto Messalina, as if it had been for the greatest gift she could bestow upon him, to do him the grace that he might have the doffing of her shoes ; and the right-foot pump [c] which he had drawn off he carried in his bosom continually between his gown and inward clothes, yea, and many times would kiss the same. The golden images also of Narcissus and Pallas he reverently honoured among his domestic gods. This was a word likewise of his, when he did congratulate Claudius at the exhibiting of the secular plays [17], *Saepe facias*, Many a time may you this do.

He died of a palsy [d], the very next day after it took him, leaving behind him two sons, whom Sextilia his wife, a woman for her virtue highly approved and of no mean parentage descended, bare unto him. Them he saw both consuls, and that in one year, yea, and the same throughout, for that the younger succeeded the elder for six months. When he was departed this life, the senate granted unto him the honour of a public funeral, a statue likewise before the Rostra with this inscription, *Pietatis immobilis erga principem* [18], Of constant devotion and irremovable piety to his prince.

3. Aulus Vitellius, the son of Lucius and emperor, was born the eighth day before the kalends of October [1], or, as some will have it, the seventh day before the ides of September [2], when Drusus Caesar and Norbanus Flaccus were consuls. His nativity [3] foretold by the astrologers his parents had in such horror, that his father endeavoured always what he could that no province while he lived should be committed unto him ; and his mother, what time he was both sent unto the legions and saluted lord-general [4], straightways lamented as if then he had been undone for ever. His childhood and flower of youth he spent at Capreae among the strumpets and catamites that Tiberius kept there ; himself, noted always with the surname of Spintria [5], was thought also by suffering the abuse of his own body to have been the cause of his father's rising and advancement.

4. All the time also of his age ensuing, stained as he was with all manner of reproachable villainies, for [1] he carried a principal sway above others in the court, grown into familiar acquaintance with Gaius for his love to chariot-running and with Claudius for his affection to dice-play ; but in greater favour he was a good deal with Nero, both in the selfsame regards aforesaid as also for this especial demerit [Aug. 57], in that, being president at the solemnity called Neroneum, when Nero was desirous to strive for the prize among the harpers and musicians, but yet durst not promise so to do (notwithstanding all the people called instantly upon him) and thereupon went out of the theatre, he, pretending that he was sent ambassador unto him from the people persisting still in their earnest request, had called him back and so brought him in the end to be entreated.

5. Through the favourable indulgence therefore of three emperors being advanced not only to right honourable offices of state but also to as high sacerdotal dignities, he managed after all these the proconsulate of Africa and executed the charge of surveying and supervising the public works [1], but with mind and reputation both far unlike. For in his province he demeaned himself for two years together with singular innocency and integrity, as who, after his brother succeeded in his stead, stayed there still in quality of his lieutenant. But in his office within the city he was reported to have secretly stolen away the oblations, gifts, and ornaments of the temples, to have embezzled and changed some of them, yea, and in lieu of gold and silver to have foisted in tin and copper.

6. He took to wife Petronia, the daughter of one that had been consul, by whom he had a son with one eye named Petronianus ; him, being by his mother [1] ordained her heir upon condition that he were freed once out of his father's power, he manumitted indeed, but soon after (as it was thought) killed, having charged him besides with parricide [2],

and pretending withal that the poison which was provided
to work that mischief he upon remorse of conscience had
drunk himself. After this he wedded Galeria Fundana, whose
father had been praetor, and of her body also begat children
of both sexes, but the male child had such an impediment of
stutting and stammering, that little better he was than dumb
and tongueless.

7. By Galba sent he was contrary to all expectation into
the Low Countries of Germany, furthered, as it is thought,
by the voice and favour of Titus Vinius, a man in those days
most mighty, and unto whom long before he had been won by
favouring the faction [1][a] unto which they both were equally
affected but that [2] Galba professed plainly that none were
less to be feared than those who thought of nothing but
their victuals only, and that his greedy appetite and hungry
belly might be satisfied and filled with the plenteous store that
the province did yield. So that evident it was to every man
that he chose him in contempt rather than upon any special
grace.

This is for certain known that, when he was to go forth,
he wanted provision for his journey by the way, and for the
maintenance of his family was driven to those hard shifts and
extremities, that mewing up [3] his wife and children (whom he
left at Rome) in a little upper lodging [4] that he rented, and [5]
let out his own dwelling-house for the rest of the year; yea,
and took from his mother's ear a pearl which he laid to gage,
and all for to defray the charges of that voyage. As for a
number verily of his creditors who waited for him as ready to
stay his passage, and among them the Sinuessans and For-
mians, whose public imposts, tollage, and revenues he had
intercepted and converted to his own use, he could not be
rid of but by terrifying them with an action of the case,
serving one of them, and namely a libertine (who very eagerly
demanded a debt) with process upon an action of battery, as
if he had stricken him with his heel, and would not withdraw
the suit before he had extorted from him 50,000 sesterces.

In his coming toward the camp, the army, maliciously
bent against the emperor and ready to entertain any revolt
and change of state, willingly and with open arms received
him as a gift of the gods presented unto them from

heaven above, the son of one thrice consul, a man in the vigour
and strength of his years, of a gentle disposition besides, and of
a frank and prodigal heart. Which opinion and persuasion,
being of old conceived and settled in men's heads, Vitellius had
augmented by some fresh proofs lately given of himself ;
kissing all the way as he went along every mean common
soldier that he met, so courteous and affable above all measure
to the very muleteers and wayfaring passengers in every
inn and baiting-place, that he would in a morning betimes
ask them one by one whether they had yet broken their fast,
and show unto them even by his belching that he had been at
his breakfast already.

8. Now when he was entered once into the camp, no suit
denied he to any man, nay, of his own accord he took off
their marks of ignomy who stood in disgrace, dispensed
with [Cal. 15] those that were obnoxious to the laws for wearing
poor and sullied garments, and forgave condemned persons
their punishments. Whereupon, before one month was fully
come and gone, without all respect either of day or time, when
the very evening was now shooting in[1], suddenly by the
soldiers called forth he was out of his bed-chamber and,
clad as he was in his domestic and home apparel, saluted
by the name of Imperator and carried round about the most
frequented and populous towns[2], holding in his hand the
naked sword of Julius of famous memory, which being taken
out of the temple of Mars was at the first gratulation presented by one unto him. Neither returned he into the
praetorium[3] before the dining-room was on a light fire [Aug.
82] by occasion of the chimney there, where it first caught.
And then verily, when all besides were amazed and in great
perplexity upon this adverse and ominous accident, " Be of
good cheer," quoth he, " it hath shined fair upon us " ;
and no other speech at all made he unto his soldiers. After
this, when the army also of the upper province consented now
by this time with the other (that army I mean which had
revolted before from Galba and sided with the senate), the
surname of Germanicus generally offered unto him he gladly
accepted ; the addition of Augustus he put off, and the style
of Caesar he utterly for ever refused.

9. And soon after, when news came unto him that Galba

was slain, having settled the state of Germany he divided his forces thus, sending one part thereof before[1] against Otho, and minding to lead the rest himself. Unto the army which was sent before there happened a fortunate and lucky sign ; for on the right hand all on a sudden flew an eagle toward them, and when she had fetched a compass[2] round about the standards and ensigns hovered softly before them as they marched on the way. Contrariwise, as himself removed and set forward, the statues on horseback erected in many places for him all at once suddenly broke their legs and tumbled down, and the garland of laurel, which most devoutly he had done about his head, fell from it into a running river. Within a while after, as he sat judicially upon the tribunal to minister justice at Vienna[3], a cock first settled upon his shoulder and anon perched upon his very head. Upon which prodigious sights ensued an event correspondent thereto ; for the empire which by his lieutenants was confirmed and established unto him he by himself was not able to hold.

10. Of the victory before Betriacum and the death of Otho he heard while he was yet in Gaul ; and without delay whosoever belonged to the praetorian cohorts he by virtue of one edict cassed[1] and discharged all, for the most dangerous precedent and example that they had given[2], commanding them to yield up their armour into the marshals'[3] hands. As for those hundred and twenty, whose supplications exhibited unto Otho he had found, such I mean as claimed rewards for their good service in killing Galba, he gave command they should be sought out and executed every one. A worthy beginning I assure you and a magnificent, such as might give good hope of an excellent prince, had he not managed all matters else according to his own natural disposition and the course of his former life rather than respecting the majesty of an emperor. For no sooner put he himself in his journey but he rode through the midst of cities in triumphant wise, and passed along the great rivers in most delicate barges, garnished and adorned with coronets of sundry sorts ; faring at his table most sumptuously and served with all manner of dainty viands, observing no discipline either of household servitor or of soldier ; but turning the outrages,

villainies, and licentious pranks of them all to a jest ; who,
not content with their ordinary diet allowed and provided for
them in every place where they came at the common charges
of the State, look, what slaves or aliens it pleased them, they
manumitted and made free, but paid as many as withstood
them with whipping-cheer [Cal. 33], blows, knocks, bloody
wounds oftentimes, yea, and otherwhiles with present
death.

When he came into the fields where the battle [4] was fought,
and some of his train loathed and abhorred the putrified corruption of the dead bodies, he stuck not to hearten and encourage them with this cursed speech : that an enemy slain
had a very good smell, but a citizen far better. Howbeit, to
qualify and allay the strong savour and scent that they cast,
he poured down his throat before them all exceeding great
store of strong wine, and dealt the same plentifully about [5]
with as much vanity as insolent pride. When he beheld the
stone under which Otho lay interred, with an inscription [6] in
his memorial, " Worthy was he of such a monument," [7] quoth
he. And the very same dagger wherewith he had killed himself he sent to Cologne for to be dedicated unto Mars. Certes,
upon the top of the Apennine hill he celebrated a sacrifice with
a vigil [8] all night long.

11. At length he entered the city with warlike sound of
trumpet, in his coat-armour and with a sword girt unto
him, among ensigns, banners, and flags [1], his followers and
dependants clad in military cassocks and the armour of
all his fellow-soldiers discovered in open view [2]. Thus
neglecting more and more from time to time all law of god
and man, upon the very disastrous day of Allia [a], he was
installed in the sacerdotal dignity of high priest. He ordained
that the solemn assembly [3] for election of magistrates should
be held every tenth year and himself be perpetual dictator [4].
And to the end that no man might doubt what pattern he
chose to follow for government of the commonweal, calling a
frequent number of the public priests about him in the middle
of Mars' Field, he sacrificed to the spirit and ghost of Nero ;
and at a solemn feast openly put the harper in mind, singing
as he did to his great contentment, for to say somewhat also
of Domitius [5] [b] ; and as he began to chant Nero's canticles

he was the first that leaped for joy and clapped his hands withal.

12. Having in this manner begun his empire, a great part thereof he administered no otherwise than according to the advice and pleasure of the basest stage-players and charioteers that could be found, but especially of Asiaticus, a freedman of his own. This Asiaticus when he was a very youth had in mutual filthiness with him abused his own body, and afterwards, loathing that abominable sin, ran his way. Now, finding him once at Puteoli selling of a certain drink made of water and vinegar[1], first he laid him by the heels and hung a pair of fetters at his feet, but forthwith loosened him and entertained him as his darling again. After which a second time being offended with his contumacy and malapert stubbornness[2], he sold him to one of these common fencers that went from market to market[3], and by occasion that he was upon a time put off to the last place in a sword-fight for to play his prizes[4], at unawares he privily stole him away, and no sooner was he gone into his province but he manumitted him. The first day of his empire, as he sat at supper, he dubbed him knight of Rome, and gave him the golden ring, notwithstanding that the very morning before, when all the soldiers entreated in his behalf, he detested [Cl. 3] so foul a blot to distain and discredit the worshipful degree of knighthood.

13. But being given most of all to excessive belly cheer and cruelty, he divided his repasts into three meals every day at the least and sometimes into four, to wit, breakfast, dinner, supper, and rere-bankets[1], able to bear them all very well, he used to vomit so ordinarily[a]. Now his manner was to send word that he would break his fast with one friend, dine with another, etc., and all in one day ; and every one of these refections, when it stood them in least, cost 40,000 sesterces[2]. But the most notorious and memorable supper above all other was that which his brother made for a welcome at his first coming to Rome, at which by report were served up to the table before him two thousand several dishes of fish the most dainty and choicest that could be had and seven thousand of fowl. And yet even this (as sumptuous as it was) himself surpassed at the dedication of that platter[3],

which for the huge capacity thereof he used to call the target
of Minerva and αἰγίδα πολιούχον, the shield of the city's
protectress [4]. In this he huddled and blended together the
livers of gilt-heads [5] [b], the delicate brains of pheasants and
peacocks, the tongues of the birds phoenicopteri [Cal. 22], the
tender small guts of sea-lampreys fet[ched] as far as from the
Carpathian sea [c] and the straits of Spain, by his captains over
galleys. And as a man that had not only a wide throat of his
own to devour much, but also as greedy a stomach to feed
both unseasonably and also grossly of whatever came next
hand, he could not so much as, at any sacrifice whensoever
or in any journey wheresoever, forbear but among the altars
snatch up by-and-by the flesh, the parched corn also and meal
even from the very hearth, and eat the same, yea, and at every
victualling-house by the way-side fall to viands piping hot,
yet reeking and not cooled one jot ; and not spare so much as
meats dressed the day before and half-eaten already.

14. Being forward enough to put to death and punish any
man what cause soever was pretended, noblemen, his schoolfellows, and playferes [1] in time past (whom by all fair means
and flattering allurements he had enticed and drawn to the
society as it were of the empire with him) by sundry sorts
of fraud and treachery he killed, and one above the rest
he made away with poison, which he raught [2] unto him with
his own hand in a draught of cold water, that he called
for lying in a fit of an ague. Of usurers, takers of bonds and
obligations [3], and publicans, who ever at any time had demanded of him either at Rome debt, or by the way as he
travelled toll and custom, he hardly spared one. And one
of them, whom even as he came to salute him and do his
duty he had delivered over to the executioner for to suffer
death, he called straightway back again ; and when all
that were by praised him for his clemency, he commanded
the said party to be killed before his face, saying withal
that he would feed his eyes. At the execution of another
he caused two of his sons to bear him company, for nothing
in the world but because they presumed to entreat for their
father's life. There was besides a gentleman of Rome who,
being haled away to take his death, cried aloud unto him,
" Sir, I have made you my heir." Him he compelled to

bring forth the writing-tables containing his last will, and
so soon as he read therein that a freedman of the testator's
was nominated fellow-heir with him, he commanded both
master and man to be killed. Certain commoners also,
for this only that they had railed aloud upon the faction of
the watchet livery [4] he slew, being thus conceited [5] that in
daring so to do they had him in contempt and hoped for a day [6].

Yet was he to none more spitefully bent than to the
wizards [7] and astrologers [a]. Was any of them presented and
informed against ? he made no more ado, but, without hearing what he could say for himself, bereaved him of his life.
Nettled he was and exasperated against them for that after an
edict of his, wherein he gave commandment that all judicial
astrologers should depart out of Rome and Italy before the
first of October, presently [Cal. 25] there was a writing or
libel set up in open place to this effect, that the Chaldeans [8]
made this edict, as followeth : " *Bonum factum* [b], etc. We
give warning by these presents unto Vitellius Germanicus
that by the kalends of the said October he be not extant [9] in
any place wheresoever [10]." Suspected also he was to be con-
senting unto his own mother's death, as if he had straitly
forbidden that any food should be ministered unto her lying
sick, induced thereto by one Chatta [11], a wise woman, in whom
he rested as in an oracle [12] : that then and not before he
should sit sure in his imperial throne and continue very long,
in case he overlived his mother. And others report how his
mother herself, weary of the present state and fearing what
evil days were toward, obtained at her son's hand poison
and that without any great entreaty.

15. In the eighth month of his empire the armies of Moesia [1]
both the one and the other as also at Pannonia revolted
from him ; likewise, of the forces beyond sea those of Judaea
and of Syria, and some of them swore allegiance unto Vespasian
who was present among them [2]. To retain therefore the love
and favour of all other men he cared not what largesses he
made both in public and private beyond all measure. He
mustered also and levied soldiers within the city with this
covenant and fair condition [3], that all voluntaries should by
virtue of his promise have not only their discharge from service
after victory, but also the avails [Cal. 44] and fees due unto

old soldiers for serving out their full time. But afterwards, as the enemy came hotly upon him both by land and sea, on the one side he opposed his brother with the fleet and young untrained soldiers together with a crew of sword-fencers, on the other, what forces he had about Betriacum and the captains there ; and in every place being there discomfited in open field or privily betrayed, he capitulated and coven-anted with Flavius Sabinus, brother of Vespasian, to give up all, reserving his own life and 100,000,000 sesterces. And forthwith upon the very stairs of the palace, professing openly before a frequent [Cal. 15] assembly of his soldiers how willing he was to resign up that imperial dignity which he had received against his will, when they all gainsaid it, he put off the matter for that instant ; and but one night between, even the next morning by break of day he came down in poor and simple array to the Rostra, where with many a tear he recited the same words out of a little written skrow.[4]

Now, as the soldiers and people both interrupted him a second time and exhorted him not to cast down his heart, promising also with their utmost endeavour and striving a-vie [Cal. 57] who should do best to assist him, he took courage again and plucked up his spirits ; so that now fearing nothing[5] at all, he came with a sudden power and violently chased Sabinus and the rest of the Flavians[6] into the Capitol, and there, having set on fire the temple of Jupiter Optimus Maxi-mus, vanquished and slew them, while himself beheld both the fight and the fire out of Tiberius his house, sitting there at meat and making good cheer[7]. Not long after, repenting what he had done and laying all the fault upon others, he called a public assembly, where he swore and compelled all the rest to take the same oath, that he and they would respect nothing in the world before the common peace. Then loosened he his dagger[8] from his side[a] and raught [14] it first to the consul, then upon his refusal to the other magistrates, and anon to the senators one after another. But when none of them all would receive it, he departed as if he meant to bestow it in the chapel of Concord. Now when some cried out unto him, that himself was Concord, he came back again and protested that he not only retained still the blade with him, but also accepted the surname of Concord.

16. Hereupon he moved and advised the senate to send ambassadors together with the Vestal virgins to crave peace, or else some longer time to consult upon the point. The next morrow, as he stood expecting an answer, word was brought unto him by his espial that the enemy approached. Immediately therefore, shutting himself close within a bearing-chair [1], accompanied with two persons only, his baker and his cook [2], secretly he took his way to the Aventine hill and his father's house, minding from thence to make an escape into Campania. Soon after, upon a flying and headless rumour that peace was obtained, he suffered himself to be brought back to the palace. Where finding all places solitary and abandoned, seeing those also to slink from him and slip away who were with him, he did about him a girdle [3] full of golden pieces of coin [4], and fled into the porter's lodge, having first tied a ban-dog [a] at the door and set against it the bedstead and bedding thereto.

17. By this time had the avant-couriers [1] of the Flavians' main army broken into the palace, and meeting nobody searched as the manner is every blind corner. By them was he plucked out of his lurking-hole, and when they asked who he was (for they knew him not) and where upon his knowledge Vitellius was, he shifted them off with a lie; after this, being once known, he entreated hard (as if he had somewhat to deliver concerning the life and safety of Vespasian) to be kept sure in the mean season, though it were in some prison; and desisted not until such time as having his hands pinioned fast at his back, a halter cast about his neck, and his apparel torn from his body, he was haled half-naked into the Forum [2]. Among many scornful indignities offered unto him both in deed and word throughout the spacious street Sacra Via [3] from one end to the other, whiles they drew his head backward by the bush of his hair (as condemned malefactors are wont to be served) and set a sword's point under his chin [4], and all to the end he might show his face and not hold it down, whiles [5] some pelted him with dung and dirty mire, others called him with open mouth incendiary [6] and patinarium [7], and some of the common sort twitted him also with faults and deformities of his body. For of stature he was beyond measure tall; a red face he had, occasioned for the most part by swilling in

wine, and a grand fat paunch besides ; he limped somewhat
also by reason that one of his thighs was enfeebled with the
rush of a chariot against it, what time he served Gaius [8] as his
henchman at a chariot-running. At the last upon the stairs
Gemoniae [9] with many a small stroke all to-mangled [Cal. 28]
he was and killed in the end, and so from thence drawn with a
drag into the river Tiber.

18. Thus perished he with his brother and son together in
the fifty-seventh year of his age. Neither falsified he their
conjecture who had foretold him that, by the prodigious sign
which befell unto him (as we have said) at Vienna [9], nothing
else was portended but that he should fall into the hands of
some Frenchman [a]. For dispatched he was by one Antonius
Primus, a captain of the adverse party, who being born at
Tolosa was in his childhood surnamed Beccus [1], which in the
French tongue signifieth a cock's-bill.

THE HISTORY OF
FLAVIUS VESPASIANUS AUGUSTUS

1. THE empire standing thus a long time in doubtful terms, unsettled and wandering (as it were) by occasion of the rebellious broils and bloody slaughter of three princes[1], the Flavii at length took into their hands and established ; a house, I must needs say, of obscure descent and not able to show any pedigree and images of ancestors to commend their race, howbeit, such as the commonweal had no cause to dislike and be ashamed of, although it be well-known that Domitian abidd[2] condign punishment for his avarice and cruelty.

Titus Flavius Petro, a burgess of the free borough Reate[3] and a centurion, siding in time of the civil war with Pompey (but whether he served voluntarily or was called forth and pressed it is uncertain) fled out of the battle[4] at Pharsalus and went home to his house ; where afterwards, having obtained his pardon and discharge from warfare, he became a bailiff under the bankers and money-changers to gather up their moneys. This man's son, surnamed Sabinus, nothing martial nor skilful in feats of arms (although some write that he had been a principal leader of the foremost cohorts, and others that, while he led certain companies, he was acquit from his military oath by occasion of sickliness[5]), came to be a publican[6] in Asia and gathered the custom or impost *quadragesima*[a] for the State. And there remained certain images which the cities in that province erected for him with this title and superscription, Καλῶς τελωνήσαντι, For him that was a good and faithful publican[7]. After this he put forth money to usury among the Helvetians, where he ended his life, leaving behind him his wife Polla Vespasia, and two children which he had by her. The elder of which, named Sabinus, was advanced to the provostship of the city ; the younger, called Vespasianus, attained to the imperial dignity.

FLAVIUS VESPASIANUS AUGUSTUS

This dame Polla, born at Nursia and descended of worshipful parentage, was the daughter of Vespasius Pollio, one that had been a military tribune [8] thrice and provost-marshal [9] of the camp besides, and sister to a man of senator's degree and promoted to the dignity of praetor. There is a place moreover even at this day six miles from [Nursia] (as men go to Spoletum from Nursia) upon the hill-top, bearing the name of Vespasiae, where many monuments of the Vespasii are to be seen, a great evidence to prove the nobleness and antiquity of that family. I cannot deny that some have given out how the father of that Petro came out of the Transpadane region [10] and was an undertaker by the great [11], to hire those labourers and hinds which were wont yearly to repair out of Umbria into the Sabine country for to till their grounds; how he planted himself and stayed in the town of Reate aforesaid and there married a wife. But myself could never find (make what search I could) any sign or trace to lead me thereto.

2. Vespasian [1] was born in the Sabine territory beyond Reate within a small village named Phalacrinae, the fifteenth day before the kalends of December [2] in the evening, when Quintus Camerinus and Gaius Poppaeus Sabinus were consuls, five years before that Augustus departed out of this world. His bringing up he had under Tertulla, his grandmother by the father's side, in the land and living that she had about Cosa. Whereupon when he was emperor he both frequented continually the place of his birth and breeding, the capital house and manor remaining still as it had been in former times, nothing altered (because forsooth his eyes should have no loss nor miss of that which they were wont to see there); and loved also the memorial of his grandmother so dearly, that on all solemn and festival and high-days he continued ever drinking out of a silver pot that was hers and out of none other. After he had put on his virile gown [3], he refused a long time the senator's robe [a], although his brother had attained thereto; neither could he be forced to seek for it at last but by his own mother. She in the end wrought perforce so much from him by way of reproachful taunts more than by fair entreaty or reverent authority, whiles ever and anon she called him in taunting wise his brother's huisher [4].

FLAVIUS VESPASIANUS AUGUSTUS

He served as tribune military in Thrace, and in quality of quaestor had the government of Crete and Cyrene, provinces by lot fallen unto him. When he sued to be aedile and afterwards praetor, he hardly attained to the former office (and not without some repulse) even in the sixth place ; but presently [Cal. 22] at his first suit and with the foremost being chosen praetor, and upon displeasure taken maliciously affected[5] against the senate, because he would by all manner of demerit [Aug. 57] win the favour of Gaius the emperor, he earnestly demanded extraordinary plays and games in honour of him for his victory in Germany, and gave opinion in the senate-house that, to augment the punishment of certain conspirators against him, their dead bodies should be cast forth and left unburied. He gave him also solemn thanks before that right honourable degree for vouchsafing him the honour to be a guest of his at a supper.

3. Amid these occurrents he espoused Flavia Domitilla, the freedwoman of Statilius Capella, a Roman gentleman of Sabrata and an African born, committed unto him sometime upon trust and enfranchised in the freedom of Latium, but afterwards pronounced a gentlewoman born and naturalised a citizen of Rome in the court of judges delegate, upon claim made by her father Flavius Liberalis, born at Ferentinum (a man that never rose higher than to be a scribe[1] to a quaestor) who vouched her freedom. By her he had issue, Titus, Domitian, and Domitilla. His wife and daughter he overlived and buried them while he was yet in state of a private person. After his foresaid wife's decease, he called home again to cohabit with him in his house Caenis, a freedwoman of Antonia and her secretary[2], whom he had fancied in former time ; and her he kept when he was emperor, instead of his true and lawful wife.

4. Under the emperor Claudius, by especial favour of Narcissus sent he was into Germany as lieutenant of a legion ; from thence, being removed into Britain, he fought thirty battles with the enemy. Two most mighty nations and above twenty towns, together with the Isle of Wight[1] lying next to the said Britain, he subdued, under the conduct partly of Aulus Plautius, lieutenant to the consul, and in part of Claudius himself, for which worthy acts he received

triumphal ornaments, and in short space two sacerdotal
dignities with a consulship besides, which he bore the two
last months of the year. For the middle time between,
even until he was proconsul, he led a private life in a retiring place out of the way, for fear of Agrippina, who as
yet bore a great stroke[2] with her son[3] and hated to the
heart all the friends of Narcissus, although deceased.

After this, having the province of Africa allotted unto him,
he governed the same with singular integrity and not without
much honour and reputation, but that in a seditious commotion at Hadrumetum there were rape-roots[4][a] flung at his
head. Certain it is that from thence he returned nothing
richer than he was, as who, not able to keep credit but grown
almost bankrupt, was driven to mortgage all his houses and
lands unto his brother, and of necessity, for the maintenance
of his estate and dignity, went so low as to make gains by
huckster's trade[5], pampering beasts for better sale ; whereupon he was commonly named Mulio, muleteer. It is said
also that convicted he was for extorting from a young man
200,000 sesterces, in consideration that by his means he had
obtained a senator's dignity even against his own father's
will, for which he had a sore rebuke. While he travelled
through Achaia in the train and inward company of Nero, he
incurred his heavy displeasure in the highest degree, for that
while he was chanting either he made many starts away out
of the place or else slept, if he stayed there still. And being
forbidden not only to converse in the same lodging with him
but also to salute him publicly with others, he withdrew
himself aside into a small city and which stood out of the
way until such time as, lying close there and fearing the
worst, the government of a province[6] with the command of an
army was offered unto him.

There had been spread throughout all the East parts an
opinion of old, and the same settled in men's heads and constantly believed, that by the appointment of the destinies
about such a time there should come out of Judaea those who
were to be lords of the whole world[b] ; which being a prophecy
(as afterwards the event showed) foretelling of the Roman
emperor the Jews[7] drawing to themselves rebelled, and
having slain the president[8] there, put to flight also the

lieutenant-general of Syria [9] (a man of consular degree) coming in to aid, and took from him the eagle [10]. To repress this insurrection, because there was need of a greater army and a valiant captain, yet such a one as to whom a matter of so great consequence might safely be committed, himself was chosen above all others, as a man of approved valour and industry, howbeit no way to be feared for the meanness of his birth, lineage, and name. Having therefore under his hand an addition to the former power of two legions [11], eight cornets of horse, and ten cohorts [12] of foot, taking also unto him among other lieutenants his elder son [13], no sooner arrived he in that province but the other states [14] likewise next adjoining he brought into admiration of him, for reforming immediately at his first coming the discipline of the camp, and giving the charge in one or two battles with such resolution, as that in the assault of a castle he caught a rap with a stone upon his knee and received in his target some shot of arrows.

5. After Nero and Galba, while Otho and Vitellius strove for sovereignty, he had good hope of the empire, conceived long before, by these presaging tokens, which I will now relate. Within a country farm by the city side, belonging to the Flavii, there stood an old oak consecrated unto Mars, which at three childbirths of Vespasia suddenly did put forth every time a several bough from the stock, undoubted signs foreshowing the destiny and fortune of each one. The first was small and slender, which quickly withered (and therefore the girl at that time born lived not one year to an end) ; the second grew very stiff and long withal, which portended great felicity : but the third came to the bigness of a tree. Whereupon Sabinus, the father of Vespasian, being confirmed besides by the answer of a soothsayer [1], brought word back (by report) unto his own mother [2], that she had a nephew born who should be Caesar ; whereat she did nothing else but set up a laughter, marvelling that her son should have a cracked brain and fall a-doting now, since that his mother had her wits still whole and sound.

Soon after, when Gaius Caesar, offended and angry with him for that, being aedile, he had not been careful about sweeping and cleansing the streets, had commanded he should be all bedaubed with mire that the soldiers gathered up and threw into the lap of his embroidered robe, some were ready to make this interpretation thereof, that the commonweal, trodden one day under foot and forlorn by some civil troubles, should fall into his protection and as it were into his bosom. As he was at his dinner upon a time, a strange dog brought into his dining-room a man's hand and laid it under the board. Again, as he sat another time at supper, an ox having been at plough and shaken off his yoke, rushed into the parlour where he was at meat ; and when he had driven the waiters and servitors out, as if all on a sudden he had been weary, laid him down along at his feet where he sat and gently put his neck under him. A cypress tree likewise in his grandfather's land, without any force of tempest plucked up by the root and laid along, the very next day following rose up again greener and stronger than before. But in Achaia he dreamed, that he and his should begin to prosper so soon as Nero had a tooth drawn out of his head. Now it fortuned that the morrow following a chirurgeon that came forth into the courtyard showed unto him a tooth of Nero's newly-drawn.

In Judaea, when he consulted with the oracle of the god Carmelus [a], the answer which was given assured him in these terms, that whatsoever he thought upon and cast in his mind (were it never so great) it should so come to pass. And one of the noblemen of that country taken captive, named Josephus [3], when he was cast into prison, avouched and said unto him most constantly, that he should shortly be set at liberty even by him, but he should be emperor first. There were moreover significant tokens presaging no less reported unto him out of the very city of Rome ; and namely, that Nero in his latter days, a little before his death, was warned in a dream to take the sacred chariot of Jupiter Optimus Maximus forth of the chapel where it stood into Vespasian's house, and so from thence into the circus. Also, not long after, as Galba held the solemn election for his [4] second consulship, the statue of Julius, late Caesar of famous memory, turned of itself unto the East [b] ; and at the field fought before Betriacum, ere the battles joined, two eagles had a conflict and bickered together in all their sights, and when the one of them was foiled and overcome, a third came at the very instant from the sun-rising and chased the victor away.

6. Yet for all this attempted he no enterprise (notwithstanding his friends and soldiers were most prest [1] and forward, yea, and urgent upon him) before that he was solicited
by the unexpected favour of some who, as it fell out, were
both unknown to him and also absent. Two thousand drawn
out of the three legions of the Moesian army and sent to aid
Otho, when they were upon the way marching (albeit news
came unto them that he was vanquished and had laid violent
hands upon himself) held on their journey nevertheless as far
as to Aquileia, as giving small credit to that rumour ; where,
after they had by vantage of opportunities offered and uncon-
trolled liberty committed all manner of robberies and outrageous villainies, fearing lest, if they returned back again,
they should answer for their misdemeanours and abide condign
punishment therefor, [they] laid their heads together and consulted about the choosing and creating of an emperor. For
worse they took not themselves nor inferior, either to the
army in Spain that had set up Galba, or to the praetorian
bands which had made Otho, or to the Germanician forces
who had elected Vitellius emperor. Having proposed therefore and nominated of the consular lieutenants as many as
they could in any place think upon, when they misliked all the
rest, taking exceptions against one for this cause and another
for that, while some again of that 3rd legion, which a little
before the death of Nero had been translated out of Syria into
Moesia, highly praised and extolled Vespasian, they all
accorded thereto and without delay wrote his name upon their
flags and banners. And verily for that time this project
was smothered, the companies for a while reclaimed, and all
brought into good order. But when the said fact was once
divulged, Tiberius Alexander, provost [2] of Egypt, was the first
that forced the legions to swear allegiance unto Vespasian,
upon the kalends [3] of July, which ever after was celebrated
for the first day and beginning of his empire. After them, the
army in Judaea took the same oath before Vespasian himself,
the fifth day before the ides of July [4].

These enterprises were very much furthered by the copy of
a letter that went commonly through men's hands (true or
false I wot not) of Otho now deceased to Vespasian, charging
and willing him now at the last cast [5] of all love to revenge

his death, and wishing him withal to relieve the distressed
state of the commonwealth ; by a rumour also spread abroad,
that Vitellius upon his victory meant fully to make an exchange of the legions' winter harbours, namely, to remove
those that wintered in Germany into the East provinces [6],
as to a more secure service and easier warfare. Moreover,
among the governors of provinces Licinius Mucianus, and of
the kings Vologaesus of Parthia had promised, the one [7]
(laying down all grudge and enmity which unto that time he
openly professed [8] upon a humour of emulation) the Syrian
army, and the other [9] forty thousand archers.

7. Vespasian therefore, having undertaken a civil war and
sent before him his captains and forces into Italy, passed
over in the meantime to Alexandria, for to be possessed of
the frontier straits and avenues [1] of Egypt. Here when he
had voided [Tib. 40] all company from him and was entered
alone into the temple of Serapis, after he had upon much propitious favour of that god obtained devoutly at length turned
himself about, him thought he saw Basilides [a], one who was
known to have had access [2] unto no man and long since for the
infirmity of his sinews scarce able to set one foot before another, and withal to be absent a great way off [3], to present unto
him vervain and sacred herbs, garlands also and loaves of
bread (as the manner is in that place). And hereupon immediately letters came unto him importing thus much, that
the forces of Vitellius were discomfited before Cremona, reporting besides that himself was killed at Rome. The only
thing that he wanted (being, as one would say, a prince unlooked for and as yet new-come to the empire) was countenance, authority, and a kind as it were of royal majesty. But
even that also came on apace by this occasion. It fortuned
that a certain mean commoner stark-blind, another likewise
with a feeble and lame leg, came both together unto him as
he sat upon the tribunal, craving that help and remedy
for their infirmities which had been shown unto them by
Serapis in their dreams ; that he [4] should restore the one to
his sight, if he did but spit into his eyes, and strengthen
the other's leg, if he vouchsafed only to touch it with his
heel. Now whenas he could hardly believe that the thing
any way would find success and speed [N. 15] accordingly,

and therefore durst not so much as put it to the venture, at the last, through the persuasion of friends, openly before the whole assembly he assayed both means, neither missed he of the effect [5]. About the same time, at Tegea in Arcadia, by the [impulse] and motion of prophets, there were digged out of the ground in a consecrated place manufactures and vessels of antique works, and among the same an image, resembling for all the world Vespasian.

8. Thus qualified as he was and graced with so great fame, he returned to Rome, and after his triumph over the Jews he added eight consulships more to that which of old he had borne. He took upon him also the censorship, and all the time of his empire esteemed nothing more dear than first to establish and afterwards to adorn the commonweal, brought almost to utter decay and at the point to fall down.

The soldiers, some presuming boldly of their victories, others in grief for their shameful disgrace [1] were grown to all manner of licentiousness and audacity. The provinces likewise and free states, yea, and some kingdoms, fell to discord and seditious tumults among themselves. And therefore of the Vitellians he both cassed [V. 10] and also chastised very many ; as for the partners with him in victory, so far was he from allowing them any extraordinary indulgence, that their very due and lawful rewards he paid not but slackly. And because he would not let slip any occasion of reforming military discipline, when a certain gallant youth smelling hot of sweet balms and perfumes came unto him, to give thanks for an office [2] obtained at his hands, after a strange [3] countenance showing his dislike of him, he gave him also in words a most bitter and grievous check, saying, " I would rather thou hadst stunk of garlic," and so revoked his letters patents for the grant. As touching the mariners and sea servitors, such of them as are wont to pass to and fro on foot by turns [4] from Ostia and Puteoli to Rome, who were petitioners unto him that some certain allowance might be set down for to find them shoes, he thought it not sufficient to send them away without answer, but commanded that for ever after they should run up and down between unshod [5] ; and so from that time they use to do. Achaia, Lycia, Rhodes, Byzantium, and Samos, first disfranchised [6], likewise, Thracia, Cilicia, and Commagene, subject until that time to kings, he reduced all into the form of a province. Into Cappadocia, for the continual rodes [G. 7] and incursions that the barbarians made, he brought a power besides of legions, and in lieu of a Roman knight he placed there for ruler a man who had been consul.

The city of Rome, by reason of old skarfires [Aug. 25] and ruins was much blemished and disfigured. He permitted therefore any man to seize as his own all vacant plots of ground and to build thereupon, in case the owners and landlords were slack in that behalf. Himself took upon him the re-edifying of the Capitol, and was the first man that did set his hand to the ridding of the rubbish and rammel, yea, and upon his own neck carried some of it away ; three thousand tables of brass also, which were burnt with the said temple, he undertook to make and set up again, having searched and sought out from all places the patterns and copies thereof [7]. A most beautiful instrument and right ancient record of the whole empire he compiled and finished, wherein were contained from the first beginning well-near of the city all acts of senate, all deeds passed by the communalty as concerning leagues, alliances, and privileges granted to any whatsoever.

9. He built also new works ; the temple of Peace, situate next unto the Forum ; that likewise of Claudius, late emperor of sacred memory, seated upon the mount Caelius, which verily had been begun by Agrippina [1] but almost from the very foundation destroyed by Nero ; item, a most stately amphitheatre in the heart of the city, according as he understood that Augustus intended such a one. The two degrees [2], wasted by sundry massacres and distained through the negligence of former times, he cleansed and supplied by a review and visitation of senate and gentry both ; wherein he removed the unworthiest persons and took in the most honest that were to be found, either of Italians or provincial inhabitants. And to the end it might be known that both the said degrees differed one from another not so much in liberty as in dignity, he pronounced in the case of a certain brawl between a senator and a knight of Rome, that senators might not be provoked first with foul language ; marry, to answer them with evil words again was but civility and a matter allowed [3].

10. Suits in law depending one upon another were grown in every court exceeding much, while the old actions by the interval of jurisdiction[1] hung still undecided, and new quarrels arose to increase them, occasioned by the tumultuous troubles of those times. He chose therefore certain commissioners by lot, some by whom the goods taken and carried away perforce during the wars might be restored, and others, who extraordinarily should determine and judge between party and party in centumviral cases[2][a] (which were so many as that the parties[3] themselves, as it was thought, could hardly by course of nature live to see an end of them), and reduce them all to as small a number as possibly might be.

11. Wanton lust and wasteful expense without restraint of any man had gotten a mighty head. He moved the senate therefore to make a decree : that what woman soever joined herself in wedlock[1] unto another man's bondservant, should be reputed a bondwoman ; item, that it might not be lawful for usurers to demand any debt of young men while they were under their father's tuition for money credited out unto them, I mean, not so much as after their decease. In all other matters, from the very first beginning of his empire unto the end, he was courteous enough and full of clemency.

12. His former mean estate and condition he dissembled not at any time, nay, he would often of himself profess the same and make it known openly ; yea, and when some went about to fetch the original of the Flavian lineage from as far as the founders of Reate and the companion of Hercules, whose monument is to be seen in the Salarian Way[1], he mocked and laughed them to scorn for their labours. And so far was he from desiring any outward ornaments in show of the world, that upon his triumph day, being wearied with the slow march and tedious train of the pomp [Cal. 15], he could not hold but say plainly that he was well enough served and justly punished, who being an aged man had so foolishly longed for a triumph, as if forsooth it had of right been due unto his forefathers[2], or ever hoped for by himself[3]. Neither accepted he so much as the tribune's authority and addition of *Pater patriae* in his style, but it was long first[4]. For[5] he had forelet [Cal. 21] altogether the custom of searching those that came in duty to salute him even while yet the civil war continued.

13. The frank speech[1] of his friends, the figurative terms and quips of lawyers pleading at the bar, and the unmannerly rudeness of philosophers he took most mildly. Licinius Mucianus[2], a man notorious for preposterous wantonness but (presuming confidently of his good deserts[3]) not so respective of [Cal. 26] him as reverent duty would, he could never find in his heart to gird and nip again but secretly; and thus far forth only, as in complaining of him unto some good friend of them both to knit up all with these words for a conclusion, " Yet am I a man[4]." When Salvius Liberalis, pleading in the defence of a rich client, was so bold as to say, " What is that to Caesar[5], if Hipparchus be worth 100,000,000 sesterces ? " himself also commended and thanked him for it. Demetrius the Cynic, meeting him in the way after he was come to his sovereign dignity[6], and not deigning once to rise up nor to salute him, but rather barking at him I wot not what, he thought it enough to call cur-dog[a].

14. Displeasures to him done and enmities he never carried in mind nor revenged. The daughter of Vitellius his enemy he married into a most noble house ; he gave unto her a rich dowry withal, and furniture accordingly. Whenas by reason that he was forbidden the court under Nero he stood in great fear and was to seek what to do or whither to go, one of the gentlemen huishers, whose office it was to admit men into the presence, in thrusting him out had bidden him *abire Morboniam*[1], to be gone in a mischief. When this fellow afterwards came to ask forgiveness, he proceeded no further in heat of anger but to words only, and to quit him with just as many and almost the very same. For so far was he from working the overthrow and death of any person upon any suspicion or fear conceived, that when his friends admonished him to beware of Mettius Pompusianus, because it was generally believed that the astrologers had by the horoscope of his nativity assured him to be emperor another day, he advanced the same Mettius to the consulship, presuming and promising in the man's behalf that he would be one day mindful of this benefit and good turn of his.

15. There is not lightly found an innocent person to have been punished but when he was absent and not ware thereof, or at leastwise unwilling thereto and deceived. With Helvidius Priscus, who only had saluted him after his return out of Syria by his private name plain Vespasian[1], and being praetor in all his edicts and proclamations passed him over without any honour at all or once naming him, he was not angry and displeased before that he had with his most insolent altercations made him in manner contemptible and little better than an ordinary person. Him also, notwithstanding he was first confined to a place and afterwards commanded to be killed, he would have given a great deal to have saved by all means possible, as who sent certain of purpose to call back the murderers ; and saved his life he had, but that false word came back that he was dispatched already. Otherwise he never rejoiced in the death of any, but rather, when malefactors were justly punished and executed, he would weep and groan again.

16. The only thing for which he might worthily be blamed was covetousness. For not content with this, to have revived the taxes and payments omitted by Galba, to have laid unto them other new and heavy impositions, to have enhanced also the tributes of the provinces, yea, and of some dupled the same, he fell openly to negotiate and deal in certain trades, which even for a private person were a shame to use ; buying up and engrossing some commodities for this purpose, only to put the same off afterwards at a higher price. Neither made he it straung[1] to sell either honourable places unto suitors for them, or absolutions and pardons to men in trouble, whether they were innocent or guilty it skilled not [N. 37]. Furthermore it is verily thought that of his procurators, if any were greedy and given to extortion more than other, his manner was to promote such for the nonce to higher offices, to the end that when they were more enriched, he might soon after condemn them. And commonly it was said that those he used as sponges, for that he did wet them well when they were dry and press them hard when they were wet.

Some write that he was by nature most covetous, and that an old neat-herd upbraided him once therewith, who being at his hands denied freedom without paying for it (which he humbly craved of him now invested in the empire), cried out with a loud voice and said, The wolf [fox] might change his hair, but not his qualities. Contrariwise there be again who are of opinion that he was driven to spoil, to pill and poll [Cal. 38] of necessity, even for extreme want both in the common treasury and also in his own exchequer ; whereof he gave some testimony in the beginning immediately of his empire, professing that there was need of forty thousand millions [£320,000,000] to set the State upright again. Which also seemeth to sound more near unto the truth, because the money by him ill-gotten he used and bestowed passing well.

17. To all sorts of men he was most liberal. The estate and wealth of senators [a] he made up to the full. To decayed men that had been consuls he allowed for their maintenance 500,000 sesterces by the year. Very many cities throughout the world by earthquake or fire ruinated, he re-edified better than they were before.

18. Fine wits and cunning artisans he set much store by and cherished them above all others. He was the first that out of his own coffers appointed for professed rhetoricians, as well in Latin as in Greek, a yearly salary of 100,000 sesterces apiece. Excellent poets, as also actors[1], he bought up[2]. Semblably, upon the workman who had repaired and set up again the giantlike image called Colossus [a] he bestowed a notable congiary[3] and endowed him with a great stipend beside ; to an engineer also, who promised to bring into the Capitol huge columns with small charges, he gave for his device only no mean reward and released him his labour in performing that work, saying withal by way of preface, that he should suffer him to feed the poor commons[4].

19. At those plays during which the stage of Marcellus' theatre newly re-edified was dedicated he had brought into request and use again even the old acroames[1][a]. To Apollinaris[2] the tragedian he gave 400,000 sesterces ; to Terpnus and Diodorus, two harpers, 200,000 apiece ; to some 100,000 ; and to whom he gave least 40,000, over and above a great number of golden coronets. He feasted continually, and for the most part by making full suppers, and those very plentiful[3] ; for why ? his meaning was to help the butchers and such as sold victuals. As he delivered forth gifts unto men at the Saturnalia, so he did to women upon the kalends of March [b]. Yet verily, for all this could he not avoid the infamous name of his former avarice. The men of Alexandria termed him still Cybiosactes [4] after the surname of one of their kings, given to most base and beggarly gain. And even at his very funeral, Favor the arch-counterfeit [5], representing his person and imitating (as the manner is) his deeds and words while he lived, when he asked the procurators openly what the charges might be of his funeral and the pomp thereto belonging, no sooner heard that it would arise to 10,000,000 sesterces but he cried, " Give me 100,000 and make no more ado but throw me into the Tiber."

20. Of a middle [1] stature he was, well-set, his limbs compact and strongly made, with a countenance as if he strained hard for a stool. Whereupon one of these plaisants [wits] came out with a pretty conceit. For when Vespasian seemed to request the fellow for to break a jest upon him also as well as upon others, " That I will," quoth he, " if you had done your business once upon the seege." [2] His health he had, no man better ; although for the preservation thereof he did no more but rub his own jaws and other parts of the body to a certain just number within the Sphaeristerium [3] [a], and withal monthly interpose abstinence from all food one whole day [4].

21. This course and order of life for the most part he held. While he was emperor he waked always very early and late in the night [1]. Then, having read through all missives and the breviaries of every office, he admitted his friends ; and while he was saluted, he both put on his own shoes and also apparelled and made himself ready. After dispatch of all occurrent businesses he took himself to gestation [a], and so to rest ; having one of his concubines lying by his side, of whom he had appointed a great number instead of Caenis deceased. From his privy closet [2], he passed into his baine [Aug. 76] and so to his refection-room. Neither was he, by report, at any time fuller of humanity or readier to do a pleasure ; and such opportunities of time as these his domestic servants waited for especially to prefer their petitions in.

22. At his suppers and otherwise at all times with his friends being most pleasant and courteous [1] [a], he dispatched many matters by way of mirth. For given exceedingly he was to scoffs and those so scurrilous and filthy that he could not so much as forbear words of ribaldry [b]. And yet there be many right pleasant conceited jests of his extant, among which this also goes for one. Being advertised by Mestrius Florus, a man of consul's degree, to pronounce *Plaustra* [2] rather than *Plostra*, he saluted him the next morrow by the name of Flaurus [3] [c]. Having yielded at length to a certain woman enamoured of him and ready as it were to die for pure love, when she was brought to his bed [4] and had given him forty thousand sesterces for lying with her [5], his steward comes to put him in mind in what manner and form he would have this sum of money to be set down in his book of accounts [6] : " Marry, thus," quoth he, " *Vespasiano adamato*, Item, given to Vespasian beloved " [d].

23. He used Greek verses also in good season and aptly applied, as namely of a certain fellow, tall and high of stature, but shrewd [N. 7] and testy withal [a], in this manner,

Μακρὰ βιβὰς κραδάων δολιχόσκιον ἔγχος [b],

and especially of Cerylus, his freedman ; upon whom, for that being exceeding rich, yet to avoid a payment sometime to his exchequer, he began to give it out that he was freeborn, and so changed his name and called himself Laches, Vespasian played in these terms :

ὦ Λάχης, Λάχης, ἐπὰν ἀποθάνῃς,
αὖθις ἐξ ὑπαρχῆς εἰρήσῃ Κήρυλος [1].

O Laches, Laches, wert thou once dead in grave,
Thine old name Cerylus again thou shalt have.

Howbeit, most of all he affected a kind of dicacity in his unseemly gain and filthy lucre, to the end that by some scoffing cavil he might put by and do away the envy [odium] of the thing, turning all to merry jests.

A minister and servitor about him, whom he loved dearly, made suit in the behalf of one as his brother [2] for a stewardship. When he had put him off to a further day, he called unto him the party himself that made means [3] for the thing ; and having exacted so much money at his hands as he had agreed for with the mediator aforesaid, without more delay he ordained him steward. Soon after, when the servitor interposed himself, " Go your ways," quoth he, " seek you

another to be your brother ; for this fellow whom you think
to be yours is become mine." Suspecting that his muleteer
who drove his carroch alighted one time, as it were to shoe his
mules, thereby to win some advantage of time and delay for
one that had a matter in law and was coming unto him, he
asked the muleteer what might the shoeing of his mules cost [4]
and so covenanted with him to have part of his gains. When
his son Titus seemed to find fault with him for devising a kind
of tribute even out of urine [c], the money that came unto his
hand of the first payment he put unto his son's nose, asking
withal whether he was offended with the smell, or no, and when
he answered " No," " And yet," quoth he, " it cometh of
urine." Certain ambassadors brought him word that there
was decreed for him at the common charges of the State a
giantlike image that would cost no mean sum of money.
He commanded them to rear the same immediately, showing
therewith his hand hollow [5] : " Here is the base," quoth
he, " and pedestal [6] for it ready."

And not so much as in the fear and extreme peril of death
forbare he scoffing. For whenas among other prodigious
signs the mausoleum [7] of the Caesars opened suddenly and a
blazing star appeared, the one [8] of them he said did concern
Junia Calvina, a gentlewoman of Augustus (Caesar's) race [9],
the other [10] had reference to the king of the Parthians, who
wore his hair long [11]. In the very first access also and fit of his
disease, " Methinks," quoth he, " I am a-deifying [12]."

24. In his ninth consulship, after he had been assailed in
Campania with some light motions and grudgings [1] of his
sickness and thereupon returned forthwith to the city, he
went from thence to Cutiliae and the lands he had about
Reate, where every year he was wont to summer. Here
having (besides the malady still growing upon him) hurt also
his guts and bowels with the use of cold water [2], and yet
nevertheless executed the functions of an emperor after his
accustomed manner, insomuch as, lying upon his bed, he gave
audience to ambassadors, when all of a sudden he fell into a
looseness of the belly that he fainted and was ready to swoon
therewith, " An emperor," quoth he, " ought to die standing."
As he was arising therefor and straining still to ease his body [3],
he died in their hands that helped to lift him up, the [ninth]

day before the kalends of July [4], when he had lived threescore
years and nine, seven months, and seven days over [5].

25. All writers agree in this, that so confident he was
always of his own horoscope and his children's, that after so
many conspiracies continually plotted against him he durst
warrant and assure the senate that either his own sons should
succeed him or none. It is said moreover that he dreamed
upon a time how he saw a pair of scales hanging in the midst
of the porch and entry of his house [on the] Palatine, with the
beam thereof even balanced, so as in the one balance stood
Claudius and Nero, in the other, himself and his sons. And it
fell out so indeed ; for they ruled the empire of both sides so
many years and the like space of time just.

THE HISTORY OF
TITUS FLAVIUS VESPASIANUS
AUGUSTUS

1. TITUS, surnamed, as his father was, Vespasianus [was called] the lovely darling and delightful joy of mankind, so fully was he either endowed with good nature and disposition, or enriched with skilful cunning, or else graced with fortune's favour ; and that, which is hardest of all, in his imperial state, considering that while he lived as a private person under the emperor his father, he could not avoid the very hatred and much less the reproof of the world. This Titus was born the third day before the kalends of January[1], in that year which was remarkable for the death of Gaius the emperor, near unto the Septizonium[a], within a poor ill-favoured house, in a very little chamber and dark withal ; for it remaineth yet to be seen.

2. His education he had in the court together with Britannicus, trained up in the like arts and disciplines under the same teachers. At which time verily, men say that a fortune-teller[1][a], whom Narcissus the freedman of Claudius brought to see Britannicus, after inspection affirmed most constantly that by no means he[2], but Titus who then stood hard by, should surely be emperor. Now were these two so familiar that (as it is verily thought) of the same cup of poison whereof Britannicus drank and died Titus also, sitting near unto him, tasted ; whereupon he fell into a grievous disease, that held him long and put him to great pain. In memorial of all which premises[3], he erected afterwards for him[4] one statue of gold in the Palatium, as also another of ivory on horseback (which at the Circensian games is even at this day carried before in the solemn pomp) he dedicated and accompanied accordingly.

3. At the very first, even in his childhood, there shone forth in him the gifts both of body and mind, and the same more and

more still by degrees as he grew in years ; a goodly presence
and countenance, wherein was seated no less majesty[1] than
favour and beauty ; a special clean strength, albeit his stature
was not tall, but his belly bare out somewhat with the most ;
a singular memory and aptness to learn all the arts, in manner
[Cal. 34] as well of war as of peace. Most skilful he was in
handling his weapon, and withal a passing good horseman ; for
his Latin and Greek tongue, whether it were in making orations
or composing poems, prompt and ready even to the performance thereof extempore. Neither was he unseen[2] in music, as
who could both sing and also play upon instruments sweetly
and with knowledge. I have heard also many men say that
he was wont to write with ciphers and characters most swiftly,
striving by way of sport and mirth with his own clerks,
whether he or they could write fastest, to express likewise and
imitate what hand soever he had seen, yea, and to profess
many a time that he would have made a notable forger and
counterfeiter of writings.

4. In quality of military tribune he served in the wars
both in Germany and also in Britain with exceeding commendation for his industry and no less report of modesty[1],
as appeareth by a number of his images and titles to them
annexed[a] throughout both provinces. After this warfare
of his, he pleaded causes in court, which he did rather to
win credit and reputation[2] than to make it an ordinary
practice[3]. At which very time he wedded [Arrecina], the
daughter of Tertullus, a gentleman of Rome, but captain
sometime of the praetorian bands ; and in the room of her
deceased he took to wife Marcia [Furnilla], and from her,
when she had borne unto him a daughter, he divorced himself. After this upon his quaestorship, being colonel and
commander of a whole legion, he brought under his subjection Taricheae[4] and Gamala, two most puissant cities of
Judaea, where, in a certain battle having lost his horse under
him by a deadly wound within his flanks, he mounted another
whose rider in fight against him[5] had been slain and was
fallen.

5. Afterwards, when Galba was possessed of the State,
being sent to congratulate his advancement, what way soever
he went he turned all men's eyes upon him, as if he had

been singled forth to be adopted. But so soon as he perceived all to be full of troubles again, he returned back out of his very journey and visited the oracle of Venus Paphia[1], where, whilst he asked counsel about his passage at sea, he was confirmed withal in his hope of the empire. Having attained thereto[2] within short time and being left behind to subdue Judaea thoroughly, in the last assault of Jerusalem he slew twelve enemies that defended the wall with just so many arrows' shot, and won the city upon the very birthday of his daughter[3], with so great joy and favourable applause of all his soldiers, that in their gratulation they saluted him emperor, and soon after, when he was to depart out of that province, detained him; in humble manner, yea, and eftsoons in threatening wise instantly calling upon him to stay or else to take them all away together with him. Whereupon arose the first suspicion that he revolted from his father and had attempted to challenge the kingdom of the East parts for himself; which surmise himself made the more, after that on his way to Alexandria, as he consecrated at Memphis the ox Apis, he wore a diadem[a], which he did indeed according to the custom and rites of the ancient religion there, but there wanted not some who construed it otherwise. Making haste therefore into Italy, after he was arrived first at Rhegium and from thence at Puteoli, embarked in a merchant's ship of burden, to Rome he goes directly with all speed and most lightly appointed; and unto his father looking for nothing less, " I am come," quoth he, " father, I am come," checking thereby the rash and inconsiderate rumours raised of him.

6. From that time forward he ceased not to carry himself as partner with his father, yea, and protector also of the empire. With him he triumphed, with him he jointly administered the censorship, his colleague he was in the tribune's authority, his companion likewise in seven consulships. And having taken to himself the charge well-near of all offices, whiles he both indited letters and penned edicts in his father's name, yea, and read orations in the senate, and that in the quaestor's turn, he assumed also the captainship of the guard, an office never to that time executed but by a gentleman of Rome. In this place he demeaned himself nothing civilly[1], but proceeded with much violence; for ever as he

had any in most jealousy and suspicion, by sending secretly
and underhand certain of purpose who in the theatres and
camp should require for to have them punished (as it were
with his father's consent), he made no more ado but brought
them all to their end. As for example, among these he commanded Aulus Caecina, a man of consular degree and a guest
by him invited to supper, when he was scarce gone out of the
banqueting-parlour to be stabbed. I must needs say that
driven he was to this violent proceeding upon an extremity
of danger, considering that he had found out his hand-writing
bearing evidence of a conspiracy that he plotted with the
soldiers. By which courses, as he provided well and sufficiently for his own security another day, so for the present
time he incurred very much displeasure and hatred of the
world, insomuch as no man lightly, when so adverse a rumour
was on foot and, that which more is, against the wills of all
men would have stepped to the imperial throne.

7. Beside his cruelty suspected he was also for riotous life,
in that he continued banqueting until midnight with the
most profuse and wasteful spendthrifts of his familiar minions ;
for wanton lust likewise, by reason of a sort of stale catamites
and gelded eunuchs that he kept about him, and the affectionate love that he was noted to bear to queen Berenice[1],
unto whom also as it was said he promised marriage. Suspicion there was moreover of his pilling and polling [Cal. 38].
For certain it was that, in the commissions and hearing of
causes which his father held, he was wont to sell the decision
of matters and to make a gain thereby. After this, men both
reputed and also reported him to be even another Nero.
But this name that went of him proved good for him and turned
to his greatest commendation, considering that no gross vice
could be found in him, but contrariwise many excellent
virtues. The feasts that he made were pleasant merriments
rather than lavish and sumptuous. He chose for his friends
such as in whom the emperors also his successors reposed
themselves[2], and whom they used especially as necessary
members both for them and also for the commonwealth. As
for queen Berenice, he sent her quickly away from the city of
Rome, but full loath they were both of them to part asunder.
Certain of his minions and darlings whom he favoured and

fancied most, albeit they were such artificial dancers that within a while after they carried the greatest praise and prize upon the stage, he forbare quite not only to huggle and embrace long together, but to behold so much as once in any public meeting and assembly.

From no citizen took he aught, and from aliens' goods he abstained, if ever any did ; nay, he received not the very contributions granted and usually paid. And yet, being inferior to none of his predecessors in munificence, as having dedicated an amphitheatre [3] and built the baines hard by with great expedition [a], he exhibited a spectacle of sword-fencers, with all kinds of furniture thereto belonging in most plentiful manner. He represented also a naval fight in the old Naumachia [C. 39], in which very place he brought forth likewise his sword-fencers to play their prizes [Cl. 21] ; and in that one day he put out to be baited 5000 wild beasts of all sorts.

8. Furthermore, being of his own nature most kind and gracious, whereas by a constitution and order that Tiberius began, all the Caesars his successors held not the benefits granted by former princes good and in force, unless they also themselves made new grants of the same again, he was the first that by virtue of one sole edict ratified and confirmed all that had passed before, neither suffered he any petition to be made unto him for them. In all other suits and requests he evermore held most constantly men's minds at this pass [1], that he would send none away without hope. And when his domestic ministers about his person would seem to tell him that he promised more than he was able to perform : " What ! " quoth he, " there ought no man to depart from the speech of a prince sad and discontented." Calling to mind one time as he sat at supper that he had done nothing for any man that day, he uttered this memorable and praiseworthy apophthegm, " My friends, I have lost a day."

The people especially in general he entreated on all occasions with so great courtesy that, having proposed a solemn sword-fight, he made open profession that he would set it forth not to please himself but to content the beholders. And verily, even so he did ; for neither denied he aught to them that would call for it, and of his own accord willed them to ask what their minds stood to. Moreover, showing plainly that he stood well-affected to the manner of the Thracian sword-fencers'[2] fight and their armature, he would many times even with the rest of the people both in word and gesture (as a favourer of that kind) jest and make sport, yet so as he kept still the majesty of an emperor, and withal judged with equity indifferently. And because he would pretermit no point of popularity, sometime as he bathed in his own baines he admitted the commons thither unto him.

There fell out in his days certain mischances and heavy accidents : as the burning of the mountain Vesuvius in Campania, a skarfire [Aug. 25] at Rome, which lasted three days and three nights, as also a pestilence[3], the like whereof had not lightly been known elsewhere at any other time. In these calamities so many and so grievous he showed not only a princely care, but also a singular fatherly affection ; sometime comforting his people by his edicts, otherwhiles helping them so far forth as his power would extend. For repairing the losses in Campania[4] he chose by lot certain commissioners to look thereto, even out of the rank of those that had been consuls. The goods of such as perished in the said mount, whose heirs could not be found, he awarded to the re-edification of the ruinated cities adjoining. And having made public protestation that in the said skarfire of the city there was no loss at all but to himself, look, what ornaments were in any of his own palaces and royal houses[5], the same he appointed to the city buildings and the temples ; for which purpose he made divers of knight's degree supervisors, to the end that every thing might be dispatched with greater expedition. To cure the sickness and mitigate the fury of those contagious diseases, he used all help of god and man, having sought out whatsoever kinds of sacrifices and remedies might be found.

Among the adversities of those times may be reckoned these promoters [N. 32] and informers with such as underhand set them a-work, occasioned all by old licentiousness and impunity. And these he commanded to be whipped and beaten with cudgels ordinarily in the open market-place ; and last of all, when they had been brought in a show through the amphitheatre, partly to be sold in port-sale [C. 50] for slaves, and in part to be carried away into the roughest and bleakest

islands that were. And because he would for ever restrain
such as at any time should dare to do the like, he made
an act among many others, prohibiting one and the same
matter to be sued by virtue of many statutes and laws
enacted in that behalf [6], or to make inquisition as touching
the estate of any man deceased after the term of certain
years limited.

9. Having professed that he took upon him the high
priesthood in this regard, because he would keep his hands
pure and innocent, he made good his word. For after that
time never was he the principal author of any man's death
nor privy and accessory thereto (albeit he wanted not sometimes just cause of revenge), but swore devoutly that he would
rather die himself than do others to death. Two noblemen
of the patrician rank, convicted for affecting and aspiring to
the empire, he proceeded against no farther than to admonish
them to desist and give over, saying that sovereign power was
the gift of destiny and divine providence. If they were
petitioners for anything else he promised to give it unto them.
And verily, out of hand [N. 44] to the mother of the one, who
was then far off (woeful and pensive woman as she was), he
dispatched his own cursitors [1] and footmen to carry word
that her son was safe ; as for themselves, he not only invited
them to a familiar and friendly supper that night, but also
the next day following at the fight of sword-fencers, placing
them of purpose near about his own person, the ornaments [2]
of the champions that were to fight, presented unto him, he
reached unto them for to view and peruse [Cal. 36] [a]. It is
said, moreover, that having knowledge of both their horo-
scopes [3], he avouched that danger was toward them both and
would light upon their heads one day, but from some other ;
as it fell out in deed. His own brother [4] never ceasing to lay
wait for his life, but professedly in manner [5] soliciting the
armies against him, plotting also and intending thereupon to
flee and be gone, he could never endure either to kill or to
sequester and confine, no, nor so much as to abridge of any
honour ; but as he had always done from the first day of his
imperial dignity, persevered to testify and declare that partner
he was with him in the sovereign government and his heir-
apparent to succeed him ; otherwhiles secretly with tears and

prayers beseeching that he would vouchsafe him yet at length mutual love and affection.

10. Amid this blessed course of life cut short he was and prevented by death, to the greater loss of mankind than of himself. After he had finished the solemn shows and games exhibited to the people, in the end and upshot whereof he had shed tears abundantly, he went toward the Sabine territory somewhat more sad than usually he had been, by occasion that, as he sacrificed, the beast broke loose and got away, as also because in fair and clear weather it had thundered [a]. Hereupon, having gotten an ague at his first lodging and baiting place, when he was removing from thence in his litter, it is said that, putting by the curtains of the window, he looked up to heaven and complained very piteously that his life should be taken from him who had not deserved to die ; for there was no act of his extant of which he was to repent, save only one. Now what that one should be neither uttered he himself at that instant, neither is any man able readily to guess thereat. Some think he called to mind the overfamiliar acquaintance that he had with his brother's wife ; but Domitia devoutly swore that he never had such dealing with her, who no doubt would not have denied it, if there had been any folly at all between them ; nay, she would rather have made her vaunt thereof, so ordinary a thing it was with her to glory in all naughtiness and shameful deeds.

11. He departed this world [a] in the very same country-house wherein his father died before him, upon the ides of September [1], two years, two months, and twenty days after that he succeeded his father, and in the two and fortieth year of his age. Which being once notified and known abroad, when all men throughout the city mourned no less than in some domestic occasion of sorrow and lamentation, the senate, before they were summoned and called together by any edict, ran to the Curia, finding as yet the doors fast-locked ; but when they were set open, they rendered unto him now dead so much thanks and heaped upon him so great a measure of praises, as they never did before at any time whiles he was living and present among them.

THE HISTORY OF
FLAVIUS DOMITIANUS

1. DOMITIAN was born the ninth day before the kalends of November [1], what time his father was consul elect and to enter upon that honourable place the month ensuing [2], within the sixth region of Rome city, at the Pomegranate [3], and in that house which afterwards he converted into the temple of the Flavian family. The flower of his tender years and the very prime of youth he passed by report in so great poverty and infamy [4] withal, that he had not one piece of plate or vessel of silver to be served with. And full well it is known that Claudius Pollio, a man of praetor's degree (against whom there is a poem of Nero's extant entitled *Luscio* [a]) kept by him a skrow [V. 15] of his own hand-writing, yea, and otherwhiles brought the same forth to be seen, wherein he promised him the use [5] of his body one night. Neither wanted some who constantly avouched that Domitian was in that sort abused even by Nerva, who soon after succeeded him.

In the Vitellian troubles [6] he fled into the Capitol with his uncle Sabinus and part of the forces which were then present. But when the adverse faction broke in and while the temple was on fire, he lay close all night in the sexton's [7] lodging, and early in the morning, disguised in the habit of a priest of Isis [b] and among the sacrificers belonging to that vain superstition, after he had passed over Tiber, accompanied with one only person, to the mother of a schoolfellow of his, he lurked there so secretly, that albeit the searchers traced him by his footing, yet could he not be found. At last, after victory obtained, he went forth and showed himself, and being generally saluted by the name of Caesar [8], the honourable dignity of the city praetor in the consular authority he took upon him in name and title only, the jurisdiction whereof he

372

made over to his next colleague. But in all power of lordly
rule [9] he carried himself so licentiously and without control
that he showed even then betimes what a one he would prove
hereafter. And not to handle every particular : having with
unclean hands offered dishonour to many men's wives, he [led]
away and married also Domitia Longina, the wedded wife of
Aelius [Lamia], and in one day gave and dealt above twenty
offices within the city and abroad in foreign provinces, insomuch as Vespasian commonly said, that he marvelled why
he sent not one also to succeed in his place.

2. He enterprised moreover a voyage into Gaul and Germany, notwithstanding the same was needless and his father's
friends dissuaded him from it, only because he would equalise
his brother both in works [1] and reputation. For these pranks
of his rebuked he was, and to the end he might the rather be
put in mind of his young years and private condition, he dwelt
together with his father ; in a litter he attended the curule
chair of father and brother, whensoever they went forth of
doors, and being mounted upon a white courser accompanied
them both in their triumph over Judaea. Of six consulships
he bore but one ordinary [2], and the same by occasion that his
brother Titus yielded unto him his own place and furthered
him in his suit.

Himself likewise made wonderful semblance of modesty ;
but above all he seemed outwardly to affect poetry (a study
which he was not so much unacquainted with beforetime but
he despised and rejected it as much afterwards) and recited
his own verses even in public place. Yet nevertheless, when
Vologaesus, king of the Parthians, required aid against the
Alans and one of Vespasian's two sons to be the general of
those forces, he laboured with might and main that himself
before all others should be sent ; and because the quarrel was
dispatched already to his hand [3], he assayed by gifts and large
promises to solicit other kings of the East to make the same
request.

When his father was dead, standing in doubtful terms
with himself a long time whether he should offer unto the
soldiers a donative duple to that of his brother Titus, he never
stuck [Cal. 25] to give out and make his boast, that left he
was to be partner with him in the empire, but that his father's

will was very much abused. Neither would he give over from that time forward both to lay wait secretly for his brother and also to practise openly against him, until such time as he gave command, when he was stricken with grievous sickness, that he should be left for dead before the breath was out of his body; and after he was departed indeed, vouchsafing him no other honour but his consecration [4], he carped also at him many a time as well in glancing figurative speeches as in open edicts.

3. In the beginning of his empire his manner was to retire himself daily into a secret place for one hour [1], and there to do nothing else but to catch flies and with the sharp point of a bodkin or writing-steel prick them through; insomuch as when one inquired whether any body were with Caesar within, Vibius Crispus made answer not impertinently, " No, not so much as a fly." After this, Domitia his own wife, who in his second consulship had borne him a son, and whom two years after he had saluted as empress by the name of Augusta, her I say, falling in fancy with Paris the stage-player and ready to die for his love, he put away; but within a small while after (as impatient of this breach and divorce) took her home and married her again, as if the people had instantly called upon him so to do. In the administration of the empire he behaved himself for a good while variably, as one made of an equal mixture and temper of vices and virtues, until at length he turned his virtues also into vices, being (so far as we may conjecture) over and above his natural inclination, for want covetous and greedy, for fear bloody and cruel.

4. He exhibited ordinarily magnificent and sumptuous shows not only in the amphitheatre, but in the circus also; in which, beside the usual running of chariots, drawn as well with two steeds as four, he represented likewise two battles of horsemen and footmen both, and in the amphitheatre a naval fight. Baitings of wild beasts and sword-fencers he showed in the very night by cresset and torch-lights, and he brought into the place not men only to fight, but women also to encounter wild beasts. Furthermore, at the games of sword-fight set out by the quaestors (which having in times past been discontinued and forelet [Cal. 21] he brought into use again) he was always present in person, so as he gave the people leave to choose two pair of sword-fencers out of his own school, and those he brought in royally and courtlike appointed in the last place. And at all sights of sword-players there stood ever at his feet a little dwarf arrayed in scarlet with a small head that it was wonderful, with whom he used to talk and confer otherwhiles of serious matters. Certes, overheard he was, when he demanded him of what he knew and what he thought of the last disposal of the provinces, and namely of ordaining Mettius Rufus lieutenant-general of Egypt. He exhibited naval battles performed in manner [Cal. 34] by full fleets and complete navies, having digged out a great pit for a lake and built a stone wall round about it near unto the Tiber ; and those he would behold in the greatest storms and showers that were. He set forth also the secular plays and games, making his computation from the year, not wherein Claudius, but Augustus long before had made them. During these, upon the day of the Circensian solemnities, to the end there might be a hundred courses [1] the sooner run, he abridged the races of every one, to wit, from seven to four.

He ordained moreover in the honour of Jupiter Capitolinus quinquennial games of threefold masteries, music, horse-riding, and gymnastic exercises, and in the same rewarding victors with coronets more by a good many than now they be. Herein the concurrents strove also for the prize in prose, both Greek and Latin ; and besides single harpers there were sets of those also that played upon the harp, yea, and consorts of such as sung thereto in a choir. In the running-place, virgins also ran for the best games. At all these masteries and solemnities he sat as president in his pantofles [2], clad in a robe of purple after the Greek fashion [a], wearing on his head a golden coronet with the image of Jupiter, Juno, and Minerva, having the priest of Jupiter and the college of the religious called Flaviales [3] sitting by him in like habit, saving that in their coronets there was his image also. Semblably he celebrated every year upon the Alban mount the Quinquatrus of Minerva, in whose honour he had instituted a society, out of which there should be chosen by lot masters ond wardens of that solemnity, who were to exhibit peculiar and especial beast-baitings and stageplays, yea, and contentions for the prize of orators and poets besides. He gave a largesse to the people thrice, to wit, three hundred sesterces apiece, and at the show of the sword-fight a most plenteous dinner [4]. At the solemn Septimontial [5] sacrifice he made a dole of viands, allowing to the senators and gentlemen fair large panniers, to the commons, small maunds [6] with cates in them ; and was the first himself that fell to his meat. The next day after he scattered among them missiles [Cal. 18] of all sorts, and because the greater part thereof fell to the ranks of the common people, he pronounced by word of mouth for every scaffold of senators and gentlemen fifty tickets or tallies.

5. Many buildings, and those most stately, which had been consumed with fire he re-edified, and among them the Capitol which had been fired again [1], but all under the title of his own name without any memorial of the former founders. Marry, he founded a new temple in the Capitol to the honour of Jupiter Custos, also the Forum, which is now called Nervae Forum, likewise the temple of the Flavian family, a show-place for running and wrestling, another for poets and musicians to contend in [2], and a naumachia for ships to encounter. Of the stone that was about which the greatest Circus [3] of all was afterwards built, by occasion that both sides thereof had been burnt down.

6. Expeditions he made, some voluntary, some upon necessity ; of his own accord that against the Chatti, upon constraint one against the Sarmatians, by occasion that one whole legion together with their lieutenant fell upon the sword ; two against the Daci, the former because Oppius Sabinus, a man of consul's degree, was defeated and slain, and the second for that Cornelius Fuscus, captain of the praetorian bands (unto whom he had committed the whole conduct of that war) lost his life. Over the Chatti and Daci (after sundry fields fought with variety of fortune) he triumphed twice. For his victory over the Sarmatians he presented only Jupiter Capitolinus with his laurel garland.

The civil war stirred up by Lucius Antonius, governor of Upper Germany, he dispatched and ended in his absence [1], and that by a wonderful good hap, whenas at the very hour of conflict the Rhine swelling and overflowing suddenly stayed the barbarians' forces as they would have passed over to

Antonius. Of which victory he had intelligence by presages
before the news by messengers came. For upon that very
day when the battle was fought, an eagle, after a strange
manner having overspread his statue at Rome and clasped it
about with her wings, made a great flapping noise in token of
much joy, and within a little after the bruit was blown abroad
so rife and common of Antonius' death, that many avouched
confidently they had seen his head also brought home to Rome.

7. Many new orders besides in matters of common use he
brought up. The dole of viands given and distributed in
little baskets in lieu of a public supper he abolished, and
revived the ancient custom of complete and formal suppers[1].
Unto the four factions[2] in former time of several crews running
with chariots at the Circensian games he added twain, to
wit, the golden and purple livery. Players and actors of
interludes he forbade the open stage, but within house,
verily, he granted free and lawful exercise of their art. He
gave commandment that no males should be gelded, and of
such eunuchs as remained in the hands of hucksters[3] he
abated the price and brought it down to a meaner. By reason
one time of an exceeding plentiful vintage and as much
scarcity of corn, supposing that by the immoderate care
employed upon vineyards tillage was neglected, he made an
edict, that no man in all Italy should plant any new young
vineyards, and that in foreign provinces they should cut them
all down, reserving at the most but the one half[a]; howbeit
he continued not in the full execution of this act. Some of the
greatest offices he communicated indifferently between
libertines and [knights]. He prohibited that there should be
two camps of the legions[4][b]; Item, that any man should lay
up more than a thousand sesterces about the camp-ensigns[c],
for that Lucius Antonius, intending rebellion in the wintering
harbour of two legions, was thought to have taken heart and
presumed more confidently upon the great sums of money
there bestowed in stock. He added a fourth stipend also for
soldiers, to wit, three pieces of gold by the poll[5].

8. In ministering justice precise he was and industrious.
Many a time, even in the common place[1], sitting extraordinarily
upon the tribunal, he reversed the definitive sentences of the
centumvirs, given for favour and obtained by flattery. He

warned eft-soons the commissioners and judges delegate not to accommodate themselves and give ear unto persuasive and rhetorical assertions [2]. The judges that were bribed and corrupted with money he noted and disgraced every one together with their assessors upon the bench. He moved also and persuaded the tribunes of the commons to accuse judicially for extortion and to force unto restitution a base and corrupt aedile [3], yea, and to call unto the senate for to have a jury empanelled upon him. Moreover, so careful was he to chastise as well the magistrates within Rome as the rulers of provinces abroad of their misdemeanours, that never at any time they were either more temperate or just in their places ; the most part of whom after his days we ourselves have seen culpable, yea, and brought into question for all manner of crimes.

Having taken upon him the censuring and reformation of manners, he inhibited that licentious liberty taken up in theatres, of beholding the plays and games pell-mell one with another in the quarter and ranks appointed for gentlemen. Defamatory libels written and divulged, wherein men and women of good mark were touched and taxed, he abolished not without shame and ignominy of the authors. A man of quaestor's degree, because he took pleasure in puppet-like gesturing and dancing, he removed out of the senate. From women of dishonest carriage [4] he took away the privilege and use of their litters ; he made them incapable also of legacies and inheritances. A gentleman of Rome he rased out of the roll and tables of judges, for receiving his wife again into wedlock, whom he had before put away and sued in an action of adultery. Some of both degrees, as well senators as gentlemen, he condemned by virtue of the law Scantinia [5]. The incestuous whoredoms committed by Vestal votaries, negligently passed over by his father and brother both, he punished after sundry sorts, the former delinquents in that kind with simple death [6], the later sort according to the ancient manner [a]. For having given liberty unto the sisters Ocellatae [7] as also to Varronilla for to choose their own deaths and banished those who had deflowered them, he afterwards commanded that Cornelia Maximilla [8], who in times past had been acquit and a long time after was called into question again and convicted, should be buried quick [9], and the parties who had committed incest with her beaten with rods to death in the Comitium ; except one alone, a man of praetor's degree, unto whom, whiles the matter remained yet doubtful and because he had confessed and bewrayed himself (upon his examination by torture which was uncertain), he granted the favour of exile.

And that no religious service of the gods should be contaminated and polluted without condign punishment, the monument or tomb, which his freedman had built for a son of his with the stones appointed for the temple of Jupiter Capitolinus, he caused his soldiers to demolish, and the bones and relics therein he drowned in the sea.

9. At the first he abhorred all bloodshed and slaughter, so far forth as that (while his father was yet absent), calling to remembrance this verse of Virgil,

> *Impia quam* [1] *caesis gens est epulata juvencis,*
> Ere godless people made their feasts
> With oxen slain (poor harmless beasts),

he purposed fully to publish an edict, forbidding to kill and sacrifice any ox. Of covetousness also and avarice [2] he gave scarcely the least suspicion, either at any time when he led a private life or a good while after he was emperor, but contrariwise rather he showed great proofs oftentimes not of abstinence [3] only but also of liberality. And whensoever he had bestowed gifts most bountifully upon those that were about him, he laid upon them no charge before this nor with more earnestness, than to do nothing basely and beggarly. Moreover, one legacy put down in the last will of Rustus Caepio, who had provided therein that his heir should give yearly unto every one of the senators as they went into the Curia a certain sum of money, he made void.

All those likewise, whose suits had hung and depended in the chamber of the city [4] from before five years last past, he discharged and delivered from trouble. Neither suffered he them to be sued and molested again but within the compass of one year and with this condition, that the accuser (unless he overthrew his adversary by that time) should be banished for his labour. The scribes and notaries belonging to the quaestors, who by an old custom (but yet against the Clodian law) used to negotiate and trade, he pardoned only for the time past. The odd ends and cantels[5] of grounds, which after the division of lands by the veteran soldiers[6] remained here and there cut out as it were from the rest, he granted unto the old owners and landlords as in the right of prescription. The false information of matters, whereof the penalty came to the exchequer, he repressed, and sharply punished such informers. And this (by men's saying) was a speech of his ; " The prince that chasteneth not promoters [N. 32], setteth them on to promote."

10. But long continued he not in this train either of clemency or of abstinence ; and yet fell he somewhat sooner to cruelty than to covetousness. A scholar of the cunning player and counterfeit Paris, being as yet of tender years and at that time very sick, he murdered, for that both in skill and also in countenance and feature of body he seemed to resemble his master. Semblably dealt he with Hermogenes of Tarsus for certain figures of rhetoric[1] interlaced in his history, and withal crucified the scriveners and writers that had copied it out. A householder[a], for saying these words, that the Thracian fencer[2] was equal to the mirmillo[b] but inferior to the setter forth of the game[3], he caused to be plucked down from the scaffold in the theatre into the plain beneath, and there to be cast before the greedy mastiffs, with this title, *Impie locutus parmularius*, The parmularius[4][c] hath blasphemed.

Many senators, and some of them which had been consuls, he killed. Among whom Civicus Cerealis, in the very time when he was proconsul in Asia, Salvidienus Orfitus and Acilius Glabrio during their exile he put to death, pretending that they practised innovation[5] in the State ; all the rest every one for most slight causes. As for example, Aelius Lamia, for certain suspicious jests (I must needs say) but such as were stale and harmless ; namely, because unto Domitian when (after he had taken from him his wife[6]) he fell a-praising of her voice[7], he said, " I hold my peace[8], alas[d] " ; as also for that unto Titus, moving him to a second marriage, he made answer, Μὴ καὶ σὺ γαμῆσαι θέλεις ; " What ! (and if I should wed another) would not you also marry her ? " Salvius Cocceianus[9], because he had cele-

brated the birthday-mind [Aug. 53] of Otho the emperor,
his uncle[10]. Mettius Pompusianus [Vesp. 14], for that it
was commonly said he had the horoscope in his nativity
of an emperor, and carried about him the map or geographical
description of the world in certain parchments, and withal the
orations of kings and brave captains written out of Titus
Livius ; for imposing likewise the names of Mago and Hannibal[11] upon some of his slaves. Sallustius Lucullus, lieutenant-general of Britain, for suffering certain spears of a new
fashion to be called Lucullean[12]. Junius Rusticus, for publishing the praises of Paetus Thrasea[13] and Helvidius Priscus[14]
and calling them most holy and upright persons ; by occasion
of which criminous imputation (charged upon Rusticus) he
packed away all philosophers out of the city of Rome and
Italy. He slew also Helvidius the son[15], for that in an interlude (as it were) and by way of an *exodium* [farce] upon
the stage, he had under the persons of Paris and Oenone
acted[16] the divorce between him[17] and his wife. Flavius
Sabinus, one of his cousin germans, because upon the election
day of the consuls, the crier chanced to mistake a little and
before the people to pronounce him (being consul elect) not
consul, but emperor.

And yet after his victory in the civil war[18] he became much
more cruel ; for many of the adverse party, even such as lying
hid a good while were found out by those that were privy
unto them[19], he by devising a new kind of torture made
to confess, namely, by thrusting fire into the passage of their
secret parts ; some also he dismembered by cutting off their
hands. And this is for certain known : that two only and no
more of the most notorious[20] among them, to wit, a tribune of
senator's degree and a centurion were pardoned ; who, the
sooner to show that they were unguilty, had proved themselves
to have been effeminate catamites, and therefore could not
possibly be of any reckoning, either with captain or soldiers.

11. Now in this cruelty of his he was not only excessive
but also subtle and crafty, coming upon men when they
looked least for it. A controller[1] of his own, the very day
before he crucified him, he called into his bed-chamber and
made him to sit down by him upon a pallet or bedside ; he dismissed him light-hearted and merry ; he deigned him also a

favour and remembrance from his own supper[2]. Unto
Aretinus Clemens, a man of consul's degree, one of his familiar
minions and bloodhounds to fetch in booty, when he purposed
to condemn [him] to death, he showed the same countenance
as beforetime, yea, and more grace than ordinary, until at
last, as he went with him in the same litter, by occasion that
he espied the informer against him ; " How sayest thou ? "
quoth he ; " Clemens, shall we to-morrow hear this most arrant
knave and varlet, what he can say ? " And because he
would with greater contempt and disdain abuse men's patience,
he never pronounced any heavy and bloody sentence without
some preamble and preface of clemency, so that there was not
now a surer sign of some horrible end and conclusion than a
mild beginning and gentle exordium.

Some that stood accused of treason he inducted into the
Curia ; and when he had premised a speech[3] that he would
make trial that day how dear he was unto the senate, he soon
effected thus much thereby that the parties should have their
judgement to suffer *More majorum*[4] ; and then, himself
affrighted as it were with the rigorous cruelty of that punishment would intercede in these words (for it shall not be impertinent to know the very same as he delivered them) :
" Permit, my good lords, this to be obtained of your gracious
piety (which I know I shall hardly obtain) that ye would
do so much favour unto these persons condemned as that
they may choose what death they will die ; for by this ye
shall spare your own eyes and all the world shall know that I
was present in the senate."

12. Having emptied his coffers with expenses of buildings
and games exhibited to the people, as also with that stipend[1]
paid unto the soldiers over and above the former [7], he assayed
verily, for easement of the charges belonging to the camp, for
to diminish the numbers and companies of soldiers. But
perceiving that hereby he was both in danger of the barbarians, and also nevertheless to seek which way to be relieved
from burdens, he made no reckoning at all but to raise booties,
to rob and spoil he cared not how. The goods of quick and
dead both were everywhere seized upon ; who the accusers
were, or what the matter was, it skilled not. Sufficient it
was, if any deed or word whatsoever were objected against

one to make it high treason against the prince. Inheritances, were they never so far off and belonging to the greatest strangers, were held confiscate and adjudged to the emperor's coffers, in case but one would come forth and depose that he heard the party deceased say whiles he lived, That Caesar [a] was his heir. But above all others the Jews were most grievously plagued in the exchequer [2][b]; unto which were presented as many of them as either professed [3] in Rome to live as Jews, or else dissembling their nation had not paid the tributes imposed upon them. I remember that myself, being a very youth, was in place when an aged Jew, fourscore and ten years old, was by the procurator [4] in a most frequent assembly searched whether he were circumcised or no.

From his very youth nothing civil and sociable he was [5]; bold of heart, audacious withal, and as well in words as deed beyond all measure excessive. Unto Caenis his father's concubine newly returned out of Istria and offering to kiss his lips (as her manner was) he put forth his hand. Taking it heinously that his brother's son-in-law [6] had attending about him his servitors also, clad in fair white, he cried out,

> οὐκ ἀγαθὸν πολυκοιρανίη[7],
> There is no good plurality
> In lordship and in sov'reignty.

13. But when he was mounted once to the imperial seat, he stuck not in the very senate to make his boast that he it was who had given unto his father and brother both the empire, and they had but delivered it up to him again. Also, when after divorcement he brought home and remarried his wife, he bashed not to give it out that she was called to his sacred bed [1]. Moreover, upon the day when he made a great dinner unto the people [2], he was well-content and pleased to hear their acclamation throughout the theatre in these words,

> *Domino et Dominae feliciter,*
> All happiness to our Lord and Lady.

Likewise at the solemnity of trying masteries in the Palatium [4], when all the people besought him with great consent and one accord to restore Palfurius Sura [3] (one in times past degraded and thrust out of the senate, but at that time crowned among the orators for his eloquence) he vouchsafed them no answer, but only by voice of the public crier commanded them silence. With semblable arrogance, whenas in the name of his procurators he indited any formal letters, thus he began, Our Lord and God thus commandeth. Whereupon afterwards this order was taken up, that neither in the writing or speech of any man [4] he should be otherwise called. No statues suffered he to be erected for him in the Capitol but of gold and silver ; and the same of a certain weight, just [5]. As for two-fronted Jani [6] and arches with their four steeds, together with the ensigns and badges of triumph, he built them stately and so many in every quarter and region of the city, as that in one of the said arches there was this mot in Greek written, ἀρκεῖ [7 a], It is enough.

He took upon him seventeen consulships, more than ever any man before him ; of which those seven in the middle he bore continually one after another, and in manner all in name and title only ; but none of them beyond the kalends of May [8], and most to the ides only of January [9]. Now after his two triumphs [10], having assumed into his style the addition of Germanicus, he changed the denomination of the months September and October, calling them after his own name Germanicus and Domitianus, for that in the one [11] he entered upon his empire and was born in the other [12].

14. In these courses that he took, being both terrible and odious also unto all men, surprised he was in the end and murdered by his friends and freedmen that were most inward with him, who together with his wife conspired his death. The last year and day of his life, the very hour also and what kind of death he should die, he had long time before suspected. For when he was but a youth the Chaldaean astrologers had foretold him all. His father also, one time at supper, when he saw him forbear to eat mushrooms, laughed him to scorn as ignorant of his own destiny, for that he did not fear the sword rather. And therefore, being always timorous and stricken into his pensive dumps upon the least suspicions presented, he was beyond all measure troubled and disquieted, insomuch as it is credibly reported, that no other cause moved him more to dispense with that edict which he had proclaimed for the cutting down and destroying of vineyards, than certain pamphlets and libels scattered abroad with these verses :

Κἄν με φάγῃς ἐπὶ ῥίζαν, ὅμως ἔτι καρποφορήσω
ὅσσον ἐπισπεῖσαι Καίσαρι θυομένῳ [1].

Eat me to root ; yet fruit will I bear still and never miss,
Enough to pour on Caesar's head whiles sacrific'd he is.

In the same fearfulness he refused a new honour and that which never was devised before, offered by the senate unto him (though otherwise most eager and greedy of all such things), whereby they decreed that so often as he was consul, the gentlemen of Rome, as it fell by lot to their turns, should in their rich and gay coats and with military lances march before him among the lictors and other serjeants and apparitors.

When the time also of that danger drew near which he suspected, he became perplexed every day more than other ; and therefore he garnished the walls of those galleries wherein he was wont to roam himself and walk with the stone Phengites [2], by the images rebounding from the brightness whereof he might see before his face whatsoever was done behind his back. The most part of prisoners and persons in duress he would not hear but being alone and in a secret place, taking hold first of their chains in his own hand. And because he would persuade his household servitors that no man should be so hardy as to lay violent hand upon his own patron to kill him, no though much good might ensue thereof, he condemned Epaphroditus the secretary of Nero, for that it was thought his lord and master (after he was forlorn and forsaken of all) had his helping hand to dispatch him out of the world.

15. To conclude, his uncle's son Flavius Clemens [a] (a man for his litherness [1] and negligence most contemptible), whose sons, being yet very little ones, he had openly ordained to be his successors, and abolishing their former names, commanded the one to be called Vespasian and the other Domitian, he killed suddenly, upon a slender and small suspicion, even when he was scarce out of his consulship. By which deed of his most of all he hastened his own end and destruction.

For eight months space together so many lightnings were seen and reported unto him, that he cried out, " Now let him [2] strike whom he will." The Capitol was smitten and blasted therewith, the temple also of the Flavian lineage, likewise his own house in the Palatium and very bed-chamber. Moreover, out of the base of his triumphal statue the title[3], being driven by force of a storm, fell down into the sepulchre next adjoining. That tree [Vesp. 5] which, being laid along, had risen up again when Vespasian was yet a private person, fell suddenly then a second time. The image of Fortune at Praeneste[4], which all the time of his empire, when he recommended unto her the new year, was wont to give him a happy answer and always the same, now in this last year delivered one most woeful and not without mention of blood.

He dreamed that Minerva[b], whom he worshipped superstitiously, departed out of her chapel and said she could not protect him any longer, for that she was by Jupiter disarmed. But with no one thing was he so much disquieted as with the answer of Ascletario the astrologer, and the accident that chanced unto him thereupon. This Ascletario, being informed against and not denying that he had delivered what by his art and learning he foresaw, he questioned with and asked what his own end should be ; and when he made answer and affirmed that his destiny was to be torn in pieces with dogs, and that shortly after, he caused him presently [Cal. 22] to be killed ; but to prove the rashness and uncertainty of his skill and profession, he commanded withal that he should be buried with as great care as possibly might be. In the doing whereof accordingly, it fortuned that by a sudden tempest the corpse being cast down out of the funeral fire, the dogs tare and rent it piecemeal, when it was but half-burnt ; and the same happened to be reported unto him among other tales and news of that day, as he sat at supper, by Latinus the player and counterfeit jester, who as he passed by chanced to see and mark so much.

16. The day before his death, when he had given command that certain mushrooms set before him should be kept against the morrow, he added moreover, " If I may have use of them " ; and turning to those that were next him he said, the day following it would come to pass that the moon should imbrue herself with blood in the sign Aquarius, and some act be seen whereof men should speak all the world over. But about midnight so scared he was[1] that he started out of his

bed. Hereupon in the morning betimes he gave hearing unto the soothsayer sent out of Germany, who being asked his opinion about the lightning had foretold a change in the State, and him he condemned. And whiles he scratched very hard at a wart in his forehead which was festered and grown to be sore, seeing blood run out of it, " Would God," quoth he, " this were all." Then asked he what was a-clock, and instead of the fifth hour which he feared word was brought for the nonce that it was the sixth. Being joyous hereupon that the danger was now past, and hastening to cherish his body and make much of himself, Parthenius his principal chamberlain turned him another way, saying there was one come who brought tidings (I wot not what) of great consequence, and of a matter in no wise to be deferred. Voiding [Cal. 58] therefore all persons from him, he retired to his bed-chamber, and there was he murdered.

17. As touching the manner how he was forelaid [C. 25] and of his death, thus much (in manner) hath been divulged. Whiles the conspirators were in question with themselves and doubtful when and how they should set upon him, that is to say, whether he bathed or sat at supper, Stephen the procurator [steward] of Domitilla[1], and at the same time in trouble for intercepting certain moneys, offered his advice and helping hand ; who having for certain days before bound up and enwrapped his left arm (as if it had been amiss) with wool and swaddling bands, thereby to avert from himself all suspicion, at the very hour interposed fraud and made a lie. For professing that he would discover the conspiracy, and in that regard being admitted into the chamber, as Domitian was reading of a bill which he preferred unto him and therewith stood amazed, he stabbed him beneath in the very share[2] near unto his privy parts. When he was thus wounded and began to struggle and resist, Clodianus, a cornicularius[3], and Maximus, a freedman of Parthenius, and Satur, the dean or decurion of the chamberlains[4] with one out of his own sword-fencers' school, came in upon him, gave him seven wounds, and killed him outright. A youth and page of his, who stood by (as his wonted manner was) because he had the charge of his bed-chamber Lares[a], and was present at this murder committed, made this report moreover ; that Domitian

at the very first wound given immediately bade him reach the dagger that lay under his pillow and to call in his ministers and servitors, but at the bed's head he found nothing at all thereof save the haft only, and as for the doors besides, they were all fast shut; also that Domitian in this mean space took hold of Stephen, bore him to the ground and wrestled with him a long time; that he one while assayed to wrest his sword out of his hands, another while (albeit his fingers were hurt and mangled) to pluck out his eyes.

Well, killed he was, the fourteenth day before the kalends of October [5], in the forty-fifth year of his age and the fifteenth of his empire. His dead body was carried forth upon the common bier by the ordinary bearers, and Phyllis his nurse burned it in a funeral fire, within a country-manor of his own near unto the city, situate upon the highway Latina. But his relics she [secretly] bestowed in the temple of the Flavian family, and blended the same with the ashes of Julia, the daughter of Titus, whom she had reared and brought up.

18. Of stature he was tall, his countenance modest, and given much to redness [a]; his eyes full and great, but his sight very dim. Besides, fair he was and of comely presence, especially in his youth; well-shaped all his body throughout, excepting his feet, the toes whereof were of the shortest [1]. In process of time, he became disfigured and blemished with baldness, with a fat grand-paunch and slender shanks, and yet they grew to be so lean upon occasion of a long sickness. For his modesty and shamefacedness he so well perceived himself to be commended, that one time before the senate he gave out these words, " Hitherto certainly ye have liked well of my mind and of my countenance." With his bald head he was so much irked, that he took it as a reproach unto himself, if any man else were either in bord [2] or good earnest twitted therewith; albeit in a certain little book, which he wrote unto a friend of his, concerning the nourishment and preservation of the hair of the head, he by way of consolation both to that friend and also to himself inserted thus much:

οὐχ ὁράᾳς οἷος κἀγὼ καλός τε μέγας τε [3];

See'st thou not yet how big and tall,
How fair I am and comely withal?

" And yet," quoth he, " my destiny[4] and fortune will be to
have the same defect of hair, and with a stout heart I endure
that the bush of my head waxeth old in my fresh youth. And
this would I have you to know, that nothing is more lovely,
nothing more frail and transitory than beauty and favour."

19. Being impatient of all labour and painstaking, he was
not lightly[1] seen to walk in the city. In any expedition
and march of the army seldom rode he on horseback, but
was carried in a litter[2]. No affection had he to bear arms or
wield weapons, but delighted he was especially to shoot
arrows. Many men have seen him oftentimes, during his
retiring abode at Alba, to kill with shot a hundred wild beasts
of sundry sorts at a time, and of very purpose to stick some of
them in the head, so as that with two shoots he would set his
shafts in their fronts like a pair of horns. Sometimes he
would drive his arrows point-blank so just[3] against the palm
of a child's right hand, standing far off and holding it forth
stretched open for a mark, as they should all directly pass
through the void spaces between the fingers and do him no
harm at all.

20. All liberal studies in the beginning of his empire he
neglected, albeit he took order [Cal. 8] to repair the libraries
consumed with fire, to his exceeding great charges ; making
search from all parts for the copies of books lost and sending as far as to Alexandria[a] to write them out and correct
them. But never gave he his mind to know histories, or to
have any skill in verse, or to write aught, though necessity
so required. Except it were the commentaries and acts[1] of
Tiberius Caesar he never used to read anything. For his
epistles, orations and edicts he employed the wits of other men
to draw and frame them. Howbeit his ordinary speech was
not inelegant, and otherwhiles you should have him come
forth even with notable sentences and apophthegms. As for
example : " Would God," quoth he, " I were as fair and well-
favoured as Mettius[2] thinks himself to be " ; and seeing one's
head parti-coloured, with yellowish and white silver hairs intermingled, he said it was snow and mead[3] mixed together.
His saying it was, that the condition of princes was most
miserable, who could not be credited as touching a conspiracy
plainly detected unless they were slain first.

FLAVIUS DOMITIANUS

21. Whensoever his leisure served, he solaced himself with dice-play, even upon the very work-day, and in morning hours. He bathed by daytime, and made his dinner so liberal to the full, that seldom for his supper he took anything, unless it were a Matian apple[1] and a small supping or portion out of a narrow-mouthed and great-bellied glass. He feasted often and that very plentifully, but his feasts were short and after a snatching manner ; certes, he never sat past sunsetting, nor admitted any rear-banquets [V. 13] after supper. For towards bedtime he did nothing but in a secret chamber walk by himself alone.

22. To fleshly lust he was overmuch given. The ordinary use of Venus, as it were a kind of exercise, he named Clinopale, as one would say bed-wrestling. The report went that himself used with pincers to depilate his concubines, and to swim among the commonest naughty packs[1] that were. His brother's daughter[2], offered first unto him in marriage whiles she was yet a maiden, when he had most resolutely refused by reason he was entangled and overcome with the marriage of Domitia, not long after, when she was bestowed upon another, of his own accord he solicited and was naught [C. 6] with her, even verily whiles his brother Titus yet lived. Afterwards when she was bereft of father and husband both, he loved her with most ardent affection and that openly[3], insomuch as that he was the cause of her death, by forcing her to miscarry and cast away the untimely fruit[4] wherewith she went.

23. That he was killed the people took it indifferently, but the soldiers to the very heart, and forthwith went about to canonise him a god and to call him divus[1] ; ready enough also to revenge his death, but they wanted heads to lead them. And yet within a whiles after they did it, calling most instantly and never giving over for the authors of this murder[2] to be executed. Contrariwise, the senate so much rejoiced, that being assembled in great frequency within the Curia, they could not rule themselves, but strove a-vie [Cal. 57] to rend and tear him now dead with the most contumelious and bitterest kinds of acclamations[a] that they could devise ; commanding ladders to be brought in, his scutcheons[3] and images to be taken down in their sight, and even there in place to be thrown

and dashed against the hard floor ; in the end, that all titles
wheresoever bearing his name should be rased and scraped out,
and his memorial abolished quite for ever.   Some few months
before he was murdered, there was a crow on the Capitol spake
these words plainly, ἔσται πάντα καλῶς, All shall be well ;
and there wanted not one who interpreted this strange prodigy
thus :

> *Nuper Tarpeio quae sedit culmine cornix,*
> *Est bene non potuit dicere, dixit Erit.*
> The crow which lately sat on top of Tarpeie news to tell,
> 'Tis well whenas she could not say, said yet, it will be well.

And reported it is that Domitian himself dreamed how he
had a golden excrescence rising and bunching behind his
neck, and knew for certain that thereby was portended and
foresignified unto the commonwealth a happier state after
him.   And so it fell out, I assure you, shortly after ; such was
the abstinent and moderate carriage of the emperors next
ensuing [b].

ADDENDA

P. 87, l. 19: "or the Circus." The latest texts for *Circove* read *circave:* "or in the neighbourhood (of the Forum)."

P. 101, l. 23. *Antony* should be *Augustus*, who was said to have desired the daughter of Cotiso for his wife.

P. 103, l. 24. The Latin in the original, following ἀπολέσθαι, paraphrased by H. in his note but omitted by him in the translation, is *nec aliter eos appellare quam tres vomicas ac tria carcinomata sua*, "and never called them anything but three boils and his three cancers" (p. 35 *n.*).

P. 116, l. 2. A. is said to have "put prepositions unto verbs (*verbis*)"; others read *urbibus*, that he put prepositions before the names of towns where grammatical usage was against it.

P. 168, l. 31. The words "impatient of . . . at Rome" are a paraphrase of the old reading *Romae dominii;* later texts have *remediorum*, "unable to bear his remedial measures."

P. 218, l. 5. "As his style framed." As his pen suited, or perhaps, as the fit took him.

P. 229, l. 7. H. here translates *exposceretur*. Read *exposcerent:* "to beg from the consuls that they (the knights) might be allowed to bear the body of A."

P. 232, l. 36. "By his grandmother" (*ab avia*). Read rather *ab viva*, "by her (his mother) during her lifetime."

P. 234, l. 30. After "the fourth year" add "the last for six, the rest for two months," omitted by H.

P. 254, l. 25: "that he was now . . . make satisfaction." H. here translates *satisfacientibus*. Reading *satisfacientis*, translate: "that he was treated by them as an ordinary person, he suddenly pardoned them, almost in a tone of apology."

P. 269, l. 29. "Proctors." The Latin word is *postulator*, better "claimants." The verb *postulare*=(1) to prosecute, (2) to ask leave to prosecute.

P. 273, l. 37. "He stuck not." Others read *dubitavit . . . an*, "he could not make up his mind whether. . . ."

P. 277, l. 24. The construction is confused: something like, "where he had won them, and whom he had defeated" is wanted. "Fabulous," of course, does not mean "feigned," but "relating to plays."

NOTES AND ANNOTATIONS UPON
GAIUS JULIUS CAESAR, DICTATOR

[1] [More familiar as Alba Longa.]   [2] Or returned unto.   [3] Or rather 265, according to the chronology annexed unto Titus Livius. [4] By the computation of Dionysius, T. Livius, Cassiodorus, and others. [5] C. Julius, or Iulus.   [6] Or Mamercus.   [7] Or 281, after the chronology aforesaid of Dionysius.   [8] More truly 303.   [9] 307, by Livius' account.   [10] 319.   [11] 320.   [12] 487.   [13] [Inscription.]   [14] So surnamed.   [15] Haply Pomptinas of the tribe Pomptina.   [16] *Caeso matris utero.*   [17] *Cum caesarie.*   [18] *Oculis caesiis.*   [19] 597, after the abovesaid chronology.   [20] 663.   [21] Consulship.   [22] *Frater patruelis.*   [23] [Docile, teachable.]

1. [1] *Sequentibus consulibus.* For at Rome they reckoned the years according to their consuls, whose office ordinarily continued one year, and began with the year upon the first day of January   [2] Or, divorce. [3] Of Marius.   [4] To flee into the Sabine country.   [5] [Place of refuge for a runaway criminal.]   [6] For Aurelia was his mother.

[a] Gaius Caesar. He died suddenly at Pisae in Italy, as he put on his shoes in a morning, when he was new-risen. Pliny, *Nat. Hist.* vii, 53.

[b] *Flamen Dialis,* that is, the great priest of Jupiter. Three flamens there were at Rome, by the first institution : *Dialis* of Jupiter, *Martialis* of Mars, *Quirinalis* of Romulus, and these were the principal ; unto whom in process of time 12 more were adjoined, attending all upon several gods and goddesses. Carol. Sigonius, *de ant. jure Civium Romanorum,* i, 19.

[c] *Ut repudiaret.* In the civil law, we observe a difference between *repudium* and *divortium. Repudium,* when the man rejecteth and casteth off the woman betrothed only unto him before marriage in this form, *Conditione tua non utor ;* and in this wise Caesar and Cossutia parted before. *Divortium,* when he putteth her away after she is his wedded wife, with these solemn words, *Res tuas tibi habeto,* or *Res tuas tibi agito.* Howbeit, in this place *repudiare* is to be taken in this latter sense, for Cornelia was his wife, and had borne him a daughter [Paulus, Modestinus, Gaius : Digest, xxiv, 2].

[d] I take it that he meaneth such inheritances as are not *testamentariae,* but *legitimae,* which, when one dieth intestate, fall unto the children first, and, for default of them, to the agnati and gentiles, *i.e.* to the next of kin, and to the name. These are called with us the right heirs at common law. *Vide* Car. Sigon. *de Judiciis,* i, 4. *De antiq. jur. civ. Rom.* i, 7.

[e] The principal of them was Cornelius Phagita, a freedman of Sulla, unto whom Caesar gave two talents for to escape his hands. See ch. 74, and Plutarch [Life of Caesar, 2].

[f] It belonged unto these votaries and nuns of Vesta, to go between parties offended and make reconciliation. See more hereof Alexander ab Alexandro, *Genialium dierum libri,* v, 12. [He was a Neapolitan jurist, 1461-1523.]

2. [1] Marcus Minucius Thermus.   [2] [Freedman.]

[a] Young gentlemen of noble blood, the better to be trained up in martial feats and the knowledge of any provincial affairs, were wont to attend the lord-deputies there, and to be entertained with them in the same pavilion, as familiar companions. Cicero, *pro Caelio*, xxx, *pro Plancio*, xi.

[b] Libertines (*libertini*) were such properly, as of bondmen were manumitted and made free, although Suetonius elsewhere, to wit, *Claudius*, xxiv, nameth the children of such Libertines, by which it appeareth that he confoundeth them with *ingenui*, that is, freeborn.

[c] Clients have a relation to their patrons ; and as these were patricians and nobles, so the others were commoners. And such a mutual and reciprocal intercourse of duty was between them that, as the patrons were ready to instruct in the knowledge of the laws, to defend and protect their clients, who had put themselves into their patronage, so these were bound to attend their patrons when they went abroad into the city and returned home, to relieve them with their purse in the bestowing of their daughters, etc. And lawful it was for neither of them to inform, to depose, to give their voices, or to side with adversaries, one against another, without the note [stigma] and guilt of treachery and perfidious prodition.

[d] Made of oaken branches, or of ilex, or aesculus, bearing mast, in defect of the oak, for saving the life of a citizen ; although generals of the field were honoured therewith, in other respects.

3. [1] Surnamed so of the people in Cilicia named Isauri, whom he subdued.

[a] Who, being consul with Q. Lutatius Catulus, went about to repeal and annul all the acts of Sulla, late deceased, and so kindled a new civil war.

4. [1] While he governed his province.   [2] [Avoid.]   [3] For calling into question so honourable a person.   [4] Moloni, not Molonis, as Plutarch taketh it, that is, the son of Molo.   [5] *Hibernis mensibus*, that is, in the winter months, which were December, January, February.   [6] Some read *dignatione* in a diverse sense [without losing any of his dignity.]   [7] Or the rest of his companions and servants.   [8] To the cities of Asia, a province adjoining.   [9] [If the talent is reckoned = 24,000 sesterces, 50 talents would = about £10,500.]   [10] [At once.]

[a] By the death of Lepidus, whom his colleague Catulus drove out of Italy into Sardinia, where he died, as some write, of a violent rheum : or, as others, with a deep thought that he took, upon intelligence that he had of his wife's adultery, in which melancholy he pined away (Plutarch, *Life of Pompey*, xvi).

5. [1] C. Cotta, M. Crassus, and Cn. Pompeius, who were the chief.   [2] A tribune of the commons.   [3] Lepidus.

[a] These tribunes military, call them colonels over a thousand footmen, whereupon they took that name first, to wit, when the Roman legion consisted of 3000, according to the three ancient tribes, Ramnes, Tities, and Luceres ; or high marshals, as Budaeus would have them to be, considering the execution of their office in the camp, not much unlike to our knight marshals in these days. Some by virtue of an act or law preferred by Rutilius Rufus, were chosen in the army by the lord-general, and named Rutuli or Rufuli, others by the voices of the people in their public assemblies for elections called *comitia*, and for distinction

sake, named *comitiati*.   And such a tribune military was Caesar in this place.

  b *Rogatione Plotia.*   A bill preferred, and the same as a law not yet enacted, was called *rogatio*, as one would say, *interrogatio ;* for that the people were demanded and asked their opinions in this form of words : *Velitisne, jubeatisne, Quirites*, etc. : Is it your will and pleasure, ye citizens of Rome, that such a thing should pass, or no ?   And of him who proposed the same, it took the name.

  6. [1] Treasurer.   [2] [Guilty of immorality.]   [3] Of the goddess Bona [Dea], which were celebrated in Caesar's house, being the pontifex.

  7. [1] Called Baetica.   [2] Antistius Vetus.   [3] In head shire towns which were called *conventus*.   [4] That is, thirty-three.

  8. [a] By the Latin colonies are meant here those beyond the Po, which, being before endowed *Latinitate*, that is, with the freedom of Latium, stood not therewith contented, unless they might be *donati civitate*, that is, enjoy the franchise and freedom of Rome.

  9. [1] That had been consul.   [2] Or rather, L.   [3] [History. He probably lived in the time of Cicero.]   [4] [There were three famous orators named C. Scribonius Curio, whose relationship was that of father and son. This is the second of the three.]   [5] So called of a river, near to which they dwelt beyond the Po [both name and locality are uncertain].   [6] Who was slain by Spanish horsemen, of whom he had the conduct.

  10. [1] *Geminis fratribus*, that is, Castor and Pollux, who commonly be called *gemini fratres.*   [2] [Phrase for fighting in earnest, with unblunted swords.]   [3] And yet he exhibited 320 pairs, as Plutarch writeth.

  [a] *Comitium* was one part of the *Forum Romanum*, wherein stood the *Rostra*, and the people used to assemble for election of magistrates, for making of laws, and hearing of public orations.

  11. [1] [Made.]   [2] That he might govern it and place the king again in his royal seat.   [3] Ptolemy Auletes, the father of Cleopatra, who many years after by Gabinius was restored to his kingdom.   [4] As Torrentius [1525-95, bishop of Antwerp, author of a commentary on the Lives of the Twelve Caesars] saith.   [5] This is by the figure prolepsis to be understood of Caesar, when he was praetor of the city, as who favoured the faction of Marius both then and before, howsoever it may seem that Suetonius speaketh this of him being aedile, or presently after his aedileship ; which, by Torrentius' leave, may well stand with the truth.

  [a] Sulla, in the time of his proscription and outlawing of the adverse faction of C. Marius, ordained two talents for every one that killed any of the proscribed and brought him his head, not sparing master or father, but that the servant might kill his master and the son his father ; nay, he made it death if they saved any such.

  [b] Of Cornelius Sulla.

  12. [1] In place of the praetor.   [2] Caesar.

  [a] T. Labienus.   Cicero and Hortensius pleaded for him.

  [b] For to kill a tribune of the commons, who were *sacrosancti* and *inviolabiles*, would bear the action *perduellionis*.   And that was laid to Rabirius a senator his charge, although indeed he slew him not,

3

but one Scaeva : marry, when he was killed, he caused his head in most ludibrious [scornful, derisive] manner to be carried about.

Now was the crime *perduellionis* all one with treason against the commonwealth or a principal person of state ; or else felony in some high degree.

c The liberty of appealing unto the people was granted by Tullus Hostilius, the third king of the Romans, as appeareth by Livy [i, 26], in the case of Horatius, for killing his own sister.

13. ¹ That is, Egypt and the restoring of the king aforesaid. ² Which [the tribes] were 35.

ᵃ Q. Lutatius Catulus and P. Servilius Isauricus.

14. ¹ But not entered yet into the office. ² *Ultimum supplicium* [extreme punishment]. ³ As if he meant by *ultimum supplicium* imprisonment, or some less punishment than death. ⁴ Quintus Cicero. ⁵ M. Tullius Cicero. ⁶ Of consul and senate. ⁷ Plutarch nameth Curio for one of them. ⁸ Of M. Tullius Cicero the consul his year, which now drew to an end.

15. ¹ That is, to Cn. Pompeius [the triumvir, more familiar to English readers as Pompey, often called the Great]. ² [Originally used of draught animals = to pull together.] ³ [Obsequious.]

ᵃ Caesar, envying such an honour unto Catulus, as to re-edify and dedicate the Capitol consumed with fire, a piece of work that Sulla the dictator took in hand but finished not, and the only thing whereby his felicity was not complete, would have put him by it [18] and conferred it upon another ; and therefore put the matter in question before the body of the people, there to be discussed and debated, whether it were their mind and will that Catulus should do it, or some other.

ᵇ A law is said to be promulged, after it is once proposed for to be considered upon, until it be fully enacted ; during which time, reasons were alleged for the convenience thereof, or otherwise, and free it was for any man who had a voice to impugn or allow it.

ᶜ *Optimates* and *populares* were in the city of Rome opposite, either against other, and are lively described by Cicero in his oration *pro Sestio* (xlv) in these words : [In this state there have always been two classes of people eager to occupy themselves with state affairs and to make a name therein ; of which classes the one desired both to be considered and really to be democratic, the other aristocratic. Those who desired what they said and did to be agreeable to the multitude were considered democrats, but those who so conducted themselves that their counsels approved themselves to all the best citizens, were considered aristocrats. Who then are the best citizens ? In number, if you ask, they are countless, for otherwise we could not hold our ground ; they are the chief of the general council ; they are the followers of the same ; they belong to the largest classes, to whom the senate-house is open ; they are the Roman provincials and peasants ; they are the business men ; there are even freedmen who belong to the aristocratic party]. Whereby it appeareth, that those were counted *optimates*, not simply of noble birth, and of great wealth, etc., but were they *patricii, equites,* or *plebeii,* if they stood for good things, or favoured those that so did ; nay, whether they were burgesses of free boroughs, yeomen of the country following husbandry, merchants and tradesmen, or very libertines, so they affected good causes, they were reckoned in the number of *optimates.* On the other side, as many as aimed only

4

at this, to please and content the multitude, were they never so well-born or otherwise qualified, they went in the rank of *populares ;* so that it seemeth, that *populares* were the *forensis factio* that Livy writeth of [ix, 46], and whom Q. Fabius reduced all into the four *tribus urbanae*, and *optimates*, the *tribus rusticae*, wherein was *integer populus, fautor et cultor bonorum.* Thus much of the strict signification of this word *optimates.* But forasmuch as commonly few of the nobility and gentry of Rome were popular, and as few of the communalty favourers of the best things, usually by these *optimates*, or the better sort, are meant the *Patricii* and gentlemen.

d Upon the kalends of January, *i.e.* the first day of the year, the consuls entered their office, on which day attended they were obsequiously by those better sort of the citizens and their friends, waiting upon them, when they went up into the Capitol for to sacrifice, and home again. On this day likewise it appeareth, that Caesar began his praetorship.

16. ¹ Surnamed Nepos, as Valerius [Maximus, ix, 14, 4] witnesseth, for his riotous life and behaviour.

a This purple robe bordered, called *praetexta*, was a garment not proper to the praetors only, but to other magistrates also. Embroidered it was or guarded about with purple. For Pliny (*Nat. Hist.* ix, 39), writeth that Lentulus Spinther, aedile curule, wore in his robe purple of a double dye, called thereupon *Dibapha ;* and thereupon it was called in Greek περιπόρφυρος. And not only city magistrates, but priests and children of gentle birth used the same. Setting aside the border of purple, it was otherwise white.

b By *Curia* simply, without any adjunction, is meant *Curia Hostilia*, as witnesseth Alexander ab Alexandro, *i.e.* a stately place built by king Tullius Hostilius in the *Forum Romanum* near unto the *Rostra*, where, as in the parliament-house, assembled the senators ordinarily to consult upon the affairs of state. For other places there were, under the name of *Curia*, wherein likewise the senate met together, as *Curia Pompeii*, in which Caesar was murdered, *Divi Augusti*, etc., but then they had their addition. I am not ignorant that other *Curiae* there were for the pontiffs and priests, to say nothing how the people was divided into *Curiae*, that is, parishes, and in every [one] of them was a *Curia*, and a superintendent or curate called *Curio.*

17. ¹ *Indice*, some read *Judice*, as if *Judex* were his surname. ² [Take stresses=distrain.]

a Superior magistrates be the consuls, praetors and censors ; the rest, as aediles, quaestors, were accounted inferior.

18. ¹ *Ex praetura*, whereby it appeareth he was Praetor Urbanus. ² [Made arrangements.]   ³ Cato [the Younger, *Uticensis*] and his followers.   ⁴ [To be prevented from obtaining or enjoying.]

a Crassus is named for one, who entered into a bond for him of 830 talents, what time Caesar, deeply indebted, said, *bis millies et quingenties centena millia nummum sibi adesse oportere, ut nihil haberet*, that is, that 250 millions of sesterces would but set him clear with the world. [Approximately, £2,200,000. It may be noted, in reference to the approximate value of large amounts of sesterces, that modern authorities reckon 1000 sesterces as=£8, 15s. and 100,000 as=£870. This should be borne in mind in reading Holland's annotations in such cases. Smith's Dict. Antiq. gives division by 100 as a rough equivalent ; this would make 100,000 sesterces=£1000.]

b By the laws none might make suit for a triumph but whiles they remained absent without the city, nor for a consulship, except they were present as private persons within the city. In these straits, Caesar made choice to be consul, and gave over his right to a triumph for the victory obtained in Spain over the Gallaeci and Lusitani.

19. [1] *Optimates.* [2] Consul.

a The manner was at Rome, that they who sued for magistracies should, for the obtaining of the people's voices and suffrages, make promise of certain sums of money to be distributed among them, and such as were appointed to deal the said largesse they called *divisores.* Now, for that the election of consuls passed by *Comitia centuriata,* that is, by the assembly of the people by their centuries or hundreds, according as Servius Tullus first ordained them, therefore was this money to be divided amongst them, as they gave their voices.

b Provinces signify three things, the countries conquered or yielded, and the same governed by Roman deputies, and this is the proper and primitive signification thereof ; also the region wherein any Roman general by commission from the State maketh war ; and last of all, what public function or affairs soever is to be administered, in which sense it is here taken.

c Either for the cutting down of trees for the best commodities, or else for a guard to be kept near unto them, to suppress the outrage committed by thieves, haunting the same and robbing and spoiling passengers.

d To amend the ways and beaten paths, where either wayfaring men or beasts should pass with more ease. And verily these were base matters and requiring no great forces to be performed ; and so by consequence the consuls employed therein could compass no great projects and [were] therefore less to be feared.

e This society bred the civil war that after ensued between Caesar and Pompey unto which the poet Lucan alluded, writing thus (*Pharsalia,* i, 84) :

> *Tu causa malorum,*
> *Facta tribus dominis communis, Roma.*

20. [1] [Precede.]　　[2] [Rather, the Forum, the common marketplace.]　[3] [Tumult.]　[4] *Turbis,* that is, trespasses or offences [rather, disturbances].　[5] *Obnuntiaret,* by pronouncing out of the augurs' learning, that the day was *nefastus et non comitialis,* that is, no law-day.　[6] *Per edicta,* some read *per lictores,* that is, by his serjeants and officers.　[7] [This district, which gave its name to one of the tribes, was in Campania, south of Cales.]　[8] At the discretion of twenty men deputed commissioners for that purpose.　[9] For that they had taken things at too high a rate.　[10] Three o'clock in the afternoon.　[11] *Indicem,* others read *Judicem,* that is, Vettius Judex : L. Vettius, according to Dio and Appian.　[12] Vettius Judex aforesaid ; for dead he was found in prison by night.

a As well to avoid tedious canvassings and consultations, as to provide for the history and memorial of every matter.

b One of the consuls only had the twelve lictors going before him with the rods and axes : to wit, each of them their months, by turn, one after the other, *Ne, si ambo fasces haberent, duplicatus terror videretur.* As Livy writeth : An ordinance as ancient well-near as the first institution of consuls.

c Accensus, an officer attendant upon a magistrate, so named *ab acciendo,* that is, of giving summons to any for appearance, or of calling any to the magistrate. [Really participle of *accenseo* = reckoned in addition.]

d Great indulgences, immunities, and privileges were granted by the Romans unto those that had *jus trium liberorum ;* but, as Appian writeth more particularly to the explication of this place [*Bell. Civ.,* ii, 10], there assembled 20,000 together, craving maintenance and food every man, for three children and more that they had.

e Publicans were they that either for a certain rent took to farm the public revenues of the city, whether it were corn, pasturage, customs, imposts, etc., or undertook by the gross to make provision for the State, or to build and repair any city works, etc.

21. ¹ Whom he promised in marriage the daughter of Pompey.

a This was not *more majorum*, for then his sentence should have been demanded first, that by the censors was elected *princeps senatus*, that is, president of the council ; but extraordinarily, as appeareth by Aulus Gellius, *Noctes Atticae*, iv, 10 ; xiv, 7.

22. ¹ [L. Calpurnius Piso.] ² Pompey. ³ [Full, as in the modern " a full house."]

a For as Livy testifieth, the Romans triumphed oftener over the Gauls than over all the world beside.

b Which Vatinius, a tribune of the commons, proposed in the behalf of Julius Caesar, that for five years together he should (without casting lots and the senate's decree) govern Cisalpine Gaul, together with Illyricum ; contrary to the Sempronian law, which provided that such provincial governors, or lord-deputies (*legati*), should yearly be chosen by the senate. Carol. Sigon. *De antiquo jure provinciarum* (ii, 1).

c Gallia Cisalpina is that which lay between Italy and the Alps, divided into Cispadana and Transpadana, according to the site thereof, either on this side, or beyond the river Po ; it carried the name likewise of Togata, either because it was much inhabited by the Romans, or for that unto this province the Roman robe *toga* was granted, or else in regard that the said province was more civil and peaceable than the other called Transalpina.

d Gallia Comata, a part of Gallia Transalpina, lying beyond the Alps, from Italy toward Spain, so called for the long hair that they wore ; and συνεκδοχικῶς [when the part is put for a whole] put for the whole Transalpine province, like as Bracata, one part of the said province, so called of a certain kind of apparel, is taken for the whole and confounded with Comata.

e This term, which they commonly use, who threaten such as they contemn, may be drawn to an obscene and filthy sense, not here to be named : and albeit Caesar hereby was galled to the quick, as privy to himself of the passive abuse of his body with Nicomedes, yet in his answer thereto he turned it to another signification.

f Warlike women, so called (as some write) of their paps which they did cut off and sear, thereby to be more expedite and nimble in fight, and to shoot at greater ease [Strabo, p. 504 ; Herodotus, iv, 110 ; Justin, ii, 1-4].

23. ¹ Whether they should be repealed or stand in force. ² [Quarrel about trifles.] ³ When he was consul. ⁴ For that he was extraordinarily absent, longer than the Sempronian law did permit. ⁵ [Written document.]

a For if his quaestor or treasurer had been condemned, it would have been a shrewd [damaging] precedent for his conviction also in the same cause.

GAIUS JULIUS CAESAR

24. [1] The bird *galerita* or *cassita*, so called of a crest upon the head. This legion, it should seem, wore plumes of feathers in their crests of helmets, whereupon it took that name. [2] Cato [Plutarch, *Cato Minor*, li].

[a] Who stood in election for the consulship, so called of the whited robe, which they put on, who sued for such magistracies and places of honour. For whereas the ordinary gown that Roman citizens daily wore was white of itself, against such a time they made it whiter with chalk; so that a difference there was between *toga alba*, and *candida*, whereupon they were called *candidati*, as appeareth by Macrobius and Livy.

[b] Supplication was a solemn honour done unto the lord general of a province upon some notable victory. For the manner was that lord governors, after they were by their soldiers saluted by the name of emperor, *i.e.* sovereign commanders, should send their letters dight with laurel unto the senate, wherein they required both to be styled by the said name, and also to have solemn processions made by the people in the temples and thanksgiving unto the gods for their good success, which solemnity at the first continued but one day, as Livy reporteth [iii, 63; v, 23] in the 304th year after the foundation of Rome, but [in] process of time it grew to four and twelve. And at length, Caesar obtained it for 15, yea, and 20 days together, as Plutarch testifieth in his life, and himself in his own Commentaries of the Gallic war [ii, 35; vii, 80].

25. [1] [Waylaid.]

26. [1] Aurelia, a dame of singular chastity. [2] *Neptem;* others read *nepotem*, that is, nephew. [It should be remembered that, in H.'s time, " nephew " and " niece " were used for " grandson " and " granddaughter." Ancient authorities differ as to the sex of this particular child.] [3] By Milo. [4] That is, a hundred millions of sesterces, and 20, as Pliny writeth [*Nat. Hist.* xxxvi, 15], if Glareanus [Heinrich Loriti of Glarus, 1488-1563, humanist and commentator on Suetonius] readeth truly, *Millies ducenties*. [5] [H. nearly always uses " gentlemen (of Rome) " to translate *equites* (knights).] [6] [To each man.]

[a] *Super HS. millies.* This character HS. standeth for a silver coin in Rome, which is the three halfpence, farthing, cue [1], the fourth part of a *denarius*, and is called *sestertius, quasi sesquitertius*, as one would say, valuing [worth] two brazen asses and the half of a third; so common a piece of money there, that *nummus*, put absolutely alone, standeth for it and no other coin, so that *millies sestertium* and *millies nummum* are both one. Now if the Roman denier be valued at *vii d. ob.* [2] with us, and 100 *nummi* arise to one pound sterling, this sum here set down, that is to say, a sesterne [3] multiplied by the adverb *millies*, amounteth by just account unto 781,250 pounds sterling; and thereto for the overdeal or surplusage *ducenties sestertium*, which is one-fifth part of the former sum, it maketh up 937,500 pounds sterling. [18, annot.] A thing that may be thought incredible, but that we read that Caesar himself said he was 250 millions in debt when he went into Spain, and P. Clodius, whom Milo slew, dwelt in a house, the purchase whereof cost him almost 15 millions. No marvel therefore, if so many houses, which

---

[1] [The sum of half a farthing, in college buttery books indicated by *q.*, that is, *quadrans*. The sesterce was then about = 2.4*d.*].

[2] [7½*d*.: *ob.* = obolus.]

[3] [= sestertium, 100,000 sesterces; sestertia = 1000 sesterces.]

Caesar must needs buy for the plot of ground aforesaid and in so populous a city, cost not so little as a hundred millions.

27. ¹ So he was great-uncle unto her, like as he was to Octavius Augustus, the emperor. ² Or patron. ³ [On every occasion, in time of need.]

ᵃ The dole given by a prince or great man unto the people was properly called a congiary, which word took name of the measure *congius* among the Romans, consisting of 6 *sextarii*, and is answerable to our gallon, by which oil or wine was given. Howbeit [by a misuse of language] καταχρηστικῶς any such public munificence, in money or otherwise, is so called ; and in this place by it are meant other gifts bestowed upon private persons.

28. ᵃ In some copies we read, *Quando nec plebiscito Pompeius postea abrogasset*, to this sense : that Caesar, being absent, was not eligible by virtue of an act made by Pompey to that effect, considering he had not abrogated the same by any ordinance of the people, but only of his own authority corrected it after it stood upon record in the city chamber.

29. ¹ [The third of the Curios : see 36.]

30. ¹ [*De Officiis*, iii, 82.] ² [*Phoenissae*, 524.]
ᵃ This hath reference unto his violent dealing with his fellow-consul Bibulus (20).

31. ¹ [=Platform, in the sense of ground-plan, plan for building.] ² [Secretly.]

32. ¹ [Posts where they were on guard.] ² [Hazard, risk everything.]

33. ᵃ The fourth finger next unto the little one, honoured especially with a gold ring, for that there is an evident artery from the heart reaching unto it (Gellius [x, 10] ; but Pliny [*Nat. Hist.* xxxiii, 6, 24] allegeth another reason).
ᵇ He would do any thing rather than his soldiers so well-deserving at his hands should not be satisfied, such a credit carried the ring upon a Roman's finger.
ᶜ Which is the state and worth of a Roman knight or gentleman according to this verse of Horace [*Epistles*, i, 1, 59] : *Si quadringentis sex septem millia desunt, plebs eris*, and amounteth to 3125 pounds sterling [rather, 3480].

34. ¹ [Completion.] ² That is, the gulf of Venice. ³ [Hindrance.]
ᵃ As if Petreius, Afranius, and Varro had no skill in martial feats.
ᵇ He meaneth Cn. Pompeius, for his military knowledge and war-like exploits surnamed Magnus, the Great, whose principal power was now overthrown at Ilerda in Spain.

35. ¹ [Ramparts.] ² [Scipio and Juba, who were endeavouring to reorganise and revive the fortunes of the Pompeian party.]

37. ¹ A street in Rome. ² [Triumphal procession.]
ᵃ *Lychnuchos gestantibus*, bearing either young men that carried links, torches, and cresset lights ; or else branches and candlesticks resembling them, and holding the said lights. Some read, *Lychnos gestantibus*, that is, bearing lights ; but to the same effect.

38. [1] Or rather *vicena*, that is, 20,000.   [2] Rather *quadragena*, that is 40,000.   By which reckoning the proportion to horsemen was double.   [There is nothing about horsemen in the text : " He gave his veteran legions 24,000 sesterces, by way of prize-money, in addition to the 2000, which he had paid them at the beginning of the civil war."]   [3] [Surplus, in excess.]   [4] [That is, for bearing so long.]   [5] *Viscerationem :* which, as some think, Persius [*Sat.* vi, 50] calleth *artocreas* and is expounded εὐφρασία, whereupon the genius of such merriments is named Εὐφραδής.   [What is the authority for this statement ?]

   a   *Super bina HS.*, that is, *sestertia* ; that is to say, £15, 12s. 6d.

   b   *Quaterna Sestertia*, £31, 5s.

   c   *Vicena quaterna millia*, £187, 10s. ; by which reckoning he gave unto horsemen four times as much as to footmen.   Look in the marginal note to the text, and you shall find this donative much more, which may seem incredible ; but consider what provinces he spoiled, and what pillage he made, in regard whereof he was called of the Greeks χρηματοποιὸς ἀνήρ [money-grubber].

   d   *Denos modios*, in round reckoning may go for ten pecks or hoops with us.

   e   *Totidem libras*, so many pints, with the better [with addition, or more].

   f   *Trecenos nummos*, 46s. [10½d.]   ⎧Which being put together make
   g   *Centenos*, 15s. [7½d.]   ⎨100 *denarii* or drachmae, that is, one *mina*, and amount in all ⎩to £3, 2s. 6d.

   h   *Bina millia nummorum*, £15, 12s. 6d.

   i   *Quingenos sestertios*, £3, 18s. [1½d.]   [*See* Anno.t 18, 26.]

39. [1] To gratify all strangers that conflowed [verb now obsolete, *cf.* con-fluence] to Rome.   [2] [In like manner.]   [3] [Fr. *à outrance*, to the death.   Tib. 7 has the French form : to the outrance.]   [4] [This must be " vaulting " (*desultorii*).]   [5] [The combatants were drawn up in battle array.]

   a   *Regionatim urbe tota*.   Rome, as Pliny witnesseth, was divided into 14 regions, and every one of these had their several stage-plays by themselves.

   b   The *Ludi Circenses* I take to be so called of the great circus or show-place, wherein they were performed ; and not of swords, wherewith they were environed, as one would say, *Circa enses*.   Indeed these games resembled the Olympic in Greece, by Elis, where the runners with chariots were hemmed in of the one side with the running river, and of the other with swords pitched pointwise, that they should hold on the race directly, and not swerve aside without danger.   Herein were performed running with horses and chariots, jousting, tilt, and tournament, baiting and chasing of wild beasts, etc.

   c   *Pyrrhica*.   Of some thought to be the same that [the Greek] *Enoplia* was, a kind of moriske [morris] dance, after a warlike manner in harness, devised in Crete first by Pyrrhus (Pliny, *Nat. Hist.* vii, 56).   In which young gentlemen were trained to exercise all parts of the body by sundry gestures as well to avoid all venues[1] and defend themselves, as to annoy and offend the enemy.

   d   This Decimus Laberius [107-43 B.C.] was a poet also, that kind which wrote wanton poems or lascivious comedies called *mimi*.   For, howsoever in all stage-plays there is represented a lively imitation in

---

[1] [Old fencing term=hit, attack, thrust.]

gesture and voice of others, yet in these *mimi*, these same are done after a more licentious manner and without all modest reverence, even in unseemly and filthy arguments ; as Ovid [*Tristia*, ii, 515] testifieth in these words, *imitantes turpia mimos*. It seemeth, therefore, that as well the poems as the authors and actors be called *mimi*.

e *Orchestra* is here taken for the most commodious place in the theatre, wherein the senators and nobles of Rome were allowed to sit and behold the stage-plays apart from the people. For so the poet Juvenal [*Sat*. iii, 178] understandeth it in these words *Similemque videbis Orchestram et populum*.

As touching this orchestra and the poet Laberius above named, Seneca in his [seventh] book of *Controversies*, and third controversy, reporteth thus. Julius Caesar, at the solemnity of his plays, brought Laberius forth to act upon the stage ; and when he had made him a gentleman, or knight of Rome, willed him to take his place among them of that degree, but as he came toward them, they all sat so close and near one another, that there was no room for him. Now, by the way, you must understand that Cicero, then in place, had gotten himself an ill name, for that he was no fast and faithful friend, either to Pompey or to Caesar, but a flatterer of them both. Again, Caesar at that time had chosen many unto the range [rank] of senators, partly to supply and make up their number, which during the late civil wars was much diminished, and in part to gratify those who had well-deserved of him and the side. Cicero[1], therefore, alluding to the extraordinary number of new senators, sent unto Laberius, as he passed by, this word merrily, *Recepissem te nisi anguste sederem*, I would have taken you to me and give you a place, but that I sit myself very straight[2]. Then Laberius returned this pleasant answer back unto him, *Atqui solebas duabus sellis sedere*, And yet you were wont to sit upon two stools, scoffing at him for his double-dealing with Pompey and Caesar.

f The Troy fight was in warlike manner on horseback, brought by Aeneas into Italy. The manner whereof is described by Virgil, *Aeneid*, v, 553-603.

g These goals, called in Latin *metae*, above which the horses and chariots ran, were in fashion broad beneath and sharp above, in manner of pyramids, steeples, or cocks of hay, and for their matter, of wood first, or of soft gritstone, but afterwards of marble and laid over with gold. Concerning this circus, why Caesar enlarged it and brought water round about it, read Pliny, *Nat. Hist.* xxxvi, 15, 102.

h To try masteries in footmanship[3], leaping, flinging the quoit or hammer, darting, and wrestling ; which game was called pentathlon of those five kinds of exercises.

i *In minore Codeta*, which was a place on the further side of the Tiber, so called of certain plots of young springs[4] or shoots there growing which resemble horsetails [*coda, cauda*]. Some read *In morem cochleae*, that is, narrow beneath and broad above, like to the shell of a periwinkle or such-like fish.

40. a This day is called *bissextus*, and falleth out to be the fifth day before the end of February, to wit, the sixth before the kalends of March, by interposing whereof we say twice Sext. Calend. Mart., of which day our leap-year hath the name *bissextilis*.

---

[1] [Quoted in Macrobius, *Sat.* ii, 3, 9.]
[2] [=Strait, pressed for room]
[3] [To try conclusions in pedestrianism.]
[4] [Sprouts, sprigs.]

41. [1] According to the Cassian law.   [2] [=so that, it being arranged that.]   [3] Contrary to the Cornelian law.   [4] Disabled them for being judges.   [5] As who best knew the number of their tenants and inhabitants in their houses.   [6] [Should be 320,000.]

[a] Which by the first institution were 300, and by occasion of the late troubles much impaired.

[b] *Patricios allegit.* For those that were *plebeii generis* might be senators ; or else, as some expound it, he advanced divers to the degree and rank of the *patricii.*

[c] All but consuls, praetors, and censors, were counted inferior magistrates.

[d] For the censors with the public notaries ordinarily took this review, and that in *Campus Martius* and *Villa publica.*

[e] By reason of so great a number receiving corn from the State, the purveyance hereof stood the city yearly, as Plutarch writeth, in 1250 talents [£262,500].

42. [1] Either by the tribunes of the commons, or the debtors themselves.   [2] In the free state before the emperors, citizens of Rome might depart before sentence pronounced, and so avoid both condemnation and loss of goods.   [3] [It is not known where this statement is made in Cicero : Casaubon would delete *ut Cicero scribit.*]

[a] For they might discontinue out of Italy eleven years.

[b] Such were called *comites,* or *quasi ex cohorte praetoria,* as it were gentlemen of the privy chamber.

[c] *Novarum tabularum.* To wit, when, the old bonds being cancelled and thereby former debts remitted, new obligations were made.

[d] *Parricidas,* that is, *Parenticidas,* such as kill father, mother, brother, sisters, and such-like, near in blood, as also any other man or woman wilfully, according to the law of king Numa, *Si quis hominem liberum sciens morti duit parricida esto.*

43. [1] Or, scarlet in grain.   [2] [By chance.]

[a] *Repetundarum convictos.* Such governors as by way of extortion pilled and polled the provinces which they ruled ; who, after their time expired, were many times called judicially to their answers.

[b] Many laws there were called *Sumptuariae* and *Cibariae,* to restrain the excess at the table, as namely, Fannia, Licinia, Aemilia, Julia, etc. Read Aulus Gellius, *Noct. Att.* ii, 24, Macrobius, *Saturnalia,* iii, 17.

44. [1] [The Pomptine marshes.]   [2] [Causeway ; Fr. *chaussée.*] [3] [The Dacians, whose territory answered to the modern Rumania, Transylvania, Wallachia, and part of Hungary.]

[a] Of whom Terentianus[1] writeth thus, *Vir doctissimus undecunque Varro.*

[b] Isthmus is a narrow strait or foreland by Corinth, five miles over, lying between the two seas, Ionian and Aegean, or as Pliny writeth [*Nat. Hist.* iv, 4] between the two gulfs, Corinthian and Saronic. The cutting through whereof was attempted before by Demetrius, and afterwards by C. Caligula and Nero, but without effect.

[c] Which Crassus before him had not done, and therefore was overthrown.

45. [1] [Well-formed.]   [2] *Inter res agendas,* that is, *cum aciem ordinaret,* while he was setting his army in battle array.   [3] Or fantastical [fastidious].   [4] [Clipped or cut short.]   [5] His attire different

---

[1] [Terentianus Maurus, end of 2nd century A.D., writer on prosody.]

from others, or of a new fashion, which the Greeks called ἐσθῆτας ἐξάλλους καινοφανεῖς. ⁶ [Carelessly.]

ᵃ *Comitiali morbo*, so called for that the assemblies of the people, called *Comitia*, were dissolved and broke up by occasion thereof, in case any one among them fell down of that disease, according as Q. Serenus Sammonicus¹ hath testified in these verses, 57 :

> *Est morbi species subiti, cui nomen ab illo est,*
> *Quod fieri nobis suffragia justa recuset.*
> *Saepe etenim membris acri [atro] languore caducis,*
> *Concilium populi labes horrenda diremit.*

[It is a kind of sudden disease, called *comitialis*, from the fact that it prevents our votes from being duly recorded. For it often happens that when a citizen has been smitten in his limbs with this horrible disease, the assembly of the people is broken up.]

As also for that they who were subject thereto fell into a fit thereof ordinarily at such assemblies, if they were crossed in their suits and businesses there. Cornelius Celsus calleth it *Morbum majorem*, a great sickness. It is named likewise ἱερὸν νόσημα, the sacred disease, either because it affecteth the head, which is the most honourable place of the body and the seat of the soul, or in regard of the greatness thereof, which the Greeks express by the ἱερὸν ; also *Epilepsia*, for the sudden invasion of it ; *Herculeus Morbus*, either for the strength of the malady, whereby a man is forced to fall, or because Hercules was troubled therewith. Pliny [*Nat. Hist.* xxxvi, 19, 142] nameth it *Sonticus*, for the hurt that it doth unto the body ; others *Caducus*, for that upon it men fall to the ground. It is called moreover *Lunaticus*, of the moon : because it keepeth time with the course of the moon, or apprehendeth them that are born in the change thereof, as the same Serenus reporteth in these verses :

> *Huc quoque commemorant dubiae per tempora Lunae*
> *Conceptum, talem, quem saepe ruina profudit.*

[It is also said that those who are subject to attacks have been conceived during the new moon.]

Lastly, Hippocrates nameth it, *Paedicon*, that is, *puerilem morbum*, for that children be subject thereto ; whereupon some term it, *Mater puerorum*.

ᵇ This manner of going so loosely girt might signify a dissolute and effeminate wanton. Hereupon Cicero made choice in the civil war to take part with Pompey against Caesar ; and when one asked him how it came to pass, that in siding with Pompey he was so much overseen [deceived], for that he had the worse, this answer he made, *Praecinctura me decepit* [Macrobius, *Sat.* ii, 3, 10], deceived I was by that loose girding of his.

46. ¹ A district in Rome much frequented. ² [The Via Sacra, or Sacred Way.] ³ In the grove of Diana, near Aricia, 16 miles from Rome. ⁴ The paving tiles of marble, etc., whereof such floors are made.

47. ¹ [Estimate their weight.]

48. ¹ Thus Turnebus [A. Turnèbe, French scholar, 1512-65] expoundeth it : but it may be meant of the meaner sort of his praetorian cohort, who were *sagati* or *palliati*, to put a difference between them and the persons of better quality, who were *togati*.

---

¹ [3rd century A.D., author of a medical poem.]

GAIUS JULIUS CAESAR

49. [1] [I will say nothing about.] [2] [Litter.] [3] *Stabulum* [=house of ill-fame; also, as here, used as a term of abuse]. [4] [Had a liking for, *i.e.* had his eye on.] [5] [Reproached, taunted him.] [6] *Deductum*, or *eductum*, that is, brought out of his own bed-chamber into the king's.

[a] Caesar derived his pedigree from Iulus, the son of Aeneas, whose mother was Venus.

[b] The grace which is in the Latin cannot be expressed well in English, because the word *subegit* carrieth a double sense; the one signifieth the conquering of a nation, and so it is taken in the former place, as it is applied to Gaul; the other, the wanton abuse of the body, in which acceptation it is to be understood in reference to Caesar, abused by king Nicomedes.

50. [1] That is, adulterer: for that Aegisthus committed adultery with Clytaemnestra, the wife of Agamemnon. [2] *Proximo;* others read *primo*, that is, first, *cum Bibulo*. [3] [Approximately, £60,000.] [4] [By auction.]

[a] In the twofold sense likewise of these two words, *tertia* and *deducta*, lieth the pleasant grace of this conceited [witty] speech.

By the one may be understood that a third part of the price was deducted; by the other Cicero meant, that her daughter Tertia was brought by her to his bed [Macrobius, *Sat.* ii, 2, 5].

51. [a] This Distich, or two verses, which his soldiers after their licentious manner in the triumph chanted may thus be Englished:

> Look to your wives, ye citizens, a lecher bald we bring;
> In Gaul adultery cost thee gold, here 'tis but borrowing.

For, as he borrowed of other men, so he lent or paid as much again, in that his own wife Pompeia, as is thought, was kept by P. Clodius.

52. [1] Of which the Egyptian kings had always ready-rigged 800, as Appian writeth. [2] [Having induced her to visit Rome.] [3] That is, Ptolemaeus Caesario. [4] *Incessu*, in his gang or manner of going. [5] *Quas et quot ducere vellet*, even an alien. [6] For otherwise, πολυγαμία was unlawful. And Antony was the first Roman that had two wives at once. [7] [Against the laws of Nature.]

[a] Such a vessel as this named here *thalamegos*, and by Seneca, De Beneficiis [vii, 20, 3], *Navis cubiculata*, Ptolemy Philopator, as witnesseth Athenaeus [204, D.], had, which carried in length half a furlong, in breadth 30 cubits, and in height little less than 40.

[b] *Impudicitiae.* I observe that, both in this author and also in other approved writers, *impudicitia* is properly and peculiarly taken for that abominable uncleanness only, which is named sodomy; like as *pudicitia*, for the integrity of the body and clearness from that detestable filthiness. And so *pudicus* and *impudicus* are to be understood.

53. [1] [Fastidiousness.]

54. [1] Tubero. [This should be " C., when proconsul."] [2] That is, in Portugal. [3] *Divenderet*, some read *divideret*, he distributed and dealt away. [4] [At the rate of.] [5] Auletes. [6] That is, of silver, after 80 pound weight the talent [more than £1,000,000]. [7] [Pilling and polling=plundering.]

[a] Which cometh to £23, 8s. 9d., and is not much more than half the worth. According to Budaeus, it was 7 pound *dim.* [=*dimidium*, half] of silver for one of gold.

^b For it was esteemed a great honour to be called allies and associates, or styled kings, by the people of Rome.

55. ¹ *Eloquentia militarique re*, after Lipsius. ² [When several accusers came forward, an examination, called *divinatio*, was held to decide which of them was best fitted to conduct the prosecution. The occasion was the prosecution of Cn. Dolabella for extortion in his province Macedonia.] ³ Take it generally for the whole action. ⁴ [Not, in defence of, but] which he wrote for, or to Metellus. ⁵ [Address to the soldiers.]

56. ¹ *Ad Brutum* [lxxv, 262]. ² [Haply, perhaps.] ³ [Hastily, without discrimination.] ⁴ Against Cicero in the dispraise of Cato Uticensis, in whose commendation Cicero had written before. ⁵ *De Analogia.* ⁶ [Completed.] ⁷ *Anticatones.* ⁸ *Iter.* ⁹ Or rather, 27. ¹⁰ A book of remembrance. ¹¹ In manner of ciphers. ¹² c for b, etc. ¹³ [Collections.]

ᵃ *Anticatones.* Whereas Cicero had written in the praise of Cato of Utica, he wrote two books against the said Cato, which he called *Anticatones.*

57. ¹ Or carroch [caroche], with four wheels, Gr. τετράκυκλος or *petoritum* [a word really of Celtic, not Greek origin]. ² In imitation hereof the Romans devised the *ascogephrus*, as if from ἀσκογέφυρα, that is, a bridge founded upon such leather bottles blown with wind or lightly stuffed with straw.

58. ¹ [*In propria persona*, in person] : yet himself writeth that he sent C. Vossenus before. ² *Hieme ;* or, in a tempestuous and stormy season, as Virgil and others use the word.

59. ¹ [Frighten.] ² Read Pliny, *Nat. Hist.* vii, 12.

60. ¹ *Non saepe.* Some read *non tantum*, that is, not only, but also.

61. ᵃ Venus, surnamed Genetrix, *i.e.* Mother, Caesar honoured as the goddess from the which he was descended, by Iulus or Ascanius, her nephew.

62. ¹ [Twisting, seizing them by, the throat.] ² [Bewildered, stupefied.] ³ *Aquilifer.* Some read *aquilifero*, as if Caesar threatened the standard-bearer. ⁴ Wherewith it was pitched into the ground.

ᵃ The principal ensign or standard of the Roman legion was an eagle of silver, reared upon a spear-top, the point whereof beneath was sharp and fastened into the ground ; and the same stood within a little shrine, not to be removed but when the army was on foot.

63. ¹ *Vectoria navicula*, a ferry boat. If you read *victor*, that is, being victor, distinguish [punctuate there].

64. ᵃ Dio (xlii, 40) and Appian (*Bell. Civ.* ii, 90), report this otherwise : namely, that he forsook the said coat-armour (it clogged him so much), and so the Egyptians got it.

65. ¹ This seemeth strange and contrary to the Roman discipline. ² *A fortuna*, πλουτίνδην ; others read *a forma*, that is, beauty, favour, and feature of body. ³ [Paying attention, heedful.] ⁴ [Ready for action, keen, alert.]

66. ¹ *Minuendo*, or *inhibendo*, that is, suppressing, which might seem

GAIUS JULIUS CAESAR

good policy. ² Footmen heavily-armed. ³ Footmen lightly-armed.

67. ¹ *Pro modo ;* or, *pro more,* that is, after the manner of military discipline. ² And the legions with him, 54 B.C. [Titurius Sabinus and L. Cotta were attacked by Ambiorix, chief of the Eburones in Gaul.]

68. ¹ Or fort, at the siege of Dyrrachium. ² According to Plutarch [*Life of Caesar,* xvi, 2], 130. ³ [At the battle of Marathon.]

ᵃ *E viatico suo.* Albeit *viaticum* properly signifieth the store and provision set by for a journey, yet here it is put for the wealth and the substance of a soldier, like as in Horace, *Ep.* ii, 2, 26 :

> *Luculli miles collecta viatica multis*
> *Aerumnis.*

In which sense ἐφόδιον likewise in Greek is taken.

ᵇ Pliny calleth it *lapsana, Nat. Hist.* (xix, 8, 41) ; a kind of wild wort or cole.

ᶜ To be tithed, *i.e.* every tenth man to suffer death.

ᵈ Which ordinarily consisted of 550 footmen, and 66 horse, whereof ten went to a legion. Some, I wot well, had more, some fewer. But for this place it may suffice that it was the tenth part of a legion.

70. ᵃ *Quirites,* that is, Roman Citizens, as freed now from their allegiance, which by their military oath they were bound unto.

71. ¹ Who laid claim unto Masintha as his tributary. ² *Stipendiarium quoque pronuntiatum :* however, some read *pronuntiavit,* as if Caesar had averred openly that he was his waged soldier. ³ [The fasces.]

ᵃ Which was a great abuse offered among the barbarians, who set great store by their beards, and suffered them to grow very long.

72. ¹ In a pallet or mattress upon the ground. ² Under the jetty of the house. ³ [Cutthroats.]

73. ¹ [The great lyric poet.] ² By saying *Nollem factum,* I am sorry for it, and I would I had not so done.

74. ¹ Two talents, according to Plutarch. ² Of *Bona Dea,* in whose chapel it was thought he did the deed, disguised in woman's apparel.

76. ¹ Censorship in deed, though not in name. ² *Imperatoris,* sovereign and absolute commander. ³ [State.] ⁴ In the Forum.
⁵ Of himself, as a god. ⁶ [Trans. of Lat. *pulvinar.*] ⁷ Juliani.
⁸ [This should be " consulships " : the word is *consulatibus.*] ⁹ [*Praefecti.*] ¹⁰ *Etiam praesente se :* some read *absente se :* clean contrary [the latter seems right]. ¹¹ The last of December. ¹² [With similar disregard of law and custom.] ¹³ Made free citizens of Rome.

ᵃ *Tensa et ferculum,* a chariot of silver or ivory, with a frame in it sustaining the images of the gods, which was drawn in most solemn and stately manner unto the pulvinar.

ᵇ *Pulvinar.* A bed-loft, or place where certain rich beds were made for the said images to be laid upon.

ᶜ *Flamen.* A certain priest, bearing the name of that god, for whose service he was instituted, as *Dialis* of Jupiter, *Martialis* of Mars, *Quirinalis* of Romulus, etc. Cicero (*Philippic,* ii, 43, 110) saith that M. Antonius was flamen to Julius Caesar.

16

^d *Luperci* were certain young men, who at the licentious feast, *Lupercalia*, instituted to the honour of Pan Lycaeus, otherwise called Inuus [or Faunus], by Romulus and Remus, ran up and down naked in the city of Rome. A new kind of these *Luperci* ordained Caesar, of his own name called *Juliani*. At this feast *Lupercalia*, M. Antonius played the part of a Lupercus, at which solemnity, when Caesar sat in a throne of gold, arrayed in a purple robe, the said M. Antonius attempted to do upon his head the royal band, called a diadem.

^e Whereas before it was called *Quintilis*, he named it *Julius*.

^f This was Caninius Rebilus, of whose consulship there go divers jests, as namely these, whereof Cicero [*ad Fam.* vii, 30; Macrobius, *Sat.* ii, 3, 6] was the author. A vigilant consul we have had of Caninius, who in all his consulship never slept wink. Also, a consul we have had so severe and censor-like, as that during his consulship no man dined, no man supped, no man so much as once slept. Pitholaus (ib., ii, 2) said of him, Heretofore we had *flamines Diales,* and now we have consuls *Diales*, playing upon the equivocation or double sense of the word *Dialis*, which, being derived of Διός, of [Zeus or] Jupiter, signifieth his *Flamen :* but of *Dies*, a day, betokeneth a day-consul or *flamen*.

77. [¹ T. Ampius Balbus, friend of Cicero and a supporter of Pompey, author of an historical work.] ² *Nam grammatici est dictare* [for it is the part of a grammarian to dictate, literally and figuratively]. ³ Should signify better fortune.

^a According to Lucan, *Omnia Caesar erat*, Caesar was all in all.

^b Well-known it is that Sulla was passing well-learned both in Greek and Latin. But in that he resigned up the absolute power of his dictatorship, which he took upon him, for a hundred and twenty years, that is to say, for ever, Caesar said he was no grammarian, *quia nescivit dictare, quod munus est grammatici ;* alluding to the ambiguous word *dictare*, to indite, or give precepts, as grammarians do to their scholars, as also to command absolutely, whereof it may seem that dictator took the name.

78. ¹ *Inexpiabilem* or *exitiabilem*, that is, deadly, and that which brought him to mischief. ² Not so much as rising up unto them. ³ Saying withal, " What, Sir ? Remember you are Caesar." ⁴ [Seats or benches (*subsellia*).] ⁵ [Took offence at.]

^a Who were in number 10.

^b Or, if I may for Pontius Aquila ; spoken by way of a scornful *ironia*.

79. ¹ Resembling a diadem. ² [Stigma, reproach.] ³ [The festival of Lupercus, the Lycaean Pan, identified by the Romans with Faunus.] ⁴ [Handed over.]

^a *Plebeio*, and not *plebi*, for the commons could not endure that name, as may appear by Cicero's words in his second Philippic or invective against M. Antonius [ii, 34, 85] : Thou showedst the diadem. The people all over the common place gave a groan thereat. Thou wert about to set it upon his head to the great grief and sorrow of the people, he rejected it, with as great joy and applause of theirs.

^b The name Optimus Maximus, wherewith the ancients styled Jupiter, signifieth most bountiful and most powerful ; wherein it is observed that bounty goeth before power, because, as M. Tullius writeth, it is better and more acceptable to do good unto all, than to have power over all.

^c In Egypt. A renowned city, built by Alexander the Great, for the

pleasant site much commended, and therefore might be affected by Caesar : at which there is no day almost through the year, but the inhabitants behold the sun shining clear upon them : and which Ammianus [xxii, 16, 7] calleth *Verticem omnium civitatum*, the chief of cities.

^d Ilium, a city where Troy stood ; the citizens whereof, as Strabo [xiii, 1, 27] writeth, Caesar, in memorial of his progenitors from thence descended, and namely from Iulus or Ascanius, the son of Aeneas, had endowed with many franchises and immunities, and therefore it carried some likelihood, that he meant there to make his abode.

^e These *Quindecimviri*, or fifteen men, were instituted in the days of Cornelius Sulla, with this addition *Sacrorum ;* unto whose charge it appertained to see that sacrifices and divine service, that supplications, and processions, expiations, and ceremonial rites should be duly performed, as also to peruse the books and prophecies of Sibylla. At first they were but two, called *Duumviri*, afterwards ten, under the name of *Decemviri sacris faciundis*. Alexander ab Alexandro, *Genialium dierum libri*, iii, 16.

80. ¹ Or bill [petition, memorial, unless it means a placard posted up]. ² Or rather, *Idem in Curiam*, for the same Caesar brought them into the senate. ³ *Bracas*, trousers, breeches ; some take them for mantles. ⁴ *Postremus :* or *postremo*, at last [*i.e.* has finished by becoming king]. ⁵ M. Brutus. ⁶ Some upon the bridge, others under it. ⁷ In which Caesar dwelt after he had been high priest. ⁸ March 15th, in honour of Anna Perenna ; and because the plays were exhibited in Pompey's theatre. Therefore the senate met also in his Court (*Curia*).

^a *Bonum factum.* A form of preface which in old time they used, *boni om[i]nis causa*, before their edicts and decrees, etc., so commonly as that these two capital letters B. F. did betoken the same as ordinarily, as S. C. stand for *Senatus consultum*. It had the same use as *In nomine Dei* with us.

^b Some take these *bracae*, whereof Bracata Gallia, a part of Transalpine Gaul, took name, for frieze rugs striped with sundry colours, which may resemble Irish mantles ; but I suppose them to be a kind of coarse breeches, much like to the Irish trousers, but that they are more full.

^c By rising up unto him, and shouting or applauding as he passed along.

^d *Utinam viveres.*

^e   *Brutus, quia reges ejecit, consul primus factus est :*
      Hic, quia consules ejecit, rex postremo factus est.

^f Certain bridges there were for the time made, upon which the tribes passed when they gave their voices in *Campus Martius*, at their solemn leets[1] and assemblies for election of magistrates.

81. ¹ Which himself promulged. ² Or *Regaviolus*, as if *rex avium*. ³ [Group or set, a number.] ⁴ [Memoranda, documents.] ⁵ [Succeed in obtaining.] ⁶ Of Pompey.

^a Some take it to be the same as regulus, or trochilus, thought to be the wren, and is likewise named king of birds, in Greek βασιλεύς, ominous therefore unto Caesar, seeking to be king.

82. ¹ *Conspicati ;* or *conspirati*, that is, the conspirators stood round about him. ² Who before had been his great friend and sided with

---

[1] [Used as a translation of Comitia.]

him [his name was Tillius, not Tullus or Tullius]. ³ *Alter Cassius*, or *alter e Cassiis*, one of the Cassii. Another reading makes it " one of the Cascas." ⁴ *Jugulum*, or the chanell-bone [cannel-bone, collar-bone]. ⁵ Out of his chair. ⁶ Which they were wont to cast over their shoulders, or tuck up slack above the waist. ⁷ Some expound this of the litter, as if one corner thereof hung down, carried as it was by three. ⁸ Whereby it seemeth he had one given him in his neck before, which the author hath omitted.

ᵃ This is diversely reported by authors, the occasion of which variety ariseth upon the affinity of these names, Cassius and Casca. For as there were two Cassii at this action, so likewise were there two Servilii brethren, both surnamed Casca. By Alter Cassius or Casca, therefore, you may understand one of the two brethren, or the second of them. For some write that the one Casca gave him in the neck a wound, but not deadly, whereupon Caesar caught hold of his dagger, crying out, *Scelerate Casca, quid agis ?* What meanest thou, O wicked Casca ? and then Casca called unto his brother for help, who came in and gave him his death wound, in the breast under the chanell-bone (Plutarch).

ᵇ Albeit *graphium* doth signify a writing punch (or steel or weir), otherwise called *stilus*, wherewith they wrote in hard matter, as wood, or bark, before the use of our parchment and paper, as also our pen made of a quill or other substance, as brass, etc., in which sense it is taken in that verse of Ovid, *Amor.* i, 11, 23 :

> *Quid digitos opus est graphium lassare tenendo ?*
> [What need to tire the fingers by holding a pen ?]

and probable it is that Caesar, sitting in council, was not without such a writing instrument : yet both Dominicus Marius upon the foresaid verse, and Perottus¹ also, the author of *Cornucopia*, expounding this place of Suetonius, takes *graphium* for *pugiunculum*, *i.e.* a little poniard, poinado, or pocket-dagger. And happily therewith Caesar wounded Cassius or Casca (whether you will) being more ready at hand, hanging at his girdle, than the style or steel aforesaid, which by all likelihood was yet in the case or sheath, called *graphiarium*, considering Caesar was but new-set. But I leave the exposition of this place *in medio*.

ᶜ Valerius Maximus under the title of *Verecundia*, commendeth this maidenlike modesty of Caesar, who, notwithstanding that he was maskered [62] with 23 wounds, for manhood sake forgot not to hide his nakedness and to die in decent manner, but as Euripides [*Hecuba*, 569] writeth of the virgin lady Polyxena,

πολλὴν πρόνοιαν εἶχεν εὐσχήμως πεσεῖν.

Where by the way it may be noted, that the Romans wore, not trusses or breeches, as we do, to cover those inferior and secret parts.

ᵈ This may have reference to that which is reported before, how in his youth he loved Servilia, the mother of this Brutus ; for his age falleth out to agree fitly with that time, insomuch as he was commonly thought to be a son of his. And yet this attribute *fili* may sort well with the familiarity that was between them.

Others read Καὶ σὺ εἶς [or εἶ] ἐκείνων. And art thou one of them ?

83. ¹ 13th of September. ² So he was their great uncle. ³ Afterwards Augustus, son of Atia, Julius Caesar's sister's daughter. ⁴ As

---

¹ [N. Perotti, 1430-80, Italian scholar.]

Postumus, born after his death.   [5] Of Rome.   [6] [Gardens.]
[7] [£2, 6s. 10½d. sterling.]

[a] *Virgini Vestali Maximae.* That nun or Vestal virgin, who in age and dignity excelled the rest, and was the mistress as it were and governess of them, they called *maxima;* much like unto the lady abbess or prioress in our days.

84. [1] His own daughter, wife to Pompey, who died of childbirth, and by special privilege was interred in Mars' field.   [2] Or, hearse. [3] Or, bier.   [4] Which was, that the magistrates and senators should go before without their badges and robes of dignity ; the knights and gentlemen follow in mourning weed ; then the soldiers, carrying the heads or points of their weapons downward : last of all, the common people marshalled according to their tribes.   [5] Or Atius, who wrote a tragedy bearing the same title. [The name should be Atilius. He translated the Electra of Sophocles.]   [6] Or, bier.   [7] Where he was murdered.   [8] They affected Caesar (it should seem) in regard of many benefits, and namely [especially] for bringing Pompey to confusion, who had forced their chief city.

[a] The argument whereof was the deciding of the contention between Ajax and Ulysses about Achilles' armour.

[b] For some of these who took part with Pompey he had pardoned.

[c] *Quicquid praeterea ad manum aderat.* Others read, *ad donum aderat :* understanding thereby those gifts which they brought as offerings to his ghost, and be called *inferiae.*

86. [1] [Ailing, sickly (a form of crazy).]   [2] [There is a lacuna in the text here.]

87. [1] [*Cyropaedia,* viii, 7.]

88. [1] In the 8th septimane [week].

[a] Which is counted one of the climacteric years, in which it falleth out that 7 is multiplied by 8, which two numbers, as Cicero hath observed [*de Republica,* vi, 3], be complete ; a revolution fatal to Scipio Africanus the younger, to Virgil also and Pliny.

[b] Appian writeth that it was in a sudden uproar of the people burnt to the ground.

[c] To signify that upon that day, The Father of his Country was killed.

89. [1] [So to say, as it were.]   [2] Cassius, as Plutarch [*Caesar,* lxix] reporteth ; and Brutus according to Dio [xlviii, *ad init.*], and the two Cascas. A notable judgement of Almighty God upon the unnatural murderers of their sovereign.

NOTES AND ANNOTATIONS UPON OCTAVIUS CAESAR AUGUSTUS

1. [1] [An ancient Volscian town, mod. Velletri.] [2] Or, to Octavius. [3] Where they were a-boiling or roasting.

2. [1] [The equestrian order.] [2] Against Hannibal and the Carthaginians. [3] Colonel of 1000 footmen. [4] [C. 2, Annot.] [5] A seller of ropes : *restionem,* not *Restionem* with a capital *R,* as if it were a proper name. [6] [Inhabitants of the (originally Greek) colony of Thurii in Lucania.] [7] *Argentarius,* an exchanger of money for gain.

3. [1] [Immediately after.] [2] [I, i, 21 ; 2, 7.]
[a] *Inter divisores operasque campestres.* This was thought to be but a base occupation, namely, to give among the tribes such sums of money as the *candidati,* or those that stood in election for offices, promised and pronounced for the buying of voices. The name also grew to be odious, howsoever Plautus in *Aulularia* [i, 2, 29] calleth them *magistros Curiae.* Likewise all such servitors as otherwise gave attendance in the *Campus Martius,* and thereby got a living, whom he termeth here *operas campestres,* were but of mean reckoning.

4. [1] [From Aricia, mod. La Riccia, a town on the Appian way, 15 miles from Rome.] [2] [Marcus Antonius, more familiar to English readers as Mark Antony.] [3] All this is spoken allegorically of his base parentage.

5. [1] 23rd of September. [2] Ox- or bull-heads. [3] [Guardian, keeper.]
[a] *Regione Palatii.* In old time Rome was divided into four principal regions or quarters : *Suburrana, Esquilina, Collina,* and *Palatina.*
[b] The manner in old time was, that the new-born babe should be set up on the bare ground to cry and call upon the goddess Ops, who so gently had received it. And the goddess forsooth, that helped to lift it up again, was called Levana. [From *levare,* to raise ; cf. Augustine, *De Civitate Dei,* iv, 11.]

6. [1] [After purification.] [2] [To test the truth of the rumour.]

7. [1] Hadrian the emperor [one of whose secretaries Suetonius was]. [2] [Proposal.]

8. [1] Otherwise called Getae [C. 44]. [2] His mother's husband [Augustus's stepfather, not father-in-law.]
[a] The virile robe [*toga virilis*] was the ordinary Roman gown, all white without purple, which they wore when they came to be past 16 years of age.
[b] To wit, bracelets, chains and collars, spear-staves without iron heads, trappings, chaplets and garlands, etc.
[c] This was the triumvirate so much spoken of, during which M. Antonius, M. Lepidus, and Augustus ruled jointly together.

10. [1] Of the commons. [2] [*Tralaticium jus :* really = traditional, customary, ordinary justice.] [3] Antony. [4] As massive and heavy as it was.

11. [1] [Nothing is known of him.] [2] [Rather, the other.]

12. [1] *Pro partibus :* of Pompey and the commonwealth. If you read *pro patribus :* with the nobility. [2] *Et tollendum.* [Used in the double sense of (1) exalted, (2) made away with.] [3] [Hardened, experienced.] [4] [Inhabitants of Nursia, a Sabine town at the foot of the Apennines.]

[a] Marcus Brutus.

[b] He meaneth Cicero, as appeareth by an epistle of D. Brutus unto Cicero [*Ad Fam.* xi, 20] in these words : *Narravit mihi, etc., ipsum Caesarem (Augustum) nihil sane de te questum nisi quod diceret te dixisse laudandum adolescentem, ornandum, tollendum : se non [esse] commissurum ut tolli possit.* In which words, as also in this place of Tranquillus, there is an equivocation or doubtful sense in this verb *tollendum ;* which in one signification is in manner equivalent with *laudandum* and *ornandum,* and betokeneth to be advanced, extolled, or lifted up, and so is to be taken in good part ; but in another, it is all one with *tollendum de medio,* or *occidendum,* that is, to be dispatched out of life, or killed. In which sense Cicero meant it, and Augustus took it, namely, in ill part. Much like to this, you shall read in Nero [39], *sustulit hic matrem, sustulit ille patrem.* The grace lieth in the ambiguity of the Latin word *tollendum* which cannot in English be so well delivered.

13. [1] [Reached, made good his escape to.] [2] Sovereign commander [*imperator*].

[a] The *Egnatii,* as Appian witnesseth [*Bell. Civ.* iv, 21 ; but the reference does not bear this out. Others refer it to two Aquilii Flori].

14. [1] [Turned out of his seat.]

[a] Which, by the Julian and Roscian laws, were allowed for the knights or gentlemen of Rome, whose estate was valued not under 400,000 sesterces [£3480]. The laws abovesaid were promulged by Augustus Caesar and L. Roscius Otho, a tribune of the commons. And these 14 seats, named *equestria,* were the next unto the stage after the orchestra, arising by degrees and stairs, as it were higher and higher, and so farther off. Above which, in the upper and more remote scaffolds, sat the common people, and thereupon they were called *popularia.* Howbeit, for all the Roscian law, many commoners of good wealth and credit used to sit indifferently in the said 14 foremost seats, until the other Julian law was enacted, which distinguished the orders more precisely. Carol. Sigonius, *De Antiq. Jur. Civ. Rom.,* ii, 19.

15. [1] Brained with an axe and not beheaded. [2] On which day Julius Caesar was murdered. [3] [Kept quiet, restrained themselves.] [4] [*i.e.* by declaring themselves, when they had the chance of getting L. Antonius as their leader.]

16. [1] When commonly it is calm in those seas. [2] A port town in Sicily [E. part of the N. coast]. [3] A harbour near Messana [between Mylae and Pelorus]. [4] Mark Antony, the triumvir. [5] For God's help [rather, to avoid looking at the battle]. [6] [*i.e.* accuse him of having cried out.] [7] [*i.e.* would not allow it to be carried in the procession.] [8] [Neither . . . lightly = and hardly.] [9] Of Italy. [10] Sextus. [11] Sextus. [12] In the triumvirate. [13] [*i.e.* The

alliance between him and Mark Antony.]   [14] Read Cn. Domitius.
[15] [The inhabitants of Bononia (mod. Bologna).]

[a] When in stately pomp the sacred chariot *tensa*, with the images of the gods in it, was devoutly drawn according to the solemn manner.

[b] A coast-town of Italy affronting Sicily, from whence it is a very short cut oversea ; so called by the Greeks, as if even there a breach [1] was made by the sea, dividing Italy from Sicily, which beforetime was a part of the continent or mainland ; and no marvel of that name, since that maritime region, wherein Locri stood, was in times past called *Magna Graecia*.

[c] In that he put down in his will the children which he had by Cleopatra, a stranger and barbarian born, which also were begotten in bastardy, as well as if they had been natural Romans and legitimate, he faulted in common civility, but much more, when he proceeded to call the sons that he had by her, Reges Regum, the kings of kings. As absurd also and immodest he showed himself, when, having by her at one birth two twins, the male infant he surnamed Sol, the sun, and the female Luna, the moon.

[d] In the custody of the Vestal nuns, or votaries, as Julius Caesar had done before him ; of such integrity and so good conscience they were thought to be, as things of greatest weight were committed unto them in trust.

[e] This forename Titus cannot truly be given to any of the Domitii, if that be true which is averred of them afterward in Domitius Nero 1.

[f] But in the behalf of M. Antonius, considering he was their patron and protector ; for other foreign states and cities usually were shrouded under the favour of gentlemen at Rome. In which regard, he laid not to their charge that they had not sided with himself, but rather taken part with their patron Antonii, considering that near bond wherewith such protectors and clients or dependants were linked together ; which Dionysius supposeth to be almost as ancient as Rome itself, and almost equal to that of allies, yea, and kinsfolk in blood.

[g] A promontory or cape in Epirus, shooting into the Gulf of Ambracia [mod. Arta], in the view whereof the sumptuous armada of Antony and Cleopatra was defeated.

17 [1] [Making a detour.]   [2] [Took steps, entered into negotiations.]   [3] *Viditque mortuum*. In some copies we read thus : *Viditque mortuam Cleopatram*, and he saw Cleopatra dead ; for he heard only of Antony's death and saw the sword wherewith he wounded himself. [4] His great uncle, indeed, but father by adoption.

[a] These Psylli are people in Africa, supposed to have bodies of a singular virtue to kill serpents, as also a special skill in sucking forth venom out of the wound made by their sting. Yet Cornelius Celsus [*De Medicina*, v, 27] is of opinion that they have no principal gift or cunning in this feat above other men, but more boldness rather, confirmed by use and practice. For the venom of a serpent, saith he, hurteth not by being tasted, but as it is infused by a wound, which he proveth by those poisons that the French use especially in hunting. And therefore a very snake or adder itself may be eaten safely, however the sting is deadly ; and if, whiles it lieth astonied or benumbed (the cast [2] whereof these mountebanks or jugglers have by means of certain medicines), one put his finger into the mouth thereof, and be not bitten or stung withal, there is no spittle or slimy humours there to do harm.

---

[1] [Gr. ῥηγνύναι, to break.]
[2] [Trick, artifice.]

So that whosoever else, by example of these Psylli, shall suck any wound inflicted by a serpent, he shall do it safely, and cure besides the party that is stung, provided always, that he have no sore or ulcer in gums, palate, or any part of his limbs.

b Some think this kind of aspis which she used was [*ptyas* (Gr. the spitter)], others *hypnalē*[1] ; for that the sting brought drowsiness upon her, and Lucan [*Pharsalia*, ix, 701] called it *aspis somnifera*. But common it is unto all the sorts to kill by sleep and stupefaction without pain, some sooner, some later, but all within the space of six hours ; so that *Hypnalē* may seem to be a general attribute to them all.

18. [1] Or *Ptolemaeos*, *i.e.* the bodies or tombs of the Ptolemies. If you read *Ptolemaeum*, it is meant of Lagus [the word *Ptolemaeum*, with *sepulchrum* understood, really means " the tomb of the Ptolemies " generally]. [2] Which stood upon the said promontory Actium.

a As if he counted those Ptolemies dead, who left no memorable acts behind them, and Alexander a king still, or worthy alone to be called king, whose memorial was yet so fresh and lively.

19. [1] Or Egnatius. [2] [Shoud be, his granddaughter's husband. In several places, *nephew* and *niece* are used for *grandson* and *granddaughter*.] [3] Begotten between a bondslave and a libertine. [4] Or, prompter of names, employed in telling of their names who came to salute and bid good morrow, and placing also of guests at the table, and in no better service.

a For that one of his parents was a Parthine, that is to say, a stranger of Illyricum, and the other a Roman.

20. [1] Or turret of wood [a drawbridge let down from besieging towers].

a Wars take the name of those that be vanquished, as *Gallicum bellum, Germanicum, Dalmaticum*, etc., in which Gaul, Germany, and Dalmatia be subdued.

b Some take this bridge to be a kind of fabric or scaffold reared for the assault of the town Metulum[2], and not an ordinary bridge built over some river.

21. [1] [Rather, the Vindelici and Salassi, Alpine peoples.] [2] Unusual in those days. [3] Or 20, rather. [4] [At Carrhae (mod. Harran) in Mesopotamia, 53 B.C.]

a This temple, as appeareth afterwards, he had vowed in the Philippian war, which he undertook in revenge of his father Julius Caesar's death, and therefore dedicated it unto Mars Revenger.

22. [1] *Tertio ;* or *ter*, thrice. [2] [*See* Annot.]

a The temple of Janus Quirinus, or of Quirinus, because it was first founded by Romulus, Numa Pompilius his successor ordained to be set open in time of war, and shut when there was peace. Whereupon Janus was termed under a twofold name, Patu[l]cius [opener] and Clusius [closer]. Once it was shut in the said Numa his reign ; and a second time, after the first Punic war ended, when M. Atilius, and T. Manlius, or Mallius, were consuls. At all times before and after it stood open until Augustus Caesar's days ; during whose empire it was thrice shut. First, upon the defeat of Antony and Cleopatra before Actium ;

---

[1] [Killing by sleep (Gr. ὕπνος) : *see* Solinus, xxvii, 28. He lived in the 3rd century A.D., and put together a work called *Polyhistor*, the chief source of which was Pliny's *Natural History*.]

[2] [The Dalmatian capital.]

secondly, after his victory in Spain over the Cantabri ; last of all, when all nations (in manner) of the earth by occasion of his victories grew to a universal peace. About which time our Saviour Jesus Christ, Immanuel, that True Peace-maker between God and us, was born. Thus Orosius reporteth, and readeth, *ter*, not *tertio*. Howbeit Livy seemeth to acknowledge but once, namely, upon the Actian victory.

b Ovation was a kind of petty triumph, wherein the captains victors rode not in a chariot, nor wore a coronet of laurel, but of the myrtle. It took the name *ab ovibus*, from sheep sacrificed, or rather all the voice, [*evoe*, or *ovoe*], which the soldiers in their acclamations resounded.

23. ¹ [Lollius in 16 B.C. by some German tribes who had crossed the Rhine ; Varus in A.D. 9 by the revolted German tribes under Arminius in the Saltus Teutoburgiensis (Lippischer Wald).] ² [The vowing of games.] ³ Which also was called *Bellum sociale*, wherein the associate nations in Italy rebelled ; of which rebellion the authors were the Marsi [Cimbrian, 105-101 B.C. ; Marsian, 90-88 B.C.]. ⁴ Upon an opinion of the paynims, that if they did injury to their own bodies they should sooner pacify the gods. ⁵ [Rather, my.]

a The Roman army consisted of legions, who were all Romans, and of *Auxilia*, aids, and those were of allies and confederate nations.

b This day was *Ante diem quartum nonas Sextiles*, the second day of August, which was also that very day of the month, wherein the Romans in times past suffered the disastrous overthrow at Cannae [216 B.C., when they were defeated by Hannibal].

24. ¹ [Cashiered.] ² [Retreated.] ³ The generals' pavilions. ⁴ Or waistcoats, without their *Sagum* [military cloak]. ⁵ Or, meeting-poles, in token of regradation [*obs.*] or putting down to a lower place.

a By which the people of Rome won their immortal fame and conquered the whole world ; as Cicero saith in his *Pro Murena*.

b December, January, and February.

c Thereby disabling them for being serviceable soldiers.

d These publicans, so called for that they farmed their cities' revenues, as customs, tolls, imposts, etc., were likewise knights or gentlemen of Rome, and, by being so earnest to buy out one of their own sort, were thought to favour him, and minded presently to dismiss him at liberty ; which was contrary to his intent.

25. ¹ [Rather, more condescending.] ² [Sudden outbreaks of fire.] ³ [Who had to supply a certain number.] ⁴ *Sub primore vexillo ;* or, *sub proprio vexillo*, under his own banner. ⁵ Trappings. ⁶ *Quicquid auro argentoque constaret* [consisted of] ; or rather, *quamquam . . . constarent*, albeit they were made of gold and silver. ⁷ [A crown for mounting a *vallum* or rampart.] ⁸ [Rather, without partiality, without any idea of courting popularity.] ⁹ [With considerable risk.]

a For his uncle and predecessor Julius Caesar had taken up that familiar term of *commilitones*, by occasion of so many troubles that followed him, and therefore was driven to speak his soldiers fair.

b Libertines were those who, having been bond, were made free or manumitted ; and these were not capable of *militia Romana*, but in time of great extremity and desperate cases.

c It seemeth by this that these vallar and mural coronets were made of some other matter than silver and gold. Yet Aulus Gellius (v, 6), writeth that both these, as also the naval, were of gold. Now, the vallar or *castrensis* coronet (for they were both one) resembled a *vallum*, the rampier [C. 35] a palisade about a camp, made *ex vallis*, from stakes or pales sharpened at the head, wherewith the bank [earthwork] or mure [wall] was the better fortified, and he received it as an honourable reward, who first mounted the said palisade, and entered the camp of his enemies. The mural was fashioned like to the battlements of a wall, given likewise unto that soldier, who approached the enemies' wall first, scaled, and climbed over it into the city. As for these *phalerae*, albeit they be commonly taken for the ornaments or trappings of horses, yet it appeareth that they be the ornaments of the men themselves ; and as well they, as torques, were *tralaticia militum dona*, ordinary and common gifts bestowed upon good soldiers. See Juvenal [*Satires*, xvi, 60], *Ut laeti phaleris omnes et torquibus omnes.*

d Such as he called before *manipulares* and *gregarios ;* although in other authors *caligati* stand for all manner of soldiers.

e In Latin *Festina lente*, much to this sense in our English tongue : No more haste than good speed [More haste, less speed] : for, The soft fire makes sweet malt[1]. This proverb the same Augustus expressed also in his coins, wherein he stamped, together with lightning or a thunderbolt, the god Terminus, representing by the one, celerity, and by the other, stayedness. Like as Titus Vespasianus the emperor joined an anchor and a dolphin together in his coin, to the same purpose.

f A verse of Euripides, in the tragedy *Phoenissae* [602] : A wary captain is better than a venturous.

g It was the apophthegm of Cato : Soon enough is that done, which is well done [in the form, *sat cito, si sat bene ;* the quotation in the text has been referred to Publilius Syrus].

26. [1] By the laws called *annales.* [2] As the triumvirate [rather, the principate]. [3] As the tribune's authority and censorship. [4] Or, casting it behind him [throwing back], *rejecto sagulo.* [5] [The Forum.] [6] The natural sons of his daughter Julia and [M.] Agrippa. [7] The elder in his twelfth, the younger in his thirteenth consulate. [8] The first of January, or New-year's day.

a By the law called *Annalis*, that L. Julius, or Villius rather, promulged, required it was that a consul should not be under the age of 43. Yet for their worthiness and demerits [57], some attain to that dignity under 30.

b Like unto this was the speech of that centurion who, being sent by Julius Caesar dictator, for to have the time of his government and conduct of an army in the province prorogued, standing before the door of the senate-house, and taking knowledge that it would not be granted, shook his sword-hilt with his hand and said, *Hic prorogabit,* This then shall prorogue it.

27. [1] That was the colour and pretence of it. [2] [Who could be prevailed upon by entreaties. Now only used with the negative prefix.] [3] [Nothing is known of him.] [4] Or Vinius, for so was his patron named. [5] [*Paganus*, a civilian as opposed to a soldier.] [6] [*Curiosus*, inquisitive, a prying person, much the same as spy ; *speculator* is properly a scout.] [7] [Disparage, speak ill of.] [8] [Folded tablets.] [9] [Released him from confinement. The noun " enlargement " still has this sense.] [10] Lustrum was a space of five years.

---

[1] [If intended as an equivalent of *festina lente*, this is hardly appropriate.]

OCTAVIUS CAESAR AUGUSTUS

28. [1] The said Antony [this should be Augustus].   [2] Augustus [long of=along of, owing to him.]   [3] *Ac senatum :* or *e senatu,* out of the senate.   [4] Or, of his acts and proceedings in the government. [5] Base, or pedestal.   [6] As if he had been a god himself, according to the saying, *Sapiens ipse fingit fortunam sibi.*

29. [1] [On the Palatine hill.]   [2] [The word decury was applied to any division of a large whole, not necessarily consisting of ten.]   [3] His daughter's children by Agrippa.   [4] *Atrium libertatis* (Gr. αἴθριον). A place where learned men were wont to meet and confer, as our merchants do in the Royal Exchange, built not unlike unto it with arched walks on every side standing upon pillars : and as this cloister was called *peristylium,* so the open yard within was called *Atrium,* or *subdival* [*sub divo,* in the open air].

[a] Three such halls there were in Rome, wherein judicial courts were held, and causes pleaded : 1. *Romanum,* which was so much frequented with lawyers and their clients that Cato the Censor delivered his opinion, that it should be paved with caltrops, to keep out that rabble which haunted it ; 2. *Julium* or *Caesaris,* that Caesar dictator built, and adjoined thereto the temple of Venus Genetrix ; 3. *Augusti,* whereto was annexed by him one temple of Mars Revenger ; for another he erected in the capitol, after he had regained from the Parthians the Roman standards and military ensigns, which they won from Crassus.

[b] An amphitheatre and a theatre differ as the full moon from the half, or a complete roundel from a semicircle.

30. [1] [Rubbish.]   [2] About £450,000 : *see* C. 18, Annot.]

[a] Pliny writeth [*Nat. Hist,* iii, 66] that Rome was divided into fourteen regions or wards, and into more than a thousand streets.

31. [1] [The so-called Sibylline oracles.]   [2] [Public health or welfare, worshipped as a goddess.]   [3] [The Lares of the cross-ways (*compita*).] [4] *Supposuit :* some read *superposuit* [placed it upon such an arched Janus or thoroughfare].   [*Regia :* not " palace," but " colonnade."]

[a] Augurs were certain priests employed about the observation of birds, and from them out of their learning gave directions.   In number at first they were but three, belonging unto the three ancient tribes of Rome.   In process of time there was a college or convent of them to the number of 24[1], namely, in the days of Sulla dictator : so that I doubt not but among these were some appointed for this ministry, either about the goddess Salus, unto whom there was likewise a temple built, or else in the name and behalf of the people, *Captare Augurium salutis,* which, as Dio [xxxvii, 24] maketh report, was in this manner : " That they should call unto god for safety, if he would permit, as if it were not lawful to crave it at the gods' hands, unless they first granted it."   And one day every year was chosen for this business, in which no army did set forth to war, no man warred against them, nor took weapon in hand to fight ; a thing that could not be during the late troubles and civil wars.   No marvel therefore if, this function being forelet [37] was now taken up again by Augustus, when by occasion of peace he did shut the temple of Janus.   And as this function was called *Augurium,* so I see no reason but the very augurship or sacerdotal dignity itself in this place might be named *Augurium,* in the same form that, presently after, the flamenship or priesthood belonging to Jupiter is named *Flaminium ;* and this I take to be the meaning of our author.

---

[1] [There were really only 15 in Sulla's time ; Caesar increased the number to 16.]

OCTAVIUS CAESAR AUGUSTUS

^b Which were solemnised once in a hundred, or, as some say, a hundred and ten years.

32. ¹ [Swaggered about.]　　² [Short swords or daggers.]　　³ In manner of bridewells or houses of correction.　　⁴ [Swashbucklers.] ⁵ Or obligations.　　⁶ *Exussit;* or *excussit,* cancelled.　　⁷ [Not necessarily immoral : Acts xvii, 5, certain lewd fellows of the baser sort.] ⁸ Or, cause.　　⁹ Law-days, or pleading time.　　¹⁰ *Liberalia, Bacchanalia, Praetoria,* or others in the honour of men living, which might be well spared.　　¹¹ For that they were valued at 200 sestertia [about £1800], whereas the other were worth 400.　　¹² Or 20 rather, for the ordinary age was 25 years, at which they were eligible.　　¹³ *Quarto quoque anno,* every fourth year.　　¹⁴ Upon certain days of those months, during which there were sports and revels and the licentious feast *Saturnalia.*

^a By which addition there were in the year 230 law-days or pleadable [days, on which causes could be pleaded].

33. ¹ [Bag, Fr. *malle ;* budget=pouch, wallet, Fr. *bouge(tte)* : in the modern use, budget apparently=the dispatch box, which the Chancellor was said to open, when introducing his financial statement.]

^a *More maiorum* ordained it was, that a parricide should first be beaten with rods, and then sewn within a leather male or budget together with a dog, a cock, a viper, and an ape, and so thrown into the sea or some running water.

^b Whereof Cornelius Sulla was the author, entitled : *de falsis,* or *testamentaria.*

34. ¹ *De pudicitia* or *impudicitia.*　　² Of living unmarried.　　³ After the decease of a former wife or husband.　　⁴ Unripe age, under 12 years.　　⁵ By means of divorces.

^a Many laws went under the title *Sumptuaria,* to repress the immoderate expense in apparel, and belly-cheer especially ; as namely, Fannia, Didia, Oppia, Cornelia, Julia, as well Caesaris as Augusti. But in the time of Tiberius Caesar, notwithstanding he did what he could to keep them in force, yet they were all abrogated.

^b *Lex Julia, Caesaris et Augusti, de Adulteriis et Pudicitia.* For albeit the law Scantinia [*Domitian,* 8] provided against the latter, to wit Paederasty, yet the penalty thereof by virtue of the said law was but *pecuniaria,* a money matter, whereas by Julia it was *capitalis,* worthy of death. And that Augustus established and enforced this law against incontinence, it may appear by this, that Sextus Aurelius reproved him because, being himself given to lasciviousness, yet he was a most severe and sharp chastiser of that vice ; as also by that answer of a young man, whom he for committing adultery with his daughter Julia smote with his own hands, who thereupon cried out, Νόμον ἔθηκας, ὦ Καῖσαρ. Thou hast made a law, O Caesar. Now as touching the foresaid law Scantinia, it was so called (as Valerius Maximus writeth [vi, 1, 7]) by occasion of one Scantinius, a tribune of the commons, who against kind [C. 52] had abused a son of Marcellus, and was therefore condemned accordingly.

^c *De ambitu.* Of which there were divers, namely, Acilia Calpurnia, Aufidia, Baebia Aemilia, Cornelia Fulvia, Maria, Pompeia, Poetelia, Tullia and Julia, Caesaris and Augusti.

^d *Lex Papia Poppaea, de maritandis ordinibus,* whereof there were many branches and chapters, not only respecting this conjunction of the gentry and commons, but also concerning penalties to be laid

28

upon those that neglected marriage, and rewards due to such as lived in wedlock and begat children, etc.

35. [1] *Abortivos* : some read *orcivos* or *orcinos, velut Orco seu terra natos,* obscure and base [Orcinos (of the dead), the reading now generally accepted = *lit.* belonging to Orcus (the lower world, or its ruler), those admitted to the senate by virtue of the dead Caesar's will]. [2] 300 [stent = stint = limit]. [3] [An historian who lived in the time of Augustus and Tiberius : see Tiberius, 61.] [4] For taking upon them that dignity. [5] Among other senators. [6] And that they should not need to come and salute him, but save that labour. [7] Haply, by reason of vintage that was not to be neglected.

[a] The badges that distinguished senators from others were, their robes purfled or embroidered with broad studs of purple like nail-heads, called thereupon *lati clavi,* and shoes with peaks resembling the horned tips or pointed ends of the moon, named therefore *Calcei lunati,* in token of their ancient nobility, as some interpret it.

[b] These solemn feasts, at which senators were allowed to be present, were *Epulum Jovis,* otherwise called *Cena Dialis* within the Capitol : likewise *Cena Triumphalis Pontificalis,* and *Auguralis,* the sumptuous suppers to the honour of Jupiter, at triumphs, given by the pontiffs and augurs.

[c] The first day of every month.

[d] The 15th of March, May, July, and October, the 13th of the rest.

36. [1] *Acta Senatus* and not *Senatusconsulta :* he meaneth *Diurna acta,* the proceedings that passed there every day of sitting [Julius Caesar had ordained the contrary]. [2] [Tents, Fr. *halles.*] [3] Ten men either chosen out of the centumvirs by lot, or created of purpose.

[a] A judicial court there was at Rome called *Centumviralis Hasta,* for that it consisted of certain commissioners or judges named *Centumviri,* the hundred men, before whom were debated civil matters and causes between citizen and citizen, of no great importance. Chosen these were out of every tribe three ; and those were in all 35, which number doth arise to 105, but in round reckoning they went for a hundred [*hasta* or spear, the symbol of legal ownership, was set up in front of the centumviral court, which decided questions of property].

37. [1] [Prefecture.] [2] An office which three men jointly bare. [3] [Renounced, abandoned.]

38. [1] Colonels of 1000 footmen. [2] [Cavalry divisions.] [3] *Transvectio* [a festal parade of the equites or knights].

[a] What these ornaments and badges were, T. Livius reporteth in the 30th book [ch. 15] of his *Roman History :* to wit, a crown of gold, and a fair golden bowl ; a curule ivory chair, with a staff likewise or sceptre of ivory ; a long robe embroidered of sundry colours, and a rich coat of needlework representing the date-tree [*palmata :* rather, embroidered with palm-branches].

[b] This solemn show or riding of Roman gentlemen was upon the ides, the 15th day of *Quintilis* (July) yearly. Instituted first by Fabius Rutilianus in the honour of Castor and Pollux, who appeared unto the Romans at the battle near the lake Regillus, what time they achieved a noble victory. [Livy, ix, 46, ascribes its institution to the censors Q. Fabius and P. Decius, 304 B.C. ; Dionysius of Halicarnassus (vi, 13) to the dictator Albinus Postumius, after the battle of lake Regillus.] They rode from the temple of Honour, as some write, or as others, of Mars without the walls, through the Forum, and by the

temple of Castor, up into the capitol, dight with chaplets of olive branches, as Pliny writeth (*Nat. Hist.* xv, 19).

39. [1] *A senatu* or *senatoribus*, out of the senator's degree. [2] Wherein were written all their faults [*pugillares*, small waxed tablets].

40. [1] Of gentlemen, or of the senators. [2] *Parentibus :* comprehending all ancestors. [3] 400 *sestertia* or 400,000 *sestertii* [about £3500]. [4] [Made up a list or register, *not* the same as taking a census.] [5] [*Curiose*, carefully.] [6] By black he meaneth cloaks or gowns of a self-russet colour ; for their gowns should be white and fair, not sullied. [7] By the trope *Ironia*, meaning those that were in cloaks or foul gowns. [8] [Virgil, *Aeneid*, i, 282.]

[a] By this it appeareth that ordinarily he might not be a tribune of the commons, who was not a senator ; for, albeit this be a plebeian magistrate, yet might a commoner be a senator.

[b] Whereupon Suidas thinketh *Annonas* to take their name, as it were ἀνὰ τὰς νώνας διδόμενας, because corn was wont to be dealt among the people upon the nones of every month, namely, the seventh day of March, May, July and October, and the fifth of the rest ; whereas indeed *Annona* is derived *ab anno*, the year, as it were *annalis alimonia*, the year's provision of food.

[c] It seemeth that Augustus held of two tribes : to wit, Scaptia, unto which the Octavii belonged, and wherein he was born, and Fabia, by his adoption into the family of the Julii.

[d] For, howsoever the Roman habit was the gown, yet permitted were they upon necessity, namely, to save the said gown in foul weather, or to defend themselves from cold, to cast over it a cloak in any frequented place of the city, as were the Forum, the common pleading courtyard or market-place, and the Circus.

41. [1] The Ptolemies. [2] Duple the worth of gentlemen. [3] [Commonly.]

42. [1] [Careful of.] [2] [*Salubrem :* rather, one who looked after his people's welfare.] [3] [Taken measures.] [4] [Put to such straits.]

43. [1] [An enclosure in the Campus Martius, where the people assemble to vote.] [2] Or, lamed. [3] His lightness was more to be noted than his short stature : for whereas the full height is six feet and the weight somewhat above 100 pounds, this levity of two feet is under that proportion the one half. [4] *Superque se :* or, behind at his back higher, and therefore farther off ; or else, in a second seat from him of the one side, but in the same rank for honour sake. [5] [Slack, disregarding rules (C. 76).] [6] [" To " is superfluous : *recepit* probably = received with due respect, although, according to an old use, " receive " might mean " made room for him " = vouchsafed a rowme.] [7] [Or, *rowme* = room.]

44. [1] Or, a rank of their own. [2] And by consequence farther off. [3] Which himself exhibited, being *pontifex maximus*, or high priest. [4] Eleven of the clock, by which hour all that sight was past.

[a] For the ordinary Roman gowns were white and fair-kept.

[b] Of these spectacles and games, some were *Matutini*, some *Meridiani*, and other *Pomeridiani*, according as they were exhibited in the morning, at noon, and afternoon.

45. [1] [The imperial box.]   [2] [Devote his whole attention to.] [3] As if he had no delight in those games.   [4] [Prove or try masteries = try conclusions.]   [5] *Pugiles*, answerable in Greece to the Roman gladiators.   [6] And so had learned the skill and feat of fighting. [7] [Deal heavy blows.]   [8] [Attack their competitors.]   [9] [This is incorrect. The meaning is, he prohibited combats of gladiators, unless they were allowed the right of appealing to the people that their lives might be spared if they were *defeated*.]   [10] By beating with rods. [11] Praetors and aediles.   [12] [The same as shorn.]   [13] Of Pompey, Balbus, and Metellus. For so many there were in Augustus's days, besides the amphitheatre of Statilius Taurus.   [14] A cunning actor counterfeiting all parts.   [15] [Made him conspicuous.]

[a] These were called likewise sacred games, as stage-plays, gymnastic exercises, and masteries in music, in Nero's time.

[b] They took that name of a spacious gallery or walking-place called *Xystos*, wherein they were wont to exercise in winter-time.

46. [a] Colonies were townships in Italy and other provinces planted with Roman inhabitants ; in which *decuriones*, as one would say aldermen, had the same authority as senators in Rome.

47. [a] Hereupon some provinces were called *Caesaris*, or *praesidiariae :* namely, which were ruled by the emperor's sole appointment, and had strong garrisons placed in them : others, *Populi*, and they were named *praetoriae*, *consulares*, or *proconsulares*, governed by praetors, consuls, or their vicegerents.

49. [1] *Superi*, called otherwise the Adriatic sea, gulf of Venice. [2] *Inferi*, otherwise Tuscus, or Tyrrhenus, the Tuscan sea.   [3] People of Spain.   [4] [Hire for pay.]   [5] Fees, pensions, land and living. [6] [According to the Ancyra monument, he gave out of his own patrimony 170,000,000 sesterces. Legacy duties and a tax on goods exposed for sale were included.]

50. [1] A cunning lapidary and graver in precious stones.

[a] There is a kind of monkey or marmoset in Ethiopia, going under the name of Sphinx, in Pliny [*Nat. Hist.* viii, 21, 72]. The poets also feign that a certain monstrous beast, so called, sometimes did haunt the city of Thebes and the territory about it ; which from a rock proposed riddles unto the passengers. This monster, by their report, carried the resemblance of three creatures, to wit, a fowl, a lion, and a maiden, according to these verses of Ausonius [Griphus Ternarii Numeri, 40-41] :

> *Terruit Aoniam volucris, leo, virgo triformis*
> *Sphinx, volucris pennis, pedibus fera, fronte puella,*
>> A three-shap'd sphinx, bird-lion-maid,
>> Aonian land did fright,
>> In wing a fowl, in feet a beast,
>> In face a virgin [bright].

Pliny writeth in the last book of his *Natural History* [xxxvii, 2, 9], that Augustus used at the beginning to sign with this sphinx engraven upon his signet. " And verily," quoth he, " in the casket of his mother's jewels two of these he found, so like that one could not be discerned from the other. And as he was wont to wear the one wheresoever he went, so in his absence during the civil wars with Antony, his friends that managed his affairs at Rome sealed with the other those missives and edicts which passed in his name. And from hence it came, that those who received any such letters or edicts containing matter of difficulty, were wont merrily to say, that the said sphinx came ever with some hard riddle or other, which could not be assoiled [solved]. Whereupon Augustus, to avoid the obloquy that arose by his sphinx, gave over sealing therewith, and signed always after with the image of king Alexander the Great."

51. [1] [Examples, instances.]   [2] *Male opinari*. The same in this author as *Male dicere* [abuse].   [3] [Hesitate.]   [4] Young : imputing his choler and cruelty to the heat of youth and hot blood, measuring Tiberius by himself.

[a] This humanity and affable courtesy, termed by Suetonius *civilitas*, was reproved in Alexander [Severus] the emperor by his mother and wife both, as not beseeming the majesty of a prince ; for they told him many times that thereby he caused his imperial power and dignity to be the more contemptible : " Yea, but it is by that means," quoth he, " both surer, and like also to last the longer " [Lampridius, *Life of Alexander Severus*, 20].

52. [1] With the money for which they were sold.   [2] *Cortinas*, otherwise called *tripodas*, standing upon three feet, from which oracles were delivered.

53. [1] *Domini*, or Sir.   [2] Or interlude, *mimo*.   [3] Or Sir. [4] [Jest.]   [5] [Deceitful, flattering.]   [6] [*Non temere*, hardly ever.] [7] [*i.e.* to avoid troubling any one to do him honour.]   [8] *Adoperta :* if *adaperta*, the sense is contrary.   [9] [Politeness.]   [10] [Reached, presented.]   [11] *Stipem*, which Quintilian [Inst. Orat. vi, *de Risu*] renders *as*.   [12] Or *nomenclator*.   [13] As birthdays and marriage-minds [commemoration].   [14] Assurance-making of a marriage [betrothal].

[a] This name *dominus* among the Romans, like as sir with us, was diversely used. In the sense of imperious and lordly command, as we sometime take it [Lord], it was odious, as having a relation to *servus*, a slave or villein. To mollify therefore the harshness of the word, they used to term householders or masters of families, *patres familias*, instead of *dominos*, as also household servants *familiares*, and not *servos*. Otherwise they used it by way of flattery or fair speech, as appeareth in Claudius, 21. Hence it is, that lovers call their sweet-hearts, *dominas*, mistresses. Also, if a man speaketh unto one, whom he either knoweth not, or hath forgotten, he saith, *domine*, Here you, Sir, according to that epigram in Martial [i, 112] :

> *Cum te non nossem, dominum regemque vocabam.*
> All while that I you kenned not, I called you Lord and King.

Last of all, by way of scorn and derision, and so the same Martial testifieth in this distich [v, 57] :

> *Cum voco te dominum, noli tibi, Cinna, placere ;*
> *Saepe etiam servum sic resaluto meum.*
> When I, O Cinna, call you sir, joy not, I you advise ;
> For even my servant I salute ofttimes no otherwise.

In which manner we speak unto our servant, or any other in contempt, by this term sirrah, to say nothing of sir knave. No marvel therefore, if Augustus could not abide this word *dominus* so doubtfully taken, and seldom in good sense.

[b] If you read [*adoperta*], close and shut, it may have reference to this, that he took not state upon him, nor sought the people's applause, which accordeth to his other behaviour reported before. If [*adaperta*],

open, it showeth likewise his courteous carriage and affability, as who was ready to accept of petitions and requests, a thing right commendable in a prince ; as it is written of king Artaxerxes surnamed Mnemon, how, riding in a carroch with his queen, he commanded her to draw open the curtains thereof, that he might the better attend upon his subjects. And this agreeth as well with that which followeth of Augustus. And hereto I rather incline.

c He looked not for their attendance at home in his own house, neither would he be thought to have conferred with any one privately, as touching the public affairs.

d It is generally a received opinion that, within seven natural days, such voluntary abstinence from food is not mortal, as Pliny writeth in his eleventh book, who reporteth also, that many have continued fasting more than eleven days, which I easily believe. For, in mine own knowledge, I may be bold to report, that a bitch lived so long, and yet died not, nor miscarried the whelps within her. Some melancholic persons, therefore, may within the latitude of health endure so long, yea, and those likewise who are fraught top-full with a balance of crude and cold humours, which may engender a quartan ague as well as melancholy doth. For I doubt not but in such chronic diseases, occasioned and maintained by gross matters, one may abide above eleven days without all manner of food. Yet Aulus Gellius saith, that beyond seven days' wilful abstinence a man is not able to live.

54. [1] [Understood.]   [2] As if Augustus by his absolute power had taken up all.   [3] *Cum vir virum*, not *triumvirum*.

55. [1] Wherein the manner was to use broad jests of any person (Casaubon).

a For, as Ulpian testifieth, l. 18, *de Testamento*, a law there was that whosoever to the infamy of any person published a libel, either in his own or another man's name, yea, without name at all, if he be convict thereof, shall be *Intestabilis*, disabled both for making a will himself, and also for to be a witness unto another man's.

56. [1] *In tribu*, or in *tribubus*, among other tribes.   [2] Called *Forum Augusti*.   [3] Than the other.   [4] Or, offender.   [5] Within the bar, among the advocates, as a well-willer.   [6] Or targeteer, *scutario ;* some take this for a proper name of some soldier of his.

a By these candidates he meaneth either such as himself recommended unto the people for any office, as Caesar his predecessor did before him, and those were called *Caesaris candidati*, or else his especial friends whom he laboured for.

b Pliny [*Nat. Hist.* xxxv, 12, 164] writeth that Cassius his accuser charged him to have killed 130 guests, with one platter of poisoned meat.

c Certain soldiers there were, going under the name of *scutarii*, as Paulus Diaconus witnesseth in his supplement upon Eutropius, writing that Valentinian of a tribune or colonel over these *Scutarii* became emperor.

57. [1] [Merits.]   [2] Into the railed or empaled place named *Septa*, where sometime was that lake.   [3] In the Shoemakers' street.   [4] In the Tragedians' street.   [5] On the Palatine hill.   [6] [*Denarius*, at this time=about 8½d.]   [7] *Faustis ominibus*, or, *nominibus*, names. [According to Murray's Dictionary, this use of osses as an equivalent of *omina* is chiefly confined to H.]

58. [1] Or, addition.   [2] Father of the Country.

59. [1] *Patres familias*, good honest citizens of Rome that were *sui juris*.   [2] Their fathers, the testators.   [3] As if he had been a demigod.

62. [1] [Shrewish, railing.]

63. [1] Her daughter's husband.   [2] It seemeth the younger.   [3] Emperor after him.   [4] Iotapas [Artavasdes, whose daughter was Iotape] the Median king of Armenia : or else he meaneth Cleopatra [p. 48].

64. [1] *Sororis*, or uxoris, his wife's nephew, and both true.   [2] [*Natare :* another reading is *notare*, to make shorthand notes.]

[a] Germanicus was the son of Drusus, and Antonia the younger. Now Drusus had for his mother, Livia, the wife of Augustus, and Antonia for hers, Octavia, the sister of Augustus.

[b] In all bargains of sale and alienations, the solemn and ceremonial form [*mancipatio*] at Rome was this : that [with] five witnesses at the least, Roman citizens and of lawful age, with one other beside of the same condition, called *Libripens* (because he held a pair of balances, etc.) the chapman or buyer should come with a piece of brass coin in his hand, and say (for example sake, if it were a bondslave to be bought and sold) these words, " This man or woman I avouch by the law of the Romans to be mine, and bought I have him or her for this piece of brass, and with this brazen balance," and therewith, striking the said balance, give the brazen piece unto the other party that is the seller, by which imaginary kind of chaffering things were alienated, and their property changed.

[c] So ordinary it was to train up youth in swimming and in grammar [1], of which the one had relation to the exercise of the body, the other of the mind, that of such as had no bringing up at all arose this proverb, μήτε νεῖν, μήτε γράμματα.

65. [1] [Unchastity.]   [2] Two of his nephews.   [3] These acts were called *leges curiatae*, made in a parliament of all the *curiae*, in number 30, into which Romulus divided the city. These laws Sextus Papirius collected into one book, and called it was *jus civile Papirianum*. [4] *Sordidum :* others read *stolidum*, and *horridum*, sottish and rude. [5] Pandataria [Tacitus, *Ann.* i, 53 ; xiv, 63].   [6] [Save, preserve. Rather, " he wished them such wives and daughters."]

[a] Gaius was sent by Augustus with an army to suppress the troubles and insurrections in the East parts, where he was stabbed treacherously, with a knife or short skene [Aug. 32], by one who presented unto him a supplication, of which wound he died afterwards. A. Lucius likewise he sent into Armenia, recommending him unto the gods in these words, that they would vouchsafe him as well-beloved as Pompey, as valorous as king Alexander, and as fortunate as himself.

[b] These he adopted, because they were out of the tuition of their fathers (deceased) in the common hall or Forum, before the high priests, and with consent of the people, by virtue of the *lex Curiata*, and this was properly called adoption ; whereas sufficient it was to adopt others abovenamed with the assent of their fathers, by the formal bargain of sale called *mancipatio*.

[c] Certain quaestors there were, named also *Candidati Principis*, whose office it was to read such missives or letters in the senate.

---

[1] Reading and writing.

[d] Happily [possibly] this he did to know thereby, whether she had been naught [C. 6] of her body with them or no, considering we learn out of natural philosophy that commonly children resemble their parents in complexion, favour, and marks. Howbeit, this Julia is reported to have brought forth children all like unto M. Agrippa, her husband, so long as he lived, notwithstanding she was known to be a common strumpet. But beside her answer to that point, unto those who made a wonder at it, which ye may see in Macrob. *Saturnal.* ii, 5, read the pleasant and witty epigram of Sir Thomas More, upon the like example.

[e] Alluding to a place of Homer, *Iliad*, iii [40], wherein Hector curseth his brother Paris, and after some opprobrious terms saith thus,

αἴθ' ὄφελές τ' ἄγονός τ' ἔμεναι, ἄγαμός τ' ἀπολέσθαι,

Would God thou had'st of women ne'er been born,
Or else had died thy wedding day befor(n)e.

Which verse, by inversion of words and using one of them in a contrary sense, Augustus transferred unto his own person. For it is to be noted that ἄγονος here in Homer hath a passive signification, and soundeth as much as μὴ γεννηθείς, not born, whereas Augustus taketh it in the active, for one that is childless, or hath begotten no children[1].

[f] These cancers be certain tumours or swellings, hard and unequal of their nature, which be called scirrhi, and of an ugly aspect, as arising from unnatural melancholy, breeding, as Cornelius Celsus writeth [v, 28], for the most part in the superior region of the body, about the face, nose, ears, lips, and women's breasts. Which our author here and the Greek writers name *Carcinomata*, for the resemblance of the crab-fish crooked claws, which the black or swart veins all about them do represent, or because they be hardly or uneth[2] removed, if they once take to a place, no more than the said fish when it settleth to a thing and claspeth it. Untoward to be healed, and commonly the worse for all the cure done unto them. These cancers, if they become ulcers once are termed wolves. In regard of which properties, aptly compared Augustus those ungracious imps of his breed unto them, as being foul eyesores, distaining his honour, and by no discipline of his corrigible [omitted in 1606 trans., as noted in Tudor Translations].

66. [1] M. Agrippa. [2] *Frigoris :* or *rigoris*, as if Augustus had looked sternly or strangely upon him. [3] Maecenas. [4] [Traffic in : *cp.* the modern termination—monger.] [5] Final or last.

[a] According to that sage precept of Solon, τοὺς φίλους μὴ ταχὺ κτῶ[3], Be not hasty in making any thy friends, and the saying of Hecuba in Euripides [*Troades*, 1051],

[οὐκ] ἔστ' ἐραστής, ὅστις οὐκ αἰεὶ φιλεῖ,

No friend, I say,
Who loves not ay ;

which two rules Propertius [II, xx, 35, 36] elegantly comprehendeth in one verse,

*Hoc mihi perpetuo jus est, quòd solus amator
Nec cito desisto, nec temere incipio,*
Late ere I love, as long ere I leave.

[b] Aesop gave this lesson, τῇ γυναικὶ μηδέποτε πιστεύσῃς ἀπόρρητα,

---

[1] Or, is unable for generation.
[2] [With difficulty.]
[3] [The folio has κάτα, which is unintelligible.]

Commit no secrets to a woman. And as for this Maecenas, he was noted to be *uxorius* more than he should, and one who (albeit his wife was a shrew and ready to go from him every day) soon admitted atonements and reconciliations. Whereupon Seneca in his Moral Epistles [114] said that, having but one wife, yet he married a thousand times.

67. [1] [This must be " detected " (*compertum*).]   [2] Clerk or secretary.   [3] Lycia.

68. [1] A kind of psilothrum [depilatory].

[a] Every word almost in this verse carrieth a double construction, without the understanding whereof all the grace is lost. For *cinaedus* in one sense betokeneth one of the Galli, priests of the goddess Cybele, named also *Ops Mater deum*, and *Tellus*, even the very earth ; which priests were gelded or disabled for generation, and took that name of the river Gallus, the water whereof, drunken, caused men to be evirate and effeminate. Now the manner of these priests in the divine service of the said goddess was to bear the taber or tamper[1] upon the timbrel, which is expressed here in these words, *Orbem digito temperat ;* for that the timbrel is round and circular, to signify the globe of the earth symbolised by Cybele. And in this sense may the verse literally be interpreted ; but, beside this signification, *cinaedus* betokeneth a wanton pathic or catamite, who suffereth himself against nature to be abused. *Orbis* also is put for the habitable world, and *digito temperat* is as much to say as he hath the world at a beck, or at his command, as if the same were ruled by Augustus Caesar, who was noted for that abominable filthiness. And in this latter sense did the people of Rome expound the said verse, and apply it unto him.

69. [1] [It made no difference.]   [2] Whom he could not forbear but marry when she was great with child.   [3] His own wife.   [4] [Outspoken.]   [5] [Examine.]   [6] Tertia, Terentia, Rufa, as lovers use to name their sweethearts.   [7] [" Not " is superfluous.]

70. [1] *Choragus*, or one to provide the furniture [and expenses] of the feasts. [*Mensa* perhaps = company, band, the choragus being Augustus.] [2] Some take this to be the name of one of the six goddesses' guests : or rather, some dame that could skill in bringing such together [or the wife of the choragus].   [3] *Thronos* [others read *toros*], beds ; or *tholos*, scutcheons in architecture.   [4] Not counterfeit, as at the supper overnight.

[a] Of twelve gods and goddesses together, alluding to those six select gods, and as many goddesses whom antiquity in heathenesse honoured above the rest ; whose names Ennius the poet comprised in these two verses,

Juno, Vesta, Minerva, Ceres, Diana, Venus, Mars,
Mercurius, Jovis[2], Neptunus, Vulcanus, Apollo.

Answerable to which number he entertained six young women attired like goddesses, and six boys (catamites) in habit of gods, as his guests at this supper.

---

[1] [Probably formed from *temperat*, and used by H. (according to Murray, the only author in whom it occurs) in the sense of " beating, tapping."]
[2] Jupiter.

ᵇ I doubt the first verse of this hexastich is not perfect, for I do not please myself in the translation of it.

ᶜ Neither is it certain what this Mallia should be. Some read Manlia, as if it were the name of a chamber within the castle or citadel of the Capitol, which this banqueting-place of his did counterfeit, and then we must admit the figure *Prosopopaea* [personification of inanimate objects}. Others take Mallia to be the name of some woman, employed in the furnishing and setting out of such a supper.

ᵈ For Augustus not only sat here among the rest in the person of Apollo, but also would sometimes be thought Phoebus, otherwhiles Phoebus his son.

ᵉ For it is not unknown what adulteries the poets talk of between Jupiter and Alcmena, etc., between Mars also and Venus.

ᶠ No marvel if Jupiter Capitolinus, with other gods and goddesses, being before possessed of the Capitol, abandoned their shrines and chapels, when they saw such in place.

ᵍ Wherein tormentors' whips and scourges were to be sold ; and thereupon he took that name of Tortor (like as before he is surnamed Sandaliarius, and Tragoedus) which Augustus seemed now to verify in himself, whipping and plaguing the people with hunger, as he did.

71. [1] [Charge.]   [2] Or murrha [murra] the cassidony [=chalcedony, from Chalcedon in Asia Minor].   [3] [Was not ashamed.] [4] Between dishes or courses of services.   [5] Or bones.   [6] [We kept things warm at the gaming-table.]   [7] Drusus Nero.   [8] [Tolerably.]   [9] [Or cockall, a game played with sheeps' bones instead of dice.]

ᵃ In which month the feast *Saturnalia* was kept, and much liberty tolerated of gaming, feasting, and revelling.

ᵇ In this game called in Latin *Lusus talorum*, or *Talarius*, there is some resemblance of our dice, but that the *tali* have but four faces or sides, and therefore yield four chances and no more. Of which the first is named *Canis* or *Canicula*, answering as some think to our *Ace*, and is the worst of all. The opposite unto it they termed *Venus* or *Cous*, and [it] is accounted the best, as which may stand for our *Sise*. The third bare the name of *Chius*, proportioned to *Trey* with us : and the last *Senio*, and is as much as *Quatre*. For in these *tali* or cockall bones there is no chance of *Deux* or *Cinque*.

ᶜ *Quinquatrus*, or *Quinquatria*, were certain festival holidays held for five days together in the month March to the honour of Minerva. See Ovid [*Fasti*, iii, 809] ; Varro [de Lingua Lat. vi, 14].

72. [1] [On which were some jewellers' or ringmakers' (*anulus*, ring) shops.]   [2] [Receipt, reception of visitors ; probably originally spacious accommodation for that purpose (*laxitas*).]   [3] Or τεχνόφυον. [4] *Xysti*, admitting the winter sun.   [5] For shade in summer.   [6] *Beluarum*, as whales, whirpooles [whirlpools, sea-monsters of the whale kind], etc.

ᵃ For pleasure therein he called it Syracuse, comparing it to that beautiful city in Sicily ; and because it served his turn for meditations and inventions, he gave it the name τεχνόφυον [study].

73. [1] Not raised up and swelling high with down.   [2] [Seldom.] [3] [Tight, close.]

74. [1] *Cena recta*, or *recta* absolutely [a regular, formal supper, when the guests reclined at the tables], in difference of *sportula* [a dole given in place of a regular meal].   [2] Restored to his blood and created a

gentleman, for he was *donatus aureis anulis ut inter ingenuos haberetur.*
³ *Speculator,* or a squire of his body.   ⁴ *Tribus ferculis,* not such as
ours be, but framed in manner of trophies, with devices that some
meats might lie flat, others hang thereupon.   ⁵ As minstrels, musicians, choristers [*acroama,* Gr. ἀκρόαμα, *lit.* something heard, hence,
performers].   ⁶ As fortune-tellers, jugglers, buffoons [trivial, *triviales,*
picked up in the street].   ⁷ *Aretalogos* [second-rate Cynics or Stoics,
who were always talking about virtue (ἀρετή)].   Or, story-tellers.

ᵃ Employed, as it should seem, in his civil wars.   Certain soldiers
there were attending upon the prince under the name of *speculatores,*
whose service he used in spying and listening.   In Greek such were
named Ὀπτῆρες, σκοποί, and κατάσκοποι.   Also in doing execution
upon condemned persons, and in sending of letters unto the senate, as
Laevinus Torrentius hath observed very well in his annotations upon
Gaius Caligula.

75. ¹ [Probably " at " should be supplied.]   ² Or fire-forks.
³ Or snippers [tongs, *obs.* form of scissors].   ⁴ [Dealing in, trafficking
in.]   ⁵ A kind of lottery.   ⁶ [Board, table.]

76. ¹ Or cheat [second quality bread : *cf.* modern " seconds "].
² Much like *angelots* [small cheeses made in Normandy], *manu pressum*
or *mane pressum,* green cheese new-made.   ³ Or German, *essedum*
[really a *Gallic* war-chariot], for they were used in both countries
indifferently.   ⁴ *Uvis duracinis,* or, with hard kernels.   ⁵ [Bath,
Fr. *bain.*]   ⁶ *Ex hac inobservantia,* or, *ex hac observantia,* upon this
due observing of his, to eat when his stomach called for it, and not else
[retchless = reckless, careless].

ᵃ *Sabbatis ieiunium servat.* If Sabbaths be put for weeks, as the
manner of the Jews was to speak, according as the publican saith
in the gospel after Saint Luke, νηστεύω δὶς τοῦ Σαββάτου, and as it
appeareth in other places of the evangelists, true it is that Suetonius
or Augustus reporteth of the Jews, as also if by Sabbaths are meant
other of their festival and solemn days.   But if you take it for the
seventh or last day of the week, it is altogether untrue, and to be imputed unto the error and ignorance of Suetonius and the Romans
in the Jewish rites and ceremonies.   For seeing them religiously to
keep the said seventh day or Sabbath holy, whereupon they were commonly called *Sabbatarii,* and observing withal their fasting, generally
it was thought of strangers that they fasted upon the Sabbath.   Also
for their devout fasting against the feast of the Passover, called by
themselves sometime the great Sabbath, as also by foreigners, as it
appeareth by Horace [*Satires,* i, 9, 69], in this piece of verse, *Hodie
tricesima Sabbata,* etc., they imagined that the Jews fasted every
Sabbath.   And in truth, reckon from September (at which month
the Jews in one computation begin their year) thirty weeks forward,
you come unto their *Pascha ;* according to which time we Christians
also do celebrate our feast of Easter.   This only is the difference between us and them, for that they observe the *Neomenia* or new moon at
the spring equinox, and solemnise their Passover in the next full moon,
and we, the Lord's day or Sunday after the said full.

77. ¹ Six measures, containing either 2 ounces apiece, or two cyathi,
3 ounces ; in all, at the most not above a good pint, or a small wine
quart, called *sextarius,* consisting of 18 ounces.   ² *Interdiu,* as we
say, betwixt meals.   ³ *Acidum,* or *aridum,* dried, but yet of a winish
taste.   ⁴ [Attaching much importance to.]

OCTAVIUS CAESAR AUGUSTUS

78. [1] [Rather, members of the household.] [2] [Business, official duties. So above, instead of "worldly affairs of his friends."]

[a] It seemeth he took but a light repast, not putting off his shoes, as the manner was, at full meals.

[b] Some copies have *retectis pedibus*, making (*re*) to be ἐπιτατικόν [intensive], as if he meant very well covered (contrary to the use of that word *retegere*, which otherwise signifieth to uncover) like as *recondere*, to lay up very fast and sure. Others, *retractis*, with his feet somewhat drawn or pulled up to him, in the same sense as Cornelius Celsus useth, *paulum reductis, qui fere jacentibus habitus est*, as he saith, which is the ordinary form of lying, whenas men be in health. Lastly, some read *rejectis*, let down or stretched out to the full length.

[c] Casaubon interpreteth *Lecticulam* as a pallet or low bed made for the nonce, to rest and study upon [by candle-light (*lucubratoria*)].

79. [1] [Daintiness, elegance, trimness.] [2] [Held back. The word in the original is *remollitus*, softened.] [3] [Attentively.] [4] Toward his forehead. [5] *Deductiore*, or as some expound it, sharp and thin [rather, bent inwards]. [6] *Inter aquilum candidumque*, somewhat tanned and sunburnt, as Casaubon seemeth to interpret it.

[a] By whose report he wanted not much of the full height of men, to wit, near six feet, according to Vegetius. Above which stature the growth is somewhat giant-like.

80. [1] Charlemagne his wain [Charles's Wain, Ursa Major, the Plough]. [2] Much like a curry-comb. [3] [Hip-bone.] [4] [Pain, ailment.]

[a] *Ad impetiginis formam.* The second kind whereof, as Cornelius Celsus (v. 28, 17) writeth (for willingly do I often cite him as the Roman Galen, in explication of a Roman writer), *Varias figuras habet*, resembleth many and sundry forms.

[b] This infirmity of his was a kind of gout, which the Greek writers call *Ischias*, and is commonly named sciatica. As for the remedy or palliative cure rather (for easement of pain) with sand, it may be meant either of some fomentations with linen bags wherein was sand, for, Cornelius Caesar [? Celsus] writeth, that millet seed, salt, and sand, or any of them put within a linen cloth, and so applied to the affected place, cure the said disease ; or of walking in sand by the seaside, or else of tumbling and wallowing therein, which remedy Q. Serenus Sammonicus in this verse : *Nec non et tepidis convolvere corpus arenis*, etc., hath prescribed and experience verified.

[c] Cato in his *Husbandry*, and Pliny [*Nat. Hist.* xvii, 28], maketh mention of curing the sciatica with a cleft of a green cane or reed, but there must be, forsooth, a charm go with all, and so it reposeth dislocations or bones out of joint. Indeed, both Dioscorides and also Galen attribute unto the rind or bark of Cane-roots, and to their ashes a desiccative virtue ; whereby they are found good for such dislocations, and so may cure the articular disease likewise, called sciatica, which differeth not much from a dislocation of the huckle-bone.

[d] Pliny reporteth [*Nat. Hist.* xxv, 3], that the disease of the bladder, and especially the strangury, pissing drop-meal[1], occasioned by gravel (which I take here to be meant) is of all others most dolorous.

81. [1] *Destillationibus jocinore vitiato.* What if we thus point and

---

[1] [Drop by drop: *cf.* piece-meal, the only survivor of numerous similarly formed adverbs.]

39

OCTAVIUS CAESAR AUGUSTUS

read ?   *Destillationibus, jocinore vitiato ;* to this sense, that he was much subject to rheums, by occasion that his liver was diseased, to wit, obstructed or stopped.   ² Under the short ribs.   ³ [Severe cold in the head and catarrh.]

ᵃ This accordeth to an observation of Cornelius Celsus : *Qui secundis aliquando frustra curatus est, contrariis aliquando restituitur.* The patient whose cure devised by art, and according to the rule of physic, some-time speedeth not well, recovereth otherwhile by a course of means quite contrary.

ᵇ Which the Greeks call *Periodical,* as the quartan ague and other intermittent fevers be so termed, because their fits return upon certain days. The falling sickness likewise, keeping time with the moon, whereupon some name it *Lunaticus.* And gouts, which are most busy in the spring and the fall, etc.

ᶜ Toward the end of September. An unequal season of the year, wherein commonly the mornings and evenings be cold, and the noon-tides hot, whereby many diseases are occasioned. But as touching the birthday here mentioned, Valerius Maximus [viii, 16] and Pliny [*Nat. Hist.* vii, 51, 172] report, that Antipater Sidonius the poet every year upon the day of his nativity only felt the access of an ague. Where-of he died in the end, after he had lived to a great age.

ᵈ No marvel if in cacochymical bodies, such as his was, the humours which lay still and quiet all winter, began to spread and swell in the spring, causing distensions and ventosities ; especially in that place where they were gathered and laid up as it were in store, to do a mis-chief when the time came.

82. ¹ [Wrapped up.]   ² [Bubbling up, gushing forth.]   ³ Or bongrace [sunshade in front of a cap or bonnet].   ⁴ [Hardly ever.] ⁵ [Slow, leisurely.]   ⁶ In hot waters.   ⁷ [Burning brightly, blaz-ing.]   ⁸ Which naturally were hot, standing upon a vein of brimstone.

ᵃ *Feminalibus et tibialibus.* Instead of our breeches and stockings, the Greeks and Romans used in those days certain loose clothes in manner of swaddling bands to cover and lap their nakedness. And long it was ere they took to any such, unless it were upon occasion of some disease. Witness hereof Philip, king of Macedonia, who, in Plutarch [*Apophthegmata,* 178 C.], when he sat in port-sale [C. 50] of certain slaves or captives, was admonished by one of them to let down his upmost garment for to hide his shame. Julius Caesar also himself, being deadly wounded, was careful to let fall the lap of his gown ¹ for to cover his privy parts when he should fall. In process of time they took to wearing the clothes aforesaid in lieu of *Bracae,* or breeches, which the French and other barbarous nations used ; but they did so in winter only. For otherwise they went ordinarily in those parts without trusses : covering all as mannerly as they could with their loose upper garment, which upon a small occasion were ready to fly open.

ᵇ Partly, to make a noise and so to procure sleep, and in part to refresh and cool the air.

ᶜ As well to cool him as to drive away gnats, for want of curtains or a canopy, which thereof took the name in Greek κωνωπεών or κωνωπεῖον. Now the manner of this winnowing or making wind was for the better and daintier sort, with plumes of peacocks' tails, much like to the fan of feathers used in these days as well as in old time, but for the meaner, with beasts' tails.

ᵈ From Rome to Praeneste or Tibur, is about one hundred *stadia :*

---

¹ [Which usually was cast over the shoulder.]

if then you reckon 125 paces to a *stadium*, it cometh to 12 miles and a half. Cato the Censor was of another mind, who said he repented whensoever he went to any place by water, if he might by land.

e The abstinence whereof in some measure is good for those that have feeble joints, and be remembered otherwhiles with any gout, as Augustus was yet, a thing that physicians in old time could hardly bring their patients unto, so ordinary it was in those days to bath.

f Which the wanton and delicate ladies of Rome, as Pliny writeth, used of silver.

83. ¹ Either on horseback, or in a litter.   ² Two feet and a half square.   ³ [*Ocellata :* small stones marked with little eyes or spots, like dice.]   ⁴ These the Romans called *Delicias suas*, their playferes [playfellows] and darlings in an honest sense ; not such as the Greeks in an unclean signification named *Paidika*, wanton baggages, catamites.

a *Ad pilam.* Whereas there were divers kinds of balls to play with, it seems that he meaneth in this place that which of all other was least and hardest, as being stuffed with hair, whereupon it took the name ; the same no doubt that our tennis-ball is sent to and fro with the racket. Named likewise it was *Trigonalis*, of a tennis-court within the baines [baths], three-square walled, from which walls the ball did rebound. Of this ball, and the exercise thereof, Galen wrote a treatise.

b *Folliculum.* By *folliculus* is meant a kind of wind hand-ball covered with leather, having within it a bladder puffed up with wind, the softest and lightest of all others, smitten, not with a racket as the other, nor with the palm of the hand, as that which they called *Paganica*, filled with wool, flocks, or yarn, but driven with the clenched fist, whereupon it took the name *Pugillatoria*.

c So Turnebus expoundeth it. But Isaac Casaubon understandeth thereby *Segestre*, in Greek στέγαστρον, a light blanket or quilt.

d By this is meant a play, that children used, and not that game of hazard resembling dice, at which, he said before, they played γεροντικῶς [like old men].

e For aught that I can gather out of the sundry conjectures of ex- positors, these *Ocellata*, made of silver or ivory, resemble the game of young gentlewomen called of some *Trol-Madame* [or Trol-my-dames, Fr. *trou madame ;* also called pigeon-holes, played with a board, at one end of which there were arches resembling pigeon-holes, into which small balls were bowled] ; or else that pastime of boys named nine- holes.

84. ¹ [A teacher of declamation and elocution.]   ² When he was hoarse, by reason of rheum.

85. ¹ *Uticensis.*   ² [Set forth, described.]   ³ xxx *Libris*, or rather xiii, according to Suïdas, and all old copies.   ⁴ Called *Ajax*. ⁵ Was wiped away or blotted out with a sponge, alluding to Ajax, that fell upon his own sword ; whereof Sophocles made a tragedy entitled *Ajax*.

a Besides the pretty allusion unto the fabulous history of Ajax, Torrentius hath observed in the word *spongia*, a double signification : to wit, a sponge called *deletilis*, which writers had at hand, either to wipe and wash out what misliked them, or to blur and blot the same, according to these of the poet Ausonius [*Epistolae*, vii, 54],

> *Aut cunctis pariter versibus oblinat*
> *Fulvam lacticolor spongia sepiam,*

whereupon Martialis saith of it,

[Delebis], *quoties scripta novare voles,*

and also a sword. Which addeth the better grace unto the conceit, considering that Ajax fell upon his own sword. But in this latter sense, I have not yet found *spongia* taken, in any approved author.

86. [1] Curled locks or feakes [dangling curls], glib [matted hair, worn on the forehead, covering the eyes] and dropping again with sweet balms [steeped in unguents]. [2] The Censor, who wrote a book of *antiquities*, so called. [3] By his daughter Julia, and M. Agrippa, the mother of Caligula.

[a] Augustus taxed Maecenas for being *cacozelos*, and found as much fault with Tiberius, because he was *antiquarius*.

[b] By these words μυροβρεχεῖς *cincinnos* Augustus noteth the affected forced phrases and curious inkhorn terms, as it were, of Maecenas, *Cuius oratio*, as Seneca reporteth of him, *Epist.* 94, *aeque soluta est ac ipse discinctus*. His manner of style might be compared to those hairs of his, curled with crisping pins and besmeared with odoriferous oils, which Cicero calleth *capillos calamistratos et delibutos*. Neither do I think that Augustus reprehendeth Maecenas for using these words, μυροβρεχεῖς *cincinnos*, because it is his own manner in writing to interlace Greek with Latin, and besides, no *cacozelon* is therein to be found. But his over-curious terms and new-devised phrases he so calleth, for that Maecenas was wont in trimming and tricking up himself to be somewhat womanish.

[c] Augustus, in a certain epistle unto Maecenas, by expressing his own nice and delicate phrases, after a sort derideth them, and dehorteth him thereto, in these words : *Vale [mi ebenum] Medulliae, ebur ex Etruria, laser Aretinum, adamas Supernas, Tiberinum margaritum, Cilniorum smaragde, iaspi figulorum, berylle Porsennae, carbunculum Italiae,* καὶ ἵνα συντέμω παντα, μάλαγμα *maecharum* [Macrobius, *Sat.* ii, 4, 12]. [Farewell, my ebony of Medullia (a small town in Latium), ivory of Etruria, asafoetida of Aretium, diamond from the Adriatic, pearl of the Tiber, emerald of the Cilnii (his name was C. Cilnius Maecenas), jasper of the potters, beryl of Porsenna, carbuncle of the Adriatic, emollients of the courtesans. Of course there were neither diamonds in the Adriatic nor pearls in the Tiber.] In which words, as in a mirror, he might see himself.

[d] As if he should say, " Never a barrel better herring." There was neither of them better than other, as offending both ways. The Asiatic orators were *Cacozeli* [bad imitators], Cimber, Atticus and Veranius, *Antiquarii*. So that it was mere folly and vanity to make any doubt, whether of them to imitate, being all stark naught.

87. [1] At the Greek kalends, *i.e.* at latter Lammas, for the Greeks had no kalends, no more than the Latins *neomenias*, *i.e.* new moons, to begin their months with. And yet the word seemeth to be derived of καλῶ [call] in Greek [now the generally accepted derivation]. [2] Read Macrobius, *Saturnalia*, ii, 4. [3] [Boiled.] [4] A fool. [5] Or *bliteolus*, from *blito*, or *blacolus* from *blax* [stupid, lazy]. [6] Or for *puleium, pulegium, pulleiaceum* [*pullus* = dark, but it is not easy to see the meaning or point of *pulleiaceus*]. [7] [Instead of *cerritus*, crazy, *vacerrosus*, block(head).] [8] [Both = to be unwell.] [9,10] [Both words are connected with vegetables : *beta*, beet, *lachanon*, cabbage.] [11] [Rows], or lines.

89. [1] In Greek.   [2] As well to cut off the expenses of sumptuous edifices, as to prevent danger by skarfires [25].   [3] Which were not so usually read and rehearsed in open audience.

[a] This Sphaerus was a deep scholar and great humanitian [humanist] as we speak, and whom the Greeks call *Philologos*.   Under him Augustus became πολυμαθὴς, skilful in history, antiquities, etc., like as, under Areus, he learned philosophy. [The latest texts omit Sphaerus, and read [s]per *i.e.* filled with learning *through* his intimate acquaintance with Areus and his sons.]

[b] The principal authors whereof Horatius comprised in this verse [*Sat.* i, 4, 1],

Eupolis atque Cratinus Aristophanesque poetae.

In this manner of comedy the vices of men and women were represented and taxed upon the stage over-boldly, and plainly to their discredit.   For which it grew to be offensive, and was laid away a long time.

[c] Who was censor in his time, and persuaded in his orations that all men of what degree soever should be compelled to marry for procreation of children.

90. [1] Or of a sea-calf, which as Pliny [*Nat. Hist.* ii, 146] writeth, checketh all lightnings.

[a] Pliny, *Nat. Hist.* ii, 55, writeth, that it never lighteneth above five feet within the ground.   Fearful persons therefore think such deep caves most safe.

91. [1] *Medici.*   Some read, *amici*, a friend.   [2] [Attack.]   [3] Doorkeeper.   [4] Or top [*fastigium*].   [5] Or chime.   [6] To rouse the porters.   [7] As beggars do.   [8] Or pieces worth about ½d. [Dodkin is a coin of little value, doit.]

[a] By this custom and gesture, as the argument and circumstance of the place naturally importeth, he thought to entreat the goddess Nemesis for to spare him ; Nemesis I say, whom the heathen imagined to attend with an envious eye upon all excessive prosperity.   To avoid therefore adverse afterclaps[1], which this spiteful goddess might bring upon him, unless they were pacified, Augustus thus debased himself superstitiously, and in some sort seemed to abridge his own felicity.   Much after the manner of Polycrates, that rich tyrant who, to be excused from this Nemesis, flung into the sea a jewel, with a precious stone of inestimable price.

92. [1] [Strange, rare.]   [2] Wherein they stood.

[a] *Nundinae* among the Romans were those days in every month whereon they kept fairs and markets.   It should seem therefore, that he held the day after them ominous and of unlucky presage, as we say in our proverb, " A day after the fair," or else because he had sometime not sped very well, whenas he did set out in his journey upon such a day.

[b] *Nonis*, as if it were *non is*, which literally osseth [signifies] as much as, You go not.   Much like to that in Pliny, *Nat. Hist.* xv, 19, when M. Crassus was ready to embark in that unfortunate expedition into Parthia where he was slain, a fellow cried certain figs to be sold with this note, *Cauneas, Cauneas* (for of that kind were those figs [from Caunus in Caria]), which ossed thus much unto him, as if in short speech he had cried *Cave ne eas, cave ne eas*, Take heed you go not this voyage.

---

[1] [Something unpleasant and unexpected.]

OCTAVIUS CAESAR AUGUSTUS

93. ^a An idol resembling an ox, which the Egyptians worshipped as a god for Serapis.

^b He did this, as it should seem, in policy, because he would not be thought addicted to the Jewish sect. For otherwise it appeareth, as well by his gracious indulgences granted unto them, as his own testimony in edicts and commissions, wherein he giveth unto their God [the true and only God]¹ the attribute of ὕψος [ὕψιστος, most high], and instituted for ever certain holocausts, or whole burnt offerings, to wit, two lambs and one bull, to be offered unto that sovereign and most high deity.

94. ¹ [Portended.]   ² [Took measures, made arrangements.] ³ [*Aerarium*, the state-treasury, kept in the temple of Saturn, where the decrees of the senate were at this time deposited.]   ⁴ Or Mendesius, bearing the name of the city Mendes in Egypt.   ⁵ Of divine discourses [or, Speculations on divine things].   ⁶ The mother of Augustus. ⁷ A famous astrologer [and writer on theology and grammar. Next to Varro, he was regarded as the most learned Roman of his time].   ⁸ And thereby the horoscope of his nativity.   ⁹ Which properly are attributed unto Jupiter.   ¹⁰ In the Appian Way.   ¹¹ [=Ingenuous (*liberalis*) : rather, noble, frank.]   ¹² [Usually kept for senators.] ¹³ Senators.   ¹⁴ Doves are consecrated to Venus, from whence the Julii are descended. By them therefore and the date-tree was prefigured perpetual felicity to that name and family.   ¹⁵ [Put up with, endure.]   ¹⁶ Or school [rather, studio, at the top of the house]. ¹⁷ Or astrologer.   ¹⁸ [Declared.]

^a Some have expounded this of our Saviour Christ, King, not of Rome only, but also of all the world, who took our nature upon him, and was born in the days of Augustus Caesar.

^b The like conception by a serpent is reported of Olympias, the mother of king Alexander the Great, of Pomponia likewise, the mother of Scipio Africanus.

^c This broad seal, wherewith were signed letters patents and other public instruments, carried a stamp representing the city of Rome ; and being thus put into his bosom, prefigured that he one day should have the government of the state and commonweal.

^d Symbolising thereby that the citizens of Rome, who beforetime might not lawfully be scourged, were in danger to lose their liberty in that behalf.

95. ¹ Or vultures (Ger. *Geier*).

^a Or, when he stood the first time for to be consul. For the manner was of the candidates or competitors of the consulship, the night before the election day, to lie without the city abroad in the open air ; and afterwards, early in the morning, to sit in a chair made of one entire piece within the precinct of a certain place therefor appointed (which thereupon was called *templum*), and there, to wait and expect until some god presented unto them a good and fortunate sign.

96 ¹ Antony, Lepidus, and Octavius.   ² [Entirely, thoroughly beat : to probably answers to the German zu in compounds, although it is sometimes written as all-to beat (all-to=extremely).]   ³ And therefore by likelihood a wizard.   ⁴ Or spectre [vision].   ⁵ Obtain the favour of the gods.

^a *Cum augeri hostias imperasset.* The manner was of the paynims, if

---

¹ [This is in the folio, and is an addition of H.]

44

they could not speed of [succeed in obtaining] their gods' favour at the first sacrifice, to kill more beasts still, until they saw some tokens thereof ; which in the soothsayers' learning was called *litare*. Thus did Paulus Aemilius for twenty together, and obtained no warrant of happy success before he had slain the one and twentieth. Yet some write, that sacrifices are then said *augeri*, when, together with the beasts, there is use of *Salsa molae* meat and salt. Which kind of ostes [1] be called *Mactae*, as if=*magis auctae* [increased].

b Significant names both, and osses [omens] of victory. Eutychus importeth lucky or fortunate ; Nicon victor or conqueror.

97. [1] Called *lustrum*. [2] [*Nuncupare*, to express a vow in words.] [3] C, in Caesar. [4] [A small islet on the coast of Latium.] [5] For Astura was a water-town with a river also of that name running by it.

a This solemnity of purging the army every five years was instituted by king Servius Tullius, and celebrated with the sacrifice of a swine, a sheep, and a bull, named thereupon *Suovetaurilia*. Hereupon, the revolution of five years they called *lustrum*. This function or office belonged afterwards to generals of the field, like as the expiation and purging of the people unto the censors. And this manner of *lustrum* is here meant.

b Writings or instruments signed, containing the said vows, whereby they bound themselves, as it were, by obligation to pay and perform the same. Oftentimes also they fastened them with wax unto the knees of those gods or idols unto whom they nuncupated those vows, according to that verse of Juvenal, *Satires*, x, 35 :

Propter quae fas est genua incerare Deorum.

c *Praeter consuetudinem.* Suetonius seemeth here to forget himself, writing that Augustus, contrary to his old wont, embarked by night, having reported before that it was his manner so to do. Torrentius would salve all, expounding it thus ; that his hasty and long journey (for it was a good stretch from Astura to Beneventum) was contrary to his wonted manner. But to speak what I think, his journey now by night was occasioned by a gale of wind that served well for Beneventum, and hath no reference at all to his accustomed travel. Some would read *pro consuetudine*, that is, after his usual manner, but they respect not the scope of our author, whose purpose in this place is to put down certain particulars that were ominous and presaging his death. Among which this may be reckoned for one, that he did a thing now, repugnant to his ordinary guise [custom]. A point, I wis, observed too much even nowadays by those that are superstitiously given. Although I am not ignorant that of this observation, in sick folk there may be a natural reason rendered out of physic.

98. [1] Of the Greeks who sometime inhabited those parts. [2] [Scrambling.] [3] [As there is no island near Capreae, it is better to interpret (with Casaubon) an island " at C." *i.e.* the island of C.] [4] [Heartily.] [5] Or if ye distinguish [punctuate] thus, *Morbo variante tamen*, etc., yet by reason that his disease altered, and himself was better sometime than other.

a *De navi Alexandrina.* By *navis* he meaneth, as I suppose, *classis* by the trope *Synecdoche* [in which part is put for the whole or vice versa], the whole fleet, like as, by the same figure, *classis* signifieth a ship. For one vessel alone arrived not into that haven of Puteoli, fraught with merchandise, considering that the same is by other writers named

---

[1] [Victims : Lat. *hostia ;* not to be confused with osse(s), omen(s).]

πορευτικὸς στόλος, and *Commeatus*. Yea, and by the figure *Catachresis* [improper use of a word], Martial [xii, 74] calleth it *Niliacus cataplus*, which properly betokeneth the fleet when it is arrived. Neither is it like[ly] that mariners and passengers out of one ship only saluted Augustus in this wise.

b *Quadragenos aureos.* Every such piece was worth fifteen shillings [really about 16s. 8d.] sterling and better, answerable to our Spur-Royals.

c These commodities were thought to be drugs and spices of all sorts, webs, or clothes in say[1], books, paper, glasses of sundry fashions, teere[2] of flax, hirds[3], or tow, sindall[4] or fine linen, twisted yarn and thread of divers colours, Babylonian and Egyptian cloth, well-favoured bondslaves, and of good education, etc.

d *Vicinam Capreis insulam.* Yet some read otherwise, *Vicinam Capreas insulam*, the island Capreae near adjoining, as if Augustus had abode all this while in the skirt and coast of Campania, or in some other of the neighbour islands. But I incline rather to the former exposition.

e The city of ease and idleness.

f This Masgabas seemeth by his name to have been an African, whom Augustus had made constable as it were of that place, and ruler over a company, that he sent thither to dwell, after he had purchased it of the Neapolitans. And for that Augustus had in mirth given him the name of founder, he was so reputed, and his year's-mind[5] after his death solemnised accordingly.

g *Morbo variante.* I take it, he meaneth that which Celsus calleth *alvum variam,* and other physicians *egestiones varias*, namely, when in a flux the excrements and humours be of divers colours, an argument that nature is not able to concoct them being so irregular, and therefore sometimes a deadly figure. Or, it may be expounded thus : that otherwhiles he seemed to be better and on the mending hand, and thereupon more venturous. Then read, *Morbo variante tamen*, etc.

h Celebrated every five years after the Greek manner, and called gymniké, because the masteries therein were performed by champions for their better agility well-near naked [γυμνός].

99. [1] [Or farce.]   [2] As the manner is, at the end of comedies, to call for a plaudite, he persisted therefore in the metaphor, and by this plaudite allegoriseth the end of this life, which he called before *Mimum vitae*.   [3] [Later editions of the text give ἡμᾶς for ὑμεῖς, and προπέμψατε for κτυπήσατε, *i.e.* send us forward on our journey.]   [4] [Usually.]   [5] [Carried off.]

100. [1] The 19th of August.   [2] About three of the clock in the afternoon.   [3] Aldermen, or senators.   [4] A thing against the old received religion.   [5] Before him called Sextilis.   [6] The Augustan age.   [7] [*Sub veteribus* (*tabernis*, shops, being understood) was the name of a street ; later edd. omit *sub*, veteribus then meaning the old rostra as distinguished from the Rostra Julia.]   [8] Dio nameth him Numerius Atticus, and saith he was hired by Livia for two millions of sesterces, to swear that of Augustus, which Proculus had sometime

---

[1] [A kind of silk or satin, Fr. *saye, soie*.]
[2] [The finest fibre of flax.]
[3] [Same as tow.]
[4] [Rich silk material.]
[5] [Solemn commemoration.]

46

sworn of Romulus. ⁹ Or true portrait. ¹⁰ Or shirts, as some would expound *tunicis*.

ᵃ This was a special honour and indulgence granted by a singular privilege, for otherwise it was against the custom and laws of the Romans to bring a dead body into a sacred place, or into the city, for fear of polluting and profaning it.

ᵇ The senators and gentlemen of Rome wore rings of gold, the commoners of iron.

ᶜ The chief colleges and societies at this time were counted four, that is to say : The pontiffs, or chief priests, the augurs, the septemvirs or seven wardens called *epulones*, for that to them belonged the charge of providing the sacred feasts, the sumptuous suppers of the pontiffs, named *cenae adjiciales*¹, as also the stately tables, in the honour of Jupiter and other gods, and fourthly, of the *quindecimviri sacris faciundis*, fifteen overseers of the sacrifices. Afterwards adjoined there was to these a fifth, *Augustalium Sodalium*, erected by order from Augustus, and others in process of time by his precedent.

ᵈ This *Rostra* was the public pulpit for orations, standing in the common market-place, called *Forum Romanum*, so called for that it was beautified with the beak-heads of ships (named in Latin, *rostra*) which, in a memorable fight at sea, the Romans won from their enemies. Near unto which were certain shops called *Veteres Tabernae*, and absolutely *veteres*, for distinction of others, known by the name of *novae*, the new shops. Yet some are of opinion, that in this place our author meaneth *Rostra vetera*, the old pulpit, to put a difference between it and another named *nova*, the New.

ᵉ You must think that the dead body to be burnt in a funeral fire was set therein, so as the ashes and bones thereof remained apart by themselves from the rest. Otherwise, the ashes of wood, the bones likewise of horses and other beasts sometimes burnt therewith, should have the honour due unto the said dead corpse. Some are of opinion that it was lapped in a linen sheet of the flax called *asbeston* or *Asbestinon*, which would not be consumed with fire.

ᶠ The sumptuous tomb that queen Artemisia built for her husband Mausolus, king of Caria, and reckoned one of the seven wonders of the world, was called *Mausoleum*, after his name. Whereupon all such costly and stately monuments are so named, and more particularly, that of Augustus. Of which you may read more, in Strabo, v, 16, for the better explanation of this place.

101. ¹ The third of April. ² [The actual word is *primos*, *i.e.* his direct heirs.] ³ For default of the other if they died [or refused to take the inheritance]. ⁴ If the second heirs failed. ⁵ Some read *quadringenties tricies quinquies ;* and then it is three millions and a half more. ⁶ Or praetorian band. ⁷ [Immediately.] ⁸ [Nuncupative bequest, oral, not written.] ⁹ *Produxitque quaedam ad vicena sestertia.* So Torrentius expoundeth it. ¹⁰ Of sesterces. ¹¹ *Quaterdecies millies*, fourteen hundred millions. ¹² Octavius and Julius Caesar. ¹³ His daughter's daughter. ¹⁴ [The Monumentum Ancyranum.] ¹⁵ *Aeneis tabulis ;* other writers say, pillars. ¹⁶ [Arrears.]

ᵃ *Depositum apud se.* Some read, *apud se, sex virgines vestales*, as if six of these Vestal virgins had the custody thereof, or at leastwise brought the same forth, being committed to them all, and the seventh,

---

¹ [Should be *aditiales*, feasts given by magistrates on entering into office (*adire*).]

named *Maxima*, the prioress as it were and governess of the rest, were left behind.

b This hath a reference unto the *As*, or pound weight Roman, consisting of 12 ounces, which standeth for the base and rule of many other things ; and namely here for the entire inheritance that Augustus disposed of by his last will and testament. For two third parts of 12 he gave unto Tiberius : and another third part unto Livia, which made up the whole.

c This was against the Voconian law, which expressly provided, that no man should endow a woman in more than the fourth part of his goods. So that if a man died seized of [possessed of] one hundred thousand pounds, his wife might not enjoy the thirds, but only 25,000 pounds and no more. Howbeit Augustus had a special indulgence and dispensation for this law.

d Albeit Tiberius had been long before adopted his son, and thereby may be thought to have assumed the names of his civil father into his style : yet this surname only of Augustus would not be communicate with him, but left it as hereditary after his decease, as appeareth in Tiberius. As for Livia, after Augustus his death she was commonly called Julia Augusta ; however some writers retain her old name Livia, and others again in Augustus his life name her Julia by the figure *Prolepsis* [anticipation], because she carried that name after he was dead.

e In most copies of Suetonius you find this reading, *Legavit populo Romano quadringenties, tribubus tricies quinquies.* In which words there may be thought a tautology, for that the people of Rome and the tribes (which were in number 35) be all one. Therefore some learned men have thought good to leave out the latter clause wholly, or at leastwise the word *tribubus.* Others again would have here two legacies to be implied, the one of 40 millions given generally in common to the whole body and people of Rome, the other of three millions and one half to be distributed among the tribes in particular, or to the poorest persons in every tribe according to the discretion of their *vicorum magistri* [overseers of townships]. And these put a distinction between *populus* and *plebs,* which *plebs* is here understood under the name of *tribubus.* But I leave it indifferent, although I am not ignorant that sometimes *populus* and *tribus* be confounded and put the one for the other, as also that *tribus* stand for the vulgar and meaner sort of the people only, expressly distinct from *populus, equites* and *senatores,* which the poet termeth *sine nomine turbam :* and T. Livius not unaptly, *ignota capita.*

NOTES AND ANNOTATIONS UPON
TIBERIUS NERO CAESAR

1. [1] Or Clausus.   [2] *Locum.*   Some read *lucum*, not in the strict signification of a sacred grove, but of a pleasant tuft of trees wherewith monuments were beautified, as you may gather by the mausoleum of Augustus.   [3] [From that time forward.]

[a] It seemeth that in his own native country, where the inhabitants beforetime were descended from the Greeks, he had to name Atta Clausus ; and being once incorporate among the Romans, changed it into Appius Claudius. Now, *Atta* savoureth of the Greek word ἄττειν, which is, in going, not to set the sole of the foot firmly upon the ground, but rather lightly to tread, as it were, on tiptoe. Hereupon, as Festus noteth, they that have that imperfection in their feet, whereby they can go no better, be called *Attae :* which was the occasion that one of the said house took that name first, and so his posterity after him. Like as among the Romans, of another accident arose the name Agrippa first, for that one was born into the world with his feet forward. And these additions, whether they were forenames or surnames in the beginning, it skilleth not : for surnames in continuance of time came to be forenames, and contrariwise.

[b] If you have recourse unto the original, Nero is as much as Νεύρων, or Νευρώδης, *Nervatus* or *Nervosus :* that is to say, well-compact of nerves and sinews : and such are strong.

2. [1] One of the ten decemvirs.   [2] [Hold in thrall, enslave.] [3] The fair.   [4] Or Ilycia.   [5] Pliny, *Nat. Hist.* vii, 35 [Ovid, *Fasti*, iv, 305].   [6] Cybele.   [7] Or bar(r)s [sandbanks, shallows].   [8] For unto this time that sex had not been indicted and attaint of treason (Valerius Maximus, viii, i).   [9] C. Fonteius.   [10] [Dress. The word, of course, survives in widows' weeds.]   [11] Claudia.   [12] Of so reverent regard were these nuns, that no magistrate might either attach [indict, charge] or cross them.

[a] Seneca reporteth in his book *De Brevitate Vitae*, xii, That this Claudius persuaded the Romans first to go to sea, and embark ; whereupon he was styled *Caudex*, which in our Latin is as much to say, as the framing, and joining together of many plants or ribs of timber, which is the very periphrasis of a bark.

[b] One of his predecessors, who had a jurisdiction there, gave it that name, as having built likewise a forum or hall of justice there, whereupon the inhabitants of it and the territory thereabout, owing service to that court, as clients and dependants to that family, afforded this Claudius a meet place for him of innovation and usurping unlawful dominion.

[c] Observing signs from birds, by their feeding, flying, or otherwise, that might give him warrant to go forward with the favour of the gods in his enterprise.

[d] Adoptions by order of law should follow the course of nature, whereby the son cannot be older than the father. The cause why

TIBERIUS NERO CAESAR

he sought thus extraordinarily to be adopted a commoner, was that he might be chosen tribune of the commons.

ᵉ The usual manner in Rome was, that those persons who were arrested for criminal causes, during all the time of their trouble and trial, should change their apparel, and instead of gowns which were fair and white, put on others sullied and foul, thereby to move mercy and compassion of the people. Whereupon such *rei* were called *sordidati*.

ᶠ These tribunes of the commons as may appear in T. Livius, were *sacrosancti*, inviolable, and such as no violent hands might be laid upon.

3. ¹ Or mother's grandfather (*materno avo*). ² Or rather, Drusus. ³ Or nephew, *abnepos*. [Really, the son of a great grandchild.] ⁴ [Dispute, dissension.]

ᵃ So called of *salinae*, the salt-pits or salt-houses. For, being censor, he set an impost upon salt, and thereby augmented the revenues of the State, little to the benefit or contentment of the people.

4. ¹ [Julius Caesar, the] dictator. ² This is that *amnestia*, which Cicero persuaded unto. ³ To wit, his six lictors or vergers, with their knitches of rods and axes sticking therein (Alexander ab Alexandro). ⁴ *Servis ad pileum vocatis :* because the cap or bonnet was the badge of freedom.

ᵃ For the manner was, that governors of provinces, who (as they were) so would be counted also more courteous than others, should unrequested allow some of their lictors unto all Roman senators that repaired unto them, for to do them honour : see Cicero, *Ep. ad Cornificium* [*ad Fam.* xii, 30].

5. ¹ Or his grandam by the mother's side. ² *Felicitatis*, or *Fecunditatis*, fruitfulness. ³ The sixteenth of November.

ᵃ In token of his nativity there, which, as they gave out, was borne to the good *urbis et orbis*, of Rome and the whole world besides, for so by way of flattery they magnified their princes.

6. ¹ *Luxuriosam*, growing apace to maturity [later reading, *Laboriosam*, full of hardship]. ² Or discovered. ³ [*lit.* Crying like a cat.] ⁴ [Youth, growing lad.] ⁵ Or spire-pole [pole or shaft of a chariot]. ⁶ See Cal. 20.

ᵃ Some read *luctuosam*, sorrowful, in regard of many hurts and dangers.

ᵇ When a chariot is drawn by a team of four steeds all in one rank or affront, as we may see them portrayed upon divers coins, it must needs be that the two middle are joined or yoked as it were to the spire-pole running between them : and these be called ζύγιοι. The other two then are without, the one on the left, and the other on the right side, called παρήοροι in Greek, and in this place by our author *funales*, because they are guided and ruled by a cord, or some reins or chain in lieu thereof. And say that these *quadrigae* or four steeds draw two by two in files, one pair before the other, those which be next unto the chariot be aptly called *jugales*, and those before them beyond the spire, *funales*, of which Tiberius rode upon one and Marcellus upon the other.

7. ¹ At 17 years of age. ² Or great market-place. ³ Livia. ⁴ Augustus. ⁵ Whom Tacitus calleth Vipsania after the surname of her father. ⁶ [Strained, tense.] ⁷ Ready as it were to run out of his head. ⁸ Who died when he was consul.

50

8. [1] Whilst he was quaestor, and but nineteen years old. [2] [Removing objectionable occupants.] [3] *Ergastulorum.* Such as bridewell and houses of correction. [4] [Take shelter.]

9. [1] Colonel of a thousand footmen. [2] *Primus :* some read *prius,* that is, *ante ovationem,* before he had ridden ovant or triumphed.

10. [1] In administration of the commonweal. [2] [This is obscure. The original is : " when Marcellus was raised to, brought into office (*admoto*)." " Them " and " their " should be him and his, unless it can be referred to A.'s children.] [3] To darken their light [stand in the way].
[a] According to the vulgar speech, *Nimia familiaritas parit contemptum.*

11. [1] [Rather, suburban villa, estate.] [2] Or public place of exercise. [3] He was then tribune of the commons and consul the second time. [4] *Aegros :* some read *agros,* as if he minded to walk the fields. [5] Rhetoricians [*antisophistae,* counter-sophists, those who take the opposite side of a question].

12. [1] [Ceremonial visits.] [2] As praetor, propraetor, proconsul, etc. [3] The son of his wife Julia by Agrippa. [4] [The day when their leave expired.] [5] Or of his friends. [6] [Messages.] [7] [Ceased.]

13. [1] The gown. [2] Pantofles or cork-shoes after the Greek fashion. [3] [The inhabitants of Nemausum (Nismes).] [4] Gaius, his nephew or daughter's son. [5] His mother's husband.

14. [1] [Stealthily.] [2] The diadem. [3] Under Julius Caesar or Augustus. [4] *Subitis ignibus* or *Subductis ignibus.* When the fire was taken from them. [5] Or cockalls, *talos.* [6] Venus or Cous, which is the best chance. [7] Which brought the messenger of his return.
[a] These dice were called *tali,* because at first they used with such cockall bones named *tali* to play ; but afterwards they were made of ivory, gold, etc. Among many sorts of sorceries and divinations, one there was by these bones or dice, and the wizards that professed their cunning in it were termed Ἀστραγαλομάντεις.
[b] For the greater light to this place and better proof of Thrasyllus' skill, Dio reporteth that, when Tiberius intended verily to throw him down headlong, he perceived him by his countenance to be much troubled and disquieted in mind, whereupon he demanded the cause thereof ; and then Thrasyllus answered, that by speculation of the stars he foresaw some present danger to himself, and so Tiberius durst not proceed to execute this intent of his.

15. [1] There to commence and show the first proof of pleading at bar. [2] Which was in the street Carina [Carinae was a district of Rome, between the Coelian and Esquiline hills]. [3] Or Exquilia, another street in Rome. [4] Of two years rather : by Velleius and Dio, and as himself hath written in Augustus. [5] One that was *sui juris.* [6] Falling unto him by the testaments of his friends. [7] A stock given and granted unto one by him under whose tuition he is, be he father or master.

16. [1] Germany. [2] Out of Germany.

17. [1] Augustus.
[a] *Septa* was a place in Mars' field railed about at first like a sheep-

pen, whereupon it was called *Ovilia*. But afterwards mounded with marble stone, beautified also with stately galleries and walks, within which cloister and precinct the people oftentimes assembled about election of magistrates and other public affairs ; yea, and with wares which were there set out to be sold, as Alexander ab Alexandro witnesseth.

18. ¹ *Deponerentur :* or *deportarentur*, transported and carried over.

19. ¹ [Commands.] ² [Had a narrow escape : Fr. *l'échapper belle*.] ³ *A Rhuteno quodam.*

ᵃ Some read *Bructero*, of which name there is a nation, as well as of the R(h)uteni in Gaul. Others, *Rutero*, as if he meant one of those horsemen or riders in Germany, which at this day be called Rutters [Reiter].

20. ¹ Augustus Caesar. ² [In a tight place, an unfavourable position.] ³ [For 3000 read 300.]

21. ¹ [Immediately.] ² [Consideration.] ³ 'Ἐμοὶ καὶ μούσαις or τοῖς σοῖς, thy friends [the passage is corrupt]. ⁴ *Si tu non valebis :* or, *si tu modo valebis*, so you continue well.

ᵃ By this enigmatic speech, Augustus compareth the state of the people of Rome unto the miserable case of one, whom some savage and cruel beast hath gotten between his teeth, not devouring and dispatching him at once, but there holdeth and cheweth him a long while in exceeding pain ; alluding to the secret malice and dreaming nature withal of Tiberius.

ᵇ It should seem that, in adopting him, he used these very words, *Hoc Reipublicae causa facio.* This do I for the commonwealth's sake.

ᶜ Alluding to this verse of Ennius in the commendation of Quintus Fabius Maximus :

> *Unus homo nobis cunctando restituit rem,*
>
> One man alone by sage delay
> Restor'd our state fall'n to decay.

[In the folio text *vigilando* (by watching) is the reading as altered by Augustus.]

ᵈ In his *Iliad* [x, 246], where Diomedes, in making choice of Ulysses to exploit a piece of service with him, giveth him this praise.

22. ¹ Colonel. ² Or warrant. ³ [Odium, unpopularity.] ⁴ [Unfavourable opinion.]

23. ¹ Which he had penned. ² For the death of Augustus. ³ That is to say, in 8 parts of twelve, or two-third parts.

ᵃ The tribunes of the commons had power to call a senate, but not whensoever they would, without a special decree granted by the nobles.

24. ¹ [Did not scruple.]

25. ¹ [Becoming his colleague in the government.] ² [Outwitted.]

ᵃ The cohort or band of soldiers which were of the prince's guard were called *praetoriani*, taking that name of *praetorium*, which signifieth the lord general's pavilion in the camp, his royal palace in Rome and elsewhere ; as also the lord deputies' house of estate [C. 76] in any province. Now those soldiers that gave attendance and served in this place about the prince or governor, were entertained in better condition than the rest, because their wages were greater and the time of their service shorter. For Augustus had set down their term twelve years, whereas the rest, before they could be discharged, were to serve sixteen.

b It may be thought that *Germaniciani*, as well by the grammatical analogy of the letter, as also by some circumstance of this very place, import a reference unto Germanicus the son of Drusus deceased, like as *Vitelliani, Flaviani*, etc. But the learned observe that, as an army lying encamped or in garrison in Germany, is properly in Latin called *Germanicus*, so the soldiers of the said army be fitly named *Germaniciani*.

26. ¹ *Paulo minus quam privatum egit :* or, little better than the port, etc. ² Or November rather, for in it he was born, of his own name. ³ Or September, of his mother's. ⁴ From the kalends or first day of January to the 15th of May.

a These solemnities were exhibited about the middle of November, whereas the other, named *Romani*, were held in the beginning of September.

b It is to be noted that the name of *imperator* in Roman history is taken three ways : first, for him who, by commission or warrant from the State, hath the conducting of an army, and in this sense it hath relation to soldiers, and is all one with lord-general of the field, or a commander, etc., and the same that *praetor* was in old time. Secondly, for a victor or conqueror, namely, when such a general or chieftain hath by martial prowess achieved many valiant exploits, and put to sword such a number of enemies, as the law setteth down ; for then the soldiers were wont to salute him by the name of *imperator*, conqueror. Lastly, for a sovereign prince, king, and monarch. In the first acceptation, it is a mere relative, in the second a surname, in the third and last, the forename of all the Roman emperors, to wit, from Julius Caesar forward. Who, although they wore not the crown and diadem, were nevertheless absolute princes, sovereigns, kings and monarchs. The want of this distinction may breed some trouble in the readers of Roman history.

c Made of oak branches, or in default thereof, of some other tree bearing mast ; which garland, by the first institution, was given to that soldier who in battle had rescued a citizen of Rome and saved his life. And afterwards it, together with the laurel, beautified the gates of the Caesars' palaces, although some of them were bloody tyrants, and made no spare of their citizens' and subjects' lives.

27. ¹ One who had been consul : Tacitus saith [*Ann.* i, 13] it was Quintus Haterius. ² Whereby the said Q. Haterius had like to have been killed by the guard. ³ Or Lord. ⁴ [He professed to regard it as an insult.]

28. ¹ *Ad vos*, or, *ad nos*, unto us. ² Such as might beseem one citizen to speak of another, and not a prince of his subjects [*percivilis*, very courteous, affable]. ³ [In turn.]

29. ¹ The senators. ² [Politeness, urbanity.]

30. ¹ Or wing. ² Whereas by course he should have had his trial before the lord-general, or prince himself. ³ [Retire.]

a The manner was, if prince or senator were carried in his litter, usually supported by eight bondservants, and thereupon called *Octophoron*, to have a company of citizens in their gowns going before, and accompanying him by his side, as also certain servitors to carry his curule chair of ivory behind.

31. [1] [Give their attention to.]   [2] Or Trebians [both Ocriculum and Trebia were towns in Umbria].   [3] [Going over to a party or person's side of the house.]

[a] This free embassage, called *libera legatio*, was granted many times to such as [were] desirous either to travel and see foreign countries, or to flee, for avoiding of dangerous troubles at home ; thereby to be better entertained abroad, and with the more honest colour, to conceal the occasion of their departure and absence, as if they were sent from the State about the affairs only of commonweal.

32. [1] As collars, chains, spears, chaplets, etc.   [2] Or read a lecture. [3] Once a week, or every seventh day.   [4] [*Deglubere*, to strip, flay ; is this a misprint ?]

[a] It was not ordinary with the emperors to accompany the corpse unto the funeral fire, but only to vouchsafe their presence at the funeral oration in the Forum or common place.   This therefore may be attributed unto Tiberius his civil humanity.

[b] It appeareth by Dio, that they had omitted to subscribe the clause which went in this form, *Vota facimus pro te, Imperator.*   We make our vows (and pray) for thee, O Emperor.

33. [1] [Rescripts, edicts, statutory enactments. The resolutions of the senate at this time were merely formal ratifications of the emperor's will, so that for any ordinances of his that proved, or were likely to be, unpopular he could throw the responsibility upon that body.]

[a] Causes were heard judicially and justice ministered, either from a superior place as the tribunal, or beneath upon the even and plain ground, *de plano*, as the lawyers speak, so that there were a chair or seat for the judge to sit upon.   And the said place of justice wheresoever, either *pro tribunali*, or *de plano posita sella*, is properly called *Jus*, as Carolus Sigonius hath observed, i, 5, *de Judiciis ;* whereupon cometh the usual phrase, *In jus vocare.*   It seemeth therefore, that Tiberius would come into the *Comitium* or hall of justice, and take his place, sometime within the tribunal (for it was a spacious room) or else sit in his curule chair of ivory beneath as a moderator, which is expressed here by the term *de plano.*

34. [1] Of sword-fencers.   [2] [Limit.]   [3] [*i.e.* he proposed that there should be a new sumptuary law.]

[a] As marchpanes, tarts, gingerbread, custards, sugared biscuit, and generally all manner of pastry-conceits [pastries of fanciful design], wrought with honey or sugar.   The workman is called *dulciarius*, and the things, *bellaria mellita*, or *pemmata.*   Toys [trifles] not only needless, but hurtful also to the body, according to that in Aulus Gellius, *Noctes Atticae*, xiii, 11, 6 (from Varro) : *Bellaria ea maxime sunt mellita quae mellita non sunt :* Πέμμασιν *enim cum* πέψει *societas infida.*   Such junkets sort not well with concoction [digestion].

35. [1] According to the manner and custom of their ancestors. [2] [Released him from his oath.]   [3] [Evade.]   [4] Juliae, etc., *de adulteriis.*   [5] As well senators as gentlemen.   [6] In sword-fight at the sharpe [C. 10].   [7] He deprived him of his senator's place.   [8] Without the city.   [9] The morrow : his levity was notable as well in making choice so slightly [without thought], as in casting her off so quickly, making but a game of marriage.

54

ᵃ Diverse statutes there were, sharply punishing the adultery of matrons or married wives. An act likewise passed in the senate, that no person of knight's degree or above should play upon the stage, perform sword-fight, or combat with wild beasts for hire ; providing all to preserve the honour of wedlock entire, and to maintain the reputation of knighthood and nobility. Those shameless dames therefore, of whom Suetonius writeth in this place, either because they would be thought unworthy to be reckoned within the censure of law, or, as Tacitus writeth, deemed to have abidden [endured] punishment enough in making profession of so base a trade and life ; these lewd persons likewise, and unreclaimable unthrifts [wastrels] suffering themselves thus to appear noted with infamy, and that upon record, made accompt [reckoned], both the one and the other, not to be obnoxious or liable unto the statutes and acts aforesaid.

ᵇ The manner was at Rome, for tenants to remove and flit out of one house into another, upon the first day of July, like as with us at the feasts of Saint Michael and the Annunciation of the Virgin Mary, which are the ordinary rent-days.

36. [1] Roman citizens.

ᵃ Josephus[1], *Antiquities of the Jews*, xviii, 3, 4, 5, writeth that Tiberius sent 4000 of them into Sardinia, an island in summer-time especially very intemperate and unwholesome, as may appear by that pretty epigram of Martial [iv, 60, 5], wherein he opposeth the healthy city Tibur to the pestilent isle Sardinia :

> *Nullo fata loco possis excludere, cum mors*
> *Venerit, in medio Tibure Sardinia est.*

No place exempt from fatal death ; for when our time is come,
Mid Tibur will Sardinia be found of all and some.

37. [1] Near unto the walls thereof, as Pliny writeth, *Nat. Hist.* iv, 5.   [2] [Rather, quarters or barracks.]   [3] [" But " seems superfluous.]   [4] [=at the sharpe : *see* C. 10.]   [5] A petty king about the Alps.   [6] Senators, or aldermen.   [7] [Town of Mysia, on an island or peninsula in the Euxine or Black Sea.]   [8] [Or Rhascuporis.]

38. [1] [Cicero, *ad Atticum*, xiii, 12, 3. The Greek proverb is Καλλιππίδης τρέχει, used ἐπὶ τῶν πολλὰ μελετώντων ποιῆσαι, ὀλίγα δὲ δρώντων. It is probable that this Callippides was an unsuccessful runner, not to be identified, as he is by H., with C. the tragedian.]

ᵃ This Callippides, who gave occasion of this byword, was a famous stage-player, or one of these mimi, counterfeiting other men's gestures, as Beroaldus supposeth. *See* Plutarch [Alcib. 32, Apophthegmata Laconica, 57].

39. [1] Adopted.   [2] His own son.

40. [1] Strangers that conflowed [C. 39, *n.*] thither to see the shows.
[2] [Kept at a distance, refused to see.]

41. [1] [To such an extent that.]

42. [1] [On every occasion.]   [2] Or Cestius Gallus.   [3] [Spendthrift.]   [4] For the devising of new pleasures.

ᵃ Biberius, from *bibendo*, of drinking ; Caldius, from *calda*, or *calida*, hot ; Mero, of *merum*, strong wine. An elegant agnomination

---

[1] [It seems the reference should be Tacitus, *Annals*, ii, 85.]

[bestowal of an agnomen or surname], whereby is shown, that he loved to drink wine hot, which is right delicate, and goeth down more merrily.

b The Italian amphora containeth 48 *sextarii*, every sextarius 20 ounces *mensurales*, which is a wine pint and half of our measure with the better [*i.e.* and more]. By which reckoning he drank at one meal a rundlet[1] of ten wine gallons well-near.

c A bird that feedeth upon grapes and figs especially, whereupon it took the name. In autumn or the latter end of summer it is so called ; at other times *melanocoryphos*, or *atricapilla*, of the black cop [crest], or hair-like feathers that it carrieth upon the head.

d Of this bird for the dainty flesh of it Martial made this epigram :

Inter aves turdus, si quis me judice certet,
Inter quadrupedes, gloria prima lepus.

Of feathered fowls, if I may judge, the blackbird is the best,
Among four-footed beasts the hare surpasseth all the rest.

e [For " one who had been censor " read T. Caesonius Priscus.]

43. a Alluding partly to the isle Capreae, and in part either to *capra* in Latin, a goat, or to καπρός in Greek, a wild boar, and that member, *Quo viri sumus.*

45. [1] [Women of high rank.]   [2] [Common informers.]   [3] [Stigma, brand of infamy.]   [4] Or shape, as the kind is of such beasts to do.

46. [1] In money.   [2] Or rank.   [3] Some read *Graecorum*, that is, Greeks, by way of contempt.

47. [1] At Rome.   [2] [Especially.]   [3] He had married a young wife, upon hope of maintenance by virtue of the Papia-Poppaean and Julian laws.

48. [1] [Publicly offered.]   [2] Or patrimony.   [3] That thereby their money might come abroad.   [4] That is, debts paid.   [5] For then it was that 20,000 were killed at Fidenae by the fall of a theatre. [6] *Publicata.* [Later edds. have *duplicata, i.e.* after double the amount had been paid.]   [7] Or guard.   [8] As of their general.   [9] With allowance of lands, fees, or yearly pensions for their service.   [10] In number twelve (Pliny, *Nat. Hist.* ii, 84 ; Eusebius, *Chronica*, 13).

49. [1] Her husband.   [2] And therefore he hoped to be his heir. [3] More than by law they might.

a Seneca reporteth thus, *De Beneficiis*, ii, 27, *Quater millies sestertium suum vidit.* He saw of his own 400 millions of sesterces.

b Provided it was by an ancient law, and the same revived by Julius Caesar dictator, that no person should in silver or gold possess above 60 *sestertia*, that is, three-score thousand *sestertii*. This may have a relation to that order set down by him a little before, that monied men and usurers should lay out two-third parts of their stock in lands and houses, etc.

50. [1] Mother of her Country.

51. [1] *Quorum nomina*, or such-like.   [2] *In antliam :* or wheel and bucket [treadmill] ; some read *in Antiliam*, or *Anticyram*, an island : or else *lautumiam*, a dungeon in the common prison.

---

[1] [A vessel of varying capacity.]

ª As we say, to make him justice of quorum, etc. : for the decuries of Judges were they *quorum nomina* were written in the commission roll.

52. ¹ Of Drusus. ² *Justitium*, as the manner was in any mournful time. ³ *Ni Sejanus secreto obstaret :* or, *Nisi ea secreta obstarent*, but that they were in secret delivered, and therefore could not be proved. [The text is corrupt.] ⁴ *Increpitum :* others read *inscriptum*, that is, this inscription was in many places set upon his statues.

53. ¹ Germanicus, his adopted son's wife and daughter to Agrippa and Julia. ² [Arranged.] ³ [And that she should be cautioned against eating it, as if it would be certain death to her.] ⁴ [Expressed his opinion.] ⁵ *Scalae* [steps, or stairs].
ª The Greek verse is read thus, Εἰ μὴ τυραννεῖς, θύγατερ, ἀδικεῖσθαι δοκεῖς, or Εἰ μὴ τυραννεῖς, τέκνον, etc.
ᵇ *Scalae Gemoniae.* A place at Rome upon the Aventine hill, into which the dead bodies of malefactors were dragged and thrown with shame.

54. ¹ [After they had assumed the *toga virilis* : *cf.* the use of the word at some universities.] ² Or largesse. ³ [In an underground dungeon in the palace.] ⁴ To famish his own self wilfully. ⁵ To strangle him and drag him to the Scalae Gemoniae. ⁶ Or bed. ⁷ Bones and ashes, which was done by him of spite.

56. ¹ Or curiously. [The meaning seems rather to be, that Zeno used some far-fetched words or expressions which made Tiberius ask what dialect it was.] ² [Solve.]
ª They speak the Greek language generally throughout all Greece, yet not after one manner. For in divers parts were different kinds of Greek called dialects, to wit, Attic, Ionic, Aeolic, etc. Like as with us in Great Britain a common English tongue goeth well-near throughout the whole island, albeit there is a diversity perceived between the Scottish or northern English, and the southern, between the Cornish and the Kentish, etc.

57. ¹ [In Palestine. He was the founder of a school of rhetoric, opposed to that of Apollodorus of Pergamum.] ² [Compare, liken.] ³ Or mire. ⁴ Clay so tempered becometh very strong, tough, and stiff. ⁵ [Laid himself out.] ⁶ A scoffing jester. ⁷ *Elato mortuo*, or *clare mortuo*, with a loud voice called upon the dead man. ⁸ [This was in the senate.] ⁹ The Pompeiani, that took part with Pompey against Julius Caesar.

58. ¹ High treason. ² Fled thither for refuge as unto a sanctuary, or otherwise howsoever. ³ Either of Tiberius or Augustus (Seneca, *de beneficiis*, iii, 26).
ª In so doing the body must needs be bared and some shame discovered, which being an impiety before the sacred images of the gods, was made treason also before the emperor's statue, unto whom divine honours were exhibited.

59. ¹ [The author is unknown.] ² [Or, if you want to know all.]
ª The last hexastich, or six verses, seemeth to make one entire epigram by itself. Every distich before carrieth a several [different] sense. And as for the first two, they seem to have a reference to the time whiles he abode in Rhodes, before he was *sui Juris*.

60. [1] Being scaly and having a couple of barbets [small beard]. [2] [Lucky, fortunate.] [3] Or [pleasure-] garden. [4] [The front line of an army.] [5] With cudgels, which punishment was called *fustuarium* [*Aug.* 96, note].

61. [1] The sovereign captain and general of the Greeks at Troy. [2] A. Cremutius Cordus : read Seneca, *Consolatio ad Marciam*, 22. [3] Who slew Julius Caesar and were accounted *tyrannoctoni.* [4] Or Calvilius. [5] Who had been sometime consul, and therefore to be credited. [6] *Inter copreas* [low, foul-mouthed jesters].

[a] At which times, both among the Greeks and Romans also, the manner was to forbear execution, yea, and to ease prisoners of their irons.

[b] As if under his person he had offered abuse unto the emperor Tiberius.

[c] He would say, The courage and generosity [noble character] of the Romans died with them, seeing that none arose to recover their liberty oppressed and trod under foot by this tyrant Tiberius.

[d] Rather, two hundred and twenty. For Tacitus [*Ann.* vi, 19, 7] reporteth that all the suspected complices of Sejanus were killed, *Jacuit immensa strages, omnis sexus, omnis aetas*, etc.

[e] The like hypocritical religion was practised during the bloody proscription in the triumvirate. A young gentleman nobly born, because he might not be killed lawfully, *praetextatus*, under age, and wearing still his embroidered garment *praetexta*, he commanded to put on his virile gown, and so he was murdered.

62. [1] Daughter of Germanicus and Agrippina, and wife to the said Drusus. [2] Among other examinates. [3] [Had taken as much drink as they could carry.] [4] The astrologer [14].

63. [1] Fortunes or chances. [2] In manner of a lottery. [3] Of Fortune at Praeneste. [4] L. Aelius Lamia and L. Arruntius. [5] Or presidents that had been consuls.

64. [1] Agrippina, his adopted son Germanicus' wife and widow, or Livilla beforenamed, wife to Drusus his own son. [2] Because they should not ask who was within.

65. [1] For he remained still at Capreae. [2] To be matched in marriage with one of his nieces. [3] Or epistle rather, written unto the senate. [4] In Rome, about Sejanus, who was so highly honoured there. [5] Or farm-house, in the isle of Capreae [rather, country-house].

66. [1] Where the senators sat to behold the plays. [2] [Extravagance, dissipation.]

67. [1] For he was wonderfully addicted to the study of astrology and such curious arts. [2] [That is, he refused to allow his acts to be sworn to.]

[a] [Is *ut imperium inierit . . . recusasse* good Latin, as H. translates ? Rather, "When he had become emperor, he refused."]

68. [1] The Claudii. [2] For such prominent eyes are not commonly quick of sight. [3] Manner of going. [4] Or downward into his bosom [*obstipus :* the lexica render " bent or drawn back "]. [5] [*Adductus*, strained, drawn tight.] [6] [Or effeminate.]

[a] The full stature of men in Italy was six feet wanting two inches ;

if men grew higher than six they were accounted exceeding tall, if to seven (and to that height men may grow, as Varro, Gellius, and Solinus do write), they went for giants. So that in musters young men were chosen soldiers, five feet high and ten inches, which was called *Justa Statura*.

b Some read *subiti*, and not *subtiles*, to signify that such pimples continued not, but arose and fell at times, much like to those that the physicians call *hidroa, sudamina*, or *papulas sudorum*, according to Pliny, proceeding of heat or sweat, if the humours be sharp.

c Such be termed in Greek βυσαυχένες. And if we may believe the physiognomy delivered by Aristotle, they be by nature deceitful and wily, given to circumvent, entrap, and supplant others.

d Cornelius Celsus, among other good rules and precepts of health, writeth thus, *Sanus homo, qui et bene valet et suae spontis est, nullis obligare se legibus debet, ac ne medico neque alipta egere*, etc. But give he what directions he will, and let us say what we can to this point, that men and women may be physicians to themselves, such is there misgovernment in diet and otherwise, that physicians shall never want employment. And as touching thirty years of age, Tacitus addeth [*Ann.* vi, 46, 9] moreover and saith, that he [Tiberius] was wont to mock those and hold them to be fools, who after the said years had need of other men's instructions, to know what was good or hurtful for their bodies. Whereupon might arise our English proverb, A fool or a physician.

69. [1] The course of the stars. [2] Or upon his head, in manner of a coronet. [3] [Pliny, *Nat. Hist.* ii, 55, xv, 40.]

70. [1] As well Greek as Latin. [2] Prose. [3] [Roman general (64 B.C.-A.D. 8) distinguished orator and writer, and a patron of literature and art.] [4] [*Morositas*, pedantry, over-nicety.] [5] One of Augustus' sons, yet some expound it of Julius Caesar, the dictator. [6] [E. of Chalcis and R. of Alexandria were grammarians and poets; P. of Nicaea, who taught Virgil Greek, wrote love-stories.] [7] [In rivalry, emulated one another in.] [8] *De his*, haply of their doing. [9] [Test and question.] [10] The daughters of king Lycomedes, in the isle of Scyros, where he feigned himself to be a maiden. [11] Androgeus.

a Such as were sung to the harp. In which kind Pindar excelled among the Greeks, and Horace among the Romans.

b One of Augustus' [adopted] sons. Yet some read Julius Caesar.

71. [1] [Another reading is *Graece*, a soldier who was examined in Greek.]

a A word usual with us in these days, for who knoweth not that monopoly is, when one man engrosseth[1] some commodity into his own hands, that none may sell the same but himself, or from him?

b It signifieth in this place a piece of workmanship set upon a cup or other vessel of gold or silver to garnish the same, so fitted as it may be put to, or taken away, at our pleasure. The ancient poets in Latin called such devices *insertae*.

c Contrary to Augustus Caesar, whose manner was ever and anon in his speeches and writings to interlace Greek words and sentences.

72. [1] With three ranks of oars. [2] [Get out of the way of; or, keep off.] [3] When he came by the river. [4] When he journeyed

---

[1] [To buy up the entire stock, make a "corner" in.]

by land. ⁵ *Venas* for *arterias*, by the trope *Catachresis* [a forced use of words], for they only beat. ⁶ Who waited upon him, or upon whom he leaned. ⁷ *Valere dicentes*, or, as they saluted him, after the Greek phrase, χαίρειν καὶ εὖ πράττε. *Gaudere et bene rem gerere*, All hail and fair cheer you.

ᵃ A place near the river Tiber, so called of a naval fight exhibited sometime there, by Julius Caesar dictator, within a spacious pit receiving water for that purpose.

ᵇ In the port highways from Rome, the manner of the Romans was, at every mile's end, to pitch down a great stone, and according thereto were the miles reckoned, like as with us in some places there stand crosses of wood or stone to that end.

ᶜ A creeping dragon. Which implieth that there be others winged, or at leastwise supposed to fly, in the common opinion of men ; for the attribute *Serpens* signifieth creeping. Now, because all of them use most so to do, the general name of dragons goeth under serpents. And as for the word dragon, it is given to the whole kind for their quick sight, coming of *draco*, in Latin, and δράκων in Greek, ἀπὸ τοῦ δρακεῖν, of seeing.

ᵈ *Recidiva pejor radice*, say the physicians. The relapse unto a former disease is more dangerous than it was before.

73. ¹ [Released from confinement.] ² With full intent, as it should seem, to be revenged of the senate. ³ Or manor-house. ⁴ Of Lucullus, who either built it, or there dwelt. ⁵ 16th of March. ⁶ Caligula, emperor after him. ⁷ Some leave out this clause, and read thus : as he desired meat, etc., a pillow was, etc. ⁸ Or cushion. ⁹ *Intellecta defectione*. Some expound this of the slinking away of his familiars and those that were about him. ¹⁰ Upon which he wore the ring.

ᵃ It took the name of L. Lucullus, the lord thereof.

74. ¹ Unto seamen and passengers by night.

75. ¹ *Tiberium in Tiberim*, into the Tiber with Tiberius.

ᵃ A town in Campania, where he took so great delight, and a place infamous for the licentious life of the inhabitants, whereupon grew the name of those lascivious and filthy comedies, *Atellanae*, a place, I say, suiting well to his beastly behaviour. As if he had been unworthy to be conveyed to Rome, the city which so long before he had abandoned.

ᵇ As poor beggar bodies were wont to be served in haste by the common bearers, and not fully burnt with leisure.

ᶜ Where malefactors ordinarily were burnt.

76. ¹ He meaneth, I suppose, a counterpair indented.

NOTES AND ANNOTATIONS UPON
GAIUS CAESAR CALIGULA

1. [1] Daughter of Antonius the triumvir (Mark Antony) by Octavia, sister of Augustus. [2] *Annariae* [more commonly *annales*]. [3] Seven [five] years after. [4] [Rather, *his* firmness and loyalty to Tiberius.] [5] [Checked, resisted.] [6] From the said army wherewith he was acquainted. [7] [Translating *dejecisset ;* others read *devicisset*, had subdued.] [8] [Tacitus, *Ann.* ii, 69, 73 ; Pliny, *Nat. Hist.* xi, 71.]

[a] Called by some *annales* or *annariae ;* of others, *comitiales.* By which provided it was, in what years of a man's age he was capable of quaestorship, praetorship, consulship, or any other like office of state ; as also it was limited, within what time between one might eft-soons bear the same office again. Item, what the term of every magistracy should be, etc. And albeit the ancient Romans had no such laws, but (as Cornelius Scipio [1] at his petition of aedileship made answer, when exception was taken against him for his young age) whomsoever the Quirites would charge to be a magistrate, he had years enough on his back, yet afterwards sundry statutes were enacted in that behalf ; although by virtue of special privileges the same were not duly observed. By the chronology it appeareth that he was but nineteen [? twenty-one] years old when he became quaestor [he was born May 24, 15 B.C., and was quaestor A.D. 7, consul A.D. 12. Originally the legal age for the quaestorship was 27-30, but in imperial times it was reduced to 24 or 25], like as Tiberius before him.

[b] Which Tiberius, envying his greatness, wrought, thereby to expose him unto greater dangers.

2. [1] Tiberius himself, or Germanicus his adopted son. [2] [Without restraint.]

3. [1] Greek and Latin. [2] The good will and affection of men, counted among the gifts of fortune. [3] For they used then no stirrups and therefore the blood and humours would descend to the legs. [4] *Triumphales ;* some read *triumphalis*, as if he gave not over pleading when he had triumphed, or received triumphal ornaments. [The latter is preferable.] [5] [His Latin translation of the astronomical poem by Aratus of Soli is still extant.] [6] [Tac. *Ann.* i, 62, says he himself laid the first sod.] [7] [Magic spells, incantations ; *see* Tac. *Ann.* ii, 69.]

[a] Well might this unseasonable exercise puff up and fill his skin with crudities and foggy [2] humours, but hurtful unto his health it was and brought upon him diseases, and namely that called *Cardiacus*, of

---

[1] [Cornelius Scipio Africanus the Younger. He was a candidate for the aedileship in 147, but the people desired his election to the consulship, which he secured although he was only thirty-seven years of age, the legal age being forty-three.]

[2] [Puffy, bloated.]

which some say he died. Let them look to it therefore, who, because they would be fat, not only fall to bodily exercise out of time, even upon full stomachs, but also every morning eat in their beds and sleep upon it, yea, and ordinarily take a nap at noon, so soon as their meat is out of their mouths.

b By this attribute, civil, in our author, ye must understand courtesy, affability, and a part not exceeding that of private citizens, without taking any state.

5. ¹ Or, the images of the gods within the temples.   ² Touching them all and every one privately.   ³ At Rome, a stay of all courts and pleas, in token of a public sorrow [*justitium, lit.* a standing still (*stare*) of law, represented by -steed or -stead].

a As if the gods, whose images were shrined within, were not to be honoured any longer as gods, suffering so good a man as Germanicus was to die. For as, in token of honour, the people used to adorn the statues and images of famous persons with flowers and green leaves, so, whom they did vilipend and despise, they were wont to cast stones at their images and statues.

b The tutelary gods of the house, which ordinarily stood within a closet, called thereupon *Lararium*.

c For to what end should they rear children any more ? since Germanicus, grown to so good proof, sped no better, but was taken away by untimely death.

d In this place the circumstance showeth, that the king of the Parthians is meant, however the Persian king and such mighty monarchs, having under their dominion other petty kings as tributaries or homagers, be so called, like as Agamemnon also in Homer.

e Which at Rome betokened a general mourning, occasioned upon some extraordinary calamity, or fear of public danger, even as with us the shutting in of shop-windows, etc.

6. ¹ [In sorrowful mood.]   ² Torches, tapers, etc.   ³ Which they had made *pro salute Germanici*, for the health and welfare of Germanicus.

a About the middle of this month began the feast *Saturnalia*, celebrated with good cheer, with revels, dances, gaming, and all kind of liberty.

8. ¹ The last day of August.   ² [Historian and poet.]   ³ [mod. Tivoli.]   ⁴ Or Ambitivum [or Ambitarvium].   ⁵ The meeting of two rivers [Coblenz].   ⁶ [Refutes.]   ⁷ [The use of nephew and niece for grandson and granddaughter was common in the 17th century.]   ⁸ [Made arrangements.]   ⁹ May 18.

a Or, his country's.

9. ¹ He was then but a child, about three or four years old.

a For common soldiers wore a certain studded shoe, named *Caliga*.

10. ¹ [The opposite of doff, to do off.]   ² [The day when degrees are conferred in certain universities ; here used of the day when the *toga virilis* was put on ; cf. Aug. 26.]   ³ [Tricks, artifices.]   ⁴ [Lat. *querelas*, complaints.]   ⁵ Passienus [P. Crispus, a well-known orator] was the author of this apophthegm [Tacitus, *Ann.* vi, 20].

a Which was later than the ordinary time, by reason of Tiberius his lingering. For usually these complements were performed at forty-seven years of age.

11. ¹ Commonly taken for a water-snake.

^a In this habit and manner of attire counterfeiting a woman, thereby to decline [avert] suspicion when he entered into other men's houses for to dishonour them and abuse their wives, whom our author termeth here *Adulteria*, for *adulterae*, as elsewhere, *conjugia* for *conjuges*.

^b The fabulous history of Phaethon is well-known, namely, how by misgovernment of the steeds which drew the chariot of the sun his father, he set the whole world on fire. By Phaethon therefore is meant a combustion (as it were) and general confusion of the provinces, like as by the water-snake the very bane and poison of the Roman State.

12. ¹ For Claudia, as Livilla for Livia, after his ordinary manner, to name women *hypokoristicos*, by their diminutives. ² A bishop. ³ Issue male, except himself, and Tiberius, a very child, the son of Drusus. ⁴ *Enniam, Naevii Macronis.* ⁵ [Written document.] ⁶ Who wrought the fall of Sejanus. ⁷ Tiberius' freedman. ⁸ [Confessed, acknowledged.] ⁹ [Filial affection.] ¹⁰ Rapier or spud [short knife or dagger].

13. ¹ [Attire : the word survives in widow's weeds.] ² [Rather, doll, darling, as a term of endearment.]

^a To do him the greater honour, they entertain him upon the way (as the manner was) with sacrifices, torches, tapers, and wax-lights.

14. ¹ Tiberius, the son of Drusus. ² [The purple-bordered toga worn by freeborn children.] ³ [Fr. *à outrance*, to the death.] ⁴ Offered to lay down their own lives. ⁵ The main standards.

^a An opinion there was, deeply settled in men's heads, that the death of one man might be excused and redeemed with the death of another.

15. ¹ [Lat. *ferculum*, barrow, litter.] ² [In crowds.] ³ [Procession.] ⁴ His cousin german, for such are called brethren. ⁵ [In republican times, the knight whose name appeared first in the censor's list ; under the empire, properly the young sons of the emperor.] ⁶ The form of oath, that any man took. ⁷ [Pardoned, condoned their offence.] ⁸ As we say, from the beginning of the world to this day.

16. ¹ [Orator and author of a history of the civil wars. His works having been condemned to be burnt, he put an end to his life by shutting himself up in the tomb of his ancestors.] ² [In the reign of Augustus he had written with great freedom on the end of the republic and the foundation of the monarchy. His books were nearly all burnt, a few copied being saved.] ³ [Orator and satirist. He had a very bad reputation, but his biting sarcasm made him greatly feared as well as detested.] ⁴ [That it was of the greatest importance to him.] ⁵ [Statement of the financial position of the empire.] ⁶ Public horses of service [purchased and kept by the State]. ⁷ Some read *centesimam* [1 p.c.]. ⁸ [C. 26, annot.] ⁹ *Octingenta sestertia.* Some read *octoginta*, 80,000, and this cometh nearer to the truth.

^a The two-hundredth part [½ p.c.].

^b His half-image downward from the head to the waist, portrayed with a shield or scutcheon ; and the same was commonly set out with the largest. Hereupon, M. Tullius Cicero [Macrobius, *Sat.* iii, 4], when he saw such a demi-personage representing his brother Quintus in the province that he governed (and a very little man he was of stature) : " My brother," quoth he, " in his half-part is greater than in the whole."

^c A festival holiday solemnised by herdsmen in the honour of Pales their goddess and patroness, upon which day the foundation of

Rome city was laid. This feast they kept the 12th day before the kalends of May, to wit, the 20th of April.

17. [1] The seventh of January. [2] *Fascias :* some expound these to be ribbons, garters, and gorgets.

18. [1] *Missilia,* small gifts [such as dried fruit, cakes, or tickets, specifying the amount the successful grabber was to receive in money, etc., Aug. 98]. [2] Or leopards. [3] Red and green [called chryso-colla in the 16th century since it was used to solder gold]. [4] [A private house belonging to a certain Gelos.] [5] *Maenianis* [first used by a certain Maenius].

[a] Maenius, a riotous unthrift [prodigal], when he had wasted his patrimony and sold his capital house in Rome, excepted in the sale and reserved to himself and his heirs one column or pillar, from which he projected and put forth into the street a jetty, and upon it built a gallery, out of which he might behold the sword-fencers in the market-place, whereunto he had a fair prospect from the said pillar. Whereupon all such galleries or buildings jutting out in the street be called *Maenianae.*

19. [1] An arm of the sea. [2] Two-wheeled war-chariots. [3] Tiberius, the son of Drusus Tiberius, the emperor's son.

20. [1] Some read *Hasticos,* as running at tilt [later readings are : *asticos,* celebrated in the city in honour of Bacchus, or *iselasticos,* public contests, the victors in which were conducted home in triumph : cf. Pliny the Younger, *Epp.* x, 119. Both names are of Greek derivation, given by Caligula in the spirit of imitation. The *ludi astici* were originally celebrated at Athens (the city, ἄστυ), in honour of Dionysus. Actiaci were the games in honour of Apollo revived by Augustus to celebrate his victory over Antony and Cleopatra]. [2] [=Ferules.] [3] *Rhodanus,* the Rhone.

21. [1] The conduit. [2] [Vanguard.]

22. [1] Usurping the attributes of Jupiter. [2] Agrippa and Antiochus. [3] [At once.] [4] Under Caesars. [5] *Principum,* for the Roman emperors were called *Principes.* [6] The portrait and proportion of his own self. [7] The palace on that mount, that stood in *Forum Romanum.* [8] To his palace. [9] Sacrifices [Lat. *hostia :* cf. the modern use of host ; the word is not to be confused with osses = omens]. [10] [He whispered to the god, or listened to him in return (*praebens in vicem aurem*) ; rounded really = whispered.] [11] [Later reading ἤ μ' ἀνάειρ' ἤ ἐγὼ σέ (*Iliad,* xxiii, 724) : " Either do thou lift me up or I thee," a term in wrestling.] [12] From the Palatium to the Capitol.

[a] The end of one verse, and beginning of another, cited out of Homer in the second book of his *Iliad* [204]. The poet ascribeth them unto sage Ulysses, in this sense :

One [Sovereign] Lord,
One King let there be.

[b] By exchanging the ensigns and ornaments of the Roman sovereign or emperor with the regal diadem, purple robe, and sceptre.

[c] Phoenicopterus (the flamingo) is a water-fowl haunting lakes and fens and the river Nilus, as Hesiod [1] writeth. The feathers be of colour

---

[1] [This should be Heliodorus, who (cvi, 3) calls the flamingo Νειλῷος.]

red or purple, whereof it taketh the name ; and the tongue is a most dainty and pleasant morsel. So said Apicius [a famous gourmand, who lived in the time of Augustus and Tiberius, and was the author of a book on cookery : cf. Pliny, *Nat. Hist.* x, 133 : " Apicius, the most riotous glutton and belly-god of his time, taught men first that the tongue of phoenicopterus was a most sweet and delicate piece of meat " (Holland's trans.)]. Of this bird Martial [xiii, 71] made an epigram :

> *Dat mihi penna rubens nomen, sed lingua gulosis*
> *Nostra sapit.   Quid si garrula lingua foret ?*

> My name I take of wings so red, but unto glutton's taste
> My tongue right pleasing is ; oh, what if it could prate as fast ?

d Some take them for bustards, birds decked, no doubt, with most beautiful feathers, as may appear by Tertullian against Marcion [i, 13] in these words : " One tiny wing of a wood-cock, I say nothing about the peacock, will of course declare to you that the Creator was a poor artificer."

e They are thought to be hens of Guinea.

f By the description of Clytus [in Athenaeus, 655 B], they be our turkeys [or, another kind of guinea-fowl].

g The pheasant called in old time Itys (which was the son of Tereus and Procne, transformed as poets feign into this bird) and afterwards phasianus or phasiana, took his name of Phasis, a river and city in Colchis, according to this epigram of Martial [xiii, 72] :

> *Argiva primum sum transportata carina :*
> *Ante mihi notum nil nisi Phasis erat :*

> In Argive ship transported first I was to foreign land :
> Foretime naught else but Phasis town I knew, or Phasis strand.

23. [1] Agrippa [made him out to be one of the imperial family]. [2] Agrippina, supposed to be the daughter of M. Agrippa and Julia. [3] *Siculasque*, not *Singulasque*. [4] Baseness of birth. [5] Aufidius Lingo, or Lurco. [6] By the father's side, to wit, the mother of Germanicus. [7] Silanus. [8] [Caligula.] [9] Tiberius. [10] [As for his uncle Claudius, he reserved him.]

a Philo [*Legatio ad Gaium*, 10] reporteth this far otherwise, and telleth a pitiful narration : how, by commission from Gaius, certain colonels and centurions came to young Tiberius, commanding him to kill himself, because, forsooth, unlawful it was for any other to murder a prince of the imperial blood. The youth, who had never seen any man killed, and by reason of his tender years was nothing at all experienced in the world, requested first of them, who were come thus to him, for to strike off his head, which he held out unto them ; but seeing his request would not be heard, he desired them yet to instruct him in what part of his body he should stab himself for the speediest death. And so by instructions from them he was his own executioner.

24. [1] [*In flagrante delicto*.] [2] To signify a solemn mourning. [3] *Per nomen*, some read *numen*, the godhead or divine power : for he equalled her with Venus, and commanded that she should be worshipped as a goddess ; and, as Dion writeth [lix, 11], named she was Panthea, and women were compelled to swear by her, as by Juno. [4] By them, to wit, Lepidus and his two sisters : or by him, for their death.

25. [1] Or sought again for the company, etc. *repetisse*. [2] Where she was with her husband aforesaid. [3] [With her hair down ; or, bare-headed.] [4] Short cloak or horseman's coat (*chlamys*). [5] Like

as Candaules, King of Lydia, did to his friend Gyges [Herodotus, i, 8].
⁶ A daughter. ⁷ Goddess of good arts and sciences : *operum haud
ignara Minervae*, Virgil [*Aen.* 5, 284]. ⁸ [Savage disposition.]
⁹ [Naughtiness, maliciousness.] ¹⁰ [Dangerous.] ¹¹ [Hesitate.]

ᵃ Romulus ravished the Sabine virgins ; and Augustus by force
took from Tiberius his wife Livia.

26. ¹ Removed. [He was the grandson, Caligula the great-grandson
of Antony.] ² [Considerate, respectful.] ³ *Essedum*, or carroch.
⁴ Or tickets. ⁵ Rooms and seats in the theatre appointed for the
gentlemen [knights]. ⁶ *Emitti ;* some read *amiciri*, to be covered
with hat, veil, bonnet of bongrace [broad-brimmed hat to keep off the
sun]. ⁷ [No better than skeletons.] ⁸ Citizens. ⁹ *Pegmatis*,
in the dative case, or frames for pageant [text and interpretation
doubtful]. ¹⁰ *Induxit :* another reading is *indixit*, enjoined, brought
upon.

ᵃ *Selene* in Greek signifieth the moon. And well-known it is that,
as M. Antonius the triumvir called himself Bacchus and Osiris, so
Cleopatra his wife took pleasure to be named *Luna*, the moon, and
Isis. Whereupon they gave to their son Alexander begotten by
them the name of the sun, and to their daughter Cleopatra the name
of the moon, or selene, which is all one.

ᵇ The consuls were reputed still (in outward show) sovereign
magistrates, although, indeed, the Caesars carried all before them, and
were absolute monarchs.

ᶜ Some read, *Tesseras decima citius*, before the tenth hour, or
four of the clock after noon, for so long continued the stage-plays
ordinarily. At which time, the emperors were wont to bestow their
tickets or tallies among the people, by virtue whereof they received
such and such gifts [Aug. 41].

ᵈ There be learned critics that expound this place far otherwise,
reading *Pegmares*, instead of *Pegmatis*, and understanding thereby
such sword-fencers, whose good hap it had been to escape with life
the fall from those frames or pageants called *Pegmata* or *Pegma*, which
with certain vices or screws were set up and let down, upon which as
on scaffolds, malefactors were brought forth, either to exhibit a show
unto the people, fighting one with another at sharpe [27], to the outrance
[14], or to make them sport, by falling down into a pit underneath,
where either wild beasts were ready to devour or fire to consume them,
a device wrought by dissolving the joints of the said *Pegmata* under
them. And in this sense they interpret the rest that followeth, concerning *patres familias*, good honest citizens, householders. [The
latest suggested reading *proque paegniariis patres familiarum notos* . . .
subiciebat is made to give the sense : " and put up well-known householders to fight as *paegniarii*," gladiators who fought only in jest.]

27. ¹ *Medios* [or *mediam*, standing in the middle of the gallery].
² [With unblunted swords.] ³ Ribbons. ⁴ [Mound, or embank-
ment] of Tarquinius, as some think. ⁵ [On all-fours.] ⁶ [Showed
contempt for.] ⁷ These *genii* are of a middle essence, between men
and gods, called therefore *medioxumi*. It signifieth here the demon,
tutelar angel, or spirit of the prince. For the manner of the Romans
was in flattering wise thus to swear, as also by the health, the life, the
honour of their emperors.

ᵃ He had espied in the multitude of those prisoners and malefactors
two with bald heads, distant far asunder, and happily [perchance] as
much as from the one end of the place unto the other : all those between,

without respect of their cause, he commanded to be put to death indifferently.

b An ordinary thing it was at Rome, to swear by the *genius*, as also by the fortune, the health, etc., of their emperors. And what a devout oath this was, *per genium*, by the demon, the spirit, or super-intendent angel of the prince, which I take to be as much as by his own good self, appeareth by Tertullian, *Apologet*. cap. 28. *Citius apud vos per omnes deos, quam per genium principis peieratur.* [" Among you there is far more readiness to commit perjury in the name of all the gods, than to swear falsely by the genius of Caesar."]

c Seneca [*de Ira*, ii, 33] reporteth the like example of Pastor, a right worshipful gentleman of Rome, whose son the same Caligula, upon very envy that the young man was a proper and beautiful person, put to death in his father's sight, and then invited the old man to supper, provoked him to carouse and be merry, which the good father was fain to endure and make semblance of contentment, for fear lest the tyrant would have done as much by another son whom he had living.

d *Catenis verberatum.* Among other chastisements of the body, there is reckoned *Vinculorum verberatio*, as Callistratus [Digest, 48, 19, 7] witnesseth, lib. 7 *de Paenis*. The ignorance whereof hath made some to read, *in catenis verberatum*, bound in chains and then beaten ; others, *habenis* for *catenis*, as if he had been well-lindged [thrashed] with leather thongs or halters' ends, as slaves were wont to be served by the lorarii [official floggers].

28. [1] Who had banished him.   [2] Where they were wont to live banished.   [3] [All to-pricked, pierced him thoroughly. To- either goes with the verb, like the German *zu-*, or with all-, the compound then meaning thoroughly, extremely : Tib. 60.]

a Albeit the proper use of these *graphia* was to cut or engrave letters only on tables of bark or soft wood, yet, because it was unlawful to wear weapons in the senate-house, some of a mischievous mind made those writing-styles or steels, so as they might kill therewith, enacted therefore it was, that no man should carry about him such writing-instruments of iron or steel, but of bone only. And yet even these, as others also of reeds and quills, were made so keen and sharp, that they were able to give a mortal wound [C. 82].

29. [1] [*Gr.* ἀδιατρεψία : a Stoic term.]   [2] Or counter-poisons. [3] By letters or friends that he made.   [A. was the name of three towns, all famed for hellebore.]   [4] Renewed.   [5] By purging.   [6] A nation mixed of French and Greeks. [After their defeat at Delphi (280 B.C.) the Gauls made their way to Thrace, crossed the Hellespont and settled in Asia Minor, their district being called Gallograecia, or Galatia.]

a For the manner of the Roman emperors was, upon displeasure, to send men and women away into some desert isles, and there to confine them.

b Hellebore that groweth in the isles of Anticyra, is of most effectual operation. The root is that whereof is made our sneezing powder ; it purgeth extremely by vomit. Thereupon ariseth the proverb, *Naviget Anticyram*, Let him sail to Anticyra, applied to one that is melancholic in the highest degree and little better than mad. See Pliny, *Nat. Hist.* [xxv, 21, 47-61] ; Horace, *Sat.* ii, 3, 166.

30. [1] Atreus [the name of a tragedy by Accius].   [2] Of charioteers. [3] For he favoured the green livery.   [4] Worthy and meet to be put to sword-fight. [5] So named of a net that they used in fight to catch their adversary with; they handled also a weapon with three tines or pikes like a trout-spear. They were called *Threces*. [6] *Gregatim dimicantes:* for distinction of those that were called *monomachi*, and employed in single fight. [7] Otherwise, *mirmillones*. These were armed, whereas the *retiarii* were lightly appointed and *tunicati*, traversing their ground nimbly, and seeming otherwhiles to flee; whereupon the others took their name, *secutores*, as following them.

[a] Some conjecture very well that this Tetrinius was not surnamed Latro, being the addition appropriate to the noble family of Rome of the Porcii, but a notorious thief or robber, such as in Latin is called *Latro*. And of that sort commonly were they that performed before the people this bloody fight with unrebated swords, without foils. And no marvel, if he termed all the citizens there assembled *Tetrinios*, thieves, considering he wished before that he could cut off all their heads at one blow.

31. [1] [Sudden outbreaks of fire : Aug. 25.]

32. [1] For this bridge was made of barks. [2] Waiting at the board. [3] Or leaf. [4] For tables in those days were laid and covered over with silver plates [Pliny, *Nat. Hist.* xxxiii, 49, etc., for various uses of silver]. [5] Or *Secutores* aforesaid. [6] [Cudgels, clubs.] [7] [Lat. *sponte*, of his own accord, purposely.] [8] [Short dagger : Aug. 32.] [9] At sacrifice.

33. [1] [Flogging, cheer being used in the sense of reception or entertainment.] [2] By cramping and torturing her therewith [*fidiculae*, a number of strings which were used as instruments of torture].

[a] He suspected that she had given him some love-drinks.

34. [1] [So to say, almost entirely.] [2] Being a poet. [3] Virgil. [4] Livy.

[a] *Praeter aequum.* How this can stand with his pride or malice, which our author hath propounded to exemplify, I cannot see. In some copies we read *praeter eum*, beside him, that is to say, otherwise than he would have them, or approve. And one critic or judicious lawyer, Franc. Hottoman, as also Coracius, read *praeter Eccum*, as if he should say, All lawyers shall give none other answer but this : Behold him, meaning the emperor Gaius, thereby referring the decision of all matters to his will and pleasure. Lastly, Torrentius concludeth : the period thus, *Ne quid respondere possint*, That they should give no answer at all. And for *praeter aequum*, etc., he putteth *praeterea*, Moreover, for a beginning of the next chapter.

35. [1] Or ensigns. [2] Or chain. [3] Who afterwards married the daughter of Claudius the emperor. [4] *Hoplomachus*, with shield and helmet. [5] To the *Threx* and *hoplomachus* [give the foil=defeat]. [6] [Rival, competitor.] [7] To wit, sword-fight. [8] *Essedario*, or champion that used to fight and play his prizes [engage in contests] out of a British or French chariot called *essedum*.

[a] Colosseros seemeth to be a word compounded of *Colossos* and *Eros*. The one importeth his tallness, resembling the stately and giantlike personages called colossi, and the other his lovely visage, representing Eros, even Love or Cupid itself.

[b] These fencers, called Threces or Thraces[1], thought to be the same

---

[1] So thinks Sabellicus.

that *retiarii*, were lightly appointed for armour and put to desperate fight, as having all parts of their bodies exposed to danger, whereupon they were called also *Tunicati*, and were matched in opposition with the *Mirmillones*, as this verse of Ausonius [*Technopaegion*, xii, 3] implieth :

> *Quis mirmilloni componitur ?*[1] *aequimanus Thrax.*

Whereas the other, named *Hoplomachi*, had for their defence headpieces and targets (Seneca, *Epp*. i, 7).

[c] The priest, called *Rex Nemorensis*, of a place where Diana Aricina was worshipped, within a temple beautified with a grove about it, by a barbarous custom of the Scythians, so long only held his place until, after one year's revolution, some one stronger than himself stepped unto him and overcame him in single fight, and so deposed him, like as by the first institution himself, foiling another in combat, attained thereto[2].

36. [1] A player counterfeiting all parts and kinds of gesture. [2] [Against nature : C. 52.]   [3] [Hardly ; also, rarely (*non temere*).] [4] [Examine.]   [5] [Perchance.]

37. [1] Or oils.   [2] [Very spacious.]   [3] [Ragstone, a dark grey sandstone.]   [4] *Vicies ac septies millies* [about £21,600,000].

[a] Seneca writeth, *Consolatio ad Helviam* [x, 4], that it was ordinary with him to consume at one supper ten millions of sesterces, and who studied himself and laid his head to others, how he might at one supper make an even hand with[3] the revenues and tributes of all the provinces belonging to the state of Rome.

[b] Some read for [*de Cedris*] *Deceres*, after the form of *Moneres*, meaning by *Deceres* a mighty galley furnished with ten ranks of oars, for such the Greeks call Δεκήρεις.

38. [1] [Plundering : often coupled with pilling.]   [2] *Deflebat ;* or *deflabat*, he rejected and [treated with contempt].   [3] [Being nominated heir . . . in consequence of the fear which he inspired. The English of the text is clumsy.]   [4] *Macteas* or *mattyas*, such as marchpanes.   [5] [To so high a price.]   [6] Or crier [auctioneer].   [7] As it were, to buy this and that.

39. [1] Livilla and Agrippina.   [2] [*Libertos*, freedmen. H. is here apparently translating a reading *liberos*.]   [3] In grinding corn and carrying bread.   [4] [*lit*. one who holds land or dwellings for a term of years ; here, simply those engaged in lawsuits (*litigator*).]

40. [1] [Proved guilty of.]   [2] [Arrived at an agreement.]   [3] [Earnings.]

41. [1] [Same as " copy."]   [2] [Basilicas.]   [3] [A slave whose business it was to name the citizens whose support his master was anxious to obtain, and to announce visitors.]   [4] [Rather, money was lent (*praebita*) to them on interest.]   [5] [Cheating.]   [6] [At once.]

[a] *Dum multa commissa fierent.* Which may be expounded otherwise thus : Whenas many things were forfeited and confiscate.

42. [1] Or laps of their clothes.

---

[1] Or, *committitur*.
[2] [*See* Frazer's *Golden Bough*.]
[3] [Took counsel with others, how he could spend.]

43. [1] [Mevania, a town, Clitumnus, a river, in Umbria. Mevania (*mod.* Bevagna) was the birth-place of the poet Propertius. The river was supposed to turn the cattle white that drank of its waters, or to cause them to produce white calves : Virgil, *Georg.* ii, 146. It ran through beautiful scenery in the midst of rich pasture lands.]

44. [1] [Who were late with their contingents.] [2] [Remote.] [3] [Remuneration.] [4] *Batavorum,* the Batavians. [Rather, *Britannorum.*]

45. [1] *De custodia :* or that were prisoners and in ward [*i.e.* either some of his own bodyguard, or some captives]. [2] [The troops.] [3] [Well-known.] [4] [*Aen.* i, 207 : *Durate, et vosmet rebus servate secundis.*]
[a] Taking the name from *Exploratores* [scouts], a military term, signifying the avant-couriers and fore-riders, to discover the enemy, and to clear the coasts.

46. [1] As if with £3, 2s. 6d. they had been made for ever.

47. [1] [= Renegades, deserters.]

48. [1] To kill every tenth man of them. [2] [Announced, proclaimed.]

49. [1] Of Senators. [2] Alexandria is Antiochea in old MSS. [3] Senators and gentlemen [knights]. [4] [Or, in his private papers.]

50. [1] [To walk.] [2] [See 29, annot.]

51. [1] Or person. [2] [Narrow way, pass.] [3] Or guarded. [4] [Maintain.]
[a] Yet Dion [lix, 28] reporteth of him, that otherwhiles, when it thundered aloft, he would seem to do the like beneath with a thunder barrel, or such a kind of device ; when it lightened, to make flashes with fireworks, and if a thunderbolt fell, to discharge likewise some stone out of an engine.

52. [1] [Like a citizen.] [2] Lawn or tiffany. [3] [*Cycladatus,* wearing a *cyclas,* a thin flowing robe, fringed with rich embroidery.] [4] Or pantofles. [5] Or pinsons [thin-soled shoes]. [6] With three grains [prongs] like an eel spear. [7] [Staff, rod.]
[a] Which ornaments belonged to Jupiter and Aesculapius.
[b] Resembling thereby Neptune, for it symboliseth his power over waters in sea, river, lakes.
[c] The ensign of Mercury, betokening his eloquence [rather, his position as the messenger of the gods].

53. [1] *Quantumvis facundus :* or, being very fair-spoken, etc. [2] [Hardly, with difficulty.] [3] [= Picked : ornate, refined.]

54. [1] [Competitions of strength and skill.] [2] *Thrax.* [3] [*Scabellum,* a musical instrument played with the foot.] [4] A laudable exercise in Rome, as may appear before in Augustus.

55. [1] A gesturer or dancer that counterfeited all parts. [2] [Was not ashamed.] [3] The said Mnester. [4] [Made a disturbance.] [5] Or *retiarii,* as some think. Others take it to be a general name of all sword-fencers. [6] A faction or crew of fencers opposite to the *Thraces* or *retiarii,* whom in respect of the *Thraces* he favoured not. [7] [" Anyhow it was found mentioned under that name among other poisons in his catalogue." This is omitted by H.]   ⁸ *Prasina factio*.   ⁹ Or lodging [quarters where they lodged and where the horses were kept]. ¹⁰ Of that green livery.   ¹¹ [Presents given to the guests at table, to take away with them (*apophoreta*, Gr. ἀποφέρειν). "Hospital" is apparently the old form of "hospitable."]   ¹² *Incitato equo, cuius causa*, some interpret it otherwise thus : To Incitatus, for whose horse sake, taking Incitatus to be the name of the master, and not of the horse, because in the poet Martial [x, 76, 9] there is mention made of Incitatus, a famous chariot-rider and a muleteer. Yet L. Verus Antoninus erected an image of gold for a horse that he had named Volucer while he lived, and a sepulchre when he was dead. And why might not this brain-sick prince be as absurd ?   ¹³ [Or poitrel : breast-piece.]

56. ¹ Caligula.   ² [Snub, jeer at.]
^a So called, because they were exhibited in the Palatium.

57. ¹ *Cinyras*.   ² The son of Amyntas.   ³ Of some house represented upon the stage.   ⁴ [Tried to rival one another.]   ⁵ Fit actors and expositors of such an argument.
^a Capitolium, although κατ' ἐξοχὴν it was the stately mount or castle of Rome, yet it became a general name of all citadels and strong castles built for the defence of any city.
^b Meaning the murder of Gaius Julius Caesar dictator.
^c Bearing the name of a notorious thief, or captain rather of thieves, crucified for his deserts.

58. ¹ January 24.   ² Or vault[ed passage].   ³ [A sacrificial phrase. The sacrificer of the victim asked the priest *Agone* (am I to do it), and the priest answered *Hoc age* (do it, *i.e.* dispatch the victim). H.'s rendering hardly expresses the idea.]   ⁴ [Made to retire.] ⁵ [Ironical, " you have appealed to Jupiter ; take what he sends you by way of fulfilment."]

59. ¹ [Orchards, pleasure gardens.]   ² [Additional formality.] ³ Which he called a vault or cloister before.

60. ¹ A new senate-house in lieu of the *Curia Hostilia*.   ² For now the name of the Caesars and their race became odious, as oppressors of the commonweal.   ³ And yet we read not so much of Gaius, one of Augustus' sons [grandsons], brother of Lucius.

NOTES AND ANNOTATIONS UPON
TIBERIUS CLAUDIUS DRUSUS CAESAR

1. [1] Augustus : and not by Tiberius Nero, his mother's husband.
[2] Or Drusianae [Tacitus, *Ann.* ii, 8. They connected the Rhine from
Westerwoort with the Isala (mod. Yssel) at Doesburg. "Straung"
is presumably a form of strange, although it might possibly=strong.
If the former, does it mean made in a foreign country, or simply extraordinary, wonderful ?] [3] Representing Germany. [4] Called Ovation [Aug. 22]. [5] The wicked and mischievous [disastrous, ill-
omened] camp. [6] Or Chancellors [rather, clerks]. [7] Which the
Greeks call *Cenotaphium*, an empty tomb. [8] Or port-way [used by
H. for a Roman road, as a translation of *via*]. [9] [That is, he thought
as much of military glory as of making himself popular.] [10] Which
he [personally] took from their generals [called *spolia opima*].
[a] Like as in Rome the gate called *Porta scelerata*, and the street
Vicus sceleratus upon some semblable unfortunate accidents.

2. [1] [The legal meaning is to institute a suit in the court of wards to
obtain possession of lands, livery being the legal delivery of property :
the original, *post tutelam receptam*, means, when his age entitled him to
be exempt from guardianship.] [2] *Olim superjumentarium*, rather a
master of muleteers.
[a] Whereas by usual custom such were brought into the Forum or
common-hall.

3. [1] Otherwise called Livia and Julia, the mother of Drusus.
[2] [Expressed her horror, wished that such a fate might be averted.]

4. [1] His grandmother's brother by the mother's side. [2] As well
good as bad. [3] Ultor, the Revenger. [4] Sufficient [sound, unim-
paired]. [5] Sound throughout and perfect. [6] Or steps. [7] To
be impaired or disabled and maimed, as well for the sufficiency [sound-
ness] of body as integrity of mind. [8] Who are wont to make good
game and scoff at such things. [9] If it be not resolved upon and
set down aforehand by us. [10] *Conspici* or *despui*, spit at. [11] A
bed-loft at the circus games, whereon the images of the gods are laid
[*see* Aug. 45]. [12] [In any case.] [13] In the absence of the consuls
attending the sacrifice upon the Alban hill. [14] [People would wonder
why some municipal office was not bestowed upon him, such as the
city prefecture.] [15] Claudius. [16] Superficially [rather, forget-
fully, absent-mindedly : *cf.* 39]. [17] [The latest texts transfer *misellus*,
the poor creature (H.'s silly soul) to the next sentence, put a colon at
ἀτυχεῖ, and read *nam ἐν τοῖς σπουδαίοις*, omitting πάνυ : the poor
creature is unfortunate ; for in matters of importance, when his mind
. . . .] [18] [Nobility.] [19] Darkly and confusedly. [20] Clearly and
plainly to be understood.

5. [1] [An empty distinction.] [2] Every one worth 15s. 7d. *ob.*
[=*obolus*, used for ½d.] or 100 sesterces. [3] [*Sigillaria*, little images

presented during the last days of the Saturnalia, also called Sigillaria.
Translate rather: "to spend at the Saturnalia and Sigillaria."]
4 [Stigma, reproach.]

6. **1** As we use to veil bonnet or do off [doff] our hats.   **2** The
emperor.

7. **1** Caligula.   **2** All hail or happiness.

8. **1** *A copreis* [Tib. 61] ; or *a tropaeis*, such as would play bopeep
and hide themselves when they had done some unhappiness [something
mischievous].   **2** For whiles they sat or leaned upon pallets at their
meat, they put off their shoes.

9. **1** Gaius Caligula's.   **2** [Calig. 8, 24.]   **3** [Entertained, admitted. The praetor was said *recipere nomen*, to receive the name of
the accused. The senate, if it desired, could refuse to admit the charge.]
4 [A fee paid on entering upon an office.]   **5** [The treasury at this
time managed by the praetors.]   **6** [Hung up the edict advertising
the sale.]   **7** His lands and goods were forfeited and so were published in table as void and vacant. [Other interpretations are : to make
up the deficiency ; without reserve, no buyer being found.]
    a By virtue of this Act [relating to the sale of estates by auction],
himself, his lands and goods were proscribed and exposed to open
sale, in a table hung up by an edict from the masters of the exchequer
or city-chamber. And if within the time appointed he came not in
to satisfy the debt, nor any chapman or surety to undertake it, he
and his whole estate fell by escheat as forfeit and confiscate into the
prince's hands.

10. **1** A garret [rather, the flat house-top or terrace, balcony. There
were curtains in front of the windows opening upon it].   **2** [Keep on
fuming : so, fare and rage.]   **3** [" Hope " of obtaining the empire
offered him, " confidence " that his life was safe.]   **4** *Armatos ;* or
armatus, himself armed.   **5** *Quina dena sestertia. See* Josephus
(*Antiq. Jud.* xix, 4, 2).

11. **1** [Important, advantageous.]   **2** Germanicus.   **3** [Mark Antony.]   **4** His uncle.

12. **1** [Sparing : acc. to Murray, peculiar to H.]   **2** Or solemnity
of nuptial contract.   **3** By applause and acclamation.   **4** [*Incessere*,
to attack, accuse.]

13. **1** Some call this a Jacob's staff.   **2** [C. 30 ; A. 58.]   **3** Ominous and unlucky signs.

14. **1** Of private matters, as praetors and centumvirs.

15. **1** And therefore, ambitious.   **2** [In a matter which affected
himself.]   **3** The plaintiff himself.   **4** As a citizen of Rome.   **5** As
a foreigner.   **6** [Another early reading, *puto, licuit* (I think that is
a valid excuse), is now generally adopted.]   **7** Or judgement-seat.
8 [Scratched, grazed.]

16. **1** *Litura tamen extet.* Some read *extat*, yet the blot remaineth,
meaning the filthiness of the fact.   **2** [Marked, or branded.]   **3** [He
was defended by Cicero in a speech still extant : the Ptolemy was
Auletes.]   **4** For these matters would bear action.   **5** [Usually.]
6 Or enhuile [anoint with oil].

17. [1] [He or Caligula had refused to give up certain deserters.] [2] [Rather, W.N.W.] [3] Where Calais standeth, or Boulogne, as some think. [4] Sixteen, according to Dion [lx, 23]. [5] [Surrendered with expressions of loyalty.] [6] [Gave them permission to return.] [7] Embroidered or worked with palm-branches ; *cf.* also C. 76.

[a] These islands are situate in the mouth of the river Rhodanus (Rhone) : and they be so called of the order in which they lie.

18. [1] Whensoever you read in Suetonius " city " absolutely, understand thereby Rome, κατ᾽ ἐξοχήν, as one would say, The city of all cities, an ordinary phrase in other Roman writers ; according as Virgil hath fitly expressed in this verse, *Eclog.* i, 19 : *Urbem quam dicunt Romam.* [2] [A building in the Campus Martius near the Septa, where votes were counted and presents distributed to the people.] [3] Or Forum.

20. [1] [Later reading : *magna potius et necessaria quam multa*, rather great and necessary than many in number.] [2] Or gott [watercourse, sluice]. [3] Or Pier. [4] The drawing of the lake Fucinus. [5] *Alterum*, the Pier at Ostia. But because there is no mention made in Julius Caesar's life of this pier or haven, some read for *alterum* in this place *ceterum ;* and then the word *alterum* before is meant of the second work of these three, denied unto the Marsians. *Ceterum*, but intended oftentimes in the design of Julius. [6] *Novi Anienis :* some read *novo opere*, within new stonework. [7] Or Cisterns. [8] [Pliny, *Nat. Hist.* xvi, 202 ; xxxvi, 70.]

21. [1] For the stage thereof was consumed with fire. [2] Or seat of state. [3] Which were solemnised once in the revolution of one hundred years or one hundred and ten, as some write. [4] [Caligula built a circus in the Vatican where the basilica of S. Peter is now.] [5] Of chariot-running. [6] [The Circus Maximus, in the valley between the Palatine and Aventine.] [7] [These goals (*metae*) or turning-posts were three conical pillars at each end of the circus.] [8] [Prize may mean either the actual contest or the reward given to the successful competitors.] [9] [The English is awkward. The meaning is : One, without the regular accompaniment of baiting, etc., was held in the praetorian camp ; the other, with these accompaniments, in the Septa.] [10] Or, my masters, *Dominos*. [11] The name of a fencer. [12] [Gladiators who gained the popular favour, or who owing to age or the number of their victories were allowed to retire, were presented with a wooden sword or rapier (*rudis*).] [13] This Verb (*Avete*) signifieth here, farewell or adieu. But the soldiers construed it in the better sense for their own turns (as they had used it before in saluting him) All hail ye also. [Another early reading is *aut non*, or not (about to die).] [14] *Duodenarum*. Some read *undevicenae*, 19, and out of Dion [lx, 33], *quinquagenarum*, 50. [15] Resembling Neptune's trumpeter.

[a] The name of this fencer, Palumbus, signifieth also in the Latin tongue a stock-dove : which gave occasion unto him to come out with this odd jest.

22. [1] Whether it were an owl, or the bird named *Incendiaria* [causing a conflagration], *see* Pliny, *Nat. Hist.* x, 34.

23. [1] That a woman under fifty years of age should not be wedded to a man that was threescore. [2] Granting that men threescore years old might marry women under fifty. [3] Wards under age. [4] [Seat or bench : C. 78.] [5] Licences to be absent a time from Rome.

ª Provided it was by the law Papia, That no woman under fifty years of age should be married to a man threescore years old or upward ; item, That no man under threescore years might wed a woman fifty years old or above. Where note that these words [*a Tiberio*], as if he added the said branch, seem to have been foisted in, considering that, as it appeareth by Tacitus [*Ann.* iii, 25], the emperor Tiberius went about to moderate the foresaid law, and not to make it more strict by annexing such a clause.

24. ¹ Who received 200,000 sesterces for salary or might dispend so much by the place. ² The senator's robe [*latus clavus*, broad stripe] studded with purple. ³ [Obsolete form of author. The Latin is *proauctorem*, distant ancestor, founder.] ⁴ Cisalpina, which thereupon was called Provincia Quaestoria. ⁵ From Augustus' days. ⁶ [This must be " while he was undergrown."] ⁷ *Latus texit*, that is, *laevus ei incedebat*, he gave him the right hand, and went on his left side.

25. ¹ [Military service.] ² Otherwise called Tiberina. ³ Without the gate Esquilina. ⁴ And his successors. ⁵ This some think is to be understood of Christians whom we find in the ecclesiastical writers to be misnamed by the ethnic infidels, *Chrestiani*, like as Christ himself *Chrestos*, in scorn. [Either referring to Christ, in which case there is an anachronism, or Chrestus is the name of some Jew.] ⁶ Or Fetials (Livy, i, 24) : they were a body of priests who ratified treaties and formally declared war after satisfaction had been refused.

ª For fear of breaking up the pavements, if they rode in coach, wagon, chariot, or on horseback.

ᵇ In divers Greek and Latin writers the names of Jews and Christians were confounded, so as by Jews they understood Christians.

ᶜ *Orchestra* was that place in the forefront of the theatre or scaffolds and nearest unto the stage, wherein the senators ordinarily sat and sometime the emperor himself.

ᵈ *Popularia* were seats within the scaffolds and theatre, most remote from the stage, wherein the common people were allowed to stand or sit. Between the said *Orchestra* and these *Popularia* were ranged the knights or gentlemen of Rome, and those ranks bare the name of *Equestria*.

ᵉ So called of the mountain Eryx in Sicily, where she was highly worshipped and where she had a temple.

26. ¹ [Really great-granddaughter.] ² Or Urgulanilla. ³ While she was empress and wife to Claudius. ⁴ The handfasters [those who make contracts, especially nuptial] or makers of the marriage [witnesses of the ceremony, who formerly took the auspices]. ⁵ [=and yet he could not keep his resolution, but immediately.] ⁶ His own niece. ⁷ [Exempted ; *cf*. Cal. 15.] ⁸ With their brothers' or sisters' daughters.

27. ¹ Emperor after him [and his stepson].

28. ¹ *Hasta pura donavit :* for his great valour forsooth. [Such spears were used as a military decoration.] ² Of this Felix mention is made in the Acts of the Apostles [xxiv]. ³ [To plunder, secure by fair means or foul : *pill and poll* were very often combined ; Cal. 38.] ⁴ [He made the apt reply.] ⁵ Narcissus and Pallas.

ª As for Drusilla his wife [daughter of Agrippa I], a Jew born, she had been married indeed before to king Azizus, as Josephus writeth [xix, 9] ; but as touching the other two queens, whosoever they were, he was acquainted with them otherwise, and not in way of marriage, so far as I can find. [A second wife, also Drusilla, was the granddaughter of Antony and Cleopatra and daughter of Juba II, King of Mauritania. Of the third wife nothing is known.]

b For every man might not so do, unless he had a knight's estate, which was four hundred thousand *sestertii*[1], or were freeborn; neither libertines nor mechanical persons living by base trades and occupations were allowed.

29. [1] *Consocerum* : so called for that their children married together, and such with us name one another brethren [joint father-in-law]. [2] The son of Tiberius. [3] Who is called also Livilla. [4] [This is interpolated by H.] [5] Tacitus writeth [*Ann.* xii, 7] that he killed himself upon that day. [6] ["On the other hand" would better express the meaning that he does not vouch for the story.]

a Other writers, as Philostratus [*Vita Apollonii*, v, 28] and Julian [*Caesares*, 310] say moreover, That without his wife and freedmen, he was κωφὸν πρόσωπον [mute, supernumerary] and δορυφόρημα [bodyguard] τῆς βασιλείας, much like to a player in a dumb show, and the bare image of a king's majesty, as Plutarch [*An seni sit gerenda*, 15] reporteth of Aridaeus.

30. [1] [A north of England form of stutter, apparently still in use.]

31. a This disease some physicians name Καρδιαλγίαν, the heartache, or *Cardiacam passionem*, seated in the orifice of the stomach, which is called Καρδία. The pain whereof Pliny [*Nat. Hist.* xxiii, 1] affirmeth to be most intolerable, next unto the passion of the strangury.

32. [1] [*Assidua*, continually, constantly.] [2] Or, at a settle at the tables' end. [3] [Secretly.] [4] Or earthen pot.

a *Flatum crepitumque ventris.* By *Flatum* understand that riddance of wind downward, *qui nares ferit, non aures*. Which in English cometh near unto the Latin word *Visio*, for that the verb *Visire* is the same that τὸ [βδεῖν]. As Cicero in his *Epistles* [*Ad Fam.* ix, 22] hath well, but covertly observed, out of the word *Divisio*, wherein he noteth *Quiddam Cacemphaton* [an unseemly expression]. Which place some interpreters, for ignorance of the said verb *Visio*, have expounded very absurdly [*cf.* Quintilian, viii, 3, 46].

33. [1] [The Forum of Augustus.] [2] Revenger, situate near to the hall, for distinction of another temple bearing that name, on the Capitol mount. [3] [Swollen, bulging.] [4] [Intoxicated.] [5] [*Gestatio* properly means being carried in a litter, but is applied generally to any mode of conveyance (carriage, ship).]

a So sumptuous were these feasts that *Pontificum Cena* and *Saliares Epulae* grew into a proverb, to express exceeding great belly cheer and most delicate fare.

34. [1] [See Nero, 49.] [2] The adverse faction to the *mirmillones* whom he favoured. [3] Which combats were usually in the morning. [4] [At these noonday fights those who fought were quite unprotected : see Seneca, *Epp.* 7, 3.] [5] Prompters of names [Aug. 19]. [6] With wild beasts or otherwise.

a Seneca, *De Clementia* [i, 23] writeth that Claudius caused more parricides to be sewn within a leather male [Aug. 33], etc. in five years' space than had been ever before his days.

---

[1] [The original here has *sextarii*.]

b Whether they were hired thereto or, presuming of their own strength, voluntarily entered upon such a combat, or forced to undergo that dangerous fight, or else exposed unto their greedy jaws for to be worried and devoured by them.

c This device called here *Automatum*, Horace [*Sat.* ii, 7, 82] by a periphrasis, prettily expresseth thus, *Nervis alienis mobile lignum* [a block of wood moved by wires worked by another, from outside (*extrinsecus*) in Persius, 5, 128].

35. ¹ [*i.e.* Passed description, or, his timorousness and diffidence surpassed every other characteristic.]   ² [Bodyguard, retainers.]
ª For with their *graphia*, as hath been noted before [C. 82], they might do a mischief.

36. ¹ [Silly, unfounded.]   ² [*Praecones*, the public criers.]

37. ¹ [Of the suspicion, *i.e.* one who prompted it.]   ² [Something to worry about, to occupy his mind.]   ³ [Foolish ideas, fancies.]
⁴ Narcissus.

38. ¹ [Aware of these faults.]   ² *Irae atque iracundiae.* The manner is of this author throughout his story to set those points down first in a word, whereon he meaneth to stand, and then in order to particularise presently upon them. By which method of his it appeareth in this place, that he meaneth by *ira*, the momentary passion of anger, which we call heat and choler, soon up and as soon down, quickly kindled and as quickly quenched; by *iracundia*, the habit of inveterate wrath continuing still until revenge be had, which we call malice and rancour. Howsoever our modern lexicographers have in their dictionaries put down the contrary.   ³ [This should be: a scribe (or clerk) to a quaestor, not, who had been quaestor.]   ⁴ The scribe.   ⁵ To intercede for them.   ⁶ The position of emperor.
⁷ [Rather, " since," " for," or simply " and."]
ª *Stultitiam neminem fingere*, or rather, *Stultitiam stultum neminem fingere*, That no fool counterfeits folly.

39. ¹ Or mistress of the house, *Domina*, δέσποινα.   ² And indeed he was her uncle.   ³ Britannicus [natural=legitimate].

40. ¹ *Rogo vos*, or I demand of you.   ² Or excessive number.
³ [Latest texts have Telegenius, old reading Telegonius. In any case nothing is known of the person.]   ⁴ [Latest texts have the old reading of Turnebus, λάλει καὶ μὴ θίγγανε, " say what you like, but don't touch me." Λογιώτατος=most eloquent or learned.]
ª It was an inconsiderate speech of an emperor and foolishly let fall, in the senate especially, tending much to his discredit and dishonour, as if he sent to the tavern for his wine by the pot or bottle, and had not his own cellarage stored therewith.
b These words without all rhyme or reason were rife in his mouth, which unadvisedly he had taken up and by use could not leave them.

41. ¹ [Livy the historian.]   ² [Squat person.]   ³ [He could not help calling to mind.]   ⁴ [Owing to his own stammering.]
⁵ [Immediately after.]   ⁶ Antonia, the triumvir's daughter.   ⁷ Octavia, the wife of Antony, or Livia Augusta herself. [The latter is right; Octavia died before Claudius was born.]   ⁸ [The son of Asinius Pollio, who had been forced by Tiberius to commit suicide: *see* Pliny, *Epp.* vii, 4.]   ⁹ [These were : Ⅎ to represent consonantal *u* ;), *bs* or

ps ; Ⱶ a sound between *i* and *u*. The first and second are found in inscriptions.]

ᵃ Some think that he devised not new letters in the alphabet, but new forms rather of the former, as namely to write for the Aeolic digamma *F* the inverted character Ⅎ, and for *ae* diphthong, *ai*.

42. ¹ [Rather, discipline = branch of learning.]   ² [Foreigner.]
³ Of Tuscan affairs.   ⁴ Of Carthaginian matters.   ⁵ Called Claudium [or Claudieum].   ⁶ [In the lecture-room, or as a recitation.]

43. ¹ *Matrimonia,* or wives, like as *Conjugia* for *conjuges.*   ² Or rather, ὁ τρώσας καὶ ἰάσεται, he that wounded will also heal; I that have done thee wrong will make amends. [This was the answer given by the oracle to Telephus, King of Mysia, after he had been wounded by Achilles and the wound would not heal. Eventually Achilles cured him with the rust of his lance.]

ᵃ For by report of Dio [lxi, 1], that is, Xiphilinus, his stature far exceeded the proportion of his years.

44. ¹ *Conscii :* some read *Conscientia quoque,* even his own conscience. [Rather, *her* conscience and informers. Another reading is *urguebant :* her conscience and the fear of informers only spurred her on.]   ² [*Repetitus :* he was attacked again with a fresh dose of poison : *cf.* Cal. 58 : *Repete !* strike again !]   ³ [The excuse was made that it was necessary to give him food to support him.]   ⁴ [The opposite of ingestion, a word still in use.]

ᵃ And yet by circumstances it may be collected that he caught his bane and died in the Palatium at Rome.

45. ¹ October 13.

46. ¹ Or blazing.   ² Or tomb.

ᵃ These were as it plainly appeareth, quaestors, aediles, tribunes, praetors, censors, and consuls. Of all these some one or other died, excepting censors, as Tacitus writeth [*Ann.* xii, 64].

NOTES AND ANNOTATIONS UPON
NERO CLAUDIUS CAESAR

1. [1] Castor and Pollux resembling two young men. [2] [At lake Regillus.] [3] Or ruddy. [4] Or copper. [5] Or ruddy. [6] [Alternately.]

2. [1] *Atavus ejus*, his grandfather four degrees off. [2] High priests [*pontifices*]. [3] Gallia Narbonensis. [4] [Suetonius confounds him with his father.] [5] Julius Caesar dictator. [6] Approbation of the gods. [7] [Summoned.] [8] The Pompeians.

3. [1] Which Quintus Paedius made against the murderers of Caesar. [2] The present state governed according to his will and pleasure. [This note is obscure. In any case, " the sovereign empire " should rather be " the chief command of the army."]

4. [1] *Dicis causa*, by an imaginary bargain of sale to have bought them to the behoof and use of the heir [Aug. 64]. [2] *Censorium*, not *Censorem*.

5. [1] [Child, offspring.] [2] Son of Marcus Agrippa and Julia, adopted by Augustus. [3] [Or, which he had bought.] [4] [Deprived of : C. 28.] [5] *Morbo aquae intercutis :* that kind of dropsy wherein water runneth between the fell and the flesh all the body over, *Leucophlegmatia* in Greek.

[a] These four factions or crews that ran with chariots for the prize, were distinguished by four colours of cloth, or liveries, and thereupon called by their names : *Alba*, white, *Veneta*, watchet or light-blue, *Prasina*, green, and *Rosea*, rose-coloured or red. Unto which were added by Domitian *Aurata* and *Purpurea*, gold-coloured or yellow, and purple. The former four Sidonius Apollinaris hath comprised in his hendecasyllables [Carmina, xxiii, 323], thus :

> *Micant colores,*
> *Albus cum veneto, virens rubensque.*

> Then shine these crews and make a gallant show
> In white, in blue, in green and roseate hue.

Proportionate they are unto the four seasons of the year : white, to the autumn or end of summer, watchet to the winter, green to the spring, and red to summer, or as some would have it to the four elements.

[b] Physicians have observed three kinds of dropsy. The first is *Ascites*, wherein the belly doth swell with much water gathered between the inner skin or rind of the belly and the cawl which lappeth the guts, and some wind withal, so named of ἀσκὸς [bottle] in Greek because, in turning of the body to a side, the water is perceived to shog [shake] in the womb, like as liquor in a bottle half-full, when

it is shaken ; the second, *Tympanites*, wherein the belly is hoven up [swollen] with wind especially and some water among, whereby it will sound like a taber or drum, if one tamper [Aug. 68] upon it, and thereof it was so called ; the third *Leucophlegmatias, anasarca, hyposarca*, in Latin *Intercus*, or *Aqua intercus*, in the proper signification[1], when the body all over is puffed up with water and wind running between the fell and the flesh.   And thereof, as should seem, died this Domitius.

6. [1] Dio saith [lxi, 2] he was compassed with the sunbeams ; and yet no sun appeared above the horizon.   [2] Forename.   [3] [Attentively.]   [4] [Jest.]   [5] Her son.

[a] To wit, the ninth day after he was born, on which they used to name their sons.   And as this day was called *Nominalia*, so there was a goddess forsooth, president of this complement and ceremonies, whom they named Nundina.   [On this day the child was purified, whence it was called, as here, *dies lustricus*.]

7. [1] *Undecimo :* some read rather *tertio decimo*, the thirteenth. [2] Caligula.   [3] [Malicious, mischievous.]   [4] [Bad friend, enemy.] [5] Or hall of justice.   [6] Or running at tilt.   [7] Drawn in large books [*maximas :* rather, of chief importance].

[a] The manner was, during these solemnities on the Alban mount (where the chief magistrates were present) to leave for provost of the city some principal young gentleman of the nobility, before whom, sitting judicially, causes of no great importance should be brought.

8. [1] Between noon and one of the clock.   [2] Of the praetorians. [3] Father of his Country.

9. [1] [(Filial) affection.]   [2] [Control.]   [3] Or *corps de guard*. [4] Or haven.

10. [1] [Good disposition.]   [2] £3, 2s. 6d. sterling [nearer £3, 10s.], a Roman pound.   [3] Annuities.   [4] More by a fourth part than the state or worth of a gentleman of Rome.   [5] [Rather, would that I could not write !]

11. [1] [*Juvenales ludi*, instituted to commemorate the first cutting of his beard.]   [2] Gentlemen and senators.   [3] *Per Catadromum*, for there were *Elephanti funambuli : see* Galba, 6 [Liddell and Scott, referring to this passage, translate καϊάδρομον " course " or " lists "]. [4] Or gifts.   [5] [Small Irish and Scotch horses.]   [6] [Rather, even tamed beasts.]   [7] [*Insulas :* detached houses or buildings : *lit.* islands.]

[a] These youthful sports *juvenalia*, or *juvenales ludi*, were first instituted by this Nero, privately in houses or gardens, and orchards. Wherein, of all degrees, ages, and sexes they danced and revelled.

12. [1] The fore-stage [the part between the background or scene and the orchestra].   [2] *Quadringentos*, rather *quadragenos*, 40.   [3] *Sescentosque*, rather *sexagenos*, 60, according to Justus Lipsius.   [4] Warlike.   [5] Or, among.   [6] [Subjects, themes.]   [7] To the likeness of that which was devised by Daedalus.   [8] Of Nero.   [9] Or pavilion [the raised seat of the emperor].   [10] Or a pallet.   [11] [*Podium :* a balcony next the arena.]   [12] Where they were wont to sit as presidents at other games and plays.   [13] *In Orchestram senatumque :* others read *per orchestram in scenam*, by the orchestra to the very stage.

---

[1] For Cornelius Celsus attributeth this name to all the kinds.

[14] [H. here translates the reading *citharam : citharae* is preferable : the garland or prize for harp-playing.]   [15] To Jupiter Capitolinus.

[a] The fabulous reports of lady Pasiphaë, wife to king Minos, how she was enamoured of a bull, as also of Icarus the son of Daedalus, who would needs attempt to fly in the air, be well enough known to them that are but meanly seen [1] in poetry.

[b] *Juxta cubiculum eius decidit.* By *Cubiculum*, he meaneth here a royal seat raised on high within that quarter of the theatre called *Orchestra*, under a rich tent or canopy, where emperors were wont to sit when they beheld such solemnities.   These pavilions were called in Greek οὐρανισκοὶ κωνωπεῖα, in some sort resembling bed-chambers.

[c] So named because they that wrestled, ran, or otherwise exercised, were naked, like as the place itself of such exercises thereupon took the name gymnasium.

13. [1] Or market-place.   [2] Resembling a cap of maintenance, or, as some think, a Turkish tuffe [tuft] or turban.   [3] Which he had laid off again as it should seem, like as when he was vanquished by Corbulo he laid [it] down before the image of Nero.

15. [1] [Immediately after one another.]   [2] [Be successful.]   [3] Somewhat before.   [4] Or rather, one piece of a day [C. 76].   [5] Or upon occasion of war.   [6] Which elsewhere be called epistles.   [7] Unto whom properly it appertained.

16. [1] *Ante insulas* [12].   [2] Foregates, or gatehouses.   [3] From the front of such edifices.   [4] Or promised, rather, to build.   [5] To bring an arm of it thither.   [6] In costly and excessive fare at the table.   [7] [*Sportulas :* rather, doles or presents of food.]   [8] [Boiled, cooked.]   [9] As pot-herbs.   [10] Cunning actors, playing all parts and resembling [imitating] all gestures.

[a] Full and formal suppers, whereto men were invited, and at which the guests sat orderly marshalled according to their worth-place, and were called *cenae rectae*, and after this manner in other princes' days were their favourites feasted.   Instead hereof came in *Sportulae*, allowances given unto them, either in money or cates, in recompense of their ordinary salutations and attendance.

[b] As there were sundry factions or crews favouring this or that colour of the charioteers, so were there likewise of actors and players, whereupon many riots, outrages, frays and murders were committed.

17. [1] Or uppermost.   [2] Or cered tables.   [3] Pews [C. 78] or seats ; some expound this of the judges' bench, as if their sentences should not be bought and sold.   [4] [The Forum.]   [5] [A small board, appointed for settling money cases and urgent legal questions generally.]

[a] It should seem that for the pleading and trial of causes such tribunal seats, pews [C. 78], benches, and bars were erected at first for the present occasion, and taken down again by certain persons, who gathered therefor a rent of those that went to law.

18. [a] Divers kings of Pontus were named Polemones as of Egypt Ptolemaei, whereupon the realm Pontus is by Vopiscus [*Life of Aurelian*, xxi, 11] called Polemonius [or Polemoniacus], like as the Alpes Cottiae of Cottius.

---

[1] [Moderately acquainted with.]

19. [1] Jag, welt, or fringe. [2] *Rastello* = *ligone*, the same as *Dikella* in Greek : with a cloven bit [the blade of an axe, spade, etc.]. This, according to some writers, was of gold. [3] *Senum pedum*, some read *senum millium peditum*, of six thousand footmen.

[a] Many had attempted this beside him, but all their cost and labour came to nought : οὕτως χαλεπὸν ἀνθρώπῳ τὰ θεῖα βιάσασθαι. [Pausanias, ii, 1, 5 : " So hard it is for man to lay violent hands on what is divine."]

20. [1] Or hoarse [husky, indistinct]. [2] At Naples. [3] Ditties. [4] Tuned and composed to the rules and measures of music [written or sung from notes] in the praise of him, by the merchants of Alexandria. [5] [*Neque segnius*, with equal energy.] [6] Or crews [companies]. [7] *Nec sine anulo laevis*, or, clean contrary, *ac sine anulo laevis*, wearing no rings at all. [H. here translates the reading *pueris*, boys ; later texts have *puris* agreeing with *laevis*, their left hands being plain, with no rings on them.] [8] A knight's living.

[a] τῆς λανθανούσης μουσικῆς οὐδεὶς λόγος.[1]

[b] In respect of a former fleet, that was wont to come before and bring news of the second laden with merchandise and under sail. Therefore those ships were called *naves tabellariae*. Seneca [*Epp.* 77].

[c] *Bombos*, resembling either the buzzing and humming noise of bees, or the sound of trumpets.

[d] *Imbrices*, much after the manner of that rattling, which a sudden shower makes upon the tiles of a house, or the sound that crest-tiles [2] or gutter-tiles may make.

[e] *Testas*, to express the crashing of potsherds or earthen pots, clattering one against another.

[f] *Insignes pinguissima coma*. In which sense we read of *pingues togae* and *Lacernae*. Yet some understand thereby λιπαροπλοκάμους, whose locks and faix [3] were so slick and glib [4] with sweet oils, that they shone again.

21. [1] Every fifth year. [*Neroneum* here agrees with a singular *agona*.] [2] [Satisfy their desires.] [3] Or colonels. [4] Wife of Amphion, king of Thebes, who priding herself in her fair issue, six sons and as many daughters, durst compare with Latona, the mother of Apollo and Diana, but she with her arrows killed them all, and turned her into a stone. [5] Four of the clock after noon. [6] Of other magistrates, who in respect of the prince are accounted private. [7] According to Xiphilinus [a 12th century Byzantine monk, who made extracts, still preserved, from the later books of Dion Cassius], his name was Larcius Lydus, a Lydian named Larcius (Dion, lxiii, 21). [8] Or masks. [9] Or, a young untrained soldier.

[a] For so would he have it to be called. And Thrasea Paetus was judicially convented [summoned] and deeply charged, because he had never offered sacrifice for that heavenly voice of his [Tacitus, *Ann.* xvi, 22].

[b] Who was with child by her own brother Macareus, whereupon

---

[1] [Cannot trace the Greek original. A. Otto, *Sprichwörter*, refers to this passage and to Aulus Gellius, xiii, 31, but does not mention the Greek, cf. Ovid, *Art. Am.* iii, 40c.]

[2] [Bent tiles for covering the ridge of a roof.]

[3] [Hair ; A.S. *feax*. The word occurs in the family name Fairfax, etc.]

[4] [Smooth and glossy.]

her father Aeolus caused the child new-born to be cast before hungry dogs, and sent a sword to his daughter to kill herself with.

c In revenge of his father Agamemnon's death, by her murdered, whereupon he fell into a furious kind of deep melancholy.

d Who unwitting killed his own father Laius, and as ignorantly wedded his own mother Iocasta.

e By putting on a garment next his skin, envenomed with the poison of Nessus the centaur, and so sent unto him as a token from his wife Deianira.

22. 1 Or sore wounded and bruised with the wheels running over him. *See* Pliny, *Nat. Hist.* xxviii, 17, 72, 238.   2 Who was likewise *Raptatus Bigis*, as Virgil writeth [*Aen.* ii, 272].   3 Or chariots, to express those games *Circenses*.   4 *Secessu*, or by way of retiring and recreation.   5 *Greges*, either *agitatorum*, of chariot-drivers : or *equorum quadrigariorum*, of steeds, both to one effect.   6 Which was their greater gain.   7 A town in Corcyra.

23. 1 Wherein he thither came.   2 Solemnised twice in the same year.   3 Thereby to make them relent and not do their best.   4 [Or apaid, satisfied.]

24. 1 [Spit up phlegm.]   2 Or sleeve, and not with any handkerchief.   3 [*Hypocrit-es* or *-a*, who accompanied the chief actor by gestures.]   4 Due to him that had the loudest voice.

a It may be thought that he then acted Oedipus or Creon or some other king, and therefore carried in his hand a regal staff or sceptre. Yet some interpret this of a laurel rod or branch, such as actors held in their hands while they sung.

b For at Olympia were games also of criers, striving who could cry loudest for the prize.

c These were called *Hieronicae*, as one would say, sacred victories [victors], to wit, at the solemn games in Greece, Nemea, Pythia, Isthmia, and Olympia.

25. 1 [Or mantle. Later texts have *veste* and *chlamyde*, in a purple robe and a cloak. In the text from which H. translates *veste* is omitted.]   2 Made of wild olive branches.   3 Of laurel.   4 Isthmian, of pine ; Nemean, of smallach [smallage], or parsley. [These were carried in procession (" pomp ") by a train of attendants.]   5 Or Minstrel.   6 *Per nuntios*, by messengers sent between.   7 When himself was present.   8 A moderator of his voice [Aug. 84].

a Five thousand were there of these gallants, as Dion writeth, ready to applaud him when he chanted.

26. 1 Or hood.   2 [The sewers.]   3 Or market.   4 Or Litter.   5 Or loft.   6 The fore-stage [12].   7 Or among.

a He meaneth either a peruke and cap of counterfeit hair, Κόμας περιθέτους [Dion, lxi, 9], thereby disguising himself, the same that in Caligula [11] he termeth *Capillamentum*, or else some hood covering his head all save the eyes. Julius Capitolinus [*Verus*, 4] calleth it *Cucullionem*, wherewith the emperor Verus played such parts by night, in imitation of Caligula and Nero.

b *Quintana* was a gate or street rather in the Roman camp, wherein was usually kept *Forum rerum utensilium*, in resemblance whereof he termed a certain place in his house *Quintana*, in which he made sale of such wares and commodities as he had got together by rifling and robbing.

NERO CLAUDIUS CAESAR

c It appeareth by Tacitus [*Ann.* xiii, 25] that this was Julius Montanus, who, albeit he had not sat in council as senator, yet was *Laticlavius* and wore the senator's robe. Such gentlemen were called *Juvenes secundi ordinis*, in distinction of those of the imperial blood or otherwise near allied unto the emperor.

27. [1] A broad place, wherein a naval fight had sometime been exhibited, but then filled up ; yet it carried the former name still. [2] Or bay.

a The manner was in old time to employ the day in business and therein to take no liberal meals, putting off the full refection and cherishing of the body until night. *Convivia de die* argued intemperance much more than feasting from noon to midnight.

b *Ambubaiarum.* These took their name (as most expositors have conjectured), *Quod circa Baias versarentur* [because they frequented the neighbourhood of Baiae]. Yet some learned men of later time fetch the same from this Syriac word *Ambubaiae* [*abub*, reed-pipe], as if such were Syrian women, who being otherwise naughty packs and callots[1], got their living also by playing upon certain instruments of music, which they brought with them out of their native country.

c *Copas imitantium.* Although *Copae* properly be such women as keep victualling houses, ready not only to entertain but also to invite and call in guests, yet because these commonly are very bold and unshamefaced, this term goeth indifferently for strumpets and courtesans. For seldom shall a man see an impudent woman that is not withal incontinent, so inseparably is modesty joined with chastity.

d The corrupt text in this place hath given occasion of much obscurity and ministered matter enough for critics to work upon, while some read *Mellita*, others *Myrtitrichila*, by which are meant certain sweet junkets, as dainty wafers, etc.

e This may be thought incredible, that banqueting conceits at one sitting should cost so much, and the aspersion of rose-water or other odoriferous liquors arise to more. Where is to be noted the observation of some, who for *ab Syrtio rosaria* read *aspersio rosaria*, that is to say, the artificial besprinkling and aromatising (as I may so say) of banqueting-rooms out of spouts and pipes, conveying odoriferous waters and oils, going under the name of *Rosaria.* Which spouts, if they were made of silver or gold (as we read they were at the feast of Otho, when he gave Nero entertainment) might soon amount to that sum, to say nothing of the costly compound distilled waters, or extracts and oils, themselves drawn out of most precious simples and spices. [The latest texts read : *indicebat et familiaribus cenas, quorum uni mitellita quadragies sestertium constitit, alteri pluris aliquanto rosaria*, *mitellita* [*mitella*, a headband] and *rosaria* both being adjj. agreeing with *cena* understood, a supper at which these *mitellae* were worn and there was abundance of perfume of roses. Possibly there may be an allusion to rose wine (*rosatum :* cf. Lampridius, *Heliogab*, 11). In the old reading *absorptio*=draught, *mellita*=flavoured with honey, *rosaria*=flavoured with roses.]

28. [1] Which had been a great disparagement. [2] [Pretended friends.]

a Him he called, as other authors write, Sabina and Poppaea, after the name of his wife deceased.

---

[1] [Or callets, lewd women.]

29. ¹ [To such an extent that.] ² Or grate. ³ I wish that both Suetonius and Dion had in this place and such-like been altogether silent. ⁴ Confessed of themselves and their own accord.

ᵃ In other writers he is named Pythagoras, so that it should seem he carried two names.

30. ¹ [H. here translates a reading suggested by Torrentius, *Panerotis faeneratoris :* later texts have the accusative : he enriched " the monkey-tailed usurer P."] ² *Quadringenis Sestertiis.* Take *Sestertium* here in the neuter gender ; otherwise it were but a mean venture for such a one as Nero, as amounting not above £3, 2s. 6d., whereas now it ariseth to £3125 [C. 18, annot.]. ³ *Aurato rete.* Orosius [vii, 7] saith more expressly, *retibus aureis.* ⁴ [In fast colours, properly the dye from Kermes.] ⁵ [Wool from Canusium in Apulia.] ⁶ Horsemen of Africa and Cappadocia.

ᵃ A great magician, whom he entertained thus royally because he would have learned magic of him [Pliny, *Nat. Hist.* xxx, 6, 16].

ᵇ Whereas Augustus, when he played at this game, ventured no more than for every *Talus*, which were four in all, a single denier. For it should seem that the game of *Tali* here mentioned was *Pleistobolinda*, who could throw most with four *Tali*, whether the same were cockall bones indeed, or made of gold, silver, or ivory, with four sides, every one representing a chance, an *Ace* or unity and *sise*, a *trey* and *quatre*, opposite one unto the other. For they wanted *deux* and *cinque*, which the *Tessera Cubus*, or die carrying six faces, hath.

ᶜ It is evident hereby, as also out of that verse of Juvenal [*Sat.* xvi, 60],

Ut laeti phaleris omnes et torquibus omnes,

that these *Phalerae* were not trappings and furniture belonging to horses, but some other ornaments, wherewith footmen and horsemen both were trimly decked.

31. ¹ As one would say, the passage from one hill to another. ² Or foregate. ³ *Porticus triplices miliarias.* If a man expound it thus : galleries with three rows of pillars, or as many isles [does H. mean blocks of buildings ?] a thousand feet in length, it would be more consonant to the truth I suppose. And yet the proportion that followeth is very strange and answerable to the vulgar and received exposition. [There were three colonnades, each a mile in length.] ⁴ Mother-of-pearl. ⁵ [=Ceiled, overlaid.] ⁶ Or heaven. ⁷ [From the sulphur springs near Tibur (Tivoli).] ⁸ Made his first entry into it after a solemn and festival manner. ⁹ *Piscinam.* ¹⁰ Or lake. ¹¹ Or walking-places. ¹² Or ditch [canal].

32. ¹ [H. is here translating *dodrans ;* the usual reading is *dextans,* five-sixths.] ² Remembered him not in their wills and made him not an heir. ³ [Informer.] ⁴ Or violet in grain. ⁵ Or fair. ⁶ Who had bought the said colours. ⁷ [*Praeclusit ;* shut up their shops.] ⁸ Julia, which Caesar the dictator made [C. 43]. ⁹ Proctors or factors. ¹⁰ Or possess. ¹¹ Apollo, Neptune, Jupiter, Juno, Minerva.

33. ¹ Or proverb. ² [Came by his death.] ³ θεῶν βρῶμα, alluding to the deification after his death. ⁴ *Bustum.* ⁵ As the manner was for certain days before the ashes and relics were gathered up. ⁶ [Popular.] ⁷ [Looseness of the bowels.] ⁸ *De Veneficiis* [the lex Cornelia *de sicariis et Veneficiis,* passed by Sulla 81 B.C.

and kept up by Julius Caesar, whence it became generally known as the lex Julia].   [9] [Taking effect instantaneously.]   [10] For her former practice of poisoning, by which she stood condemned.

[a] In this verb *Morari*, there is couched a double sense, which gives the grace unto this pleasant scoff. For being a mere Latin word and having the first syllable by nature short, it signifieth to stay or to make long abode ; and taking it thus, Nero might be thought to imply thus much, that Claudius was now departed out of the company of mortal men and ranged among the heavenly wights. But take the same word, as Nero spake it, derived of μῶρος in Greek, which signifieth a fool and hath the first syllable long, it importeth that Claudius played the fool no longer here in the world among men. Read the little pamphlet of Seneca entituled ἀποκολοκύντωσις [the Pumpkinification of Claudius], if ye would see Claudius depainted in his colours and in a fool's coat ; which he, as it may appear, composed of purpose to gratify Nero in that humour of his.

[b] The Greeks call this Καύστραν or τύμβος. And the Romans in honour of their princes were wont to compass the same all about with a wall of flint, or other durable stone, as marble.

34. [1] As if she were the cause thereof.   [2] *Militum et Germanorum :* Hen dia duoin [hendiadys : rather soldiers (*i.e.* Roman) and Germans].   [3] [Persecute.]   [4] [*Camera :* a vaulted roof.]   [5] [Day for settling a quarrel.]   [6] [Draw on, entice.]   [7] A feast in the honour of Minerva, beginning five days before the ides, the 11th of March.   [8] Or pinnace [light galley].   [9] Or to the stairs.   [10] Between his feet [Tac. *Ann.* xiv, 7].   [11] About midnight it was.   [12] Domitia, by his father's side.   [13] *Ex duritia alvi, alias enim cibum non transmittit*, as Pliny writeth [*Nat. Hist.* xxvi, 8, 43].   [14] As if she would say, If I might see thee once a man grown, etc., for he came to be emperor before he was eighteen years old.   [15] You must suppose he sent for the barber first, etc.   [16] As purging was the cure, so it was the colourable means whereby she was killed.

[a] It may be it was in the same form that Justin Martyr [*Cohortatio,* 18] citeth out of *Orpheus :*

θύρας δ'ἐπίθεσθε βεβήλοις,
Fortes opponite profanis.

Which Virgil [*Aen.* vi, 258] in some sort hath expressed thus :

Procul este profani.

And Claudian [*De Raptu Pros.* i, 4] after him :

Gressus removete profani.

35. [1] The daughter of Claudius.   [2] Or Pompeia, as some read.   [3] Titus Ossius [Ollius].   [4] [Rufrius Crispinus.]   [5] In the right line of descent.   [6] Statilius, who in Augustus' time built the great amphitheatre in Rome bearing his name [she was the daughter of Statilius Taurus, consul A.D. 44].   [7] Who had brought him up in his childhood.   [8] Or spurn.   [9] [Stepson, not son-in-law. The praenomen is now spelt Rufrius. He was the son of Poppaea, by another Rufrius Crispinus, her former husband.]   [10] *Ducatus* or captainships.   [11] To cut the master-veins of arms and legs and so to bleed to death.   [12] Seneca.   [13] Ἔπαρχος τῶν δορυφόρων [praefect of the praetorian guard].   [14] A squinancie [quinsy].   [15] Namely, Doryphorus and Pallas ; Tac. *Ann.* [xiv, 65].

36. [1] And his friends, *Pisoniana*. [2] And his adherents, *Viniciana*. [3] And by name Sulpicius Asper. [4] [The *capsarii* were slaves who carried the books, etc., of school-children in a box (*capsa*).]

37. [1] [Mattered.] [2] [H. here translates the reading *restituisset* ; others *retinuisset*, had kept.] [3] *Polyphago cuidam*, or glutton. [4] [That no previous emperor had realised the extent of his power.] [5] [Destroy, blot out.] [6] In Achaia, near Corinth [C. 44, Cal. 21, N. 19]. [7] Comprising therein the gentlemen's degree : not *Senatui populoque Romano*, as the manner had been.

[a] The like example is reported by Vopiscus in *Life of Aurelian* [50], who took wonderful delight in a mighty eater [1], that in one day before his own table devoured a wild boar full and whole, a hundred loaves of bread, a wether mutton, and a pig.

38. [1] *Cubicularios* : the grooms of his [bed-]chamber. [2] [In the act.] [3] [Tow.] [4] Or lodgings. [5] [Take shelter.] [6] Against the Carthaginians.

[a] This iambic verse, as Dion [lviii, 23] writeth, was rife also in Tiberius Caesar's mouth.

[b] Albeit this word *Insula*, beside the common signification of an island, is taken for a house standing entire by itself apart from other, yet in this author I observe that it is put elsewhere for other houses also and tenements let out to tenants by the owners and landlords, who are called *Domini Insularum*. And even in this acception it may well go in this place.

[c] This tower Horace describeth [*Odes*, iii, 29, 10] in these words,

Molem propinquam nubibus arduis, etc.

39. [1] As we say, in the church-book. [2] In whose temple were to be bought or hired, whatsoever pertained to funerals and burials : Varro [*Ling. Lat.* vi, 47]. Plutarch [*Quaest. Rom.* 23] taketh her for Venus. [3] *Camulodunum et Londinium coloniae*. Maldon [more probably Colchester] and London, two colonies ; and together with them, Verulamium, a borough free town, in the ruins whereof St Albans now standeth [Tac. *Ann.* 32, 33], in which places 7000 (by report) were slain of citizens and allies. [4] [Reproaches.] [5] To wit, Agrippina. [6] [Νεόνυμφον. The latest texts adopt a reading suggested by F. Bücheler, *Rheinisches Museum*, lxi, 1906, p. 308, νεόψηφον = a fresh, numerical interpretation of Nero's name. Νερων = 1005, ιδιαν = 75, μητερα = 454, απεκτεινε = 476, also making 1005. Thus, the name Nero = matricide.] [7] Anchises. [8] Hexameter and pentameter. [9] Philosopher. [10] Which were very lascivious and licentious. [11] Whose son he was by adoption ; for some report he took his poison in a cup of drink and not in a mushroom. [12] Who was thought to have perished in the sea ; and indeed she hardly escaped drowning by swimming [34]. [13] [Displeasure.]

[a] Which number ariseth to ten thousand a month, a mortality nothing comparable to that which, as Eusebius [*Chronicon*, ii] reporteth reigned at Rome in the days of Vespasian, in which there died of the pestilence ten thousand a day, nor to that in Constantinople, when many days there were likewise ten thousand dead bodies carried forth. Procopius, *de Bello Persico* [ii, 21].

[b] Such a rumour indeed ran rife, but untruly [Tacitus, *Ann.* xiv, 2 ; cf. Dion, lxi, 11].

---

[1] Phago.

^c Orestes, to revenge his father Agamemnon's death wrought by Clytaemnestra his mother and Aegisthus the adulterer, murdered her.

^d Alcmaeon, son of Amphiaraus and Eriphyle, killed her, because she had contrived his father's death.

^e Aeneas carried his old father Anchises upon his shoulders out of the fire of Troy when it burned. Here is to be noted the duple sense of the verb [*Sustulit*] in one and the same Latin verse : for in the former place it signifieth to kill or make away, as Nero did his mother, in the latter, to take up and carry, as Aeneas did his father. This yieldeth an elegant grace in Latin and cannot so well be expressed in English.

^f Apollo was surnamed *Paean* of παίειν in Greek, which signifieth to strike, or of παύειν, to ease and allay pain, as being a god that both sendeth diseases and also cureth them[1]. But commonly the Romans term him so in this latter and better sense. He is styled likewise Hecatebeletēs in Greek, which is as much as shooting or wounding from afar. In these abstruse significations and obscure terms therefore this epigram implieth thus much : that whiles Nero in the habit of Apollo playeth upon the harp and would seem to be a mild and gracious prince, the Parthian king, with bow and arrows representing Apollo likewise, endangered the empire of Rome, and all through the supine negligence of Nero given to his music and other vanities excessively.

^g This is meant by that huge house of Nero's building, and hath a reference to that desolate estate of Rome, when it was sacked and fired by the French [Gauls], after the unfortunate battle of Allia [July 18, 390], what time the Romans were in consultation to abandon the city and depart to Veii, there to inhabit.

^h It seemeth that Nero in his poem entitled *Troica*, had used to chant of Nauplius, the father of Palamedes, who abode many calamities himself, and in revenge of his son's death wrought much mischief to others. The cynic therefore noteth Nero for his singing, as also for abusing his own good parts in perpetrating all wickedness, or else for misspending his treasure so dissolutely.

ⁱ Ἔρρωσο δὲ καὶ ὑγίαινε οὔτε λέγειν οὔτε ἀκούειν ἀγαθόν· οὔτε γὰρ προσιόντες ἀλλήλοις οὔτε μέλλοντές τι πράττειν ταῦτα λέγουσιν οἱ ἄνθρωποι, ἀλλὰ ἀπαλλαττόμενοι ἀλλήλων καὶ πρὸς ὕπνον τρεπόμενοι [Artemidorus, *Oneirocriticon*, i, 82 : "The words good-bye and farewell are neither good to utter nor to hear ; for men do not use them when meeting one another nor when they are about to do something, but only when taking leave or going to rest"].

^k By Orcus, or Pluto, taken for the god of hell or the grave, is understood death in this place, ready to seize upon the senators, whose overthrow Nero had intended. Now, well-known it is that the manner was then among the Romans, as at this day with us, to carry forth their dead with the feet forward.

40. ¹ Of Gaul. ² [Later readings ἡμᾶς διατρέφει or διαθρέψει, a poor art supports us (a general statement), or, will support me.] ³ As they did to Polycrates, that mighty tyrant of Samos ; but it was not long before his fall and destruction. ⁴ Public place of exercise. ⁵ *Malum*, an emphatic and significant word in this place : like as in Livy iv [49], *Malum militibus meis nisi quieverint*. As if he had said, A mis-

---

¹ [Probably originally the god of the triumphant song of victory or paean and distinct from the healing god, but afterwards identified with him.]

chief take these rebels ; or, mischief will come to them.   ⁶ *Descissent ;* others read *dedissent*, as if mischief would fall upon the authors' heads.

^a It should seem this answer was delivered in these words :

Ἑξηκοστὸν ἔτος τρισκαιδέκατόν τε φυλάττου.

Of sixtieth year (I do thee rede)
And thirteenth more, see thou take heed.

Whereby Apollo (for his oblique answers rightly of the Greeks termed Loxias) or the devil himself, whether you will, playing with him in a twofold and ambiguous construction (as his manner was) deluded him. For whiles he rested secure, dreaming still of the 73rd year, which he supposed was meant of his own age and which he was far short of, he fell into the hands of Galba, a man indeed of those years.

41. ¹ An inflammation or swelling in the throat.   ² *Citharaedum*, a singer to the harp.   ³ Which was the name of his family, and so had he been called before his adoption.   ⁴ Nero Claudius Drusus. ⁵ Which it seems he spake ironically ; if simply, he meaneth, in case Vindex interrupted not his sports and the public felicity.

42. ¹ In that he played without a concurrent, whereas himself but for his businesses would have put him down.

43. ¹ Occasioned by the commotions and revolts abroad [*tumultus :* here used in its special sense of insurrection, sudden uprising]. ² [Phrase originally used of draft-horses pulling together.]   ³ As sometime Gnaeus Pompeius Magnus was, for the like exploit.   ⁴ The consular authority [C. 71].

44. ¹ [At once.]   ² Surliness [*fastidio :* it is not easy to see the meaning of this word.   Does it mean he was very particular about the kind and condition of the money ?]   ³ [Harshness.]   ⁴ [*Pustulatum, lit.* blistered.]   ⁵ [*Ad obrussam*, the assaying of gold by fire.]

45. ¹ Cornmongers, *lucrantium* [others read *lucranti*, referring to Nero himself].   ² Or the fleet itself, *navis* for *classis*, as *classis* for *navis* by the figure synecdoche.   ³ Alluding to his chariot-running [later reading *cirrus*, ringlet, lock of hair].   ⁴ [Motto, inscription : Ital. *impresa.*]   ⁵ A satchel, *ascopera.*   ⁶ *Ego quid potui ?* ⁷ *Culleum* [another form of budge is bouge (O. Fr.), Lat. *bulga*]. ⁸ *Gallos et eum cantando exci*(ta)*sse* [or *etiam Gallos*, even the Gauls].

^a Rome was wont to be served of corn from Alexandria in Egypt, in the time of dearth especially, when Sicily, otherwise reckoned *Horreum populi Romani*, the people of Rome's garner, was not able to furnish them.   Now, when instead of corn long-expected there arrived certain sail from thence fraught with dust and sand for the sports of his gallants, no marvel if all the discontentment and heart-burning of the people conceived against cornmongers and such as made gain by the scarcity of grain redounded upon Nero and his courtiers.

^b Νῦν γὰρ ἐστ' ἀγών.   The end of some trimeter or senarian iambic verse in a tragedy.

^c Νῦν δεῖ ἐλαύνειν ἢ ἕλκειν, Now 'tis high time to drive or draw. In both which impreses, by a tart and bitter *Sarcasmus*, is taxed his excessive love of charioteering.   [*Traderet* is translated by some " give up, hand himself over."   The latest reading of the passage that follows, suggested by A. A. Howard, *Harvard Studies in Classical*

NERO CLAUDIUS CAESAR

Philology, vii, 1896, is : *alterius collo ἀσκὸς praeligatus simulque titulus : ego egi quod potui, sed tu culleum meruisti*, " on the neck of another was fastened a leather bottle (bag, sack) with the inscription, I have done my best, but you have deserved the sack." W. Chawner, *Classical Review*, ix, 1895, punctuates : *ego quid ? potui ; sed tu culleum meruisti*, translating : What am I ? a sack to drink from (dative of pōtus), but you have deserved a sack of another kind."]

d The speech of the people, or of his mother, who could not reclaim him.

e As a parricide or killer of parents, etc., whose judgement was to be sewn quick within a leather budge [Aug. 33], etc.

f There is not only a homonym in the word [*Gallos*] signifying the French nation and the crowing cocks, but an amphibology also in the sentence ; whereby it may be understood, either that Nero with his chanting had awakened the French, who began now to revolt, as not able any longer to endure his songs, or that the French awakened him, to bestir himself and look better about him ; as if they were the cocks indeed, to raise him out of his drowsy security.

g The ambiguity of this word [Vindex] implieth both a private chastiser of servants for their faults, and also Gaius Julius Vindex, a revenger of public injuries and a maintainer of the common liberty, who now had taken arms against Nero.

46. 1 [The punctuation is doubtful : (*a*) comma after mother, " once " being=when once, as soon as ; (*b*) comma after once=at last, but this reads rather oddly. The Latin word is *demum*, then and not till then, or it may be used without any idea of time and merely emphasise the preceding word.]   2 The stately sepulchre of Augustus.
3 All this happened upon the New-year's day.   4 *Decidisse ;* or *desisse*, stayed and gave over [or, ended up with].

a *Auspicia*, albeit they properly do signify presaging tokens delivered by birds, yet the sequence and circumstance of this passage lead us rather to some other uncouth prodigies and strange sights.

b Nero was semblably distained [sullied] in another kind, as having murdered his father Claudius[1], his mother Agrippina, and his two wives Octavia and Poppaea.

47. 1 See the annotation.   2 [In the S.W. of the city : not Servitii, as in H.]   3 [Hesitated and shuffled.]   4 And to suffer him for to enjoy the empire.   5 To the Rostra.   6 Or starting out of his sleep.   7 [Cut-throat.]

a *A caelatura carminum Homeri*. Which if we strain a little, may be Englished thus, for the workmanship and engraving upon them out of Homer's verses, alluding to that standing massy [massive] cup of Nestor's, described by Homer [*Iliad*, xi, 632].

b A half-verse out of Virgil, *Aen.* xii, 646, the words of Turnus unto his sister Juturna.

c Although there were divers *Praefecturae* in Egypt, called *Nomi*, as one would say shires or divisions, as appeareth in Pliny [v, 9, 49], yet by this place is to be understood the presidency over all Egypt, which by the institution of Augustus was ordinarily conferred upon some gentleman of Rome. By which it appeareth he would play at small game rather than sit out.

48. 1 [Revoked, changed.]   2 Single waistcoat.   3 The rest

---

1 Who adopted him.

were Phaon, Epaphroditus, and Neophytus.   [4] [Not a proper name, but=one who had been discharged from the service, retired.]   [5] For fear either of pricking his feet, or of being heard to go.   [6] Or into my grave [quick=alive].   [7] Or sodden. Pliny reporteth (*Nat. Hist.* xxxiii, 3) that Nero devised to seethe water first, then within a glass to let it stand in snow, whereby it became exceeding cold, partly by the snow, and in part by the former decoction. A delicate drink in the heat of summer.   [8] [The nearest *cella*, a small, mean room for slaves and servants.]

49. [1] [Rather, to which at any time he might be subjected (*impendentibus*).]   [2] Meaning his singular skill in music, for which pity it was he should ever die.   [3] Or else, What manner of artisan am I now become, thus to prepare mine own funeral ?   [4] [Perhaps formalities may express the meaning here : cf. Cal. 59.]   [5] Or footman. [6] Or set.   [7] [A piece of wood shaped like a fork which was placed round the neck of slaves and criminals marked out for punishment.] [8] Homer, *Iliad,* x [535], spoken by Nestor.   [9] Or his master of requests.   [10] By Nero.   [11] Occasioned by the rebellion in Gaul and Spain.   [12] For he might do all in all with Galba (*see* Galba, 14).

50. [1] [Remains, ashes.]   [2] [A stone coffin, sarcophagus.]   [3] [In Etruria : Carrara marble.]   [4] [From the island of Thasos, off the Thracian coast.]

51. [1] Within a little of six feet.   [2] [Handsome but wanting in grace or attractive expression.]   [3] [Rows, tiers.] As you may see in the coins and pictures of Otho the emperor ; Statius [*Silvae*, i, 2, 114] calleth this *suggestum comae*.   [4] Haply in imitation of Apollo (who was *Intonsus*, and is called by Homer therefore ἀκερσεκόμης), because there especially he professed music, whereof Apollo is the patron. [5] [Partly undressed.]

53. [1] [At the next lustrum.]   [2] Or the lists.   [3] Or couples matched.   [4] [*i.e.* his custom was to, he would.]

55. [1] Nero's city.

56. [1] Atargatis or Astarte ; the same some think, as Juno [or Cybele].   [2] Her image.   [3] [Protection.]

57. [1] Or bonnets, to testify freedom recovered [caps of liberty]. [2] Namely, to Calpurnius Asprenas, to be executed for a lying counterfeit [Tacitus, *Hist.* i, 2, ii, 9].

NOTES AND ANNOTATIONS UPON
SERVIUS SULPICIUS GALBA

1. [1] Or line.　[2] Which proved white, as also the whole brood of them : Dion [xlviii, 52].　[3] [At the Hens, or, the Fowl-house.] [4] And branches which they held in their hands [Pliny, *Nat. Hist.* xv, 14].　[5] [Plant in small holes.]　[6] [Wither away.]　[7] [Immediately after the temple . . . was. This temple is perhaps the temple of Augustus built by Livia (Pliny, *Nat. Hist.* xii, 94), later called *templum divorum* from the deified emperors. As to the sceptre of Augustus, since the sceptre was never a distinguishing mark of the imperial power, a triumphal statue must be meant, the sceptre being a token of triumph. As a sign of divinity, however, it would find a place on statues of the gods.]　[8] Pliny saith the very same. [The editor is unable to find this reference.]

[a] [It is possible that the note in the text, which is one of the marginal " glosses," may really be meant for the withering of the bay-trees and the dying of the hens, which is mentioned in *Dion Cassius*, lxiii, 29. The ed. may have missed the reference in Pliny, but the concordance to the Delphin ed. of the *Nat. Hist.* does not give it.]

2. [1] Or pedigree.　[2] *Pronepotem* [really, great-grandson].　[3] Or courtyard.　[4] [Of direct as opposed to collateral descent.]

3. [1] A gum or hardened juice issuing out of the root (when it is wounded) of a plant called *ferula*.　[2] Like unto those round rolls, which women instead of farthingales use under their clothes beneath the waist, called in Latin *galbei*.　[3] Resembling maggots.　[4] [Oak-trees bearing edible acorns.]　[5] *Perfidia* according to M. Tullius Cicero in his *Brutus* [23]. Some expound it otherwise, namely, for their treachery [Livy, xlv, 35].　[6] 7000 as Valerius Maximus saith [ix, 6, 2].　[7] Of Viriathus the captain thereof.　[8] [Or crouch-backed, hunchbacked.]　[9] When his time by course came.

[a] The like narration is reported of Hipparchia and Crates the Theban, a Cynic philosopher [Diogenes Laërtius, vi, 5, 7].

4. [1] *Supposita*, or rather, as some read, *Superposita*, upon.　[2] Livia Ocellina.　[3] Or Ocellaris.　[4] As the manner was in kissing young children.　[5] [*v. l.* παρατρώξῃ, " have a bite at."]　[6] Galba. [7] For some be fortunate and signify good.　[8] For some be fruitless. [9] Or the outward court-gate.　[10] Or door-sill [threshold].　[11] Or wake.

5. [1] The father of Nero.　[2] *Quingenties* HS. ; some read *quin-quagies*, 5,000,000 [C. 18, annot.].　[3] *Ad quingenta*, sc. *sestertia*.

6. [1] Either in honour of Flora, the goddess of flowers, or else in thankful memorial of a famous courtesan named Flora, who made the people of Rome her heir and gave the city a great sum of money, out of the yearly increase whereof were the charges defrayed that went to these licentious plays. [2] Not substituted in the room of another deceased. [3] Caligula. [4] Or under. [5] Or Mandilions [soldier's cloak]. [6] Or laborious.

[a] *Tessera data.* However this word [*Tessera*] in our author hath other significations, to wit, of a watchword, a signal, a tally or ticket, etc. Yet here verily it seemeth to be put for a precept or command, whether it were delivered by word of mouth unto those that stood next, or in writing, and so passed through the camp, it matters not.

[b] It may appear that Gaetulicus their former general had allowed his soldiers more liberty and pastime.

7. [1] Licences or permits to be absent from camp. [2] [Hardened, experienced.] [3] [Raids, inroads.] [4] Caligula. [5] [Made an excellent impression or appearance.] [6] Much about our peck. [7] £3, 2s. 6d. sterling. [8] [Ownership : also=owner.] [9] As some horse or mule. [10] [Supply " it was."] [11] Covered all over the head.

8. [1] *Sacris faciundis*, or *Sibyllinis libris inspiciendis*, to oversee sacrifices and divine service or to peruse the prophetical books of Sibylla. They were in number fifteen. [2] Carrying in a light litter or chair. [3] [*Rerum*, of affairs, conditions.] [4] Or dint [stroke] of lightning. [5] *Lacum ;* others read *Lucum*, a grove.

[a] These were also called Titii, by Tacitus [*Ann.* i, 54 ; *Hist.* ii, 95], instituted by Tatius, king of the Sabines.

[b] They took their name of Augustus, like as other orders afterwards, as Flaviana, etc., of the emperors following.

9. [1] And therefore not to be crucified. [2] *Solatio et honore*, or comfortable honour (hendiadys). [3] For they be stirring spirits, that are looked into in a State. [4] Or Lieutenant [governor]. [5] [Of distinguished family.]

10. [1] Enfranchising. [2] Some nobleman's son of Rome. [3] By Nero. [4] Or lord-general [*imperator*]. [5] As if they had served their full time, and were now called forth again by way of honour. [6] Who usually wore rings of iron. [7] *Dertosam* [a town in Spain, on the left bank at the mouth of the Iberus (Ebro)] *appulit :* others, *Decursa appulit*, hulled down the tide : or, as the wind did drive it. [8] *Omitterent*, or *amitterent*, lose.

[a] In habit of a woman and with wings, holding forth a garland in the right hand, and bearing in her left an olive branch, as is to be seen in many antique coins.

[b] A trunk of a tree, or post erected, upon which hung the armour and apparel of enemies slain and despoiled.

11. [1] Notwithstanding that upon the death of Nero he was declared emperor at Rome.

12. [1] Either by waste in melting or by the crafty conveyance of the gold-founder. [2] *Ordinario dispensatori ;* or thus, one Ordinarius his steward. [3] As of pease or beans. [4] [Or Canus.] [5] Or pence, 3s. 1d. *ob.* [=*obolus*, ½d.] English.

13. [1] *See* Turnebus, *Adversaria*, v, 2. [2] [Well-known.] [3] Hush or whist, an interjection of silence [latest texts omit St, and read Onesimus for Io Simus]. [4] [Or simply, carried out the singing and repetition with suitable gestures (*egerunt*).]

14. [1] Or Vinius. [2] [*Assessor*, a judge's assistant.] [3] [Laziness.] [4] Knighthood. [5] *Summae equestris gradus*, or *summi equestris ordinis.* [6] Seventy-three. [7] Gentlemen and senators.

SERVIUS SULPICIUS GALBA

^a During which time were held the festival days of the *Saturnalia*, New-year's tide and others.

15. ¹ Which amounted, according to Tacitus [*Hist.* i, 20] to *bis et vicies milies sestertium*, 2200 millions.   ² Tacitus saith thirty.   ³ [In a position, had not enough means.]

16. ¹ [Nearly all classes.]

17. ¹ [The midst of.]   ² *Semper ;* or *super*, besides.

18. ¹ [Besprinkled ; *see* note Tib. 60.]   ² To avert the harm prognosticated thereby.   ³ Like a mourner.   ⁴ Ominous tokens, presaging his brittle state.   ⁵ Or chair of estate [C. 76].

19. ¹ Of the praetorians.   ² Cuirass [here, a coat of quilted leather, sometimes plated with iron].   ³ [Deluded by false reports.]

^a They used in old time such cuirasses (instead of breastplates) made of linen webs, folded eighteen times and more. For so Nicetas Acominatus, *Rerum Isaaci Angeli*, writeth [i, 8], ἠριθμοῦντο δὲ εἰς ὀκτωκαίδεκα καὶ πλείω τὰ τοῦ ὑφάσματος συμπτύγματα ; which folds being throughly steeped and soaked in vinegar or austere wine, with salt put thereto, and afterwards well driven and wrought together in manner of felt, became so stiff and an armour of so good proof, ὡς καὶ βέλους εἶναι παντὸς στεγανώτερον, as that it would check the dint of any dart or shot whatsoever.

^b As touching the soldier thus reproved by Galba, it was Julius Atticus, as Tacitus writeth [*Hist.* i, 35], one of those who went under the name of *Spiculatores*, billmen [watchmen armed with a pike] : or *Speculatores* rather, as some would have it, employed in espial, executions, etc., as hath before been noted.   Here also in the clause, *Dimota paganorum turba*, is to be understood the multitude of the people and common sort, who were not soldiers ; for so *Pagani* are taken, as in opposition to *Milites*.

20. ¹ [Properly a small flag or ensign, or the officer carrying it ; then, generally, a body of men serving under it.]   ² The place where sometime that lake was [in the middle of the Forum].   ³ Or water-bearers and wood-purveyors for the soldiers.   ⁴ Homer, *Iliad*, v, 254, Diomedes to Sthenelus.   ⁵ Patrobius.

^a These *Aurei* among the Romans were valued at one hundred *Sestertii* apiece, so as in round reckoning they may go for our old Edward Star-Reals¹, or fifteen shilling pieces. For by exact computation one of them ariseth to fifteen shillings, seven pence halfpenny, the fourth part just of the Roman pound (containing one hundred deniers or Attic drachmae) which maketh three pounds, two shillings, six pence sterling.

^b This place where Patrobius was executed, and into which they flung their heads, who by command of the Caesars were put to death, was called *Sestertius*².   Plutarch [*Galba*, 27].

21. ¹ Or bunch [wen].   ² Or swathing-band.

22. ¹ [He ate so much at supper that the remains of the dishes were enough to make a meal for the attendants.]   ² Made smooth.

23. ¹ [=marketstead, market-place, *i.e.* the Forum.]   ² [Holding the opinion concerning him.]

---

¹ [=Spur-rial, -royal, so called because the reverse bore a sun like the rowel of a spur.]

² [Instead of Σηστέρτιον, Σεσσώριον, Lat. *sessorium*, is now generally read.]

NOTES AND ANNOTATIONS UPON
MARCUS SALVIUS OTHO

1. [1] [Descended.] [2] Or his, Camillus's [Cl. 13]. [3] Otho.
[a] Not without the rampart and precinct of the camp, where was the ordinary place of execution, nor by the ministry of a centurion, who by order was deputed to see justice done ; but in the very face and most frequented quarter of the camp called *Principia*, not far from the lord-general's pavilion, and where the principal captains quartered and lodged ; wherein also the main standard named the eagle and other military ensigns of the bands and cohorts were kept, even in his own sight, being general, whose manner was not to be present.

2. [1] April 28. [2] [Or swinged = thrashed.] [3] [Who enjoyed great favour there.] [4] [*Tantum potentia valuit*, had so much influence. " Bare such a side " somewhat resembles the modern slang use of " side."] [5] For pardon. [6] Restoring to his former state. [The senate could condone such offences, but the emperor alone had the privilege of granting restitution of rights.]
[a] This rude and gross kind of sport was thereupon called *Sagatio*, not unlike to that pastime with us in some places called the canvassing, and elsewhere the vanning of dogs [tossing in a canvas sheet or winnowing-fan].

3. [1] Rufrius Crispinus. [2] Until he could put away Octavia. [3] So writeth Plutarch [*Galba*, 19], but Tacitus [*Ann.* xiii, 45] differeth from this narration. [4] Partner with him in love of that mistress. [The account in Tacitus, *Hist.* i, 13, agrees in the main with Plutarch and Suetonius, but in the *Annals* her connexion with Otho is spoken of as *matrimonium*.] [5] Pledge or gage, to wit, Poppaea. [6] How Nero had been excluded and shut out of doors, etc. [7] [*Mimum*, farce, comedy.] [8] [As a rule only those who had been consuls or praetors were appointed provincial governors.] [9] Without severity. [10] Without pillaging, polling, and extortion.
[a] For after that by command of Nero he and Poppaea were in some sort put asunder, he solicited her as being his own wedded wife to keep him company, which, in regard of her marriage with Nero, was held adultery.

4. [1] On Nero. [2] [*Repromittens ;* rather, promising in addition, as no mention is made of his having promised the throne to Otho on a previous occasion.] [3] Galba. [4] 15s. 7d. *ob.* in English.

5. [1] [Swindled out of.] [2] *Speculatoribus* [bodyguards]. [3] 100 Aurei : every aureus being 15s. 7d. *ob.*

6. [1] Religious scrupulosity. [2] January 15. [3] Or close chair, wherein women use to be carried. [4] [Where the general's quarters were.]

MARCUS SALVIUS OTHO

a A column erected in the upper end or head of the *Forum Romanum*, at which all the principal highways in Italy began, with directions thereon engraven, to every gate of the city leading unto the said highways.

7. [1] Which either were of wax, or painted. [2] Commonly of brass, stone, or such solid matter. [3] Or ghost. [4] By observing the sacred birds.

a Some read ἀσύλοῖς for αὐλοῖς, to no good sense at all. But the latter accordeth well with Juvenal, *Sat.* xi, 34, 35, who to the same effect saith

Buccae
Noscenda est mensura tuae,

and proverbially implieth thus much, that he was not able to manage the empire. [Later texts of Juvenal do not agree with H. either textually or in punctuation. *Cf.* also Cicero, *ad Att.* ii, 16.]

8. [1] For Fabius Valens and Aulus Caecina were come with a power out of Germany into Italy. [2] By Otho and the senate. [3] *Classiarii.* [4] [Rather, arms] with which the 17th cohort, sent for out of the colony Ostia before to Rome, should be armed. [5] The praetorian or guard soldiers. [6] Who, to the number of fourscore, with many ladies were at supper that night with Otho, and by the soldiers suspected to have plotted his death. [7] [The accounts in Tac. *Hist.* i, 80-82 and Plutarch, *Otho*, 3, should be compared with this.] [8] Of Mars. [9] Galli. [10] The infernal god so named as if *dives*, rich as Pluto, from Ploutos (πλοῦτος, riches), because all things arise out of the earth and fall into it again. [11] [At the twentieth milestone.]

a *Germaniciani exercitus.* Which served in camp or as garrison soldiers in Germany, whether they were Romans, Germans, or any other auxiliaries from associate nations, it skilled not.

b The manner was, that whosoever enterprised a war-voyage should enter into the chapel of Mars, where hung the sacred scutcheons or shields called *Ancilia*, and first stir them, after that shake the spear also of Mars, and say withal *Mars, Vigila*, Awake, Mars. This had Otho done, but according to the religious ceremony not bestowed them quietly again in their places.

9. [1] Tacitus [*Hist.* ii, 24] calleth it *Castrorum*, or rather *Castorum*, of Castor and Pollux. [2] [H. has omitted *apud Betriacum*, " at Betriacum," also spelt Bebriacum, Bedriacum.] [3] By the name of *Commilitones : in ipsa consalutatione.* Some read *in ipsa consultatione*, as they were in consultation. [4] [Body of men, force.]

10. [1] [Later texts Laetus.] [2] Or colonel. [3] *Angusticlavius* [a plebeian tribune, who only wore a narrow stripe, as distinguished from the sons of nobles, who wore the *latus clavus*].

11. [1] The senators [whom he had ordered to leave the camp]. [2] For fear his head should be severed from his body, etc.

12. [1] Or counterfeit cap of false hair.

a This bread was made of bean and rice flour, of the finest wheat also, a very *Psilothrum* as the physicians term it, or a depilatory, to keep hair from growing, especially being wet and soaked in some juice or liquor appropriate therefor, as the blood of bats, frogs, or the tunny fish, etc. To this effeminacy of Otho alludeth the satyric poet Juvenal [ii, 107] in this verse :

Et pressum in faciem digitis extendere panem.

NOTES AND ANNOTATIONS UPON
AULUS VITELLIUS

1. [1] [Faunus, an old Italian rural deity identified with the Greek Pan, is also represented as a legendary king of Latium.] [2] Or causey [C. 44]. [3] [A hill on the left side of the Tiber, adjoined to Rome by a bridge. Here the old god Janus was supposed to have built a town or citadel.] [4] [By the Romans.]

[a] This Quintus Eulogius was the freedman of the said Quintus Vitellius. [This is a conjecture of Casaubon. Nothing is known of such a person. Others read *elogii* and take it with *libellus,* a pamphlet eulogising the family history of the Vitellii. *Elogium* is properly an inscription under an ancestral bust.]

2. [1] *Sutorem veteramentarium* [one who patched up old shoes]. [2] *Sectionibus* [sale by auction of confiscated goods] *et cognituris* [the office and emoluments of an informer]. [3] Or proscribed and outlawed. [4] [In Campania, mod. Nocera.] [5] Which as Onuphrius [Onofrio Panvinio (1529-68), Italian antiquarian and historian] saith, was Nepos. [6] [Tac. *Ann.* ii, 48, where his name is mentioned.] [7] Of Germanicus Caesar. [8] Aulus [Tac. *Ann.* v, 8]. [9] Or restraint of liberty and duress. [10] Or President [*praefectus*]. [11] A Collution [mouth-wash]. [12] *Arterias,* windpipe. [13] [Wheedling, flattering.] [14] Or salute after a devout manner. [15] Caligula. [16] Which be the reverent gestures used in worshipping the gods. See Pliny, *Nat. Hist.* xxviii, 25. [17] So called because they were solemnized but once in a hundred, or a hundred and ten years. [18] A man of . . . .

[a] Some read *Sectionibus et Suturis,* expounding it thus, as if his son had been not a cobbler but a shoemaker indeed, occupied in cutting of new shoes and sewing them together.

[b] These kind people, so double diligent about the feminine sex, be fitly called good women's men, and, doting overmuch upon their wives, *Uxorii* in Latin, as one would say bridegrooms still. Such a one Seneca [Frag. 83] makes report he knew, who could not endure to be without his wife's company one minute of an hour ; and if upon necessity he went abroad into the town, yet would he take with him a stomacher of hers and wear it ever next his heart, etc.

[c] No doubt the same was garnished with gold, rich stones, and precious pearls [Pliny, *Nat. Hist.* ix, 35, 114].

[d] It may be gathered it was *Hemiplegia,* which we call the dead palsy, taking the one side of the body and most commonly ensuing upon an apoplexy, if it were not the very apoplexy itself (which is none other but a universal palsy) considering the quick dispatch it made.

3. [1] September 24. [2] September 7. [3] Or fortune by the horoscope of his nativity. [4] Or emperor (*imperatorem*). [5] A deviser of new fashions and forms of filthy uncleanness.

21

AULUS VITELLIUS

4. [1] [" For " is superfluous.]

5. [1] [These curators were two in number, one of whom looked after public works, the other after sacred edifices, although the former often included the latter.]

6. [1] Deceased.   [2] [That is, with an *attempt* at parricide.]

7. [1] *Venetae* [the Blues], which Galba likewise with them favoured. [2] [Had it not been that.   To break up this long sentence, a semicolon might be put after " affected " and " that " omitted, with a comma after " yield " : or, " But as " . . . " yield," omitting " so that."] [3] [Confining, properly of hawks in a coop : " mews " are so called because the king's falcons were originally kept in the Mews near Charing Cross.]   [4] For in such tenants dwelt, whereas the owner himself kept beneath.   [5] [For " and " read " he."]

[a] He meaneth the crew, or faction of charioteers holding of the blue or watchet colour, which Vitellius and Galba both affected.

8. [1] [Coming on apace.]   [2] *Vicos*, or streets : of Colonia Agrippina [Cologne] where all this was done, as some [Tac. *Hist.* i, 57] write. [3] The lord-general's lodging.

9. [1] Under the conduct of Fabius Valens by the Alps, and of Caecina over the Apennines.   [2] [Encircled, flew round about.]   [3] In Gaul, within the province Narbonensis [mod. Vienne].

10. [1] [Cashiered.]   [2] In betraying Galba their sovereign.   [3] Or tribunes.   [4] Before Betriacum.   [5] Some conclude the former period here, and begin a new sentence thus, *Pari vanitate*, With like vanity, etc.   [6] Plutarch, *Otho*, 18.   [The MSS. reading here is Δηλώσει Μάρκου Ὄθωνος, but it is difficult to see what this means, unless it is intended as a translation of Memoriae. Lobeck suggests Δαίμοσι, *i.e.* Dis Manibus.]   [7] Or mausoleum.   [8] Or wake.

11. [1] Or among the standards and other ensigns, *inter signa et vexilla*.   [2] [With unsheathed swords.]   [3] Or folkmote (*comitia*). [4] [Rather, consul.]   [5] Nero.

[a] So called of an unfortunate battle fought that day near the river Allia, in which the Romans were overthrown by the French, who following the train of their victory, advanced their ensigns to Rome, forced the city, and put it to the sack.

[b] Some read *De Dominico*, out of Dominicus, for so it may seem was the book of Nero's Canticles entitled, alluding to himself, who would be called *Rerum Dominus*, Lord of the world.

12. [1] *Poscam, oxycraton* [ὀξύκρατον].   [2] *Ferocitatem;* or *furacitatem*, thievery.   [3] [A trainer of gladiators.]   [4] [Engage in a public contest : Cl. 21.]

13. [1] [Or banquets ; a collation after dinner or supper ; here rather " orgies " (*comissatio*).]   [2] [Should be 400,000.]   £3125 sterling [cf. C. 18, annot.].   [3] Or charger.   [4] Minerva.   [5] *Scavorum*.

[a] Cornelius Celsus [i, 3] findeth no fault with Asclepiades[1], who condemned vomiting, *Offensus eorum consuetudine, qui quotidie ejiciendo vorandi facultatem moliuntur*, as utterly disliking their manner, who by daily casting up their gorge seek to enable themselves for beastly

---

[1] [Of Prusias in Bithynia (124 B.C. ——), a famous physician who settled in Rome.]

gormandise. And to the same purpose he saith : *Istud luxuria causa fieri non oportere*, that this ought not to be put in use for to maintain riotous excess. He admonisheth also, *Ne quis qui valere et senescere volet, hoc quotidianum faciat*, That no man who desireth to live long and in health would make it a daily practice. But Seneca [*Ad Helviam*, x, 3] reproveth such very aptly in these words :

> *Edunt ut vomant, vomunt ut edant.*
> They eat to vomit, and they vomit to eat.

ᵇ If Scarus were not the gilt-head, a delicate fish, no doubt it was in those days, and better esteemed than the acipenser, the sturgeon. It cheweth cud and hath plain teeth to grind withal, not indented like a comb or saw.   ᶜ [Later texts have *a Parthia*.]

14. ¹ [Playfellows.]   ² [Reached, held out.]   ³ As our scriveners and attorneys do, for other men [*stipulator*, one to whom verbal acknowledgment of a debt is made in the presence of witnesses].   ⁴ Of chariot-runners *venetae factionis*.   ⁵ [Having an idea.]   ⁶ [*Nova spe*, that is, had hopes of a revolution.]   ⁷ [H. is here translating *veraculis*. Later edd. have *vernaculis*, lit. home-bred slaves, here used = buffoons. Madvig suggested *genethliacis*, those who calculated nativities.]   ⁸ Astrologers.   ⁹ Or be seen [lit. in existence].   ¹⁰ Not in Rome and Italy only, as before he denounced unto them.   ¹¹ Or by a wise woman of that country where the people Chatti inhabit, in Germany.   ¹² [Something like " who had foretold " must be supplied here.]

ᵃ *Veraculis* or *vericulis*, or *divinaculis :* all to one sense, Such as will take upon them to tell fortunes, etc. Women of this profession Apuleius [*Met*. ix, 129] termeth *veratrices*.

ᵇ *Bonum factum.* The usual preface or preamble premised before edicts and proclamations, *Boni ominis causa*.

15. ¹ Upper and lower.   ² [H. has omitted *in absentis verba*, some swore allegiance to V. in his absence, others in his presence.]   ³ Or offer.   ⁴ [= Scroll, document.]   ⁵ *Nihil iam metuens ;* some read *metuentes*, to this sense, that he chased them fearing no such thing.   ⁶ The faction of Flavius Vespasianus.   ⁷ For ye must remember how much he was given to gormandise.   ⁸ *Pugionem* or rapier, *a pungendo, quia punctim potius quam caesim vulnerat* [because it wounds rather by pricking than cutting].

ᵃ By this ceremony he seemed to resign up his empire.

16. ¹ Or litter.   ² That made his dainty pastry-works and sweetmeats, meet grooms to accompany such a glutton.   ³ Or bandolier.   ⁴ Fifteen-shilling pieces and better.

ᵃ Making semblance thereby that he was fled and gone ; for the manner was, at the porter's lodge door, if nobody were within, to tie up a mastiff dog, for to give warning abroad if any man came. And not far from the said lodge, such a dog with a chain was usually painted upon the wall with these words in great letters :

> *Cave, Cave Canem*, Beware, Beware the Dog.

17. ¹ Or the vaward [Cal. 21].   ² Or market-place.   ³ *Sacra Via* [C. 46] reacheth from the palace to the Forum.   ⁴ As a gag.   ⁵ [At one time . . . at another time.]   ⁶ Or firebrand, because he burnt the Capitol.   ⁷ Or platter-knight, for his gormandise and huge platter aforesaid [13].   ⁸ Caligula.   ⁹ [Tib. 53.]

18. [1] Or *Becco*, a beak in English, which may somewhat confirm the learned conjecture of him, who guesseth that both our ancient nation and language were extract from Gaul. [The word, of course, still exists in mod. Fr. *bec*.]

[a] He meaneth that *Gallus Gallinaceus*, or dunghill cock, that before had perched upon his head and shoulders, alluding to the French, who are likewise named *Galli*.

NOTES AND ANNOTATIONS UPON FLAVIUS VESPASIANUS AUGUSTUS

1. [1] Galba, Otho, Vitellius. [2] [Abided, suffered.] [3] [Old Sabine town, mod. Rieti.] [4] Or, after the battle, fled from him. [5] Such be called *Causarii*. [6] *Publicanus*, or *publicus*, both to the same effect. [7] Or customer [custom-house officer]. [8] Or Colonel. [9] Or camp-master [*praefectus castrorum*]. [10] Beyond the river Po in respect of Rome. [11] [In bulk, or at a fixed price, by contract.]
[a] The fortieth part [2½ p.c.]. [Perhaps] the fortieth penny of all bargains of sales that were unlawful.

2. [1] The emperor. [2] November 17. [3] In the seventeenth year of his age. [4] [*Anteambulonem*, a slave or client who went before his master or patron to clear the way.] [5] [Others, *infensum*, that is, Gaius.]
[a] Which had a border or broad guard about it, embroidered with purple studs like nail-heads, and therefore was called *Latus clavus*, and thereupon Senators themselves *Laticlavii*.

3. [1] Or notary. [2] Or keeper of her books and accounts.

4. [1] [Vectis.] [2] [Had great influence.] [3] Nero. [4] Or turnips. [5] *Mangonicos quaestus*, which extendeth also to slaves and old wares or thripperie [=frippery, old clothes]. [6] Judaea. [7] Who then looked for their Messias and do so still. [8] Or governor, Sabinus. [9] Gallus. [10] The main standard. [11] Roman. [12] These cornets and cohorts seem to be auxiliaries. [13] Titus. [14] Or provinces rather in the East part.
[a] In lieu of φυλλοβολία ; for in token of love and affection they should have heaped upon him gay flowers, green leaves, and pleasant fruits.
[b] This no doubt had relation to the prophecy of the True Messias and Saviour Jesus Christ. The very words imply no less, according with these out of Holy Scripture : Ἐκ σοῦ ἐξελεύσεται ὁ ἡγούμενος, etc. Read Josephus, vi, 31, of the destruction of Jerusalem.

5. [1] One of those that pry into beasts' bowels. [2] Tertulla, the grandmother of Vespasian. [3] Who wrote the Jewish history. [4] Vespasian's [? Galba's].
[a] There is a hill of that name in Judaea. And because answers had been given from thence and nothing there was to be seen, neither image of a god, nor temple, but a bare altar, and the reverence only of the place, both Tacitus [*Hist.* ii, 78] and Suetonius by the name of Carmelus call that unknown god unto them, who reigneth for ever.
[b] This sight and the other following betokened sovereignty unto Vespasian, who warred then in the East countries Judaea and Syria.

FLAVIUS VESPASIANUS AUGUSTUS

6. ¹ [Ready : Fr. *prêt*.]   ² Or governor.   ³ The first day.   ⁴ The 11th of July [Tac. *Hist.* ii, 79, makes it the 3rd].   ⁵ [When in extremities, or near his death ; unless *extrema obtestatio* = urgent entreaty.] ⁶ No marvel then if the armies there inclined to Vespasian.   ⁷ Mucianus.   ⁸ Unto Vespasian.   ⁹ Vologaesus.

7. ¹ [*Claustra*, defences, key.]   ² [Rather, to have been admitted by nobody.]   ³ Eighty miles ; happily [perhaps] the same whom Tacitus [*Hist.* ii, 78] reporteth to have been the priest of Carmelus. [They are different persons.]   ⁴ Vespasian.   ⁵ [Both proved successful.]

ᵃ This Basilides seemeth rather to have been some priest, or principal man of note, and not libertus, his freedman, as some copies have.   But whoever he was, to the setting forward of this design of Vespasian, *Nomen et omen erat* [Gr. Βασιλεύς, king].

8. ¹ In taking part against him [the defeated Vitellians].   ² Or charge [according to Casaubon, *praefectura alarum*, a cavalry command : Aug. 38].   ³ [Unfriendly, stern.]   ⁴ *Per vices ;* some read *per vicos*, along the towns and villages.   ⁵ Bare-footed.   ⁶ Whereas they had been free states.   ⁷ For in them were engraven the public evidences and records, etc.

9. ¹ Claudius his wife.   ² Of senators and gentlemen.   ³ [Was the right of a citizen (*civile fasque*).]

10. ¹ The vacation during the civil troubles.   ² Which pertained to the centumvirs' court : to wit, civil causes between private persons, as probates of testaments, etc. [Cicero, *de Orat.* i, 36, Aug. 36.] ³ Plaintiffs and defendants.

ᵃ Out of the 35 Tribes of Rome were chosen certain Judges or Commissioners, named Centumvirs, to wit, out of every Tribe three, and albeit their number arose to a hundred and five, yet roundly they went for a hundred, and so were called.   These I say, being ordained *Stlitibus judicandis*, determined private and civil matters between man and man, *de Testamentis, Stillicidiis*, and such like of no great moment.   They put forth or erected a spear in the place where they sat in jurisdiction, whereupon their court was named *Hasta Centumviralis* [see Aug. 36].

11. ¹ *Si junxisset*, as Sabellicus expoundeth it ; or, at large [in a general sense], carnally.

12. ¹ By which salt (*sal*) was brought out of the Sabine country to Rome.   ² Who were but of mean calling.   ³ Being three-score of age, and therefore past the ambitious desire of such glory.   ⁴ [The English is obscure, and the reading doubtful.   The meaning must be that it was a long time before he would accept these honours.] ⁵ [*Nam* merely introduces a new subject.]

13. ¹ *Libertatem*, which the Greeks call παρρησία.   ² His friend. ³ For he was the chief helper of him to the empire.   ⁴ Whatsoever you are, noting him for that he was *Pathicus*.   ⁵ Noting Vespasian, as if he had a longing eye after his wealth and therefore sought his condemnation.   ⁶ *Post dominationem ;* others *damnationem*, after he was condemned ; for Vespasian had banished all philosophers out of Rome and confined this Demetrius to an island [Dion, lxvi, 15].

ᵃ Alluding to the name Cynicus.   For these philosophers took this denomination Cynics, either of their dogged and currish demand, or of a place where they taught and disputed, called *Cynosarges*.

14. [1] Or *Morboviam*, according to which phrase we say, The foul ill [*morbus*] take thee ; the Greeks εἰς κόρακας, the crows eat thee ; the Latins *in malam crucem*, Go hang.

15. [1] Not Caesar nor Augustus nor Imperator.

16. [1] [=Strange ; he did not hesitate, made no difficulty about.]

17. [a] Which in Augustus Caesar's time amounted to 1,200,000 sestertii, triple to the worth of a Roman knight.

18. [1] Artificers, for so Livy [vii, 2] termeth *ludios et histriones*, stage-players. [2] Or hired. [*Artifices* is rather sculptors or painters. " Bought up " is the old reading *coemit*, for which Graevius conjectured *Coae Veneris*, to be taken with *refectorem*, " the restorer of the Coan Venus and also of the Colossus," the colossal statue of Nero in the Golden House. Pliny, *Nat. Hist.* xxxvi, 5, 27, says the artist is unknown : *Ignoratur artifex ejus quoque Veneris, quam Vespasianus imperator in operibus suae Pacis dicavit.*] [3] Or reward. [4] To allow them wages for their painful labour in such works rather than to have the same done without them and, as we say, to keep poor people at work.

[a] This Colossus Zenodorus, a famous workman, made beforetime for Nero.

19. [1] Ear delights, as players, musicians, etc. [Aug. 74]. [2] [Later texts, Apelles.] [3] *Recta :* in opposition to *sportulae* [Aug. 74]. [4] [A dealer in salt fish, *salsamentarius*, ταριχέμπορος. The fish was salted in square slabs or κύβοι ; or the first part of the compound may be from κύβιον, Lat. *cybium*, tunny-fish ; σάκτης is one who loads an animal with wares for sale. The king was the false Seleucus, who became the husband of Berenice, the daughter of Ptolemy XIII Auletes, who soon put him to death : Dion. xxxix, 57 ; Strabo, xvii, 1, 11.] [5] [A famous mime.]

[a] As namely, *Pueros Symphoniacos*, etc., choristers or quiristers with most sweet breaths and pleasant voices, etc.

[b] For then had women their *Saturnalia*, like as the men in December. Those festival holidays were called *Matronalia*, in memorial of lady Hersilia and other noble dames, who in old time upon that day interposed themselves as *Mediatrices* between the Romans and Sabines ready to strike a most bloody battle.

20. [1] [*Quadratus*, Gr. τετράγωνος, full-square, neither too tall nor too short.] [2] [=Siege, Fr. *siège*, privy.] [3] A round place of exercise belonging to the baines. Some would have it to be a tennis-court. [4] Natural, 24 hours.

[a] This is reprehended by Cornelius Celsus, ii, 14, in these words : *Neque audiendi sunt, qui numero finiunt, quoties aliquis perfricandus est ; illud enim ex viribus hominis colligendum est.*

21. [1] Or arose before day, *de nocte vigilabat*. Sextus Aurelius [Victor, *Epit. de Caesaribus*, ix, 15] writeth of him that he watched all night. Pliny [Pliny the Younger (*Epist.* iii, 5, 9) in an account of his uncle, says : " Before daybreak he used to visit the emperor, for he too (Vespasian) made use of the night " (*nam ille quoque noctibus utebatur*), but the ed. is unable to find *ut . . . trajiceret*] also saith *Nocte uti*

FLAVIUS VESPASIANUS AUGUSTUS

solitum : ut dierum actus noctibus, et nocturnos diebus trajiceret.   [2] A secret, or retiring place.

[a] To be carried between men in a chair or seat called thereupon *Sella gestatoria,* or *Lectica.* Celsus reckoneth sundry sorts of this gestation, to wit, *Navi, Lectica, Scamno, Vehiculo.*

22. [1] *Et semper alias cum amicis ;* others read, *et super aleas communissimus,* and whiles he played at hazard, etc.   [2] A word in Latin that signifieth carts or wains.   [3] And not Florus.   [4] *Cum perducta,* etc., not *perductae,* in a quite contrary sense, as if he had given her so much.   [5] *Quadraginta Sestertia,* or *quadringenta sestertia,* 400,000.   [6] To wit, in the page of receipts.

[a] For it was an ordinary matter in supper-time, between the services and several dishes, to cast the Dice or cockall bones by fits.

[b] *Praetextata verba* by the figure antiphrasis [use of words in a sense opposite to their real meaning] are put for such words as beseemed not either the mouth or the ears of *Praetextati,* youths well-born and of gentle blood descended, who in truth should be modest and maiden-like ; and in like manner *praetextati mores* signify such behaviour. [*Praetextatus,* as applied to manners and language=immodest (cf. Juvenal, ii, 170, *Sic praetextatos referunt Artaxata mores,* they take back to their native Artaxata the immodest manners of Rome), apparently with the idea of being disguised or veiled (*praetexere*), of equivocal meaning, Fr. *double entente.*]

[c] Noting him for his ridiculous vanity, which φλαῦρος in Greek doth signify.

[d] Or, if ye read before *perductae,* it must so stand in the page of expenses, to this sense, laid out for or to Vespasian beloved ; as if he had given her a reward for loving him, whereas she should have given unto him.

23. [1] [These lines are from Menander's Θεοφορουμένη, the god-possessed or prophetic girl. Latest texts give them as follows :

ὦ Λάχης, Λάχης,
'Επὰν ἀποθάνῃς, αὖθις ἐξ ἀρχῆς ἔσει
Σὺ Κήρυλος.

The meaning is, after death you will become the freedman Cerylus, and so your money will be forfeit to the treasury ; see Kock, *Comicorum Atticorum Fragmenta,* iii, p 63.]   [2] [*Quasi :* he was not really his brother.]   [3] [Solicited.]   [4] The party that came to solicit his own cause.   [5] For to receive the money.   [6] Meaning his hand.   [7] Monument or sepulchre.   [8] The Mausoleum.   [9] Whereas himself was not of that line.   [10] A blazing star [comet].   [11] Whereupon is called *Stella Crinita* and *Cometes* in Greek.   [12] Am a-dying, and so grow to be a god.

[a] Some read instead of *Improbius irato, improbius nato,* that is to say, of no good making but ill-shaped to his height.

[b] A piece of a verse in Homer, *Iliad,* vii, 213, spoken there of Ajax, advancing forward to fight with Hector, unto whom or to whose long pike rather he likeneth this gangrel [slim, lanky, ungainly fellow].

[c] Either of fullers, walkers [=fullers], and dyers, who gathered and occupied much thereof about their cloths, or else, for the tubs that commonly stood in odd corners and nooks of the street, to receive every man's water that he made as he went.

24. [1] [Twinges and symptoms.]   [2] These waters of Cutiliae [sulphurous springs in the Sabine country] as Pliny writeth [*Nat.*

104

Hist. xxxi, 2] were exceeding cold.   ³ To avoid the ordure of the guts.   ⁴ June 24.   ⁵ *Superque mensem ac diem septimum.* [This agrees with Dion. Others take it to mean "a month besides"; but he was born Nov. 17 and died June 23.]

NOTES AND ANNOTATIONS UPON TITUS FLAVIUS VESPASIANUS AUGUSTUS

1. [1] December 30.

[a] A place in Rome so called of a building there, which stood upon seven courses of columns or pillars, arising all round and higher every one than other, in manner of so many circles or girdles [not to be confounded with that built later by Septimius Severus].

2. [1] *Metoposcopum* (μετωπόσκοπος). [2] Britannicus. [3] [Previous circumstances.] [4] Britannicus.

[a] He meaneth not a physiognomer, who hath taken upon him by inspection of eyes, forehead, face, etc., to tell one's nature and disposition (such a one as Zopyrus was, who noted Socrates for to be by natural inclination a wanton lover of women), but a fortune-teller by looking on the forehead only [Pliny, *Nat. Hist.* xxxv, 10], such as in these days, by the art of palmistry forsooth, can assure folk, how long they shall live, and what not, [who] if they do but see lines in the palms of their hands, or by feaxe[1] on the forehead, will say how many wives a man shall have, etc. As vain as those who, by counting the letters of the husband's and the wife's name, will confidently pronounce whether of them shall bury the other.

3. [1] *Auctoritas*, which Tacitus [*Hist.* ii, 1] calleth *majestas*. [2] [Unskilled.]

4. [1] Temperate behaviour. [2] In undertaking causes of greater importance. [3] In entertaining all matters whatsoever. [4] Near to lake Gennesaret. [5] [Or, near him, by his side.]

[a] By titles in this place and many others of Suetonius are to be understood inscriptions, testifying for what considerations such statues were erected. Such also were usually set up at public executions, to show the offences and causes why any suffered. A thing usual among the Romans in their government, in what province soever, as may appear by that which stood upon the Cross of our Saviour Christ.

5. [1] In Paphos, a city within the isle of Cyprus. [2] [Not the empire, but the hope aroused by the elevation of his father to the throne.] [3] September 8 (Josephus, *De Bello Jud.* vi, vii).

[a] That is to say a white band or ribbon, such as the royal diadem at first was.

6. [1] [Unlike a citizen.]

---

[1] Another form of faix (Nero, 20, annot.).

TITUS FLAVIUS VESPASIANUS AUGUSTUS

7. [1] The sister, as some think, of Agrippa Minor, and wife for a while of Polemon, king of Lycia [Pontus and Cilicia] ; others say she was the wife first of Aristobulus, afterwards of Antipater [*Acts of the Apostles*, xxv].   [2] [Were satisfied with, content to rely upon.]   [3] At which solemnity 5000 wild beasts were killed, as Eusebius [*Chronicon*, ii] and Eutropius [vii, 21] write.

[a] Of these baines, with what speed and celerity they were finished, Martial [*de Spect*, ii, 7] writeth thus :

Hic ubi miramur velocia munera, thermas.

8. [1] [He firmly adhered to the rule.]   [2] Who were opposite to the *Mirmillones*, that were armed after the French fashion.   [3] Wherein there died ten thousand a day [Eusebius, *Chronicon*, ii].   [4] By the burning of Vesuvius which consumed many towns and much people. [5] In the country, as columns, statues, painted tables, etc.   [6] [So that the delator or informer might not be able to shift the ground of action from one law to another.]

9. [1] [Couriers.   The word is used in modern times of a clerk in the Court of Chancery who makes out original writs.   Cursitor Street is so called from Cursitor's Inn, founded by Lord Nicholas Bacon, the father of the famous Lord Bacon.]   [2] As their armour, weapons, etc. [3] Ascendants of their nativity.   [4] Domitian.   [5] [Almost openly.]

[a] Doing them thus much credit in the eyes of the world, as to give the allowance and approbation, or otherwise, of the weapons wherewith they should fight.   For in this sense may ornaments be taken, the rather because some copies have *Ferramenta*.   Or this place may be understood of other furniture as well as arms, wherewith they should come appointed into the lists.

10. [a] This hath been observed in all ages to forerun the death of some prince.   Thus before the end of Julius Caesar, as Virgil [*Georg.* i, 488] writeth,

Non alias lato occiderunt plura sereno [1]
Fulgura.

Horace [*Odes*, i, 34, 7] likewise,

Per purum tonantes
Egit equos volucremque currum.

Our own chronicles [2] also exemplify no less ; to say nothing of the fresh resemblance of that which happened with us three years since, in July.

11. [1] September 13.

[a] Some write [Philostratus, *Vit. Apol. Tyan.* vi, 32] and Tzetzes [this is not in his *Chiliades*] by name, that he was poisoned with eating of sea-hares.

---

[1] [Read, non alias *caelo ceciderunt*, etc.]
[2] A little before the death of king Henry the second.

NOTES AND ANNOTATIONS UPON
FLAVIUS DOMITIANUS

1. [1] October 24. [2] January. [3] A place so called like as before, *ad capita Bubula* [Aug. 5] and *ad Gallinas* [G. 1]. [4] For his impure life. [5] Or abuse rather. [6] Between Vitellius and his father Vespasian and their factions. [7] [*Aedituus*, sacristan.] [8] The emperor's son and heir apparent of the empire. [9] As being a young prince and a Caesar.

[a] This was some satirical poem, of which Juvenal [iv, 106] writeth thus :

Improbior satiram scribente cinaedo [Nero].

[b] A vestment of white linen after the manner of a surplice ; for such priests thereupon were named *Linigeri*.

2. [1] *Operibus*, deeds and exploits [others, *opibus*]. [2] Which began the first of January, in his own right and not in the vacant room of others. [3] Peace concluded between the two nations [*Discussa*, settled. " To his hand " seems to mean, without his having anything to do with it]. [4] Canonisation for a god.

3. [1] *Horarium*, or for a certain time of the day : some say three hours [rather read *horarum*, a partitive genitive, some hours].

4. [1] *Missus*, every of which ordinarily consisted of seven races. [2] Or slippers. [3] [College of priests instituted by him, similar to the Augustales.] [4] Xiphilinus [Dion, lxvii, 1]. [5] So called of the seven hills, whereupon the city stood. [6] Or [wicker] baskets.

[a] *Toga Graecanica*. Which is spoken καταχρηστικῶς, for *chlamys*, a cloak or loose cassock. For *Toga* was *Romanorum*.

5. [1] In Vespasian's days. [2] [The Odeum.] [3] [The Circus Maximus.]

6. [1] By Norbanus Appius, who slew the said Antonius [before Domitian arrived].

7. [1] Whereas contrariwise under Nero, *publicae caenae ad sportulas redactae*. [2] White, Blue, Red, Green. [3] Who gelded, pampered, and set them out to sale. [4] *Geminari castra*, the greater and the less, as we read in Livy, etc. [5] Every one about 15s. 7d. *ob.* sterling [rather, about £1. He added three aurei to the nine formerly given].

[a] Philostratus [*Vit. Apol.* vi, 17] allegeth another reason of this edict, namely for that many seditious broils and commotions were occasioned by drunkenness.

[b] Or rather, as Casaubon expoundeth, that two legions should not encamp in one leaguer [camp]. For the policy of war found the same always dangerous in regard of mutinies, that by occasion thereof

might arise. Soldiers, as Dion writeth [xlix, 13], πρὸς τὴν ὄψιν τοῦ πλήθους σφῶν θρασύνονται, Seeing their own numbers great, grow to be stout and malapert.

c For beforetime it was thought good policy that soldiers should lay up a portion of their donative about the ensigns within the camp and not spend all their stock (which commonly they are given unto), whereby they might be put in mind to fight more valiantly and not to forsake their colours, so long as they had somewhat to save or lose.

 | 8. ¹ [The Forum.] ² Of such bondmen, as against their lords' and masters' right claimed freedom and used therein the plea of orators [assertiones perfusoriae, really, claims for freedom that were unauthorised, obtained by fraud. Perfusorius appears to mean by which the master was " swamped," cf. Cic. pro Roscio Amerino, 29, perfundere judicio. On the recuperatores, cf. Nero, 17]. ³ Who by taking money exercised his office otherwise than he ought. ⁴ [Of immoral character.] ⁵ Against the filthy sin of paederasty or Sodomy. ⁶ As to lose their heads. ⁷ Surnamed so of a family in Rome. ⁸ Or Maxima, sc. Vestalis, the chief of those nuns, as lady prioress or abbatess. ⁹ [Alive.]

a Namely, to be buried quick [alive] under the ground, that is to say to be let down into some grot or vault, and there to be starved to death.

9. ¹ Georgics, ii, 537. This hath relation to the last word (ante) in the verse precedent. [The allusion in the original is to the Golden Age.] ² Cupiditatis quoque atque avaritiae. By covetousness he meaneth the greedy desire of other men's goods : by avarice, in this place the pinching expense of his own. ³ [Moderation, self-restraint in regard to the property of others.] ⁴ [Those whose names had been posted up as debtors in the treasury five years before : cf. Cl. 9.] ⁵ [Remainders or pieces of land.] ⁶ Old soldiers who had served out their full time. [For " by " read rather " among."]

10. ¹ As Ironia and Antiphrasis, etc., whereby he seemed to glance at him. [Not to be confused with H. of Tarsus, the famous rhetorician of later date, fl. c. 170.] ² Who was armed with a buckler. ³ I.e. Domitian. ⁴ The favourer of the armed fencer Thrax abovesaid. ⁵ [Molitores rerum novarum, aiming at revolution.] ⁶ Domitia Longina. ⁷ Vocem suam, or Lamia his voice, as some expound it. ⁸ As if he had uttered these words : This is mere injury, but I must say nothing. [H. translates the reading heu taceo. Reading εὐτακτῶ, the sense is : when his voice was praised, Lamia said, I have no wife since you have taken mine ; therefore I can control my passions, which preserves the voice.] ⁹ Understand here, and in the other following (he slew or put to death). ¹⁰ For his father Lucius Salvius Titianus was Otho's brother. ¹¹ Two most renowned warriors of the Carthaginians and mortal enemies of the Romans. ¹² Of his own name. ¹³ Who being persecuted by Nero cut his own master-veins. ¹⁴ The son-in-law of Thrasea, even another Cato or Brutus and a man of most free speech in the behalf of the commonwealth. ¹⁵ For the father Vespasian had slain before. ¹⁶ Tractasset, handled ; or taxasset, taxed or reproved. ¹⁷ Domitian. ¹⁸ Of the Flavians and Vitellians. ¹⁹ Dudum latentes, per conscios investigatos [later text, dum etiam latentes conscios investigat, in his search for hidden conspirators]. ²⁰ [Distinguished : not, as now, used in a bad sense.]

a Patrem familias. A good honest citizen of Rome, such as came to behold the games.

FLAVIUS DOMITIANUS

^b Under these tyrannical emperors of Rome, that favoured, some this faction of fencers and chariot-riders, others that, it was high treason and impiety for men to speak a word, not in open place only and in the theatre, but also at home in their houses, even in table talk, in commendation of the adverse faction, by way of comparison. Martial [x, 48, 23] inviting a friend to his board and promising that no mirth and free speech at meat should turn him to any danger and displeasure, writeth thus unto him,

> *De prasino conviva meus vomitoque*[1] *loquatur ;*
> *Nec facient quemquam pocula nostra reum.*

Now, it is to be understood that Domitian affected the fencers called *Mirmillones* against the others named *Thraces* or *Threces*, whom his brother Titus favoured.

^c By Parmularius understand him that speaks favourably in the behalf of those fencers named *Parmularii* of the little bucklers, wherewith they were armed : otherwise called *Threces* (as one would say Thracians, whose armature they had), in opposition of others which were the *Mirmillones*, who were otherwise appointed after the French fashion, and therefore took the name otherwhiles of *Galli*, and so is that verse of Horace [*Sat.* ii, 6, 44] to be expounded, *Thrax an Gallina Syro par ?* As touching blasphemy, no marvel if these tyrants, taking upon them to be gods here upon earth, held every word derogatory anyways unto their majesty high treason and impiety.

^d Domitian and other such monstrous tyrants, as namely Caligula, envied all persons and things that were excellent. It behoved therefore Lamia to be silent, and to dissemble what he thought, as well as he might, although for grief of heart happily [haply] he could not choose but fetch a secret sigh to himself with a *Heu, Helas,* alas ! [For the reading εὐτακτῶ, cf. Aelian, *Var. Hist.* iii, 30.]

11. [1] *Actorem summarum* [one who managed his property and looked after his accounts]. [2] A dish of meat, etc. [3] [Had given notice.] [4] [According to the ancient custom.] To have their necks fast-locked in pillory, and so to be beaten with rods to death.

12. [1] Of 3 *aurei*. [2] [*Judaicus fiscus,* the tax paid by Jews into the imperial treasury. *Deferebantur* (" unto which were presented ") is difficult. Does it mean " were informed against, denounced ? " then *ad quem* (fiscum) must mean the treasury officials.] [3] [*Professi* : others, *improfessi,* those who lived as Jews without professing that religion, that is, certain Christians.] [4] Or Master of the Exchequer. [5] But proud and scornful. [6] Who married Titus his daughter Julia. [7] A hemistich out of Homer, *Iliad* [ii, 204], Ulysses' words : as if he should say, I like not so many Caesars.

^a I observe a double acception of this word Caesar in this history penned by Suetonius. First, for a noble house in Rome whereof Julius Caesar dictator was descended, whose line, either in blood or by adoption were called Caesares. And in this sense it is truly said that *Progenies Caesarum in Nerone defecit,* that the race of the Caesars was extinct in Nero ; and in this sense the heirs-apparent of the emperors in that line were named Caesars. Secondly, for all the sovereign emperors of Rome after Julius Caesar ; so Galba and the rest his successors were styled Caesares.

^b This exaction levied of the Jews, which he calleth *Judaicus*

---

[1] [This should be *veneto*.]

fiscus, was for the profession and exercise of the religion within Rome ; who, as Xiphilinus witnesseth [Dion Cassius, lxvi, 7], were permitted before by Vespasian his father to observe the rites and ceremonies of their own religion, paying a yearly tribute, to wit, a didrachm, two Roman deniers, or fifteen pence with us. And so the Christians afterwards for a time had the same indulgence. [*See* Merivale, *Hist. of the Romans under the Empire*, vii, p. 150.]

13. [1] *Pulvinar suum*, as if he had been a god ; for their gods and goddesses they bestowed in certain bed-lofts called *Pulvinaria* [Aug. 45]. [2] During the solemn games exhibited unto them.   [3] To his senator's place.   [4] Common talk.   [5] *Ponderis certi.* Sabellicus readeth *centeni*, of a hundred pounds, according to Papinius Statius of Domitian's statue, *Da Capitolinis aeternum sedibus aurum, Quo niteat sacri centeno pondere vultus Caesaris* [*Silvae*, i, 189].   [6] [Arches which spanned the markets and frequented streets, all covered passages being associated with the Italian god Janus. There were three arches dedicated to him in the Forum, in the middle one of which money-lenders congregated.] [7] [A pun on *arcus*, arch.]   [8] Not above four months.   [9] Not a fortnight full.   [10] Over the Chatti and Daci.   [11] September. [12] October.

[a] In some copies are inserted these words, *Aream et Calvitiem*, to no sense unless ye would have him thereby noted for his baldness and fall of hair, which some physicians call *Area*.

14. [1] Alluding to the like verses of the poet Evenus [Anthol. Pal. ix, 75, where the reading is σοί, τράγε for Καίσαρι, enough to pour on thee, O goat], which Ovid seemeth to express [*Fasti*, i, 357] in Latin thus, *Rode, caper, vitem, tamen hic cum stabis ad aras, In tua quod spargi cornua possit, erit.*   [2] [Pliny, *Nat. Hist.*, xxxvi, 22. It was a translucent stone from Cappadocia, used for window-panes, of Greek derivation (φέγγος, light).]

15. [1] [*Inertiae*, laziness ; lither also=pliant, yielding.]   [2] Jupiter. [3] Or Inscription.   [4] Where was an oracle.

[a] This Flavius Clemens is thought to have been a proselyte and convert to the Jewish religion[1], by reason whereof, being somewhat mortified and making conscience to do evil, he was reputed baseminded, and as Suetonius saith, *contemptissimae inertiae*,—imputations charged by pagans upon Christians and the true servants of God for their quiet carriage and modest behaviour.

[b] Whose son, he would not else, he would be thought, as who put one to death, because in his public prayers he had not made mention of him as the son of Minerva (Philostratus, *Vit. Apol.* vii, 24).

16. [1] He dreamt haply that Junius Rusticus, whom he had killed, came upon him with a naked sword [Dion Cassius, lxvii, 16].

17. [1] Whom Eusebius [*Chronicon*, ii] reporteth to have been niece by the sister of Flavius Clemens and a Christian, therefore confined to the island Pontia.   [2] [Groin.]   [3] Certain soldiers were so termed [leader of the wing of a small division of troops].   [4] [The headchamberlain. *Decurio* has not necessarily anything to do with a body of ten.]   [5] September 18.

[a] Little images, which paynims devoutly kept and worshipped (as the tutelar gods of their bed-chamber) within a certain closet called *Lararium*.

---

[1] Or Christianity rather.

FLAVIUS DOMITIANUS

18. [1] *Restrictiores*, drawn inward.   [2] [Or board = joke.]   [3] Homer, *Iliad*, xxi, 108.   Lycaon the son of Priam unto Achilles.   [4] *Eadem me manent*, some read *te*.

[a] It may be thought by the circumstance of this place that this *Rubor vultus* in Domitian was a tincture of virtue and modesty.   But there was nothing less in him, so that it was rather a hypocritical vizard and mask, under which was couched a most fell and cruel nature, as being by the judgement of Tacitus [*Agricola*, 45] more sanguinary than Nero.   For whereas Nero *subtraxit oculos, jussitque scelera, non spectavit, sub Domitiano praecipua miseriarum pars erat videri et aspici, cum denotandis tot hominum palloribus, sufficeret saevus ille Domitiani vultus et rubor, quo se contra pudorem muniebat.*   A flushing red therefore is not always a sign of grace.

19. [1] [Rarely.]   [2] Upon men's shoulders.   [3] [*Tanta arte :* with so accurate an aim.]

20. [1] [Tib. 61.   The *acta* were either the transactions of the senate or the official daily chronicle.]   [2] [10 and Vesp. 14.]   [3] A kind of delicate drink among the Romans.

[a] At Alexandria in Egypt was that famous library of king Ptolemy Philadelphus and the other Ptolemies his progenitors and successors, containing to the number well-near of 700,000 books.   [This library was destroyed in Julius Caesar's Alexandrine War (Aulus Gellius, vii, 17), and the reference here is probably to the library of Pergamum, presented to Cleopatra by Antony and removed to Alexandria.]

21. [1] It took the name of one Matius who loved a hortyard well ; like as *Appiana* and *Scaptiana mala* of Appius and Scaptius.   [A friend of Augustus, a great gardener, and wrote on cookery.]   [2] [Of wine.]

22. [1] [Immoral women.]   [2] Julia.   [3] As his wedded wife. [4] Conceived, as some say, by her former husband, others, by Domitian in her widowhood ;   and hereto accordeth Juvenal (ii, 32) : *Quum tot abortivis fecundam Julia vulvam Solveret, et patruo similes effunderet offas.*

23. [1] A saint or of sacred memory.   [2] Petronius and Parthenius [Aurelius Victor, Epit. xii, 14].   [3] Coats of arms.

[a] Acclamations must be restrained here to the worse sense, for all manner of curses and detestations, such as before were taken up by the people in this tune, *Tiberium in Tiberim*, and afterwards by the senate against Commodus, that wicked emperor, in these terms, *Hosti patriae honores detrahantur, parricida trahatur, hostis deorum, carnifex senatus unco trahatur, in spoliario ponatur, etc.*   [Lampridius, *Vit. Commodi*, 18.]

[b] Nerva, Trajan, Hadrian, etc.   Of whom Aurelius Victor writeth thus : *Quid Nerva prudentius aut moderatius ?   Quid Trajano divinius ?   Quid praestantius Hadriano ?*

INDEX TO SUETONIUS

INDEX

1 The reference number followed by *n*. indicates the page of the Notes and Annotations at the end.

115

INDEX

116

INDEX

INDEX

Sextilis, month, 79.
Social war, 25 *n*.
Speculator, 38 *n*., 94 *n*.
Spelunca, 157.
Sphaeristerium, 360.
Sphinx, 94.
Sportula, 81 *n*.
Stature of men, 112, 174.
Subdival, 27 *n*.
Subura, 32.
Sulla proscribes the M arian party, 3 *n*.;
 his opinion of Julius Caesar, 5.
Sumptuary laws, 12 *n*., 28 *n*.
Suovetaurilia, 45 *n*.
Superum Mare, 31 *n*.
Supplication, 8 *n*.
Supra numerum, 245.
Syracuse, retiring place of Augustus,
 109.

Tabellariae naves, 82 *n*.
Tali, 37 *n*., 85 *n*.
Templum, 44 *n*.
Tertia, d. of Servilia the mother of M.
 Brutus, 35.
Tessera, 93 *n*.
Testae, 273.
Tetraones (birds), 194.
Tetrinius, 202.
τεχνόφυον, 37 *n*.
Thalamegos, 35.
Theatralis lex, 86, 22 *n*.
T(h)ensa, 16 *n*.
Thraces, Threces, 68 *n*.
Thrasea Paetus, 82 *n*.
Thrasyllus, astrologer, 142, 193.
TIBERIUS Nero Caesar, emperor, 131-
 179.
Tiberius the younger, his pitiful death,
 195.
Tigellinus, 317.
Tillage, supported by Augustus, 88;
 regulations of Domitian, 377.
Tiridates, king of Armenia, 269; 85 *n*.
Titles, 106 *n*.
TITUS Flavius Vespasianus, emperor,
 364-371.

Toga Graecanica, 108 *n*.
Togata Gallia, 7 *n*.
Tribunes of the Commons, created from
 the Knights by Augustus, 86; their
 persons inviolable, 3 *n*.
Tribunes, military, 2 *n*.
Tribus rusticae and *urbanae*, 5 *n*.
Triumphal ornaments, 29 *n*.
Triumvirate, 84; 21 *n*.
Troica, poem by Nero, 88 *n*.
Trojan game, 28.
Trophy, what it was, 93 *n*.
Tunicati, 68 *n*.

Vallar coronets, 25 *n*.
Varro, M., 31.
Varus, his overthrow, 72.
Vatinian law, 16.
Venus, throw of dice, 37 *n*.
Venus Genetrix, 15 *n*.
Vespasia, Polla, mother of Vespasian,
 346.
VESPASIANUS, Flavius, emperor, 346-
 363.
Vestal virgins buried alive, 379.
Viaticum, 16 *n*.
Vindex rebels in Gaul, 292.
Vineyards, decay of, 377.
Vinicius, conspiracy of, 288.
Visceratio, 10 *n*.
VITELLIUS, Aulus, emperor, 332-345.
Vitellius, Lucius, 334.
Vitellius, Publius, 333.
Vitellius, Quintus, 333.
Voconian law, 48 *n*.
Vologaesus, king of Parthia, 304.
Vomiting, 98 *n*.
Vonones, king of Parthia, 162.

Wine, its use disapproved by Augustus,
 88.
Women as hostages, 71.

Xystici, 92.

Zeno (or Xeno), Greek professor, 166.
Zopyrus, physiognomist, 106 *n*.

PRINTED IN GREAT BRITAIN BY
THE EDINBURGH PRESS, 9 AND 11 YOUNG STREET, EDINBURGH.